WORLD MENTAL HEALTH

WORLD MENTAL HEALTH

Problems and Priorities
in Low-Income Countries

Robert Desjarlais

Leon Eisenberg

Byron Good

Arthur Kleinman

With contributions from

Alastair Ager, Myron Belfer, Ruth Fischbach,
Mary-Jo DelVecchio Good, Kris Heggenhougen,
Ladson Hinton, Sue Levkoff, Shubhangi Parkar,
Jamie Saris, Norma Ware, and Mitchell Weiss

New York   Oxford
OXFORD UNIVERSITY PRESS
1995

Oxford University Press

Oxford   New York
Athens   Auckland   Bangkok   Bombay
Calcutta   Cape Town   Dar es Salaam   Delhi
Florence   Hong Kong   Istanbul   Karachi
Kuala Lumpur   Madras   Madrid   Melbourne
Mexico City   Nairobi   Paris   Singapore
Taipei   Tokyo   Toronto

and associated companies in
Berlin   Ibadan

Library of Congress Cataloging-in-Publication Data
World mental health : problems and priorities in low-
income countries / Robert Desjarlais ... [et al.] ; with
contributions from Alastair Ager ... [et al.].
p. cm.   Includes bibliographical references and index.
ISBN 0-19-509540-5
1. Mental health–Developing countries.
2. Mental illness–Developing countries.
3. Mental health services–Developing countries.
I. Desjarlais, Robert R.
[DNLM: 1. Mental Health.
2. Developing Countries.
3. Social Problems.
WA 305 W927 1995]
RA790.7.D44W67   1995   362.2′09172′4–dc20
DNLM/DLC   for Library of Congress
94-31615

1 3 5 7 9 8 6 4 2

Printed in the United States of America
on acid-free paper

Acknowledgments

This book is the product of a two-year collaborative research effort by members and associates of the Department of Social Medicine, Harvard Medical School. The effort was supported by funding from the Carnegie Corporation of New York, the MacArthur Foundation, the Rockefeller Foundation, and the Milbank Memorial Fund. We especially wish to thank David Hamburg, Denis Prager, Robert Lawrence, John Evans, Daniel Fox, and Elena Nightingale for their personal contributions to the planning and development of the report. Without their vision, concern, and commitment, there would have been no report. Arthur Kleinman's contributions were supported, in part, by the Guggenheim Foundation, the Center for Advanced Study in the Behavioral Sciences, and the Center's Foundations' Fund for Research in Psychiatry.

Many scholars and policy experts wrote working papers and brief reports, directed us to research, offered advice, read various drafts, questioned our assumptions, and encouraged us to go farther in our work. Without their help, the book could not have been completed. They are too numerous to acknowledge each by name here, but we appreciatively note members of the Advisory Board, consultants to the project, additional readers, and the authors of the various working papers in the appendices. Of the thirty-one members of the Advisory Board, several scholars went beyond the call of duty in helping us to work through the issues and problems posed by the report. We wish to express our sincere gratitude to Veena Das, Mamphela Ramphele, Violet Kimani, Naomar Almeida-Filho, Julio Frenk, Li Shichuo, Sermsri Santhat, and Julius Richmond for their invaluable efforts.

At the World Health Organization in Geneva, Norman Sartorius, John Orley, J.M. Bertolote, Giovanni de Girolamo, Walter Gulbinat, and Anne Yamada of the Division of Mental Health, and Hans Emblad and Mario Argandoña of the Programme on Substance Abuse were instrumental in providing us with data and insights on mental health and substance-abuse issues. Felton Earls, Stanley Tambiah, and William Beardslee helped us to think through issues pertaining to ethnic conflicts and mental health. Chapter 3 builds on a preliminary draft written by Shubhangi Parkar; Chapter 6 is based on a working paper by Alastair Ager. Many of the boxed inserts draw on working papers and brief reports contributed by various scholars (as noted in the appendices). B. D. Colen of the Public Affairs Office at Harvard Medical School helped us to rewrite sections of the manuscript, and Kathleen Much of the Center for Advanced Studies in the Behavioral Sciences offered editorial advice on each chapter. Virginia Angell and Juliana Ekong wrote many of the boxed inserts, and Elizabeth Donnelly and Ann Seymour helped with a range of editorial tasks. Thanks, as well, to Vicki Webster, Susan Grosdov, Anne Fitzgerald-Clark, Joan Gillespie, Peggy Zalvidar, and Amber Crenetz for their assistance in the project's many research and administrative tasks. Finally, we want to express our gratitude to Jeffrey House, vice president, and Susan Hannan, development editor, at Oxford University Press, for their assistance, as well as two anonymous readers for their critical assessments of an earlier draft.

Foreword to World Mental Health Report

"Mental health represents one of the last frontiers in the improvement of the human condition. In the face of wide-spread stigma and inattention, mental health must now be placed on the international agenda." With this bold statement, the report that follows issues a call to action for individuals, communities, governments, and international agencies to take the steps necessary to stem the growing personal and social burdens due to mental illness and behavioral problems, worldwide.

Globally, in developed and developing countries alike, mental illness and health-damaging behaviors exact a tremendous toll in human suffering, evident in the distress and despair of individuals and the anguish of their families, and in social and economic costs due to lost productivity and increased use of medical and welfare services. The tragedy is even greater because much of it could be avoided were we to commit ourselves to applying what we know and learning what we don't about prevention and treatment.

Even those who acknowledge the public health importance of mental illness in industrialized nations all too often dismiss the problem as a relatively unimportant one in the developing world where overall health is so much worse. The information summarized in this volume makes clear just how wrong that position is: Unless we act now, the unprecedented gains over the past 40 years in reducing child mortality, improving physical health, and increasing life expectancy, worldwide, are in jeopardy of being offset by a steady growth in mental and behavioral problems.

A major barrier to progress is the tendency to categorize and label these problems in ways that preclude the most effective action by the most appropriate actors: we identify schizophrenia and depression as mental illness, but we stigmatize the individuals who suffer from them and fail to recognize that they can be treated; we regard alcoholics as ill, yet we dismiss heroin and cocaine users as criminals; we define violence against women (when we acknowledge it at all) as a "criminal justice" issue and see refugees, who now number in the millions, as a "political" problem; we take account of the physical destruction associated with natural disasters but fail to see the enormous psychological harm they cause; and our medical services separate physical from mental problems as if they do not occur at the same time in the same persons, and as if one can be easily separated from the other. As this report makes clear, such labels applied to complex health problems, the epidemic of violence against women, the resurgence of ethnic conflict and forced migration, and the global epidemic of substance abuse obscure their common underlying mental, emotional, and behavioral causes; mask their cumulative societal impacts; and militate against the kind of concertered and coordinated action that will be necessary to reduce those impacts.

This report represents the most comprehensive and authoritative statement to date on the state of mental and behavioral problems around the globe. Guided by a distinguished international editorial board drawn from many countries, the authors have culled essential information from public health and scientific reports published in world literature and from papers prepared by individuals knowledgeable about the nature and magnitude of these problems in their countries and about efforts to address them. The weight of evidence documenting the extraordinary personal and social burdens that mental and behavioral problems impose on all the peoples of the world is balanced by reports of local programs that demonstrate that, by applying what is known or can be found out through research, real progress can be made in ameliorating those burdens through appropriate prevention and treatment. Indeed, that there is humane and effective care for a number of mental health problems is important news that needs to reach many more people in low-income societies.

That is the challenge, the opportunity. Progress will not be made by pretending that these problems don't exist or by labeling them as belonging to someone else. Progress will be made when the world community openly acknowledges them as problems, develops a blueprint for addressing them, and works together in a focused and coordinated way to implement that blueprint.

This report does not attempt to prescribe how to face the challenge or seize the opportunity. That must be determined by those who are closest to the problem as it exists locally. However, the report does represent a compelling call to action. We urge all who read this powerful document to heed that call.

Jimmy and Rosalynn Carter

Contents

WORLD MENTAL HEALTH

Introduction

In the past fifty years, the world beyond North America and Western Europe has seen improvements in health care and living conditions as breathtaking in their sweep as the technological changes experienced in richer areas of the Northern Hemisphere. Average life expectancy in low-income nations such as Zaire, Egypt, and India has risen from forty to sixty-six years; smallpox, which once killed millions of people annually, has been eradicated; average infant mortality rates have fallen from 28% to 10% of live births; and close to half the adults in the world are now literate. Average real incomes have more than doubled, the percentage of rural families with access to safe water has increased from less than 10% to almost 60%, and more than three quarters of children now attend school.[1] Control of water and sewage, effective vaccination campaigns, and the availability of primary health care services have eased the lot of many people. The burden of pain and suffering from chronic diseases such as asthma and diabetes, but also leprosy, epilepsy, and depression, has been lessened by medical interventions. This century has also witnessed the attainment of nationhood by many former colonies, which has meant a marked reduction in the worst of economic and racial abuses in Asia and Africa.

Other positive developments have occurred in economics and technology, in agriculture and health services, in education, and in opportunities for employment. Communication technologies have become readily available to many groups, rich and poor. There have never been greater opportunities to respond to certain problems—infectious diseases for which effective vaccines exist, disabilities that low-level technologies can ameliorate, population control, treatable mental disorders, identifiable behavioral sources of chronic diseases for which behavioral interventions are effective. More is now known about how to mount successful community intervention programs, how to apply technology to improve health and nutrition, and how to formulate useful social and environmental policies than even the wealthiest of nations could have imagined four decades ago.

As for global conflicts, only two decades intervened between the devastation of World War I and the vast destruction of World War II, with 50 million people killed, several hundreds of millions displaced, and entire nations terrorized. Against that history, it is impressive that almost five decades have passed without a similar global conflict. Seen in the context of long-term historical processes, our times have seen many gains, even in impoverished societies. Many societies are now in a posi-

3

tion to improve significantly the quality of life and to advance the human potential of their populations.

But just as in Western Europe and North America, there is a downside to these remarkable improvements in the measures of daily survival and societal function. Along with the increase in life expectancy has come an increase in depression, schizophrenia, dementia, and other forms of chronic mental illness, primarily because more people are living into the age of risk. Along with economic growth and various social transformations have come a marked increase in rates of alcoholism, drug abuse, and suicide. And while there has been declining maternal mortality, the incidence of violence against women, young and old, has increased sharply.

In other words, in many parts of the world economic progress and gains in overall longevity have been accompanied by an increase in the social, psychiatric, and behavioral pathologies that have become a part of daily life in North America and Western Europe. Although poorer countries have made great progress, they are plagued by continued infectious diseases and by chronic medical, mental, and behavioral conditions. Many in these poorer nations face the worst of both worlds: they continue to suffer from high rates of parasitic and infectious diseases at the same time that they are being afflicted by a growing burden of chronic diseases and new social pathologies.

Mental, behavioral, and social health problems are an increasing part of the health burden on all parts of the globe. According to a recent World Bank study, mental health problems (including self-inflicted injuries) are, in the aggregate, one of the largest causes of lost years of quality life, accounting for 8.1% of all such lost years (See Figure I.1).[2] In turn, 34% of all disability is due to behavior-related problems, such as violence, diarrheal diseases, malnutrition, tuberculosis, sexually transmitted diseases, and motor vehicle and other unintentional injuries. Hundreds of millions of women, men, and children suffer from mental illnesses; others experience distress from the consequences of violence, dislocation, poverty, and exploitation. Substance abuse and other behavioral problems affect the lives of countless adolescents, young adults, and the elderly. Women and children suffer an appalling toll of abuse.

Yet despite the importance of these problems, they have received scant attention outside the wealthier, industrialized nations. In many poorer nations, government and health officials recognize the existence of these problems; faced with the choice of reducing deficits or establishing community health programs, they opt for the former. Meanwhile, social and neuropsychiatric problems are missing from the consciousness and official agendas of many international agencies and ministries of health. International agencies and national ministries have shown relative indifference toward mental health issues and, until recently, international health professionals excluded much of this domain from standard assessments of global health. As a result, allocations in national health budgets for preventing and dealing with these problems are disproportionately small in relation to the hazards to human health they represent.

Though the burden of illness resulting from psychiatric and behavioral disorders is enormous, it is grossly underrepresented by conventional public health statistics,

Percentage of DALYs Lost*

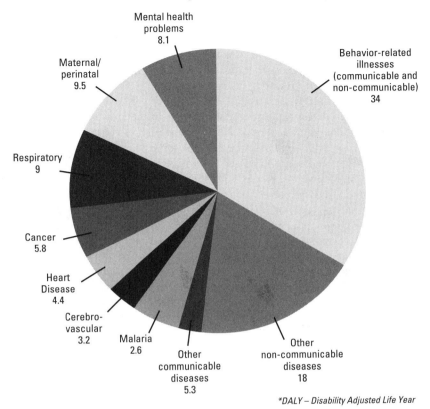

Figure I.1 Global Distribution of Health Burdens, 1990 (*Source*: Adapted from the World Bank, 1993). * DALY = Disability-Adjusted Life Year

which have tended to focus on mortality rather than morbidity or dysfunction. Deaths have traditionally been ascribed to their proximate causes, rather than to the behaviors or underlying disease states that lead to the final crisis; thus, a death is attributed to liver failure, although the underlying cause for the failure is alcoholism. National and international health statistics do not reflect the enormous toll of misery from mental disorders because these conditions are not the immediate cause of death. For instance, even when suicide represents a death due to depression or schizophrenia or drug addiction, it is tabulated as suicide.

Until quite recently, counting deaths was the only way to determine whether public health programs were succeeding. The first challenge was to reduce the number of excess deaths in order to create conditions for a better life. Having accomplished much in this respect, we have been slow to appreciate that greater longevity has been accompanied by an increasing burden of chronic disease and social and behavioral health problems. In part, the increase comes about simply because more people live to later ages, when heart disease, arthritis, stroke, dementia, and other chronic diseases first appear. In part, the increase has resulted from changes in diet, exercise, drinking patterns, drug use, and the like. The new morbidities that have resulted from these changes have brought personal suffering, impairment in role functioning and social relations, diminished quality of life, and the substantial monetary costs associated with mental illness and behavioral problems. (Few studies have mapped the specific economic costs of mental illness, but a recent study by Professor Dorothy Rice estimates that total costs for the United States in 1990 for mental illness were \$148 billion, for alcohol abuse \$99 billion, and for drug abuse \$67 billion.[3] One yardstick for cost comparison is that the cost burden from depression is about the same in the United States as that from heart disease.)[4]

Of course, these problems are not new. But some are more common than they were a century ago, and some have taken on additional force in our time. As for mental illness, the number of persons with major mental illnesses will increase substantially in the decades to come, for two reasons. First, the numbers of men and women living into the ages of risk for certain illnesses are increasing because of changes in demographics. Thus, the number of persons with schizophrenia will increase by 45% between 1985 and the year 2000 because of a 45% increase in the population between age 15 and age 45 the world over.[5] Similarly, there will be a substantial increase in the senile dementias, again by virtue of the increase in the numbers of people living to age 65 and beyond. The second reason for the overall increase in mental illnesses is that rates of depression have increased in recent decades; depression is now being seen at younger ages and in greater frequency in countries as different as Lebanon, Taiwan, the United States, and the nations of Western Europe.[6] Relative risk for depression has increased from one ten-year birth cohort to the next (i.e., those born between 1925 and 1934 versus those born between 1935 and 1944, etc.) by a factor of 1.3 in New Zealand, 1.6 in Taiwan, 1.9 in the United States, and 2.6 in Italy.[7]

In general, mental, social, and behavioral health problems represent overlapping clusters of problems that, connected to the recent wave of global changes and new morbidities, interact so as to intensify each other's effects on behavior and well-being (see Figure I.2). One cluster is made up of substance abuse, violence, abuses of women and children, and the psychiatric sequelae of such aggression. Another cluster links health problems with biological bases such as heart disease, stress, and depression to changes in social behavior, interpersonal support, and personal coping. Clusters such as these are more prevalent and more difficult to cope with in conditions of high unemployment, low income, limited education, stressful work conditions, gender discrimination, unhealthy lifestyle, and human rights violations. These social conditions are influenced by the powerful global transformations of our era. Many conditions, from violence to suicide to the trauma of disaster, as well as certain mental illnesses such as depression, often relate to the same constellation of social forces. Some of the forces are global, some differ by region and by nation. Some are acute crises, others are continuing sources of distress. All work through the local worlds in which we live—communities, neighborhoods, networks—to affect lives and relationships.

World Mental Health represents the first systematic attempt to survey the burden of suffering related to these clusters of problems. It brings together information

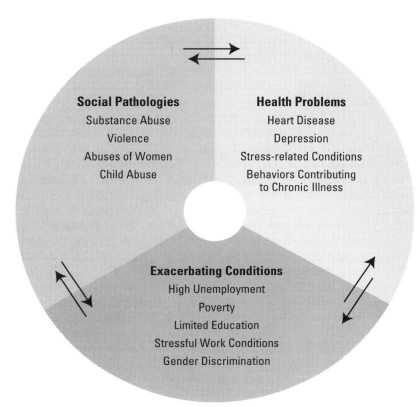

Figure I.2 Model of Overlapping Clusters of Problems

on mental illness and behavioral disorders, on behavior (normal or abnormal) that influences health and the potential for human development, and on the promotion of mental health as defined by the World Health Organization. There is no single "mental illness." Rather, there are many different ones, such as schizophrenia, depression, and dementia, each with its own symptoms and signs. Mental health is not simply the absence of detectable mental disease but a state of well-being in which the individual realizes his or her own abilities, can work productively and fruitfully, and is able to contribute to her or his community.

The book also examines the personal and social sequelae of suicide and substance abuse and considers the social and cultural aspects of these problems. It reviews the mental and social health consequences of violence and dislocation. And it identifies the concerns of certain groups—particularly children, women, the elderly, minority populations, and poor communities—that are especially at risk for these problems. We do not develop a systematic analysis of the social origins of psychiatric and social morbidity, in part because there is no single theory to account for such morbidity, and in part because we believe that the various problems at issue relate to a diverse range of political, cultural, and social forces.

To best attend to this diversity, this book provides local examples of the myriad problems and describes global patterns and international linkages of problems and solutions. It shows how people in different settings deal with these problems and points to concrete opportunities for developing more appropriate interventions. It also reviews local strengths and discusses how they can be further developed.

Rather than being simply a compilation of statistics, this volume includes case studies as illustrations of how seemingly small interventions, and efforts that appear minor when viewed in a global context, can have an important impact on the lives of individuals. For example, a program that did something as basic as teaching the proper disposal of solid human waste dramatically reduced infant illness in a village in Bangladesh; the reduction contributed to the mental health of families by reducing suffering and saving lives. As another example, the commercialization of beer drinking in areas of central Africa has led to the erosion of age-old social customs and the widespread abuse of alcohol, with its associated violence and other negative consequences. We refer to problems in specific societies not to find fault, but rather to illustrate situations that many regions face and to identify ways of confronting them. Indeed, the fact that such data exist shows that some governments are actively confronting these problems.

The primary focus of this book is low-income countries in Africa, Latin America, Asia, and the Pacific. However, since mental health and associated problems are shared by all societies, it is important to understand their human costs in suffering and their financial costs, and to develop programs for dealing with them worldwide. If we are to find such broad solutions, we need a domain of policy that draws on the social sciences as much as it does on the health sciences, and that applies what we have learned about mental health to both low-income and high-income societies.

Throughout our analysis, we emphasize the social context in which mental and behavioral health problems occur, the suffering they produce, and the consequences for the health of individuals and populations. In emphasizing social context, we do not imply that social problems are the sole or even the principal cause of mental disorders. There was a time of simplistic sloganeering and grandiose claims for mental health as the lever for social change, claims that have left a residue of distrust. We disavow those slogans.

Social context cannot be ignored, however. Indeed, a brain disorder like epilepsy can run in families, can result from a cyst caused by a parasite, or can be produced by a scar left by a blow to the head. Whether the infection is treated before it leads to epilepsy, whether the blow occurs because of a civil riot, or whether the family can obtain anticonvulsant treatment for the children and thus avoid complications, all are influenced by social factors, though none is the immediate cause of the disease. We call attention to social context despite acknowledging that psychiatrists and other mental health workers have no specific expertise in avoiding war or ending poverty. Nonetheless, the connection between the social context and public health is real; it must be acknowledged; it can be studied and there is a growing knowledge base to guide interventions; and citizens and leaders in all countries must address such problems if we are to do more than apply bandages to gaping wounds. As the report published in this volume demonstrates, there are points of entry.

Contents of the Report

In the twelve chapters, we review the range of mental health and behavioral problems, the major social challenges of violence and displacement, and the problems of special populations (women, children, and the elderly). We examine the issue at three levels: the individual, the community, and the greater society.

Chapter 1 explores the social, political, and economic forces contributing to the increase in the worldwide incidence of mental health problems. It examines the interaction of local, national, and global events, and it provides the conceptual framework necessary to begin to understand the impact of the major social transformations of our time on communities and individuals. Through the examination of local, seemingly isolated, events and problems, we demonstrate how, even when global forces are similar, local outcomes differ because of the particular histories and realities of a population. At the local level, combinations of class, gender, age, ethnicity, and political factions place some persons in the category of victim in some communities, whereas the same characteristics provide protection in other communities.

In Chapter 2, we consider the extent of the burden resulting from the major mental illnesses, including schizophrenia, depressive disorders, dementia, and the anxiety disorders. It has been estimated that two common types of mental illness—depressive disorders and anxiety disorders—account for 20%–30% of all primary care visits worldwide. If they are neither recognized nor treated effectively, these illnesses lead to avoidable suffering and repeated, fruitless, and costly medical visits. A review of the data suggests that there are effective treatments that can help to overcome social stigma and neglect. The development of appropriate services, laws, and policies for low-income countries is our emphasis.

Chapter 3 examines the patterns of suicide, which vary greatly among societies. The fact that suicide is on the increase in many transitional societies may be an important indicator of the negative impact of a myriad of sociopolitical changes, and, as such, requires careful interpretation. Is suicide an index of social or moral decay, an unavoidable "downside" of development, or the result of some other play of forces? Research suggests that many acts of suicide are deeply related to social stresses that trouble people, many of whom have limited political resources to ward off these troubles. Fortunately, there are potentially effective interventions for this problem.

In Chapter 4, we survey the burden of alcohol and drug abuse, which has severe consequences for mortality, morbidity, and social breakdown. For example, the Pan American Health Organization estimates that substance abuse is the underlying leading cause of adult mortality and related violence and injury in Latin America (see Table I.1). Thus, attempts to control substance abuse and to cope with its ravages are central to the overall well-being of the population of Latin America (roughly 9% of the world's population). There and elsewhere, substance abuse is often rooted in social problems and often associated with corruption and organized criminality. We examine the varying patterns of substance abuse around the world, comparing areas in which it is and is not a major problem, and programs that do and do not appear to be successful.

Table I.1 Population, Number of Deaths, and Crude Death Rates in Latin America, 1985–2000

Population and Causes of Death for the Region and Its Subregion	Number of Deaths			Crude Death Rate (per 100,000)		
	1985	2000	Percent Change	1985	2000	Percent Change
	Latin America & the Caribbean					
Population	**248,563,000**	**336,672,000**	35.4			
Nutritional deficiencies	19,349	26,016	34.5	7.8	7.7	−1.3
Cerebrovascular disease	90,822	137,887	51.8	36.5	41.0	12.3
Cirrhosis	33,733	53,695	59.2	13.6	16.0	17.6
Suicide	8,364	11,836	41.5	3.9	4.1	5.1
Motor vehicle accidents	39,864	58,513	46.8	18.7	20.3	8.6
Homicide	42,077	64,318	52.9	19.6	22.2	13.3
Total of above causes	**234,209**	**352,265**	**50.4**	**100.1**	**111.3**	**11.2**

Source: Levav et al., 1989.

Chapter 5 considers the public health consequences of the violence that arises from political oppression, civil war, and widespread trauma in a range of societies. By discussing this violence in a social health context we seek neither to trivialize it nor to medicalize its origins. Rather, we believe that it is necessary to understand the political and cultural forces that maintain it. The task is to consider violence as a broad social problem, with traumatic effects that are collective as well as personal, not one that health professionals can manage alone.

The violence considered in Chapter 5 contributes to displacement and the refugee experience, the subjects of Chapter 6. Ninety percent of the more than 20 million refugees in the world live in Africa, Asia, and Latin America; as many as two-thirds may be suffering from post-traumatic stress disorder and related conditions. In Chapter 6 our major focus shifts from local scenes to national and international forces whose control requires an entirely different level of response: we consider the displacement that results from political and ethnic violence, natural disasters, and economic deprivation. In general, the problems reviewed in Chapter 6— and throughout the volume—have become central to discussions of peace, security, protection of the environment, and human rights, as well as to the development of effective international structures to control societal breakdown and international conflicts. To engage this subject effectively, however, the notion that trauma is rooted in individuals or individual families must give way to an understanding of the collective impact of social harms.

Chapter 7 is devoted to a consideration of the well-being of children and youth. Children in economically marginal areas are three to five times more likely to suffer from epilepsy or mental retardation than are their counterparts in wealthier areas. Conduct disorders and adolescent delinquency are prevalent in the world today. In many nations, children continue to be exploited economically and sexually. In areas of Latin America, Africa, and Asia, millions of children live in the streets, foraging for survival.

Chapters 8 and 9 are devoted to a discussion of the special needs of two groups at particular risk—women and the elderly. Epidemiologic and anthropological data informing the prevalence of psychological distress are presented in their social context. Quite often women's suffering originates in the marked gender inequalities characteristic of most poor countries and the many disadvantages that follow from low social status. These disadvantages include a disproportionately heavy burden of work; sexual, reproductive, and other forms of violence; and discriminatory practices that result in denied access to valuable, but scarce, resources (such as education, employment, food, and the benefits of economic development). We conclude that health policies that address the negative consequences of gender inequalities for women's mental and physical well-being as well as "healthy" policies designed to empower women and enhance their social status, provide the two essential components of initiatives directed toward the improvement of women's lives.

The growth in elderly populations in the world and social changes in the care of the aged point to increased needs for mental health care in this population. For example, the number of demented elderly in Africa, Asia, and Latin America (estimated at 25 million in 1990) may exceed 80 million by 2025.[8] Specific steps can be taken by governments and communities to enhance the psychological and social welfare of the elderly, as well as that of children and women.

Chapter 10 returns to the larger question of the social, cultural, and behavioral determinants of well-being. We focus here on the ways in which culturally shaped behaviors, such as smoking, sexual practices, and diet, can contribute to poor health. Behavior contributes to general health and mental health so closely that they must be considered together. In Chapter 10 we also discuss behaviors that place populations and individuals at risk for parasitic and other infectious diseases. These are areas in which changes in behavior can have a positive impact on health. But they are also areas in which behavior is so inseparable from social, cultural, and political dynamics that we consider social (rather than simply individual) behavior as the primary target for treatment, prevention, and policy programs.

In the final chapters of this report we draw together the chief conclusions from our review to examine their policy and research implications. Chapters 11 and 12 define a series of issues so that discussions about what needs to be done may begin among researchers, practitioners, policy experts, and administrators (national and international). Our review demonstrates that alongside the great pressure of lasting troubles is evidence of local strengths, promising projects, and innovative responses. The problems in societies with constrained resources are serious and sometimes overwhelming, but there are local initiatives, some of them greatly impressive, as many existing programs suggest. And there is much that can be done by international agencies if they give mental health the priority it deserves and the financial resources it requires. What is needed beyond specific policy recommendations is an international campaign that raises the priority of mental health problems and policies at both the local and global levels.

The agenda for essential research, outlined in the final chapter, raises questions that provide a next step in the development of international mental, behavioral, and social health as a substantial subject matter. We outline a domain of inquiry that can be the basis for the development of international policy centers and research programs throughout the world. Although much of the expertise in the past has come from North America and Western Europe, there is now a critical mass of researchers in some countries in Asia, Africa, Latin America, and the Pacific. Strengthening the capacity for research essential to improving mental and social health must become a major goal for the 1990s.

The social aspects of mental health raise a question about human rights. To what degree are mental and social well-being a fundamental human right? What policies at international and local levels can best promote the most promising human conditions? Which actions, programs, and traditions—from austerity programs to gender inequalities—impede a person's or a community's quest for health and the development of human potential?

Obviously, no government can guarantee health to each of its citizens (for one thing, most hereditary disorders are not detectable before birth nor curable by present methods). What citizens can claim is a right to an environment compatible with health and a right to decent care when illness occurs. Such an environment is one where the air is breathable and the water drinkable, and one where shelter is available, where each person is free from assault and treated with respect, and where the community provides health care to all with illness and suffering. Those ideals have yet to be attained in many countries of the world; this report insists that none of us can rest secure until these basic human rights have been assured for all. Asserting the right to a healthy environment and to decent care does not assure universal respect for these rights. But it does establish a standard against which these rights can be measured, and toward which men and women of goodwill the world over can strive.

We have written this report for a broad and diverse audience, from ministers of health to officials of nongovernmental organizations to participants in international policy discussions and to citizens broadly. We address a broad audience in order to launch a debate over issues that, in the past, have never been considered within a single framework. Previously, discussions of physical and mental health, social well-being, economic development, international security, and human rights have followed distinct and isolated paths.

The time has come to develop a forum in which these issues are seen as being inextricably linked. It is counterproductive to evaluate development programs without considering their impact on the quality of life in the community. We can no longer maintain strict, artificial divisions between physical and mental well-being.

We hope this report, which ultimately is more a provocation to action than a final word on the subject, contributes to the creation of such a forum by proposing a series of initiatives that can help to change the ways we think about health and prosperity. These initiatives can also make a substantial difference to the lives of many. What is needed is the political will to put them into effect.

1

The Global Context of Well-Being

World mental health is first and foremost a question of economic and political welfare. Although the links between social forces and ill health are complex and varied, close inspection suggests that mental health concerns almost always relate to more general concerns that have to do with the economic welfare of a family or community, the environment in which a person lives, and the kinds of resources that he or she can draw upon. In general, enduring political and economic structures—both within and between societies—contribute to the perpetuation of poverty, hunger, and despair. Demographic and environmental pressures spark regional and intrastate conflicts, which in turn lead to personal trauma, social demoralization, and dislocation. And the mental health problems associated with natural disasters, environmental scarcities, urbanization, and physical illness generally take a greater toll on poorer communities because of a lack of programs and services to lessen their impact. At first glance, these pressures and problems might appear to have distinct origins and histories. But a closer review suggests that they typically relate to the economic and political disadvantages facing poor communities in the world today.

Economic and Political Concerns

The 1980s, a time of true global interdependence, was a lost decade for many economically disadvantaged countries. Despite consistent reductions in mortality rates and other disease burdens, a marked deterioration in living conditions occurred in many countries. In several regions, most notably Latin America and sub-Saharan Africa, advances in health care and education eroded. Unemployment rates rose in many parts of the world, as did the global poverty rate. By 1989, one out of five people was living in "absolute poverty," which the World Bank defines as suffering from malnutrition to the point of being unable to work.[1] By the end of the 1980s, low-income countries had accumulated a debt of 1.3 trillion.[2] Crippled by massive debt burdens, many countries saw their growth rates slow and living standards decrease. For every $100 that Africans earned in 1977, they made about $82 in 1992.[3] Several other regions, most notably Latin America, the Caribbean, the Middle East, and North Africa, also saw their GNPs per capita decline since 1980 (see Table 1.1).

World Mental Health

Table 1.1 GNP Per Capita and Growth of GNP Per Capita

Country Group	1991 GNP Per Capita ($ U.S.)	Average Annual Growth of GNP Per Capita (%)					
		1965–73	1973–80	1980–90	1989	1990	1991[a]
Low-and Middle-income Economies	**1,010**	**4.3**	**2.7**	**1.2**	**1.1**	**−0.1**	**−2.1**
Low-income economies	350	2.5	2.6	4.0	2.9	2.9	2.1
Middle-income economies	2,480	—	—	0.5	0.7	−1.0	−3.4
Severely indebted	2,320	5.2	3.4	−0.8	−0.6	−5.4	−2.5
Sub-Saharan Africa[b]	350	1.7	0.9	−1.3	0.5	−1.4	−0.6
East Asia and the Pacific	650	5.0	4.8	6.2	4.5	5.3	5.0
South Asia	320	1.2	1.7	3.2	2.9	3.3	−0.7
Europe	2,670	—	—	1.4	1.4	−2.7	−9.8
Latin America and the Caribbean	2,390	4.6	2.2	−0.4	−1.1	−1.4	1.7
Middle East & North Africa	1,940	6.0	1.7	−2.5	−0.2	−0.2	−1.3
High-income Economies	**20,570**	**3.7**	**2.1**	**2.3**	**2.7**	**1.6**	**0.3**
OECD members	21,020	3.8	2.1	2.3	2.7	1.6	0.1
World	**4,010**	**2.8**	**1.3**	**1.2**	**1.6**	**0.5**	**−0.1**

[a] World Bank Projections.

[b] Excludes South Africa.

Source: Adapted from World Bank, 1993a:199.

Impoverished countries have not fared much better in the 1990s. Economic growth among low-income countries was weak at the start of this decade, and GNP per capita has actually declined.[4] The deterioration in living standards and a continuing increase in the global population have led to unprecedented poverty. More than one billion people in the world still lack adequate food, clean water, elementary education, and basic health care.

Despite the economic disparities between countries like Zambia and the United States, the greatest inequalities are often found *within* the borders of certain nation-states. In countries of both low and middle-range GNPs, stark economic disparities divide rich and poor social groups. In Brazil, for instance, the top 20% earn 26 times what the bottom 20% earn.[5] More often than not, global economic policies reinforce the economic status of the richest peoples of a nation-state.

The economic weakening of poor countries and communities in the last fifteen years is linked to a range of global economic forces. An overall downslide of productivity growth in industrial countries, and the current global economic slowdown, have impaired the markets of some countries and limited the aid available to them. Failed economic policies in a range of low- and middle-income countries led to a situation in which governments could not afford to fund schools, clinics, or services of any kind. The international "debt crisis" of the early 1980s, the domestic austerity programs implemented to tame the crisis, and the sharp rise in real interest rates have limited the growth potential of many nations. The abundance of low-wage labor in many countries is being countered by a sluggish world demand for manufacturing and a steady reduction in the relative importance of labor costs in manufacturing. Real food prices in Asia, Africa, and Latin America have generally increased, whereas the price of raw materials—a main source of revenue for many societies—has fallen sharply. Between 1980 and 1987, for instance, the prices of 33 raw materials fell by 40% on average.[6] The fall in prices led to a deterioration of terms of trade between rich and poor countries, with net financial resource flows reversing in direction. Until 1984, industrial countries lent more money to their "underdeveloped" counterparts than they took back in interest and principal payments. The flow then reversed, so that by 1988, countries of the "South" (Latin America, the Caribbean, Africa, Central and South Asia, and the Pacific islands) were paying those of the "North" (Western Europe, Russia, Japan, the United States, Canada, and Australia) $50 billion a year.[7]

Some regions, such as East and Southeast Asia, are dealing with the challenge quite successfully. In part as a result of industrial, export-oriented economies, political stability, and significant educational opportunities, the countries of these regions (including coastal China) are growing economically at the fastest rate in the world, and they are redefining international development and global economic relations. This economic boom has resulted in improved educational and health services; in Taiwan, for instance, it has led to a substantial expansion of the mental health care system.[8]

In contrast, other regions, such as sub-Saharan Africa and impoverished parts of Latin America, face a deterioration of living standards. For these poor regions, the ability to improve their economies is limited by economic stagnation, a paucity of resources, and dependence on industrial and postindustrial economies. Commodity prices are expected to remain near present low levels, and the need for inexpensive manual labor will probably decrease in the coming years. In fact, the manufacturing services that many industrializing countries possess are growing increasingly obsolete. As Head notes, many impoverished countries are "condemned for the foreseeable future to pursue outmoded, low-valued economic activity of a kind that is increasingly irrelevant to world market demand."[9]

The irrelevance of economic activity in many African countries underscores the fact that these countries are largely dependent on forces "exogenous" to their economies: the principal elements of the global economic environment—industrial-country growth, world trade, real interest rates, and commodity prices—largely *affect* poor countries but are largely *unaffected* by them.[10] These countries can wield several bargaining chips, from oil prices to debt defaults to "debt-for-environment" swaps, but they are generally unable to damage richer economies without doing significant harm to their own interests.[11] The irony is that, in general, when local production decisions are not dependent on world markets, local economies prosper; but when decisions are dependent on world markets, they can be disastrous for producers. Lacking political or economic clout, poor countries have largely been reduced to petitioning for assistance.

It is becoming increasingly difficult for these countries to replace traditional sources of external finance. During the Cold War, most nations could count on drawing financial or military support from either the United States or the Soviet Union if the support was seen to be in the security interests of the superpowers. In the 1990s, however, the United States has not been inclined to beef up the economy of a country outside of its immediate region, and the former Soviet Union lacks the resources to do so. Although the United States is still quite concerned with political instabilities in Central America, and the European Community is compelled by its own self-interest to assist market transitions in Eastern Europe, the bulk of Africa and parts of South Asia have lost superpower support except for basic humanitarian aid. As for such aid, the World Bank warns, "donors now find it less expedient to overlook economic mismanagement and poor governance by recipient countries."[12]

The prudence is not bad in itself. Several countries that have demonstrated successful economic reforms (such as Mexico and Argentina) point to the need for reforms in the economic and political machinery of other countries. With reform comes the hope of renewed growth and investments. In fact, there are signs that capital investments in low- and middle-income countries are beginning to increase substantially, with investments going to private industries much more than to government projects.[13]

Although the need for sustained economic prosperity is crucial to well-being, most countries, even those receiving foreign aid, have not been able to reduce poverty on a significant scale, because of internal instabilities and inadequate command over resources. Several studies have found that economic slowdowns hinder poor nations most, and within those countries, have a magnified impact on poor people.[14] For example, the largest fall in incomes in Latin America in the 1980s occurred in the urban informal sector, where extremely poor families are concentrated.[15] Children and women are particularly affected by economic downturns and accompanying declines in average per capita income.[16] Poor people were also disproportionately hurt by the "structural adjustment" measures that countries with heavy debt burdens undertook in the 1980s; case studies show a deterioration in general health, education, and living standards since the adoption of such measures.[17] Governments, international banks, and nongovernmental agencies are paying heed to this situation. Faced with the difficulty of improving the economic status of a society without harming its poorest members, they are trying to launch programs that promote economic development without causing more poverty and distress.

The general political context in which these efforts are being enacted is quite different from what it was ten years ago. Today, international politics and policies hinge less on tensions between communism and capitalism (and the various economic and political repercussions that these tensions produced) than on a complex range of economic and political links and tensions between wealthy nation-states of the North and impoverished ones of the South. The significance of this new political axis was most evident at the "Earth Summit" in Rio de Janeiro in the summer of 1992, where participants met to develop a concerted international policy on pressing environmental concerns. The Summit exposed the problems that must be faced in developing international policies in the next century: the emergence of regional economic superpowers (Western Europe, the Pacific Rim, and North America) that define the economic activities of lesser powers in those regions, the interdependence and lasting inequality between rich and poor nations, and the need to develop a working relationship between different nation-states that goes beyond the needs and welfare of individual governments.

Many issues on the international agenda now flow across borders largely outside of state control. These problems, along with the growing importance of global economic markets and transnational corporations and communications, are diminishing the autonomy of the nation-state as a bounded, sovereign entity. States are becoming more permeable, international allegiances shift with the economic tides, and nationalist movements in Eastern Europe and Africa are threatening the traditional (and often arbitrary) borders that divide nation-states. The concept of the nation-state as we have known it is increasingly anachronistic, with the Rio Summit pointing to the need for policies based on transnational concerns and global interdependence.

Poverty, Hunger, and Malnutrition

Given that one-fifth of the world's population—an estimated one billion people—lives in abject poverty, the current global economic slowdown, which is projected to continue, bodes ill. Poverty of such magnitude takes a considerable toll on the well-being of its victims. It creates the conditions for malnutrition, illness, social strife, political instability, and despair.

Although urban poverty is growing, the rural poor still account for over 80% of the total number of poor people in the world.[18] The largest number of these live in Asia (some 633 million), followed by 204 million in sub-Saharan Africa, 76 million in Latin America and the Caribbean, and the rest in the Near East and North Africa. The groups most vulnerable to rural poverty are smallholder farmers, the landless, nomadic pastoralists, ethnic populations, small-scale fishermen, displaced and refugee populations, and households headed by women. The rural poor face problems of reduced access to fuel, weak infrastructure, seasonal unemployment, a lack of education and training, and isolation. They are vulnerable to exploitation, disease, natural calamities, drought, acute regional food shortages, and famine. Because they lack productive assets and suffer from physical weakness and illness, population pressures, and powerlessness, poor people, like poor countries, almost always stay poor.

Poverty translates into hunger and malnutrition. Though the farms of Asia, Africa, and Latin America produce more than half of the grain harvested in the world, at least half a billion people in those regions lack enough food to eat, and thus live with chronic energy deficiencies; another half-billion live at constant risk of hunger.[19] About 15 million people die each year of hunger, and malnutrition affects the lives of almost 24% of the global population each day.[20] The great majority of the hungry live in rural areas; many of these are children. Serious protein-energy malnutrition is pervasive among preschool children in countries such as Bangladesh, Bhutan, Botswana, Nepal, and Zambia. In Nepal, for instance, 50% to 75% percent of children under five suffer from some degree of protein and calorie deficiency.[21] The World Bank estimates that the total direct and indirect damage from malnutrition is at least 20%–25% of the disease burden in children, and at least 4%–5% of that for the general population of the world.[22]

Some of the hunger and malnutrition is caused by famines, which are typically due to poverty, landlessness, and sudden surges in the price of food, rather than to shortages of food. As the economist Amartya Sen notes, it is the loss of the ability of people to obtain food to which they are "entitled" that is responsible for most famine, not overall shortage of potentially available food.[23] Famines wreak havoc with the human, social, and economic welfare of impoverished countries, but even more devastating are the consequences of day-to-day hunger. Prolonged hunger and malnutrition can result in chronic energy and protein deficiencies, inactivity, disease, cognitive impairments, constraints on normal child development, stress, and demoralization.

Malnutrition during pregnancy can result in congenital abnormalities that directly affect the central nervous system or result in conspicuous cosmetic abnormalities and/or physical disabilities. Iodine deficiency, one of the most common microdeficiency states worldwide, can, during pregnancy, result in cretinism, a condition in which the newborn suffers from irreversible mental retardation and neurological impairment. Early malnutrition can lead to attentional deficits, which can contribute to problems in behavior and academic performance later in life. Iron-deficiency anemia, for instance, can affect cognition and behavior by decreasing the ability of the child to attend to his or her environment, which can lead to a kind of functional isolation of the child. Malnutrition can also exacerbate the medical consequences of substance abuse.

The phenomenology of hunger is complicated by local political and social realities. In her ethnographic study of a Brazilian *favela*, the American anthropologist Nancy Scheper-Hughes shows how the local medical category of *nervos* or "nerves," is used to interpret the bodily and psychological distress associated with chronic hunger.[24] Local physicians treat the symptoms of *nervos* with psychotropic and other medications but fail to address the sources of the problem: chronic hunger resulting from extreme poverty.

Chronic hunger occurs in the context of tremendous uncertainty about the future. At stake is life itself or the lives of family members or neighbors, a fact that can cause continued stress. When large segments of the population are threatened by death due to famine and starvation, uprooting and mass migration, mass violence, and the breakdown of local moral, social, and economic structures can ensue. Wherever chronic hunger becomes endemic, demoralization can result.[25] "Even if you work 24 hours a day in Nepal, you do not get enough to eat," says Manju, a 20-year-old Nepalese woman who works as a prostitute in Bombay.[26] "One can endure anything except hunger. If I were a man, maybe I would have committed murder to fill my stomach. But as a woman, I became a prostitute."

Box 1.1 Forced Labor

Most people believe that slavery was abolished from the face of the earth decades ago. Anti-Slavery International reports, however, that there may be as many as 200 million people who work in conditions of forced labor.[27] Almost half of these are children. Some are chattel slaves, viewed, in places like Mauritania, as pieces of property to be bought, sold, and used as their "owners" see fit. Others, in places like Haiti and the Dominican Republic, are forced laborers, made to work in deplorable conditions for substandard wages. Still others are captives of the practice of debt bondage, in which a creditor unscrupulously makes it impossible for the debtor to pay off his debt, and thus retains the services of the debtor or his family indefinitely.

In India, for instance, poor villagers are often recruited by the promise of well-paying jobs. Once at their place of employment, they must borrow money for food, rent, and whatever tools they need to work. They immediately fall into debt. The wage is not as good as promised, and barely enough to pay for food, making it impossible to repay the debt. To make matters worse, the employer often levies a high interest rate and may falsely increase the debt by doctoring the loan documents. The laborers are not allowed to leave until the debt is paid and can be killed for trying to escape. In addition, they are subject to severe beatings, torture, and rape if they displease their employer. Upon the death of an adult bonded laborer, his children inherit the debt and must continue to work to pay it off.

Bonded laborers are among the poorest people in their countries; they are plagued by hunger and malnutrition. They often work twelve-hour days at physically demanding jobs, under the constant threat of violence. Many live in crowded, unsanitary conditions that are conducive to the spread of disease. They are under enormous stress, which is strongly associated with behavioral and emotional disturbances. In addition, the disruption of family ties and traditional values removes important social supports necessary for stability. Bonded laborers and their families are thus highly susceptible to mental distress and physical disease. They have no easy access to a doctor and are usually unable to afford her services or the drugs she may prescribe. Indeed, bonded laborers may have some of the worst morbidity and mortality rates in the world.

Anti-Slavery International estimates that there are more than 35 million bonded laborers in the world today, in places as diverse as Haiti, South Africa, Brazil, Chile, Bolivia, the Dominican Republic, Pakistan, and the United States. In most of these countries, including India, debt bondage is illegal. In spite of official prohibition, however, the practice continues to thrive.

One reason for the survival of debt bondage is that it is a profitable practice that supplies employers with cheap labor. A second reason is the existence of millions of people living in extreme poverty, too destitute to refuse an offer that may help provide food—even an offer that might lead to debt bondage. There are few alternatives for those who are illiterate, having worked full-time before they were old enough to have completed the first few years of school.

Several solutions have been suggested to halt debt bondage and forms of forced labor. If governments are to limit these practices, they will need to enforce antislavery laws and institute strong penalties for offenders. They will also need to help the poor by providing agricultural subsidies and low-interest loans and otherwise attempting to stimulate the domestic economy. And they will need to make provisions for free and compulsory education of all children, with special attention paid to the children of those enslaved by such practices. Finally, the international community can help limit bondage and forced-labor practices by refusing to buy products from companies that depend on such practices in the production of goods.[28]

Urbanization and Social Change

Seventy-nine percent of the population of Addis Ababa lives in extreme poverty; roughly half of the urban population in "developing" countries live at the level of extreme poverty.[29] Although poverty as measured by low income tends to be at its worst in rural areas, poor city-dwellers suffer more than rural households from certain aspects of poverty.

The number of people living in urban settings and the extent of poverty in cities have been rising at unprecedented rates. As a result of high fertility rates, falling death rates, and rapid cityward migration, most countries in Asia, Africa, Latin America, and the Pacific have been transformed from rural to urban societies in two to three decades, which suggests an astonishing rate of social change. Between 1950 and 1985, the portion of the population living in urban areas on these continents doubled. By the year 2000, nearly half of the population in these regions will reside in urban areas, and 50 of the world's 66 largest cities—each with more than 4 million inhabitants—will be in these regions. In cities of this sort live an estimated 100 million homeless adults and perhaps as many as 80 million homeless children, many of whom sleep on the street. During the 1990s alone, cities in poor countries of the world will grow by an aggregate of over 160,000 persons per day, with much of the growth due to population increases rather than rural-urban migration. Several megacities dominate this urban landscape. Mexico City, for instance, contained 3.1 million inhabitants in 1950 but should exceed 24 million by the end of this decade (which was the total population of Mexico as a whole in the 1950s). São Paulo, which held 2.8 million people in 1950, is expected to reach the same mark by the year 2000. At present, 150 cities in the developing world contain a million or more residents (there were 31 in 1950), with a projected 279 in the year 2000.

Since urbanization in Latin America, Asia, Africa, and the Pacific has generally occurred without any surge in prosperity through industrialization, there is considerable urban poverty in the major cities of these regions. Almost half the residents live in unplanned and illegal settlements, in substandard housing and environmental conditions. The residents of "slums" or "shantytowns" face uncertain prospects for employment and the threat of eviction, as well as a lack of sanitation, clean drinking water, and basic hygiene. Many work in the informal sectors of urban economies, and approximately 10% of the labor force in many cities is unemployed at any given time. The percentage of people who are underemployed is undoubtedly much higher.

A lack of financial resources, infrastructure, and basic services need not translate into apathy, anomie, or social disintegration. Many poor urban communities are locally organized and relate, in complex ways, to the political economy of the larger urban environment. One way that poor urban communities vary is in the ways they deal with crowded, cramped conditions. Early research tended to argue that crowded living conditions unequivocally led to stress and mental distress. More recent work suggests, in contrast, that a variety of cultural and social factors affect how communities deal with dense living conditions. In some communities, for instance, crowded households do not necessarily translate into stressful conditions because families (particularly children) spend a great deal of time outdoors. What seems to matter most is the quality of life in urban settings, which often hinges on the strength of social and familial ties: children who live in crowded urban settings risk being marginalized to some extent, and single male factory workers who bed down in "sleeping hotels" in India (where they rent a room for one-third of a day to sleep) risk social isolation.

In general, poor urban residents are less healthy than those living in more prosperous settings. Researchers through the years have attempted to determine rural-urban differences in rates of mental illness and the reasons for these differences. Neither rural nor urban domicile alone is a reliable predictor of mental health, but poverty is.

Recent research in Brazil, for instance, has tried to clarify the links between residence, economic status, and mental health. Mari, working in the city of São Paulo, Brazil, where spots of high income and modernity coexist with shantytowns and slums, found that poor families living in irregular housing showed higher psychiatric morbidity than those living in better conditions.[30] And Santana found that the lower the income of residents of a poor-income district of Salvador, Brazil, the higher the prevalence of psychiatric morbidity, especially for neurotic and psychosomatic disturbances.[31]

These studies suggest that poverty is one of the prime indicators of mental illness. Indeed, recent research suggests that one's changing economic situation is a better indicator of well-being than any social changes that one might undergo. Earlier research theorized that forms of social change or acculturation, as brought on by rural-urban migration, led to increased mental distress. Although situations of cultural instability or rapid and involuntary social change (as encountered by refugees) show such a correlation, more recent data suggest that employment status is a better indicator of well-being than the residential changes involved with relocation. In several studies conducted in Bahia, Brazil, for instance, the Brazilian psychiatrist Naomar Almeida-Filho has found that employment status is a clearer indicator of psychiatric morbidity than residential status.[32] Although migrants were more distressed than nonmigrants in 1982, the reason for their distress related more to lack of stable work than to where they lived. "Displaced" people, belonging to the urban reserve army of labor, had higher levels of stress than did people who held jobs in the formal labor market. In 1993, however, the situation was reversed, at least for lower-class men: men who held jobs in the formal economy suffered more neurotic disorders than those working in the informal sector. Almeida-Filho theorizes that profound changes in Brazilian economic life between the times of the two studies account for the shift. Whereas the formal sector was a more secure and prosperous place to work in the early 1980s in view of the exploitative and impoverished conditions of underemployed labor forces at that time, a decade later the formal sector had lower earnings and opportunities and was under greater social control and pressure compared to being part of the more dynamic informal sector of the economy. The informal sector now offers a "protective" function that the formal sector no longer does.

Occupation and income, as well as age, gender, education, social mobility, and ethnicity, thus appear to be more important for psychiatric disorder than whether one lives in a rural or urban setting.[33] Indeed, recent studies of psychiatric morbidity in urban settings demonstrate that certain groups within these settings—the urban poor, exploited workers, uneducated women and men, the homeless, street children, and the elderly—are more at risk than others. Women are especially vulnerable; several studies show that women in urban settings typically suffer more distress than men.[34] Given that women work long hours for little compensation and head the majority of families in slum settings, the poor mental health of women appears to be intimately tied to their social and economic status. The "feminization of poverty" currently sweeping the globe will therefore probably lead to greater psychological distress among women (see Chapter 8).

Though poverty is linked to mental ill-health, economic prosperity does not translate directly into either personal or social well-being. Epidemiological data on adolescents from Western Europe and the United States in the past fifty years show an increase in psychosocial disorders (antisocial behavior, alcohol and drug abuse, depression, suicide, and eating disorders) during the very time interval (1950–1973) when social and economic conditions were improving most rapidly.[35] In the past forty years, crimes per capita increased on average by a factor of five, although variations between countries should be noted. Over the same interval, alcohol consumption has increased markedly. Although alcohol consumption and alcohol abuse are not identical, substantial evidence demonstrates that as total consumption increases, alcohol-related disorders increase. Epidemiologic surveys in the United States show an enormous increase in the use of illicit drugs during that period; European data, though less comprehensive, are similar. Rates of depression among adolescents showed a steady increase, as did suicide rates in the United States and most European countries (with the exception of West Germany) between 1970 and 1980.

The challenge to conventional wisdom is the increase in disorders during a time interval when living conditions were improving, even though cross-sectional data show that social disadvantage per se is associated with disorder. Affluence itself is unlikely to play a substantial role except in that it increases opportunities for crime and for substance abuse. Increasing violence in the media is often invoked as a cause, but it is more likely to reflect changing social values than to initiate them. Increasing levels of family discord and breakup may well have had an effect. Although the increasing divorce rate is the focus of attention because it is so visible, marital discord rather than the breakup is likely to be the significant factor.

A recent report of the Academia Europaea Study Group calls attention to the apparent paradox of the increase in psychosocial disorders during the very period when the economies of OECD countries were growing at an unprecedented rate.[36] Yet it should be noted that economic prosperity does not benefit all segments of the population equally. Antisocial behavior and substance abuse are disproportionately represented among segments of the population with the greatest persisting disadvantage. How far these phenomena in industrial countries parallel or predict similar events in low-income countries is uncertain. Relative poverty in Scandinavia (that is, being at the low end of the economic distribution in countries with effective social welfare nets) describes a very different set of circumstances from absolute poverty in Asia and Africa.

Violence

Violence also plagues many societies. With the notable exception of Eastern Europe, most major conflicts in the world now occur in Africa, Asia, and Latin America. They typically involve regional warfare between weak states or conflicts within the border of a single state; in recent years, the number of classic interstate wars has been decreasing and the number of intrastate conflicts increasing. Civilians, rather than soldiers, are most often the casualties in these conflicts. By all accounts, both the number of conflicts in the world and the percentage of civilian casualties are on the rise. Most observers believe that the present era of global politics will be marked by a diffusion of threats throughout the world. Many of these threats will spring from nationalist movements, ethnic rivalries, political insurgencies, and regional disputes over economic and environmental resources. We appear to be beyond the age of large, international wars between military superpowers; future conflicts will most often be local, bloody, and directed at civilians.

The reasons for the nature and severity of conflicts are many. During the Cold War, the ability or willingness of impoverished nations to go to war against one another was dampened because the Soviet Union and the United States restrained, as well as offered security to, their satellite clients. With the end of the superpower era and the rise of mutual insecurity between nation-states, it is now less difficult to follow through on threats of aggression. Furthermore, the superpowers left behind a legacy of armaments employed by local governments, warlords, and rebel groups.

The end of Cold War constraint has also unleashed a wave of nationalist ideologies, ethnic disputes, sectarian tensions, and separatist movements throughout the world, particularly in Eastern Europe. In contrast to the Cold War era, governments now lack the political and military might to tame or appease rival factions. In Africa, a series of arbitrarily drawn colonialist boundaries has augmented tensions between rival political factions and tribal groups living uneasily within the same nation-state. In India, political groups are involved in a bloody dispute over the religious and cultural identity of the nation. Ethnic disputes elsewhere involve the same levels of violence and terror to the extent that "animosity among ethnic groups is beginning to rival the spread of nuclear weapons as the most serious threat to peace that the world faces."[37] Although ethnic conflicts are by no means new, their import, range, and severity have become more pronounced since the end of the Cold War. To date, the international community has generally been unable to prevent or lessen such conflicts when they occur. "In this century," Maynes notes, "when two or more populations have been reluctant to live with one another in a single state, the options open to the international community have turned out to be either unconscionable or unpalatable: ethnic cleansing, repression, partition, or power sharing."[38] In the 1990s, those in power have most often resorted to the first two options.

The loss of superpower support has underscored the fact that many post-colonialist nations are "weak states" whose governments are threatened with conflict and collapse. Many governments are on the verge of "failing," to use the language of the United Nations, as Somalia, Cambodia, and Liberia have failed: Sudan, Zaire, and Peru are challenged by powerful insurgencies, and Colombia is racked by civil violence.[39] The fragility of nation-states is partly due to poverty and economic stagnation; their demise is often marked by violence, civil strife, the breakdown of food and health systems, refugees, and widespread human rights violations that affect other states. In fact, most human rights abuses occur today in places, like Bosnia, where there is no effective central government (with the abuses often being committed against allies or representatives of the government). There are two principal threats when nations fail: the division, or "Lebanonization," of a country into rival factions when power is relatively balanced, and genocide when one group dominates another.

Some nation-states have maintained a strong central government by relying on repressive techniques; others are tempted to turn to militarism and oppression to maintain order. In South Africa, the apartheid regime wielded power over the impoverished townships through pervasive structural violence. In Iraq, Haiti, and Guatemala, the dominant regimes rely on fear, terror, and torture to control citizens and repress minority populations. Throughout the world, nation-states are engaged in conflicts against nations who live under, but actively resist, the political will of the state; at times, the mandate of the state is active genocide.[40] Harff and Gurr report that "state-sponsored massacres of members of ethnic and political groups are responsible for greater loss of life than all other forms of deadly conflict combined. . . . On average, between 1.6 and 3.9 million unarmed civilians have died at the hand of the state in each decade since the end of World War II."[41]

In recent years, government-sponsored attacks on unarmed civilians have typically taken the form of "low-intensity" conflicts geared toward the control of populations rather than of territory. A distinctive feature of low-intensity conflicts is the persistent assault on the lives and lifeways of villagers and farmers. For more than a decade, government forces in El Salvador terrorized the civil society in an attempt to maintain power over it; the methods of violence included death squads, disappearances, massacres, and the targeting of teachers, health care workers, and church officials. A parallel conflict has erupted in Mozambique, where RENAMO, a South African–supported rebel group, has terrorized the civilian population in an attempt to destabilize the socialist government. The effects of the violence, like the methods, are similar: trauma, the disintegration of families and communities, distressed children, the destruction of economic infrastructures, and the imposition of a general culture of fear (see Chapter 5).

Along with the traditional causes and parameters of conflict, tensions within and between nation-states are now commonly sparked or worsened by a range of forces, such as economic stagnation, debt, drug trafficking, environmental degradation, population increases, and the influx of refugees. Many observers predict that conflicts will soon break out over ever-scarcer environmental resources, such as water, fertile land, and energy sources.[42] Many also worry about the predicted rise in populations in economically stressed countries and uncontrolled mass migration.

Refugees, Migrants, and Populations

One of the major tragedies of collective violence are the refugees who flee from violence and hunger in the wake of war. There were 2.7 million refugees throughout the world in 1976, and 10.3 million in 1982. Today, there are nearly 20 million refugees, with at least 20 million more displaced within their own countries.[43] Many of these refugees are destitute people from poor countries who travel within or to other impoverished countries. These displacements can destabilize the host countries, aggravate regional tensions, and increase rates of environmental degradation. Meanwhile, established nations that have traditionally offered asylum are increasingly unwilling to open their doors to massive refugee flows.

There are approximately 20 million official refugees, as recognized by the United Nations, but there are countless other economic and environmental refugees in the world today. More than 70 million people around the world have left their native countries, primarily in search of work. At least 10 million of these have fled from environmental decline, land degradation, and diminishing agricultural and water resources.[44] Whereas refugees from conflict or starvation typically remain in their native regions, economic refugees most often travel to live and work, often illegally, in Europe, East Asia, North America, or more prosperous regions closer to home.

In addition to regional and civil conflicts, two other seemingly inescapable forces—an unprecedented rise in the world's population and continued environmental degradation—point to an increase in displaced populations in future years. There are about 5.4 billion people in the world today.[45] Between 90 and 100 million people are being added every year during the 1990s. The World Bank estimates that there will be as many as 8.4 billion people in the world by the year 2025.[46] No less than 95% of the global population growth by 2025 will occur in Africa, Asia, and Latin America; Europe and North America will constitute less than 9% of the world's population by the year 2025.[47]

Most of the population increase will occur in the world's poorest countries, those least equipped to handle the economic, nutritional, housing, and environmental needs of their growing populations. The changes that the population pressures will bring include continued urban growth, high rates of labor force growth, degradation of land and water resources, continued deforestation, desertification, food shortages, and the spread of infectious disease. Population growth alone can threaten, or diminish, the economic welfare of a society. In India, for instance, economic growth has averaged 6% for the past decade, compared with population growth of 2.4% a year. "The trouble," Maddox notes, "is that inflation accounts for much of the difference and the enlargement of the middle classes may have eaten up what is left, leaving nothing to benefit the poor. . . . India's economic growth is regularly cancelled out by population growth."[48]

Population increases, combined with harmful industrial practices, are taking a toll on an already overburdened global environment. Evidence of weather instability, greenhouse gas–related climate change, the thinning of stratospheric ozone, a reduction in genetic and ecosystem diversity, and acidification of waterways and soils are detected throughout the world. Water shortages, the deterioration of farming lands, and other forms of environmental degradation are changing the way many communities live; many of these problems are primarily affecting countries unable to respond quickly and effectively. In China, for instance, there is concern that increasingly limited water resources will hinder the food and economic resources of the country.[49]

Degraded living conditions in various regions may quite possibly force impoverished peoples to move to more prosperous regions in search of work, food, land, and housing. Along with the constant flow of political refugees, many of these "environmental refugees" will be at risk for economic exploitation, substandard living conditions, social isolation, and psychological distress (see Chapter 6). Those who remain will need to contend with poverty, urban congestion, social instabilities, and environmental and social degradation.

Societies and communities are confronting these problems through a variety of means and with varying degrees of success. One ominous development is the increase in anti-immigration sentiments in European and North American societies, which are geared more toward isolationist policies than efforts to deal directly with the roots and problems of dislocation. In turn, as a result of the ways agencies like the United Nations work, there is clearer consensus on the rights and benefits owed to refugees who flee their countries in wartime than to either those who do not leave their country or those who are displaced because of economic problems. The needs, rights, and political dilemmas of internal refugees, migrant workers, and economic refugees must gain greater visibility on the international agenda before significant advances in their health care can be made.

Disasters

Social and environmental changes (typically brought on by increased populations and urbanization) will lead to more natural and industrial disasters in poor countries. Of the almost 3 billion people affected by disasters from 1967 to 1991, about 85% lived in Asia. Roughly 11% lived in Africa, and 4% in the Americas. Only 0.4% lived in Europe (see Table 1.2). More people are affected by disasters in poor countries, and a greater percentage of people die from natural disasters and industrial accidents in these countries (see Table 1.3). As is the case with famines, poverty is a vital ingredient, for the poor are the most vulnerable to the effects of disasters. They live in the most precarious environments, possess the most limited

Table 1.2 Total Number of People Affected by Disasters per Region, 1967–1991

Region	Number	Percentage of Total
Africa	324,339,545	10.9
Americas	115,364,673	3.9
Asia	2,509,142,168	84.7
Europe	12,559,751	0.4
Oceania	2,007,353	0.1
Total	2,963,483,490	100

Source: International Federation of Red Cross and Red Crescent Societies, 1993. World Disasters Report 1994. Kluwer Academic Publishers, 101 Philip Drive, Norwell, MA 02061, USA.

Table 1.3 Natural Disasters Worldwide by Region, 1945–1986

Region	Number of Disasters	1000s of Deaths	Deaths per Disaster	Deaths per Million Population
East Asia/Pacific	401 (400)*	977 (277)	2,435 (691)	5
Latin America/Caribbean	239	239	999	21
Southern Asia	234 (233)	808 (308)	3,452 (1,321)	10
North America	149	15	104	2
Europe/U.S.S.R.	127 (126)	166 (56)	1,308 (444)	2
Middle East/North Africa	86	129	1,505	24
Sub-Saharan Africa	45	9	201	1
Total	**1,267 (1,264)**	**2,343 (1,033)**	**1,849 (837)**	

* Numbers in parentheses exclude the three worst disasters.

Source: Glickman et al., 1992. World Disasters Report 1994. Kluwer Academic Publishers, 101 Philip Drive, Norwell, MA 02061, USA.

resources, and have the least access to health services. Much of Bangladesh's population, for instance, lives in areas of repeated flooding; they therefore must contend with recurring natural calamities as an expected (and highly feared) part of the annual cycle of life, which is already constrained by poverty. The residents of poor regions must also contend with externally induced industrial and environmental practices that place them at greater risk for ecological hazards.

Indeed, although a disaster may be primarily local in its effects, it can result from larger global economic and environmental factors. The disaster at Bhopal, India, for example, was due to the poor safety procedures of an American corporation and the negligent industrial policies of the Indian government. Other, more "natural" disasters, such as droughts, famines, and floods, might themselves be linked to decisions made by humans within and beyond the regions affected. Increased flooding in Bangladesh, for instance, is in part the consequence of deforestation in Nepal, and famines in Africa largely relate to local and international food entitlement practices.

The suffering typically ranges from economic devastation to the loss of housing to psychological distress. Mental health care, along with basic humanitarian care, is essential in the wake of disasters. Roughly 36% of those affected by disasters suffer some form of mental distress.[50] But few of those living in disaster-prone areas presently receive the kinds of services required (see Box 1.2).[51]

Global Networks and Local Worlds

Given that most impoverished countries and communities are dependent on richer economies (which derive part of their strength from labor and resources in poor countries), there is no unilateral way to achieve economic and social prosperity. Whether in the foothills of Nepal or Mayan villages in Guatemala, the common by-products of stagnation are poverty, hunger, ill health, political instability, violence,

Box 1.2 Disasters and Mental Health Care

The town of Armero, Colombia, was destroyed in November 1985 when a volcano erupted in the Colombian Andes, creating an avalanche of gray ash, steaming mud, rocks, and tree trunks. The resulting damage from the mile-wide mud slide, traveling up to 90 mph, killed 80% of Armero's population of 30,000 and left more than 10,000 in the area homeless, half of them injured. The 160-bed town hospital and a psychiatric hospital was demolished.

Initial rescue work was undertaken by a fleet of helicopters; survivors were transported to regional hospitals, where their injuries were treated. The Colombian government set up emergency units in six surrounding towns. The units included medical facilities and camps and shelters for the homeless. Physicians, nurses, and rescue personnel were brought in from all parts of Colombia. The Red Cross and other public and private agencies were also involved in the relief efforts.

Disaster relief work and humanitarian aid usually center on direct medical assistance, rescue operations, and infrastructure rebuilding. What is frequently overlooked in disasters is the mental health needs of the victims. After the Armero tragedy, mental health consultants were brought in to work with health care professionals to treat survivors' initial trauma.

But mental health care is needed over an extended period as victims of disasters confront subsequent feelings of grief and loss and the daunting task of rebuilding their lives. The time required to confront the cycle of psychological responses to a severely traumatic event is often underestimated.

Studies of victims from Armero and from a less devastating earthquake in Ecuador showed that they suffered from anxiety and major depression six months to a year after the tragedy. In addition, the victims' problems affect family and social relationships; disaster victims can suffer from alcohol and drug abuse, marital problems, and violent or maladaptive behavior. Although the frequency of symptoms was higher among the Armero victims, the victims in both studies showed similar forms of emotional distress.

In principle, local medical practitioners and primary health care workers are better able to respond to immediate needs of affected populations than expatriate teams, particularly if they are trained in disaster care. In addition, the local health system is far better adapted to common local problems. Local practitioners are culturally integrated, with an extensive knowledge of typical symptoms. They are also more able to ensure that treatment schemes are followed up.

Unfortunately, established mental health resources are often limited in disaster-prone areas and cannot meet the long-term mental health needs of the victims. In addition, victims and family members frequently do not seek mental health treatment on their own, even if it is available.

One means of filling the gap between resources and needs is to train primary health care workers in identifying and treating the mental health problems of disaster victims. A preliminary training course developed for primary care workers and nurses in Colombia and Ecuador confirmed that local health workers can provide needed mental health care to their patients. With initial training using basic screening techniques, the primary care workers were better able to determine the emotional state of victims and to recommend appropriate care.

Crucial to the training was the development and use of a manual that profiled methods to evaluate the victims' emotional health, outlined the identification of the most frequent mental disorders (anxiety states, depression, suicidal behavior, adjustment reactions, psychosomatic disorders, and drug dependence), and underscored the social aspects of disasters and the emotional problems of children.

A series of activities and strategies were then proposed in Colombia to provide wide-ranging mental health care—preventive, therapeutic, and rehabilitative—to the disaster victims. Mental health specialists contributed supervision and consultation for the primary care workers.

As a result of the training project, the National Plan for Primary Care and Mental Health of Colombia has incorporated many of its findings. It outlines mental health services that primary care workers can offer to populations in disaster-prone areas. These include the identification and treatment of people in distress, the inclusion of mental health care activities in overall disaster-relief efforts, the coordination of mental health activities with other mental health professionals and relief workers in the community, and the development of rehabilitation and public awareness programs.[52]

and dislocation. Within societies as well, inequalities between rich and poor, men and women, and different social groups create pervasive harms and tensions.

The links between structural violence and mental health are more often indirect than direct. The lack of satisfaction of basic health needs, such as nutrition and environmental sanitation, can cause significant damage to the central nervous system, with impairments in cognition and psychological functioning. Other environmental stressors, such as urban crowding, endless poverty, or poor working conditions, can lead to anxiety, depression, or chronic stress. Still other problems have a detrimental effect on the quality of life of families and individuals. For instance, rural poverty in some parts of Thailand may force indebted parents to sell their daughters to work as prostitutes in Bangkok; the daughters are then at risk for sexual slavery, physical abuse, and sexually transmitted diseases such as AIDS. Forces that trouble societies at large, such as chronic hunger, sexual exploitation, or pervasive underemployment, can devastate families and destroy the way of life of a community. These problems, rooted in the everyday structure of societies, can take as great a toll on mental health as does the acute stress of a major life crisis such as bereavement, with which mental health professionals are more familiar. To think about mental health, then, we must consider a range of interrelated forces that, at first glance, might not appear to be "mental health" problems.

We must also examine how these forces work at the local level. The forces that constrain, or contribute to, personal welfare and opportunities are as much local as national and international. Communities, neighborhoods, social networks, and families stand between regional politics and economics and the everyday lives of real people. Political violence can traumatize a neighborhood but leave some untouched. Local relationships and resources protect some while placing others at risk. Although characteristics of the person such as genetic endowment, early-life experience, and behavioral style influence relative risk and protection, the social system of class, ethnicity, gender, age cohort, and social networks is especially powerful at deflecting or intensifying the consequences of broader societal forces. Being female in most of India, for instance, results in greater risk of neglect and in fewer educational opportunities; in the Indian state of Kerala, in contrast, the situation of women is better than in areas of northern India.

Opportunities for effective coping are also often local. Community leadership can organize more successful networks of communication and action to respond to a disaster such as famine. Neighborhood organizations can work as advocates for slum residents. And resilient kinship networks can mobilize resources to assist a family undergoing a social crisis or a major mental illness. Indeed, because of the regional and cultural specificity of many social problems, preventive and treatment strategies often work best at the community, rather than national, level. A network cannot mobilize resources that do not exist, as many communities in impoverished countries are painfully aware. Local leaders might resist promising innovations because such changes threaten their privileged political status. And larger economic and political forces, such as serious economic scarcities or a campaign of political violence, can overwhelm local responses. Yet when viewed at the level of the village, the street, or the family, the possibilities for controlling the potentially harmful effects of global social change seem more apparent.

The search for solutions at the local level warrants more optimism than the dismal statistics that are aggregated for mental health problems nationally or by regions of the world. One reason is that it is often possible to identify strengths and resources at the local level that can motivate intervention programs. In Kenya, for instance, local credit agencies have offered economic support to families during times of economic hardship. In Nepal, unpaid social workers helped to develop village infrastructure, health care posts, and grade schools. And in China, some workers' collectives fare better than others through the political skills of local leaders. Indeed, when one considers the dynamics of well-being at the level of everyday action, the alarming picture of global and regional forces begins to look less frightening. In each of the following chapters, we therefore emphasize specific ways that communities are dealing with a range of health problems.

Conclusions

- The 1980s was a lost decade for many low-income countries. Many of these same countries have not fared much better in the 1990s. As a result of a range of factors at both the global and regional levels, economic growth remains weak, living standards continue to deteriorate, and millions still lack adequate food, clean water, elementary education, and basic health care. Rapid population increases, particularly in urban regions, and environmental degradation have the potential to further diminish the quality of life for many living in economically disadvantaged countries.

- Because of a variety of economic, political, and environmental forces, poor countries in Asia, Africa, Latin America, and the Pacific must contend with a greater burden of problems—from disasters to low-intensity conflicts to dislocated peoples—than wealthier countries. These problems are themselves often exacerbated because of a lack of economic and political means to provide sufficient health care and humanitarian aid.

- Poverty and economic stagnation have both direct and indirect impacts on social and mental well-being. Poverty translates into hunger and malnutrition, inadequate living conditions, greater risk of ill health, and, often, limited health care services. Urban crowding and poor working conditions can lead to anxiety, depression, or chronic stress, as well as have a detrimental effect on the quality of life of families and communities. Problems such as chronic hunger, sexual exploitation, and pervasive underemployment can take as much a toll on mental and social health as does the acute stress of a major life crisis such as bereavement, with which mental health professionals are much more familiar. To think about mental health, then, one must consider a range of interrelated forces that, at first glance, might not appear to be "psychiatric" problems.

• Because of the regional and cultural specificity of many social problems, the most successful strategies to improve the basic social and economic conditions that contribute to well-being often involve work at the level of communities, rather than at the national level. The reason is twofold. One, it is often possible to identify local strengths and resources that can help spark community programs. And two, programs that pay heed to local traditions and cultural values are usually more successful than programs that neglect local realities and concerns.

2

Mental Illness and Psychiatric Services

The past several decades have seen a sizable investment—of capital, research, and programs—in problems of health and health care throughout the world. Nevertheless, although infectious diseases, family planning, and the health of infants have been the focus of active programs in the international health community, mental illnesses have not received attention proportionate to the suffering they produce. Several factors account for this.

First, much of the burden of mental illness is relatively invisible to current forms of accounting. Because mental illnesses do not produce a large increase in the death rate, mortality rates (the most frequently cited public health statistic) fail to record the suffering they actually cause. For societies with high infant and maternal mortality rates, the apparent contrast between infectious diseases and mental illnesses is therefore deceiving.

Alternative ways of accounting for the burden of mental illness are more complex and the results more difficult to compare across societies, particularly between highly industrialized societies and the poorer countries of the world. For example, the monetary cost of providing health care is a poor indicator of burden for societies with relatively few mental health workers, few psychiatric facilities, low use of psychiatric medications, and relatively inexpensive hospital day rates. Measuring costs in quality of life and burden on families is difficult. Yet we know that major mental disorders take an enormous toll, in *all* societies, in human suffering, disability, and the loss of community resources.

A newly developed indicator supports this view. As noted earlier, the 1993 World Development Report estimates that mental health problems the world over produce 8.1% of the Global Burden of Disease (GBD) measured in Disability-Adjusted Life Years (DALYs), a toll greater than that exacted by tuberculosis, cancer, or heart disease. The burden from neuropsychiatric disorders ranges from 3.4% in sub-Saharan Africa to a high of 8% in China and the Latin American and Caribbean region. For adults aged 15 to 44, neuropsychiatric disorders are estimated to account for 12% of the GBD; when "intentional, self-inflicted injuries" are added, the total constitutes 15.1% of the GBD for women, 16.1% for men.[1] Of the disorders considered, depressive disorders, self-inflicted injuries, Alzheimer's disease and other dementias, and alcohol dependence cause the largest burden, followed by epilepsy, psychoses, drug dependence, and post-traumatic stress disorder (see Figure 2.1).

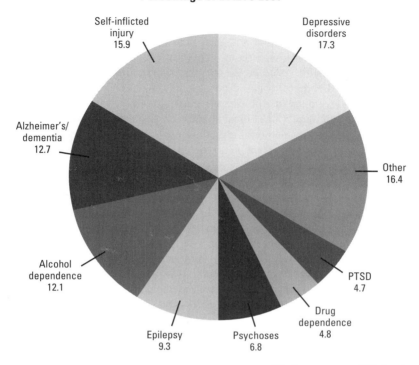

Percentage of DALYs Lost*

Depressive disorders 17.3

Self-inflicted injury 15.9

Alzheimer's/ dementia 12.7

Other 16.4

Alcohol dependence 12.1

PTSD 4.7

Drug dependence 4.8

Epilepsy 9.3

Psychoses 6.8

*The figure represents 8.1% of total DALYs (Disability Adjusted Life Years)

Figure 2.1 Disability From Mental Health Problems (*Source*: Adapted from the World Bank, 1993). * DALY = Disability-Adjusted Life Year

A second widespread misconception is that psychiatric conditions are not "real" illnesses, amenable to the kind of definition, identification, evaluation, treatment, and research that is possible for other medical conditions. This general perception was reinforced by psychiatric researchers in the 1950s and 1960s, when the contrast between approaches to investigating infectious diseases and psychiatric illnesses could hardly have been greater. In those years, the "interesting" mental illnesses were understood as constellations of neurotic symptoms, to be treated through intensive dynamic psychotherapy. Psychiatric epidemiologists attempted to measure levels of mental illness using diagnostic categories with vague criteria, resulting in unreliable measurements, or using scales that record the overall level of psychological symptoms suffered by individuals. These approaches to research tended to reinforce the belief held by many—including international health researchers—that, with the exception of psychotic disorders like schizophrenia (about which little could be done anyway), "mental illness" is a vague domain of psychological distress and general human unhappiness. Concerns about the legitimacy of attempting to treat mental illnesses in other societies were deepened by claims that psychiatrists are often used by oppressive regimes to "medicalize deviance" or suppress political dissent.

Dramatic changes in approaches to psychiatric research over the past two decades provide a basis for rethinking mental illness in a global, multicultural context. Psychiatric classification—as represented in the International Classification of Diseases (ICD) and the Diagnostic and Statistical Manual (DSM) of the American Psychiatric Association—has undergone important changes since the early 1970s. Categories of illness with specified diagnostic criteria, linked to particular treatments, have replaced categories based on psychological etiology. And psychiatric epidemiology has developed instruments for making both diagnostic judgments and severity ratings in community or clinical studies (particularly in North America and Europe). These changes in methodology allow new questions to be asked—about prevalence and burden of illness, the neurobiology of psychiatric disorders, and the efficacy of particular interventions.

Unfortunately, the majority of research has focused too narrowly on biological and genetic aspects of mental illnesses, and too little on the social and cultural factors so crucial to our understanding of the distribution, burden, and treatment of such conditions in a global context. Since the mid-1970s, the "brainless" social psychiatry of the 1950s has too often been replaced by a "mindless" biological psychiatry, deflecting attention from the social factors so obviously important to understanding the burden of mental illness.[2] Research methods now available in psychiatric epidemiology, if combined with approaches from medical anthropology and cross-cultural psychiatry, provide an opportunity to address these issues in a new way.

Third, a widespread perception that there are few or no effective treatments for mental illnesses has furthered neglect of mental illnesses in the international health community. In the past, this view was largely justified. Many mental health services in Europe and in North America—such as large, understaffed public hospitals or asylums—actually made suffering worse rather than relieved it. All too often these institutions were reproduced in their worst forms in Asia, Africa, and Latin America as part of colonial medicine (see Box 2.1).

Box 2.1 Psychiatric Care in the Americas: Argentina and the Dominican Republic

The Padre Billini Psychiatric Hospital, the Dominican Republic's sole public psychiatric hospital, is located in the community of Pedro Brand, thirty kilometers from the capital city of Santo Domingo and on the site of one of the most notorious prisons administered by the secret police of the late Dominican dictator Rafael Leonidas Trujillo. Although the hospital is described as a 130-bed facility, it has not always had "beds" in any recognizable sense. Many of its patients, for example, were forced to sleep on floors slick with human wastes during lean economic times. Nor has its population stayed within official limits: in the period leading up to the celebration of the Quincentennial of Columbus's discovery of America, Dominican security personnel swept the homeless mentally ill off the streets of the capital (lest they negatively impact tourism) and into the crowded hospital.

Although the hospital is staffed primarily by hardworking and enthusiastic residents, the therapeutic resources available to these practitioners are limited. Shortages of essential medications, as well as insufficient personnel for outpatient services and time-intensive therapies, lead to the overuse of electroconvulsive therapy, which is administered in substandard conditions. There are no provisions for the treatment of somatic comorbidity, life-threatening emergencies, infections, and the like. Because of malodorous and filthy conditions, psychiatrists are often unable to effectively evaluate inpatients. And food for patients and house officers on duty is cooked outdoors over wood fires because modern kitchen facilities remain half built.

In weighing the costs and benefits of admitting someone to the hospital, Dominican psychiatrists must first ask several nonclinical questions. Does the patient appear to have been successful in obtaining enough food on the city's streets? If so, it might be better for him or her to remain outside the institution instead of exposing them to the malnutrition, tuberculosis, and conjunctivitis that ravage the wards. Is the patient a frail, elderly, or extremely passive person? If so, he or she will be an easy target for more aggressive patients and frustrated patients. Is the patient an attractive woman or a virgin? If so, she will almost certainly be attacked by male patients and staff and men from the surrounding community who, with assistance from hospital employees, can sneak on the grounds at night in search of sex.

That these are relevant factors when plotting a therapeutic course reflects the problems of mental health care in the Dominican Republic. In this insular Latin Caribbean nation, care stands hostage to the relentless proliferation of local political conflicts, rampant graft and corruption, and the devastating impact of structural adjustments. The politicization of labor conflicts, and the economic dependence of the surrounding community of Pedro Brand on hospital resources, have thwarted many initiatives on improving conditions at Padre Billini. Despite intermittent efforts to integrate mental health care—known as the "the Cinderella of public health care"—into primary health care centers, delivery of psychiatric care remains limited to the custodial and acute intervention services provided at the national hospital. Plans to make health care personnel available in rural areas and to experiment with deinstitutionalization are subverted through government underfunding and a lack of continuity in health care development leadership.

Argentina, like the Dominican Republic, has tried to maintain a health care system that covers most of the population. In the late 1980s, however, a decline in public money has affected the quality of health care, particularly for the poor. The mentally ill are especially at risk.

In 1990, thirty-two women at Moyano Hospital, a state-run psychiatric institution that houses 1,650 women outside of Buenos Aires, died of malnutrition. Initial reports from hospital officials said the deaths occurred as a result of old age and other natural causes. Further investigations discovered that a number of the women were in their forties and fifties; lack of funds and poor management of government funds led to starvation of some patients. According to kitchen workers, the daily diet given to patients was subsistence level. It was estimated that about two-thirds of the patients at Moyano did not require permanent hospitalization but had been abandoned by their families and had nowhere else to go. Public outcry about the deaths resulted in dismissal of hospital administrators and major reforms at the institution.

Further abuses were brought to light in 1992 in a series of newspaper articles about excessive deaths and misappropriation of funds at Colonia Montes de Oca, a psychiatric colony near Buenos Aires. According to newspaper accounts, from 1976 to the end of 1991 1,321 patients died and 1,395 disappeared from the institution. Among those who "disappeared" was a young woman doctor who had been looking for her two brothers-in-law who had also vanished. The ensuing investigation led to the dismissal of top staff members for mismanagement and substandard care and for embezzling money meant for running the institution.

In both Argentina and the Dominican Republic, many of the problems of poor psychiatric care are caused by political and economic circumstances. Even under optimum circumstances, however, the mentally ill in most countries are often powerless; and they become even more disenfranchised during times of political or economic upheaval. To prevent abuses, there is an urgent need to improve the quality of mental health care, to strengthen the management of institutions to prevent corruption, and to closely monitor the rights of the mentally ill.[3]

However, treatments for mental illness have changed dramatically since the 1960s, when effective pharmaceutical treatments and new forms of psychosocial interventions began to be available. In little more than two decades, advances in psychopharmacology have radically altered the treatability of most mental illnesses, and health services research has placed our knowledge of the effectiveness of particular forms of care on a more scientific foundation. Evaluation research suggests, for example, that when combined with appropriate medications, brief psychotherapeutic interventions are beneficial and that community rehabilitation programs for patients with serious mental illness can be provided in a cost-effective manner by nurses, social workers, and trained local citizens.[3] In spite of this progress, the worst aspects of the antiquated mental health systems of Europe and the United States persist in societies that have limited services even today. It is a great challenge to translate what *has* been learned about the treatment and organization of services into widely distributed and sustainable community-based services, particularly in the poorest societies.

One other change in our understanding of mental illness in a global context is worth noting. The social psychiatry of an earlier generation focused primarily on the relation between level of psychological symptoms and social status (including poverty), suggesting broadly that adverse social conditions are the primary cause of mental illness, a grossly oversimplified theory of cause. Cross-cultural psychiatrists of the same era attended almost exclusively to exotic syndromes found in non-Western societies—the so-called culture-bound disorders. In the last twenty years, stimulated in part by innovative approaches to cultural psychiatry and cultural epidemiology in Africa and Asia,[5] research in medical anthropology and cross-cultural psychiatry has provided foundations for a "new cross-cultural psychiatry."[6] New theoretical models and empirical studies have transformed our understanding of the role of culture and social forces in shaping *all* psychiatric symptoms and mental illnesses, in producing vulnerability and triggering illness episodes, in organizing the classification and behavioral response to illness, and in providing indigenous forms of care.[7]

These dramatic changes in psychiatry and psychiatric research paradigms provide an opportunity to reevaluate the place of mental illnesses and their treatment in the context of international health. What do we know about the burden of mental illnesses globally—about incidence and prevalence, about risk factors and social distribution, and about the burden to individuals, families, communities, and societies? What forms of treatment are available? How can they be employed effectively in economically burdened societies? What are the benefits of formulating mental health problems as "biomedical" problems, and what are the potential hazards? How effective are folk and family-based treatments, as well as existing medical services? What are the specific challenges and priorities for improving mental health services? Although we can only sketch out answers for some questions, with an indication of how much more we need to know, we hope to suggest new ways for thinking about mental illnesses and services in the context of international health care and social policy.

The Burden of Mental Illnesses: An International Perspective

Of the varieties of human suffering reviewed in this book, mental illnesses are the most clearly amenable to "medical" interventions. Throughout history, madness and some less severe forms of emotional distress have been experienced and understood as "illness" and treated by popular, folk, and professional healers. Since the end of the last century, mental illnesses have been "medicalized" in a more restricted sense: they have come to be viewed as a special category of medical diseases (neuropsychiatric disorders), have been subject to clinical and basic science research, and are the domain of a significant sector of health services.

During the past three decades, mental illnesses have come to be viewed within psychiatry as a set of discrete disorders (therefore "illnesses" in the plural), acute or chronic in form, which can be more or less successfully treated (as are other diseases) by specific drugs, by psychosocial interventions, and by rehabilitative care. The extent to which the "causes" of these conditions are either specific and biological (genetic, neuroendocrinological, viral, etc.) or are more general, social, and psychological (trauma, chronic forms of environmental stress, or oppressive social arrangements) remains a matter of controversy. And the cross-cultural validity of particular categories of illness—their "universality" versus "cultural specificity"—is far from certain.[8] Nevertheless, these general categories provide a framework for reviewing the sources and burdens of mental illnesses in a global perspective.

Schizophrenia

The schizophrenias are a group of severe mental disorders that first appear in late adolescence or early adulthood.[9] These illnesses are devastating, not only because of the emotional turmoil and the confusion and fear they produce, but because of their social consequences for patient and family. In nearly every society, whatever theories people hold about its causes, psychosis, or madness, is highly stigmatized. In some societies, madness is thought to be contagious or to be passed through a family. As a result, patient and family are shunned and chances for marriage are limited. Stigma leads to isolation and neglect. Patients are often hidden and mistreated by families or institutionalized under deplorable conditions (sometimes caged in groups, without clothing, on starvation rations). Others are ridiculed in public or left without food or shelter as part of a homeless population. Others are treated with care, involved in community and family activities, and regarded as possessed or ill but not isolated from daily life.

According to Kramer, there were about 23 million people with schizophrenia in the world in 1985, three-quarters in the less developed countries.[10] By the year 2000, projected demographic profiles suggest that the absolute number in these countries will have risen from 16.7 to 24.4 million, a 45% increase. This increase, like the increase in the dementias of old age, is a consequence of the increase in the number of persons living into the age of risk, which in this instance is the age cohort between 15 and 45.

In acute schizophrenia, the manifest clinical signs and symptoms include delusions (false beliefs), hallucinations (disembodied voices or visions), jumbled and incoherent thoughts, a mood out of keeping with thoughts, and lack of awareness of being ill. Because of the patient's strange and excited behavior, he or she is often disruptive and disturbing to the community. In chronic schizophrenia, the "positive" symptoms of the acute syndrome (delusions and hallucinations) are replaced by "negative" symptoms of underactivity, apathy, lack of drive, and social withdrawal.

"Brief reactive psychosis," which can mimic acute schizophrenia, is a transient disorder with good prognosis, commonly seen in patients with an acute medical condition. Because of the importance—and difficulty—of distinguishing schizophrenia from acute and transient psychotic disorders, ICD-10, the tenth revision of the International Classification of Diseases, requires that delusions, hallucinations, and other symptoms be present for a minimum of *one month* to make a diagnosis of schizophrenia.[11] In DSM-IV, the fourth revision of the Diagnostic and Statistical Manual, continuous signs of disturbance must be present for at least *six months*.[12] (Thus, patients whose symptoms remit before the end of the six-month period would be classified as schizophrenic by ICD-10 and not by DSM-IV.) Evidence suggests that the ratio of brief reactive psychoses to schizophrenia might be greater in some nonindustrial societies than in Europe and North America.

Prevalence estimates of schizophrenia from studies in low-income countries vary from a low of 0.8 per thousand reported from rural China to a high of 5.9 per thousand in Calcutta, India (see Table 2.1). European epidemiologic studies show a more restricted range of prevalence from 2.5 to 5.3 per thousand.[13] The most comprehensive study undertaken in China reported a point prevalence of schizophrenia of 6.06 per thousand in urban and 3.42 per thousand in rural areas. With a population of 1.1 billion and a rural-to-urban ratio of 3 to 1, the reported prevalence leads to an estimate of 4.5 million people with schizophrenia at any given time. Less than 2% are hospitalized in the nation's 414 psychiatric hospitals; about 3.4% live on their own; less than 4% are to be found in prisons, in nursing homes, or on the streets. More than 90% live with their families, more than double the percentage who do in the United States. Nevertheless, changes in China over the past several decades (smaller families, reduced availability of free health care, greater competition for jobs, and the higher value placed on personal autonomy) are making it increasingly difficult for families to cope with schizophrenia in the family.[14]

Because the specific cause of schizophrenia is unknown, so too there is currently no known form of prevention. Familial aggregation is evident in multigenerational studies; concordance is higher among identical than fraternal twins, but heritability accounts for less than half the variance. Despite the strong evidence for a

Table 2.1 Prevalence Studies of Schizophrenia

Author/Year	Region	Area	Population Size	Rate per 1000
		Africa		
Baasher, 1961	Sudan	Rural	3,984	2.0
		Asia		
Nandi et al., 1975	India	Rural	1,060	2.8
ICMR, 1986	India	Rural	146,380	2.2
Verghese et al., 1973	India	Urban	1,887	2.6
Padmavathi et al., 1987	India	Urban	101,229	2.5
Sen et al., 1984	India	Urban (Calcutta slum)	2,168	5.9 4.5 (M) 6.6 (F)
Wijesinghe et al., 1978	Sri Lanka	Semi-urban	7,653	3.8 2.9 (M) 4.7 (F)
Shen et al., 1981	Mainland China	Mixed	190,000	1.9 1.2 (M) 2.6 (F)
Shen, 1981	Mainland China	9 Urban areas 8 Rural areas		1.4–5.6 0.8–4.6
Lin et al., 1989	Taiwan	Taiwanese Chinese		1.4 2.5

M = male; F = female; ICMR = Indian Council of Medical Research.

Source: Jablensky, 1993.

familial disposition, what is inherited is unknown.[15] There is no single gene for schizophrenia.[16]

Epidemiologic studies in Europe and North America find schizophrenia more prevalent in lower than in higher socioeconomic classes. For decades, some have argued that adverse or stressful living conditions increase the risk of onset of schizophrenia. Others have contended that disproportionate numbers of people suffering from schizophrenia are to be found among the poor, in cities, and among some immigrant populations because of "drift" rather than "stress." That is, those who suffer schizophrenia become disabled and are thus likely to *become* poor, "drifting" into poverty or moving to cities to seek services. Bruce Dohrenwend and his colleagues have concluded that social drift rather than stress explains the increased prevalence of schizophrenia in lower socioeconomic strata.[17] (By contrast, their research suggests that differential levels of social stress account for higher rates of depression in lower social classes.) No current data provide a clear model of (preventable) social or biological factors that account for the onset of schizophrenia. Further research will need to identify such sources if efforts at prevention are to be undertaken.

If research has provided little evidence for understanding social origins of schizophrenia, it does provide strong support for the hypothesis that social and cultural factors affect the course and prognosis of schizophrenia. In 1976, a World Health Organization team published results of a two-year follow-up study of people diagnosed as suffering from schizophrenia in nine countries. To the surprise of the researchers, outcome varied enormously. Sufferers in low-income countries did far better than those in North America and Europe. For example, two years after the first treated episode of schizophrenia, 58% were reported to have recovered in Nigeria and 50% in India, whereas only 8% were reported as recovered in Denmark.[18] These findings were startling, because schizophrenia was generally considered a chronic illness with severe, persisting symptoms leading to an almost certain decline over time. Comparability of samples across countries was immediately suspected, with critics suggesting more severe cases were selected in North America and Europe. To investigate possible sources of variation in outcome, the World Health Organization launched a second study that used more rigorous diagnostic criteria and obtained a more complete sample of first admission cases.[19] Although less striking, results were similar (see Table 2.2).

Research now shows that there are numerous patterns of the course of illness for people suffering an initial episode of schizophrenic illness, ranging from a single episode followed by complete remission of symptoms to a chronic, deteriorating course without any remissions. These findings of the international studies are now matched by results of longitudinal studies in North America and Europe.[20] For example, a review of five long-term studies of American patients followed for more than twenty years found that at least half and arguably two-thirds of the 1,300 subjects studied "achieved recovery or significant improvement."[21] The implications are clear: the "natural course" of schizophrenia need not produce deterioration and

Table 2.2 Five-Year Outcome of WHO Study of
Schizophrenic Patients: Cities in "Developed" versus
"Developing" Countries

Location	Percentage with Best Outcome	Percentage with Worst Outcome
Developed Countries		
Aarhus, Denmark	6	40
London, UK	5	14
Moscow, Russia	6	21
Prague, Czechoslovakia	9	23
Washington, DC, USA	17	23
Developing Countries		
Agra, India	42	10
Cali, Colombia	11	21
Ibadan, Nigeria	33	10

Source: Jablensky et al., 1992b.

chronicity for all sufferers. Some investigators credit differences in prognosis to different subtypes of the disease; however, leading researchers now argue that chronicity has "less to do with any inherent natural outcome of the disorder and more to do with a myriad of environmental and other psychosocial factors interacting with the person and the illness."[22]

Given the enormous human and financial costs of serious mental illness, we have much to learn from investigating social, cultural, and other environmental factors that influence the course and outcome of major mental illness. Studies of particular social environments can thus have crucial implications not only for the development of mental health services, but for anticipating the impact on the mentally ill of some aspects of economic change and for devising psychosocial interventions that might prove useful in other societies.

There are several important hypotheses about how social and cultural factors might contribute to a less severe course of mental illness. First, anthropological and cross-cultural studies have found that conceptions of the cause and course of schizophrenia held by members of a society or social group (including mental health professionals) strongly influence their response to people who are ill and both directly and indirectly influence the course of illness.[23] Where such illness is considered an essential part of the self that cannot be expected to change (e.g., "the schizophrenic" as opposed to "the patient with schizophrenia"), it is more likely to *be* chronic. In contrast, other understandings (e.g., that the ill person is possessed by spirits that can be exorcised) can set the scene for recovery.

Second, the extended families present in many countries can provide a supportive environment that lessens the severity of mental illness. The "extended family" is far from uniform across societies, and families are not uniformly supportive of a mentally ill member. However, the influence of family supports on the course of illness is important and remains a significant area for research and for psychosocial interventions.[24]

Third, severity of illness course seems to be linked to work environments and level of involvement in the wage economy. Greater opportunity for people who suffer mental illness to engage in meaningful labor in some nonindustrial countries can contribute to better outcomes.[25] Implications of this hypothesis for rehabilitation programs are quite significant.

Finally, characteristics of treatment settings, as well as specific treatments, can influence outcomes both positively and negatively. Psychosocial interventions aimed at rehabilitating mentally ill patients can unwittingly produce dependency, and mental health systems are often subtly encouraged (through reimbursement policies) to maintain a population of patients rather than promote empowerment and independence from systems of care.[26] Basic research on treatment settings and mental health policy is thus needed if we are to understand the social course of mental illness and design more effective systems for promoting recovery.

What are the most effective forms of treatment for schizophrenia? There is no current medical treatment that can "cure" the disease. However, a combination of medications and community- or family-based psychosocial interventions is now considered the best form of treatment for those suffering from schizophrenia, and improvement and recovery are quite common.[27] Neuroleptic drugs, of which chlorpromazine was the first and remains the prototype, can reduce the acute symptoms that interfere with vocational and social activities. Gradual programs of return to work (beginning with sheltered workshops for the most handicapped patients) can facilitate resumption of social roles. Studies in many societies, including the United Kingdom, the United States, and China, have demonstrated that the likelihood of relapse after remission of an acute episode can be diminished by supportive counseling and advice to the families to whom patients return. These services can be delivered by psychiatric nurses after appropriate training courses.[28]

Extensive experience has demonstrated that prolonged hospitalization in understaffed large institutions interacts with the schizophrenic disease process to produce a social breakdown syndrome no less devastating than the disease itself.[29] Consequently, mental health programs now emphasize treatment in the community, unless the patients are a danger to others or themselves. Such treatment is often augmented by short-term hospitalization when needed and rapid return to the community with appropriate plans for follow-up care, including supervised medication, vocational rehabilitation, and support for the family.

Mood (Affective) Disorders

The World Health Organization notes that, with mood disorders, "the fundamental disturbance is a change in mood or affect, usually to depression . . . or to elation."[30] Most are recurrent. They typically take the form of either bipolar affective disorders or depressive disorders.

Bipolar affective disorder (manic depressive disorder) is characterized by repeated episodes in which the patient's mood, energy, and activity are markedly disturbed, at times in the direction of elation and overactivity (mania) and at others of lowered mood and decreased energy (depression). While there are periods of normalcy, the episodes tend to recur. Manic episodes are characterized by elevated mood varying from carefree joviality to uncontrollable excitement accompanied by incessant talking, decreased sleep, and loss of normal social inhibitions. Mania can be accompanied by delusions and hallucinations. Acute manic episodes can be halted by neuroleptic drugs and the likelihood of recurrence diminished by taking lithium salts daily.

Depressive episodes have the same clinical characteristics as those found in unipolar depressive disease. Depression, as currently understood in psychiatry, is a mood disorder that can occur as a single episode in a lifetime (uncommon), as one of many episodes (most common), or as part of an alternation with mania (bipolar disorder). Patients suffer intense emotional and physical anguish; their illness disrupts their ability to function in family, job, and social life. The worst consequence of depression is suicide. It is estimated that between 40% and 70% of all suicide victims in the United States suffer from major depression.[31]

Whereas schizophrenia is a low-prevalence but high-severity disorder, depression is of high prevalence and moderate to high severity. For example, one-year prevalence was ten times higher than that for schizophrenia in a large population study in the United States.[32] Surveys of patients attending primary health care clinics in sub-Saharan Africa, in Latin America, and in other countries indicate that for as many as one-fifth to one-third of cases, depression is the principal or a secondary reason for seeking care—findings similar to those of repeated research in North America and Europe.[33] In the aggregate, therefore, depression produces far more morbidity in the community than does schizophrenia. In addition, because suicide is a far greater risk in depression, depression has a greater impact on premature mortality. In the United States, depression produced a cost to the nation in 1990 of about $44 billion, about the same as the costs resulting from heart disease and some 30% of the total cost of $148 billion for all mental illness in that year.[34] The World Bank report estimates depression ranks fifth in illness burden among women, and seventh among men in the developing countries surveyed.

Depression is characterized by sadness, diminished pleasure in daily life, weight change, disturbed sleep patterns, fatigue, feelings of worthlessness and self-blame, diminished ability to concentrate, indecisiveness, and changes in motor patterns (retardation or agitation). Chronic depression (dysthymia) is characterized by the persistence of such symptoms over several years.

Many people experience depression as a disabling set of physical symptoms, including chronic pain, incapacitating fatigue, and persistent headaches. In some societies, physical complaints are the preferred idiom for expressing psychosocial distress, including depression and anxiety; in others, depression is more commonly experienced and expressed in psychological or emotional terms.[35] The results have important implications for care. Researchers have found that when depression is presented as physical symptoms, it is less likely to be recognized and treated appropriately by health workers.[36]

Costs to the health care system rise as resources are expended on searching for the causes of, or "treating," nonexistent physical conditions. Despite the high prevalence of depression, only a minority of depressed patients receive appropriate treatment.[37] Primary care health workers often fail to recognize and diagnose depression. The opportunity to make use of effective pharmaceutical and psychological treatments is thus often missed.

Depressed patients suffer as much disability and distress as patients with chronic medical disorders such as high blood pressure, diabetes, coronary artery disease, and arthritis.[38] Recovery from individual episodes of depression is readily stimulated by appropriate treatment, but relapse is common and care over the long term is essential.[39] Depression runs in families, reflecting an inherited vulnerability. There is equally strong evidence, however, that childhood experiences, such as loss of a parent, also produce vulnerability to depression, and that losses experienced in adulthood can precipitate depressive episodes.[40] Depression is thus both biological and social in its origin.

Researchers have reported sizable increases in rates of depression in Taiwan over a thirty-year period during the island's rapid modernization.[41] Evidence is accumulating that rates for depression have been increasing in the United States, Western Europe, Puerto Rico, Lebanon, and Taiwan in recent decades; depression is now seen at younger ages and in greater frequency.[42] In spite of the considerable evidence about the general social correlates of, and the psychosocial risk factors for, depression, we do not know the specific causal pathways that transform social experiences into psychopathology. Nor do we know the specific links between changing socioeconomic development and changing rates of depression, although the correlation of job loss and recession and increased rates of suicide and hospitalization for psychiatric disorder indicates a link between the two. Similarly, there is a documented tie between depression, social uprooting, and refugee status.

Both medication and psychotherapy have been shown to be effective in relieving depression. The major classes of drugs include the tricyclic antidepressants, the monoamine oxidase inhibitors and the serotonin reuptake inhibitors, as well as lithium, which acts to prevent recurrence. In severe depression, electroconvulsive therapy (ECT) can lead to recovery in patients who fail to respond to drugs. Two types of psychotherapy (cognitive behavior therapy and interpersonal psychotherapy) have been shown to yield rates of recovery similar to that produced by drugs in patients with moderately severe depression. In one five-year study, continuing antidepressant drug treatment *plus* interpersonal psychotherapy yielded the best results.[43] Unfortunately, little is known about whether the kinds of psychotherapy shown to be effective in Western societies are effective in other societies.

To make the best gains in public health, it is essential to train primary care health workers to recognize depression and to treat it appropriately with drugs and counseling. This has been shown to be feasible. The cost of effective treatment of depression is offset by the reduction in inappropriate medical visits.[44] In poorer societies, in which the cost of drugs is a much greater proportion of overall medical costs, the offset effect should also apply. Nevertheless, research on rational and effective use of psychoactive drugs in specific settings is necessary.

Anxiety Disorders

Anxiety disorders are characterized by symptoms of anxiety and avoidance behavior. They are subclassified into panic disorder, phobias, obsessive-compulsive disorder, generalized anxiety disorder, and post-traumatic stress disorder. Epidemiologic studies in Latin America have identified a high prevalence of anxiety disorders, with an excess of cases in lower socioeconomic strata. A census of the mental health status of villagers in the area of São Francisco, Bahia, Brazil, noted a prevalence of 14% for anxiety disorders; rates for women were twice as high as those for men.[45] Highly prevalent idioms of distress—"nerves" (*nervios*) or "attacks" (*ataques*), for example, in Hispanic cultures, or elaborate somatic idioms ("heart distress" in Iran, the "fatigue and dizziness" characteristic of "neurasthenia" in China)—make direct translation of categories across cultures difficult.[46] Nonetheless, anxiety in its various manifestations produces suffering and disability for many persons worldwide.

Panic disorder is marked by episodes of intense fear or discomfort, which occur unpredictably and for no apparent reason, last for minutes to hours, and include shortness of breath, dizziness, palpitations, tremor, sweating, and often a fear of dying or "going crazy." *Agoraphobia* is present if the patient is fearful of being in situations where escape would be difficult in the event of panic; as a result, the person is unable to leave home or is able to leave only if accompanied. *Social phobia* is a persistent fear of one or more social contexts because of the anticipation of embarrassment and humiliation. So persistent is the fear that the need to avoid such exposure interferes with work and social activity. *Simple phobias* are uncontrollable fears of particular stimuli, such as dogs, snakes, insects, blood, or heights. *Obsessive compulsive disorder* is characterized by intrusive, distressing, and senseless thoughts and by behaviors (such as hand-washing) that are repetitive, illogical efforts to ward off misfortune through ritualized performance (compulsions). *Generalized anxiety disorder* is manifested by motor tension and overactivity of the autonomic nervous system (shortness of breath, palpitations, dry mouth, dizziness). The patient is beset by constant fears and worries about impending misfortune in the absence of visible threat. Lifetime prevalence rates for generalized anxiety disorder vary from 5% to 12% in urban and rural communities in Taiwan and from 5% to 10% in regions of the United States.[47]

Anxiety disorders can have serious effects on social function, work, personal well-being, and use of health services. Agoraphobia can render a patient housebound. Panic disorder can be misdiagnosed and result in fruitless medical test procedures, risky and ineffective treatments, and frustration for patient and practitioner. With proper diagnosis and treatment, psychopharmacologic agents and psychotherapy have been shown to be effective in treating anxiety disorder.

Post-traumatic stress disorder (PTSD) is a persistent response (which often occurs after a delay) to a catastrophic experience, one that causes distress to all victims but persists long after the event and interferes with function in only some of those exposed to the event or series of events. Typical symptoms include flashbacks and dreams of the traumatic events, numbness and blunting of emotional responsiveness, detachment from other people, and an avoidance of activities and situations that reawaken memories. There is usually a state of autonomic hyperarousal, hypervigilance, an enhanced startle reaction, and insomnia. PTSD is common among victims of natural or man-made disasters (floods, industrial explosions, etc.), torture, and repression, and among civilian populations subjected to bombardment and war, refugees forced to evacuate their homes, and soldiers after combat (see Table 2.3). Clinical research in the United States suggests that suffering and disability associated with the syndrome can often be relieved to some extent by treatment.

Controversy has arisen about applying the diagnosis of PTSD to the victims of political violence and torture. The objections are clinical and political. The first is based on the contention that the prolonged length of time and the deliberate social degradation associated with repression and torture result in a different psychological and physiological aftermath from that produced by an acute disaster. The second objection is based on the argument that applying a medical label to victims of political repression pathologizes people, some of whom have been heroes of the resistance to tyranny. The first argument will ultimately be answered by further empirical research to establish whether or not clinical syndromes differ significantly under the two circumstances. The second objection reflects a value judgment but one that also has a pragmatic component. Does it stigmatize victims to classify their distress as PTSD any more than it stigmatizes them to classify the skin burns or the rib frac-

Table 2.3 Prevalence Rates of Post-Traumatic Stress Disorder (PTSD)

Country	Author and Year	Sample Studied	Sample Size (N)	Assessment Methods	Diagnostic System	Prevalence Rate of PTSD	Notes
Cambodians in the U.S.	Kinzie et al., 1986	Cambodian young refugees (14–20 years old) resettled in U.S.	40	DIS (parts) SADS (parts)	DSM-III	50%	Mild but prolonged depressive symptoms were also common.
Colombia	Lima et al., 1991a	Consecutive patients attending two primary health care clinics from a disaster area	500	Clinical assessment	DSM-III	24%	Among the victims the rate was 32%, as compared to 11% among the nonvictims.
Colombia	Lima et al., 1991b	Victims of the Armero disaster from two shelters	104	Clinical assessment; symptom checklist	DSM-III	42%	PTSD and major depression accounted for 80% of all diagnoses made.
Fiji	Fairley et al., 1986	Victims of a cyclone	75	GHQ-28; PTSD questionnaire	DSM-III	66% (partial PTSD)	Those who lost more than 35% of body weight had higher rates of PTSD and other psychiatric disorders.
Laos	Moore and Boehnlein, 1991	Laotian refugees resettled in the U.S. and attending an Indochinese psychiatric program	84	Clinical assessment	DSM-III	88%	All patients with PTSD also had a diagnosis of major depression.
Lebanon	Saigh, 1991	Children exposed to war-related trauma episodes	840	Children's PTSD inventory	DSM-III	27%	6.9% were traumatized through direct experience; 15.2% through observation; 1.5% through verbal mediation; 3.6% by a combination thereof.
Mexico	Conyer et al., 1987	Victims of an earthquake	524	DIS, SCID	DSM-III	32%	

Location	Study	Population	N	Assessment	Criteria	Rate	Findings
Nicaragua	Summerfield and Toser, 1991	Former refugees still living in a war area	43	Clinical assessment; GHQ-28	DSM-III-R	25% (men); 50% (women)	62% of men and 91% of women were positive on the GHQ. Sustained sleep disturbance, hyperalertness and other anxiety-based symptomatology and poor concentration were frequently found.
Puerto Rico	Canino et al., 1990	Victims of a flood	321	DIS/DS	DSM-III	4%	The prevalence rate of PTSD in the unexposed control group (n = 591) was 0.7%. Other common disorders among the exposed were depression and anxiety.
Southeast Asians in the U.S.	Kinzie et al., 1990	Refugees in the U.S. attending a psychiatric clinic	40	Clinical assessment; PTSD checklist	DSM-III-R	75% (lifetime); 70% (current)	High chronicity of PTSD symptoms. Most cases never diagnosed before the start of the study.
	Kroll et al., 1989	Refugees in the U.S. seen at a psychiatric clinic	404	Clinical assessment	DSM-III	14%	15–30% of the surveyed subjects reported specific traumatic experiences either in their homeland or during their escape.
	Mollica et al., 1987	Refugees in the U.S. attending an Indochinese psychiatric clinic	52	DIS	DSM-III	50%	Each patient had experienced a mean of 10 traumatic events and 2 torture experiences. Many had a concurrent major affective disorder.
Vietnamese in the U.S.	Hinton et al., 1993	Refugees in the U.S. attending a health screening clinic	209	ADIS	DSM-III-R	3.5%	Refugees who reported more traumatic events were significantly more likely to have one or more DSM-III-R disorders.

ADIS = Anxiety Disorder Interview Schedule; DIS = Diagnostic Interview Schedule; DS = Disaster Supplement; DSM-III = Diagnostic and Statistical Manual of Mental Disorders; GHQ = General Health Questionnaire; PTSD = Post-Traumatic Stress Disorder; SADS = Schedule for Affective Disorders and Schizophrenia; SCID = Structured Clinical Interview for DSM III-R.

Source: de Girolamo and McFarlane, In Press.

tures produced by torture as pathological? Should a medical diagnosis be avoided
even though it will legitimate useful rehabilitation programs and compensation
from the state? A medical diagnosis is never a complete account of the distress a
person experiences; in the same sense, PTSD is like the diagnosis of post-traumatic
bone fracture, merely one of the many bad results of an evil event destructive of
human rights.

Summary: The Biosocial Origins of Mental Illnesses

No single model accounts for the role of social, environmental, and biological factors causing mental illnesses. Current research provides strong evidence that all
mental disorders are biosocial and that whatever physiological processes are
involved, the quality of a person's social environment influences both vulnerability
to mental illness and the course of that illness. Mental disorders are not simply
symptoms of broader social conditions; nevertheless, poverty, lack of security, violence, the lack of healthy family relationships during childhood, and trauma or
significant losses—all described throughout this report—are crucial factors for
mental illness. Indeed, although mental illnesses can be categorized and diagnosed,
they most often are found in constellations that bind together biological forces,
social conditions, cultural responses, and particular illness forms.

The interrelation between tropical disease and mental disorder is a case in point. A
tropical disease can lead to neuropsychiatric impairment; infestations of cysticercosis
(tapeworm) result in brain cysts that give rise to epileptic seizures. It can also affect
the psychological well-being of a person afflicted by the disease; infestations of dracunculiasis (guinea worm) and ascariasis (roundworm) lead to chronic fatigue and
limited work capacity. The effects of malaria, which can result in coma when the
brain itself is infected, can serve as biological, psychological, or social stressors operating in a cultural context that precipitate or shape the features of specific psychiatric
problems.[48] At the same time, the risk of being infected by those parasitic agents is
closely related to patterns of water-use behavior and of using (or not using) mosquito-
proof netting. In India, meanwhile, the social stigma associated with lymphatic filariasis contributes to psychological distress and social discord among its victims.[49]

Specific models account for how social factors influence the onset and chronicity
of particular neuropsychological conditions. For example, micronutrient deficiency
in childhood, associated with malnutrition, poverty, and dislocation, can lead to neurological deficits and brain dysfunction (see Chapter 7). Although schizophrenia has
no known social etiology, social and cultural factors strongly influence the likelihood
of recovery. Trauma in childhood, such as the loss of a parent, increases vulnerability for depression; significant losses, violence and trauma, particularly when suffered
by people who are relatively powerless and have few personal and social resources,
are important triggers of depression. Acute trauma can result in depression, generalized anxiety, or serious psychophysiological distress. Programs of prevention and
care thus require classic public health interventions (immunizations of children, iodination of salt), strategies based on our knowledge of specific conditions (violence
toward women), rehabilitation programs for persons with major psychotic disorders,
and long-term efforts to interrupt vicious cycles of poverty and violence.

The Treatment of Mental Illness:
Global Challenges, Local Responses

Review of the current status of mental health care in the societies of Asia, Africa, the Middle East, and Latin America must begin not with professional services but with "ethnomedical systems." This approach might seem paradoxical to some, but there is a good reason for it. Mental illnesses are always experienced and treated in local health care systems—local systems of cultural knowledge, local family structures, communities, and systems of popular and folk healing, as well as local medical services. Societies have multiple healing traditions that are drawn on not only to treat mental illnesses and psychosocial problems, but to make sense of them, categorize and explain their causes, and organize personal and community responses. Any effort to provide mental health care or clinical services must therefore begin with an understanding of local forms of distress and illness, systems of signs and meanings used to interpret illness and organize responses, and local systems of care.

The influence of local medical knowledge on the experience and expression of mental illness is recursive; how illness is understood and responded to actually shapes the illness itself, organizing symptoms, interpretations, and care-seeking activities in behavioral pathways that differ across societies and ethnic groups.[50] Families, healers, and physicians are not faced with "schizophrenia" or "depression" or "anxiety," each overlaid with particular cultural beliefs. They are approached with complaints of *nervios*, or "soul loss," with problems caused by "fright" or shocking traumatic experiences, with troubled dreams or feelings of weakness that suggest neurasthenia, witchcraft, or sorcery, or with recurring symptoms suggesting a possessing spirit. And each of these is treated by local therapeutic activities (see Box 2.2).

Every local system of medical knowledge and healing must cope with prolonged sadness and withdrawal, with violence and irrational anger, and with seizures, emotional distress, and acute and chronic forms of madness. However, traditional systems do not divide off such conditions as "mental" disorders to be treated in a separate sector of health services. In fact, although every known society has labels and treatments for types of madness, each society also has indigenous processes of "normalization," of resisting the label of "madness" for oneself or a kin member, in order to avoid the stigma and implications of a social consensus that one is mad, and of offering less stigmatizing explanations that offer practical approaches to treatment and hope for cure.

The role of diverse ethnomedical systems in the management of mental illness can be summarized by several observations.[52] First, all societies experience, recognize, and treat neuropsychiatric disorders. Although some forms of experience and behavior—anger, sadness and withdrawal, disordered thinking, memory loss—are more troubling in some societies than others, in no society is madness or emotional distress glorified or treated as normal. In most ethnomedical systems, however, there is no domain of "mental illness" that is the equivalent of the one identified in current medical theory and practice. In communities in the United States and France, Indonesia and Kenya, illness is experienced as nerves or nervous breakdowns, or as weakness, spells, or periods of madness, and care is sought from a wide range of available resources. As a consequence, careful research is needed to

Box 2.2 Spirit Loss and Shamanic Healing in Nepal

The Yolmo Sherpa, a Tibetan Buddhist people who live amid the foothills of the Helambu region of north-central Nepal, believe that individuals and families suffer distress for a variety of reasons. Physical pains can trouble the body, ghosts can haunt a family's household, or a person's business can suffer from an unfortunate astrological alignment. One of the most common forms of illness is a malady that can be translated as "spirit loss." Yolmo wa, or the "Yolmo people," possess several kinds of life-forces, each of which can depart from the body. The *bla*, or "spirit," is one such force. Most often, a sudden fright causes the *bla* to vacate the body and wander about the countryside, prey to malevolent ghosts, demons, and witches. If the spirit "leaves" the body, a person loses the volition to act in life: the body feels "heavy," lacks energy or "passion," and the afflicted person does not care to eat, talk, work, travel, or socialize. Thoughts become "dull" and unbalanced. The person can also have trouble sleeping and is prone to further illnesses.

If a villager suffers from spirit loss, the family summons a shaman. If the shaman deems that the malady is a serious one, he conducts an elaborate, all-night healing ceremony in which he performs a variety of rites. With sacred chants, the healer calls deities to "fall" into his body in order to have them tell about the causes of his client's illness; he sacrifices a chicken or goat to appease any gods; and he removes poisonous "harms" from the client's body and household. Toward the end of the rite, in the early-morning hours, the shaman performs a "spirit-hooking" ceremony in which his own spirit journeys on a magical flight to the land of the dead to track down the patient's lost "spirit." The shaman scavenges like a hawk, circling the skies, until he spies the spirit. Once he "hooks" the spirit, he returns to the house and deposits the spirit in several foods (milk, meat, egg, curd) set in bowls upon a tray before the patient. By eating from each of these foods, the patient reincorporates the lost vitality.

The characteristics of spirit loss among the Yolmo, and the shaman's healing rites, throw into sharp relief the profound cultural underpinnings of illness and health. One cannot really speak, in more than general terms, of the "mental health" of the Yolmo wa, primarily because they themselves do not make a strict division between bodily and mental aspects of human agency. Yet the phenomenon of spirit loss bears a close resemblance to what we call "depression." It could be argued that when a Yolmo wa loses her spirit, she is "actually" depressed, with the features of spirit loss merely the cultural dressing on a more basic, biologically based disorder. And yet the absence of some of the defining features of clinical depression (such as feelings of guilt or worthlessness, recurrent thoughts of death, and suicidal ideation) suggests that spirit loss among the Yolmo is similar to, but not equivalent to, depression. In other words, spirit loss and depression bear a family resemblance to one another, without one being more basic than the other, with the nature of each deeply tied to a distinct cultural setting. Clinicians would therefore need to take care great care, in this corner of the world, in finding, diagnosing, or treating depression in the Western psychiatric manner.

Yolmo shamans possess a vast repertoire of ritual techniques that serve a variety of implicit and explicit functions: the oracular divinations, for instance, help to identify social tensions within a family or community, and the spirit-calling rites help to change the sensory underpinnings of a patient's body. By changing what a patient knows, thinks, and feels, a shaman is often able to heal. At the same time, shamans are unable to effectively treat some illnesses, such as tuberculosis, amoebic dysentery, and most forms of "madness." And while shamans are most adept at healing illnesses related to personal distress or social conflicts, some patients repeatedly fall ill, primarily because shamans can readily address the symptoms of malaise, but not their underlying causes.

A comparison of the shaman's craft with other therapeutic practices points to key similarities in healing traditions worldwide. And yet the rites can only be fully appreciated when understood within the context of Yolmo ways of life, from the nature of social interactions to the cultural construction of bodies and selves. Indeed, much of the efficacy and value of the rites relates to the fact that they are deeply tied to a cultural tradition. The introduction of new cultural practices or of new medical technologies, without efforts to conserve important traditions, could have unfortunate and irreversible consequences.[51]

enable clinicians or epidemiologists to translate between the categories and theories of contemporary psychiatry and local cultural systems. The difficulties associated with training primary care practitioners to make appropriate use of psychiatric medications and counseling should not be underestimated.

Second, mental illnesses are treated by folk healers and specialists in every society we know, whether or not medical practitioners or psychiatrists are available. The nature of healers and therapies—elaborate ritual dramas, herbal medicine specialists, possession rituals—varies by medical tradition and region. However, there is no distinct group of "folk psychiatrists." Healers treat a variety of conditions, some classified as neuropsychiatric disorders by contemporary medicine; but as there is no clear category of mental illnesses, so too there is no separate folk sector of psychiatry.

Third, families manage the greatest burden of caring for the mentally ill, worldwide. What constitutes the family in a given society and what resources families have available for responding to mental illness vary greatly. But every health care system includes and is deeply dependent on families. Families are thus at the core of managing the care of persons suffering mental illnesses. These illnesses are a profound burden for families, causing great suffering. The family's meager resources are often consumed in search of care, and enormous time and energy are diverted from other domains of life.

Fourth, we know that there is great cross-cultural diversity in the nature and efficacy of the treatment of the mentally ill, by families as well as healers. Studying "outcomes" of the treatments of folk healers—or families—is complex, given the diversity of illnesses they attend to and the difficulty of establishing "controlled" experimental conditions without completely altering the treatment context. However, in many parts of the world, particularly in Africa, healers provide the great majority of all treatment for the mentally ill and often do so with compassion and cultural force.

There is a considerable body of research on healing and healers.[53] The few empirically grounded studies are consistent in their findings that folk and shamanic healers are generally effective in alleviating malaise spawned by psychological and social distress.[54] Many healers are charismatic and draw on culturally sanctioned healing rituals that radiate power, inspire confidence, and attend to their clients' experience. Many are successful in remoralizing their clients, giving the sufferers and families a sense of control over their illness, and providing great benefit to certain classes of patients. Some patients are resistant to any treatment, whether medical, folk, or family-based. Data are available for some societies on the types of patients for which certain indigenous healers are most successful, and we know that healers often engender greater satisfaction than physicians or mental health workers or psychiatric facilities. It should be recognized, however, that some healers are abusive, and some indigenous "asylums" are as bad as the worst psychiatric asylums.

Research on particular forms of family response to the mentally ill across cultures is more limited. Recent work suggests that the emotions expressed toward the mentally ill by other family members can influence the course and prognosis of their illnesses. For example, hostile responses of family members predict rehospitalization for patients with schizophrenia and depression.[55] Recent programs in China show that the development of psychoeducational interventions with families has the potential for great benefit.[56]

In sum, local healing systems—from families to popular and folk healers to a variety of nonphysician personnel—provide the vast majority of care and support for those who suffer from mental health problems. Planning for the application of current psychiatric knowledge in local communities in societies in Asia, Africa, and Latin America should first strive to "do no harm"—that is, to enhance existing local strengths rather than attempt to eliminate what might be viewed as irrational or traditional from the perspective of contemporary biomedicine. The development of psychiatric services should be undertaken with careful attention to local ethnomedical systems (see Box 2.3). It should also be recognized, however, that efforts to provide a *full* integration of professional mental health services and traditional healing systems have seldom been successful and should be avoided. At their best, efforts to bring healers and psychiatrists together—in Senegal, Nigeria, and Mali, or with the Navajo—have increased the understanding of mental health professionals for the work of healers and improved coordination of mental health care. At worst, efforts at integration have sometimes been designed to eliminate the work of healers or to allow professionals to abandon responsibility to provide medical care. Neither glorification nor control of traditional healers has benefited mental health services. And a primary focus on healers has often led to the neglect of the most crucial community resource for the mentally ill, which is the family.

Mental Health Services in International Perspective

The formal sector of "Western" or "cosmopolitan" mental health services varies greatly across regions and societies of Asia, Africa, Latin America, and the Pacific. In China, there are three mental health workers for every million citizens; all of Fiji has one psychiatrist. Other Western Pacific countries report a paucity of psychiatrists (see Table 2.4). In rural Tanzania it is estimated that the ratio of physicians to population is 1 to 20,000, while that of traditional doctors is 1 to 25.[58] With psychiatrists numbering fewer than twenty, and total spending on health as little as 5 U.S. cents per person annually, biomedicine provides strictly limited mental health care in that society.[59] In Taiwan, on the other hand, a society not long ago considered part of the "developing" world, the annual budget for mental health care reached 28 million

Box 2.3 Mental Health in Amerindian Populations

In April 1993, the Pan American Health Organization held a consultative meeting on "Indigenous Peoples and Health" in Winnipeg, Canada. It soon became clear that indigenous peoples attending the meeting did not share the same notion of "health" as conceived by official health agencies and member states of the World Health Organization. Whereas the latter spoke of psychiatric disorders and risk factors, representatives of indigenous nations stressed the importance of respecting the sanctity of life on earth and the holistic character of health.

The contrast underscores the serious differences found in many South American countries between national health policies and how Indians themselves see the problems and their potential solutions. The differences are pressing ones, given the mental health problems of Latin American Indians today, which are inseparable from their continuing subjugation, forced acculturation, deteriorating local ecosystems, and invasions of their land by loggers, miners, and herders. The majority of indigenous peoples in Latin America live in abject poverty, occupying the lowest social and economic echelons in their national societies. Most Indians are powerless under the threat of being assimilated into the dominant culture or nation-state. National austerity programs, limited economic opportunities, and armed conflicts have led to additional health risks. Indigenous peoples in Latin America have a consistently shorter life expectancy than the mainstream populations, a higher mortality, and a different and changing morbidity profile.

These changes have led to new and greater health needs. The frequency of mental illness among Indians is greater than in the mainstream of national populations. Developmental disorders, depressive and anxiety disorders (including culture-bound syndromes such as *nervios*), maladaptive behavior associated with alcohol abuse, and acculturative stress–related problems (including suicide and accidental and violent death) are of pressing concern among indigenous peoples. The gap between increasing health needs and existing health services is so large that neither the official health system nor existing primary health care services are able to deal with cultural differences and the beginning health transition. Nor can traditional healing practices deal effectively with the global challenges and the emergence of diseases such as cholera and AIDS.

If mental health services for indigenous peoples continue to be based on Western values, there can be only modest success in modifying the prevailing patterns of mental health care. Asylums and custodial hospitals tend only to increase chronicity, isolate patients, and provide a poor repertoire of alternative therapies. By underscoring the importance of local values, differences in meaning systems, and plural categories of illness, a culturally salient approach can help to provide a better understanding of the forces that affect health and medical care. Such an approach can also help indigenous peoples to better express their views of mental health problems and develop health services founded on those views. With the active participation of indigenous groups, and an understanding of the distinct needs and cultures of these groups, governments can implement programs that more successfully attend to the mental health of aboriginal peoples.[57]

U.S. dollars in 1993 (compared to $6,300 in 1980), spurred not only by great economic growth but also by the emergence of a new commitment to mental health care in the 1980s.

The diversity of these systems of mental health care has several sources. First, it reflects local experiences with colonial medicine and the differential influences of

Table 2.4 Mental Health Data: Western Pacific

Country	Psychiatrists per 100,000 Population	Beds per 100,000 Population
Australia	9.2	7.4
China	0.3[a]	0.73
Fiji	—[b]	2.56
Hong Kong	1.24	7.3
Japan	7.08	35.7
Korea	1.58	2.86
Malaysia	0.28	2.28
New Zealand	5.64	8.55
Papua New Guinea	—[b]	0.59
Philippines	0.034[c]	1.13
Singapore	1.49	11.06
Vietnam	0.09	0.78

[a] Including nonqualified mental health workers.

[b] One psychiatrist for the whole country.

[c] There has been a massive "brain drain" to the United States.

Source: Shinfuku, 1993.

particular historical moments of psychiatric theory and treatment. Colonial administrators built asylums that reflected British, French, German, or Dutch theories of madness and its management. Indeed, a large mental hospital, along with a central bureaucracy, a national school system, and a police force, was often part of the legacy of a retreating tide of colonialism.

"Western" psychiatric theory and institutions have been appropriated in quite distinctive ways, elaborated in relation to local psychologies, and put at the service of particular state powers. In Japan, German theories of "neurasthenia" served as a beginning point for the development of an elaborate Japanese theory of neurosis and for Morita psychotherapy; professional psychiatry in China elaborated neurasthenia in relation to Russian behaviorist psychology and local Chinese psychological concepts. In Thailand, royal patronage of mental health services lent them prestige, whereas treatment of the insane was largely devalued and often inhumane in many other societies. In South Africa and the former Soviet Union, governments abused psychiatric institutions in order to confine political dissidents and manage "antisocial" thought and behavior. In Nigeria and Tanzania, on the other hand, the asylum concept was elaborated into a local mental health "village" system for care and management of those with severe chronic mental illnesses.

The influence of mental health policies developed in Europe and North America or in the World Health Organization have continued to the present, with "dispensary"—or outpatient—care, crisis services, the "deinstitutionalization," "decentralization," and "privatization" of health services, the provision of psychiatric treatment as part of primary health care systems, and the integration of indigenous healers into systems of health services each having their day. All of these reflect episodes in the history of available therapeutic technologies and thinking about the organization and financing of health services. In many societies, mental health specialists are well-versed in the most recent of this plethora of policy models, but do not have the resources to implement particular strategies, even as new strategies are being developed.

The international diversity of mental health systems also reflects broad regional patterns. Sub-Saharan African nations face desperate economic problems, a crisis of the authority of the state, failing bureaucratic infrastructures, and a scarcity of personnel and resources. On the other hand, many have rich and diverse traditions of ritual healing and knowledgeable healing specialists. Efforts to develop innovative mental health services relying on primary care workers and traditional healers have been undertaken, but some of the most exciting—such as that in Mali—have been cut short by economic restructuring policies.[60]

Mental health services in Central and South America are marked by fragmentation and enormous disparity of services for rich and poor, even where overall funding levels are less desperate by world standards. Mexico, for instance, has psychiatric beds and hospitals under the jurisdiction of the Department of Health and Public Assistance (SSA), Social Security, the Army, and the Navy, along with many psychoanalytically trained practitioners in private practice, severely complicating any general assessments of the access of Mexicans to mental health services. Brazil struggles with the problem of providing adequate care for rural areas, the urban poor, and indigenous populations, even with its 6,000 psychiatrists, 60,000 psychologists, and 100 psychiatric hospitals.[61] Similarly, while Chile has a psychiatrist-to-population ratio quite close to WHO standards, underserved populations are still a problem because a substantial number of psychiatrists are in private practice.

Asian societies, although increasingly linked in trade and industrial development, have wide variations both between and within nations. However, many continue to struggle to provide even basic mental health services. Bangladesh, in 1984, had a mere 500 psychiatric beds for a population of nearly 100 million.[62] Malaysia relies on forty psychiatrists and 800 nurses to serve a population of 15 million people, while Bhutan apparently lacks formal mental health services entirely.[63] India has great internal diversity by region. For example, the Indian psychiatrist Narendra Wig describes an active and seemingly adequate community-oriented psychiatric program in Kerala, whereas other states (such as Himachal Pradesh) are apparently without formal psychiatric services.[64]

In spite of regional variation, practitioners and planners in Africa, Asia, and Latin America face common difficulties in efforts to make the benefits of contemporary psychiatry available to people suffering mental illnesses. In nearly all societies, rich and poor, a lack of sustained public investment in mental health services mirrors the low priority given to psychiatric care by national governments, aid agencies, and the international public health community. Although reliable figures are nearly impossible to find, Kilonzo's estimate that 4% of Tanzania's small health budget goes to psychiatric services is indicative. (In the United States, estimates have remained at approximately 16% for some years.)[65] Failure to place mental health care on national and international agendas has severely limited efforts to develop basic mental health services and often left prevention and rehabilitative care almost entirely unaddressed.

The burden of servicing national debts and the imposition of economic restructuring, particularly when combined with corrupt governance, has had important consequences for already poorly funded services. A letter from a Nigerian psychiatrist speaks for many in impoverished nations. Given "some 12 years of mismanagement, corruption, etc.," he writes,

> services in the realm of education, health and other social services have virtually ceased to have any meaning or direction in this country. . . . Until the early '80s, there were some services mainly in forms of psychiatric facilities scattered all over the country. . . . With the run-down of the facilities consequent on the neglect due to severe under-funding, what was subsidized (cost of drugs, bed fees, feeding etc.) was completely passed to the families of our patients. As most of these families were poor, most of the patients who would have opted for orthodox forms of treatment (mainly medication anyway) were either left to roam about as vagrants or kept at traditional and faith-healing centers. . . . The low priority accorded mental health in overall health planning does not help the situation in developing countries like Nigeria where competing claims made by infectious and parasitic diseases are difficult to ignore.

Lack of financial resources thus constantly threatens to undo efforts to build even basic services.

Many countries also face critical shortages of psychiatric facilities and trained personnel to staff a mental health system. The contrast between high- and low-income countries is staggering. The United States has more than 42,000 fully trained adult and child psychiatrists, plus 5,000 to 6,000 in training at the end of 1993.[66] There are also 60,000 psychologists, 85,000 social workers, and 75,000 psychiatric nurses for a population of just 260 million.[67] These figures are to be compared with Nigeria's 60 psychiatrists, several hundred psychiatric nurses, and less than 100 psychiatric social workers for a population of 100 million, and Zimbabwe's 10 psychiatrists for a population of 10 million. The ratio of psychiatrists to population in the United States is approximately 170 times higher than that in Nigeria. This problem is exacerbated by the lack of psychiatric training given to general medical practitioners and by the absence of a psychosocial approach to medical practice. Where primary care visits often last only a few minutes and extended conversations between patient and physician are expected by neither party, efforts to introduce psychiatric assessment and counseling into primary care medicine are made virtually impossible.

The inadequate supply of psychotropic medications in national dispensaries, and the lack of training of medical personnel in the rational use of such medications, adds to the difficulties of promoting quality treatment of those with neuropsychiatric disorders. Virtually all accounts of local health services stress the cost, availability, and appropriate use of pharmaceuticals as a critical problem for the development of mental health services.

Finally, the lack of resources and personnel devoted to mental health care is matched by the low esteem in which the mentally ill themselves are held in many societies. The "mad" are widely feared as dangerous or held up to ridicule, and even in societies (such as Taiwan) where families care for the mentally ill, the burden and stigma to families has led to a thriving sector of folk asylums. With urbanization, changing employment patterns, and increased geographic mobility, the care of the mentally ill within networks of family and community is threatened. When they become "vagrants," they are even more likely to be viewed as less than fully human; the desire to isolate the mentally ill thus undercuts those social practices that have permitted a less severe course for schizophrenia in nonindustrial countries.

These processes thus join to threaten the basic human rights of the mentally ill. Argentina, classified by the World Bank as an upper-middle-income country at a GNP per capita of almost $2800 in 1991, tolerates deplorable public mental hospitals. The enormity of the problem became visible in the summer of 1990 when thirty patients died from severe malnutrition in the Moyano Hospital in Buenos Aires, a state-run 1,600-bed asylum for women. More than official neglect was responsible. The tragedy could only have happened because families had abandoned their relatives as completely as though they were already dead (see Box 2.1).[68]

Directions for Mental Health Services: A Challenge to Action

In the face of these profound challenges to the development of services for persons suffering neuropsychiatric disorders, the World Health Organization and the international mental health community have devised a number of innovative strategies that have fostered quality health services in even some of the poorest countries. From more than a decade of demonstration intervention projects, there is a general consensus on the basic principles that ought to guide those who would improve mental health services.

First, although national plans are only as valuable as their implementation, national and regional commitment is necessary if mental health care is to be made a priority and if limited resources are to be put to their best use. Mental health services need to be recognized as a priority of national health and social policy; this recognition must be conveyed to important institutions and to the general public and the commitment must be sustained. Care for the mentally ill must be specifically discussed in national health programs, with a clear description of appropriate budgetary allocations and of activities that will be undertaken to help the mentally ill and their families. This commitment requires the support of international financial agencies who today exert great influence on the allocation of public funds in many poor societies.

Second, it is now widely agreed not only that the old insane asylum is a blueprint for dehumanizing treatment, but that many of the practices associated with such asylums are violations of basic human rights.[69] The United Nations Commission on Human Rights concluded that medical treatment should be a basic right for those suffering mental illnesses; further, in providing treatment and in protecting sufferers and others from potential danger, basic human rights must also be protected. Legal safeguards are therefore a prerequisite to humane care.

The introduction of new legislation in Kenya points to the significance of changing laws regarding the care of the mentally ill. As with other sub-Saharan countries, the economic crisis and increasing rates of urbanization in Kenya have led to a situation in which people are threatened with neglect or abandonment. While its neighbors are trying to tackle similar problems, Kenya has gone the furthest in implementing new legislation. Whereas the former legislation only covered the handling of patients with mental illness (e.g., their hospitalization, discharge, repatriation, and the management of their property), the new legislation is also concerned with efforts to decriminalize, demystify, and destigmatize mental illness, with making mental health care more "communal" and less centralized, with simplifying admissions, and with integrating mental health services within the nation's general governmental services. As a result of the 1991 Mental Health Act, over half of all government general hospitals opened their doors to psychiatric patients, psychiatric nurses were deployed equitably in general hospitals around the country, general medical officers became involved in mental health care, outpatient mental health clinics were set up in general hospitals, and some outreach services were established. In addition, the Kenya Board of Mental Health has begun to meet regularly, regulations for the administration of the Act have been formulated, and financial provision adjustments continue to be made. Thus, new and quite commonsensical legislation has sparked a veritable revolution in mental health care.[70]

Third, there is increasing optimism about the potential for a new community psychiatry for many countries. A study group of the World Health Organization concluded a review of mental health research and demonstration projects with what has come to be a central conviction of mental health planners:

> Economic constraints should not be accepted as a reason for abandoning mental health planning, since in the long run reduction of chronic disability in any population must be economically advantageous. The Study Group was also convinced that a policy of basing mental health care in the community, as far as possible as an integral part of primary health care services, offers the best hope of developing effective national programs at relatively low cost—and certainly more cheaply than any development of hospital and institutionally based programs.[71]

With the support of the World Health Organization, demonstration projects have been conducted in countries as diverse as India, the Philippines, and Tanzania to "extend mental health care" into both rural and urban communities.[72] These programs depend on successful training (or retraining) of primary health workers and general practitioners, the management of pharmaceuticals, the provision of consultants and referral sites, and the use of primary care auxiliary staff. Despite difficulties in these projects, they have been shown to reduce hospitalization and the unnecessary use of district outpatient services, and to provide quality care (see Box 2.4 and Box 2.5).

Fourth, the development of specialized hospital units in district hospitals, rather than continued support for large central psychiatric hospitals, is now considered most appropriate. Understanding such units as extensions of community-based programs, rather than as the heart of a mental health system, maintains the emphasis on community-based care.

Box 2.4 A Village-Based Mental Health Service in Nigeria

In 1954, Dr. Thomas Lambo, then a professor of psychiatry at the University of Ibadan, and some colleagues initiated a pilot experiment in community psychiatry at Aro, a rural suburb of the ancient town of Abeokuta, sixty miles from the federal capital of Western Nigeria. A therapeutic unit to accommodate several hundred patients was grafted onto four large traditional villages inhabited by Yoruba tribesmen and their extended families. The four villages surrounded the Aro Hospital.

Each patient admitted to the treatment program had to be accompanied by at least one member of his family who could cook for him, wash his clothes, and accompany him to the hospital for treatment. Patients, their families, and the villagers themselves regularly attended church services, plays, dances, and social functions held at the hospital.

In the second phase, outpatient services were developed in two smaller villages in full consultation with the village elders. Clinics were equipped to provide all forms of modern therapy, including a small laboratory for routine investigations. In addition, a mobile clinic was used to penetrate to more distant villages in the area.

Program developers made sure that the ratio of normal villagers to the patient population was maintained at six villagers to four patients. Small villages in the vicinity of the clinics were encouraged to take new patients into their homes. As a quid pro quo, loans and grants from the hospital helped to improve local water supply and sanitation. A major feature of the program of care was collaboration with traditional healers. Most of the healers had considerable prior experience in the management of African patients. They supervised and directed the social and group activities in the villages under the guidance of mental health workers.

Lambo identified social, medical, and economic advantages of the village scheme. The social advantages are that care becomes an integral part of the community; community attitudes about mental illness become more positive; the scheme permits assessment of the social competence of patients in the natural environment of the village rather than the artificial setting of a hospital. Medical advantages include an optimal therapeutic environment that combines treatment and rehabilitation, the promotion of a spirit of collaboration with behavioral scientists, and the creation of an environment that fosters community. The economic advantages include relatively low cost and the ability to deploy meager human and material resources in the most strategically effective way.

In his summary of the status of the program in 1963, Lambo noted that "such a scheme can operate in non-industrial agrarian communities . . . where the threshold of community tolerance is high; . . . with the advent of social change, difficulties may ensue."[73] Regrettably, they did.

Professor Olatawura of the University College Hospital in Ibadan reports that Aro Village has been completely swallowed up by the sprawling expansion of the city of Abeokuta.[74] Although the practice of admitting patients with their relatives into the "village" still exists, the involvement of the community is much less active than before. The previous program is now reduced to occasional group activity involving nursing aides, patients, and their relatives. The patient population has contracted from an average daily presence of thirty to forty to an average of ten. The active involvement of traditional healers and shrine nurses, which formed part of the initial reports, has not been part of the program for the last two decades.

Professor Olatawura concludes that "the Aro Village scheme has been a victim of Western style modernity that has characterized the health care system of the country over the recent years." Modernization of the system in the Western model elsewhere in the country made it impossible for the Aro scheme to take off in other parts of the country. For all of the exciting features of the program, it proved to be unsustainable in the face of larger social forces.

Box 2.5 Community Mental Health in Swaziland

How does one organize effective mental health services for a dispersed population in a country with few resources to commit to mental health concerns?

In Swaziland, a small but innovative Community Mental Health Program was initiated by using new treatment concepts and already established health networks. Before 1980, mental health care in Swaziland was centered around a single custodial mental hospital, inaccessible to many and feared by the general public. Most admissions were for people with violent behavior; the police brought in many of the 500 yearly admissions. Because of a lack of staff (six trained nurses and thirty untrained orderlies), violent cases were controlled by physical restraints, and patients restrained in cells often burned or battered down the doors. Given its negative image and the stigma attached to it, the hospital had few advocates in the Ministry of Health and was a low priority in the health budget.

In contrast to a centralized mental health custodial system, the general health services had branched out to the dispersed rural population. District hospitals had been set up and staffed by general medical officers; the hospitals were connected to a network of primary care clinics headed by diagnostic nurse practitioners. In addition, village health workers, who received three months' training in basic health and first aid, were assigned to forty homesteads that they visited regularly, providing basic health care and sending the seriously ill to the clinics.

The Community Mental Health Program, developed by Dr. E. A. Guinness, a British psychiatrist, was established to meet mental health needs unmet by the central mental hospital while also working within the primary health care network. Since the demands of primary care would continue to make mental health a low priority, the community program trained a cadre of community psychiatric nurses rather than train primary care health workers in mental health issues.

The program applied a number of concepts that were new to Swaziland at the time. Using the existing community health structure and tapping into the extended family network, it identified major mental illnesses and advocated treating them at the community level. This was important because early treatment could help to reduce relapse. The program also promoted a multidisciplinary role for the community psychiatric nurses. The nurses incorporated the nursing skills of ward and clinic management and the diagnostic and prescribing skills of a doctor; they also served as counselors, teachers, and advisors. The program concentrated on a number of other areas that were critical to its success. For example, the nurses were given a one-year intensive training program that involved not only theoretical issues but on-site diagnostic experience and apprenticeships under the supervision of Dr. Guinness. The job of community psychiatric nurse was supported with an adequate salary and identified by the Manpower Commission in the career structure. In this way, it was given a status within the labor hierarchy so that it would attract qualified nurses.

Five areas of mental health—psychosis, epilepsy, alcohol and drug abuse, depression and child psychiatry—were identified as the most common illnesses ineffectively handled at the central hospital. The nurses were instructed to identify these conditions and, after training in basic pharmacology, could dispense medicine to treat them. A series of workshops and seminars were conducted at all levels in the health hierarchy to inform and instruct people about mental illness and the community program. As a result, the nurses worked closely with local healers and village chiefs to gain both acceptance in communities and to help identify illnesses.

The psychiatrist (Dr. Guinness) was fundamental in the ongoing development of the program. He acted as an advocate and negotiator on behalf of the program and the nurses, and supervised the nurses' in-community clinical training and pharmacology instruction and helped streamline the diagnostic process by designing a history-taking form and diagnostic and treatment protocols. He also trained a team to eventually assume his responsibilities.

The Community Mental Health Program emerged as a successful and well-received service. In 1983, there were fifteen community health clinics treating the mentally ill. By 1986, there were fifty, many of them mobile. The treatment of outpatients rose from 2,000 in 1982 to 12,000 in 1986. Although admission to the central hospital continued to rise, there was a more rapid turnover in bed occupancy, indicating a reduction in chronicity. The program was still in place and operating in 1990. Although there had been some attrition of the original thirty nurses, many were still practicing and were highly respected and sought out in the local communities.

The shortcomings of the program became evident after a number of years. The multiple demands on the psychiatric nurses contributed to the attrition rate. Further, after the departure of Dr. Guinness, there was no single advocate of the program or ongoing support in the Ministry of Health. Clinical supervision and the training of new psychiatric nurses suffered under the lack of a central authority. Transportation to the rural areas remained a problem, as did the competition for resources between the hospital and the communities. Nevertheless, the strengths of the program—a constructive role for the psychiatric nurses, effective tools with which to address unmet mental health needs, acceptance in the local communities, and organization within an existing health structure—were established. Despite continuing problems, the core of the program remained intact.[75]

Fifth, associated with this general strategy is a shift in functions of various personnel. In particular, psychiatrists act as teachers and consultants, rather than as front-line mental health care providers; nonphysician personnel become the primary providers.

Sixth, community-based psychiatric rehabilitation services can help to improve the quality of care and the quality of life for the mentally ill. The recent development of such services in China serves as a particularly important example (see Box 2.6).[76] Evaluation studies demonstrate the clinical benefits of such community-based services and their cost efficacy.

Seventh, the family is recognized as the key to the mental health system. In societies such as India, families not only provide care in the community, but provide crucial aspects of hospital care (see Box 2.7).[79] Research indicates the benefits of psychoeducational work with families—both in managing the burden families experience and in increasing the effectiveness of their role as care providers.[80]

Finally, it is clear that both public health interventions and broad policy considerations are needed to prevent neuropsychiatric disorders, to prevent unnecessary impairment and disability, and to promote mental health. Depression and anxiety are more common amid acute stress, chronic conditions of deprivation, losses that overwhelm resources, defeat and despair that assault self-identity, and conditions of insecurity and violence. Policies and programs directed toward families, children,

Box 2.6   Innovations in Community-Based
Rehabilitation Services in China

Although China developed outpatient rehabilitation services in several major cities in the late 1950s, much of the mental health care in the country today conforms to a narrow medical model of psychopharmacological treatment with limited outpatient services and without systematic rehabilitation efforts to engage the family and the community. In recent years, however, an impressive number of experiments in community-based rehabilitation services have sprung up in both urban and rural settings.

Many of the experiments in urban settings integrate a wide range of services, including local hospital outpatient clinics, home-care programs, family education, counseling service, sheltered workshops, and welfare factories with tax relief if a certain percentage of workers are disabled. The emphasis on occupational rehabilitation relates to the fact that employment in Chinese society is essential for access to resources from income to housing, medical insurance, retirement pensions, and other social services. In Shanghai, almost 4000 clients with schizophrenia participate in 141 rehabilitation workshops, with 8 to 90 clients per workshop. The workshops are run by community administrators, retired workers, and nonpsychiatric health workers. Start-up funds are provided by the welfare departments of the urban district government, including salary for the station director, and the station is approved as a tax-free institution. The income of clients is based on the economic value of the products they produce. Most of the work is secondary processing on subcontract to local factories. Occupational therapy is combined with medical treatment, recreation, and some psychosocial education. In at least one controlled clinical trial, these services were shown to improve functioning and reduce symptoms and serious episodes in schizophrenic patients compared to those receiving standard medical treatment only.

In Shenyang, China's fourth-largest city, a community program organizes stable funding of rehabilitation services through development of a profitable welfare enterprise that also provides work for mentally ill clients who are unable to obtain other employment. This program provides work placement, occupational rehabilitation, training in social skills, and medical supervision via alternative treatment venues from day hospitals, factory clinics, and home visits by medical teams to patients with more serious relapses. Although much of the focus is on social control of patients, which helps to alleviate the burden on families, the program appears to have improved social functioning of patients and clearly has improved the delivery of mental health care. Similarly, in Nanjing, a case-control study demonstrated improved outcome of schizophrenic patients who participated in enterprise-based sheltered workshops.

In Shashi, Hubei Province, Xiong Wei and his colleagues developed a family counseling model that involves regularly scheduled outpatient sessions with family members (quite uncommon in China), home visits, a large family group meeting, a newsletter, and ongoing assistance to patient and family in the management of the illness.[77] The family sessions focus on practical and common problems encountered by patients and families from stigma to difficulties in marrying and at work to compliance with medical regimens. The meetings are an opportunity to share experiences, vent frustration, and find solidarity among families who are otherwise stigmatized and marginalized. They also provide education on drugs and their side effects, and on strategies for dealing with common and expectable behavioral and social problems. In a randomized clinical trial with blinded evaluators, follow-up until 18 months showed better functioning and lower rates of rehospitalization in the treatment group compared with controls.

This intervention was so cost-effective it could, were it applied to China's 1.5 million urban schizophrenic patients and their families, save tens of millions of dollars, which could then be used to upgrade China's mental health services substantially.

In rural areas where most Chinese live, important local experiments involving guardianship networks have been undertaken. The guardianship network, unique to China, has replaced the commune and neighborhood committees in the earlier era of collectivization. Usually a group of three individuals—a family member, a health worker, and a community member—acts as a case-management team to assure needed treatment, to intercede on the patient's behalf when social problems arise, and, where feasible, to help integrate services for the patient. Several studies have shown that rural guardianship networks of this kind can lower rates of hospitalization, decrease symptoms and psychosocial distress, and contribute usefully to improved social functioning. The method has also been shown to be affordable.

Unfortunately, with the great current pressure for economic success in China, there is considerable difficulty in developing and sustaining such voluntary networks. Another issue is how to prevent these networks from limiting the rights of patients. Nonetheless, in poor regions with limited medical services and almost no mental health services, rural guardianship networks, together with the use of small county-level psychiatric hospitals, village paramedical practitioners, and home-care services, form a promising program. In general, the chief issues are whether these and other innovative programs can be sustained in a period of surging socioeconomic change, and if they can be generalized and applied throughout this vast nation. Those questions are unanswered, but the innovative experiments noted here show how communities in low-income countries can successfully use a range of rehabilitation programs to respond to the tremen-

migrants and refugees, employment, and the prevention of ethnic conflict can help ameliorate those social sources of illness.

Current strategies for fostering mental health services suggest a broad program of interventions and research that can significantly improve the quality of medical care for those who suffer mental illnesses. Many of these strategies are effective even under conditions of scarce resources. Ultimately, however, a redistribution of resources and a broad commitment to human rights is required to provide adequate support for innovative and sustainable programs of mental health care.

Conclusions

- Mental illnesses constitute a huge burden throughout the world. The World Bank estimates that neuropsychiatric diseases make up 6.8% of the Global Burden of Disease (GBD), measured in disability-adjusted life years (DALYs). For adults aged 15–44 in "demographically developing economies," neuropsychiatric diseases are 12% of the GBD; when "intentional, self-inflicted injuries" are added, the total constitutes 15.1% of the GBD for women, 16.1% for men.
- Depressive disorders are the most prevalent neuropsychiatric disorders, con-

---

Box 2.7   Families in Indian Psychiatry

It is nine in the evening at the psychiatric hospital in Lucknow in Northern India. Patients and family members are engaged in lively conversations, occasionally punctuated by laughter. Family members reside with a hospitalized patient. Referred to as "attendants," the family members fill the wards with conversation, talking to patients, staff, and each other.

The family is intimately involved in a patient's mental health care. Unlike Europe and North America, where the family has too often been viewed as part of the patient's problem, the Indian family is often seen as part of the solution. Family members are expected to help provide therapy for the patient and to take responsibility for his or her cure.

Family involvement is rooted in Indian cultural understandings which dictate that someone other than the sick person make decisions about care. Once the family has determined that a person needs treatment, a family member is chosen to oversee the care. This attendant brings the patient in for outpatient consultations, receives prescriptions, and makes sure the patient complies with the doctor's orders. If the patient is admitted to an acute care hospital, the attendant is expected to stay in the hospital throughout the patient's treatment.

Due to a shortage of nurses, attendants fulfill practical duties rarely provided in Indian psychiatric hospitals. They look after the patient's hygiene, ensure the patient does not run away, take the patient to therapy sessions, make certain that the patient takes his medications, and keep the doctor apprised of day-to-day changes. If the attendant is a woman, she also cooks meals.

Attendants are involved throughout the patient's illness—from consultations through the hospital stay to follow-up treatment—and thus help to ensure patient compliance. Family involvement in a patient's care does not guarantee a cure and, in some cases, the family can be a source of conflict. However, attendants can provide the patient with social and emotional support and are a continual link between the patient and the outside world. Because the patient remains tied to his or her social roots, he or she often has less difficulty adjusting to nonhospital life upon leaving.[81]

---

stituting the largest proportion of community burden. The World Bank's 1993 World Development Report estimates that depression ranks fifth in burden among women, seventh among men.

- Since the most common neuropsychiatric disorders begin during adulthood, the demographic transition will result in a sharp increase in overall burden of such disorders. For example, it is estimated that the total number of cases of schizophrenia in "less developed" countries will increase from 16.7 million in 1985 to 24.4 million in 2000.
- No single model accounts for the role of social, environmental, and biological factors in the etiology of all mental disorders. Current research provides strong evidence that all mental disorders are biosocial and that the quality of a person's social environment is closely related to risk for mental illness and the likelihood that an illness will become chronic. Specific models account for how social factors influence the onset and chronicity of particular neuropsychological conditions, and these suggest specific strategies for prevention and for health services.

- Formal mental health services vary greatly in low- and middle-income countries, as well as by region. In many societies, they are profoundly inadequate. Classic insane asylums not only provide dehumanizing treatment but often abrogate fundamental human rights. With a few exceptions, trained mental health workers—psychiatrists, psychiatric nurses, and other care providers—are too few to meet even the most basic needs of the community. Primary health care workers are often poorly trained to recognize and treat mental disorders. Basic psychiatric medications are often unavailable.

- Many neuropsychiatric illnesses can now be effectively treated. Significant advances have been made in the development of both psychoactive medications and psychosocial therapies. When used properly, medications are effective in the treatment of many patients; when used improperly, they are ineffective and can have dangerous side effects. Treatments that combine appropriate medications with family- or community-based interventions have been shown effective with even serious, chronic mental illnesses.

- There is a broad consensus among specialists worldwide about the basic principles that should guide the organization of mental health services in low-income countries. Mental health services should be decentralized (rather than focused in large centralized hospitals), multifaceted (focusing on the most important mental health problems facing particular communities), culturally relevant (rather than narrowly medical), and sustainable. Explicit priority should be given to developing mental health care as part of primary health care services. Nonmedical agencies, support groups, and service providers should be recognized as important resources, and efforts should be made to enhance their effectiveness. Rational drug use programs should be extended to include psychiatric medications.

- The human rights of the mentally ill should be a significant concern at all levels of policy and services, and should be reflected in mental health legislation.

- Successful demonstration projects have been conducted in many parts of the world, indicating that these principles are practical and relevant to the improvement of mental health services in even the poorest countries. Nonetheless, demonstration projects, even when successful, have too often remained isolated rather than being generalized to whole systems of care. Particular attention should be given to evaluating innovative programs and to extending successful innovations.

- Economic constraints, particularly those resulting from mandated efforts to restructure economies, have placed extreme limits on governments' abilities to develop new services or extend successful programs. In the context of scarcity, mental health services are seldom given high priority by national governments or by international aid programs. The importance of addressing the wide-ranging problems of mental and behavioral health described in this report should be recognized as crucial for both human and economic development. Global development agencies and local governments should make investing in health and mental health a part of all development strategies.

3

Suicide

Suicide continues to be an urgent problem in all countries in the world, especially among youths. More than 1.4 million people committed suicide in 1990, which accounts for roughly 1.6% of the world's mortality for that year.[1] Rates of attempted suicide could be ten to twenty times higher.[2] Suicide is among the top ten causes of death in most countries that report rates and is one of the top two or three causes of death among the young.

Deliberate self-harm often arises from a complex mix of intolerable burden, inability to cope, and social anomie. Acts of suicide relate to a range of social, political, and psychological factors, from sentiments of despair and worthlessness associated with unemployment in Western countries to culturally sanctioned forms of self-annihilation in several Asian societies. Despite the fact that ideas about suicide are deeply rooted in cultural traditions, social-policy makers and mental health workers can take several important steps to prevent many suicides.

Global Trends in Suicide Rates

Because suicide is an event that is highly stigmatized, troubles survivors so deeply, and is illegal in many places, statistics are notoriously unreliable. Only 39 of the 166 member states of the United Nations provide mortality statistics for suicide, but even for those that do provide data, official statistics might underestimate true rates by 30 to 200 percent.[3]

Quite often, selected samples might be more accurate than efforts of most countries to report for the entire country. Indeed, field research that carefully scrutinizes a population can identify more cases, estimate a higher incidence, and reduce biases that selectively influence official statistics. Epidemiological field research in both rural and urban areas of India supports this idea (see Table 3.1). In a study of suicides in 1978 in a village cluster 50 km west of Calcutta, 58 cases of suicide were identified, indicating a rate of 43.4 per 100,000, with roughly three women killing themselves for every man who takes his life.[4] An urban study of suicide in Jhansi, Uttar Pradesh, over a two-year period, 1986–1987, identified 187 suicides, indicating an annual rate of 29 per 100,000. One hundred and three were women.[5]

Although comparative studies based on reported rates serve as a useful approximation, in some cases the statistics are clearly misleading. For example, the state of

Table 3.1 Suicide Rates among Youth and Elderly in Select Countries

Country	Year of Most Recently Available Data	Rate Per 100,000 (Age 15–24)	Rate Per 100,000 (Age 65–74)	Ratio Youth/Elderly
Sri Lanka	1986	62.3	48.6	1.3
Canada	1990	15.0	12.6	1.2
Thailand	1987	9.8	8.4	1.2
Australia	1988	16.4	16.7	1.0
United Kingdom	1991	7.0	7.9	0.9
Ireland	1990	9.3	12.1	0.8
United States	1989	13.3	18.0	0.7
Chile	1989	6.7	9.6	0.7
Costa Rica	1989	6.1	9.6	0.6
Venezuela	1989	6.9	11.3	0.6
Mexico	1990	3.1	5.1	0.6
Korea, Rep. of	1987	8.1	15.9	0.5
USSR	1990	13.9	30.4	0.5
China	1989	21.3	47.8	0.4
Germany, Fed. Rep.	1990	9.9	23.7	0.4
Uruguay	1990	8.2	22.7	0.4
Singapore	1990	10.6	31.5	0.3
Argentina	1989	5.2	19.2	0.3
Japan	1991	7.0	27.6	0.3
Israel	1989	4.9	20.0	0.2
Puerto Rico	1990	6.1	26.1	0.2
Hungary	1991	12.6	61.5	0.2
Hong Kong	1989	6.0	33.6	0.2

Source: WHO Division of Mental Health, Unpublished Statistics except China.

Source for China: WHO, 1991a.

Chapter discusses overall rate for Sri Lanka for 1991—47 per 100,000—but gender-specific rates not available.

Kerala, which has been touted for its exemplary literacy programs and health services, has the highest suicide rate in India (26.3 per 100,000 in 1990), whereas Bihar, the state notorious for poverty, corruption, and inadequate services, reported a low rate (1.7), second lowest to Jammu and Kashmir (0.9). Such differences probably reveal more about the ability of local institutions to collect these data than real differences in suicide rates.

Despite the limited accuracy of national and regional statistics, the estimates point to several global trends and noteworthy exceptions to these trends. To begin with, the common belief that suicide is a problem only for industrialized countries is unfounded. Sri Lanka now has the highest rates in the world. Both the high rates and the predominance of women among suicides in China make that country

Table 3.2 Suicide Rates and Gender Ratio in Select Countries

Country	Year of Most Recently Available Data	Rate Per 100.000			Male/Female Ratio
		Total	Male	Female	
Hungary	1991	38.6	58.0	20.7	2.8
Sri Lanka	1986	33.2	46.9	18.9	2.5
USSR	1990	21.1	34.4	9.1	3.8
China***	1989	17.1	14.7	19.6	0.8
Japan	1991	16.1	20.6	11.8	1.7
Germany, Fed. Rep.	1990	15.8	22.4	9.6	2.3
Australia	1988	13.3	21.0	5.6	3.8
Singapore	1990	13.1	14.7	11.5	1.3
Canada	1990	12.7	20.4	5.2	3.9
United States	1989	12.2	19.9	4.8	4.1
Hong Kong	1989	10.5	11.8	9.1	1.3
Puerto Rico	1990	10.5	19.4	2.1	9.2
Uruguay	1990	10.3	16.6	4.2	4.0
Ireland	1990	9.5	14.4	4.7	3.1
India**	1988	8.1	9.1	6.9	1.3
Korea, Rep. of	1987	7.9	11.5	4.4	2.6
United Kingdom	1991	7.9	12.4	3.6	3.4
Israel	1989	7.8	11.0	4.6	2.4
Argentina	1989	7.1	10.5	3.8	2.8
Costa Rica	1989	5.8	9.3	2.1	4.4
Thailand	1985	5.8	7.1	4.5	1.6
Chile	1989	5.6	9.8	1.5	6.5
Venezuela	1989	4.8	7.8	1.8	4.3
Mexico	1990	2.3	3.9	0.7	5.6

Source: WHO Division of Mental Health, Unpublished Statistics, except India and China.

** Source for India: National Crime Records Bureau, Government of India, 1992.

*** Source for China: WHO, 1991a.

Chapter discusses overall rate for Sri Lanka for 1991—47 per 100,000—but gender-specific rates not available.

unique. Reported rates in India rose from 6.3 in 1978 to 8.9 (per 100,000) in 1990, an increase of 41.3%; during the decade from 1980 to 1990, the rate of suicides increased by a compound growth rate of 4.1% per year.

Reported rates throughout the world are consistently higher among men than women regardless of age group. China is the only exception, although the gender ratio of male to female suicides in most Asian societies is lower than elsewhere (see Table 3.2).[6] In China, women have a higher incidence of suicide than men from youth through middle age (see Table 3.3), with the ratio of rates for males to females reaching as low as 0.5 for 15- to-24-year-olds. These statistics for 1989 are based on a sampling of 118.8 million people, about 10% of the total population.

Table 3.3 Suicides in China by Urban/Rural Status and Age Group, 1989 (Rates Per 100,000 Based on Selected Sampling)

Urban/ Rural	Gender	All Ages	5–14	15–24	25–34	35–44	45–54	55–64	65–74	75 +
Total	All	17.1	0.6	21.3	16.7	17.3	17.4	26.5	47.8	78.5
	Male	8.3	0.3	6.5	7.7	9.1	8.7	13.4	30.2	59.7
	Female	10.5	0.6	12.5	10.2	9.9	9.8	14.2	26.7	47.4
	M/F Ratio	0.8	0.5	0.5	0.8	0.9	0.9	0.9	1.1	1.3
Urban	All	9.4	0.4	9.4	8.9	9.5	9.2	13.8	28.4	52.3
	Male	8.3	0.3	6.5	7.7	9.1	8.7	13.4	30.2	59.7
	Female	10.5	0.6	12.5	10.2	9.9	9.8	14.2	26.7	47.4
	M/F Ratio	0.8	0.5	0.5	0.8	0.9	0.9	0.9	1.1	1.3
Rural	All	27.2	0.7	35.2	29.8	28.8	30.4	46.9	75.2	114.0
	Male	23.1	0.6	23.1	22.0	24.6	30.2	50.2	85.4	141.2
	Female	31.5	0.9	47.7	37.1	33.2	30.7	43.5	66.2	97.5
		0.7	0.7	0.5	0.6	0.7	1.0	1.2	1.3	1.4

Source: WHO, 1991a.

Overall rates in the rural areas were nearly three times higher than urban areas, but the gender ratios are about the same. These data, unusual among official reports, point to the relatively low status of women, the deeply frustrating constraints on their life chances, and cruelty toward them. Suicide, and the threat of suicide, is one of the few traditional levers of domestic power and forms of protest that Chinese women have available.

Although previously believed to be more of a problem in urban, heavily industrialized settings, suicide rates do not appear to be related directly to economic and technical development. They vary markedly among rich and poor countries (see Table 3.π2), reflecting both real cultural differences as well as variation in motivation and methods of collecting data. Thus, modernization is not directly related to suicide in any clear and simple way; urban areas do not necessarily have higher rates than rural areas within a country. In China, for example, rural rates are higher than urban rates of suicide (see Table 3.3).

Though poverty and social class are associated with important stressors, they are not necessarily associated with suicide. In the United States, the rate for some minorities is lower than that for the general population; for others, it is higher. The rate for African-American males (12.5 per 100,000) is significantly lower than the rate for their Caucasian counterparts (19.6), and the ratio of rates for African-American females (2.4) to Caucasian females (4.8) is even lower; absolute levels are also much lower. Among American Indians, rates are typically higher, though significant differences distinguish tribal groups. In New Mexico, the rate for the Apache remains the highest, but it is decreasing. Suicides per 100,000 in 1986 were 36.5 for the Apache, 15.8 for the Navajo, and 23.2 for the Pueblo. Several investigators have discussed the relationship between alcoholism and death by suicide or other violent means among many North American Indian groups.[7]

The typical age distribution of suicides, usually described as highest among the elderly, is contradicted by countries such as Thailand, Costa Rica, and Sri Lanka, but also by Canada and among African-Americans in the United States. Changes in the structure of traditional societies, including receding joint family systems, can help to explain this pattern in some countries, but a lack of consistent findings implies that the matter is more complex (for instance, although Canada has low rates for the elderly, Japan, Singapore, and Hong Kong—all societies with strong gerontocentric traditions—have high rates of suicide among their elderly).

High rates of suicide among youth have become a matter of increasing concern in many countries (see Table 3.1). The years between 1960 and 1989 were notable for a 160% increase in rates of suicide among young people in the United States. A recent survey found that 60% of teens surveyed in the United States knew another adolescent who had attempted suicide, and 6% had themselves made such an attempt.[8] The increasing rates of suicide coincide with both increasing availability of handguns and with increasing rates of depression and substance abuse.[9] As for depression, a longitudinal study of adolescents in the United States demonstrates a relationship between suicidal ideation and prior depression.[10] As for firearms, firearm suicides increased from 1984 to 1988 by 31% among white males and doubled among black males between 15 and 19 years of age.[11]

Although Hong Kong had not experienced high rates of suicide in the 1980s, the last several years have produced a dramatic increase in student suicides: During the 1989–90 school year there were 26 reported attempts and one fatality; the following year brought 35 attempts and three fatalities; in the first five months of 1993, the South China *Morning Post* reported 55 attempts and 15 fatalities. The preferred method, jumping from high-rise buildings, has a high rate of success.[12]

In Micronesia, Polynesia, and Melanesia, suicide has reached almost epidemic proportions among adolescent men. Suicide is the leading cause of death for these men, with disproportionately fewer suicides among adolescent women (see Box 3.1). In Truk, Micronesia, where rates are highest, the aggregated annual rate based on data from 1978 to 1987 for 15- to-24-year-old Trukese males was 207 per 100,000. The comparable rate for white males in this age group in 1987 in the United States was 22.7 per 100,000. Effective responses to this critical situation must combine clinical services, education in the community, and suicide prevention programs that target youth and challenge acceptance of the phenomenon as an immutable feature of life in Micronesia.

Mini-epidemics or cluster suicides have also begun to attract attention in recent years, often characterized by an adolescent suicide, publicity about it, or a film that

---

Box 3.1 Suicide in the South Pacific

Two suicide epidemics have recently been reported in South Pacific island populations—one among adolescent males in Truk, Micronesia, and the other among child-bearing-age women of the Gainj in New Guinea. There has been an eightfold increase in suicide rates among Micronesian males in the years between 1960 and 1980,[13] peaking in Trukese 15-to-24-year-old males, whose mean annual suicide rate soared to 200 per 100,000 between 1974 and 1983.[14] Among the Gainj of Papua New Guinea, the mean annual suicide rate for the period 1978–79 for women aged 20 to 49 was a staggering 1,200 per 100,000, accounting for approximately 57% of all deaths among the women in this group.[15] Data from other areas in the South Pacific indicate that these two regions lead an apparent trend in high suicide rates in the South Pacific.

Whereas Western psychiatric interpretations of suicide seek to contextualize it as a complication of mental illness or character pathology, ethnographic analyses of suicide suggest that, in the South Pacific, suicide typically represents a response to untenable social conflict with limited traditional means of resolution. Both the potential for conflict and the difficulties in mediating it are heightened by social change in Westernizing economies and lifeways in these areas.

For example, local explanatory models formulate the often impulsive act that ends in a completed suicide of a Micronesian teenager as soliciting support and nurturance.[16] Apparently this generation has become alienated against the backdrop of the development of a wage economy and the elimination of traditional clubhouses and men's organizations, thereby enhancing certain intrafamilial authority conflicts without providing an appropriate outlet for defusing them. Given limited legitimated channels to express discontent or anger toward elder kin, adolescents become *amwunumwun*, which communicates through social withdrawal and self-abasement that offense has been taken. Suicide is seen as *amwunumwun* in its most extreme form, signaling both despair in the context of a strained relationship and a wish to rectify it. The act thus is locally interpreted as not only angry and vengeful, but also conciliatory.[17]

In Samoa, direct expression of dissatisfaction with an elder is similarly constrained and is indirectly expressed in one's becoming *musu*, or socially withdrawn. Likewise, Samoan suicide is understood as an indirect solution to intolerable social conflict. Moreover, in neighboring Tonga, where the youth are considered to be particularly vulnerable to stressors that have followed in the wake of socioeconomic change, suicidal behavior is most likely to be rooted in interpersonal conflict.[18] Suicide is also portrayed as a strategy in negotiating social conflict in subpopulations within New Guinea. Particularly among women, it is seen as a calculated revenge against a perpetrator of abuse—often within a marital relationship—insofar as the suicide necessitates social restitution from the party perceived as precipitating the suicide.

Motives for suicide in the South Pacific may parallel those proposed by Western psychiatric accounts in some ways, but the local meanings of self-destruction in the South Pacific appear to derive from the shifting relationships among self, kin, and community undergoing socioeconomic change. In general, the subpopulations that have suffered epidemics of suicide are relatively powerless and invoke suicide as a complex idiom of anger, revenge, and appeasement. Although no formal studies have yet to be done, the conclusions above have several implications for treatment. First, any mental health services undertaken to combat epidemics of suicide in the South Pacific must account for the local meanings of suicidal acts in each community. In particular, clinicians will need to attend to stressors as well as conflicts and associated sentiments that arise when people perceive themselves as alienated from their social milieu. It will be essential that clinicians, together with families, teachers, and community leaders, be educated to anticipate cases in which suicide may be perceived as an option for conflict resolution in order to intervene with locally appropriate safety precautions and to recognize the behavioral precursors to suicide. Last, and perhaps most important, it will be crucial for communities to explore alternatives to resolution of social conflicts generated with changing lifeways.[19]

triggers others to act in similar ways. While these so-called imitative suicides have been documented among youth in the United States and England, among inpatients in Finland, and for the general population of Baden-Württemberg, Germany, the impact of suicide stories motivating suicide appears to be greatest among teenagers.[20] Cultural influences can produce remarkably different patterns of cluster suicides. In India, for example, the death of popular public figures, such as the chief minister of the state of Tamil Nadu, M. G. Ramachandran, who died of natural causes in 1987, and the assassination of Prime Minister Rajiv Gandhi in 1991, sparked a rash of suicides among their followers. Imitative suicides have led public health officials to warn against sensational press coverage.[21]

The Determinants of Suicide

There are several main determinants of suicide, which typically relate to either psychopathology or to social forces.

Psychopathology is important in many suicides. Clinical research indicates that 90% or more of suicides have been diagnosed or retrospectively meet criteria for a psychiatric disorder—usually, substance abuse, depression, or psychosis. The risk of suicide among people with alcohol abuse or dependence is 60 to 120 times greater than that for the general population.[22] A review of the records of all suicide victims in Finland over one year revealed that 93% could be assigned a psychiatric diagnosis; depression and alcohol abuse were the most prevalent.[23] Substance abuse has been an important factor in the almost threefold increase in suicide rates among people under 30 in the United States since 1950.[24] In a study of all autopsy and toxicological records of suicides in New York under age 61 for the year 1985, one in five had used cocaine in the few days before their death.[25]

Mental distress, like substance abuse, often contributes to suicide. Goldacre and colleagues recently showed that in an era of diminishing resources for inpatient psychiatric hospitalization, standardized mortality ratios (SMR) for suicide in the four-week period immediately following discharge was 213 times higher for men and 134 times higher for women compared with the general population; the SMR, defined more broadly for suicide and accidental death, was also 7.1 and 3.0 times higher for men and women, respectively, in these first four weeks than in the remaining forty-eight weeks of the year following discharge.[26] Finally, a review of 17 follow-up studies conducted in North America found that about 15% of patients with affective disorder end their lives by suicide, thirty times the general population risk.[27]

Since prompt detection and effective treatment of depression could prevent some proportion of these suicides, assessing suicidal risk is a top priority for mental health professionals. In fact, there was a significant reduction in suicide in the year following an education program for all general practitioners on the Swedish island of Gotland; the education program increased the rate of detecting and treating depression.[28] Similarly, Rimer and his colleagues have found a significant negative correlation between suicide rates and rates of treated depression in various administrative regions in Hungary.[29] However, in countries where mental health services of any kind are a rarity, subspecialty clinics and treatment groups focusing on suicide prevention have only recently begun to emerge in the most urbanized areas. Hotlines run by the Samaritans and Befrienders provide support and crisis intervention in some major cities, which can be the only available source of help in a crisis.

In many instances, severe stressors, painful terminal illness, or overwhelming events can lead to suicide without apparent, or any, prior psychopathology. Here a focus on disorder can obscure a dynamic relationship between a person's social context and the pain he or she feels. Reflecting on various ways of characterizing the basis of suicide, Schneidman found that intense psychic pain, that is, "psychache," from whatever source—psychopathology, social stressors, or some mix— was a least common denominator for all suicides.[30] Simply put, personal troubles might be less important than social problems.

In non-Western societies, completed suicides are less likely to have a psychiatric diagnosis. Official statistics for India, for instance, highlight social stressors; in 1990 only 3% of suicides were attributed to "insanity," the only category of mental disorder on the list (see Table 3.4). In settings where police officials, coroners, or physicians without mental health training are recording data about the principal cause of suicide, they tend to focus on social and situational factors in the death. Only the most severe and apparent psychopathology, such as someone screaming insults at passersby, is likely to be seen as a "psychiatric" problem. More subtle indications of psychiatric disorders, especially depression, can be dismissed as sadness arising from stressful circumstances, rather than a treatable condition.

Table 3.4 Specified Causes of Suicide in India, 1990

Specified Cause	Number	Percent
Dreadful disease (leprosy, etc.)	9,463	12.8
Quarrel with in-laws	4,592	6.2
Quarrel with spouse	4,312	5.8
Love affairs	3,475	4.7
Insanity	2,315	3.1
Poverty	1,871	2.5
Dowry dispute	1,405	1.9
Unemployment	1,305	1.8
Failure in examination	1,254	1.7
Dispute over property	1,060	1.4
Bankruptcy/Sudden financial loss	928	1.3
Fall in social reputation	539	0.7
Bereavement	443	0.6
Illegitimate pregnancy	149	0.2
Cause unknown	11,949	16.2
Other causes	28,851	39.0
Total	73,911	100.0

Source: National Crime Records Bureau, Government of India, 1992.

Despite evidence of the powerful role that social factors play in suicidal acts, mental health professionals throughout the world tend to emphasize the role of psychopathology, especially those forms of distress that can be treated to prevent suicide. Thus, mental health workers who learn to recognize cultural patterns of distress are more effective in reducing mortality from suicide than if they attended solely to psychiatric factors.

Social Determinants

Several important social forces have been linked to suicide; these include unemployment, domestic and collective violence, social and political protests, and a general sense of meaningless in life. As for the latter, a landmark study of social conditions associated with suicide rates by the sociologist Emile Durkheim, distinct from clinical efforts to identify psychopathology associated with suicides, made a major contribution to social research in the last century. Durkheim, who drew primarily from available social survey findings, found three types of suicide based on levels of social integration and the effect of social change: "egoistic suicides" result from a failure to integrate into society; "altruistic suicides" result from a hyperintegration that left people without the capacity to resist overly burdensome demands of society; and "anomic suicides" result from social change leading to moral instability and the loss of familiar norms.[31]

Durkheim also held that there would be a correlation between unemployment and suicide. As predicted, modern studies of unemployment statistics and suicide rates in countries of Western Europe and North America reveal a positive relationship between the two.[32] A range of cultural and social forces tend to influence the relationship, however. A recent study of Australian data, for instance, emphasizes the changing nature of this relationship. From 1966 to 1990 in Australia, for instance, unemployment has been associated most with increasing suicide rates for 15- to-24-year-old males; for middle-aged males, in contrast, who appear to have been affected more in the economic depression of the 1930s, rates have been stable or decreasing.[33] These trends might provide an imprecise indicator of the effect of adverse changes in family structures, constricted opportunities, and diminishing expectations among youth. In the years from 1962 to 1971, the suicide rate fell in Britain as unemployment increased, a paradox resulting from gas detoxification during that period, when suicide by means other than domestic gas was highly correlated with unemployment.[34]

In the United Kingdom, some have advocated efforts to counsel employment agencies and community service agencies to recognize depressive reactions to joblessness, which can precipitate suicide in extreme cases.[35] Although unemployed men in Italy have been found to be at 3.4 times greater risk for suicide than employed men, individual-level studies and case control methods are needed to specify risk more precisely and to inform service providers of ways to respond effectively.[36] Ultimately a much broader approach is required to address the links between depressed economies and depressed people.

A study of suicide by the anthropologist Dorothy Counts points to the pervasiveness of domestic violence and the paucity of effective responses to it in a community in Papua New Guinea.[37] Five of the twelve suicides she encountered in the course of fieldwork occurred shortly after these women had been beaten. Although most women who are beaten do not kill themselves, a person living in the community explained the suicides: "A woman who is beaten unjustly and who is struck repeatedly when she attempts to speak has *ailolo sasi* [literally, "a bad stomach"], which signifies self-pity. This condition is a mixture of anger, shame, and despair. If not relieved by either more gentle treatment from her husband or support from her relatives, it can result in a woman's suicide."[38]

In India, similar family tensions contribute to social dynamics that can lead to suicide. "Quarrels with spouse" and "quarrels with in-laws" together accounted for 12% of suicides in the statistics of the Indian Ministry of Home Affairs for 1990 (see Table 3–4), nearly as many as those attributed to "dreadful diseases" (such as leprosy or terminal cancer), the highest single specific category. Banerjee's study in West Bengal identified quarrels with spouse and in-laws as the main factor in 45.7% of female suicides, and a study in Jhansi, Uttar Pradesh, identified "domestic strife" among 38.3% of all suicides.[39] Typically, these involved harassment, beating, or torture from in-laws, husband, or both. Mental illness, distinguished from the social stressors, was noted as the primary cause in 23.5% of cases.

In 1990, the number of suicides attributed to "dowry dispute" in India was reported as 1,405. This is a difficult statistic to assess with confidence, since some dowry deaths, which are homicides, are recorded as suicides or accidents if families have enough influence to have the records list them as such. Dowry deaths refer both to homicides and suicides; these deaths are the end result of harassment by in-laws and husband arising from demands for additional material goods as dowry payment. This harassment may be either an effort to obtain more dowry or an effort to be rid of a bride whose family cannot meet the demands. A 1991 review by India's Parliament of dowry deaths found a total of 11,259 dowry-related deaths registered in 1988, 1989, and 1990; 4,038 of these were counted as suicides.[40] Awareness of the problem has increased reporting, up to 4,835 in 1990 from 2,209 in 1988.

War and the social disruption it produces can result in dramatically different effects on suicide rates in different settings; World War II led to lower rates in England and higher rates in Japan. Sri Lanka has recently acquired the highest national rates of suicide of any country in the world, 47 per 100,000 in 1991, with most victims between the ages of 14 and 30.[41] This figure is 22% higher than the rate of 38.6 for Hungary, next highest in 1991 among those for which WHO statistics are available. The significance of this statistic for a country that previously reported low rates of suicide (6.5 per 100,000 in 1950) points to the profound effects of the violence and social upheaval in Sri Lanka. According to social scientists Robert Kearney and Barbara Miller, the dramatic increase in suicide rates relates to anomie resulting from "destructive and destabilizing societal changes" and unemployment concentrated among youth.[42] They find that suicide in Sri Lanka often relates to an unfortunate mix of educational opportunities frustrated by limited career options and population growth, as well as large-scale internal migration, which by disrupting families imposes stress and limits support. Even when suicide rates in Sri Lanka were low for the country, however, they had been relatively high in Tamil communities in both Sri Lanka and India.

The hypothesis that social and political factors are responsible for Sri Lanka's high rates of suicide is both compelling, in view of recent history, and limited, in view of relatively modest rates in countries confronted by similar social disruptions, such as Northern Ireland. Even in 1953, an analysis of suicide, homicide, and social structure of Ceylon (the name by which Sri Lanka was then known), identified high rates of homicide that complemented low rates of suicide.[43] The Sri Lankan anthropologist K. T. Silva argues, however, that the nature of recent political violence and suicide are closely related, referring to the role of Durkheim's theory of anomie and implicitly supporting Freud's explanation of suicide as violence turned inward.[44]

Political aims constitute another powerful motive. Terrorist members of the Liberation Tigers of Tamil Elam (LTTE) exploded concealed bombs strapped to their bodies to kill Prime Ministers Rajiv Gandhi, Ranasinghe Premadasa, and other high officials. LTTE terrorists also wear a cyanide amulet around their neck; many of them have used the cyanide when captured, motivating some soldiers in the Sri Lankan security forces to do the same.[45] A third political group participating in this "cyanide war" includes militant members of the Sinhalese Janatha Vimukti Peramuna (JVP), who employ self-destructive violence to promote their political agenda.

Although each of these groups has glorified suicidal self-destruction that represents an ideal, the high rates of suicide in Sri Lanka are largely composed of deaths in response to more mundane stressors. A field study by K. T. Silva and W. T. Pushpakumara investigated all deaths over a five-year period in 27 settlement units of the Mahaweli Development Program in East Central Sri Lanka, the site of a massive resettlement program.[46] Suicide was the most frequent cause of death (68.5%); the most frequently recorded reasons were infidelity, shattered romance, and poverty (see Box 3.2). Mental illness was cited in only two of the forty-five deaths they studied, probably referring only to psychosis and listed only if no other precipitating factor could be identified. A clinical study of 22 patients admitted to the hospital before they died of suicide at a hospital in Jaffna diagnosed a psychiatric disorder in 14 of the patients.[47]

Suicide as social protest or as a feature of political terrorism purports to make a social, rather than a personal, statement. Suicides of this nature may seek to influence a political decision or demonstrate the magnitude of the victims' commitment to a cause. For example, when India's Prime Minister V. P. Singh announced he would implement a plan to reserve a higher proportion of government jobs and educational entitlements for members of "other backward castes" (as they are technically known), dozens of high-caste students, who thought these opportunities would be provided at their expense, committed suicide, many by public self-immolation. Suicides were also a feature of the language riots of 1965 in Tamil Nadu, protesting the imposition of Hindi and loss of English as a national link language. More recently, activists protesting the proposed Narmada Dam project, which will inundate village and tribal lands as the price for development, threatened mass suicide to persuade policymakers to drop the project, though negotiations with concerned government officials led to the withdrawal of the threat a week later.

Box 3.2 Suicide in Sri Lanka

Rani, a 26-year-old mother of two young children who had been abandoned by her lover, killed herself in front of her youngest child by swallowing a bottle of insecticide. At the time, she was living away from her family as a squatter in the Mahaweli resettlement district in Sri Lanka.

Suicide is the leading cause of death in Rani's area of the resettlement district; suicide by insecticide, readily available in agricultural communities, is the most common method. The suicide rate in the Mahaweli district parallels the high rate in Sri Lanka as a whole, one of the highest in the world. The accumulation of difficulties and social stresses that can lead to suicide (as in Rani's case) is a common theme in the country.

Rani was one of twelve children in a poor family struggling to get by. Because of economic difficulties, she left school after the tenth grade. Eventually she became involved with Pala, a migrant farm worker living near her family's home in Polonnaruwa.

Marriage relationships, arranged by families in the past, are a means for young people, particularly women, to build a better life for themselves. In this instance, Rani's family disapproved of Pala because he was involved with other local women. Rani continued the relationship nonetheless, without getting married, over her family's protests.

After the birth of their first child, the couple moved to the Mahaweli resettlement district, where they became squatters, building a small hut on a secluded piece of land illegally. Life became increasingly difficult for Rani: a second child was born, Pala spent most of his small earnings from farm work on tobacco and alcohol, there was barely enough money for food, and Mahaweli officials harassed the family to leave the hut.

Rani's plight worsened when Pala became involved with a settler's daughter. When the new woman became pregnant, her family urged Pala to marry her, and he went to live with her family. Unable to inspire any community or legal sanction that would prevent Pala from abandoning her, she returned to her parents' home to ask for their assistance, bringing her youngest child and leaving her eldest with a neighbor.

Her parents refused to help and Rani had to return to the Mahaweli district. While she was gone, Pala's new in-laws informed Mahaweli officials that her hut was "abandoned" and the officials bulldozed it to prevent reoccupation. When Rani learned of the destruction of her "home," she purchased the insecticide in a nearby town and swallowed it by the roadside.

The Accelerated Mahaweli Development Program (AMDP) was started in 1977 to harness the waters of the Mahaweli, the longest river in Sri Lanka. One of the largest development and resettlement programs ever undertaken in Sri Lanka, the program has affected nearly a million people. Although efforts were promised to re-create social arrangements such as kinship and neighborhood ties in settling people in the district, few of these arrangements have crystallized. Instead there has been an increased centralization of authority over formerly independent peasants. The Mahaweli Ministry and its administrative arm, the Mahaweli Authority of Sri Lanka (MASL), have acquired massive totalitarian power over the physical infrastructures and the settlements.

The majority of the population consists of families officially settled on Mahaweli land by the MASL. Squatters, migrant farm workers, and construction laborers also inhabit the area. The squatters illegally occupy Mahaweli land and have little influences in the hierarchy.

Like other squatters illegally occupying land, Rani had no right to hold on to her home. Her social status as an unwed mother gave her little influence in the local community, so she had few options. The easy access to insecticides offered a convenient means to kill herself. Rani's death illustrates the social and personal factors behind a suicide: poverty, social rejection, and powerlessness on the one hand; faithlessness, despair, and family abandonment on the other.[48]

Sanction, Stigma, and the Moral Contexts of Suicide

The links between suicide and political ideologies, cultural values, and oppressive practices underscore the fact that the meanings of suicide and social events vary considerably in different societies. Although some aspects of suicide are considered problems wherever they occur, the degree of condemnation that suicide evokes, as well as acceptance of alternative forms of suicide not considered problematic, reflect cultural beliefs and values. For instance, Catholic and Muslim theologies fiercely condemn suicide (predictably, studies of South Asian Hindus and Muslims show higher rates for Hindus).[49]

In Japan, where ritualized suicides have been sanctioned, rates of suicide remain relatively high. In fact, while there were fewer suicides in England during World War II than expected, there were high rates of suicide in postwar Japan.[50] The Japanese suicides might have related to the cultural sanctioning of ritualized forms of suicide as a response to humiliation. After the peak in the postwar years, rates dropped in Japan, in marked contrast to rates in the rest of the world, where they have risen.[51] In contrast with Western views that tend to pathologize it, cultural sanctions for ritualized forms of suicide in Japan, such as *hara-kiri*, which confers honor rather than stigma, idealize suicide.

Cultural forms of suicide in India, which have also been conceptualized as ideals rather than stigmatized behavior or psychopathology, include the self-immolation of a Hindu widow and religious suicides at the end of life. A study of suicide pacts in Bangalore, India, found they usually involved friends, and generally these double suicides employed less violent methods.[52] The Hindu practice of a virtuous widow, known as *sati*, burning herself on her husband's funeral pyre might be viewed as a one-sided variant of a spousal suicide pact, though far more violent and not restricted to the elderly. The practice was believed to confer merit on a devout, recently widowed woman, her deceased husband, and family. Widely condemned, a publicized case of *sati* in 1988 in Rajasthan generated an impassioned debate, indicating the practice still has a few powerful proponents.[53] Instances of *sati* to some extent resulted from a complex mix of feelings generated by bereavement and social pressure to express grief in this particular way. In many cases, however, the notion of ennobling choice was a fiction; death resulted from coercion, including physical restraint employed by families who profited from the economic benefits when the place of self-immolation becomes a pilgrimage site. Even when the act appeared to result from choice, the motivation to become a *sati* by self-immolation for some, perhaps many, reflected the misery a woman could expect from life as a widow.[54]

Morality and ethics are thus inextricably related to the personal and social meanings and responses to all suicides. However, religious suicides and other culturally defined forms of suicide, whether sanctioned or not, present ethical dilemmas in Asia that invite comparisons with questions about "rational" suicide in Europe and North America. A rational decision based on unendurable burden or inability to live in accord with values that one's personal life history documents as essential to self-worth presents dilemmas that challenge the letter and spirit of religious, medical, and legal doctrines. The capacity of health services, as well as social values that make resources available to address special needs for the care of the aged and people with terminal illnesses, are factors in the equations that ultimately motivate suicide or endurance.

Questions about the wisdom, humanity, and dangers of sanctioned or assisted suicide are complex and controversial. The ongoing debate about euthanasia in Holland and the notoriety of Dr. Jack Kevorkian, the Michigan physician who assists patients who are chronically ill to carry out suicide (and thereby challenges traditional medical teaching that suicide should always be prevented[55] by arguing that assisted suicide should become accepted medical treatment), indicate the intensity and complexity of concerns about sanctioning any form of suicide. The danger of the "slippery slope" that medical ethicists warn about, from concern for the potential of abusing policies for convenience or gain, and the need to safeguard the reasoned self-interest of a patient's decision that leads to a sanctioned or assisted suicide, is especially poignant in settings where other abuses are commonplace.

Concerns based on reports of possible abuses from the Netherlands, where assisted suicide is controlled and permitted, provide grist for arguments against assisted suicides.[56] The proliferation of places where ultrasound is commercialized for gender-specific abortions,[57] or where brokers earn their livelihood by arranging organ transplants from unrelated live donors,[58] underscores the need to ensure that cultural values and personal choices are not manipulated for the convenience or profit of others.

Means of Completing Suicide

Cultural values and social policy also influence preferences for methods of suicide. Associations of purity and cremation help to explain why self-immolation is frequently employed in Hindu and Buddhist cultures, especially when suicide expresses an element of social protest. In many agrarian societies, especially in South Asia, pesticides are readily available and constitute the most popular means of suicide. Insecticides were the most common means by far of completing suicide in Silva's field study in Sri Lanka (91%), and all but one of the Jaffna hospital group died of poisonous ingested substances. In a study of all suicides in Colombo in 1981, totaling 4,401, 53% of autopsied victims were found to have died from pesticide ingestion.[60] The detoxification of cooking gas in England, which had offered a popular means of suicide, dramatically reduced suicide rates; a similar campaign to control the availability of pesticides in Sri Lanka would probably help to reduce the world's largest national suicide rate.

In Western Samoa, paraquat was used in 80% of suicides in 1981[61]; in India, poisoning is the most common means of fatal self-harm (33.3% in 1990), followed by hanging (24.3%) (regional variation is significant, however, and in Punjab 55.3% of suicides were attributed to "railways"). Where readily accessible, toxic plants and fruits provide a convenient substitute for insecticides[62]; in Ethiopia *kosso*, also used medicinally as a vermicide, serves as a suitably lethal poison.[63] The sachasandia fruit, which ripens in December, is commonly used by Matako people of Gran Chaco, Argentina, and their suicide rate is highest in December.[64] Where

Box 3.3 Sallekhanā: Is the Willful Death of a Jain Sage Suicide?

Acharya Shantisagar Muni Maharaja, a Jain saint of modern India left his body on September 18, 1955 at 6:50 A.M. at the holy place of Kunthalagiri, Osmanabad District, Maharashtra State, India. Born in 1873, he had no interest in the family cloth business, and by age 18 he had started reading religious texts, embarked upon pilgrimages, and experienced an intense desire to become an ascetic. His mother died in 1912, his father shortly before that, and after a pilgrimage to Shravana Belgola in the South, he was initiated into a holy order in 1918 and then as a naked monk in 1922. His disciples conferred upon him the title "Emperor of Good Character" (*cāritra cakravarti*).

He carried the message of Jainism throughout India and awakened thousands of Jainas and others spiritually inclined to the path of purity and piety. Dr. Radhakrishnan, then vice president of India, described him as "the very embodiment of India's soul." In April 1955 he was camping at Baramati, Poona District, and suffering from defective eyesight. He decided to go to Kunthalagiri when his devotees pressed him to stay on because of his failing vision. He told them they should allow him to have his own life. On 5 July, 1955, after completing the morning scriptures, he said: "Recently, the weakness of my eyesight is growing. I had come here two years before. During my stay here then, there was some improvement in the eyesight. But this time, I do not feel so. Since I have to depend on others, even to walk, transgressions of my vows are increasing every day. I have been therefore feeling that I should adopt the vow of *sallekhanā*." On July 7 he fasted in silence.

Two eminent doctors from Sholapur came to examine his eyes and concluded he was developing cataracts, but it might take seven or eight years before they would be amenable to surgery, and his eyes were growing weak from a poor blood supply. The Acharya decided to prepare to quit his body by *sallekhanā*. He took the vow by which he was to avoid food gradually. On August 10 he stopped taking any food and drank only almond water. On August 14 he announced his *niyama sallekhanā* would last only a week. He took almond water that day and nothing but water after that. He asked pardon of all assembled, and he told them he had forgiven everyone. From August 28 he gave up water and became deeply engrossed in meditation, and his devotees began to gather at Kunthalagiri.

On the twenty-fifth day of his complete fasting he gave a religious discourse, concluding that "Compassion is the basis of religion; non-injury (*ahimsa*) and truth are the foundation of Jainism. We speak of all this but few of us practice the principles in actual life." The Acharya breathed his last as he recited, "Obeisance to the perfected souls" (*om nama siddhebhya*). Thus ended the life of this saint.

Can the Acharya's death be considered a suicide? The Acharya firmly believed the soul and the body are different, that the body that had become old was not assisting him in living the life of a saint because his sense of dependence was increasing day by day; the only way to stop further transgressions of the vows of an ascetic was to adopt the vow of *sallekhanā*. In short, his express intent was to save himself from lapses in the observance of religious rules and vows.

As Mahavira said, enunciating the authorized collective meanings of his community, there are two ways of death: death with one's own will and death against one's will. The latter is for "ignorant men" who are attached to pleasures and amusements, suffer ills and diseases in life, and die in dread of their future. But the virtuous and the learned, the monks who have controlled themselves and subdued their senses, achieve on their death either "freedom from all misery or godhood of great power." Even at death, they are "calm through patience and an undisturbed mind."[59]

In this case, self-willed death would seem not a health problem but an affirmation of moral and spiritual commitments that enrich the mental health of the person and the community. Thus, taking the cultural meaning of "suicide" or any other mental health condition into account is essential.

barbiturates are readily available without prescription, as they are in Nigeria, they are used for self-poisoning.[65]

The availability of firearms typically strengthens the link between impulsive self-destructive behavior and death.[66] In the United States, the availability of firearms accounts for their frequent use in suicides. Even among the elderly, guns have become the most common method of suicide, accounting for 66% of such deaths in 1980.[67] Social policy restricting access to guns would be an effective measure to reduce rates of suicide.[68]

Presenting another kind of challenge, potentially lethal features of urban or rural landscapes appeal to those at risk by virtue of symbolic associations and effective means of completing suicide. Tall buildings in Singapore and Hong Kong are popular and lethal for suicidal jumpers. Mountaintops, like the Jain pilgrimage site at Shravana Belagola or the waterfall at Hogenakal in South India (a resort which first became a backdrop in the Indian cinema for ill-fated lovers to kill themselves, before real lovers began to follow the example of their screen idols), show how features of the landscape, such as high places and bridges, become morbid symbols.[69] In one attempt to confront such geographical hazards, the Dutchess County Department of Mental Hygiene and New York State Bridge Authority installed a suicide prevention telephone on the Mid-Hudson Bridge in Poughkeepsie, New York, that provides a hotline to a twenty-four-hour-a-day psychiatric emergency service. The service was used about thirty times over a two-year period.[70]

A Call for an Interdisciplinary Approach to Suicide

Consideration of the social and psychological determinants of suicide, the cultural values that shape social attitudes toward suicidal acts, and the reason for, and method of, such acts contributes to a fuller understanding of its determinants, meanings, and practical significance as a health problem and as an indicator of the quality of social environments. Too narrow a focus on psychopathology can obscure the social determinants of suicide and produce programs that fail to respond both to perceived needs and important causes of suicide in a community. For this reason, health planners and government leaders must think seriously about the impact of public policy, which can result in the glorification of violence that promotes both homicide and suicide, and its effect on the relationship between suicidal behavior and completed suicides.

Public health workers, social scientists, and clinicians tend to look at death and suicide in different ways. Their concerns range over a spectrum, respectively emphasizing summary categories and classification of types and means of suicide, the social forces that influence local patterns, and the personal strengths and deficits that a clinical consultation must confront. Both social forces and personal distress must contribute to an account of suicide that is capable of guiding policy and practice.

In sum, whether suicides be judged a reflection of cultural values, abdication of responsibility to endure, or mental illness, the range of settings reveals much about the values, strengths, and shortcomings of people and the social worlds in which they live. Mental health programs concerned with suicide need to recognize interactions between social stressors and the psychological strengths and weaknesses that determine one's ability to confront them. Since the question of whether suicide is, by definition, psychopathology might be less important than the social and personal contexts that motivate it, health professionals must recognize not only diagnostic categories, but also a person's life circumstances. Dowry deaths, domestic strife, quarrels with in-laws, physical abuse, and other social sources of personal despair count high, both in official statistics and among the priorities of mental health professionals, other clinicians, and community health workers in such settings where they are called upon to formulate a helpful strategy to intervene. Interventions responsive to these priorities, empathy, and appreciation of the suffering and struggles of another person are required to make contact and establish an alliance that makes a helper credible.[71] Yet principles based on research are also required to guide assessment of risk and appropriate treatment.

Conclusions

- According to the World Development Report for 1993, approximately 1.6% of an estimated 88.9 million deaths from all causes worldwide in 1990 were classified as intentional and self-inflicted. Even more difficult to assess, rates of attempted suicide might be ten to twenty times higher.[72] Completed suicides, more than 1.4 million, represent an immense toll of potentially preventable mortality that reflects a mix of social stressors and psychopathology. Psychopathology is emphasized in countries with more resources to support a mental health system. The relative emphasis on psychopathology in Western Europe, and social stressors in Asia and Africa, might also reflect broader cultural differences that emphasize personal, rather than social, agency.
- To the extent that suicide can be explained as treatable psychopathology, it underscores the need for mental health professionals to formulate programs for prevention and treatment. In countries where psychiatry plays a minor role (if any) in medical curricula, it is essential that doctors and health workers be trained to identify locally relevant risk factors and typical themes and stressors associated with suicidal behavior. Training should ensure that clinicians and health workers can recognize and treat depression, routinely assess suicidality, and identify and help in social contexts that pose high risks.
- Planners should assess needs for resources to provide for some form of crisis management and suicide prevention in what the World Bank's 1993 World Development Report calls "essential clinical services" and higher-level facilities. Hotlines are meaningless where few people have access to telephones. Identifying and working with institutions and leaders in local communities can ensure that policies are sensitive to the limitations of actual conditions. Effective health education messages need to be developed and disseminated through mass media to advise people of available services and the transient nature of many self-destructive impulses. For services to be effective, espe-

cially where suicide is not regarded as a health or medical problem, understanding the way people explain it will enable clinical and community programs to increase awareness of typical social contexts and to provide acceptable, effective interventions.

- To the extent that psychopathology is an artifact of social circumstances and cultural meanings, it might overstate the capacity of even the most effective mental health services to reduce the number of suicides if a medical treatment model obscures critical social forces. In general, changing patterns of suicide may reflect broader processes of social transformation. For example, the age-related impact of unemployment indicates the increasing vulnerability of youth in societies where the safety net previously afforded by family supports has become ineffective. Persisting violence and civil war have been associated with a transformation of low rates into high rates of suicide, exemplifying Durkheim's theory of anomic suicide. Nevertheless, reasons for high rates of suicides for some ethnic groups (e.g., Tamils in India and Sri Lanka) and low rates among African-Americans in violent American inner cities remain for the most part unexplained.
- Because the social contexts of suicide differ dramatically from Micronesia to Sri Lanka and from Uganda to Peru, regional centers of suicide research to study variation in the contexts of suicide should be established. These centers need to complement improved record-keeping (to provide more reliable regional and national statistics) with focused research on local correlates, contexts, and meanings of completed and attempted suicides. Interdisciplinary field surveys are needed to identify relationships between suicidal behavior and cultural beliefs and practices. Research activities in clinical settings should study attempted suicide, and field studies should study attempts that do not routinely come to the attention of health professionals. Psychological autopsies of completed suicides, and the particular features of bereavement resulting from suicide and its impact on family, friends, colleagues, and health professionals, would take social research on suicide well beyond routine statistics and provide practical information for prevention activities.
- Evidence suggests that domestic violence, harassment for dowry, and the devaluation of women constitute an array of stressors that result in more suicides among women than men in many countries. The growing number of recorded dowry deaths in South Asia suggests that awareness of the problem is increasing. Programs that might increase the equality and autonomy of women (noted in Chapter 8) hold great potential for preventing these suicides.
- Specific social policies have been shown to influence suicide rates, especially in societies where popular means of suicide can be controlled. Restricted access to handguns would substantially reduce suicides and homicides where they are widely available and used. In agricultural societies, access to lethal insecticides poses a comparable challenge for basic science research to develop less toxic alternatives, and for social policy to minimize their use for suicide. Health education for clinicians and laypersons who work with agricultural chemicals should ensure that expertise and antidotes are available to respond to ingestions as promptly and effectively as possible.

- Highly publicized suicides can motivate suicidal behavior in others, the so-called "imitative suicides." Adolescents in particular appear to be at risk. Better understanding of this phenomenon would enable school officials and mental health professionals to recognize situations that impose risk and respond with supports and appropriate education to counteract it.
- Although suicide is regarded, at least to some extent, as a problem everywhere, associated stigma and condemnation are not absolute. Culturally sanctioned suicides in response to humiliation, widowhood, and infirmity, or in order to manipulate political events, show that the act has many meanings and consequences. Questions about sanctioning and assisting suicides in special circumstances have generated an intense debate. This debate must consider the significance, effects, and ethics of sanctioning suicides on those considering it, their families and friends, professionals responsible for their welfare, and society. It presents a broad challenge for ethicists, policy makers, and clinicians to scrutinize particular needs arising from local contexts.

4

Substance Abuse

Substance abuse is a pervasive problem that is taking an increasing toll on the world's population. The 1993 World Development Report finds that alcohol-related diseases affect 5% to 10% of the world's population each year, and accounted for approximately 2% of the global burden of disease in 1990.[1] Although it is difficult to draw conclusions about the burden of other substances, such as heroin and cocaine, the social consequences of abuse are apparent in an increasing number of countries. Social factors (including the speed of social change, rapid urbanization, and growing disparity between social groups) relate to, if not directly cause, drug use.

The money involved in the sale of illicit drugs (let alone tobacco and alcohol) rivals the income of the oil industries. Sales are by no means primarily to industrialized nations of the North; an increasing proportion of the "market" for illicit drugs is now in Asia, Africa, and Latin America. The pervasive use of tobacco, especially by youth, and of anabolic steroids by athletes and bodybuilders also represent public health problems, as do the potential for the abuse of prescribed and illegally sold psychoactive drugs and traditional drugs (such as khat) commonly used in certain societies.

The human and economic costs associated with the morbidity and mortality of drug and alcohol abuse offsets any monetary gain that governments might reap through taxation or other economic measures. Substance abuse takes its toll through the potential years of human life lost due to accidental or violent death, by anesthetizing youth who, in turn, cannot work productively, by placing a burden on what may be an already inadequate health care system, and by facilitating the breakdown of society. The depletion of human and economic resources in the long-term far outweighs any short-term profit.

What Is Abuse and What Are Its Causes?

It is easier to describe the parameters and extent of the *use* of drugs, alcohol, and tobacco than it is to define the nature, extent, and consequences of substance *abuse*. Where does use end and abuse begin? Substance abuse occurs in a social context. A person's readiness for use and response to use is influenced by factors such as availability of substances, cultural norms concerning use, societal response, and financial arrangements, but is also related to frustration, lack of fulfillment, and a need to escape intolerable situations of social inequity.

Substance abuse is present when: (1) the social and economic function of the user is compromised; (2) use leads to severe and potentially irreversible medical consequences; (3) people are coerced into use for purposes of exploitation; (4) the level of use threatens to undermine social institutions; (5) cessation of use causes drastic physical and psychological withdrawal symptoms and other morbidity; and (6) users seek the drug even when they acknowledge its harmful effects. Substance abuse, in other words, implies functional impairment.

The World Health Organization, through the development of ICD-10, has focused attention on drug dependence as the crucial element in the health morbidity associated with substance abuse. The International Statistical Classification of Diseases (ICD-10), a diagnostic manual used to define and classify physical, mental, and behavioral disorders, devotes a section exclusively to the identification of use, abuse, and dependence of psychoactive substances including alcohol, prescription, and nonprescription drugs. These diagnoses are classified with five character codes to pinpoint the extent of a person's involvement with alcohol, opiates, cannabinoids, hypnotics, stimulants, hallucinogens, volatile solvents, and polysubstances (see Box 4.1).

Despite these relatively objective and measurable parameters, it is frequently difficult to convince individuals, policymakers, and others that abuse may be present. People throughout the world often deny that substances are being abused when it can be demonstrated that the user can or could control use. This rationale is most frequently employed when discussing the harmful consequences of tobacco use, which is legal almost everywhere in the world, is often sold by state monopolies or marketed by international corporations with the support of governments, and causes far more deaths than all other psychoactive substances combined.[3]

The "abuse" of substances often conveys to the medical community, policymakers, and society a very negative view of the drug user. Broader support for prevention and treatment efforts is often impeded by the sense that the "abuser" is a bad or morally suspect person. Thus, the World Health Organization's emphasis on the health consequences of dependence (primarily in reference to ICD-10) could encourage the allocation of more resources for prevention and treatment.

The use of naturally produced drugs is deeply rooted in many cultures. For example, the regular chewing of coca leaves by Quechua and Aymara Indians in the Andean Highlands, and the periodic chewing (and smoking) of opium by the Karen, Akkah, and other "hill-tribe" people of Thailand, Laos, and Burma, must be seen as use rather than abuse. Use of psychoactive substances makes it possible for certain people and groups to endure the hardships of everyday life. This use may often lead to a dependence that is not recognized or addressed. Other use of psychoactive substances to celebrate social interactions, and participate in culturally salient religious and other activities, such as shamanism and ritual healing, do not necessarily imply dependence or abuse.

Use is not always voluntary. Although the tradition of providing laborers with substances to ameliorate harsh working conditions was once accepted in many societies, the use of psychoactive substances to facilitate the endurance of long and

Box 4.1 Definition of ICD-10 Terms

Acute intoxication is considered a temporary condition following the ingestion of a substance, with accompanying symptoms of disruption of cognitive processes, affect, or behavior. The effects of a substance decrease over time following cessation of use, with a subsequent abatement of symptoms. There are eight specific categories of acute intoxication listed in the ICD-10, ranging from "uncomplicated" to more serious mental and physical complications such as delirium, coma, or other bodily injury.

Harmful use has been classified as an habitual pattern of involvement with a substance that is damaging to health. The damage may be physical, as in hepatitis or cirrhosis, or mental, as in the case of triggering a depressive episode following heavy consumption of alcohol.

Dependence syndrome is classified as an intense, overwhelming desire (compulsive need) for a substance, accompanied by an inability to control one's intake or to determine level of use. In the presence of these criteria, a person will experience an increased tolerance of, and to, a selected substance. A person who is dependent on a substance places an urgency to obtain their next "fix" at the expense of other personal needs, especially in order to gain relief from the unpleasant effects of withdrawal syndrome. A physiological withdrawal state is present shortly after the substance has ceased or been reduced, and there is a marked increase in the amount of time required for a person to recover from the effects of the substance. In spite of such unpleasant consequence, there is continued use of the substance.

Withdrawal syndrome is present when one is physically dependent upon a substance. Withdrawal is classified as a group of symptoms of varying severity and occurring on absolute or relative withdrawal of a substance after repeated, and usually prolonged, and/or high dose, of the substance. Onset and course of the withdrawal state are time-limited and are related to the type of substance and the dose being used immediately before abstinence. Distinctive symptoms vary according to the substance being used. The ICD-10 classification codes include uncomplicated withdrawal, withdrawal state with delirium, accompanied by psychotic disorder (this category lists seven specific symptoms). Psychological disturbances include anxiety, depression, and sleep disorders. In alcohol withdrawal, delirium tremens is present and is typically seen in severely dependent users with a long history of alcohol use. Associated symptoms include insomnia, tremulousness, and fear.[2]

strenuous (and poorly paid) work is no longer viewed as a voluntary deed, but rather a forced use necessitated by economics. Indeed, frank psychopathology and psychiatric morbidity is more likely under conditions of stress when people rely on substances to cope with boredom, the demands of hard labor, and squalid living conditions. This is seen in many parts of the world where the illegal introduction of heroin or cocaine into populations of adolescents or those who are marginally employed wreaks havoc. The introduction of nontraditional substances into certain populations has also led to epidemics of abuse. When viewed from a policy perspective, and in terms of demonstrable morbidity and mortality, the substances of potential abuse—illicit drugs, alcohol, and tobacco—must be approached with differing perspectives on the approaches to prevention, treatment, and policy development. The economic impact, the opportunity for exploitation, the nature of the traffic in illegal substances, and the medical and psychological consequences of use and abuse are quite different.

Drug abuse is often a consequence of rapid social change (even social turmoil) brought on by factors such as rapid modernization and urbanization, civil strife, disease epidemics, and extreme economic hardships. For instance, the residents of many countries experience a destabilizing process by which adolescents and young men move from largely rural, traditional village settings to urban, cosmopolitan, and "modernizing" environments. Culture shock, conflict, loss of values, and a sense of being marginal—all associated with a crisis of identity—are frequent results of such movements. Rural youth are attracted by what they imagine to be cosmopolitan values and lifestyles but are often unable to "make it" in such settings and have few of the necessary supports and resources to fall back on when faced with lack of achievement.[4]

In addition, a move to the city can weaken preexisting family ties and contribute to the gap between generations. Many suffer tremendous stress as they struggle in limbo, finding that they are no longer part of a traditional village-based culture (and a supportive social network), but that they are also not fully and functionally integrated within the (often enticing) modern urban environment. Thus, the migration to shantytowns and slums or even more hospitable settings results in uncertainty and conflicts about personal identity and "belongingness" that have frequently been linked with initiation into drug taking and, later, drug abuse.

Those who do not migrate to cities, but grow up in shantytowns and other urban settings, face similar pressures. In several Southeast Asian countries, one of the pastimes of unemployed youth is to "hang out" in shopping arcades. The omnipresence of alluring commodities frustrates through tantalization. Peers become the most significant influence in these environments. Drugs are often easily and (at first) cheaply available, and opium, heroin, and other substances offer an escape from the frustration of not being able to obtain what is desired. Sheer boredom of existence leads others to seek an escape through drugs. This frustration can contribute to substance abuse and antisocial acts.

Often particularly vulnerable populations are directly targeted for media campaigns that play to people's aspirations and frustrations (though the detrimental effects of alcohol, tobacco, or other drugs go unnoted). The financial opportunities associated with development in some societies, and the migration of populations into settings that disrupt traditional ties, have also contributed to the criminalization of drug use and abuse. The international illegal drug dealers view many communities as markets for potential exploitation. The poor and the marginal are easy targets for the drug trade, as are impressionable youth and young adults from all backgrounds who are influenced by peer pressure.

Economics play a powerful role in rates of abuse. Brenner found that an increase in wine and beer sales occurs during periods of economic recession and rising unemployment: consumption rates go up as economic stability goes down, and the negative effects of national recessions on personal income and employment "are consistently followed in two or three years by increases in cirrhosis mortality rates."[5] Friedrich Engels, writing in the nineteenth century, described a causal chain linking alcohol availability to consumption rates, which, meanwhile, were related to the prevalence of health and social drinking–related problems.[6]

Mexico illustrates the situation of many countries where the drug abuse problem is diverse and multidrug use is the norm.[7*] Estimates show that the drug abuse problem in Mexico is essentially an urban one; drug abuse is not considered a public health problem in rural areas. The majority of urban drug abusers range in age from 12 to 21 years. The younger lower-class children use inhalants and solvents; older, more affluent adolescents usually use marijuana. The use of barbiturates and amphetamines is apparently on the increase, with barbiturates and tranquilizers preferred by young adults. Along the northern border of the country, an increase has been observed in the number of Mexicans taking heroin.[8]

Alcohol

Alcohol acts as a depressant in the central nervous system. The effects of alcohol on the user range from creating feelings of disinhibition, relaxation, and peacefulness, to maladaptive behavioral changes that can manifest as depression, aggression and violent conduct, slurred speech, stupor, and the inability to function coherently. It is well known that prolonged and excessive drinking gives rise to serious and irreversible psychotic states, delirium tremors, and alcoholic hallucinations.[9] We lack reliable data on the severity and consequences of alcohol problems in non-Western cultures using ICD criteria, but several studies point to the magnitude of the problem. Every indicator shows that the growth in alcohol use in non-Western countries continues unabated.[10] David Coombs and Gerald Globetti have estimated, for instance, that 15% to 20% of the adults in Latin America are alcoholics or excessive drinkers.[11]

Beverage alcohol has become a commodity in many evolving market economies.[12] Alcohol conglomerates in the West and some non-Western countries have made strong moves to gain a large share of foreign markets, as well as to acquire foreign distilleries, bottling plants, and retail outlets. Big distillers push for tax laws that will work to their advantage. The expansion into, and domination of, alcohol markets in low-income countries is advancing swiftly. The countries of Africa, Asia, and Latin America now constitute one of the fastest-growing import regions for both hard liquor and beer, with 15% to 25%, respectively, of the global import totals.[13] In addition to Western countries, China and Chile are two of the world's largest producers and exporters of alcohol. All of the import and export figures must be added to local manufacture, which is increasing at a rapid pace as national and transnational corporations seek to develop additional alcohol markets.

The economic aspects of alcohol extend beyond the formal commercial market, where companies push for as little regulation as possible, and where possible suppression of the noncommercial production of alcoholic beverages ensues. There has been a commercialization of even the rural, "home brew" enterprises. In some places, village members agree among themselves who will be allowed to brew beer on specific dates, since if only one person did so all the time, only one family would benefit. In some areas, brewing is more competitive and less collaborative. For example, East African "Pombe shops" have become established where the home brew is for sale outside of the traditional setting of use. This has become a major economic force, with detrimental social consequences, in some rural areas.

In general, governments are aware of the negative effects of alcohol abuse on national development, but because of the economic benefits to governments through taxes and to merchants through profits, legal and illegal, little is done to reduce the availability and consumption of alcohol and its contribution to social problems, such as automobile accidents, family dislocations, violence, and malnutrition. The threat of the latter is increasingly being felt, for example, in Nigeria, as food grains, especially corn, are being diverted into beer making, and as choice farmlands, man-power, and other resources are used in the cultivation of grains for the beer industry. Although governments may recognize the detrimental effects in both human and social terms, they might be prodded into action if they could be shown that the eco-nomic costs of alcohol and tobacco (e.g., increased hospital and prison stays, lost work hours, and damaged equipment as well as damaged lives) parallel, or may fre-quently surpass, the amounts collected through taxes (especially, of course, for those countries truly concerned with providing their citizenry with social services).

Alcohol as a means of controlling labor is well known. African migrant workers drink to alleviate personal suffering and escape the monotony of their labor, and many employers actually encourage drinking despite its negative effect on labor productivity.[14] These employers believe that the presence of a local brewery is a "useful mechanism for stabilizing the work force."[15] By absorbing a worker's wages, alcohol makes laborers more dependent on their jobs.

In Africa, the breakdown of traditional social and political life, along with the destruction of the tribal system, was a top administrative priority of colonial pow-ers. Thus, colonialism and its prevailing legacy contributed directly to problems of alcohol abuse. Wolcott reports that in Bulawayo, Rhodesia (now Zimbabwe), the white settler regime organized municipal beer gardens for use by urban black work-ers; beer-garden drinking "facilitated rapport and prompted social solidarity; it dis-sipated some pent-up hostility and frustration; it enhanced gaiety and exuberance; and it contributed to accepting things as they were."[16]

Chinese culture emphasizes social drinking and discourages solitary drinking.[18] Chinese drinking occurs almost exclusively with eating and embodies a belief in the medicinal value of alcohol derived from traditional Chinese medicine. The almost ritualistic toasting at dinner tables contributes to promoting social interaction and cementing bonds of friendship, and it helps to regulate the frequency and amount of drinking. Yet, given this background, it is interesting to note emerging data from China that show steadily increasing urban prevalence rates of alcohol use since 1982, as well as variability among regions.[19] The discrepancy between urban and rural rates is striking and may suggest a relationship between the ability to maintain traditional social bonds in rural areas but their disruption in urban settings. The most recent prevalence rates of alcoholism in Han communities reported by the Institute of Mental Health, Beijing Medical University, are 6.61% for urban and 0.83% for rural areas.[20] A 1991 study of 44,920 subjects age 15 to 65 in nine cities in China showed an average prevalence for alcoholism of 3.7%, with a significant variation by occupation: a 6.88% prevalence among laborers compared to a 1.769% prevalence among professionals (the peak age group for prevalence was 40–60 years).[21] These findings suggest that people in rural settings who are less educated and have lower incomes may be at higher risk for alcoholism.

Box 4.2 Drinking and Drunkenness In East Africa

The development of a European market economy and increased use of money in areas of Central and East Africa has had the effect of transforming social customs into commercial ventures, thus creating a new set of societal problems.

In Southeastern Uganda, for instance, until recently when an adult male spoke of "telephoning," it was understood that he had been sitting around with friends sipping thick millet beer from a common pot. The reason the drinking is called "telephoning" becomes instantly apparent to an outside observer: the men sip the beer through long straws with filtered ends; like the cables of an old-fashioned switchboard, the beer tubes connect the people who sit, sip, and converse, passing the tubes back and forth. This form of communication, communion, and alcohol consumption has long been widespread in East Africa, where friends and neighbors—mostly old and mostly male—share the brew, prepared by women. Although the beer is consumed for mundane social pleasures, it also plays a special role in important rituals where communication with ancestors is sought or required.

But the spread of money and commercial markets through the region has, not unexpectedly, commercialized "telephoning" as well as drinking in the towns. There is still some domestic and reciprocal beer drinking, but most alcohol is consumed as part of a cash transaction. Regular drinking places, village "taverns," and impromptu beer-and-supper shops that spring up on market days are fast replacing the "telephone."

There are no reliable estimates of the effect of alcohol abuse in East Africa, but it has become apparent that as the society has become more mobile and more commercial, the village "telephone" session has been replaced by the equivalent of the after-work "happy hour." The consumption of distilled alcohol has become increasingly common, and drinking and drunkenness have become more obvious social problems. Both men and women appear to be aware of the potential harmful effects of drinking and drunkenness. Drinking parties may lead to conflicts and eruptions of physical violence; domestic quarrels and violence often explode when men return home drunk. Occasional drunkenness appears to be accepted as a norm in some East African societies, but some men get drunk, and the women in their lives come to resent the fact that the men spend too much money on drinking and neglect basic household needs. Some simply leave the household when drinking gets out of hand, and the separation creates a situation in which the drinker becomes dependent on others for his survival. These days both men and women also worry about AIDS and the connection between drinking and casual sex.

In East Africa, alcoholism is still considered a sign of weakness or "bad character," rather than a disease. Indeed, in English, East African problem drinkers are still called "drunkards," and although medical professionals are aware of the psychological and organic risks of excessive alcohol consumption, "drunkards" are simply viewed as weak characters who merit no community respect. Thus, few East Africans consider alcohol abuse a major public health issue.[17]

Studies from other societies suggest that alcohol dependence and its associated problems occur at rates that are significant for public health. For example, it is estimated that 5% to 10% of all admissions to hospitals in Sri Lanka are alcohol-related. The evidence suggests that young people and older women are increasingly involved in experimentation with a variety of intoxicants.[22] In sub-Saharan Africa, the abuse of alcohol by women is on the increase, even in Islamic countries, where alcohol is religiously proscribed, yet there are problems of secret drinking. Although most of the physical and mental health or neuropsychiatric effects of alcohol abuse are seen in African men,[23] if women in Africa continue to drink at the same rate, they are likely to suffer more than men because of their reported increased vulnerability to the toxic effects of alcohol intake.[24]

Alcohol use amounting to abuse can lead to a variety of ill effects. Ray and Chandrashekhar examined 1,984 consecutive admissions to the male psychiatric wards at the National Institute of Mental Health and Neuro Science, Bangalore, India, for evidence of alcoholism by administering to them the Michigan Alcoholism Screening Test.[25] During the period of study, 6.1% of all admissions to that hospital were due to alcohol-related problems. Nevertheless, study results indicated that 19% of the patients were indeed alcoholics. The alcoholics had more first-degree relatives afflicted with alcoholism, sociopathy, and depression than the nondrinkers.

A recent report by the Royal College of Physicians documents the effect of alcohol on the nervous, gastrointestinal, and endocrine systems, with special effects on the pancreas, heart, lungs and liver, among other problems.[26] In addition, borderline nutritional states, which would not otherwise be evident in frank medical or mental illness, may become apparent in a person who drinks excessively. There is also a relation between excessive drinking and pellagra, "periodic psychoses," spontaneous hypoglycemia, and liver cirrhosis. While cirrhosis is not an absolute indicator of alcohol intake and consumption, comparisons in levels of cirrhosis mortality between various countries in the Americas and the Caribbean, demonstrate the startling consequences of the adverse effects of alcohol (see Table 4.1).[27]

In the Middlebelt Study, Nigerian drinkers reported more cases of social, psychological, and occupational problems than nondrinkers.[28] In a study of records in four psychiatric hospitals in Nigeria for the period 1984–1988, alcohol is identified as a significant precipitant of organic psychosis.[29] Alcohol was involved in most cases of polydrug use and is surpassed only by cannabis as a pervasively perceived hazard to mental health.

Complex congenital disorders such as fetal alcohol syndrome—which can be easily prevented—result in both cognitive and physical problems that severely compromise the capacity of affected persons to be productive citizens. The negative consequences of alcohol use among women and men of childbearing age have been well studied in Western countries, but have not received much attention in the scientific literature elsewhere. The impact of such congenital disorders on the productivity of populations must be considered.

In the public health domain, the prevalent consequences of alcohol abuse include accidents, homicide, and suicide.[30] Acuda, who found a strong link between alcohol use and prostitution and theft in East Africa, suggests that the linkage seen in Western countries between drug use and crime, and its associated violence, is probably also apparent in East Africa.[31] Prostitution and theft not only lead to risk-taking behavior, but are the very thing itself. These behaviors have wide-ranging morbidity and mortality consequences, such as STDs, AIDS, violence against others or self, and the psychological consequences of various trauma.

Table 4.1 Deaths from Cirrhosis in the Americas

Country	Year of Report	Total Per 100,000*	Standardized Mortality		
			Males	Females	M/F Ratio
Mexico	1990	48.6	72.5	21.8	3.3
Chile	1989	46.2	67.5	26.5	2.5
Puerto Rico	1990	29.7	47.2	13.5	4.0
Ecuador	1988	21.7	28.7	14.1	2.0
Costa Rica	1989	20.4	26.7	13.1	2.0
Venezuela	1989	19.4	28.6	9.6	3.0
Argentina	1989	13.3	20.1	6.4	3.1
Trinidad and Tobago	1989	13.2	19.6	6.7	2.9
Cuba	1990	12.4	13.3	11.3	1.2
Panama	1987	11.6	14.2	7.7	1.8
United States	1990	11.6	15.2	8.0	1.9
Uruguay	1990	11.5	17.5	6.8	2.6
Canada	1990	9.3	12.7	5.8	2.2

* Living with age standardization for European population.

Source: Edwards et al., 1994, with statistics supplied by WHO, Geneva.

Alcohol is probably responsible for more violent behavior than any other drug.[32] The association between drinking and violence is well established in a number of studies from different societies. This observation is applicable to both intentional acts of violence and nonintentional, accident-related injury. In Papua New Guinea, beer consumption doubled every four or five years during 1962–1980; the increase was accompanied by a 400% increase in road traffic fatalities and a notable increase in the death and serious injury rates from methanol consumption, blunt injury, and knife and bullet wounds. Nigeria, which has witnessed a marked increase in alcohol consumption, has the highest automobile accident rate in the world.[33]

Homicide rates are rising in many countries, often as the consequence of drug and alcohol use, especially in poor urban communities and among minority ethnic populations.[34] These homicide rates reflect the behavioral consequences of substance abuse. In Colombia, homicide is the number one cause of death, to a large extent as the direct result of violence associated with the illegal trade in drugs.[35] Family members and bystanders are often the victims of these outbursts.

Wife-battering by alcoholics is common. In Asia, parents and siblings of the batterers (who, in one study at least, are not violent while sober) are also victimized, though children less so.[36] Elsewhere as well, the local cultural context largely determines who is assaulted, and why. Anthropologist Kaja Finkler finds that in Mexico, for instance, it is not uncommon to see a drunken man beat his wife, but never his mother, sister, or children.[37] Married women residing in nuclear families were more likely to report violence by spouses than those living in extended families. While residential arrangements mitigate against wife abuse in the context of substance use, women are also spared when they share in complementary economic roles.

Box 4.3 Alcohol Abuse in Chile

Alcoholism and excess alcohol consumption are two of the most serious public health problems in Chile. The death rate from cirrhosis of the liver, the third-leading cause of death in the country, has remained high (about 30 deaths per 100,000) over the past 25 years. In 1989, the rate stood at 46 deaths per 100,000 inhabitants, one of the highest in the world (see Table 4.1). (In the United States, the death rate from cirrhosis of the liver is 11.6 per 100,000.)

The indirect economic costs of alcoholism, which accounts for about $2 billion a year or 5.5% of Chile's GNP, exceed the government's yearly contribution to elementary, high school, and college education, and to Ministry of Health programs. These costs include the value of the annual production that is lost or not earned as a result of problem drinking, reduced productivity from excessive alcohol intake at work, premature deaths, and medical-social expenses.

Both alcoholism and excessive drinking affect males almost exclusively, with a higher prevalence among the lower socioeconomic groups. Prevalence is highest in those aged 22 to 55—adults in their most product years.

Because many of its costs are indirect, alcohol abuse is not perceived as a serious economic problem. Instead, the focus has been on the direct and substantial contribution of alcohol production to the national economy and the government's tax rolls. The industry, which employs about 5% of the population, is a major source of revenue. The wine-growing sector generates 30% of the tax income the government receives from the industry. Wine production ranges from 350 million to 600 million liters per year, which amounts to about two-thirds of the domestic alcoholic beverage production. The remaining third is beer and spirits.

Virtually all of the alcoholic beverage production goes to domestic consumption. The average per capita consumption of alcohol per year is 13.8 liters among people over 15 years of age. Only France and Italy have higher per capita consumption rates. Recently, consumption has been on the rise, partly as a result of government policies that lowered import tariffs for a number of items, including spirits.

In addition, the law restricting the agricultural area used for grape growing, in effect since 1939, was repealed in 1974 to increase wine production for export and to enhance the national economy. Initially, only 2% of the domestic wine production was exported; most was consumed in Chile at low prices resulting from overproduction. The government also allowed the production of new types of wines using hybrid grapes, which led to increased production of less expensive wines.

The consumption of *pisco*, a highly popular local spirit, increased more than 315% between 1969 and 1979. The increase was the result of the government's reduction, from 45% to 25%, of a special tax on *pisco*. The reduction sharply reduced its price, making it an affordable drink for young people.

Research, identification of the issues, and public education campaigns have done little to curtail Chile's alcohol problem. Most education and awareness programs have had little informative substance in them and have been limited in scope. Recent new initiatives have included additional public education campaigns to the general public and high-risk populations, regulation of alcoholic beverage advertising, promotion of standards, and resources for early intervention and rehabilitation of problem drinkers, as well as substantial changes in the Alcohol Act.

These initiatives will have little impact on the problem overall, because of the health sector's inability to implement primary prevention measures. The problems of alcoholism and excessive alcohol consumption involve numerous powerful sectors of Chilean society—those of economics, agriculture, and labor. These sectors have a vested interest in maintaining production.

Government policy must address the problem at all levels. At present, the incumbent government advocates a free-market policy and is unwilling to take the unpopular stand of increasing the price of wine, limiting its production, and restricting the public's access to alcoholic beverages. Unless taxing and regulatory powers are used to restrict access to alcoholic beverages, the industry, which contributes much to the national economy, will, at the same time, deplete it.[38]

Cocaine and Heroin

The use of cocaine and heroin causes serious health and social problems, and because it occurs covertly and is socially unacceptable, leads to delays in intervention and prevention efforts. Users run the risk of death from overdose, infection, violence, AIDS, and circulatory, respiratory, and digestive diseases. The association of injection heroin use and AIDS is of great public health concern, as it pertains particularly to young males. Users of cocaine, especially in the form of "crack," can suffer from acute cardiovascular problems that require emergency services, while the children of pregnant users of cocaine can be born with severe health problems. Aside from the more obvious effects of drugs on the user or passive recipient (in the case of the infant), more long-lasting and often chronic disability, including neuropsychiatric disorders, ensues (see Box 4.4).

The striking increase in the worldwide production of coca leaf in the early 1980s and in the illicit importation of cocaine into the United States, Canada, and Europe between 1983 and 1985 occurred at the same time that rates of cocaine-related deaths were reported in North America and Western Europe (and most dramatically manifested in Florida's Dade County epidemic). In turn, the stabilization of the frequency of cocaine-related deaths between 1982 and 1983 in Bolivia happened just as the country was suffering a major drought that caused a reduction in cocaine production. We can anticipate similar correlations between cocaine production and human deaths in several low-income countries where cocaine is now a major substance of abuse. Cocaine is a new drug in Africa, for instance. From one mention of cocaine use in an expatriate group in Nigeria in 1981,[43] reports on the substance have become familiar in popular Nigerian periodicals, just as Nigerians have moved up to the top level of international trade in illicit drugs.

Cocaine and heroin are also involved in many cases of multidrug use. There is, in fact, a natural tendency for the two drugs to be taken together, because one is an "upper" and the other is needed to "bring down" the high. This evolving pattern has serious implications for mental health and social welfare.[44]

The cardiotoxic effects of cocaine are a leading cause of sudden death. The toll on children from intrauterine exposure to cocaine, especially from the "crack" form, remains to be defined, but maternal abuse can yield a chronic morbidity affecting the child's cognitive development. Some reports ascribe a teratogenic effect to the intrauterine exposure to cocaine metabolites. Cocaine as a contributor to aggressive behavior and violent acts is well documented.

Box 4.4 Heroin Addiction in Pakistan

Although heroin was first introduced in Pakistan less than twenty years ago, the country now has the highest reported per capita usage of heroin in the world, with at least 1.5 million drug addicts in the country. Conservative estimates report that 2.03% of the urban population and 1.36% of the rural population are active drug users. Since heroin addiction appears to be an exclusively male activity, a National Survey of Drug Abuse concluded that every nineteenth male in the country is consuming drugs regularly.[39] Despite this chilling statistic, the number of people who use and become addicted to heroin continues to skyrocket, and the narcotic has emerged as "the first drug used on a national level by all ethnic groups, all age groups, at all times and occasions," according to Asif Aslam, a Pakistani psychiatrist.[40]

Heroin addiction is more prevalent in urban areas, due to the relative abundance of users and drug dealers, who have few other outlets for earning money. Although everyone is an easy target for the drug dealer, there are factors that exacerbate a person's chances of using heroin, including easy accessibility of the drug, unemployment, breakdown of stable families, homelessness, and peer pressure.

Addicts use heroin in a variety of ways. Use often begins with smoking heroin that has been laced in cigarettes; this practice typically escalates to "chasing the dragon," a euphemism for inhaling the smoke from heroin. As users become dependent on the drug, more-alarming methods of taking heroin become routine. Users make incisions in their flesh and put the heroin on the wound so it will be absorbed quickly into the bloodstream. Those who have mastered the use of the hypodermic needle mix heroin powder with lemon and water and inject the substance into their veins.

A hard-core user often shares a contaminated syringe with several addicts at a time. This unhealthy practice promotes the prevalence of tetanus, endocarditis, hepatitis, and infectious disorders of the blood vessels. And the imminent hazard of the spread of HIV has given new cause for alarm. Drug addiction is also taking its toll on Karachi society with the rise of drug-related crime and violence and the massive drug trafficking across international routes.

The Pakistani government appears to be stymied by the epidemic proportion of heroin addiction. Since the sharp increase in the rate of addiction had not been anticipated, the government and local communities did not adequately protect against its use. In the city of Karachi, however, attempts to reduce the demand for drugs have taken shape. The squatter community of Essa Nagri, in conjunction with the Aga Khan University, has developed a program, funded by the government, that emphasizes a reduction in the demand for drugs. The activities, principally aimed at educating youth against the hazards of heroin addiction, include involving high-risk groups in indoor games, theater activities, athletic activities, and support group meetings. These activities reach a broad audience, appear to be adequately functioning on a low budget, and enlist the support of the community in the development of its services.[41]

Another successful program aimed at preventing drug abuse is the Green December Movement. Founded in December of 1983, this voluntary organization targeted its antidrug-abuse campaign in Peshawar and Mardan, two provinces in North Western Pakistan. The Movement enlisted men and women from these communities to develop and run two major treatment and rehabilitation centers where addicts get counseling for their drug-abuse problems free of charge. Specially designed drug literature is circulated to encourage the participation of teachers, students, and out-of-school youth in the community efforts. Religious leaders are instrumental in providing spiritual and psychosocial support for detoxified addicts, which helps them avoid further drug use. The Movement has been collaborating with government agencies and nongovernmental organizations on researching the nuances and magnitude of the drug-abuse problem in Pakistan. Because of the success of the Green December Movement, the organization has earned a national reputation and has recently established programs in Karachi and Quetta.[42]

In brief, Pakistan has begun to address its population's vulnerability to heroin use and abuse, and the community programs targeting preventive interventions appear to be working. Hopefully, continuous efforts to reduce the morbidity of heroin addiction in Pakistan will benefit all segments of the society.

Amphetamines

Drugs that stimulate the central nervous system are generally consumed for the sense of added energy, positive sensation, or euphoria that they produce. Students, truck drivers, farmers, and housewives swallow "brain pills," chew kolanut, or take a variety of amphetamines for wakefulness, alertness, or maintenance of energy.[45] In addition to their desired effect, however, these stimulants also induce psychological symptoms such as irritability, anxiety, and a feeling of apprehension. High doses are associated with paranoia, and with auditory and visual hallucinations.[46] Younger people tend to use amphetamines and to combine amphetamines and barbiturates.

Inhalants

A special pattern of drug behavior, associated with social deviance and delinquency, is the inhalation of certain volatile substances, such as gasoline in Sudan, and paint thinner, plastic cement, shoe dye, and industrial glue in Mexico, Brazil, and elsewhere in Latin America.[47] Inhalant abuse constitutes one of the worst problems of drug addiction in Mexico. Solvent use has also been found on Canadian Indian reservations and among Australian aboriginal groups.[48]

In Mexico, three of every thousand people between 14 and 24 years of age (0.31%) use inhalants on a regular basis.[49] These figures, however, do not include two high-risk groups, the homeless population and those less than 14 years old, where inhalation is much greater. Several community studies carried out in different areas of Mexico show that starting ages are as young as five or six years.[50] More recent data point to several trends: inhalants are used commonly by youngsters in increasing doses; the percentage of young people using inhalants decreases as age increases and other substances (principally alcohol and marijuana) are substituted; inhalant use decreases as schooling increases, with age and years of schooling closely related.[51]

Habitual inhalation of volatile substances causes severe damage to the central nervous system, liver, kidneys, and bone marrow. In addition, there is the strong possibility of sudden death as a result of just a single episode of volatile solvent-inhalation.[52] Among 8-to-15-year-old Chilean children from lower socioeconomic classes, an estimated 3% to 5% are addicted to glue sniffing.[53] A study by Solis and Wagner showed statistically significant differences between subjects who had used only inhalants and those who began their drug use with inhalants, but moved on to use other drugs as well.[54] Interestingly, the study showed that 76% of single-drug users seek treatment before they have used inhalants two years, whereas 68% of polydrug users seek treatment only two or more years after drug use.

Anabolic Steroids and Prescription Drugs

Anabolic steroids entered the arena of substance abuse through athletes and others, who take them to enhance muscle development and performance. Use led to abuse for some, with significant medical and psychological consequences. The World Health Organization, which has launched a program to monitor the abuse of prescription drugs worldwide, surveyed in depth the consequences of nontherapeutic anabolic steroid use, along with other medications of potential abuse.[55] Of particular importance is the violence associated with anabolic steroid use. A complex interaction exists between anabolic steroid use and existing personality traits and can lead to violent behavior.[56]

Psychoactive drug abuse, through inappropriate prescription practices or the street sale of illicitly obtained prescription medication, has been noted for decades. Such abuse was noted earlier in relation to the use of barbiturates and the opioids. In more recent times, evidence for overprescription came with revelations about mild tranquilizer abuse, which may or may not have an addictive effect. Better documentation of abuse of benzodiazepines, through both inappropriate prescription practices and illegal sales, heightened the awareness of more widespread patterns of prescribed or illegally sold psychoactive drug abuse. Benzodiazepines, rapidly acting sleep medications, traditional barbiturates, and tranquilizers have all been associated with abuse.

Cannabis

A number of psychiatrists in Nigeria suggest that between 20% and 50% of male admissions to psychiatric wards are suffering from psychosis associated with cannabis use.[57] Toxic psychosis (associated with cannabis ingestion) accounted for more admissions to psychiatric wards than did schizophrenia.[58] If this is true, one should expect a very high rate of the use of cannabis among young males, who account for the highest number of hospital admissions because of psychosis. In Uganda, cannabis was reported to cause varying degrees of abnormal behavior, including frank psychotic disturbances,[59] though later studies did not confirm this expectation.[60] Various factors influence cannabis intoxication, including the potency of the locally available preparation, and they must be considered when assessing the differences in the toxic effects of cannabis as reported in various countries.[61]

Khat

Until recently, khat (*catha edulis forsk*) was not considered as harmful as alcohol or narcotics.[62] Khat is an important crop economically for East African countries, and export markets exist in other African countries and in the Middle East. In Somalia, Ethiopia, and Kenya, khat is used by all levels of society from about age eight, and it has been reported to be used by more than 85% of the people in Ethiopia. Between 10% and 25% of the regular khat users in Somalia are female. Khat as a drug is said to induce mild euphoria and excitement, often accompanied by loquacity or even logorrhea, and sometimes progressing to the stage of hypomania. To break this "khat mood," people may turn to alcohol and sedatives or tranquilizers. After observing several hundred khat chewers in Kenya, researchers M. Dhadphale and O. E. Omolo found that psychosis per se occurred only if the habitual user exceeded his usual khat consumption by a considerable amount; the effect thus appears to be dose-related.[63] In Kenya, the typical khat psychosis among traditional khat chewers occurred under the conditions of increased life stress, which occasioned their increase in khat chewing.[64] Subjects reverted to their normal state after stopping khat use. Khat is traditionally seen as producing "beneficial" effects such as increased output of work, and its deleterious side effects are associated only with grossly excessive chewing, which leads to paranoid type psychosis. Some anthropologists maintain, although recognizing the possibilities of certain negative health and economic effects, that because of the way khat is handled in public settings there is little evidence of widespread and outright abuse.[65]

Factors that contribute to khat psychosis are poor appetite leading to malnutrition and increased susceptibility to infections, dehydration, opportunistic infections, sleep deprivation, irritability, constipation, and restlessness. In addition, khat may cause buccal ulcerations, amphetaminelike cardiovascular side effects, and gastrointestinal disorders. An increase in vehicular accidents by drivers under the influence of khat are reported. Alcohol use along with the chewing of khat can produce more virulent psychiatric symptoms and is life threatening. Investigators argue for distinguishing between moderate and heavy users of khat, with only the latter being more at risk for psychiatric symptoms.[66] Nevertheless, since the khat habit may be costly, it has led to corruption, family instability, and prostitution.

Data on Morbidity and Mortality

Use of alcohol and other drugs has significant consequences for morbidity and mortality, but does not necessarily lead to dependence. Ambivalent attitudes toward abuse and the abuser, the stigma associated with substance abuse, and the criminal nature of the drug trade have led to a serious and pervasive lack of systematic, objective, comparable, and precise data-gathering among countries.[67] In addition, the results obtained from many country epidemiological surveys cannot be compared because of differences in sampling and research methods, and the lack of a standard nomenclature such as ICD-10. Consequently pure distinctions between varying levels of use and dependence are not clear.

Drug seizures are all too often used to define the scope of the drug trade, and this information is often used to make assumptions about the extent of drug use and abuse. This does not constitute the type of data collection that yields useful public health or clinical insight into the nature of the drug-abuse problem.

For a number of substances, the social marketing of drug use tends to obscure the distinction between use and abuse.[68] This is most evident in the marketing for tobacco products and alcohol, where sensitivity to abuse is rarely an issue. To address this problem, the World Health Organization is developing a global monitoring system on the health implications of substance use and abuse. The Abuse Trends Linkage Alerting System (ATLAS) will provide surveillance data relevant to the formulation of national and global strategies directed toward the prevention and control of substance abuse.[69] A drug surveillance system was recently implemented in Central America, Panama, and the Dominican Republic according to guidelines established by the Pan American Health Organization (PAHO) and the Inter-American Drug Abuse Control Commission of the Organization of American States (OAS).[70]

Economically, it is difficult to define the scope of the substance-abuse problem since most of the costs and profits derived from substance abuse are illegal. Quite often we think of economic profit being derived by "marketeers" who sell illicit drugs to populations in Europe and North America. Although such profits are no doubt substantial, one must also consider that, in the economics of the illicit drug trade, the link between "first-world" policies and influences on low-income countries is extremely important. The "dumping" of low-cost tobacco products, the excessive production of alcoholic beverages, the transshipment of the means of production of narcotics, and the distortion of market forces to encourage the production of opium and coca leaf are all part of a global economy of drug use that tends to benefit those in control and harm both users and their societies. As is evident with the recent influx of heroin into the Indian subcontinent, which has brought with it great economic gain for a few, but severe abuse, violence, and economic disruption for many, an established use of drugs in accepted cultural contexts can be severely distorted by economic forces and the coercion that is fostered.

In sum, measures of the magnitude of substance abuse throughout the world involve, at best, crude estimates. In the United States, for instance, the National Narcotics Intelligence Consumers Committee (NNICC) produces annual estimates of trafficking activity based on the amount of movement in the traffic, the number of users, seizure data, and estimates of cultivation and production.[71] But these estimates are not subjected to retrospective validation or statistical sampling techniques. As Michael Montagne cautions, "Some estimates used in calculations are out of date, data concerning price and purity is insufficient, background data used to develop the estimates are not published, and the whole methodology has been criticized as 'analysis by negotiation' with final estimates resulting from a bargaining process among the member agencies."[72]

It is also extremely difficult to establish with accuracy the costs of drug use in morbidity, mortality, and human suffering. Drug use is associated with family violence, child abuse, suicide, property crimes, gang violence, and other forms of violence. The linkages to economic issues, family disruptions, and local community dynamics are well established. In one specific example, dysfunctional families often force children to move away from home and to value behaviors that run against the grain of the conventional society.[73] These youngsters often feel rejected by abusive parents and join groups in which they feel accepted, where "bad" is "good."[74] Membership in these groups frequently involves the use of drugs, especially alcohol and inhalants.[75]

Illegal drug use is taking its toll on high-income societies and low-income societies, as illustrated by the report that Pakistan has as many as 1.5 million heroin addicts; this represents a dramatic increase from the 1970s.[76] Twenty-four percent of the children in a Brazilian school sample reported that they had used solvents in the past month.[77]

Reductions in Supply or Demand

In the debate on how to control substance abuse, opinion is often polarized over whether efforts should be directed toward reducing the supply of drugs or reducing the demand for them. Efforts must obviously be made on both fronts, but we are convinced that the primary emphasis must be on demand reduction. Demand sustains the markets that make the drug trade profitable, even when interdiction and crop-destruction efforts lead to increased costs to the traffickers. A reduction in demand implies a series of actions on the personal and community level that make people aware of the dangers of substance abuse and build a personal "set," or psychological propensity, to resist substance use.

A reduction in supply most often has the support of national criminal justice systems and implies interdiction, crop destruction, and severe penalties for those caught engaging in substance distribution and use. However, there is a strong consensus among the providers of substance-abuse treatment services, the prevention community, and many who are involved in substance-abuse policy, that no amount of effort devoted to supply reduction can or will result in the eradication of substance abuse. In general, efforts to reduce supply do not work.

The pattern of use and supply influences the development of policies to deal with drug use and abuse. If people are dependent on a particular drug and it is not perceived as deleterious, then there is usually a limited commitment to restrict use. If, on the other hand, morbidity and mortality are associated with use, and no clear economic advantage is be gained by those in power, then the stage is set for policy initiatives to curb use.

Cigarette sales, for instance, are an important component of international trade. Although tobacco consumption is falling in Western Europe and North America, it is rising in many other parts of the world. Tobacco companies based in the United States actively pursue markets overseas, with the support of the government, as a means of increasing exports and reducing trade imbalance. Tobacco consumption is rising in sub-Saharan Africa about 2% annually and in other regions of the world at even greater rates. This trend is due to largely uncontrolled, aggressive advertising campaigns. The morbidity and mortality that ensue are devastating. Increasing mortality is now being reported from India, Hong Kong, China, and South Africa.

Countries have pursued strategies for substance-abuse prevention or reduction in a variety of ways. In a number of Islamic countries, for example, prohibition of alcohol, as prescribed fourteen centuries ago, is legally in force.[78] Djibouti, besides its national efforts, supports regional and international collaboration for collective action against the use of khat. The complexity of addressing the issues of supply and demand is demonstrated by what followed the introduction of a law to prohibit the use of opium in Pakistan in 1973. Prohibition proved ineffective and opium-derived heroin soon dominated the scene of drug abuse. A number of factors led to this result. Efforts to control drug traffic and use were not closely coordinated and linked to related institutions and agencies, and communities were neither prepared for, nor involved in, the implementation of these measures. Therapeutic and rehabilitation services were incapable of coping with the enormous load of drug users seeking help. Drug trafficking across the borders pushed the use of heroin, thus aggravating the situation.

It was recognized in the late 1970s that Colombia and Bolivia, and other South American countries as well, had a great potential for expanding their cultivation and production of coca and cocaine. Peru and Bolivia are the only two countries currently authorized under international agreements to grow coca legally for the pharmaceutical market. These two countries are also the source of most of the illicit coca leaves and paste used in making cocaine. Processing of coca into cocaine occurs mostly in Colombia. Table 4.2 (from NIDA) shows coca leaf production and eradication in South America. Table 4.3 shows worldwide coca leaf production.

Most recent reports are on illicit cocaine trafficking and accompanying social problems, such as crime. This same pattern is now emerging in relation to heroin. The networks used to traffic in cocaine are better organized than the organizations that traffic in heroin or marijuana, and they can also be rather dispersed geographically. The international cocaine trade has reached a point where it is becoming diffi-

Table 4.2 Coca Leaf Cultivation and Eradication in South America (in hectares)*

	1979	1980	1981	1982	1983	1984	1985	1986
Peru								
Cultivation	30,000	50,000	50,000	50,000	60,000	60,000	70,000	110,000
Eradication	—	—	0	0	680	3,180	5,350	2,675
Bolivia								
Cultivation	25,000	35,000	35,000	35,000	40,000	55,000	38,000	38,000
Eradication	—	—	0	85	0	2,000	30	135
Colombia								
Cultivation	3,000	3,000	2,900	5,000	13,000	15,000	18,000	18,000
Eradication	—	—	400	1,970	2,000	3,414	2,000	760

* 1 hectare = 2.47 acres.

Source: Montagne, 1991:282.

Table 4.3 Worldwide Coca Leaf Production (in metric tons)

Year	Metric Tons
1963–69 (average)	13,514 (S.D. = 859)
1970–77 (average)	16,063 (S.D. = 1330)
1978	19,500
1979	25,000
1980	25,230
1981	120,000
1982	135,000
1983	135,000–150,000
1984	135,000–270,000
1985	125,000–137,000
1986	152,000–188,000

500-kg coca leaf = 1 kg cocaine; S.D. = standard deviation.
Source: Montagne 1991:283.

cult to separate the source countries from the processing countries, and transit countries from the consumer countries. Cocaine use has become more popular in Europe, parts of the Middle East, and even in some African countries such as Nigeria. Some have argued that the increased use of cocaine in the past fifteen years is due to controls placed on other stimulant drugs, especially in the United States, such as the amphetamines.[79]

Governmental efforts to reduce the supply of cocaine and heroin into Africa have been problematic. Nigerians and other Africans have been involved in cannabis trafficking both locally and internationally for many years. Beginning in the early 1980s, Nigerians entered the heroin and cocaine trade.[80] Although the country initially served only as a transshipment point from producing countries of South America and Southeast Asia to Western Europe and North America, much of the trade now stays in the country and a local clientele has developed. Today, the use of cocaine and heroin by young people in Nigeria remains unabated.

Laws to control the drug problem in Nigeria have been promulgated since the late 1950s; however, effective interdiction has not occurred. Drug laws stipulate penalties such as death and long-term imprisonment for sale, possession, or use of opium, cocaine, and other dangerous drugs. The mere presence of laws, even when they are enforced, often does little to deter drug abuse. For example, prison terms have failed to discourage Nigerians from trafficking in dangerous substances. The complexity of the organization and the forces (most powerfully, the drug cartels) associated with the drug trade throughout the world evoke a control response (that is, interdiction and crop destruction) in order that governments can be seen as "doing something" without any particular confidence in the effectiveness of their measures.

As attempts are made to control the supply of drugs, adversaries seek newer ways to evade the barriers to continued distribution. An example of this pattern comes from a recent report of a shift in the drug trade between India and its neighbors. Indian drug smugglers have for years conveyed heroin to the West, but, with more effective interdiction of heroin, they have turned to supplying the materials needed to make heroin in countries where interdiction has yet to stop production. The regional demand for acetic anhydride, which is needed to manufacture heroin, is the result of successful pressure on the Golden Triangle of Laos, Thailand, and Myanmar (formerly Burma) from local and Western drug enforcement agencies. The smugglers are now supporting the drug cartels in Pakistan, Afghanistan (where political chaos makes control impossible), and Myanmar (where the government itself is reported to be deeply involved) by supplying them with large amounts of acetic anhydride. The chemical goes by camelback across the Thar Desert to Pakistan and is then transshipped to other countries. The routes used are the same as those used centuries ago to smuggle gold, weapons, and spices. Troops find it difficult to patrol the terrain, and air surveillance is not yet used (indeed, the economic gains from the trade support rebel factions in the border areas of India). Although heroin seizures on the border with Pakistan have dropped over the past two years, the seizures of acetic anhydride have soared, indicating that the economic incentives make the risks worthwhile.

Comparative research on the effectiveness of socio-legal preventive and control measures on the interaction between criminal behavior and drug abuse was carried out by the United Nations Social Defense Research Institute.[81] The study involved Argentina, Brazil, Costa Rica, Japan, Jordan, Italy, Malaysia, Singapore, and the United States. A close association was found among drug abuse, criminal behavior, and social attitudes to such problems. Both drug abuse and the socio-legal systems varied greatly in the countries involved. The primary drug abused, viewed as a stimulus to crime, varied from one country to another (e.g., cannabis and psychopharmaceuticals in Argentina and Costa Rica, amphetamines in Japan, hashish in Jordan, heroin in Malaysia and Singapore, and cocaine in other countries). No correlation was found between the harshness of the socio-legal system and the seriousness of drug abuse and its associated criminality. In the majority of countries, the direct impact of informal control systems, such as the family, church, school, and work environment, did not seem to influence the close association between drug abuse and criminal behavior. Social factors appear to have greater impact on the association than psychological factors. This finding is counterintuitive to the assumptions made by many countries who develop prevention programs.

Nigeria, for example, seems determined to fight the spread of illicit drug supply, but little attention is paid to the menace of licit drugs, especially alcohol, as noted earlier. There is no national alcohol policy in Nigeria today. There is also no concerted effort by the government to support programs of demand reduction and research on the problem. From a health perspective, the relationship between the abuse of licit drugs, including alcohol, cannot be separated from the development of any progressive plan to deal with the problem of the abuse of illegal substances.

Legalization of substances of abuse, notably heroin, cocaine, and marijuana, has frequently been proposed as a means of addressing the problem of drug abuse, and especially drug-related criminality, when other means of demand-and-supply reduction are seen as ineffective. It invariably arouses strong political, legal, and social concerns. Removing the financial incentives for the illegal drug trade offers a "safer" means for access to drugs for those unable or unwilling to reduce their use. In addition, decreasing the spread of illnesses such as AIDS and tuberculosis is typically cited as a reason for the adoption of legalization strategies. Legalization per se is rarely adopted universally, and when adopted it usually occurs where the society is rather homogeneous and where adequate treatment and social service resources exist (such as the Netherlands and some parts of Switzerland). Although legalization may not offer the answer to drug abuse, it still deserves serious consideration before it is ruled out.

Most recently, "harm reduction" has been proposed as both a philosophy and strategy to address drug abuse. This public health approach emphasizes treatment while retaining laws that have penalties for trafficking or illegal activities associated with drug use. Under various systems, addicts may be permitted access to drugs, usually with some control over the means of distribution, and with active encouragement to get the user into treatment. Law enforcement is reserved for traffickers or those who engage in clearly illegal activities associated with drug use. Needle exchange and methadone maintenance are part of harm-reduction strategies. Among the benefits reported by advocates of harm reduction are reduced criminal activity by users to support their habits and a reduction in the spread of HIV infection and tuberculosis.[82]

Some countries have emphasized demand reduction and, to that end, the treatment and rehabilitation of drug users. An interesting example is found in a report of the Singapore heroin-control program.[83] Along with an expansive enforcement strategy, all drug suspects with positive urine tests were committed to Drug Rehabilitation Centers. Active programs for instilling "discipline, social responsibility, and sound work habits" were applied together with two years of compulsory supervision on release with a five-day cycle for reporting and urine analysis. Though there was some evidence of drug substitution with cannabis, psychotropic drugs, and alcohol, the heroin epidemic apparently was controlled. Singapore, a prosperous and politically authoritarian city-state, may not represent a generalizable example. But it is a provocative one. Certain countries, such as Thailand, have made special efforts to promote primary health care and to integrate the control and treatment of drug abuse within the framework of the general health system.[84] In general, the success of these programs is often the subject of debate due to a lack of adequate, objective evaluation.

Despite the inadequacy of supply-reduction policies, efforts to decrease the demand for substances of potential abuse remain almost universally underfunded and undersupported. Although treatment and prevention services are offered, and sizable amounts of money are spent on demand-reduction programs, the comparatively small amounts of resources allocated reflect a lack of priority given to demand reduction in almost all countries. The relative imbalance speaks to a lack of knowledge about the potential effectiveness of demand-reduction strategies, the conflicting political forces that reign in the area of substance-abuse control, and the quasimilitary approach that sees substance abuse as unrelated to health and human services. Effective demand reduction requires valuing the cohesiveness of communities, recognizing prevention as an important part of the continuum of services, empowering people, and developing finer-grained culturally relevant programs to foster the reduction or prevention of the use of substances of abuse. When this occurs, both policy and practice may move to limit the use of drugs.

The demand for drugs and alcohol can be nurtured by practices that glamorize its use, that promote enhanced accessibility to vulnerable populations, and that subsidize drug and alcohol use. These practices must cease. It is clear that social, political, and economic policies must coincide to limit the use of drugs and alcohol and not to foster its abuse. The economic incentives for exploitation through drugs and alcohol must end. The traditional use of drugs and alcohol in various cultures need not be intruded upon, nor need an ethos of repressive prohibition be created, to effect the change in drug and alcohol consumption that would reduce morbidity and mortality associated with the consequences of its use.

Approaches to Therapy

The field of substance-abuse treatment, like that of demand reduction, is in a state of evolution. Even in wealthy countries in the West, substance-abuse treatment rarely fits in a comprehensive system of health care; it relies on special interests and variable funding and lacks a coherent theoretical framework. The stigma of substance abuse often thwarts the mainstream development of treatment programs. The World Health Organization has proposed a schema defining successive stages of the organization of services for alcohol and other drug problems.[85] The plan acknowledges that, since governments must be concerned with providing the greatest good for the greatest number to the extent of the available fiscal resources, most services to persons with alcohol and drug problems are more palliative than curative.

Substance-abuse treatment does not exist in isolation from other components of the human services system or the criminal justice system. As in many Western countries, the criminal justice system is all too often the primary venue for the "care" of substance abusers, but without facilitating treatment or rehabilitation. To be effective, however, planning of services must take place at all levels of government and societal groupings—communities, families, and individuals.

In most low-income countries, even where substance abuse is a major and publicly acknowledged problem, the "official" treatment and rehabilitation centers are inadequate and, as in high-income countries, have proven to be ineffective when measured by recidivism rates of "treated" addicts who do not enter sustained comprehensive programming. Frequently such facilities are merely detoxification centers; many of their "beneficiaries" are back on drugs within a short time. The only tangible, temporary benefit is that the amount of drugs the "treated" addict needs for a "high" for the next several months is less than before, as is the daily cost of sustaining the habit.

The most promising efforts involve "treatment matching," which requires a precise delineation of the client's problem so that therapies or interventions that most precisely address the problem can be tried. For instance, a client with an addiction to heroin may be best served by methadone maintenance combined with individual counseling. A client with alcoholism may benefit most from detoxification followed by vocational rehabilitation and family counseling. Matching clients to specific treatments should introduce a body of knowledge that will support efficacious treatments that can gain public support.[86]

"Self-help" movements and their associated programs are emerging as a mainstay of treatment. In many localities, official or orthodox methods of substance abuse treatment coexist with self-help programs. Self-help movements often are inexpensive, provide sustained help, offer a group identity and support, and are perceived as less stigmatizing. The unofficial sponsorship of most self-help programs and their voluntary nature generally ensures acceptance, cultural relevance, and a personal fit with any other treatment that a client has accepted.

As a result of the inadequacies of official treatment services, as well as for sociocultural reasons and concerns about confidentiality, so-called alternative therapeutic interventions have become widely used by addicts in many countries. Acupuncture is often used in Asia and elsewhere as a treatment for addiction. Faith healing, meditation, yoga, and other traditional and folk treatment methods are also extensively used.[87] Formally trained Yunani Hakkims (Muslim traditional healers) treat addicts in Pakistan. Folk healers treat heroin and opium addicts in Burma, as they do in Laos, Malaysia, and elsewhere.[88] Religious sheikhs treat addicts and other mental patients in special mejids in the Sudan. Other kinds of religious interventions in the rehabilitation of addicts are widespread throughout the world.

One example of religious concern and intervention was the treatment of addicts in Buddhist wats or temples by monks in Thailand.[89] The monks' therapies combined religious teachings with use of traditional Thai medicine. Many monks were trained at the Center for Traditional Thai Buddhist Medicine at Wat Pho, the royal Buddhist temple in Bangkok. Monks have been treating patients for a variety of social, psychological, and spiritual ailments in Thailand for centuries, and recently their therapies have included the rehabilitation of addicts. The Wat Tam Kraborg, a hundred miles north of Bangkok, was especially renowned in this regard. A charismatic abbot began a treatment program there in 1960. The therapy lasted a minimum of ten days, often longer, and included the drinking of herbal concoctions producing vomiting and sweating, as well as counseling and religious lessons by the monks. Before their release from the temple, the patients were made to swear in the name of the Buddha that they would no longer use drugs. In view of the success of this work, it is unclear why this means of treatment has been temporarily curtailed.

The ability of acupuncture to minimize craving and withdrawal symptoms during, and subsequent to, detoxification, through stimulation of the "lung points" in the patient's ear, was first discovered by Dr. Wen and colleagues in Hong Kong in the early 1970s.[90] Acupuncture reduces the pain of detoxification for addicts and is thus used widely for that purpose in a range of countries.[91] By itself, however, acupuncture is not particularly effective in the rehabilitation of addicts, as measured by high abstinence rates following treatment.

In Malaysia, as elsewhere in the world where medical pluralism is the rule, a variety of traditional and folk therapies are still in use, and some have been used for more than a century to treat opium addicts.[92] Recently, however, the Malay bomohs (folk healers) have been in the forefront of the treatment of drug addicts, especially heroin users. Although each bomoh uses a unique therapeutic procedure, there are

Box 4.5 Alternative Therapy for Addicts

Few official preventive, treatment, or rehabilitation programs for drug addiction have proved particularly successful, and in the search for effective treatment options, some attention has focused on the therapeutic practices of acupuncturists in many parts of the world, of Buddhist monks in Thailand, of "curanderos" in the U.S. and Mexico, and of folk healers in Malaysia. An interesting example of such alternatives is the practice of folk healers, or "drug bomohs," in Malaysia.

Since the mid-1970s, many of the 20,000 Malaysian "bomohs" have focused their therapeutic efforts on the detoxification and rehabilitation of heroin addicts. The addicted patients usually live in a controlled environment within the bomohs' compounds during the treatment period. During this time, the patients are carefully monitored to prevent any chance for ingestion of addictive substances.

Most of the "drug bomohs" require their patients to drink one or more vegetal concoctions over a specific period of time in order to minimize the addicts' withdrawal pains during detoxification. Many bomohs give their patients "cleansing" baths and do massage as well as perform charms (pembenci hatred rituals) on their patients to make them detest drugs. The bomohs also perform spiritual rituals, teach Islamic religious lessons, and ask their patients to read aloud Koranic verses and to participate in ritual incantations. Some bomohs even write Koranic verses on the body of the patient or make the patient eat the ashes of a burned piece of paper on which Koranic verses are written.

All bomohs are said to have their own special helping or "familiar" spirits ("hantu raya" or "pelisit"), and some former patients have indicated that their continued abstinence is due to their fear of the bomoh's "familiar," which can wreak havoc in their lives if they return to drug use.[93]

The degree to which bomoh therapy and rehabilitation is effective, in terms of sustained abstinence, is not firmly established. However, and despite the fact that most of the bomohs' patients are self-selected, there are indications that bomoh treatment is at least as effective as, and perhaps more effective than, orthodox methods. Since most patients had used a variety of different treatment modalities, the data was of limited value. Thus additional, and particularly prospective, studies are needed to establish efficacy. What can be said, however, is that a sizable number of heroin addicts are resorting to bomoh therapy. Addicts who believe in the benefits of this therapy may have better treatment outcomes.

Follow-up studies of patients of both the Buddhist monks in Thailand and of a number of the bomohs in Malaysia indicate that, when measured in terms of abstinence rates (as confirmed by urine analysis), these therapies appear superior (for some bomohs quite significantly superior) to the more orthodox interventions. It is still unclear why this should be so, but some have suggested that the Malaysian bomohs' treatments are successful because of their foundation in the traditional past and their ability to reconfirm traditional values and reestablish a distinct personal identity for the patient.

Some of the bomohs' detoxification vegetal mixtures have been tested in laboratory experiments and were found to suppress withdrawal symptoms in morphine-addicted mice. A follow-up study of 388 former addicted patients of five "drug bomohs" showed that abstinence rates could be as high as 50% a year after treatment. Since not all patients could be contacted, it could be assumed that all of those not contacted were recidivists, and in this strictest interpretation of data the overall abstinence rate was 13% (on a par with most treatment programs) and 30% for two of the bomohs.

similarities among them. Almost all insist that the patients should live in the bomoh's compound for the period of treatment. They all use an herbal concoction (albeit with different recipes) for the period of detoxification and, for some, up to a month thereafter. Experimentation with some of the bomohs' herbal concoctions on morphine-addicted mice has established that some are biologically effective in reducing withdrawal symptoms.

Creative programs for abandoned substance-abusing children have emerged in some countries. For example, Mexico has a foster care program for children who inhale solvents.[94] Under this program, adopted children are supplied with homes, food, schooling, and support. The treatment pattern works along behavioral lines, and the child is encouraged to stop inhaling solvents. The program lasts for one year, after which a child is returned home or to an alternative setting. In Brazil, a similar behaviorally oriented program is offered under the auspices of a mental health program, though the magnitude of the problem and the lack of possible family support has made the effort ineffective except for children who have a preexisting support network.

Prevention

Just as interdiction can never eradicate all of the incentives for drug use, treatment will never meet the needs of all those affected by drug abuse. Thus, prevention is an essential strategy for reducing drug abuse. The politics of prevention are complex. A World Health Organization statement describes crucial issues in prevention: "Prevention at the local level," it holds, "is not a substitute for national policies. Local activities, developed within existing legislative and organizational frameworks, complement action at the national level by encouraging full and effective implementation of national policies. In addition, local prevention activities can set the agenda for further national developments by identifying specific problems, generating information, [and by] raising and providing models of good practice."[95]

Many consider primary prevention to be the best way to combat the use of drugs. Some have tried mental health education: first informing, orienting, and counseling, and then training. The goals of the process are to protect individuals and families from use leading to abuse and to involve the community in preventing and reducing the problem.[96]

Public education about the dangers of substance abuse is an essential component of any prevention effort. For example, programs must include messages about the consequences of alcohol, tobacco smoking, and anabolic steroid use, as well as messages about drugs more commonly identified as illicit drugs of abuse. Unfortunately, understanding which prevention messages are most effective requires further study. It is clear, however, that the messages must be culturally appropriate and relevant. Messages that evoke fear do not necessarily lead to effective action. Education can lead to an increase in knowledge without producing the desired behavioral change. This is also true of substance abuse-related behaviors, including risky sexual behavior leading to HIV infection.

In some cultures, leisure time is often associated with "risk behavior" among teenagers (for example, potential alcohol or drug use), and this is a message frequently found in the commercial media the world over.[97] This perception is true across classes. The consequence for middle- and upper-class children may be an attempt to occupy the children fully as a means of preventing substance use and abuse. Only in the case of involvement with religious activities has this strategy been shown to have any demonstrable preventive efficacy, and even there the association was weak. This does not mean that providing time-filling activities is not potentially important as part of a larger prevention strategy, nor that public pressure or control of the messages the media aim at youth will be without effect.

Work place education and preventive interventions are currently being developed. For these programs to be successful, there must be an investment on the part of the employer/government to ensure sustained productivity on the part of workers and a true commitment to eliminate the stigma associated with substance-abuse problems.

Reaching people who have been marginalized by society, including homeless populations, street youth, and incarcerated and institutionalized people, presents an even greater challenge. Outreach activities are needed to communicate prevention messages to the population at large, and are well known and well practiced in many countries. The challenge to successful outreach program implementation is to find sufficient numbers of workers, to train them adequately, and to support them in their functions. Ultimately, without efforts to change underlying, and probably causative, social factors, specific educational or other intervention efforts are at best palliative.

Conclusions

- Alcohol and drug use must be seen as a public health problem of the first order. The abuse of heroin and cocaine is complicated by the fact that, since these substances are illegal and therefore socially unacceptable, treatment for addiction often goes unaddressed. There is a direct link between intravenous drug use and the spread of HIV as a result of users sharing contaminated needles. Sex for drugs and unprotected sex under the influence of alcohol is a major contribution to the heterosexual spread of AIDS. Heavy users of cocaine and "crack" suffer from a wide range of health problems, including cardiovascular abnormalities and serious neuropsychiatric disorders. Prostitution, theft, and exploitation are in direct correlation to drug use, leading to a decay in the cultural and moral fabric of developing countries.

- Supply-reduction strategies appear not to have significantly reduced drug and alcohol abuse. Although they should not abandon such strategies, governments must develop their complement: stronger policies to reduce the demand for drugs and alcohol. Effort should be targeted through public education campaigns and include messages on prevention that are meaningful to youth, and include the dangers associated with the more casually accepted use of tobacco and apparently less potent liquors. The naive attempts at substance-abuse education in schools that marked the "war on drugs" in the United

States must be replaced by programs that are culturally meaningful, provide factual information that can be retained and used, and that are supported by parents, teachers, and others important to youth. It is equally important to support educational programs that affect those youth not in school, but who reside on the streets, are not engaged by traditional organizations, and often are the largest consumers of substances of abuse. There is emerging evidence that substance-abuse education is best carried out in the context of general health education.[98]

• Treatment strategies that focus on the reduction, and eventual cessation, of unsafe drug-taking practices must be developed. Although several treatment options are now available, the capacity for treatment must be expanded to incorporate the best available and most readily accepted interventions. Treatment is essential to provide a means to help those who seek help and thus prevent the type of resignation that perpetuates drug use. Much needs to be learned about effective treatment. While both traditional and nontraditional treatment approaches appear to be effective, they must be better evaluated in a culture-specific manner. In addition, there must be commitment from a person's social system composed of government, educational, religious, community and family levels, to foster relapse prevention. Ideally, programs should include educational campaigns that convey an emphasis on healing rather than social condemnation or criminalization.

• A focus solely on interventions at the personal level cannot effectively solve the problem of substance abuse. Research and policy must be directed at etiologically significant factors that involve the complex economic and social forces that support the initiation and sustenance of substance abuse. Coalition building for the purpose of coordinated preventive intervention is essential. The coalitions must include the politically, religiously, and economically powerful, as well as those who represent the interests of individuals or specific groups. Little progress can be foreseen, however, unless underlying social and economic factors and related human rights and social equity issues are exhaustively confronted.

• The transshipment of drugs of abuse and the chemicals needed to manufacture them takes place in the absence of either coordinated interdiction or intergovernmental agreements that could provide a disincentive for this illegal trade. The financial incentives associated with the criminal enterprise of illegal and legal substance distribution can be negated by the development of more effective taxation, control of monopolization, and the regulation of the transshipment of substances of abuse or their precursors. There is, therefore, a need to target identified areas of high transshipment and negotiate the agreements necessary to effectively stem the tide of transshipment.

• Distinguishing among use, abuse, and dependence in relation to alcohol and drugs is a complex task. Factors that determine the nature, extent, and detriments of substance abuse include a person's receptivity to use, availability of drugs and alcohol, cultural attitudes toward alcohol and drug use, and whether or not a person will be stigmatized as a result of substance abuse. Conversely, many societies condone the use of naturally occurring drugs for religious ceremonies and social interaction. Since use of alcohol and drugs may not evolve into full-blown dependence, determining a direct connection between casual use and harmful use is equally challenging. There is a pressing need for precise epidemiologic study using a recognized nomenclature such as ICD-10.

• Reliable, systematic data on substance-abuse problems are lacking. The fragmentation of data-gathering has undermined effective policy development and impeded the understanding of the severity and magnitude of the problem. In addition, methods must be developed to aid in the distinction between "use," "abuse," and dependence in order to gather data that yields useful information. International agencies must therefore enhance their capacity for meaningful, comparable data-gathering on substance abuse. The ATLAS system and others will address many of the current weaknesses in the systematic gathering of data. But even these surveys leave gaps in integrating the complex nature of substance abuse as a social and economic problem. Governments must elucidate the negative economic and social consequences of substance abuse in terms that will stem the tide of drug production and distribution in their countries. This will require a coordinated effort between government agencies and the political will to address the problem. It must be understood that the economic and social costs of the consequences of addiction often far surpass the income from alcohol and tobacco taxation, or the profits that devolve to a few.

• The consumption of alcohol in low-income countries is steadily increasing. Research shows that 15% to 20% of adults in Latin America use alcohol excessively; urban areas in China show a significant prevalence for alcohol use; and the number of women using alcohol in sub-Saharan Africa and Islamic countries has become exceedingly common. A focus on alcohol use, as a dominant contribution to morbidity and mortality, must become a part of mainstream substance-abuse policy formulation.

• The adverse consequences of excessive alcohol use include traffic accidents, homicide, and suicide, suggesting that alcohol is a direct cause of physical trauma and violent behavior. Cirrhosis, esophageal varices, and other gastrointestinal consequences of chronic alcohol abuse mean that alcohol is an important cause of serious chronic medical conditions that contribute to mortality, morbidity, and health care costs. Prolonged alcohol use may eventually trigger an underlying mental illness such as depression, or an even more severe psychological condition such as psychosis. Research has shown that admissions to psychiatric wards are increasingly alcoholics. These patients typically have family members who are alcoholic, demonstrate sociopathic tendencies, and suffer depression. Programs that adequately treat alcohol abusers must be implemented as a part of public health and public safety planning. The economic costs warrant a priority status.

• Drug and alcohol abuse are exacerbated by rapid social change, repressive social institutions, and lack of employment opportunities. In addition, using drugs and alcohol is a way to alleviate boredom, frustration, and intolerable living conditions. Adolescents and young adults, in particular, are vulnerable to the messages conveyed through advertising and amplified through peer pressure—that using drugs and alcohol promises to create what for them may be an unobtainable lifestyle. Controls on seductive and exploitative advertising must be implemented.

- Although many governments are aware of the detrimental effects of alcohol abuse on the development of national resources, there appears to be no incentive to reduce the availability and consumption of alcohol. Economic gain from the sale and taxation of alcohol are encouraged both directly and indirectly by governments despite the negative social problems caused by alcohol abuse, such as family dislocation, violence, and malnutrition. It is essential, therefore, to demonstrate that the indirect costs of substance use and abuse more than offset the direct economic gain to governments. Thus, other cost-benefit analyses must be performed with the support and involvement of governments. Based on findings, governments would have incentive to direct monies to the development and expansion of treatment programs.
- Inhalant use must be treated as a health problem as serious as any other associated with drug abuse. The inhalation of volatile substances by people between the ages of 14 and 24 years constitutes one of the worst problems of drug addiction in Latin America. Adverse effects from "sniffing" paint thinner, shoe dye, and industrial glue include damage to the central nervous system and major organs. The impact of inhalant use on the health of young people represents a health emergency.

5

Violence

The ubiquity of collective violence is one of the most disturbing features of the late twentieth century. In the past two decades, the low-intensity conflicts in Nicaragua, Angola, and Mozambique, the repressive regimes in Myanmar, Guatemala, El Salvador, South Africa, and Indonesia, the "dirty wars" of Argentina and Chile, the wars in Indochina, and the civil, ethnic, and religious conflicts in Latin America, South Asia, Eastern Europe, Central Asia, Northern Ireland, and the Middle East constitute a new wave of violence, torture, and repressive techniques.

Wars, prolonged conflicts, and state repression lead to a flood of social and economic problems that affect well-being. The assault on communities disrupts the production of food, transportation services, and economic infrastructures; the loss of food and income leads to increased poverty and malnutrition. An additional stress on the economic base results from increased spending on arms. The violence committed against health care workers often causes a severe and lingering stress on health services. People are forced to leave their homes and communities; the dislocation breaks ties of reciprocity and sociality, increases the marginal (or illegal) status of refugees, and leads to additional trauma, the inability to mourn, and a further deterioration of standards of living. Families break up and children are orphaned or abandoned.

Alongside the loss of life, the fragmentation of families, the displacement of populations, and the disruption of social and economic institutions exists a range of trauma. The problems include fear, pain, loss, grief, guilt, anxiety, hatred, sadness, and the dissolution of everyday forms of sociality, language, and experience. In turn, the breakdown in economic, social, and political systems and the weakening of a society's moral fabric often coexist with domestic, civil, and ganglike conflicts.

Studies on the mental health of civilians affected by the classical forms of war in Europe and elsewhere have generally found that although the frequency of mental distress increases during conflict, the distress is usually acute and temporary (with the notable exception of torture survivors, prisoners of war, and the survivors of the Nazi death camps). A very different pattern of distress is evident in recent studies of survivors of political violence, ethnic strife, and low-intensity conflicts that have plagued the residents of Cambodia, Vietnam, Africa, Haiti, and Central and South America. The traumas of war and terror in these territories, which often take the form of generalized but pervasive fear and anxiety experienced at a bodily level, are usually severe and long-lasting.

These changes in the frequency, structure, and duration of trauma relate to three main factors.

First, the nuclear stalemate and the dissolution of totalitarian regimes of recent years has led to a situation in which low-intensity conflicts in impoverished countries have become the most frequent forms of large-scale conflict. Table 5–1 shows the number of armed conflicts in the world in 1987, according to the calculations of Bernard Nietschmann, a professor of geography at the University of California, Berkeley: whereas 72% of the conflicts were between a centralized political system, or "state," and an ethnically distinct people, or "nation," only 3% of the conflicts were between states (such as Iran and Iraq). In all, 82% of the conflicts involved politically marginal, "fourth-world" peoples. Most of these conflicts pitted states against indigenous nations, and guerrilla insurgencies against state government.[1]

The objective of low-intensity warfare is control over a population, not a territory, through terror and destruction. With these conflicts, civilians are often targeted rather than simply being incidental victims of fighting between combatants; they are usually villagers who do not belong to any formal organization or political party, and they die from either direct war actions or war-induced starvation. Those who do survive are commonly victims of dislocation, hunger, social upheaval, civil violence, and unattenuated grief.

A principal feature of "low-intensity" conflicts is that everyday life is subject to continued and fearful tension. In Nicaragua, the mass terrorization of civilians, the lingering threat to one's life and welfare, the trauma of the "disappeared," unpredictable acts of violence, and massive population displacements created an atmosphere of stress, fear, bereavement, and uncertainty. Research conducted in Nicaragua and Mozambique suggests that survivors suffer from a range of bodily ailments and emotional troubles.[2]

The second defining feature of violence today is the ubiquity of deadly weapons. The international arms sale, and the busy market for such weapons, has contributed to the severity of conflicts once they occur. Land mines are particularly hazardous because they are still a threat even in peacetime. The Arms Project of

Table 5.1 Armed Conflicts in 1987

Type of Conflict	Number	Subtotal	Percent
State-state	4		3
State-insurgency	18		15
State-nation	77		
State-multination	5	86	72
Foreign state occupation	4		
Nation-nation	5	12	10
Insurgency-nation	7		
Involving nations		98	82
Total	**120**		

Source: Nietschmann, 1987.

Human Rights Watch and Physicians for Human Rights reports that some 85 to 90 million land mines threaten civilians in 62 countries.[3] Roughly 150 people around the world—mostly civilians—are killed or injured by land mines each week; in Cambodia alone, some 30,000 people have lost limbs, most of them because of land mines. Physical wounds often require traumatic or surgical amputation. Those who survive the initial trauma often require intensive hospital care, physical therapy, and prosthetic devices. Some people are horribly disfigured or are unable to lead productive lives. The presence of unexploded land mines renders large tracts of land uninhabitable, which leads to significant economic and social consequences.

The third defining feature of the new wave of collective violence is that the brutality against civilians is often governed by a profound and devastating "aesthetics of terror."[4] Das and Nandy note that what most disturbed Indians during the bloody partition of India, Pakistan, and Bangladesh was the style of violence at that time: the murder of neighbors and atrocities committed against women solely because of religious affiliation.[5] Repressive regimes terrorize by employing a similar style of violence. Santiago reports that there are two distinct styles of killing in El Salvador.[6] Whereas the guerrillas kill as many soldiers as possible, as quickly as possible, the Salvadoran armed forces "do not just kill; they kill with a certain style." He writes: "People are not just killed by death squads in El Salvador—they are decapitated and then their heads are placed on pikes and used to dot the landscape. . . . It is not enough to kill children; they are dragged over barbed wire until the flesh falls from their bones while parents are forced to watch."[7]

The Methods of Violence

Some styles of destruction result from the mandate of a political or military force to demoralize a population. Indeed, with many acts of political violence, the correlation between violence and mental distress is direct and causal. When the control of populations, rather than of land, is being contested, as is so often the case with political violence, then the mind becomes one of the key battlegrounds. Political groups often try to terrorize a population through violence, detentions, torture, disappearances, and the disruption of health services, and those affected by violence struggle to maintain a sense of normality, well-being, and social cohesion.

Political violence can take many forms, from the assassinations and "disappearances" enacted by repressive regimes to the structural violence effected by severe inequities in opportunities for housing, water, food, jobs, land, waste disposal, education, and health care. The different forms of violence often produce related, but distinct, consequences. The repressive techniques used in the past two decades by the military regimes of Argentina, El Salvador, and Guatemala contributed to a pervasive climate of fear, uncertainty, and unrest. In turn, the poverty, malnutrition, and social segregation experienced daily by the marginalized residents of such countries as Brazil, Peru, China, and the United States are a direct result of the systematic violence enacted upon them. At times, repressive and structural violence go hand in hand. In South Africa, victims of the apartheid regime have suffered from arbitrary arrest, beatings, raids, and torture. At the same time, the structural violence that defines the apartheid regime contributes to the poverty, malnutrition, inferior education, urban crowding, and social strife in the African townships.[8] The latter forms of violence appear to have the most devastating, if not the most dramatic, impact on the welfare of South African children.[9]

Everyday, institutionalized racism, ethnic conflicts, and religious persecution often exact a similar toll on the welfare of politically marginal people. The racism and religious persecution evident in places like the United States, South Africa, and Europe contribute to limited life choices, poverty, social stresses, and violence.

A common perception is that many ethnic conflicts, such as the riots that followed the assassination of Indira Ghandi in India, result from unorganized acts of mob violence. Recent research shows that there is often planning and direction to ethnic riots, with notions of "ethnicity" created by and for political interests (see Box 5.1).[10] Local politicians and leaders of criminal gangs mobilize crowds, distribute liquor, and provide transportation, arms (including kerosene or gasoline for arson), and the names and addresses of victims' businesses and homes. The police often contribute to the violence by making no effort to prevent it. Violence is frequently directed toward reducing another group's alleged economic well-being and margin of advantage: homes are destroyed and businesses looted. Men are killed to reduce the occupational and working strength of others; women are assaulted through rape, the destruction of their homes, and the hardships of widowhood. Some of the most important repercussions of this kind of violence are social: all parties involved try to make sense of the cultural implications of neighbors fighting against neighbors and of well-known government officials who fail to stop the bloodshed. By failing to protect their citizens, and even withdrawing from the public spaces of killing, governments create crises of delegitimation that further erode legitimate authority and create widespread apathy, despair, and alienating cynicism.

At times, the aim of violence is not to gain control over a population or a territory but to eradicate an entire nation. The ethnic cleansing of Croats and Muslims in Bosnia and the extermination of aboriginal peoples in South America, Africa, and the Pacific all work to destroy nations and cultures. In Bosnia, Serbian troops rely on killings, massacres, and systematic rape to eliminate Croatian and Muslim populations and create ethnically pure territories into which Serbs then settle.

Cultures of Fear

The aim of authoritarian regimes from South Africa to Myanmar is to induce a climate of fear and confusion among civilians through a process of intensive repression. Fear is a critical instrument of social control. For populations in general, repressive regimes strive to induce a sense of fear and helplessness. For individuals held in detention, they try to effect a "personal dismantling."

Everyday life in repressive regimes during the most intense periods of violence is marked by "disappearances," rape, arrests, encounters with corpses, uprooting, house searches, censorship, dismissal from work, and economic or social deprivation. Often, there is the continued presence of what Agudelo aptly calls "grey violence": the sporadic, unpredictable arsenal of assassinations, murder, bombings,

Box 5.1 The Colombo Riot of 1983: The Complicity of Police and Government Officers

In late July 1983, the ambush of an army truck carrying eighteen Sinhalese soldiers in North Sri Lanka, and the cremation of their dismembered bodies at Colombo's chief cemetery at Borella, triggered thirteen days of riots in and around Colombo. The death toll was between 350 (the government figure) and 2,000 (the Tamil estimate). Large numbers of refugees fled their homes: in Colombo itself the number of refugees ranged from 80,000 to 100,000. Arson and property destruction were extensive.

Soon after the mortuary rites, violence broke out in several towns, in the form of street thuggery, stopping of traffic, and physical attacks, and almost a whole day passed before the army and police were called on to intervene. From the second day on, the mob violence was organized and for the most part purposeful. The riots then took a form that was decidedly more destructive and homicidal and showed firm evidence of planning and direction, of participation by politicians and government employees, and of the use of government vehicles and buses. The crowds—typically composed of Sinhala men from the urban working class—came armed with weapons, such as metal rods and knives, and carried gasoline that was frequently confiscated from passing motor vehicles. They carried voter lists and addresses of Tamil owners and occupants of houses, businesses, and other property. They also had access to transportation; they arrived mostly in government-owned trucks and buses or were dropped off at successive locations by the Colombo coastline trains. Less "visible" in the riots, but active in their initiation and organization, were certain Sinhala politicians and their local managers and bosses, entrepreneurs of organized crime, and small businessmen and their henchmen.

The victims in Colombo were Tamil shopkeepers, Tamil homeowners (especially of the middle-class and administrative and professional categories), large Tamil business capitalists and entrepreneurs, and Indian merchants, both Tamil and non-Tamil. Tamil houses, shops, mills, and factories in central market and business zones and middle class residential areas were methodically burned, destroyed, and looted.

Many Sinhalese sheltered and protected beleaguered Tamils, but members of the police force and security forces stood by during the riots—unwilling to restrain the rioters, showing sympathy for their actions, and at times actively participating in the work of destruction. One man, who was the honorary warden of the hostel of Hindu College, a school patronized by Tamil children, located in a suburb of Colombo, tried, on the first day of the riots, to telephone a police station and asked, in English, for the officer-in-charge. His assistant answered him in Sinhalese, an act that revealed his political allegiance. "Three houses in the neighborhood were on fire and a crowd was collecting and I was making frantic calls to the police," the man recalls.

Indeed, middle-class Tamil frequently complain of the lack of police action to prevent attacks and police tardiness in accepting urgent telephone calls, let alone respond to their pleas. In both the Colombo riots of 1983 and the Delhi riots of 1984, the police failed to take firm action: some took no action, others in one way or another colluded, and it was only after the worst violence had been unleashed that the army as an "outside" agent was called in as a deterrent.

Several steps can be taken to prevent such situations. Wherever there is evidence that the central government or local government agencies are implicated, those agencies must be held responsible. The police should be multi-ethnic in composition and be required to take a strong public stand against violence; prior knowledge on the part of the public that the police will not tolerate rioting is a strong deterrent. When it is suspected that violence might erupt because of certain well-known "triggering" events, the police must anticipate and make their purposive presence felt in the streets. A strong showing of police is necessary at the most frequent sites of violence: bazaars and business centers, bus depots, railway stations, and locations where a vulnerable minority is concentrated.

The importance of these suggestions is underscored by the fact that no subsequent riots have occurred in Colombo since the riots of 1983, despite a succession of assassinations and bombings. A primary deterrent has been the firm stance taken by the governments of Presidents Jayawardene and Premadasa that there shall be no repetition in the capital of the events of 1983. The police and the army, it is thought, are firm in this resolve. The absence of riots in Colombo since 1983 suggests that, with the government's support, riots are neither inevitable nor spontaneous eruptions of anger.[11]

executions, torture, and the destruction of homes, businesses, and villages.[12] The constant threat of violence ruptures the routines of everyday life; that which was commonsensical loses relevance when violence becomes an element of the everyday. Violence is not accepted as part of everyday life but rather produces an uncanny and unsettling dis-ease. As with the "psychological war" in El Salvador, an "unhinging" of social relations can occur in which a society is polarized between opposite extremes; a general atmosphere of tension and mistrust is the rule.[13]

Similarly, the civil violence that has racked Colombia for two decades has created a situation of fear, mistrust, apathy, and demoralization. Violence throughout the country most often takes the form of death squads, kidnappings, assassinations, and random killings; murder has consistently been the leading cause of death in the cities of Cali and Medellín. In one of the few studies of the mental health consequences of civil violence outside of Northern Ireland, León finds that, as a result of the sporadic, deadly violence in these cities, residents initially respond with shock and outrage followed by numbness and apathy.[14] Depression and collective demoralization are also common. This pattern of distress appears to be common to a variety of places in which continued military, civil, or drug-related violence upends civilian life without any prospects of lasting peace. The growing influence of several transnational drug markets in the Americas, Asia, and South Asia suggests that both organized and disorganized drug-related violence will have an increasingly important effect on human welfare throughout the world.

Violence and repression can lead to a profound rupture in the uses of language and cultural meanings that constitute the life of a person or people. Communities lose their grasp of the meanings, understandings, and moral sensibilities that would ordinarily define their lives. The ruptures of language and meaning often conform to the desires of the violent, for those in power want both to undermine the ability of civilians to act and to suppress the willingness of survivors or witnesses to speak out. At times, the rupture of sense and sensibility is of a forced, symbolic nature; Bourque and Warren note that journalists in Peru were killed and their bodies left without eyes or tongues.[15] Nordstrom writes of a similar "disembodiment" in Mozambique, where RENAMO, a South Africa–supported rebel group, terrorizes by maiming civilians, cutting off their sense organs (ears, noses, lips), and returning them to the community as a reminder of the powerlessness and senselessness that engulfs civilian life.[16]

The state production of fear in the Southern Cone and in El Salvador has led researchers to speak of "cultures of fear" or "frightened populations."[17] Struggling to survive in a culture of fear produces a unique structure of experience, for fear loses its protective function and becomes embedded in a person's or family's way of life. It is less a question of "post-traumatic stress disorder" than of continuous traumatic stress syndrome, which, as Straker notes, contributes to greater distress among children than do specific episodes of trauma.[18] Through their clinical work with survivors of state violence in Chile, Salimovich et al. have identified three core features of persistent fear among this population: there is a sense of personal weakness and vulnerability and a feeling of powerlessness; sensory perception remains in a permanent state of alert; and one's perception of reality becomes distorted with the impossibility of testing subjective experience against reality.[19] Fears of this intensity have physiological correlates. Martin-Baro cites a study conducted among 350 people of all ages living in a refugee camp in El Salvador; the researchers found that the presence of the army in the vicinity of the refuge was sufficient to cause 87% of those questioned to experience fear, 75% to feel an accelerated pulse rate, and 64% to be overcome by generalized bodily trembling.[20] Other common features of persistent fear in El Salvador include stomach disorders, diarrhea, headaches, bodily pains, weakness, and fatigue.

Detention, Torture, and Disappearances

Since *los desaparecidos*—people abducted by state regimes without legal propriety or formal public recognition—were first documented in Guatemala in the 1960s, there have been more than 30,000 cases of "disappearance" in South America alone. Other regions where disappearances have been known to occur frequently include the Philippines, Afghanistan, and many African countries.

The entire family suffers the consequences of the abduction. The normal psychological process of mourning is arrested (mourning is difficult without a corpse), and families can experience social anomie, disorganization, marginality, and encapsulation or isolation. The disappearance can produce contradictory sentiments, from a faint hope that the person abducted remains alive, to acknowledging the likelihood that he or she will die, to the fear that other members will be abducted as well. Families often experience a depression marked by confusion and a denial of mourning. Families are faced with continued uncertainty and lack of knowledge, but those who try to seek information about missing kin risk death or disappearance.[21]

Children appear to be particularly vulnerable to disappearances. Common symptoms observed among children of disappeared persons include withdrawal, depression, intense generalized fear, sleep disturbances, gastrointestinal and speech disorders, regression in behavior and school performance, and developmental, affective, and behavioral disorders, including loss of orientation and the evasion of reality. Allodi, writing about Latin America, notes that the severity of the symptoms varies according to the children's age, the duration of the trauma, the extent of social isolation, and the degree to which they find the explanation for the parents' absence convincing.[22]

Many of the disappeared are killed; others are detained and tortured along with other political prisoners. In detention, women, men, and children are subject to rape, interrogations, food and sensory deprivation, systematic humiliation, lack of medical care, mock executions, torture, solitary confinement, censorship, threats against self and family, and the forced use of tranquilizers and other psychotropic drugs. "My face was covered for several weeks," recalls a Chilean trade leader who was arrested two years after the military coup and accused of collaborating with the resistance movement. "They forced me to be naked, standing. I could not move, in silence. I thought I was alone in that room. I tried to move my legs and, at that moment, I was beaten repeatedly, and again there was the pain, my body started to feel overweight, to bother me. . . . I don't remember how long this lasted. Minutes? Hours? Days? I remember that they threatened to bring my wife and do the same to her. . . . It seemed I saw her in my confusion. . . . It was impossible to maintain coherence, to distinguish between reality and hallucinations."[23] Often the intent of jailers is not simply to detain or to extract information but to achieve the psychological destruction of prisoners and their families. Consequently, jailers inflict a range of punishments, harassments, and physical and psychological hardships in a systematic attempt at "personal dismantling," to use the words of a released political prisoner in Uruguay.[24]

The limited reports on the experiences of political prisoners in Latin America, South Africa, and the Philippines (limited because jailers often deny access and because many prisoners do not survive) suggest that prisoners are at high risk for psychiatric illness.[25] Studies of former detainees in South Africa, for instance, report that detainees typically experience problems related to stress, anxiety, depression, cognitive functioning, suicidal preoccupations, and psychosomatic problems.[26] Life after detention is often marked by social difficulties, depression, and sleeping difficulties with concomitant exhaustion.[27] Many of the difficulties relate to the distressful process of trying to return to daily life.

Torture, which currently occurs in over a third of the world's nations, is one of the most pernicious forms of abuse during detention. Although the methods vary— the infliction of pain by, say, beatings or electric shocks; sensory deprivation; solitary confinement; sexual harassment and rape; deprivation of food, water, or sleep; forced standing; submersion in water; false accusations; mock executions; threats to friends and family members; the forced witnessing of violence and mutilation to others—there is usually no clear division between physical and psychological methods of torture. The blurring of methods relates, at least in part, to the specific purpose of torture, which often centers on the creation of fear in family members and the destruction of the basic humanity of the individual.

Essential to the act of torture is that the interrogator controls everything, even life itself. A person's lack of control over basic bodily functions, the trauma of being detained indefinitely, and the constant violence to body and mind typically devastate his or her health. In their work with torture survivors in Denmark, Vesti et al. have found that the infliction of pain and distress on political prisoners commonly causes them to go through predictable stages of psychological dysfunction: prisoners become exhausted, confused, and disoriented; hallucinations, depersonalization, and derealization follow; torturers feed misinformation and undermine ideals, belief systems, and self-identities.[28] As a result of torture, prisoners commonly experience anxiety, depression, guilt, shame, humiliation, a loss of self-esteem, distrust, and dissociation. The body loses its ability to function properly and a person loses his or her identity as a human being. Although the physical symptoms of torture tend to lessen over time, psychological, behavioral, and social problems often persist for years. Torture survivors tend to suffer more severe psychological symptoms than do other victims of repression who have not experienced torture. The most commonly reported symptoms include sleep disturbances and nightmares, anxiety, impaired concentration and memory, depression, numbness, feelings of general fatigue or lethargy, generalized fear, social withdrawal, and sexual dysfunction.

The fact that a vast range of methods of torture have so similar an effect has led researchers to discuss the possibility of a basic torture syndrome. To date, however, a clear etiology that convincingly accounts for a single syndrome has yet to emerge. In general, it appears that the pain, trauma, and humiliation suffered contribute to a nonspecific final common pathway of anxiety, fear, guilt, withdrawal, bodily distress, and psychological dysfunction. For women in particular, rape and sexual abuse suffered during detention often affect their sexual and emotional well-being for years after the abuse. The sexual trauma is often compounded by sentiments of humiliation, shame, and guilt, especially in societies where women cannot talk about their experiences for fear of being stigmatized by the community.

The long-term health status of torture survivors, as with other victims of violence, must be understood within the larger social context in which they come to live. Safety in a different place or country, the specific measures of personal support to survivors, and the availability of community and mental health resources can help to lessen anxiety and distress. Allodi and Rojas found that the spirit of commitment to an ideology or integration into a political program were significant factors in the outcome and coping of Latin American torture survivors residing in Canada.[29] At the same time, many refugees from torture face considerable difficulties when resettling in a new society.

Often an entire family suffers directly or indirectly from the torture of family members. Family members can suffer indirectly from the persecution of parents, children, or siblings, feeling fear, anxiety, uncertainty, and grief.[30] They can also be affected by the direct consequences of torture. For instance, the Comité de Defensa de los Derechos del Pueblo, a multiprofessional health team in Santiago de Chile, found that torture survivors often experienced difficulties in communicating with, and relating to, other family members.[31] Families often had difficulties reflecting collectively on the experience of torture and often encountered profound changes in family roles. At times, family members are divided by different political interests; children may become soldiers or may decide not to side with a parent's political affiliation. These conflicts can effect a prolonged disturbance in the welfare of a family or community.

The Mental Health of Children

Acuna reports that the children of survivors of detention in the Philippines display a number of psychological symptoms irrespective of whether they were born during or after the parent's imprisonment and torture.[32] A series of studies of Chilean children whose parents were tortured have come to similar conclusions.[33]

Children with adequate support systems in the family and community are not likely to exhibit serious clinical disturbance beyond short-term acute reactions to particular stress events. But, as Dawes sums up the findings of several studies, "in the absence of support, without some form of ideological belief structure and in the face of severe overwhelming stress such as torture, repeated harassment or witnessing the death or brutal treatment of those close to them, clinical disturbance may result."[34] The need for familial support leads Kanji to stress the importance of keeping children in places like Mozambique in communities rather than in orphanages or resettlement camps.[35]

Clinical disturbances among children have been a constant threat in places of chronic violence like Guatemala, El Salvador, Cambodia, Mozambique, Eritrea, and South Africa. The dominant emotion reported by Guatemalan Mayan children living in resettlement camps in Mexico and Guatemala is *miedo*, or "fear."[36] Many of the Khmer children who lived in refugee camps along the Thai-Cambodian border suffered from emotional distress, nightmares, and fear; the trauma resulted not simply from the war in Cambodia, but from lack of food, water, and shelter, and from shellings near or in the camp itself. The wars in Mozambique, Zimbabwe, and Eritrea have led to the orphaning or dislocation of thousands of children who have been witness to the bloody conflicts. In Mozambique, children who are now in orphanages and foster families appear withdrawn, apathetic, regressed, and fearful. For children and youths suffering in the wake of violence, we need to better determine the duration of the distress, its concomitant features, and ways to alleviate it. We also need to study resilience and repair.

Violence Begets Violence

Violence begets violence. The "boy soldiers" of Mozambique who return to civilian life are likely to be aggressive, aloof, agitated, and restless.[37] Martin-Baro finds that the low-intensity conflict in El Salvador tends to "criminalize children's minds" through the creation of aberrant and destructive moralities.[38] Jenkins reports that many women flee El Salvador to escape domestic violence as well as state violence, although it remains unclear whether the latter violence has increased the frequency and severity of the former (see Box 5.2).[39] Rebels who apparently kill less for political motives than for the sake of destruction continue to terrorize the countrysides of Sierra Leone and Mozambique; the propensity for violence among rebels, the inability of civilians to prevent it, and the disintegration of everyday sensibilities has led to a general state of demoralization.[40]

One of the most significant concerns about the youth of South Africa is the emergence of acts of violence and criminal activity not directly related to political

Box 5.2 Women and Violence in El Salvador

Although violence and civil warfare have been common in El Salvador throughout this century, the period 1979–1992 represents the most intensive sustained conflict to plague the country. Since 1979, a wave of warfare and terror devastated the population by death and emigration. Of a population estimated at 5.2 million in 1979, some 75,000 persons were killed, several thousands more were "disappeared," 500,000 were displaced within its borders, and a million more have fled north to other countries.

Women suffer from the violence in several ways. Emigrants now living in a metropolitan area of New England say they fled from the violence for three main reasons: to escape from economic conditions, to escape from domestic violence, and to escape from *la situación*, as the violence is locally known. Women regularly encountered brutal evidence of the war: mutilated bodies lying on the roadside or on the doorstep to their homes, family and friends who had disappeared, and the terror of military troops marching through their towns shooting at random and arresting others who would be incarcerated. "In my country I had *un susto* [a fright] when a man was dying," says a 36-year-old married woman. "Already the man couldn't speak [but] he made signs to me with his eyes. It was during the daytime, and I was going to get some chickens for a baptism. He could barely move his eyes. He had been shot in the forehead. It was the time of the fair in November. When I came back he was already dead. I returned home with a fever, and it wasn't something I had ever experienced. Since it was carnival time, strangers came. They kill strangers. They saw *him* throwing away some papers. Yes, I have seen various dead bodies. Since then, I became sick from *nervios*. *Nervios*, upon seeing the dead bodies."

Nervios, or "nerves," is the chief complaint of Salvadoran refugee women who attend a mental health clinic in New England. According to psychiatric criteria (DSM-III-R and the SADS), nearly all of these women had suffered one or more major depressive episodes within the past two years, and some have struggled with either chronic depression or dysthymia. The women voice a variety of themes of sadness and sorrow in relation to loss and bereavement, helplessness and hopelessness. The loss and mourning are often communicated through somatic means, as insomnia, lack of appetite, fatigue, or psychomotor agitation or retardation. Many of these women also report symptoms of post-traumatic stress disorder (PTSD), including recurrent nightmares of traumatic violence, a sudden feeling that the traumatic event is recurring, and irritability or outbursts of anger.

Many women who attend the clinic suffer from illnesses related to domestic violence and abuse. Some say they feared their husbands and fathers would kill them if they did not escape their regular physical, and often sexual, abuse. A 27-year-old married woman says she felt a "fright" when her husband was "drinking a lot, already before he would arrive home. Then I would feel my heart, pum-pum-pum. If you are fearful it can make you sick because it can cause you a *crisis de nervios*. I feel that my body isn't me. It can cause a person to go crazy. It makes me have stomach pain, shaking of my body, and it makes me cold."

"I was pregnant at that time, when my husband started drinking," says a 34-year-old married woman, mother of two. "He beat me. I was very fat [in a very advanced stage of pregnancy], and he mistreated me. But later, he regretted it because the baby was born unhealthy, with a problem of *nervios*. He mistreated me for no reason when he was drunk. . . . When the baby was born, he had like a yellow color in his skin, and the doctor told me it was necessary for my baby to remain in the hospital for some time because he was ill. But when my husband found out about the baby's illness he blamed me as well; so you know, I was guilty for everything . . . and then when my baby was born I started to have nightmares . . . my daughter was ten years old by then, she noticed all what was happening and she cried, she became sick from *nervios*, she became very ill. My daughter, sick with *nervios*, was screaming, throwing things around. . . . I couldn't say a word to him because he would beat me." This woman was ultimately compelled to flee El Salvador to escape her husband's violent abuse.

Although domestic violence preceded the recent civil warfare in El Salvador, a general culture of violence in the country has augmented it. Women often suffer and express the pains of domestic violence in the form of *nervios*, but it would be futile to care for these women within a purely medical model. The pains are not simply physiological ones; they are rooted in larger social problems. And a singular focus on psychological or physiological distress places the burden of responsibility on the women themselves. A more helpful way of thinking about violence lies in addressing the social forces that contribute to, and legitimate, such violence.[41]

action. In effect, a general culture of violence has emerged alongside the repressive violence of apartheid and the rebellions in the townships.[42] Violence—murder, rape, assaults—is now both a cultural and a statistical norm; in a twelve-month period, 83% of young respondents in the Alexandra township had either observed an assault or been assaulted themselves.[43] Many, but not all, of these youths are at risk for violent lives, physical wounds, disability owing to blighted education and work, and emotional distress. Many of these youths are best skilled in the arts of defiance and violence; these skills put them at a disadvantage in peacetime. The individual attributes of youths, and the nature of the households in which they live, contribute greatly to whether or not adolescents become embroiled in the violence and despair that surround them.[44] Ramphele finds, for instance, that intelligent and attractive adolescents are more successful in school and life than aggressive misfits.[45] In addition, youths who live in coherent and supportive households have a better chance of living a reasonably successful life (see Box 5.3).

Though relatively underreported, domestic and civil violence are two of the main features of collective violence. As Nordstrom notes for Mozambique and Sri Lanka, "Terrorized civilians thus may increasingly come to absorb and, more dangerously, accept fundamental knowledge constructs that are based on force."[47] Violence can thus become a dominant way of being in the world for children and adults alike. In Colombia, for instance, decades of guerrilla warfare, military repression, and organized crime have created "a general state of demoralization, both in the sense of a weakening of the morale and a corruption of the morals."[48] Acts of violence can work their way into the practices of everyday life; violence relates both to effective ways of acting in a community and to a reworking of the moral sensibilities that define those ways of acting.

Witnessing, Healing, and Rehabilitation

Despite the suffering experienced by the victims of repressive violence, a combination of social and political processes often contributes to the deligitimation of suf-

Box 5.3 Children and Violence in South Africa

Adolescents in New Crossroads, a residential township outside Cape Town, South Africa, have to negotiate the complexities of violence and human interaction with minimal resources. New Crossroads, a poor, conflict-ridden community built in 1982, is part of Cape Flats, where most of the black townships are located. In 1991, the total population of New Crossroads was 10,340. Thirty-two percent of the households were headed by women, and children under 16 made up 36% of the total population. The average monthly income was $190 U.S.

Violence is part of daily life in New Crossroads. Beating children at home is a routine disciplinary measure, and corporal punishment at school is frequent, random, and often severe. Much of the violence is played out in the streets. Although family discipline and street committees help to keep gang formation to a minimum, gangs continue to regroup, and economic disputes and political strife add to the specter of street violence.

Despite the violence, New Crossroads has maintained neighborhood cohesiveness through close relationships in extended families and ties between neighbors and street committees. The presence or absence of these kinds of supports can have a significant effect on the welfare and futures of local youths.

Mthetheleli, age 12, has known poverty and violence most of his life. He frequently goes all day without food. From infancy on, he has been severely beaten by his father and bears scars from some of those batterings. His mother rarely intervenes in disciplinary measures; sometimes she provokes the beatings, which pit father against son.

Both of Mthetheleli's parents work, bringing home a combined monthly income of $333 U.S. His home bears the stamp of poverty—cold, dirty, and rank. Mthetheleli and his cousin are responsible for basic household chores. Mthetheleli also looks after his younger sister and helps his uncle tend his nine goats. He rebels against these responsibilities, which further incurs his father's anger.

School provides little relief. A careless student, Mthetheleli is beaten by his teachers for not knowing his lessons, for disrupting the classroom, and for provoking fights with his peers. Discipline has had little effect on Mthetheleli except to make him increasingly aggressive and hostile.

Dumo, on the other hand, has managed to escape much of the day-to-day violence. He is part of a close-knit and supportive extended family of twelve. The household monthly income is $366 U.S. Dumo's uncle, the household head and sole wage earner, has assumed responsibility for Dumo. His mother left him with her brother because of the social pressure of not being married when she gave birth. A great-aunt also provides "parental" guidance.

Dumo's home is neat and orderly, despite its poverty. Although Dumo misses his mother, he feels accepted in his extended family and willingly helps out with household chores. Because he does well at school, he has been able to avoid beatings there. He also joined an after-school soccer club to keep off the streets. Most gang members, he says, are teenagers who have been expelled from school and have nothing to do. Dumo aspires to be a lawyer when he grows up so he can help poor people.

The differences in the lives of Mthetheleli and Dumo show that violence does not always beget violence. While a violent society can predispose children to violent behavior, personal attributes and supportive relations with adults (not just parents) can provide protection and reduce the risks of further violence. Several effective programs can also reduce those risks. Economic initiatives can alleviate families' dehumanizing poverty. Reform of the educational system with more qualified staff and more resources can lessen the culture of violence. Programs for uneducated young people can offer job training. And facilities for children from troubled homes can provide a supportive environment with responsive adults.[46]

---

fering. Martin-Baro observes that the "systematic screening of reality" produced by the Salvadoran state, including the creation of an "official story" that ignored crucial aspects of the violence, led civilians to question their understanding of the truth and their political allegiance.[49] A further delegitimation can occur in the systematic denial of asylum for political refugees[50] or the denial of specific harms. The political position of women in Uganda, for instance, caused their experiences of rape during the recent wars to be dismissed as unimportant. For the most part, rape and sexual abuse have globally been treated as an unremarkable aspect of war.

Reality is screened out by a pervasive denial on the part of a population that atrocities are being committed. Several writers have observed that, during the height of violence and disappearances in Argentina in 1976 and 1977, many Argentines refused to believe that hundreds of people were disappearing daily.[51] The relatives of the disappeared found themselves abandoned by friends and relatives afraid of being associated with them. In the face of continued reports, the widespread "percepticide" eventually gave way to rationalization as the main strategy for coping with the terror: a person disappeared only because she or he "must have been involved in something."[52] Terror creates a surreal environment of confusion, mistrust, and fearful silence. In such an environment, testimonies are often silenced, discredited, or ignored. The silence is compounded by two facts: some of those in contact with victims are compliant in the silence, and victims, once they reach a safe location, are often unable or unwilling to talk about traumatic experiences.

Although silence often lingers in the immediate wake of violence, and violence often takes the form of denial or forced silence, the healing process almost always involves talking about pain and suffering. In the years following the "dirty war" in Argentina, a "horror show" of testimonies, newspaper accounts, exhumed corpses, and confessions by torturers attested to the violence and disappearances of the preceding years. Through this vast "elaboration of terror," Argentineans were able to talk about what was formerly denied or ignored.[53] A similar turn to storytelling has given force to the testimonies of Holocaust survivors and victims of repression, with individuals and families stressing the need to let others know of the violence enacted upon them.

The same need apparently drives many therapies for victims of torture and political repression. Since the 1970s, treatment centers have been set up in several countries. Although the therapeutic philosophies of these centers produce a heterogeneous mix of techniques, from psychodynamic and cognitive approaches to the use of psychopharmacology, most therapies build on the notion that victims need to verbalize and gain insight into their experiences. Psychodynamic ideas undoubtedly influence this process, but it also appears to arise from the "joint discovery," on the part of therapists and clients, that the detailed recall and reporting of traumatic events under appropriate conditions can alleviate symptoms and facilitate social reintegration.[54] Cienfuegos and Monelli, for instance, ask their Chilean clients to record a "testimony" of their persecution that serves to elaborate and integrate traumatic experiences.[55] Mollica notes, in turn, that he and his colleagues help refugees from Indochina to develop and share a "trauma story" that works to "liberate the patient from the past."[56] Therapists working with victims of political repression in South and Central America pursue the detailed reporting of harm, with beneficial results.[57] Somnier and Genefke offer the most detailed explanation for their efficacy: through a detailed reconstruction of harmful experiences, victims are able to assign meaning to their persecution and understand that the harms inflicted on them were *intended* to destroy them psychologically.[58] They are then able to generalize their personal suffering and move beyond the role of victim.

There are several caveats to these talking cures. One is that there can be an undue emphasis on torture. As Willigen cautions, "Too great an attention to or emphasis on those with a history of torture may, by relegating other forms of organized violence and their psychological impact on the individual to a position of secondary importance, inadvertently result in the neglect of people who, though not tortured, are nevertheless highly traumatized."[59] The warning is particularly apt in the care of non-Western peoples, where a singular focus on torture and psychological functioning might be largely irrelevant. A Cambodian might understand that it is best not to talk about the sorrows of the past, whereas her American therapist might be directed to help her articulate traumatic events. Indeed, some evidence suggests that detailed inquiries can intensify symptoms.[60] This is particularly true for some refugees from Africa and Southeast Asia, who tend to experience trauma and recovery in ways distinct from the narrative frames of many Western societies, which are often linked to Judaic-Christian notions of catharsis, confession, reparation, and redemption. At times, however, the willingness or unwillingness of survivors to speak of traumas may relate less to cultural sensibilities than to their appraisal of the political risks involved: some cannot afford to speak out. In either event, several studies underscore the fact that social testimonies or "reparations" must be made before wounds begin to heal.[61] Others suggest that "healing" is an optimistic term, that what people learn to do is live with their unassimilable memories.

The sociopolitical nature of the wounds and memories creates a situation in which the personal testimonies of therapy relate directly to the legitimation of suffering. Therapy is, at least in this case, a political act integral to a social context. Indeed, some of the most promising of therapies for survivors of violence seize on this fact in developing programs that attend not simply to psychiatric symptoms but to social and moral harms. Lykes and her colleagues, for instance, have developed a mental health program in Guatemalan Mayan communities that attends, through creative workshops, to the silence and fear effected by the war: through the use of play, art, and drama, mental health workers are able to help children validate their experiences of terror and loss, and help the wider community to restructure social ties ruptured by war.[62] Beristain and Riera have developed similar community-level mental health programs in Latin America, as have Shaw and Harris in Mozambique.[63] With these programs, it becomes clear that therapy involves a social contract of testimony and witnessing.

Research into rehabilitation services generally concludes that people may recover from specific psychological and medical symptoms, but the repercussions of fear, terror, and torture often continue to haunt their lives. The damage is often persistently social: as with the survivors of the Cambodian genocide and the Chinese Cultural Revolution, families dissolve, cultural roots are lost, suicides and survivor guilt occur, and a readjustment into a normal way of life is an unrealistic goal. Children sometimes display a remarkable resilience, particularly when they are able to remain within a context of familial and social support. Children who are placed in orphanages (or turn to the streets) are at much greater risk for continued psychological distress.[64] The most helpful rehabilitation services are therefore those that help not simply to ameliorate psychiatric symptoms but to reintegrate members of a community (if one still exists) in a meaningful, durable, and politically valued way.

Interpersonal Violence

Although this chapter has focused on the forms and consequences of collective and political violence, interpersonal violence cannot be neglected. Violent deaths (from accidents, suicides, homicides, etc.) rank third among the major causes of death in most high-income countries and in some low-income countries with reliable data.[65]

In the region of the Americas, mortality from causes associated with violence is alarmingly high and clearly on the increase. In Mexico, for example, violent acts accounted for 5% of total deaths in 1982, and for 8% of the total years of potential life lost. In El Salvador, violent deaths accounted for 9% of total deaths in 1984, and for 21% of the total years of potential life lost. In Colombia, the rate of homicide increased by 50% between 1972 and 1982 and tripled between 1983 and 1992. In 1990, homicide was the leading cause of death in Colombia among those under 20 years of age.[66]

In the United States, homicide is the twelfth-leading cause of death in the total population, accounting for 22,032 deaths in 1988.[67] Among both black males and black females aged 15 to 34, it is the leading cause of death. In young people, homicide accounts for more years of productive life lost than suicide for whites and blacks.

Given these alarming rates of mortality from violence, public health workers have begun to tackle the problem from a public health perspective, which contrasts with orientations within the judicial system. These health perspectives attempt to (1) reduce the risks for violence, and (2) create a social and cultural context that promotes nonviolence and other constructive behaviors.

A 1992 panel organized to develop guidelines for the prevention of violence in the United States concluded that "the strategies most likely to produce immediate reductions in mortality from violence are those related to reducing firearm violence."[68] Statistics underscore the importance of this conclusion. In 1986, firearms were used in 60% of all homicides and suicides in the United States.[69] Eighty-five percent of adolescent males in a representative state sample had immediate access to firearms; 49% of these teenage males indicated that they owned a gun.[70] Psychiatrist Felton Earls and his colleagues point out that one way to reduce violent assaults in the United States would be "the adoption of more stringent regulations on weapons availability, accompanied by a shift in societal values about the seriousness of firearm ownership and use, particularly among adolescents."[71] Other ways to reduce risk are to provide timely crisis intervention for families under stress and at risk for violence, and to improve the recognition, referral, and treatment of people at high risk for violence or violent injury, including battered spouses and victims of child abuse or neglect (see Chapter 8 for a discussion of domestic violence).[72]

As for confronting the broader social forces that contribute to violence, there are several possibilities in "health-promotion" programs. These include the development of prevention and intervention programs for communities with high rates of violent injury; educational interventions for children (including the promotion of nonviolent social skills and appropriate norms of nonviolent behavior); community-based programs to reduce the acceptability of violence and the promotion of nonviolent lifestyles; and media programs that foster nonviolent behavior. These efforts aim to reduce the high cultural tolerance for violence and promote healthier ways of dealing with conflicts.[73] Finally, since violent behavior is often linked to poverty, community deterioration, and the systematic withdrawal of services and resources, social and economic infrastructures need development.[74]

Research Needs

Studies of collective violence and its consequences must go beyond the analysis of specific psychiatric symptoms to account for a range of social and political forces. To date, most research in this field reflects Europeanist understandings of, and concerns for, the antipodal relationship between the state and the individual. There is a large body of literature on the mental health consequences of repressive regimes in Latin America and South Africa, wherein the state takes a devastating toll on the mental health of individuals. Interest in the well-being of individuals or families in the wake of repression, torture, detention, or disappearances has also dominated research agendas, but at a certain expense. We now know more about the effects of violence on individuals than on communities and societies, more about the psychiatric sequelae of violence than its behavioral and social aspects, and more about repressive regimes than situations of ethnic or civil violence.

The last point is particularly relevant in the 1990s, when many weak states are threatened with conflict and collapse. Although we can now clearly anticipate the mental health consequences of a repressive regime, we lack a conceptual framework to understand what happens to families and communities in a place like Somalia, Liberia, or Bosnia, where the state has ceased to exist and no single polity is running the country. In turn, there is remarkably little literature on the psychological and social aspects of civil violence despite prolonged situations of civil unrest in Colombia, Peru, and Sri Lanka. There is slightly more research on the social and cultural repercussions of ethnic violence, but much more needs to be known.

The focus on individual welfare, which is an understandable priority of psychiatrists and therapists, has led us to pay less attention to the societal aspects of violence. We have yet to adequately answer several important questions. What are the lingering effects of large-scale conflicts on the sensibilities, mores, and ways of life of a society or nation? What are the lasting behavioral consequences resulting from cultures of violence in places like Mozambique and South Africa? To what extent does domestic and street violence result from prolonged repression and conflict? What happens to the soldiers, the torturers, and the violent when they return to community life? What kinds of psychological and social difficulties do they encounter in civilian life? What happens to communities or societies after the fighting dies down? What happens when former enemies live next door to one another in places like Nicaragua, India, or Sri Lanka? What kinds of social memories or testaments get created in the wake of violence? In other words, what kinds of lives will the children of Cambodia, Guatemala, Mozambique, Somalia, and South Africa lead? The words of an 80-year-old Mozambican healer remind us of what is at stake. "This is not like being mad," he told Nordstrom of the refugee children for whom he cares. "That we can treat. No, this is from what they have seen—it is a social problem, a behavioral problem, not a mental problem. They beat each other, they are disrespectful, they tell harsh jokes and are delinquent. You can see it in their behavior toward each other: more violence, more harshness, less respect—more breaking down of tradition. There is no medicine for this."[75]

Future research must confront this problem. Many societies become demoralized when subjected to continued violence; is it possible for a people to remoralize? If so, how? How do people get on with their lives? How can the recovery process be best facilitated? How can we prevent the most damaging, long-term effects of violence from occurring? More also needs to be known about the social conditions that lead to cultures of violence if we are to try to prevent generations from living in societies where physical force takes precedence. To quote another Mozambican healer, "People have just seen too much war; too much violence—they have gotten the war in them. We treat this, we have to—if we don't take the war out of the people, it will just continue on and on, past RENAMO, past the end of the war, into the communities, into the families, to ruin us."[76] We must learn how to "take the violence out" of war survivors, as the people of Mozambique are trying to learn.

In sum, although a concern for trauma and psychiatric symptoms is important, mental health professionals, anthropologists, and others must be prepared to deal with the lingering social damage caused by forced exile, poverty, hunger, detention, lasting fear, and the ubiquitous presence of death, torture, and disappearances. Attempts at healing, insight, or reparation must be placed in the context of these misfortunes and the problems they occasion. We must also question what we mean by mental health, a concept typically defined in terms of normality. With fear, violence, and dislocation now the norm in places like El Salvador, notions of normality are thrown into question (see Box 6.2 in Chapter 6). What is a healthy way of acting in a refugee camp? To what extent do traditional notions of well-being apply in situations of extreme distress? Is mental health a realistic goal for communities devastated by violence?

Conclusions

- Wars, prolonged conflicts, ethnic strife, and state repression often lead to a flood of social, economic, and psychological problems that undermine well-being. Damage ranges from physical disabilities to psychological trauma to the breakdown of local ways of life. Current international services designed to attend to these problems are extremely helpful but inadequate. Similarly, health and mental health services in many poor countries are severely limited in terms of finances and potential manpower.

- Some of the most damaging aspects of violence relate to the aftermath of conflicts: the disruption of local economies, shortages of food and drinking water, separation from family members, and dislocation. To ameliorate these problems, trauma from violence can be better attended to by anticipating regional or intrastate conflicts, quickly aiding those who are victimized by the violence, and developing culturally sensitive treatment centers in refugee camps and other safe havens.

- Therapy for individuals is rarely available to many residents of poor countries, where most conflicts now take place. Community-oriented programs are therefore the most realistic options in many settings. They may also be the most effective. The benefits that community-oriented programs offer to torture survivors, the relative success of mental health programs for communities in Guatemala and Mozambique, and the positive effect of educational programs for black youths in South Africa attest to the importance of working at the community level.

- The ethos of fear and violence that persists in many communities suggests that therapeutic interventions must work at the cultural as well as the psychological level to reestablish a secure moral ground for everyday life. Indeed, an undue emphasis on individual trauma may lead to the neglect or delegitimation of social harms, from the demoralization of a society to the dislocation of entire communities.

- The traumas that threaten personal well-being put the ways of life of an entire culture at stake. Communities, like individuals, struggle in the wake of violence. The response often assumes a similar form: a community works to reestablish the language, meanings, and moral sensibilities so often undermined by violence. Although it is possible to facilitate this process, interventions must work in tandem with local values. For instance, some communities might be best served by programs that help to express in words traumatic events and the consequences of violence, whereas the cultivation of a new reality, rather than of former traumas, might be the best approach for others.

- When communities maintain a sense of coherence and durability in the wake of violence, the effects and consequences of violence are generally less severe. It is therefore extremely beneficial to help families, villages, and social networks to stay intact whenever possible. Programs need to be developed that help families to stay together when possible and enable parentless children to stay in communities rather than orphanages.

- Violence often begets violence. State repression and prolonged conflicts can effect an economy of morals in which the imposition of force is the most effective vehicle of power. Intensive research must take place to determine how to prevent generations from living in societies where physical force takes precedence. These strategies of prevention must then be effectively implemented.

- Interpersonal violence is a growing problem in many societies, particularly those of South and North America. The immediate risk of violence could be reduced if governments developed more stringent regulations on weapons and provided timely crisis intervention for families under stress and at risk for violence. The broader social context that contributes to violent behaviors can be changed by developing "health-promotion" programs that reduce the high cultural tolerance for violence and promote healthier ways of dealing with conflicts.

- Contrary to common perceptions, there is often planning and direction to ethnic riots and religious conflicts. While local politicians and leaders mobilize crowds, provide transportation, and supply arms, the police often contribute to the violence by making no effort to prevent it. Several steps can be taken to prevent such actions. The police should be multi-ethnic in composition and be required to take a strong public stand against violence; prior knowledge on the part of the public that the police will not tolerate rioting is a strong deterrent. The police should also try to anticipate conflicts and make their purposive presence felt in the streets. Finally, wherever there is evidence that the central government or local government agencies are implicated, those agencies should be held responsible for the violence.

- One of the most pernicious aspects of violence is the delegitimation of experience that sometimes occurs when survivors try to speak about what they have gone through. If the traumas of war for individuals, communities, and select groups (women, children, ethnic minorities) are to maintain legitimacy, they need to be kept to the fore of public consciousness. At the national and international level, researchers and politicians cannot remain silent.

6

Dislocation

In the camp I am not content. I have many worries. I can not clothe my family properly. I have no voice in the situation we are in. I feel deeply about my home. I want to advise the government and rebels simply to stop so that we can go home in peace. I won't go, though, until there is real peace . . . if someone tried to pressure us to go we just couldn't . . . we'd say "just shoot us here."[1]

The fear, uncertainty, and despair voiced by Mozambican refugees are increasingly common concerns among other peoples throughout the world. The various wars and conflicts in Asia, Africa, and South and Central America have forced millions from their homes. Economic problems in poor countries and regions have sparked a new wave of economic refugees. While some of these forced migrants live and work in rich, industrialized nations of Europe and North America, many more end up working within exploitative settings in slightly more prosperous regions elsewhere. The causes of dislocation, the nature of the journeys, and the conditions of life where a person or family resettles all pose dangers for personal and social well-being.

There are nearly 20 million "official" refugees in the world today—that is, people who have fled to another country to seek refuge from war or starvation (see Figure 6.1). Globally, the largest numbers of refugees are found within the continents of Asia and Africa. There are close to 7 million refugees in Asia (hosted predominantly in Pakistan and Iran) and close to 5 million in Africa (predominantly across Central and Eastern regions). Thus, while much has been written about refugees resettled into industrialized nations in the West, such refugees are atypical in global terms. Less than 17% of the world refugee population resides in the countries of Western Europe, the United States, Canada, and Australia. Another 70 million people around the world have left their native countries, primarily in search of work. Many are at risk for economic exploitation, poor living conditions, and prejudicial treatment.

There are at least another 20 million people who are displaced within their own countries. Since these dislocated peoples have not crossed the border of a nation-state, the United Nations plays no official role in formally recognizing or providing humanitarian care for them. Internal governments do play a role, however, which means that the fate and welfare of many dislocated families and communities are deeply tied to regional politics. Government policies, from environmental projects

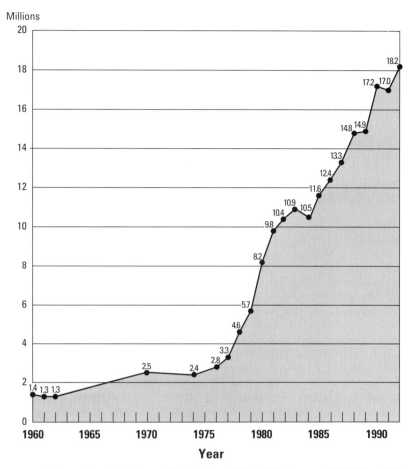

Figure 6.1 Number of Refugees Worldwide, 1960–1992 (*Source:* UNHCR, 1993)

to forced relocations, force many groups to leave their homes; quite often, these are aboriginal groups who receive little compensation in exchange for the dislocation and turmoil they must undergo (see Box 6.1).

Migration alone does not necessarily lead to poor mental health. Rather, a number of forces, from employment status to housing conditions to traumatic events before, during, or after dislocation, can lead to psychological distress.[3] The key factors that determine a migrant's well-being include: whether one adapts well to the changes brought on by migration, whether one is living in a safe and healthy environment, and whether one can live a productive, meaningful, and culturally integrated life (see Box 6.2). Two groups are therefore at great risk for distress: those who travel to live and work in another location only to end up living in isolated, exploitative conditions; and those who seek refuge from starvation, violence, and political turmoil.

Box 6.1 Displacement

Different kinds of environmental changes can drastically alter the lives of larger numbers of people who find themselves uprooted and displaced from their homes. Major hydroelectic-dam projects, for instance, with their new lakes and irrigation canals, along with involuntary resettlement schemes, continue to affect the lives of hundreds of thousands of people.

The Aswan High Dam project displaced 120,000 people in Egypt and the Sudan, Pakistan's Kalabagh project uprooted 124,000, and Brazil's Itaparica project forced 45,000 to leave their homes. The Three Gorges project in the People's Republic of China, with a proposed generating capacity of 13,000 megawatts, will make it the largest single hydroelectric project in the world. Other hydroelectric projects in China, such as the Danjiangkou and the Sanmenxia have displaced 10 million people since the 1950s. An additional one million will be relocated when the Three Gorges project is completed.

The common consequences of dislocation include impoverishment, malnutrition, increased morbidity, dependency, and the breakdown of community norms and mutual support systems. Dam and resettlement projects mean not only a loss of home and the identity that comes from a sense of place; they can obliterate generations of practical cultural knowledge and effort. To this is added insecurity, nutritional deficiencies, sanitation risks, poor water supply, insufficient or infertile land, alcohol abuse, increased risk of illness, and barriers to health services.

While guidelines on the health consequences of resettlement now exist, little is said about the mental health consequences of dislocation and resettlement. Governments frequently fail to consult with the peoples most affected by the construction and operation of such projects. The issue of compensation is often unfairly handled, if compensation is provided at all. If administered promptly and well, due "compensation" is not merely an unwelcome "cost" to the planners and a "payment" to the resettlers. Rather, it is an instrument of social justice that provides validation and healing for the displaced's sense of loss and ensures tangible support for resettlers' early efforts in their new setting. If delayed, withheld, inadequate, or poorly distributed, lack of compensation leaves painful memories, exacerbates loss and feelings of impotence, fuels distress and discontent, and can haunt a project with a rankling sense of grievance.

There has been little pre-health data collection and few long-term studies of health consequences of massive relocation projects. Most pre-project health surveys are limited in scope and insufficient in size. As a result, much about the full array of possible health and mental health consequences of resettlement are still unknown.

It is impossible to eliminate all the health consequences of massive relocation projects, but many can be alleviated by viewing health as an ongoing and integral priority in planning large-scale projects. In addition to due compensation and incorporating a health dimension into planning, other policies can lessen the impact of dislocation. For example, alternatives should be fully explored before a project is too far along in the planning to be stopped. Human rights and social justice issues, not just economic ones, should be taken into account. A full range of local opinions should be assembled to ensure full representation of all those affected. Baseline surveys and long-term health data collection are essential.

Resettlers should also be included in any benefits that result from the project. To protect against the worst ravages of dislocation in the future, current projects need to develop legal systems that guarantee and safeguard human rights, as well as sound economies and environmental policies that focus on environmental regeneration rather than degradation.[2]

Box 6.2 West African Women Migrants to France

Hawa, a Mali immigrant, has lived with her husband in France for sixteen years. She is unhappy with her marriage, and worries about it so much that she cannot sleep at night. Her husband beats her, goes out with other women, and accuses her of trying to prevent him from taking a second wife. Hawa explains that in Mali a family member would intervene, but in France no one will do so.

Between 1980 and 1992, the number of West African women immigrating to France has increased by roughly 80%. The relocation is not without its problems. As with Hawa, migration often removes opportunities for challenging the authority of husbands and fathers, which accentuates female subordination and powerlessness. And while West African women come to France with high hopes, expecting a better life than the one left behind, they also bring with them West African practices and beliefs, which often conflict with French cultural and structural systems. This can result in psychological distress.

In Africa, for instance, co-wives are accustomed to living in separate quarters. In France, they find that they must often share a single room or two. The crowded conditions and lack of privacy exacerbates preexisting rivalries, leading to jealousy, domestic violence, depression, and other kinds of distress. A Senegalese woman was hospitalized for anorexia nervosa. The disorder was eventually traced to extreme jealousy of her co-wife. She was cured (temporarily) when her husband rented separate apartments for herself and her co-wife. Unfortunately, most West African immigrants are unable to afford separate housing for each wife while in France, and the situation is not easily resolved.

For many West African women, the situation is made worse by their inability to read or write French. This makes them completely dependent on their husbands, who may ban them from leaving the home because of concerns about exposure to Western practices. Dependent and isolated, these women often suffer from depression.

Contradictions between French and West African ideas of parenting also contribute to the distress of immigrant women. For instance, corporal punishment is the standard and accepted practice of child discipline in most West African communities; in France it is tantamount to child abuse. An Ivorian woman had been living in Paris with her husband and two children. She was his second wife and he had two other children in Ivory Coast by the first wife. When they were teenagers, the stepchildren came to France to live with their father. They became involved in street hustling and petty thievery. After they stole leather jackets, the woman beat one of the sons in an attempt to discipline him, and he reported her to the police. As a result of the complaint, both her children and the stepchildren were taken away and put into juvenile residences. By French standards, she was abusing her children, though she felt she was being a good mother.

French and West African cultures also clash over female circumcision, a practice that is central to the social identity of women in many African societies. In France the practice is now a criminal offense: mothers who have their daughters circumcised, and those who perform the operation, have been charged and sentenced in highly publicized proceedings. This puts West African mothers and their female children in a bind: if they do not perform the procedure, they risk ostracism from West Africans; if they perform the procedure, the mother risks criminal proceedings and her children risk stigmatization by the French.

Several grass-roots organizations, catering to West African immigrants, address issues of multicultural identity and family conflicts. They are a source of support and provide an arena for discussion. In addition, they attempt to inform the public of the issues surrounding the cultural conflicts faced by West African women. The hope is that, in time, an increased understanding will allow for more effective solutions to the problems of dislocation.[4]

The Phases of Refugee Experience: Pre-Flight

The psychosocial consequences of displacement may be usefully considered with respect to distinct phases in the refugee experience (see Table 6–1). The *pre-flight period* refers to time leading up to the decision to seek refuge. The *period of flight* is the experience of migration from one place to another. The *reception phase* is that period (which may extend into years of residence in refugee camps or similar settings) that elapses before an individual returns to his or her home region, settles formally within a country of first asylum, or resettles in some third location. These options represent the final resettlement phase of the refugee experience.

Many refugees flee from the forms of violence noted in the previous chapter. The physical, psychological, social, and economic effects of violence spill over into the refugee experience. For instance, Cambodian refugees who lived in camps along the Thai border suffered from a variety of harms more than a decade after the collapse of the Khmer Rouge regime. One recent study notes that more than 80% of adults interviewed said they were in fair or poor health, felt depressed, and had a number of somatic complaints despite good access to medical services. Fifty-five percent had symptom scores that correlate with Western criteria for depression, and 15% for post-traumatic stress disorder.[5] The highest-reported symptom was a depressive state called *bebotchit*, "a deep sadness inside oneself."

While collective violence is one of the main causes of dislocation, it is by no means the only thing that refugees must worry about. Indeed, there is a tension that an overemphasis on discrete experiences of trauma can encourage an acutely individualized and decontextualized view of refugee experiences. For instance, in the period leading up to flight, many households suffer major hardships as the result of disruption of income-generating activity or a shortage of food. Such hardships may relate to the more frequently recognized factors of political persecution or armed conflict, but they can also serve in their own right as major stressors threatening well-being. Athey and Ahearn note the likelihood of cognitive and emotional impairment in refugee children as a result of economic deprivation, though the report they cite—of physical and mental delay in Korean children malnourished during the course of the war—is one of the few empirical studies pertinent to this concern.[6] A comprehensive study of a probability sample of Indochinese refugees in the United States that examined the relationship between present symptomology and reported motives for migration indicated escape from harsh living conditions (famine, poor economic conditions, inability to make a living, etc.) as a significant predictor of psychological distress.[7]

Social disruption, like economic hardship, also impacts pre-flight refugee mental health both directly (acting as a source of stress) and indirectly (reducing resources that may buffer the impact of stressful external events). Concern with the direct experience of persecution or violence can blind appreciation of the profound consequences that factors such as restricted mobility or school closure can have on community mental health. The psychological impact of such disruption of civil society has received little empirical attention in the refugee literature, despite clear evidence of the impact of natural disasters and social disruption on mental health. The fragmentation of families is the only factor to have been considered with any vigor in the context of refugees, and here primarily with respect to the direct impact

Table 6.1 The Health Dimensions of Dislocation

Phases of Dislocation	Precipitors of Distress	Health Consequences	Recommendations for Policy
Pre-flight	Environmental scarcities Environmental degradation Poor economic conditions Food shortages Famine, drought Inability to make a living Violence Political persecution Sexual assault Social upheaval Family loss	Hunger Malnutrition Trauma Physical disability Depression Anxiety Fear	Anticipate and prepare for refugee movements Advance political capital of marginal groups Create advocacy groups for potentially dislocated
Flight and Separation	Familial separation Separation from one's home society Violence Sexual assault Collapse of social supports	Grief Depression Fear Anxiety Trauma	Develop better assistance programs Provide international support for internal refugees Assure just compensation for forced relocation
Asylum	Threat of forced return to home Inhospitable living conditions Unemployment Food shortages Inadequate health services	Malnutrition Illness Learned helplessness Depression Despair	Improve camp conditions Provide gainful employment Provide adequate health and mental health services (including liaisons with traditional healers) Assure education of children and safety of women Foster greater participation in decision-making processes Help to establish asylum
Resettlement	Unemployment, underemployment Social isolation Acculturation problems Limited social ties Prejudice Language barriers Intergenerational conflicts Marginalization and minority status	Depression Anxiety Suicide Delinquency among adolescents Violence Familial, generational conflicts	Provide employment and housing options Maintain social and community ties Provide support programs and youth programs Create legal advocacy groups Provide community work interventions Develop mutual assistance programs Develop family reunification programs

of military conflict.[8] McCallin observed that 24% of a sample of 109 Mozambican refugee women had been separated from their children prior to their flight to Zambia.[9] Close to 50% of the Indochinese refugees sampled in 1991 by Rumbaut lost a family member in the immediate pre-flight period, with nearly 20% reporting imprisonment of a family member during the same period. This study found that family loss was a significant predictor of psychological distress in the resettlement environment.

Flight and Separation

Flight from one's homeland represents a major life event that, even if accomplished safely and swiftly, is likely to prompt major emotional and cognitive distress. Across samples of Cambodian refugees resettled within Australia and the United States, Eisenbruch found anger regarding separation from one's homeland to be one of the strongest and most widespread responses.[10] For those leaving family members behind in Cambodia, separation had a clearly tangible focus. Even those who did not experience family separation commonly reported a sense of "unfinished business" in Cambodia and a wish to return. The strength of such reactions to separation from one's home society leads Eisenbruch to propose recognition of the phenomenon of "cultural bereavement" as a discrete diagnostic condition of major prevalence and impact within refugee populations.[11]

The emotional burden of flight is frequently exacerbated by the experience of extreme danger. Women are particularly vulnerable to sexual abuse while traveling to a point of refuge. Political refugees can be understandably fearful or suspicious of anyone they encounter during their journey, including government officials.

Those refugees who arrive in another country are generally faced with some form of registration procedure. Establishment of official status as a "refugee" can be crucial with regard to receipt of food assistance and other support. The experience of new arrivals at reception centers can frequently be harrowing. Refugees may go through an extensive period when they justifiably fear being forced to return to their home to face war and/or persecution once again. Especially with large influxes of refugees, where treatment can be impersonal and threatening, refugees may quickly assume roles of dependency and helplessness. Refugees must also deal with the loss of status brought about by uprooting, unemployment, and dependency.

A significant portion of the world's refugees do not reside in camps on arrival in the country of first asylum. Throughout Africa, large numbers of refugees have settled among local populations. This pattern seems especially prevalent where there are close kinship ties between the refugee group and the local population. There appears to be significant advantages to self-settlement, despite the fact that such refugees will generally receive less (or nothing) in the way of assistance from governmental and nongovernmental agencies and may, in some contexts, appropriately fear action by the authorities with regard to their informal status. Compensations include greater opportunity for income-generation, increased socialization, and a greater sense of belonging and independence.

For most refugees, however, camp life represents an extended and difficult period of waiting in harsh, inhospitable environments. A study by Beiser and his colleagues partially isolated the impact of camp experiences by comparison across three settings that varied in the harshness of their regime.[12] Stressful camp conditions led to an increase in depressive symptoms, though the effect was transient: differences between those interned in the harsh and less harsh camps decreased on subsequent resettlement in Canada. A WHO mission to camps on the Thai-Cambodian border linked observed increases in attempted suicide, domestic violence, apathy, hopelessness, and depression to camp conditions; the refugees living in the camps still had to contend with limited resources, military assaults, and shelling attacks.[13] A number of writers have noted how conditions within camps approximate the form of "total institution" identified by Goffman as encouraging authoritarianism in those with power and dependence in those without it.[14] To the extent that camps facilitate an attitude of learned helplessness among refugees, they may also significantly increase the likelihood of depression. As Jareg notes in general, "One becomes aware of the ongoing psychological catastrophe: almost everybody is silent, even children. . . . People's faces wear a dazed, distant or constantly distressed look. People sit motionless, staring ahead, or with their faces covered, as if trying to hide within themselves. Children sit as close up to their mother or father as possible, they do not play. They do not smile or giggle shyly, but look at you with large, serious, anxious eyes."[15]

Resettlement

Resettlement in North America, Europe, and Australia involves fewer than 20% of the world's refugees. Yet given the political and social agendas of industrialized nations receiving refugees, this group has received considerably greater attention than the majority resettling in other parts of the world. Refugees who do resettle in North America, Europe, or Australia frequently confront greater problems than those who remain within their native region. Most often, these problems have to do with cultural differences, acculturation, and social ties. In general, refugees stand a better chance of being psychologically healthy if they maintain strong social and community ties and a sense of cultural identity.

Differential rates and strategies of acculturation within families clearly create major stresses. Children typically acculturate faster than adults as a result of school socialization. Women and the elderly, who have a greater chance of being isolated at home, may commonly adjust behavior and expectations far more slowly, if at all. Intergenerational conflict is, as a consequence, generally a phenomenon that is likely to *increase* rather than *decrease* over time from resettlement. Acute difficulties may arise after many years in the new setting, long after specific sponsorship supports have been withdrawn. Crises can occur precipitously and outside the expectation of the host community, as in the case of a Hmong father who hanged himself when his son bought a car without first seeking his father's permission.[17] Role reversals within families, such as children assuming adult roles as a consequence of their relative facility with language and procedure within the host culture, can produce powerfully destructive dynamics within families. Schools, which are a

---

Box 6.3 Mental Health among Displaced Khmer
on the Thai-Cambodian Border

How do we talk about mental health when the conditions necessary for emotional and psychological equilibrium are lacking for an entire population?

The question is especially salient for displaced Cambodians who lived on the Thai border in the 1980s and early 1990s. Not only had these refugees endured the traumas and deprivations of the Khmer Rouge from 1975 to 1979; they subsequently found themselves in a situation of physical danger, political and social instability, and uncertainty when they fled their own country for what seemed like greater safety at the Thai-Cambodian border. Together with their displacement to camps in Thailand itself, these factors combined to create a "normal" situation of ongoing insecurity and intermittent terror.

While the border camps provided displaced Khmer with some protection from an ongoing guerrilla war, they constituted an anomalous political and social space in which the prevailing mood was one of anxiety, frustration, and deep collective mistrust. Unlike official UNHCR refugee camps, in which the populations are maintained under the protection and control of the United Nations, these camps were made up of civilian Khmer associated with a coalition of Cambodian resistance factions involved in a guerrilla war with the Phnom Penh government. The Thai government had agreed to give these Khmer temporary sanctuary when they were forced across the border by heavy fighting in 1985, but refused to recognize them as official refugees under the United Nations refugee conventions or to provide them with material support. A special agency of the United Nations unaffiliated with the UNHCR provided this support until a solution to the conflict was reached that would allow the displaced Khmer to return to Cambodia.

Until a peace agreement was concluded in Cambodia in 1992, the camp populations remained under the political control of the leaders of the Khmer resistance, who continued to pursue their military objectives from other locations along the border. The civilian camps thus constituted important bases of "popular support" for the resistance leaders, which the camp populations had little choice but to provide. Even in the most "democratic" of the camps, authority was ultimately maintained through force or the fear of it, promoting an ethos of violence and coercion.

Families had been divided in the years under Pol Pot and in the flight to the border. Social support was patched together in the border camps with what was available to these de facto refugees: surviving relatives, former neighbors from the same village, strangers met along the road. But family ties and the longstanding patron-client relationships of an earlier era had been badly damaged in the years since 1975, and it was difficult to rebuild reliable structures of social support in the chaotic conditions of the border. Secrecy, mistrust, and false information were the strategies of survivors, and these strategies continued to be employed in the camps, where people were typically thrown together with strangers about whom they had no reliable information. Needs were great and resources were extremely limited. People had little choice but to narrow their circle of concern to the few people with whom they had the most reliable and enduring relationships.

With little to support traditional forms of reciprocity and respect and so much to encourage looking out for one's own interests, even the best efforts to maintain "proper" social relationships often fell by the wayside on the border. Living in crowded residential sections, on food rations designed for emergency use rather than long-term subsistence, with chronic fuel and water shortages which made proper sanitation a virtual impossibility, tensions ran high and small irritations often exploded into violent conflicts. It was not uncommon to hear that a neighborhood argument had ended with a grenade being thrown from one house to another.

In Site II, the largest of the six border camps (which housed as many as 195,000 people in less than seven square kilometers), there was a Khmer-run program called the Khmer Peoples' Depression Relief Center (KPDR) that provided assistance to many people who had broken down under the pressure of life in the camp. While serious cases of psychosis were referred elsewhere, the KPDR treated many suicide victims, people suffering from acute or chronic depression, and people who required protection from abusive family situations.

The center provided counseling, herbal treatments, massage, and hospice care. Since their patients' crises were usually precipitated by an especially difficult life situation, treatment almost always involved an attempt to improve the circumstances in which a patient was living as well. But these circumstances were often intrinsic to camp life and were frequently complicated by long histories of trauma.

For instance, a 14-year-old girl tried to hang herself after receiving a public beating from her mother for ignoring a curfew and walking outside alone after eight at night. The mother was very angry: walking alone at night had serious consequences in the camp of which the girl was apparently unaware when she disobeyed her mother. "Here in the camp we have to be careful," said the head of the KPDR, to which the girl was referred after the suicide attempt. "We should not walk outside after eight, particularly not alone, and particularly not if we are female. Only soldiers walk around at night, and prostitutes. Whether or not anything happens to you, people will assume things about you.

"We talked to her," the director said of the girl, "and explained why she could not go out at night. We explained to her mother that she had not been deliberately bad and should not be beaten. But in Site II mothers are afraid for their daughters. It has always been important for a young women to have a good reputation if she wants to find a good husband. But in Site II it is much harder to maintain the *impression* of a good reputation, because there are so many dangerous situations that we cannot avoid. In Cambodia, no man would think of accosting a woman; he would be afraid of the consequences. Here, there might not be any consequences at all."

Small, concrete changes could be made to improve individual situations, and that was what the KPDR focused on in addition to providing restorative care. Under the existing camp arrangements, however, there was no way to ameliorate the underlying conditions of insecurity and fear that exacerbated the distress of this already traumatized population. Although there were compelling reasons for setting up the camps in the first place, long-term displacement to such an insecure environment ultimately exacerbated the emotional and psychological difficulties of the Khmer survivors of the Pol Pot regime.[16]

major agent of socialization of refugee youth into the mores of a host society, play a pivotal role in monitoring potential conflicts within families as a result of such acculturation.

Difficulties in gaining appropriate employment can provide an additional long-term stressor. Without employment, financial and personal pressures can be considerable. Those successful in gaining employment will typically experience substantial downward mobility, with consequential threats to self-esteem as well as standard of living.

Social Supports

While refugees are clearly at risk of psychological distress, a range of personal and social factors modulate such risks. Freud and Burlingham found that children exposed to the bombing of London generally remained well-adjusted if they stayed in the care of their mother (or a familiar substitute).[18] This emphasizes the value of maintaining daily routines in establishing resilience. The increased potential for the positive modeling of coping behavior within intact families may also be a crucial factor. Ressler and his colleagues summarize a number of studies regarding war-affected children and draw the firm conclusion that organized evacuation programs, which intentionally separate children from their families to protect them from potential psychological or physical harm, are mistakes.[19] The benefits of an integrated family as a "buffer" to stress do not only apply to children. McCallin and Fozzard found those Mozambican refugee women living with their extended family to demonstrate significantly better psychological adjustment than others.[20]

Social linkages outside the family also tend to ameliorate the effects of psychological stressors. Shisana and Celentano found social support functioned as a protective factor in mitigating the impact of stress on depression among Namibian refugees.[21] McCallin and Fozzard reported factors such as having friends live nearby and seeing family members as a source of support as predictive of better psychological adjustment among Mozambican refugees.[22] McSpadden found the psychological well-being of Eritrean refugees resettling in the United States to be significantly better among volunteer-assisted refugees than among refugees resettled through formal governmental agencies; he attributed much of this difference to the broader social networks commonly established with the former strategy.[23] Overall, it makes some sense to propose that social support, by enhancing a sense of identity and belongingness, protects against the stresses of sociocultural adjustment rather more potently than against the effects of trauma and deprivation.[24]

The common proposal that religious affiliation can serve as a protective factor with regard to experienced stressors has won some empirical support.[25] While such affiliation may be seen to represent another source of social support, its primary effect may rather be concerned with the provision of a form of ideology with respect to which psychological coping mechanisms may be structured. Based on anthropological study with refugees on the Thai-Kampuchean border, Reynell notes that people who are confident in Prince Sihanouk and the resistance movement appear to be more healthy than those who are not.[26] Regarding her work in the Occupied Territories in Palestine, Punamaki noted evidence that "psychological processes of healing . . . drew strength from political and ideological commitment."[27] Cambodian youths resettled within the United States and Australia reported traditional religious beliefs and ritual as powerful resources in combating painful memories of the past.[28] Kanaaneh and Netland found symptoms of anxiety and withdrawal to correlate negatively with the degree to which individuals expressed nationalistic identity.[29]

Behavioral Health

Refugee populations may be particularly vulnerable to behavioral health problems such as alcoholism, drug abuse, and delinquency. Within camp settings, adult males tend to view alcohol or drugs as a temporary means of escape from personal anguish, uncertainty, and boredom. The loss of a productive role, typically enforced upon men within refugee camp settings, can create both incentive and opportunity for such activities. Reynell also noted high levels of alcohol consumption among Cambodian women whose husbands had taken mistresses within the camp, making them vulnerable to both extreme poverty and social humiliation.[30]

Within resettlement environments, evidence is increasingly emerging of the risk of male adolescent refugees' engagement in antisocial behavior and substance abuse. Kinzie and Sack, for example, observe a growing trend in their work with Cambodian refugees in Oregon of teenage refugees—resettled in the United States for some considerable time—developing such behavior.[31] They note that such individuals typically experienced considerable disruption in early attachment relationships with caregivers during the Pol Pot era. Despite subsequent stability following resettlement in the United States, lack of security and adaptive restraint at such a crucial period is thought to have predisposed these individuals toward antisocial behavior. Westermeyer notes the difficulties that teenage refugees may more generally have in identifying appropriate role models for culturally appropriate prosocial behavior.[32] Those resettled in isolation from ethnically similar peers, and those resettled in areas with high rates of delinquency, will face major, if distinct, challenges in identifying patterns of behavior acceptable to both families and the broader society.

To the extent that drug use is a common feature of youth behavior within a particular society, substance abuse by teenage refugees can be a common component of the process of acculturation. Westermeyer suggests, however, that substance abuse among refugees resettling in the United States is at a level that indicates specific adjustment difficulties for this group. Youths may be particularly vulnerable to substance dependence and a career in dealing drugs if their social role in the culture of resettlement is narrowly proscribed by social isolation, poor academic attainment, and/or unemployment. Such social determination of substance abuse is supported by research that indicates that the prevalence of such behavior among recently resettled refugees is generally low.[33]

While alcoholism and drug abuse is a concern among refugee youth, clinical impression, if not hard data, suggests that it may also be a major issue among the adult refuge population in resettlement countries. Westermeyer proposes that growth in alcoholism and opium addiction among Southeast Asian refugees in the United States has been a major contributory factor in the upturn in child abuse and neglect within refugee communities.[34]

Treatment

Psychiatric services generally distinguish between prevention and treatment with regard to whether clients are considered at risk for, or are actually suffering from, a specified disorder. Within the field of refugee mental health, such clear distinctions will frequently be problematic. With fieldwork programs targeted at specific groups, such as war-traumatized refugee children, the aims and scope of provision typically span both preventive and therapeutic action.

While individual therapy is not a viable treatment option for the vast majority of the world's refugees, therapeutic approaches used with individuals resettling in Europe and North America can nonetheless highlight processes of healing that may be capitalized upon in more socially oriented assistance. There is little clear consensus regarding the efficacy of particular treatment strategies, however. For example, the appropriateness of the ventilation of emotions and thoughts regarding experienced trauma—a keystone of established therapeutic approaches to traumatization—has been called into question in work with refugees.[35] Such a strategy may clash with individuals' cultural beliefs and practices (Mozambican refugees commonly describe *forgetting* as their normative means of coping with past difficulties). Further, there is evidence that, following severe experiences, such discussion of the past may intensify rather than reduce existing symptoms.[36] Punamaki reports a Palestinian mother as saying, "If I would sit down and start to think of my feelings, I could break down. . . . You, the Europeans can enjoy the luxury of analyzing your feelings. We simply have to endure."[37] Others may find it politically unwise to speak openly of their troubles.

Yet working through the experience of trauma remains a key component of the psychodynamic therapy for victims of torture commended by Bustos.[38] Silove advises that the key therapeutic task is to "help the patient compartmentalize and examine in tolerable doses elements of the trauma experience," hinting at a means of facilitating a degree of ventilation without overwhelming the person.[39] This clearly demands considerable clinical sensitivity. Facilitating self-understanding of this nature is not only a goal of more psychodynamic therapies. Behavioral treatments of trauma frequently involve a controlled exposure to recollections of traumatic events, and cognitive therapies facilitate integrative understandings of one's life situation.[40]

While all refugees are at clear risk of mental ill-health, three groups have consistently been identified as being particularly vulnerable: women, children, and the elderly. The special needs of refugee women are generally related to their lack of power in relations with men; women are at greater risk of experiencing certain forms of violence such as rape, have poorer access to assistance resources in camp and related settings, and are more likely to remain dependent and isolated following resettlement. The special needs of refugee children are principally related to stressors impacting at a foundational stage in individuals' development, and so threatening long-term psychological adaptation. Unaccompanied children—orphaned or otherwise separated from family during flight—are a particularly vulnerable group, for whom fostering and family-reunification programs can play a key protective role.

The needs of elderly refugees have been considered with considerably less vigor. The elderly may be left behind by the mass migration, are more easily separated from more mobile family members, often end up in inadequate housing, and tend to receive less food and provisions in refugee camps.[41] Godfrey and Kalache found that older adults displaced by the Sudanese war were threatened by loss of social status, physical disability, and diminished capacity for productive activity.[42] For refugees in general, age has been identified as a risk factor for psychological difficulties, especially depression. The loss of a productive role is important, as is the increased tensions that may develop within families over time as a result of differential rates of acculturation.

Community Approaches

While specific refugee groups have particular needs, the development of specific programs targeted at each group may often be less effective as a strategy than a broader community-focused approach that aims to facilitate mechanisms of social support and community integration. Community work interventions have been implemented most commonly with refugee groups resettled within Western Europe and North America and have also increasingly been adopted by programs in countries of first asylum. They typically involve a blend of preventative and curative actions, commonly featuring three major elements: (i) facilitation of group contact, discussion, and the sharing of experiences, (ii) practical assistance for refugees in such areas as child care and income-generation, and (iii) provision of more intensive, individual assistance (usually by referral) for those in need. Group discussion can help in the development of a shared account of the refugee experience, though extensive personal revelation may be acutely threatening for refugees whose culture does not encourage speaking openly about personal problems and feelings. Even when open sharing of experience is not a major feature, groups are likely to bring benefits at the level of increased socialization and provision of a supportive environment.

Refugee mental health workers, acknowledging the cultural salience of traditional healing practices, are now frequently encouraged to collaborate with the work of traditional healers. While cultural sensitivity is to be applauded, reconciliation of biomedical and "traditional" approaches to health is not without conceptual difficulty. It is frequently managed by a symbolic "reading" of traditional practices (noting their social function within traditional societies), while retaining a very decontextualized view of biomedicine (its social function within Western society unacknowledged). Given the potential resource of traditional medicine as a means of fostering refugees' psychosocial adjustment, it is important to establish a more conceptually coherent framework for collaboration with traditional healers.

Drug treatments for mental ill-health in refugees have received little attention in the literature, although some clinicians have supported their utility within broader psychosocial interventions. A recent manual on refugee mental health, produced jointly by the World Health Organization and the United Nations High Commissioner on Refugees, also recognizes the value of medication in specified circumstances.[43]

Internal Refugees

To date, much more thought has been devoted to the care and welfare of official refugees than to the millions of internal refugees throughout the world. Research agendas have followed political agendas in focusing on international rather than national concerns. Yet these people, who receive little or no support from the United Nations, face, at times, more deleterious conditions than refugees who leave their countries to seek asylum in another. Quite often, the risks to well-being relate to political factors. Governmental policies, from relocation projects to reorganizations of the environment (as with the construction of large-scale dams), may uproot entire communities and nations from their homes. The peoples uprooted typically possess little power or authority in regional or national governments, have little say in the decisions that force them to abandon their homes, and are at risk for receiving inadequate compensation for the hardships that result from dislocation. Quite often, they receive no legal support or health care.

Work must be done on both the research and policy aspects of this problem. The world scientific community needs to know more about the health consequences of forced relocation, the potential ameliorating factors in dislocation, and the social and political forces that lead to dislocation. In turn, national governments and international agencies must develop less ad hoc policies toward peoples who are dislocated. At a minimum, these policies must guarantee just compensation, provide adequate health services during and after the relocation efforts, and safeguard, in specific legal terms, the human rights of dislocated peoples. In effect, these policies must enable peoples threatened with dislocation to have a legitimate role in the decision-making process.

Research Needs

While recent years have clearly seen a burgeoning of literature on refugee mental health, the conceptual analysis of mental health issues presently afforded by this literature generally remains fundamental and generalized in nature. Research has established a number of factors that may either predict psychological-adjustment difficulties or serve to ameliorate such difficulties, but the complex manner in which such influences may interact is poorly understood. To facilitate such understandings, more-empirical research is needed. Toward that end, Jablensky and his colleagues propose a "tentative research agenda" on refugee health issues of relevance to policy studies, methodological issues, and ethical issues in refugee care and provision.[44]

While the relevance of pre-flight experiences to subsequent mental health status is widely acknowledged, study of this phase in refugee experience has been severely limited. While there clearly are major practical constraints on such work taking place within the country of origin of major refugee population movements, recent studies within Mozambique that document the social and political factors determining refugee behavior during the course of the civil war show the potential explanatory power of such fieldwork.[45] Retrospective analysis of pre-flight experience is less powerful but may still provide valuable insights. The studies of Rum-

---

Box 6.4 Migrant Workers and Health Care

"One time I was working very hard," a farm laborer told anthropologist Leo Chavez. "We had to lift some heavy equipment and I was trying to please my patrón [boss]. I pulled so hard I hurt my back. For two days, I could barely move. Then my patrón took me in his truck, and I thought he was taking me to a doctor. But imagine my surprise when we arrived at the border and he told me to get out and go back to Mexico or he'd call the Border Patrol."[47]

Despite strict immigration laws, "special provisions" in the law and the need for seasonal labor have contributed to establishing migrant workers as an integral part of the American workforce. Estimates of undocumented migrant workers in the United States range from 3.5 to 6 million, with about half coming from Mexico. These workers often suffer from feelings of alienation because of language differences, the loss of family and other social support systems, the disorganizing effects of trying to adjust to a new culture, and adhering to health beliefs that differ significantly from American practice. Undocumented workers also have a fear of deportation and legal uncertainty, and so tend to use health care facilities only as a last resort; they typically rely on traditional remedies or do not seek medical treatment at all.

Undocumented workers are more likely to use local clinics that offer special paying arrangements and hospital emergency rooms, particularly if the workers are new arrivals. However, clinic and emergency rooms are less accessible in rural areas. Undocumented workers frequently work in unsafe or unhealthy environments but are reluctant to ask for safety measures for fear of deportation or for fear of losing their jobs. Those who are injured on the job often try to hide the injury and continue to work. They are also less likely to seek preventative care.

Confusing public policies further complicate the issues and point to a number of pressing questions. Most undocumented workers pay taxes. Should they be eligible for public benefits such as health care? Many employers continue to hire undocumented workers because of the need for seasonal and low-wage labor. What is their responsibility to their workers? Migrant and seasonal farm workers are one of the most underserved and understudied occupational populations in the United States. How can known barriers to care be ameliorated so that their health needs and concerns do not continue to be ignored or detrimentally underserved? Finally, the stress of alienation and dislocation experienced by immigrants and refugees has rarely been addressed in undocumented workers. What are their mental health needs and how can they be met?[48]

---

baut and Westermeyer, which related Southeast Asian refugees' pre-migration experiences to post-resettlement adjustment, are examples of the form of study required in far greater number.[46] In general, an ongoing research agenda that enables primary health care workers to quickly identify refugees with depression, anxiety, and other treatable psychiatric problems is crucial.

Another essential task is to better evaluate the potential ameliorative factors for refugee mental health. In particular, we need to refine our understanding of, first, those circumstances where social support is and is not an effective ameliorative factor and, second, the most appropriate forms of coping strategies in specific circumstances. The effectiveness of community work interventions, as well as specific therapies, must also be studied empirically. Further work is also needed to clarify the factors identifying those at greatest risk at different periods following initial resettlement. There is also an acute need for study of the psychological distress among displaced persons who remain within their native countries. Here it is important to determine why some groups successfully adapt to new circumstances and others do not. This knowledge would help governments and agencies to devise more effective and supportive relocation programs.

In particular, several questions need to be answered. To what extent can we assist refugees to "make sense of" their frequently painful and traumatic experience as a means of assisting their psychological adjustment? What is the potential role for groups of refugees to come together in countries of resettlement to discuss and interpret the past? To what extent does such co-ethnic bonding—reflecting on a shared past—serve to usefully preserve a sense of personal identity, or does it impede future adaptation to the host country?

In general, the dissemination of accurate data regarding the effect of displacement on mental health is a necessary, though clearly insufficient, condition for putting the psychosocial needs of refugees on the world political agenda. Indeed, if subsequent studies of dislocation outside of Europe and North America confirm the extent of psychological distress resulting from forced migration, funding bodies and assistance agencies should give such research high priority. Appropriate commitment is also required from the research community itself, as the required approaches will necessarily involve extensive periods of fieldwork in areas of major social disturbance. The existing literature too often demonstrates the weakness and superficiality of research based on brief and decontextualized study of refugees in poor countries.

Conclusions

- There are nearly 20 million official refugees in the world today, most of them from Asia and Africa. Another 20 million people are displaced within their own countries. Many of these people suffer from some form of mental distress as a result of problems and difficulties encountered before, during, or after the flight from their home regions. At each step in these journeys, specific steps can be taken to lessen the risk for ill health.
- The majority of refugees and internal migrants lack services that can attend to their mental health needs. Services must therefore be developed that help health care workers to identify and treat mental distress among dislocated peoples. To identify the mental health needs of refugees and other dislocated peoples, culturally sensitive mental health assessments need to be developed and used. Since it is unrealistic to provide individual therapy to the majority of refugees, community work programs must be consistently implemented in refugee settings as the first therapeutic option. Programs that deal with the trauma of political violence must also be systematically employed in refugee camps.
- To identify the mental health needs of refugees and other dislocated peoples, culturally sensitive mental health assessments need to be developed and used.

The World Health Organization and the United Nation's High Commissioner on Refugees (UNHCR) have recently collaborated on the production of a refugee mental health manual for use in refugee camps.[48] The manual also features sections on helping victims of torture and of rape. The manual has yet to undergo field testing, and there is, as yet, no data regarding its efficacy.

- The UNHCR estimates that close to 80% of refugees are women and children. Yet few health services are in place that attend to the special needs of women and children. If the health status of women refugees are to be improved, there will need to be services that help women to develop educational and employment skills, increase their political capital, and establish a safe and meaningful life in exile. These services must also help women who have suffered sexual assault. Similar programs need to be developed to attend to the concerns of children, particularly in terms of establishing a secure environment and the means to attend to fears or traumatic experiences. In general, mental health workers need to be sensitive to the specific concerns of women (who may be reluctant to talk of sexual assaults) as well as those of children and the elderly.

- Rather than respond to needs only when difficulties arise, the major thrust with regard to refugee mental health must be to anticipate risk and to put in place actions considered likely to reduce the likelihood of the onset of such difficulties. Preventive approaches seem the only sustainable means of addressing such needs. Likely refugee movements can be frequently predicted some time in advance, making possible anticipatory, preventive strategies.

- While circumstances leading up to flight commonly result from the deliberate and hostile acts of political groups within the country of origin, many subsequent stressors are within the clear control of states and/or agencies purporting to be sympathetic to the needs of refugees. Even where governments and agencies appear genuine in offering assistance, they are commonly insensitive to aspects of their policies that negatively impact refugees. National and international agencies must therefore work more closely with refugee leaders to provide food, shelter, protection, and medical care. Greater participation by refugees in decision-making not only helps to improve the quality and reliability of decisions made, but indirectly encourages a sense of personal control in refugees likely to foster positive mental health.

- Many people resettling in a new society must contend with a range of conflicts and adjustments. Improved communication (including a greater deference to the expressed needs of refugees) and better advanced planning by sponsoring organizations can eliminate many of the initial conflicts and adjustments. In general, programs that assist refugees in establishing asylum and a secure political status in resettled countries are helpful, as are programs that help migrants and refugees to find productive and nonexploitative employment. Facilitating better access of children to schooling (particularly within camp environments) can serve to minimize disruption to cognitive and intellectual development and, equally important, maintain a key social routine and means of socialization. Schools, community work programs, and refugee assistance programs must be prepared to deal with issues of cultural assimilation, particularly when members of families and communities assimilate at different paces.

- Any formal assistance programs should consider building upon existing mechanisms that foster coping and adjustment. Programs can seek to directly foster social ties and supports by developing community programs and Mutual Assistance Agencies (as promoted among Indochinese refugees in the United States). Refugee assistance programs can deter passivity and foster active coping by allowing refugees to take greater responsibility and initiative in their own affairs. Family reunification programs, in turn, can encourage the healing processes associated with family integration and attachment.

- Refugees' understanding of their experience within some integrative narrative framework appears crucial in helping refugees adjust to a new social and political context. The benefits of a supportive, co-ethnic social network may indeed stem from the negotiation and definition of meaning afforded by access to a community with a shared cultural and linguistic framework. While governments and agencies may fear encouraging ideological zeal that might be at variance with their own, they must take into account the fact that commitment to a cultural, religious, or political charter helps to promote mental health.

- To date, there is greater attention to the care and welfare of official refugees than to the 20 million internal refugees throughout the world. And yet these unofficial refugees, who receive little or no support from the United Nations, face, at times, more harmful conditions than those who seek asylum in another country. To address this situation, more effort needs to be put into developing programs that support the health and legal status of internal refugees.

7

Children and Youth

Gains in child health the world over during the past several decades have been impressive. A combination of family planning and low-cost health measures (vaccines, the promotion of breast feeding, growth monitoring, and oral rehydration therapy) has saved lives and decreased morbidity. UNICEF estimates that immunization programs prevent some 3 million deaths each year; yet shortfalls in immunization result in 1.7 million vaccine-preventable deaths each year. Between 1975 and 1990, mortality in children under five (5Q0) decreased in sub-Saharan Africa from 212 per 1,000 live births to 175, from 195 to 127 in India, from 85 to 43 in China, from 174 to 111 in the Middle Eastern Crescent, and from 104 to 60 in Latin America and the Caribbean. Despite these impressive gains, 5Q0 rates for the least-developed countries (180) are ten times greater than those for industrialized countries (17). Averages obscure substantial differences among countries. Some countries have made little or no progress. In 1960, one child in five died before reaching age five in Indonesia as well as Ghana. By 1990, that rate had been halved for Indonesia but remained the same for Ghana; during the 1980s, Gross National Product per capita grew by 3.9% per annum in Indonesia but fell by 0.3% per annum in Ghana.

The major medical causes for the under-five mortality differential among countries are deaths from diarrhea and pneumonia, the former avoidable by rehydration, the latter by chemotherapy. The extent to which effective therapies are made available to children is determined by the political commitment to rights of children, the economic priority assigned to meeting their needs, the emphasis given to primary care for women and children in national health planning, and the way economic resources are distributed within the country. Brazil, which is classified by the World Bank as an "upper-middle-income" country, has a GNP per capita of $2,940. However, 35 million of Brazil's 151 million people live on less than $1 per day and 65 million on less than $2 per day.[1] Thus, it is not surprising that its infant mortality rate is 58, that 13% of its children under five suffer from malnutrition, and that only 39% of its adolescents are enrolled in secondary school.

Paralleling world gains in child health, the percentage of children enrolled in school has increased from under 30% in 1960 to more than 70% in 1990 in low-income countries.[2] Yet, of those children, only 45% reach grade four of primary school, as compared to more than 80% in East Asia. Once again, regional averages conceal as much as they reveal. The first-year school failure rate even in neighboring countries varies from 4% in Niger to 43% in adjacent Chad. Among countries in southern Africa, literacy varies from just over 20% in Malawi and Botswana to 40% in Namibia and Angola, and has reached 67% in Zimbabwe; yet per capita income is four times greater in Botswana than it is in Zimbabwe.[3]

Despite the general gains in child health and schooling, tens of millions of children are victims of misfortune, becoming refugees, displaced persons, casualties of war, or street children (see Box 7.1, Box 7.2). The United Nations High Commissioner for Refugees has estimated that the number of refugees and asylum seekers

---

Box 7.1 The Care of Orphans in Eritrea

Until the early twentieth century, Western countries traditionally placed orphans and abandoned children in large, impersonal, and often psychologically sterile group settings. Many children cared for in institutions suffered inordinate, and sometimes irreparable, physical and psychological damage. From such experiences grew the widespread belief that group rearing of children is inherently incompatible with normal psychological development, and causes "permanent damage to the emotional health of a future generation."[4]

Institutional care has improved considerably over the past thirty years. A number of studies have shown that group care even for young children is entirely compatible with normal social and cognitive development, provided the institution is organized to meet the needs of children and not for economic efficiency or the convenience of society. Some child-development experts question whether, when adoption is not a viable option, foster care is necessarily in the child's best interest.[5] Nonetheless, many countries regard adoption and foster care as the only socially acceptable means of caring for unaccompanied children.

Most orphans and other unaccompanied children are now concentrated in war-torn or impoverished countries where they have been permanently separated from both parents and dislocated from their homes. It is estimated that over half a million Sudanese and Ethiopian children, orphaned by the recurrent wars and civil disorders in the Horn of Africa, are forced to live in primitive shelters in the Eastern Sudan. The plight of unaccompanied children in other regions is probably even more desperate. Most of these children will probably never be reunited with extended families, and they will probably not be adopted or placed in foster homes in countries that have no tradition of caring for children not related by blood. Since group care will be the only hope of survival for virtually millions of unaccompanied children in poor countries, it is imperative to reexamine how group care can best serve the needs of children in regions of the world where technical and financial resources are limited. As a step in this process, Peter Wolff, of Children's Hospital in Boston, and his Eritrean colleagues compared orphans in Eritrea who had lost both parents and were living in an understaffed, overcrowded, and ill-equipped institution, and a matched group of accompanied children living with at least one parent in a nearby refugee camp.[6]

Eritrea is a small country that fought for its independence from Ethiopia for thirty years. Throughout the war, the Ethiopian Air Force controlled the skies over Eritrea; the entire economic and social life of the population had been forced underground. The orphanage and the refugee camp were hidden in the deepest canyons in Northern Eritrea to protect the children from air raids, but this safeguard exposed them to harsh living conditions.

The orphanage was located in a dry riverbed encircled by deforested and rocky cliffs. The orphans slept in poorly ventilated tents with two to four children to a bed. Despite their geographic isolation, orphans and refugee children lived with the constant threat of aerial bombardment. After six years of relentless drought, they also lived with chronic food and water shortages; despite the protein-enriched supplementary diets and specialized foods grown by the staff for the children, many of the orphans (and other children in Eritrea) were probably suffering from nutritional deficiencies.

Recognizing that the social and psychological conditions at the orphanage were incompatible with normal development, the Eritrean Department of Social Affairs (DSA) requested two independent surveys of the psychological and physical status of the orphans as well as detailed recommendations for changing the social organization of the orphanage. Two years after these changes had been implemented but while the war was still in progress, Wolff and his colleagues began to determine the emotional status and cognitive development of the orphans.

A group of seventy-four orphans who had lost both parents was compared to a matched group of refugee children living under the same environmental conditions with at least one parent in their own homes. Both groups were examined by standardized behavioral questionnaires modified for use in Eritrea to assess their social emotional status, and by "culture-fair" modifications of standardized psychological tests, including the Raven Progressive Matrices, the Leiter International Scale, a short version of the Token Test, a culturally appropriate version of a naming test, and by an informal sociometric procedure for measuring their social interaction.

Sleep disturbances, nocturnal enuresis, and psychosomatic complaints were more common among orphans than refugee children. The orphans were more aggressive in their social interaction with peers and staff, and showed more idiosyncratic food habits; the refugee children, in contrast, were more fearful of the dark, wild animals, and the like. Group differences were statistically significant but of small magnitude, and could be explained by group differences in the physical-social environment.

By contrast, the orphans outperformed the refugees on several test measures. The differences were again statistically significant but relatively small; most of them could be explained by the fact that while both groups of children attended regular classes after the age of six, only the orphans attended regular kindergarten classes. There were no group differences in nutritional status, physical illnesses, minor neurological signs, or fine motor manual skills. The remarkably small differences between orphans and refugee children take on added significance when one considers that at the time of the first survey before the orphanage was restructured, at least 25% of orphans had exhibited symptoms of major psychiatric disturbances as well as significant developmental delays in cognition and language acquisition.

A cross-sectional study carried out under less than optimal conditions with measures not standardized on Eritrean children does not warrant firm conclusions that the orphans will maintain their relatively stable emotional status and normal cognitive development in later years. They do suggest, however, that a dedicated if undertrained staff can, despite relatively little financial assistance and expert advice, provide humane group care for severely traumatized children that will enable them to develop normally.

The success of the Eritrean experience almost certainly depended in large part on the full support of the larger community and on the special sociological conditions that frequently emerge during protracted wars of liberation. While each country must translate the Eritrean experience in keeping with its own current historical conditions, local traditions, and values, group care organized on basic principles of human decency can be a viable alternative for the millions of children orphaned every year by war and civil unrest, when adoption or foster care are not viable options.[7]

Box 7.2 Street Children

At the age of nine, Giovani Soto left his mother's two-room shack and his sixteen siblings to live in the streets of Guatemala City. He befriended a group of street children, with whom he played, slept, traveled, sniffed glue, and shared food and warmth. They obtained the basic necessities by begging, stealing, or the occasional odd job. Giovani kept in touch with his family, visited them sporadically, and offered help when he could. He was determined to keep his younger siblings off the streets.

In 1989, at the age of 17, Giovani Soto was picked up in a police sweep and put into an adult prison. He was sexually abused by the adult prisoners, who etched their names into his skin using knives, nails, and ink. The police eventually released him and warned him to stay off the streets or suffer the consequences. Frightened and demoralized, he started sleeping at his mother's and began to search for a job. On 1, October 1989, a day before he began his new job at a textile industry, he disappeared. His body was found three days later. According to the autopsy report, he had been tortured for seven to twelve hours and then shot through the head, the signature of Guatemala's death squads.

Giovani was one of the first children to be executed in this manner in Guatemala. Since then thirty to fifty children have been murdered each year by the police and security forces in Guatemala, Brazil, and Colombia. Hundreds more have been beaten and tortured. Recently the security forces of South Africa, Haiti, Peru, Honduras, and El Salvador have joined in this brutal assault on the street children of their cities.

Despite repeated protests by local groups and international agencies, the governments involved have failed to halt the assaults on street children. The general public often views street children as symbols of the crime and social decay that plague their cities. As the social conditions worsen, the public becomes more accepting of the killing of street children. In Brazil, for instance, shantytown store owners openly pay death squads and police to "exterminate" the children.

Yet the population of street children continues to grow and has been estimated to be as high as 100 million. Some of these children have been abandoned or orphaned and have nowhere else to go. However, the majority of the children, like Giovani, know of family members who could house or care for them. They are on the streets to avoid abuse, poverty, or parental authority, or to find excitement and see the world. For them street life, even with the risk of torture or murder, is a better alternative to what they left at home.

The circumstances of street children are diverse even within a single country. Partly for this reason, large-scale governmental efforts to deal with the issue have been unsuccessful. However, a few grass-roots attempts have been surprisingly effective on a small scale. Most of these, such as the Salesian Center for Minors and Salão de Encontro in Brazil, have tried to provide well-paid jobs in protective environments as well as food, shelter, and health benefits. Others, such as the Bosconia program in Colombia, provide food, laundry services, medical services, and bathing facilities to all the children, and shelter those who agree to abide by its rules and go to school.

These attempts are not enough. Public misperceptions need to be corrected, and the urgency of the situation communicated to the public. In addition, governments need to actively find and prosecute those who murder and assault children like Giovani. Most important, governments and international organizations need to look more closely into finding ways to solve the crisis of the urban family that results in street children. Of note is the fact that Giovani's mother believed that none of her other sixteen children had achieved as much as he had.[10]

in the world has increased from under 3 million in 1976 to more than 19 million in 1993, most of them families with children, some of them children without families. To this number must be added an additional 25 million persons who have fled their homes for various reasons. Because they are still inside their country boundaries, they have no legal protection through the United Nations. Of these displaced persons, approximately 16 million live in Africa. Crude death rates (CDR) among refugees and internally displaced persons soar to levels not less than three times, and as high as fifty times, the baseline CDR in their own home areas.[8] Most of these deaths occur among young children; 63% of the deaths among displaced Kurds in northern Iraq occurred among the 17% of the population younger than five.[9]

Armed conflict is endemic in many parts of the world. The strategy of "low-intensity" warfare, characteristic of the insurrections in Africa and Latin America, aims at the destabilization of a society rather than victory through large military engagements. It is devastating for civilian populations. In Mozambique, deliberately chosen targets have included rural health units and schools, health workers, teachers, and local officials. Two to 3 million of the total Mozambican population of 16 million have been internally displaced; another million have become refugees in neighboring countries; more than 200,000 children have been separated from their parents, orphaned, or abandoned. Because of the civil war, the health of children has been endangered by economic stagnation (which has reduced already marginal food intake) and lack of access to health care. Schools targeted by the rebels have had to be closed; the assassination of teachers has been commonplace. Accurate mortality data are unavailable; surveys in some areas reveal an infant mortality rate of 200 per 1,000 and an under-five mortality of 370 per 1,000. Fifty percent of the children under five show stunted height (below the 3rd percentile for age) and 7% wasting (weight for height below the 3rd percentile). Epidemics of cholera and measles have spread rapidly among overcrowded displaced populations camped in areas without sanitary facilities.[11]

Children captured by the guerrillas in Mozambique have been trained to become killers. Others have witnessed brutality and suffered beatings, threats, and starvation. Many have seen their parents killed in front of their eyes; some have been forced to do the killing. One survey of 50 displaced children showed that 42 had suffered major family losses and that 29 had been eyewitness to murders. A mental health assessment revealed that two-thirds of those children suffered from unremitting anxiety, living in fear of another raid. One quarter of the children were markedly handicapped by their psychological distress.[12] Official rehabilitation policy is to avoid the hazards of institutionalization at all costs and to place abandoned children with substitute families in the community, despite the risk of exploitation under such circumstances (especially of female children). Training programs are being established to help teachers to recognize signs of distress and to encourage victimized children to express their feelings. The project also is designed to help teachers, themselves targets of attack and in need of support, to verbalize their experiences.[13]

Tens of millions of children and adolescents are out of school before legal leaving age; they work, beg, or thieve on city streets in places like India, the Philippines, sub-Saharan Africa, and Latin America. While some are on the streets as a result of war or displacement, most are there because of rural migration to urban slums, inadequate housing and public services, family breakdown, and school failure. Some have given up on school, others have no school to go to, and still others have been pushed out of school as "problems." The schools themselves are often grossly inadequate; increasingly, families see schooling as irrelevant because there are no jobs available at graduation; the regimentation and the bureaucratization in poorly run schools is the antithesis of the ways children live and learn in traditional communities. For families, the cost of keeping a child in school is no longer offset by higher wages after school completion. Early indenture of children into wage-earning roles is increasingly common in families that require additional income for their very survival. Children may be sold into virtual slavery in rug-weaving factories where their small fingers permit them to do fine work, or as jockeys for camel races in distant countries, or as prostitutes for organized sex rings (see Box 7.3, Box 7.4). Some escape to city streets; some are thrown on the streets when ill health, increasing size, ineptness at the job, or insubordination makes them undesirable.

The number of youth who live on the streets in Brazil alone have been estimated in the millions. Some observers challenge these estimates as many times too high. Without disagreeing that very large numbers of children are out of school and on the streets during the day, they conclude that most of them remain part of their families, contributing earnings, eating, and sleeping at home. Their income comes from the "informal" market sector, much of it illegal, hazardous, and poorly paid. Street youth take to stealing and exchanging sex for money. Many are initiated into sex by early adolescence; many have same-sex as well as opposite-sex partners. Few use condoms, most use drugs and alcohol, and many contract sexually transmitted diseases. They live in a world where sex meets multiple needs (survival, solidarity, pleasure, and dominance), where multiple partners are frequent, and where sexual practices, such as anal intercourse and gang rape, are daily risks. Most of their sexual encounters are exploitative or coercive. They are at high risk for HIV infection in a sexual culture where male bisexuality is compatible with being macho.[18] Adding to the tenuousness of their lives is victimization by illegal police action. There have been many episodes in which off-duty and out-of-uniform police, at the behest of, and in the pay of, local merchants, have summarily executed street youth in retribution for theft, alleged or real. According to Human Rights Watch/America, 5,644 Brazilian children aged 5 to 17 were murdered by death squads between 1988 and 1991.[19]

Developmental Attrition

The problems that are disproportionately large among children in low-income countries, especially those in the throes of civil war, are developmental attrition, seizure disorders, and aggressive and antisocial behavior disorders frequently associated with substance abuse.

Developmental attrition results from the failure to reach normal developmental landmarks year after year, so that cumulative defect becomes ever larger. It is the result of inadequate intake of nourishment vital for body and for mind: proteins,

Box 7.3 Child Labor

In 1980, the International Labor Organization estimated that there were 52 million children under the age of 15 that were economically active. Today, millions more labor daily all around the world, in all sectors of the economy. In poorer areas, child laborers may provide an essential portion of their families' income. In some cases they provide the only income. Yet they are abused, exploited, and typically ignored by economic and social reports.

Amaranth is a child worker from Udar Pradesh in India. At the age of eight, Amaranth's father sent him to weave carpets. The middleman who recruited Amaranth told his father that the boy would be clothed, fed, and paid 350 rupees (about $12.50 U.S.) a month. "I took two months to learn," Amaranth recalls. "No money was paid to me. All day we had to weave, even to midnight. We were not allowed to rest during the day. If we became slow . . . we were beaten with sticks . . . on our backs. He used to lock us up at home, in a room. There were nine of us in the room. For one and a half years we never had green vegetables, not to talk of milk. He did not even allow us to have a bath."[14]

Amaranth's case is not unusual. Employers often pay child workers a fraction of what they pay an adult worker for similar work—if they pay anything at all. They might also subject the children to mental and physical abuse. Fortunately, Amaranth was able to escape relatively unscathed after almost two years of employment. The rest of the estimated 300,000 child carpet weavers in India are rarely so lucky. They often remain with the employer until their early teenage years, working in dark, cramped huts for twelve hours or more daily. As a result, they often suffer poor eyesight and severe back problems for the rest of their lives.

Unfortunately, a large number of child workers are faced with such serious health risks. Some 50,000 children work in the glass and bangle industry of India, near furnaces of 700°C and 1400°C, breathing in smoke and dust. Burns and respiratory problems are common. In Brazil, where children as young as eight work with machetes harvesting bananas, it is not uncommon to hear of accidental amputations. And in Bogotá, children routinely unload and carry hot brick in the brickyards and work with explosives in the quarries.

But all of these dangers are minor when compared with the potential for mental trauma faced by child workers. Many reportedly suffer symptoms of severe depression, withdrawal, and inferior status identity. In addition, as they have time for nothing but sleep and work, their intellectual and social development is limited, and creativity is stifled. Lacking in education and social and intellectual skills, the children are doomed to a life of toil and poverty.

Most countries have legislation prohibiting or restricting child labor, but very few are able to successfully enforce these laws. Effective enforcement requires extensive and dedicated manpower, for which most counties are unwilling to pay. In addition, the industries in which these children work often bring in well-needed foreign revenue, and many governments are thus willing to ignore the exploitation. Finally, such regulations are absurd for parents who, though working, are unable, on their own, to provide enough to keep their families alive.

Some believe that child labor will become unnecessary as the per capita income of countries increases. They advocate that governments legalize child labor and accord it the rights and status of adult labor. While this approach would help to improve wages and enhance job security and employment benefits, it would not remove the potential for physical and mental abuse. The idea that child labor is a necessary evil in the path to economic development should not permit us to disregard the dangerous circumstances and unconscionable treatment of the working child today.[15]

Box 7.4 Child Prostitution

In recent years child prostitution has increased dramatically, partly because of the belief that child prostitutes are less likely to have AIDS. Rough estimates put the number of child prostitutes between hundreds of thousands to millions. The areas with the greatest number are Thailand, India, Brazil, and the Philippines. In these countries, most of the customers are tourists, a high proportion of whom are married, middle-class men from wealthy countries, including Japan.

The boys and girls whose services they buy may be as young as six years old. Some are street children who have learned that sex with tourists will get them the money they badly need to survive. Others have been kidnapped from their homes and sold to madams, with whom they will remain as sex slaves till they are too old to attract customers. And then there are those whose parents sent them to the city with a trusted recruiter, believing that their child would be provided with a well-paying job as a secretary or a barmaid. There have recently been reports of parents who voluntarily prostitute their children.

A recent report in *The New York Times* quoted a Vietnamese pediatrician, a Dr. Hoa, who was appalled and astonished as more and more fathers brought their prostitute children for treatment. "One father came with his twelve-year-old daughter," Dr. Hoa recalled. "She was bleeding from her wounds and as torn as if she had given birth. He told me: 'We've earned $300, so it's enough. She can stop.' "

On another occasion, Dr. Hoa asked the father of an 11-year-old how he could allow his child to prostitute. "First of all," the man answered, "we are very poor. And this is a good age to do it. She is still too young to get pregnant." When Dr. Hoa asked about the child's future, she received the following answer: "She is very young now. She will grow up and she will forget."

The severity of the physical and psychological trauma that these children experience is further compounded by a high incidence of sexually transmitted diseases. One survey found that more than 50% of Thai child prostitutes are HIV-positive. And the numbers for other venereal diseases are believed to be just as high.

Some customers want more than sex from these children. The following exchange occurred over the phone between a Los Angeles police undercover agent and an Italian pedophile.

"I want a child of ten years."
"A little girl of ten years?"
"Yes. Perfect. Also one of eight years, six years. What you say . . . ?"
"I think a girl of ten, but if I can find someone younger I will try."
"OK."
"OK. And you want to have sex with her?"
"Yes. Yes. And I want to have, if possible, hard sex."
"Very hard sex."
"OK. We can do all of this?"
"You can do anything you want with her."
"After she make love, she die."
"Do you want to kill the girl?"
"Yes. What happen when she die?"
"We would have to find a way to get rid of her body."
"Aha. And how much it cost?"

Fortunately, this man was arrested, convicted, and sentenced to life imprisonment.[16] Most are never caught.

Organizations such as ECPAT (End Child Prostitution in Asian Tourism) have begun to combat child prostitution and increase public awareness. The Task Force to End Child Exploitation in Thailand, a coalition of twenty-four government and private agencies, is dedicated to exposing links between Europe and the child sex trade in Bangkok. In 1992, the coalition successfully shut down one airline ticket agency catering to European pedophiles.

In this vein, the most effective solution may be to halt the flow of customers. The Australian government has declared war on illicit sex tourism, and the federal police have been targeting travel agencies catering to pedophilia. In France and the Scandinavian countries, it is against the law to patronize child prostitutes whether they are foreign or national. François Lefort, a French priest who has fought child prostitution throughout the world, makes the point succinctly: 'This problem is not just Bangkok's, Colombo's, Manila's. It's Paris', Brussels', Rome's. It's the nice, respectable white man who goes down there to molest these kids.'[17]

calories, and micronutrients; perceptual and cognitive stimuli; and social relations and interactions. Attrition manifests itself in three ways: physically, as height and weight well below norms for age; in school settings, as learning failure and retarded mental development; and behaviorally, as psychiatric disorder and social deviance. Although height is governed in part by genetic controls (no diet will enable Japanese to attain Watusi height norms), a given child needs proper diet, health care, and living standards in order to reach his full potential height. Thus, the average height of Japanese schoolchildren was well below that for first-generation Japanese growing up in California in 1940. Now the same levels are attained by Japanese growing up in either country, because Japanese living standards match those in the United States.

Similarly, for a child to attain his or her full potential requires both emotional support and intellectual stimulation. While moderate childhood deficits are reversible if they are repaired, severe and prolonged malnourishment leaves permanent damage. UNICEF estimates that one in five children in low-income countries suffer chronic malnutrition and a like number subsist on diets deficient in one or another nutrient. Protein-calorie and micronutrient deficiency conjoin to produce stunting of physical growth.

The disadvantage to which the poor child in low-income countries is subject begins before conception. Intergenerational effects of malnutrition are reflected in a mother's short stature and smaller pelvic outlet; the result is a greater likelihood of disproportion between the size of the infant's head and the outlet provided by the mother's pelvis. This is associated with higher rates of maternal, fetal, and infant mortality and morbidity. Poor nutrition and limited health care during the pregnancy increases the likelihood of poor outcomes. If, in addition, children born of a complicated pregnancy are reared under adverse social conditions, they will suffer from long-term retardation in cognitive development. Malnutrition, by depressing immunologic defense mechanisms, renders children more vulnerable to gastrointestinal infection; this decreases nutritional intake at the very time that metabolic demand increases, thus worsening the original malnutrition. This results in apathy, unresponsiveness to the environment, and lost opportunity for learning. Malnutrition conjoined with unsatisfactory family life and inadequate intellectual stimulation results in test performance far below expected levels. On the other hand, prompt renourishment accompanied by appropriate social and cognitive stimulation can lead to a resumption of normal development.[20]

Mental Retardation

Mental retardation is defined in the International Classification of Diseases 10 as "a condition of arrested or incomplete development of the mind."[21] It has its onset in childhood and is characterized by impairment of the skills that make up intelligence: cognitive, language, motor, and social abilities. It is subdivided by severity into four categories: mild, moderate, severe, and profound.

Mild mental retardation manifests itself primarily in school settings because academic abilities are well below par. Many such youngsters can be helped by special school instruction, but they will not attain average levels. However, many will be capable of practical unskilled or semiskilled labor as adults and all should be competent in self-care. When standardized IQ tests are used, the range for this group is from 50 to 69.

Moderate mental retardation is evident in impaired and limited language development. Persons so afflicted require supervision for their lifetimes. Neurological signs and symptoms and physical handicap are common. The majority have detectable organic disease of the brain. The IQ range is from 35 to 49.

Severe (IQ 20 to 34) and *profound* (IQ less than 20) mental retardation are almost always associated with marked neuromotor impairment, manifest central nervous system pathology, and detectable organic disease. Severely or profoundly retarded individuals acquire little or no understanding of language. They require care during their lifetimes in settings adapted for their physical handicaps.

The prevalence of mental retardation is estimated to be from two to eight times greater in low-income than in industrialized countries.[22] Table 7.1 provides prevalence data on severe mental retardation in seven developing countries, and Table 7.2 on mild, moderate, and severe retardation in China. As a comparison, the rate of severe mental retardation in Western countries varies from 3 to 5 per thousand children.[23]

Table 7.1 Serious Mental Retardation (SMR) in Children Three to Nine Years Old

Country	Number of Children Surveyed	SMR Rate Per Thousand Children
Philippines	1,000	5.0
Bangladesh	987	16.2
Sri Lanka	966	5.2
Malaysia	981	11.2
Pakistan	995	15.1
Brazil	1,050	6.7
Zambia	1,139	5.3
Total	**7,118**	

Source: Stein et al., 1986.

Table 7.2 Prevalence Rates of Mental Retardation in China (per 1,000, by level of severity)

Place	Population Investigated	Severe	Moderate	Mild
Shanghai	463,202	0.29	0.98	—
Nanjing	116,522	0.21	1.31	1.84
12 Districts	51,982	0.40	2.60	—
Changquao area of Beijing	7,150	0.70	2.24	4.90
Sichuan	287,981	0.46	2.1	2.8

Source: Tao, 1988. American Journal on Mental Retardation, a Publication of the American Association on Mental Retardation.

The environmental hazards that produce retardation are much more widespread in poor countries. The principal causes of mental retardation can be classified by the time at which they affect the developing fetus and child; thus, they can be divided into prenatal, perinatal, and postnatal causes (see Table 7.3).

Of these causes, many are largely preventable. Fetal alcohol syndrome consists of cognitive impairment, growth retardation, and craniofacial abnormalities.[24] It results from excessive alcohol consumption in the first trimester of pregnancy. The severity of the mental retardation appears to correlate with the extent of the facial abnormalities. The risk for alcohol effects on the fetus are about 10% for mothers averaging 2 to 4 drinks per day, and 19% for those averaging more than 4 drinks per day.[25] Incidence has been estimated at 2 per 1,000 live births in the United States and Europe, which makes it more common than Down's syndrome. This is an entirely preventable disaster. It can be reduced by public education on the hazards of drinking during pregnancy,[26] by warning labels on alcoholic beverages, by higher taxes on alcohol to limit access, and by prenatal counseling.

The incidence of neural-tube defects can be reduced by increasing maternal intake of folic acid during pregnancy.[27] Mass immunization can control congenital rubella syndrome by eliminating maternal susceptibility to rubella infection. Cretinism can be prevented by depot injections of iodized oil for pregnant women living in iodine-deficient areas. Perinatal risks can be reduced by trained birth attendants with backup local hospital facilities for management of high-risk deliveries. Postnatal damage can be reduced by measures to improve the safety of the environment.

Families at risk for such congenital disorders as Down's syndrome, Fragile-X syndrome, neural-tube defects, and Tay-Sachs disease can be offered an opportunity to abort impaired fetuses and, correspondingly, to bear their own normal children by prenatal screening tests followed by diagnostic confirmation of the health status of the conceptus. The goal of genetic counseling is to provide the information parents need to make personal choices. PKU, galactosemia, and hypothyroidism can be controlled by neonatal screening and appropriate dietary and medical care for affected infants. However, screening programs for these disorders, though cost effective, require the investment of significant initial resources and have been beyond the means of low-income countries.

Table 7.3 The Main Causes of Mental Retardation

---

1. Prenatal
  1.1 Genetic
  1.1.1 Chromosome abnormalities
      Down's syndrome
      Fragile-X syndrome
  1.1.2 Metabolic disorders affecting:
      amino acids (e.g., phenylketonuria, homocystinuria)
      lipids (Tay-Sachs disease)
      carbohydrate (galactosemia)
      purines (Lesch-Nyhan syndrome)
  1.1.3 Brain malformations
      Neural tube defects
      Hydrocephalus
      Microcephalus

1.2 Antenatal Damage
  Infections (rubella, cytomegalovirus, toxoplasmosis)
  Fetal alcohol syndrome
  Physical damage (injury, radiation, hypoxia)
  Placental dysfunction (toxaemia, nutritional growth retardation)
  Endocrine disorders (hypothyroidism)
  Deficiency states (iodine)

2. Perinatal
  Birth asphyxia
  Complications of prematurity
  Kernicterus
  Intraventricular hemorrhage

3. Postnatal Damage
  Injury (trauma from automobiles, machinery; child abuse)
  Intoxication (lead, mercury, household chemicals)
  Infections (encephalitis, meningitis)

Source: Adapted from WHO, 1993a.

Aggressive and Antisocial Behavior

Many nations face an epidemic of violent behavior by adolescents and young adults. Risk factors for such behavior, all highly intercorrelated, include poverty, limited education, residency in slum neighborhoods, single-parent families, a history of child abuse, a prison record in other family members, and adolescent gang membership. Crime increases as opportunities for legitimate employment decrease. Additional risks arise in countries under severe oppressive rule. Adolescents, initially recruited for resistance movements, may turn to lives of crime when the battle seems hopeless. This is a major problem in townships in South Africa where unprovoked violence from the police breeds a violent response among youth. Too often, their rage turns on fellow Africans rather than against their oppressors, whose firepower is awesome. The largest single component of adolescent mortality among black South Africans, from ages 10 to 14, was from assault, much of it from police forces.

As noted in Chapter 5, the South African physician Mamphela Ramphele argues that the impact of violence on a person reflects the interaction between the experience of violence and the coping strategies adopted by that person.[28] Peer pressure helps to maintain gang coherence because of the importance of a sense of belonging in a world where youths are not the focus of adult concerns. Corporal punishment is widely administered in South African schools; children complain about the randomness and severity of the beatings. Some respond by threatening teachers; gang activities on occasion spread into the classroom. Of the variables that influence the response of individual adolescents to the poverty and violence surrounding them, Ramphele's data suggest that individual attributes, such as intelligence and social attractiveness, and the dynamics of the youngster's family, are significant (see Box 5.3).

Adolescent criminality arising from apartheid will not automatically disappear simply because a democratic multiracial society has been created. One of the many challenges facing the new South África will be the rehabilitation of a generation cheated of educational opportunity, possessing limited vocational skills, and embittered by the brutal mistreatment to which they were subject.

Epilepsy

A seizure (fit) is the clinical manifestation of abnormal and excessive discharge from nerve cells in the brain. Seizures are classified as provoked (that is, secondary to another disease such as a parasitic infestation or a brain tumor) or as unprovoked idiopathic (that is, without an identifiable precipitating disease or injury). Epilepsy is a disorder of recurrent unprovoked seizures. The prevalence of epilepsy is 4 to 8 per 1,000 population in industrialized countries; in developing countries where prevalence has been studied (Latin America and Africa), rates have been as much as three to five times higher. However, there is striking variability in reported prevalence. For example, in one study in four areas of India (Bangalore, Baroda, Calcutta, and Patiala), prevalence varied from 1.28 per 1,000 in Baroda to 7.82 per 1,000 in Bangalore.[29] It is unclear how much of this variance reflects unreliable survey methods and how much reflects real differences in prevalence.[30]

Risks associated with higher rates of epilepsy include cerebral palsy and mental retardation, abnormal pregnancy and parturition, a family history of epilepsy, postnatal CNS infections, and brain injuries. The higher rates found in developing countries reflect more adverse events *in utero*, higher likelihood of injury, lack of access to treatment, and parasitic diseases (see Box 7.5). The majority (70%) of individuals with unprovoked epilepsy can remain seizure-free after medication has been discontinued. Contrary to popular myth, intelligence is not impaired by epilepsy per se.[31] However, childhood epilepsy is associated with a fourfold increase in risk for psychiatric disorder. Matuja reported that 60% of 230 consecutive referrals for epilepsy to a neurology clinic had a psychologic disturbance warranting treatment.[32] Those persons whose epilepsy was attributable to a brain lesion were four times more likely to exhibit psychopathology. In turn, brain lesions and psychological disturbance were strongly associated with social disadvantage. Epileptic people subject to frequent seizures often seek health care because of severe burns from falling into cooking fires. Indeed, epilepsy has been termed "the burn disease." In a thirty-year

Box 7.5 Epilepsy and Infection in Ecuador

Epilepsy is a major neuropsychiatric problem in much of the developing world. It can be treated effectively and inexpensively with phenobarbital; about 80% of those who suffer from generalized seizures, the most common form of epilepsy, can become seizure-free with this one drug. Yet, despite its low cost, treatment is often unavailable to poor populations. Not only do the seizures continue, with drownings, burns, fractures, and bruises as common consequences, but those with epilepsy can be stigmatized as "possessed" and excluded from local society.

The frequency of epilepsy in developing countries is many times that in the industrialized world because of higher rates of complications of pregnancy and parturition, bacterial and parasitic infections of the brain, and physical injuries to the central nervous system. Control of symptoms by medication is the only remedy when the cause of epilepsy is unknown, but when it is secondary to an underlying condition, treatment and prevention of the primary condition is the key. The neuroepidemiology of epilepsy is unique to particular countries. Careful study of the causative factors in a given country is an essential first step in the design of an epilepsy-prevention program for that country.

A compelling instance of such a program is provided by the neuroepidemiology of cysticercosis in Ecuador. The prevalence of epilepsy in rural areas in Ecuador is 2% to 3% (four to six times greater than in the industrialized world). A careful population study (employing computed tomography as the diagnostic standard) in rural villages near the capital city revealed that at least 50% of the cases of epilepsy result from invasion of the brain by larval stages of *Taenia solium*, the pork tapeworm. Human beings are the definitive hosts in the life cycle of the pork tapeworm; human excreta provide the source of infection for pigs. The pig, in turn, recycles the parasite to people when infected pigs are consumed as food. Human or pig taeniasis can be effectively treated with praziquantel; toxicity is minimal.

Drug treatment provides the basis for short-term control programs in areas where the disease is endemic. For long-term disease control, waste management and modern pig-rearing practices must be put in place along with effective meat inspection, improved sanitary facilities, and a primary health care system that can diagnose and treat individuals. That demands time and resources not available in many developing countries.

In a public health short-term prevention program, Dr. Marcelo Cruz and colleagues in Ecuador treated 10,000 persons in two villages with praziquantel. As a measure of effectiveness, they determined the rates of infection in pigs before and one year after the treatment. The prevalence of infection in pigs had decreased from 11.4% to 2.6%. The cost for deworming one person was about $0.10 U.S., 1/150 of the cost of medicating a case of cysticercosis.

Many important research questions remain. What is the optimal interval for mass worm eradication in villages? Why are the manifestations of the disease so remarkably different in India, Africa, and Ecuador? Calcification in muscles is prominent in India, skin nodules in Africa, and cerebral forms in Ecuador. How much of epilepsy in India and sub-Saharan Africa results from cysticercosis? We do not know. Population-based CT-scan studies have yet to be undertaken.

Much can be learned from careful cross-national comparisons of the incidence and prevalence of neurological diseases, as in this one instance. Correlations between regional differences and relevant environmental variables could shed light on causal factors and permit the development of disease-control programs.

follow-up of patients with epilepsy among the Pogoro people of Tanzania, Jilek-Aall and Rwiza found that survival rates were well below Tanzanian norms.[33] The most common causes of death were status epilepticus (17%), drowning (13%), burns (6%), and other causes related to epilepsy (33%). The authors conclude that patients and their families in rural Africa need safety education in connection with simple daily activities such as drawing water from a well, cooking on an open fire, and fishing.

Clinical research has identified anticonvulsant medications that permit the successful management of most people with seizure disorders. The efficacy of particular drugs for particular types of epilepsy (i.e., generalized versus partial seizures) requires titration of drug type and dose. However, the least-expensive medication, phenobarbital, permits successful control of seizures in most children with epilepsy. Phenobarbital can be administered by primary care health workers following a specified protocol. However, it has toxic effects, such as provoking overactivity in children, and is often in short supply. In consequence, Shorvon and Farmer recommend that other drugs such as phenytoin should be available even though they are more costly.[34] In a study carried out in a rural and semi-urban area in Kenya, half of 250 epileptic patients became seizure-free and another 25% had substantially fewer seizures after six months of treatment by primary care health workers.[35] The principal risk associated with phenobarbital is withdrawal seizures if the drug is suddenly discontinued; this is a serious problem because of the unreliability of drug supply in countries with marginally financed health systems. Those who are unresponsive to management at the village level must be referred to more expert care at the district hospital level.

Control of seizures is important for both the social and the physical health of the child. In many countries, epilepsy is severely stigmatized. It may be attributed to spirit possession or transgression of ancestral taboos. A person with epilepsy may be shunned and barred from all social intercourse. Marriage may be proscribed for the patient and other family members. Because of the stigma associated with the disease, families often hide afflicted children. In an area of central Ethiopia with an epilepsy prevalence of 5.2 per thousand, a door-to-door survey of 1,500 households revealed that 45% of those interviewed believed the disorder could be transmitted by physical contact at the time of an attack; three-quarters would not allow a family member to marry a patient with epilepsy and would not employ such a person.[36] A similar study in Henan, China, pointed to similarly negative attitudes: 87% against marriage; 57% against allowing their children to play with an epileptic person; and 53% against employment. Sixteen percent believed epilepsy was a form of insanity.[37]

It is therefore important to identify epileptic children. Even when children are brought into care, compliance with medication may be intermittent or cease altogether. One reason is the time required (and hence lost work hours) for follow-up visits even when there is no charge for medication. Another is the cost of drugs if prices are allowed to rise so that they become a significant fraction of family income. A third stems from the intermittent nature of the seizures. If the patient becomes free of fits for a few weeks, patient and parents may not understand the need for continuing medication. Arthur Kleinman and his colleagues portray the

Chinese experience in the following terms: "The moral crisis of epilepsy occurs because of the delegitimation of the person and the family in the structure of social relationships that affects marriage, livelihood and all aspects of social life. The moral capital of the family and the network is spent down."[38]

Primary health care workers need training on educating parents and patients and on checking for compliance on return or home visits. Countering stigma by public education, providing a reliable supply of appropriate medication for the person, counseling the family, and demonstrating that patients can resume a normal role in the community with appropriate treatment are essential components of health care for this disorder (see Box 7.5).

The size of the gap between the prevalence of epilepsy and the number of those receiving treatment for it is staggering. Table 7.4 illustrates the deficit for three countries: Pakistan, the Philippines, and Ecuador.

Epidemiology of Childhood Mental Disorders

Over the past twenty-five years, studies to investigate the prevalence and distribution of child mental disorders in general population samples have been conducted in many parts of the world.[39] The techniques used to define disorders have differed considerably. Yet, despite variations reported in rates, there are some consistent patterns in the distribution of disorders.

Preadolescent boys are nearly always reported to have higher rates of disorder than girls. The types of disorders contributing to this sex difference are primarily confined to intellectual disorders (mental retardation, specific learning disabilities, and autism) and behavioral disorders (hyperactivity and poor conduct). During adolescence, the gap in prevalence between boys and girls is closed by an increasing incidence of emotional (anxiety and depressive) disorders in girls. There has also been a consistent pattern by geographical area, with rates of ascertained disorders among city-dwelling children being higher than rates among children living in rural areas.[40]

The results of local-area studies have been more useful than aggregate data accumulated from total populations. Such studies, done in different parts of the world, have provided a varied picture of the burden of mental disorders in children and adolescents.

In a large sample of elementary-school children in districts in and around Bei-

Table 7.4 Epilepsy Treatment Gap in Three Countries

County	Estimated Prevalence	Patients in Treatment	Treatment Gap (%)
Pakistan	450,000	22,000	94
Philippines	270,000	14,000	94
Ecuador	55,000	11,000	80

Source: Shorvon and Farmer, 1988; Ellison, 1987.

jing, the prevalence of attention-deficit disorder varied from 3% in urban areas to 7% in suburban and rural areas.[41] This reversal of the typical urban/rural contrast was associated with the higher educational and occupational status of the parents in urban families. Despite this substantial effect of geographical area and parental education, the sex ratio and symptom pattern of the disorder was similar to that found in surveys in the United States and Western Europe.

Khartoum, Sudan, has been the setting for a study demonstrating the effects of urbanization and cultural change on the prevalence of psychiatric problems in cross-sectional samples of children between the ages of 3 and 15 over the 15-year period between 1965 and 1980.[42] Although the standard of living and the physical health of the children clearly improved over this interval, the prevalence of psychiatric problems increased. The proportion of children with severe disturbance increased from 8% to 13% in the total population, whereas the proportion of children rated as well-adjusted decreased from 63% to 47%. The authors attributed their findings to modernization, with new values and higher educational expectations of children.

Both the Beijing and the Khartoum studies underscore the importance of the interactions between geographical setting, culture change, parental education, and sex of the child in determining the observed prevalence of psychiatric disorders. If one extrapolates from these two studies to other cities in Asia and Africa, the expectation is that rates of psychiatric problems in children will continue to increase as these areas become more fully modernized.

In a cross-national prevalence study of children with emotional and behavioral problems,[43] teachers and parents evaluated primary-school children by means of standardized questionnaires in Japan, China, and Korea (2,000 or more in each country). The prevalence of children with high scores on parent ratings was 12% in Japan, 7% in China, and 19% in Korea; high scores on teacher ratings were reported for 3.9% in Japan, 8.3% in China, and 14.1% in Korea. The prevalence of deviance was higher in boys, especially those with poor school achievement, and in children from one-parent families. Deviance of the antisocial type was more frequent than the neurotic type in Japan and China; they were equally frequent in Korea.

The investigation of youth suicide in different parts of the world offers another way of approaching the multifactorial contribution of gender, social setting, and cultural change to pathological behavior. Contrasts in the frequency of completed suicide between West Africa, Algeria, Sri Lanka, and Malaysia offer a complex picture in which it appears that influences from changing social norms and institutions are more important than psychopathology.[44]

Setting Priorities

The current knowledge base in child mental health leads to general principles that should prove useful by governments and agencies committed to developing, or expanding existing, services.

1. Prevention, family support, and early detection should be emphasized.
2. Mental health services for children must become an integral component of

primary care. Rather than having mental health distinguished from physical health in the organization of services, it should be viewed as an essential part of pediatrics. Psychological problems make up a significant part of the reason for visits in child primary health clinics in low-income countries.[45] Particularly in countries where resources are limited, the reproduction of distinct psychiatric services for children, based on Western models of child-guidance centers, makes little sense.

3. A population-based approach to the development of services is required.
4. Considerable caution should be exercised before transplanting diagnostic systems from one culture to another. Rather than relying solely on symptom clusters (the basis in most classification systems for the definition of disorders), it is important to go beyond the presence of symptoms to levels of impairment. School failure, inability to conform to cultural and school norms, lack of self-confidence, rejection by peers, and violent behavior are the types of dysfunctional patterns that can be expected to be associated with psychiatric disorder.

Preventing Mental and Behavioral Disorders

The public health approach to prevention distinguishes among three levels of disease prevention.

Primary prevention is designed to preclude the development of disease among susceptible populations. It employs health promotion (i.e., the teaching of hygienic practices, universal education to promote cognitive development, the provision of optimal nutrition to enhance disease resistance, social support for family life, peer programs in public schools to diminish rates of onset of health-injurious habits, etc.) and specific protection (i.e., immunizations, iodination of salt, tetanus-toxoid injections during pregnancy to prevent neonatal tetanus, etc.).

Secondary prevention is designed to shorten the duration of illness once it occurs, reduce the likelihood of contagion, and limit sequelae by means of early diagnosis and prompt treatment (i.e., the use of psychotropic drugs and psychosocial measures to abort acute psychotic states). Treatment (secondary prevention) of the first disease in a causal series constitutes primary prevention for those conditions that would otherwise follow in its wake—i.e., treatment with anticonvulsants and psychosocial care for people with epilepsy to minimize accidents and personality difficulties or treatment of congenital hypothyroidism to avoid cretinism.

Tertiary prevention is directed at those with irreversible disease. Its goals are to limit disability (i.e., placing abandoned children in foster or adoptive homes to avert the developmental attrition caused by orphanages), to minimize exacerbations of the underlying disease (i.e., psychosocial education for the families of those with schizophrenia), and to promote rehabilitation (i.e., social-skills training, vocational guidance, sheltered workshops for retarded adolescents).

In the first instance, the goal is to prevent the development of disease; in the second, to shorten its duration after it has occurred; and in the third, to preserve function as far as possible when no effective treatment for the disease itself is available.

An alternative way to conceptualize prevention methods was used in a recent report by the Institute of Medicine that emphasizes reducing the prevalence by a spectrum of interventions designed to reduce risk factors and enhance supportive factors.[46] This scheme, as set out in Figure 7.1, stresses the continuity between prevention, treatment, and maintenance.

Prevention is divided into three sectors: universal, selective, and indicated. *Universal* interventions are directed at the entire population; examples are prenatal care to reduce the complications of childbirth and immunization to protect against central nervous system infection. *Selective* interventions are targeted at individuals at risk; an illustration is a nurse home visitor for a teenage mother living under conditions of poverty in order to improve the care she provides her child. *Indicated* preventive interventions are targeted at high-risk individuals with early signs or symptoms of impending disorder; an illustration is school-based peer counseling on the risks of substance abuse in the fifth, sixth, and seventh grades of schools serving neighborhoods where youngsters are about to experiment with substance use.

Indicated prevention overlaps with the "treatment" part of the spectrum of mental health interventions. Public health programs in this sector are aimed at early case identification and prompt and effective treatment to reduce the duration of the distress and to limit chronicity. The final component—"maintenance"—is designed to ensure long-term compliance in those with chronic disorders and to provide rehabilitation programs to reach enhanced function and to reintegrate the person into the community.

Action for Child Mental Health

The available database suggests that effective plans for child mental health have components with general applicability. But they will require different emphasis from one country to another, and will be more feasible in some countries than oth-

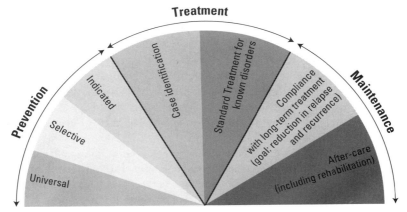

Figure 7.1 The Intervention Spectrum for Mental Health Problems (*Source:* Adapted with permission from *Reducing Risks for Mental Disorders: Frontiers for Preventive Research.* Copyright © 1994 by the National Academy of Sciences. Courtesy of the National Academy Press, Washington, D.C.)

ers because of cultural, political, religious, or other considerations. These components include:

1. *Family Planning.* The more numerous and the more closely spaced the
   pregnancies in the reproductive lives of women, the greater the risks for
   maternal and infant mortality and the worse the developmental outcomes
   for the children. In Bolivia, Brazil, Ecuador, Guatamala, and Peru, infant
   mortality rates are *twice* as high for an interbirth interval of less than two
   years as they are when the interval is four years or more.[47] The larger the
   number of children in a family (other variables having been controlled for),
   the lower their educational attainment. Unplanned and unwanted teenage
   pregnancies are associated with high risk for mother and child.[48] Taken
   together, these findings indicate the importance of family planning services
   to delay the age of first pregnancy, to reduce the number of offspring, and to
   lengthen interbirth intervals in order to optimize the ability of parents to
   care for their children. The health risks associated with modern contraception are *far less* than those associated with pregnancy and childbirth.[49]
   Because enabling parents to control family size is essential for the health of
   mothers and children, every nation should introduce sex education in the
   schools, including information about contraceptive methods and their reliability. Sexually active individuals should have access to contraceptives.
   Safe abortion should be available when contraception fails.

2. *Prenatal Care.* Inadequate nutrition, cigarette smoking, alcohol consumption, drug abuse, and inadequate prenatal care during pregnancy are all associated with increased hazards to the fetus, including higher rates of low-
   birth-weight infants. Low birth weight is associated with higher neonatal
   mortality rates and developmental impairment among survivors. Provision of
   comprehensive prenatal services, trained birth attendants, and backup hospital services for pregnancies at high risk will reduce psychiatric morbidity
   among infants.[50] Researchers have shown that the presence of a supportive
   female companion during labor and delivery significantly reduced the need
   for cesarian section; this simple remedy diminished maternal morbidity on
   an obstetrical service in Guatemala.[51] Where resources permit, newborns
   should be screened for PKU and congenital hypothyroidism.

3. *Immunization.* To protect against brain damage and death, the World Health
   Organization's expanded program of immunization should be extended to
   all infants and children. Reducing morbidity and mortality in childhood will
   in turn enable parents to plan for fewer births because of greater confidence
   their children will survive to adulthood.

4. *Optimal Nutrition.* Deficits in the intake of specific micronutrients, as well
   as in overall protein-calorie intake, can impair brain development, with
   major consequences for cognitive and emotional function.

   Iodine-deficiency disorders (IDD) constitute the most pressing class of
   micronutrient deficiencies that lead to brain malfunction. IDD affects more
   than 400 million people in Asia alone.[52] Clinical manifestations include
   stillbirths, abortions, and congenital anomalies; endemic cretinism, character-

ized by mental deficiency, deaf mutism, spastic diplegia, and other forms of neurologic defect; and impaired mental function associated with goiter. IDD in those at risk can be prevented for 3 to 5 years with one injection of 2 to 4 ml of iodized poppy seed oil, a treatment that can be given by primary care workers. To prevent fetal IDD, iodized oil must be administered before conception; treatment even as early as the first trimester of pregnancy is not fully effective. Oil injections are both feasible and practical as an immediate means to control endemic IDD. For reasons of costs and convenience, the long-term goal must be the introduction of an iodized salt program for the entire population.[53]

High-dose vitamin A supplementation has been shown to reduce mortality and morbidity in children with subclinical nutritional deficiencies.[54] Iron-deficiency anemia leads to impaired cognitive development. Children who had iron deficiency anemia in infancy are at risk for long-lasting developmental disadvantage.[55] Worm infestations retard development, both physical and cognitive. Nineteen out of the 23 major human helminth infections can be treated effectively with one of three drugs taken orally: albendazole, praziquantel, or ivermectin.[56]

The conjunction of chronic malnutrition with disadvantageous family circumstances results in retarded cognitive and social development. Simultaneous biological and social insults multiply the individual negative effects from each and lead to permanent damage.[57] Grantham-McGregor and her colleagues have shown that nutritional rehabilitation plus social stimulation for hospitalized malnourished children, maintained after hospital discharge by parents educated by home visitors, resulted in greater developmental gains than did a program of renourishment alone.[58] Effective remediation must be targeted at the entire complex of social and nutritional deprivation.

Monitoring the growth of young children, a simple method well within local resources, permits the early detection of developmental failure. It is one of the four components of the UNICEF "GOBI" initiative: growth monitoring, oral rehydration, breast feeding, and immunization. Growth monitoring of infants and toddlers is essential if malnutrition is to be intercepted.

5. *Child Safety*. Non-intentional injuries are the leading cause of Years of Potential Life Lost (YPLL) in many countries. YPLL is defined as the number of deaths from a given cause multiplied by the difference in years between age at death and age 65 for each case. The YPLL statistic gives emphasis to conditions that cause death at an early age and ignores conditions that cause death after 65. Vehicular accidents are a major source of head and spinal-cord injuries among survivors. Such injuries are preventable by vigorous enforcement of lower speed limits,[59] by better highway design, traffic regulations, vigorous prosecution of drunk driving, automatic seat belts, child safety seats, and air bags. Bicyclists wearing helmets have an odds ratio for brain injury after accidents of 0.12, compared to those without helmets.[60] Children at special risk for non-intentional injury include those with mental retardation and those subject to epilepsy.

Poisonings in children can be minimized by requiring childproof safety caps on bottles of medication and toxic chemicals for domestic use. The levels of lead in the blood of children can be reduced by effective controls on the lead content of gasoline for motor vehicles. To avoid head injury and consequent brain damage, every country should invest in injury-prevention programs.

6. *Family Support, Home Visiting, and Day Care.* Preservation of child health begins with measures to support family life and to maintain living standards above poverty levels. European countries invest a higher portion of their social resources in sustaining parents and children than does the United States. A program providing pre- and postnatal home visitation, transportation for health care, and sensory and developmental screening is effective in preventing abuse and neglect among children born to socially disadvantaged new mothers.[61] The women visited by nurses made better use of community services, experienced greater social support, improved their diets, and reduced their smoking. Length of gestation and newborn birth weights were improved and there were fewer verified cases of abuse among poor, unmarried teenage mothers.

Children growing up amid deprived circumstances exhibit deficits in cognitive development, lower levels of academic achievement, and increased rates of behavioral and antisocial disorders.[62] These disastrous outcomes can be made less likely through enriched day-care programs that involve parents as active participants. Several long-term outcome studies have demonstrated better occupational history, fewer out-of-wedlock pregnancies, and lower rates of academic and behavioral pathology.[63]

Day-care programs can facilitate the attainment of a second goal: the teaching of parenting skills to adolescents by having them participate in the care of toddlers under supervision. Experience in child care within the family, the traditional way such skills have been transmitted, is becoming ever less available. With smaller family size, fewer children have siblings. With both parents working and more single-parent families, it can no longer be taken for granted that family life education in the home is available to all children. Infants and toddlers in homes at risk (characterized by poverty, low education, unwed teenage mothers, histories of difficulties with older siblings) will benefit from home visiting by nurses at periodic intervals to advise mothers on infant care, monitor the progress of the child, and mobilize additional community services where they are required. Such children will benefit from enriched day-care programs that not only stimulate cognitive development but also serve as a vehicle to teach skills to parents.

7. *School-Based Programs.* Programs to enable children to succeed in school enhance self-esteem and reduce psychopathology. Public schooling provides an opportunity for age-appropriate education about health promotion, human sexuality, and substance abuse. However, program effects gradually dissipate if they are not reinforced in later grades by age-appropriate peer group interaction.[64] Attaching day-care centers and nursery schools to pub-

lic secondary schools will provide a natural "laboratory" for instructing adolescents in parenting skills and at the same time will increase day-care resources for the community.

8. *Mental Health in Primary Care.* Iatrogenic disease resulting from inappropriate prescribing practices can be reduced by training primary health care workers to recognize and manage psychosocial disorders. Such training will not only reduce unnecessary diagnostic studies and inappropriate medication but also make effective mental health care available. Giel and his colleagues have documented the high prevalence of mental disorders in primary child health care in low-income countries.[65] Psychological morbidity is a common accompaniment of chronic physical disease; it often persists into adulthood.[66] A program of combined comprehensive biomedical and psychosocial pediatric home care produces long-term mental health benefits five years later.[67]

9. *Child neglect and abuse*, major problems the world over, demand prompt and effective intervention. Schoolteachers and health care workers can be taught how to recognize neglect and abuse and how to initiate referral to community agencies charged with management. In some instances, visiting homemakers and social workers can help to salvage families as safe places for their children; in others, rapid removal from the home will be essential for the child's very survival, let alone mental health. But that is only the first step. Foster care can suffice in the short term if the child's family of origin can be reconstituted and the child returned to it (for example, when neglect has resulted from an acute family crisis, hospitalization of a parent, eviction from the home, etc.). Foster care is unsatisfactory over the long term. Once it becomes clear that the family is incapable of fulfilling its responsibility, the child should be legally freed for adoption and placed in an adoptive home.

10. The incidence of *epilepsy* can be reduced by better obstetrical care, more-effective accident prevention, and prompt treatment of CNS infections.[68] Greater skills in the recognition of the disorder and the appropriate use of anticonvulsant medication can markedly diminish the prevalence of seizures and the psychosocial handicap of epileptic children.[69]

11. *Teaching mental health principles* to all child health workers will enable earlier recognition and more effective treatment of developmental and behavior problems in young children. The care of children with chronic physical disorders should include measures to prevent psychological morbidity.

Conclusions

• Although there have been substantial improvements in child survival during the past two decades, trends in child mental disorders in both rich and poor countries have worsened. The limited effectiveness of existing child psychiatric treatments as well as their costliness emphasize the strategic importance of prevention through support for family life. Mental health services for children stressing early detection must be integrated into primary health care. Priority should be given to providing services that meet local needs and that are cost effective.

- The prevention of child mental disability is achievable through measures that support the family: birth planning; the provision of prenatal and perinatal care; immunization; the provision of optimal nutrition (in terms of calories, protein, and micronutrients); home visiting and day care; child-safety measures; school-based programs on family life and human sexuality; and appropriate treatment for common childhood neuropsychiatric disorders, such as epilepsy.
- Because the educational system has failed many adolescents and young adults, they are illiterate and vocationally incompetent. The economic future of many countries may rest on developing post-school programs to provide young adults with basic literacy, mathematical, and marketable skills.

8

Women

When the world of policy and public health considers the health of women, one tendency is to first and foremost link the well-being of women to that of children and the family and, at times, to the health of a society. Maternal and child health, or "MCH," has been a common focus for health programs throughout the world; however, these programs have often defined women's health as reproductive health, or even women's *children's* health. Family planning efforts, inspired by the theory that overpopulation is a major impediment to development, have dispensed contraceptives in the interests of reducing fertility, but largely ignored women's needs for information about, and control over, reproductive processes.[1]

Questions about these trends are beginning to be raised as women exercise greater influence over health policy formation. Where is the "M" in MCH programs?[2] What about programs designed to address women's needs as women as well as mothers? Traditional definitions of women's health should be broadened to reach beyond the reproductive and the maternal, incorporating mental and physical health across the life cycle. We need more definitions like the following: "A woman's health is her total well-being, not determined solely by biological factors and reproduction, but also by the effects of workload, nutrition, stress, war, and migration, among others."[3]

Epidemiologic and anthropological data point to different patterns of psychiatric disorder and psychological distress among women than among men. The origins of much of this pain and suffering can be traced to the social circumstances of women's lives. Hopelessness, exhaustion, anger, and fear grow out of hunger, overwork, violence, and economic dependence. Understanding the sources of ill health for women means understanding how cultural and economic forces interact to undermine their social status. If the goal of improving women's well-being from childhood through old age is to be achieved, "healthy" policies aimed at improving the social status of women are needed along with "health policies" targeting the entire spectrum of women's health needs.

Psychiatric Disorder and Psychological Distress in Women

Comparative analysis of empirical studies of mental disorders reveals a consistency across diverse societies and social contexts: symptoms of depression and anxiety as well as unspecified psychiatric disorder and psychological distress are more prevalent among women, whereas substance disorders are more prevalent among men. The disability-adjusted life years data recently tabulated by the World Bank reflect these differences.[4] Depressive disorders account for close to 30% of the disability from neuropsychiatric disorders among women, but only 12.6% of that among men. Conversely, alcohol and drug dependence accounts for 31% of neuropsychiatric disability among men, but accounts for only 7% of the disability among women (see Figure 8.1).

Studies of psychiatric disorders carried out over the past several decades in Africa, Asia, the Middle East, and Latin America have identified gender differences in various regions throughout the world (see Table 8.1). Working in East Africa, for example, Orley et al. assessed the prevalence of psychiatric disorders among 206 Ugandan villagers and found depression to be more widespread among females than males.[5] A decade later, Gureje, Obikoya, and Ikusan found that the prevalence of major depression (as defined by DSM-III-R criteria) was found to be three times higher for women than for men in an urban population from Ibadan, Nigeria.[6] Community surveys of psychiatric disorders carried out over the last twenty years in Brazil consistently reveal higher morbidity in females.

More general studies focusing on psychological distress rather than psychiatric diagnoses reveal a similar pattern. For example, a large-scale community study of the prevalence of mental health problems in Calcutta reveals a higher frequency of "psychoneuroses" in women than in men.[7] Finkler interviewed women and men at a traditional healing site in rural Mexico and found women were more likely than men to report emotional symptoms suggestive of depression.[8]

When assessments of substance disorders are included in prevalence studies, it becomes clear that whereas depression appears more frequently in women, alcohol and drug dependence are more common in men.[9] This has led some to contend that men tend to externalize their suffering through substance abuse and aggressive behavior, resulting in an underreporting of psychological distress. Women, in turn, more often suffer distress in the form of depression, anxiety, "nerves," and the like.

Ethnographic research and case descriptions enrich these quantitative findings, elaborating on the social context of depression, dependency, and hopelessness. Das, for example, recounts events in the life of an Indian woman following the loss of her husband and three sons in a riot, showing how her family's subtle communication of responsibility for the disaster converged with her own guilt to culminate in despair and eventual suicide.[10] Links between economic hardship, child death, emotional deprivation, and psychological distress in women have been traced in anthropological studies in Brazil, Mexico, and Pakistan.[11]

Anthropology also offers an alternative approach to understanding the experience and expression of emotional distress. Complementing an epidemiological or clinical perspective with an ethnographic one, we find psychological pain realized not as "depression" or "anxiety" but in local "idioms of distress"—"nerves," "attacks," "heaviness of the heart," and intrusions by unwanted "spirits." For instance, a generation of ethnographic studies of "nerves" in South and North America, the Mediterranean region, and in Middle Eastern societies consistently shows higher prevalences for females.[12] Careful attention to social and cultural

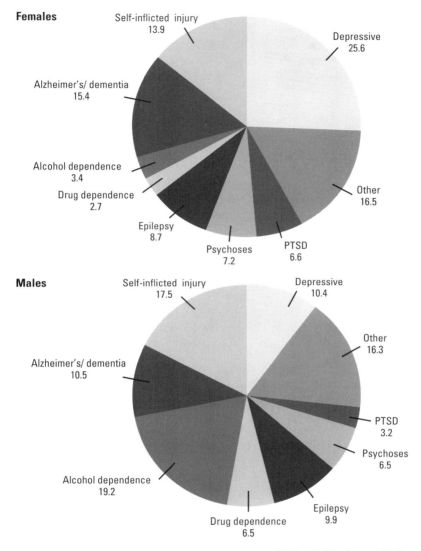

Percentage of DALYs Lost*

Females

Self-inflicted injury
13.9

Depressive
25.6

Alzheimer's/ dementia
15.4

Alcohol dependence
3.4

Drug dependence
2.7

Epilepsy
8.7

Other
16.5

Psychoses
7.2

PTSD
6.6

Males

Self-inflicted injury
17.5

Depressive
10.4

Other
16.3

Alzheimer's/ dementia
10.5

PTSD
3.2

Psychoses
6.5

Alcohol dependence
19.2

Epilepsy
9.9

Drug dependence
6.5

*DALY – Disability Adjusted Life Year

Figure 8.1 Mental Health Problems of Males and Females Worldwide (*Source:* Adapted from the World Bank, 1993)

meanings associated with complaints of nerves often points to power conflicts in families and communities.[13] "Heart distress" has been found to be 2.4 times more common in adult women than in men in an Iranian community, where it served to articulate specific experiences of poverty and confinement and difficulties associated with sexuality and reproduction.[14] The reasons for these observed gender dif-

Table 8.1 Prevalence of Psychiatric Disorder and Psychological Distress for Women

Study	Place	Disorder	Methods	Findings
Orley et al., 1979	Rural Uganda: 2 villages	Major depression	Community survey using present state exam; N = 206	Women: 22.6%; men: 14.3%
Gureje et al., 1992	Ibadan, Nigeria, primary care clinic	Major depression / Dysthymia	Patient survey, Composite International Diagnostic Interview; N = 187	(1) Major depression 3 times higher in women than men; (2) Dysthymia more than twice as high
Ullrich, 1988	Village in Karnataka State, South India, Havik Brahmin women	Major depression	Clinical interview, DSM-III-R criteria; N = 17	59% of widows met criteria for lifetime diagnosis
Ullrich, 1987	Village in Karnataka State, South India, Havik Brahmin women	Major depression	Clinical interview, DSM-III-R criteria; N = 45	55.5% of married and single women met criteria for lifetime diagnosis
Taub, 1992	Rural Mexico, Zapotec Indian women	Major depression	Community survey; N = 40	41% met criteria for lifetime diagnosis
Jablensky, 1993	China, India, Sri Lanka	Schizophrenia	Review of empirical research literature	Higher prevalence for women in 3 of 4 studies
Chakraborty, 1990	Calcutta, India	Psychological distress	Community survey; N = 13,335	Higher frequency in women
Finkler, 1985	Rural Mexico, patients seeking treatment from spiritual healers and physicians	Psychological and somatic distress; N = 879	Cornell Medical Index, socioeconomic interview, anthropological techniques	Women more likely than men to report emotional symptoms suggesting depression at spiritualist healing sites
Santana, 1982	Urban Bahia, Brazil	Psychiatric disorders	Community survey, 2-stage cluster sampling, ICD-8 criteria; N = 1549	Significantly higher overall morbidity in women, mainly "neurotic and psychosomatic disorders." Women: 21%; men: 8%
Barbosa and Almeida-Filho, 1986	Rural Bahia, Brazil, 4 neighboring villages	Anxiety disorders	Community survey; N = 1006	Prevalence 2.2 times greater in women
Mari, 1987	São Paulo, Brazil	Minor psychiatric morbidity	Survey, primary care clinic	Higher proportion of females with minor psychiatric morbidity
Almeida-Filho, 1993	São Paulo, Brasília, Porto Alegre, Brazil	Psychiatric disorders	Community survey, 2-stage cluster sampling; N = 6471	Higher prevalence of nonpsychotic disorders in women

ferences are unclear. Further research is needed to determine whether women tend to fall ill more frequently than men or fall ill in different ways.

The same questions apply to spirit possession. The vast worldwide literature on this phenomenon is connected by at least one common thread. Although both men and women may be possessed by unwanted, intrusive spirits, women in various cultures become "possessed" more frequently than men.[15] The classic ethnographic work of I. M. Lewis details both the conditions that give rise to spirit possession and its function as a legitimate mode of resistance. He reports that among Somalis he studied:

> The stock epidemiological situation is that of the hard-pressed wife struggling to survive and feed her children in the harsh environment, and liable to some degree of neglect, real or imagined, on the part of her husband. Subjected to frequent, sudden, and even prolonged absences by her husband as he pursues his manly pastoral interests and affairs, to the jealousies and tensions of polygamy here not ventilated in accusations of sorcery or witchcraft, and always menaced by the precariousness of marriage in a society where divorce is frequent and particularly easily obtained by men, the Somali married woman's lot offers little stability or security.[16]

Possession is more than passive suffering in face of oppressive conditions; it is also a form of power. For Lewis, spirit possession is a means by which "women and other depressed categories exert mystical pressures on their superiors in circumstances of deprivation and frustration when few other sanctions are available to them."[17] That is to say, possessed women are authorized by their experience of possession to voice criticism and demand retribution that is denied to them in everyday life.[18] While this may be true, the anthropologist Bruce Kapferer has pointed out that in places like Sri Lanka, women suffer from spirit possession more than men because that is the way they are supposed to fall ill.[19]

Social Origins of Distress

Social science, epidemiologic, and clinical research confirm that multiple forces contribute to women's psychological and psychiatric distress. To assemble these factors into a coherent theoretical account of women's suffering is one of the next challenges to be confronted. Table 8.2 presents, on a study-by-study basis, proposed explanations of observed gender differences in psychiatric morbidity. A review of these interpretations points to several themes, which, when taken together, illuminate the quality of women's lives. Poverty, domestic isolation, powerlessness (resulting, for example, from low levels of education and economic dependence), and patriarchal oppression, are all associated with higher prevalence of psychiatric morbidity (exclusive of substance disorder) in women. In short, a considerable body of evidence points to the social origins of psychological distress for women.[20]

In developing this basic proposition, and taking account of the many dimensions it involves, it is helpful to consider in turn several specific issues that have their roots in women's powerlessness and inequality and their consequences in the suffering of everyday life, such as hunger, work, and sexual, reproductive, and domestic violence.

Table 8.2 Social Origins of Gender Differences in Psychiatric Morbidity

Study	Country & Population	Disorder	Social Origins
Ullrich 1987, 1988	India; Havik Brahmin women	Major depression	Hypothesized explanation: devaluation of women's needs and abilities; dependency of women hypothesized explanation with depression
WHO, 1992a	World survey	Substance abuse	Hypothesized explanation: unequal social status; marital stress; isolation of domesticity
Almeida-Filho, 1993	São Paulo, Brasília, Porto Alegre, Brazil, community sample	Nonpsychotic Disorders	Housewife role shown to be risk factor for psychiatric morbidity; interaction with marital status, education, and occupation
Mari, 1987	São Paulo, Brazil, primary care clinic patients	Minor psychiatric morbidity	Housing conditions, living quarters shared with nonfamily, associated with distress
Reichenheim, 1988	Rio de Janeiro, Brazil, mothers of young children in squatter settlement	Depression, anxiety and "psychosomatic" symptoms	Low income, poor housing, low education, associated with psychiatric morbidity
Finkler, 1985	Rural Mexico, patients seeking treatment from physicians and spiritualist healers	Psychological and somatic distress	Hypothesized explanation: socioeconomic deprivation, child death and associated feelings of responsibility
Mari et al., 1993	São Paulo, Brazil, community sample from 3 urban areas	Psychotropic pharmaceutical drugs (tranquilizers)	Higher rate of psychotropic drug use for women; women take more tranquilizers than men
Naeem, 1992	Karachi, Pakistan, female psychiatry outpatients	Depression	Lack of intimate, confiding, relationship with husband
Brown and Harris, 1978	London suburb, working-class and middle-class women	Depression	Class differences in depression (23% versus 6%) explained by four vulnerability factors: loss of parent; three or more children at home; lack of confiding, intimate relationship; unemployment
Pearlin and Johnson, 1977; Radloff, 1975	Community surveys	Depression	Poverty and responsibilities for young children
Hall et al., 1985	Survey low-income mothers	Depression	Single-parent status and unemployment associated with symptom severity

Hunger

Nancy Scheper-Hughes, an anthropologist working in Brazil, interprets women's complaints of "nervousness" less as symptomatic of psychological distress and more as an expression of chronic hunger and hunger anxiety.[21] Throughout the world, nutritional, physical, and environmental deprivations suffered by female children and adults threaten women's well-being. Where there is scarcity, and where females are dependent on and less valued than males, women are more likely to suffer malnutrition and clinical anemia, even when they are not pregnant.

The World Health Organization estimates that more than 60% of women in "developing countries" are undernourished.[22] Other recent reports offer as a conservative estimate the figure of 500 million (out of 1.1 billion) women living in poor countries in 1985 who were stunted as a result of protein-energy malnutrition in childhood.[23]

Nearly two-thirds of pregnant women in Africa and Southern and Western Asia, and half of those who are not pregnant, are believed to be clinically anemic.[24] The prevalence of anemia in sub-Saharan Africa is increasing. More than a third of non-pregnant women of reproductive age living in this region were estimated to be anemic in the mid-1970s to 1980s. By the late 1980s this estimate had grown to almost half. Ten to twenty percent of deaths in childbirth in sub-Saharan Africa have been attributed to anemia.

The results of empirical research carried out in Asia provide evidence of sex differences in nutritional status. In analyzing anthropometric data from a sample of 882 children in Bangladesh, Lincoln Chen and his colleagues found malnutrition to be markedly higher among girls.[25] A comparison of daily energy expended with estimates of calorie intake among adults in rural Karnataka state, India, revealed a calorie deficit for women but a surplus for men.[26] Systematic sex bias in child nutrition was also found in a study of two villages in West Bengal, where girls under five were more likely than boys to be malnourished[27] (see Table 8.3).

Scarcity leads not only to malnutrition and illness but even, indirectly, to female deaths. Over half of 1,250 women surveyed in Madras, India, reported killing an infant daughter.[28] "In a rural village in the Indian state of Tamil Nadu," Anderson and Moore write, "a woman explains why she killed two of her infant daughters by forcing them to swallow scalding chicken soup. 'I have two living daughters already,' she says, 'and no land and no salary. My mother-in-law and father-in-law are both bedridden, and my husband met with an accident and cannot work. I need a boy. Even though I have to buy food and clothes for a son, he will grow on his own and take care of himself. I don't have to buy him jewelry or give him a 10,000-rupee dowry.'"

Work

Work contributes to mental health.[29] The ability to earn income in the informal economy, in the agricultural sector, or in wage-paying jobs can help women increase their independence and maintain self-esteem. Control over financial

Table 8.3 The Effects of Hunger on Women's Well-being

Study	Country & Population	Findings
WHO press release, 1993d	Estimates from developing countries	60% women are undernourished; anemia, protein-energy malnutrition most prevalent in females
UN, 1991d	Africa and Southern and Western Asia, estimates	Clinical anemia: two-thirds pregnant women, 50% nonpregnant women
Amazigo, Institute of Medicine Report, forthcoming	Sub-Saharan Africa	Anemia: 46% nonpregnant women, reproductive age; 10% to 20% of deaths in childbirth are attributed to anemia
Amazigo, Institute of Medicine Report, 1994, forthcoming	Sub-Saharan Africa	Body Mass Index less than 18.5; approximately 20% women underweight
Chen et al., 1981	Bangladesh; 882 children	Malnutrition markedly higher among girls and associated with morbidity and mortality
Sen and Sengupta, 1983	India: West Bengal villages; children	Girls under five more likely to be malnourished
Batliwala, 1983	Karnataka State, India	Calorie deficit for women, surplus for men

resources enables women to manage household affairs and provide for their children without the support or cooperation of male partners, if necessary. Having money also means escape is possible if life within the household becomes intolerable.

Much of the work available to women is poorly paid and labor intensive, however. Working conditions are often dangerous and benefits nonexistent. Under these circumstances, work contributes to oppression rather than independence.

Typically, women contribute to the economic support of the household while also retaining full responsibility for domestic chores, child care, and the care of aging relatives (see Box 8.1). Women, then, work a "double day" performing multiple roles. This means that they spend many more hours working than men from the same social class. For example, time-allocation studies show that when housework and child care are considered, women in Africa work an average of 67 hours per

---

Box 8.1 A Day in the Life of a Kenya Woman

Wanja wakes up at around five in the morning. It is still dark and only the sounds of the earliest birds break the silence around this hilly area in Central Province, Kenya.

Wanja lights a paraffin lamp, brings out firewood from the storage just above the fireplace, splits it into small pieces, and builds a fire. As the water for washing the cows' teats warms, she sweeps the kitchen. Today is a coffee-picking day and some casual workers will be arriving soon to pick her family's coffee for wages.

She fetches the dairy meal for the cows to feed on while she does the milking. She carries the steaming water, the milking cans, the dairy meal and the lantern, and walks to the cowshed. After milking the two cows, she feeds the calves and places the twelve-liter milk can in a large container ready to be carried on her back to the Dairy Cooperative Society offices, three kilometers away.

It is getting light, and she can now see a few meters away without the help of the paraffin lantern. Back in the kitchen she places a large bowl of water on the fireplace to warm for her husband's bath, and prepares porridge from sorghum and millet flour, and tea with the milk boiled the night before. She empties the hot water into a bucket, carries it to the bathroom outside the house, and calls her husband to get up and take his bath. She feeds the chicken and cuts up fodder for the cows.

Soon it is time to help the younger children to wash their faces and dress in their school uniforms. Wanja serves porridge and tea, and packs the food left over from the night before for the children's lunch. Her husband, who is the head teacher in the local primary school, does not carry food. He will order roast meat and ugali and share with other teachers at school. He rides a bicycle to school. The children walk with friends.

Today Wanja must take her milk to the dairy early in order to prepare for coffee picking. She carries the milk on her back and walks with the children, since the dairy is in the same direction as the school.

At around seven in the morning, she is back from delivering the milk. She washes the breakfast dishes and the milking cans and piles them on the drying rack outside her kitchen. She has to fetch water from the river just down the valley. About six twenty-liter jerry cans will fill the drum to provide enough water for the two cows, the chicken, and for domestic use. Wanja counts herself lucky that the river passes less than a kilometer below her home. Some women walk much farther to get water. Since the slope to the river is steep, the cows cannot go down to the river to drink.

She prepares dry maize and beans and puts it on the fire in a big earthen pot. This food will be for both lunch and dinner. It takes several hours to cook and requires a lot of firewood. She splits more firewood and rekindles the fire in between trips to the river.

When the coffee pickers arrive, Wanja gives them baskets and gunny bags and takes them to the coffee plantation nearby. When they begin work, she goes back to fetching water. By eleven, the drum of water is full. She waters the cows and the chicken, rekindles the fire, and joins the coffee pickers. This exercise continues until about three in the afternoon, when they must take all the coffee beans home, spread them on a big plastic sheet, sort them out, and divide them into small loads to be carried to the factory, located three kilometers away.

Wanja feeds the coffee pickers and pays them their daily wages before they depart for the coffee factory. She lines up with other farmers to get her coffee weighed and get recorded on her card. At six in the evening she returns home, warms the water, and milks the cows again. She measures the milk into bottles to sell to her neighbors and boils the rest for domestic consumption.

She fetches vegetables from the shamba, peels potatoes, and mixes them with the maize and beans boiled earlier. She warms more water and helps the children to wash themselves. She serves the food and washes the dishes. She lights the charcoal iron and presses her husband's shirts. As the children do their homework, she sorts the eggs for the market the following day.

She takes her handicraft to the women's self-help project and works on it for two hours before retiring at eleven in the night. This is a regular day in Wanja's life, about nineteen hours of work.[31]

week, compared to men's 54 hours. In the Philippines, women's average work week is 70 hours; men's, 57 hours. Data from the International Labour Organization indicate that, in general, women living in rural areas of poor countries routinely work 12 to 16 hours per day.[30]

Women express the effects of the burden of work in many different ways; the language of "nerves" is one. Maria das Dores, who lives in a remote village in the poor state of Pernambuco, Northeast Brazil, speaks for many. "I'm very nervous," she apologizes to a visitor. "When my nerves get really bad, I cry a little and it helps." She takes Valium to ease her nighttime worries about getting water, which must be fetched from many miles away. Others refer to lack of rest. Sixty-two-year-old Izabel Maria do Nascimento of Pernambuco, Northeast Brazil, comments: "I can honestly say I've never had a day's rest in my life."[32] On the other side of the world, researchers from the Center for Science and the Environment in New Delhi conclude from their study of rural women's lives in a Himalayan village: "It doesn't matter if a woman is young or old or pregnant, she has no rest, Sunday or otherwise."[33]

Sexual and Reproductive Violence

On July 13, 1991, at St. Kizito's boarding school near Nairobi, Kenya, male students organized a strike in protest over fees. When girls at the school declined to take part, the boys attacked them. Seventy-one girls were raped; nineteen were crushed to death. The school's deputy principal deplored the deaths, explaining that "the boys never meant any harm against the girls; they just wanted to rape them."[34]

Although this brief story hardly captures the complexity of the event, this comment epitomizes an attitude toward rape that is widespread throughout the world, especially in situations of societal breakdown and political violence. Rape is a masculine prerogative, an act of violence in which women figure not as victims but as objects. Women are either regarded as a form of property, such that anger and frustration may be vented upon their bodies with impunity, or they serve a sordid instrumental function, a means of enabling men to commit offenses against other men.

Thus, throughout history, rape has been part of war and civil strife. Recent events in Mozambique, Bosnia, Somalia, South Africa, and El Salvador present us with all too many cases of systematic and repeated rape of civilian and refugee women in this context. One indication of how widespread such assaults on refugee women are comes from investigations by the United Nations of crimes against Vietnamese boat people: 39% of women had been abducted or raped by pirates while at sea.[35] Forcible impregnation by aggressors also inscribes political domination and civil strife upon the bodies of women. Sharp increases in reported rape have appeared in Bangladesh, India, Malaysia, and South Africa.[36] Estimates for South Africa in 1988 placed the prevalence of rape at 34 per 1,000 women.[37] The personal sequelae of rape may include emotional trauma, depression, pregnancy (which in many poor countries may not be terminated safely), sexually transmitted disease such as HIV, and death.

The psychological consequences of rape in societies where a young woman's worth is equated with her virginity are particularly ruinous. A study of rape survivors in Bangladesh showed that rape led to psychiatric disorders, severe injury, or death in 84% of the sample.[38] A recent report on causes of death among rural Bangladeshi women points out that women who are raped are "socially wasted. Their ruined reputation cannot be amended. . . . A pre-marital sexual relation is said to spoil something intrinsic in their physical and moral person."[39] In Fiji, the Philippines, Thailand, Mexico, and Peru, women who have been raped are forced, at times, to marry their rapist in order to legitimate the action and erase the stigma of "spoiled goods."[40]

The stigma of "spoilage" may lead women to turn to prostitution to survive; others choose suicide. Such sequences of events occur generally in cultural settings where enormous social value is placed on women's virginity at marriage and where women are held responsible when their virginity is lost. Community and family responses to rape under these circumstances tend to focus on repairing family honor. This leads frequently to blaming the victim rather than punishing the perpetrator. Criminalization of the rape victim is an extreme form of this. In 1979, for example, legislation was passed in Pakistan that eliminated the distinction between rape and adultery; hence in a recent case involving a young woman's rape by a married neighbor, encouragement by police to press charges resulted in the victim's being jailed for adultery, while the rapist paid a minor fine and went free.[41] Women, so publicly despoiled, may even be killed by male family members to cleanse the family honor.

A comprehensive discussion of violence against women must consider involuntary prostitution, or "female sexual slavery."[42] Involuntary prostitution has a long history. In its present form, it involves the abduction of women under false pretenses with promises of marriage or a job. Recently, such entrapment has been especially widespread in the Philippines, Thailand, Nepal, Burma, and India, where women are transported to wealthy countries or distant cities in their own countries. Upon arriving at their destination they are sold to bars or brothels and required to provide sexual services for clients. If they resist, they are beaten or raped; reprisals may also be initiated against their families. There is little chance for escape, since the victims are forced to turn over money earned as repayment of "debts" owed their new "bosses" for plane fare, food, clothes, and even their "purchase price." The future and options for livelihood are bleak at career's end, when sexual slaves are no longer attractive to customers (see Box 8.2).[43]

Sexually transmitted diseases, including AIDS, may be viewed as a form of violence against women as a result of lack of control over their sexuality. African women, for example, are often not in a position to refuse sexual relations, and they are dependent on their partner for protection from disease through condom use.[45] If a marriage is polygamous, or the husband has taken an "outside wife" or is otherwise sexually active, the risk of disease transmission is increased. Wives are typically blamed by their husbands when they become infected, though in most cases married women acquire STDs from their spouses. Some women are devising strategies to protect themselves; in East Africa, older women with children have succeeded in avoiding a spouse they suspect is infected by surrounding themselves with their children.

Box 8.2 The Trafficking of Women in Asia

Maria, a 24-year-old Filipina, arrived in Japan in 1986. Expecting to work as a waitress, she was soon forced into sexual slavery. When she escaped five months later with two other women and found a job in another city as a bar hostess, she had an affair with a Japanese man, who was abusive to her. Less than a month after giving birth to their son, she became depressed and anorexic. Because she was an undocumented alien, her child would be stateless unless she remained with this man and he acknowledged his paternity; at that, the documentation could take years.

Maria felt she had nowhere to go. She remained addicted to a "cold medicine," which she had used in large quantities when doing sex work. Dissociative episodes began to occur: she would let out a bloodcurdling scream, her body would tense up, her eyes would open wide and move back and forth. She felt herself surrounded by strange men, all jeering at her, and the scariest face of all would turn into her boyfriend's face. These episodes happened several times a week; unable to pay any hospital bills, she hesitated to seek medical care. She has now returned to her family home. "The sickness has not gone away yet," she writes. "I wonder if I will ever be happy."

Trafficking in women like Maria is profitable, and the penalties are far less than dealing with drugs. This highly developed system of trafficking and sexual slavery ensures a steady source of sexual labor, which is inexpensive and easily controlled. The system has historical precedents in Asia, including the recruitment of impoverished Japanese women to engage in sex work in Japanese outposts in Asia in the prewar era, as well as the Taiwanese and Korean "comfort women" seized from occupied territories to service the Japanese soldiers. In the 1970s, because of shifts in organized-crime relations, improved status of living in Korea and Taiwan, inexpensive sex tours to Bangkok and Manila, and the relative ease with which visas could be obtained, the Philippines became the principal recruiting site. Thailand is now the primary source, with perhaps as many as 50,000 Thai women workers in Japan.

The marketing of women to Japan has developed into an elaborate system. Women are generally recruited from their villages. Most hope to make enough money to support their families, whether to pay off loans, help finance a sibling's education, or purchase a home. While some know that they will be engaging in sex work, most are told that they will be waitressing or working in a factory. A recruiter brings the women to Japan and delivers them to gangsters, who take their money and passports away. The women are then distributed to shops, where the owners inform each woman that she owes about $40,000 in loans, which is to be paid back by performing sex work, requiring at least a year of indentured servitude. Such "loans" are considered illegal according to the labor laws, as is failure to pay a salary, but enforcement is minimal. The women, unaware of their legal rights, may resign themselves to working until they are "free."

The women are threatened verbally and physically if they appear reticent to work, even when they are menstruating. The owners threaten to hurt the woman's family if she tries to escape. The woman are usually housed in a single-room apartment, are brought to a shop (usually a bar) in the evenings where they are expected to "hostess," and then go to a hotel with a customer. Women who have escaped tell stories of verbal threats, physical abuse (by owners and customers), starvation, rape, druggings, and murders. One woman described being forced to watch as the owner cut off a breast and an ear from a woman who unsuccessfully tried to escape. The stakes are extremely high, but, as one woman said, "I would rather die trying to escape than die there continuing to do that."

Although feminist groups in Thailand, the Philippines, and Japan have spoken out against the trafficking in women (to Japan and Europe in particular), little official action has been taken to protect women migrant workers in Japan. The mental health consequences of such systems of sexual slavery are obvious. The women, who lack the means to protect themselves, are also at high risk for contracting HIV and other diseases.

To stop the trafficking in women requires confronting violence against women, gender inequalities, and the political economy that makes it a profitable business. There needs to be better enforcement of existing labor laws. As things currently stand, women are most often the ones penalized, while the owners and recruiters are simply reprimanded or handed minimal fines. Along with stricter curtailment of organized-crime activities, the Japanese government must openly acknowledge and accept the presence and importance of migrant workers in Japanese society, which means more-concerted efforts at job training and better job security. Finally, international condemnation of the human rights abuses against women migrant workers in Japan is imperative.[44]

Untreated sexually transmitted diseases are widespread among women throughout the world, and the consequences are very serious. Pelvic inflammatory disease (PID) may cause infertility, ectopic pregnancy, and low birth weight or fetal death. Childlessness, whether due to infertility or problems in pregnancy, is devastating for African women for example, whose social status is in large part dependent on their demonstrated ability to produce offspring. The rampant spread of HIV infection in Africa is, or course, well recognized.

Violence against women may originate in planned state policies or symbolic cultural practices with long-standing traditions. Involuntary abortions, forced sterilizations, and female circumcision (or genital mutilation) are among the sanctioned societal practices that may be viewed as forms of reproductive violence against women.

In China, involuntary abortions have been used to enforce the "one-child" policy. In the early 1980s, local officials, held responsible by their superiors in the central bureaucracy for meeting population targets, relied on persuasion, then "mobilization," to keep women from exceeding birth quotas. "Mobilization" was a euphemism for coercion. Women with unauthorized pregnancies were sequestered until they agreed to abortions or were arrested for the "offense" of pregnancy and then required to undergo the procedure.[46]

A recent report suggests that forced abortions are now being replaced by involuntary sterilization as the method of choice for enforcing birth quotas. The number of people sterilized in China increased by 25% in 1991, the year in which the second wave of strict enforcement efforts began.[47] Those who do not conform face stiff fines, confiscation of valuable goods, or destruction of their homes.[48]

Accumulating evidence also indicates that amniocentesis and ultrasound examination are increasingly being used as a means of determining the sex of a fetus for purposes of selective abortion. The Indian government reports that of 8,000 abortions performed at a clinic in Bombay, 7,999 involved female fetuses.[49] Until forced by public protest to desist, "sex selection" clinics in India advertised their services by declaring openly that "it is better to spend $38 now on terminating a girl than to have to spend $3,800 later on her dowry."[50] A *New York Times* report on China's recent "crackdown" on births quotes a prominent Chinese demographer as stating that one of several factors contributing to that country's 900,000 "missing girls" each year is the growing use of ultrasound equipment in Chinese hospitals. Patients learn the sex of their unborn child from the attending physician and, not wishing, or daring, to "waste" their allotted quota of children by delivering a girl, decide to abort the fetus and "start again."[51]

One of the most highly contested cultural traditions is female circumcision or "female genital mutilation," performed by mothers and adult women upon female children as part of ritual initiation into the status of womanhood. Countries where the practice continues to be found are clustered in sub-Saharan (Nilotic) Africa, but also include Egypt, United Arab Emirates, Bahrain, Oman, Indonesia, South Yemen, Pakistan, Malaysia, and some parts of Russia. The extent of circumcisions varies from culture to culture and class to class, and ranges from removal of the tip of the clitoris to infibulation, in which the entire clitoris and labia minora, together with parts of the labia majora, are removed and the remaining tissues sewn together, leaving only a small opening for urine and menstrual blood to pass through.[52]

Negative health consequences of circumcision range from high rates of infection (urinary tract infections, greater risk of transmission of the HIV virus) to vaginal tearing, fistulas, and damage to the vagina and urinary tract during childbirth and sexual intercourse. In light of this, public health departments and women's movements have recently sought ways to curtail the practice, and have brought about changes at both local and international levels. While the health risks are undeniable, the consequences of ending circumcision for women's overall well-being are uncertain. In many places, circumcision is the standard way of preparing for marriage and adult status. Still, women from Egypt, India, Kenya, and elsewhere, who were themselves circumcised, are beginning to question the policy and to develop alternative ways for their daughters to be initiated into womanhood. In countries where female circumcision is practiced, educated women especially recognize the potential serious health problems circumcision can cause.

Domestic Violence

Domestic violence—behavior intended to physically harm an intimate partner—occurs most often in private household settings. Although it is by no means just a

Box 8.3　Domestic Violence in Mexico

Domestic violence worldwide has reached epidemic proportions. It cuts a wide swath through different countries, cultures, classes, and economic backgrounds. In Mexico, one survey indicates that 61% of Mexican housewives are physically abused by their husbands or partners. In a small survey in an exurb of Mexico City, one in five women reported blows to the stomach during pregnancy. These statistics underrepresent the true picture. Complex and multidetermined reasons prevent women from reporting abuse, reasons such as bias against women, an unresponsive legal system, and a health care system unprepared to cope with the unique traumas of domestic violence.

Anselma, at 53, lives with her ten children and one grandchild in a cinder-block house near a large garbage heap. She left her husband after twenty-five years of marriage and twenty-five years of physical abuse. Anselma, who was at one time proud of her good health, now complains of "a pain in her heart" and "fright" and is subject to bouts of shivering and ringing in her ears. Doctors have been unable to identify the pain; they have been able to diagnose, over the years, a number of other ailments, including high blood pressure. Anselma also cannot move the fingers in her hands, because her husband some time ago cut the nerves with a knife. Fear of his retaliation prevented her from leaving before.

"People told me to leave him. I was all swollen from the beating. He used to grab me and beat me as if I were a man. . . . He pursued me relentlessly. When he didn't like something, he poured water over me. He kicked me. I washed and sewed daily to maintain my children. I never had any rest. He was like that from the time we married. When we lived together, he never left me in peace. I could not speak to him, he always got angry and drunk. There were fights daily."

Anselma returned to her own parents for a year when the abuse became too much to bear, but went back to her husband and their home in Mexico City when her health improved. As the primary wage earner for her children, fearing poverty, fearing prison, fearing repercussions from her husband, fearing social stigma, fearing her marital obligations, and lacking any other resources, she remained in the marriage.

Only when a doctor assured her she would not go to jail for abandonment did she take action. "I hemorrhaged all the time I was married. The doctor insisted that I leave my husband because otherwise I would not recover and that I may even get cancer. When I left him, I got well and the doctor recommended that I don't live with him. I didn't leave him until the doctor told me I should, because I was afraid he would accuse me of abandonment."

Anselma's story is typical: fear of what might happen if she left and no knowledge of support services left her with no other option but to stay.

Recent initiatives in Mexico demonstrate what can be accomplished and how much more needs to be done. Public-sector agencies and Mexican feminist organizations have brought more awareness to the issue of rape and domestic violence through public education, direct political lobbying, publication of statistics, and direct services. Initially, the focus of these initiatives was on rape victims and resulted in the establishment of a rape crisis center in 1979. However, services have expanded for domestic violence to include legal training programs and battered women's organizations.

In 1988, the head of the Commission on Violence, centered in Mexico City, established "specialized agencies" that offered integrated legal, medical, and psychological care to rape victims. There are plans to expand these agencies to assist victims of family violence and to extend them to other Mexican state capitals. Other significant actions included the 1990 reform of laws regarding rape and battering, calling for more stringent penalties.

Policies and programs in other countries are frequently used as models for Mexican initiatives and then tailored to fit the needs and situations there. Given the pervasiveness of domestic violence, Mexico's actions barely reach those in distress. Much more is needed for substantial change. Further actions must include epidemiological research, the expansion of services (particularly to rural areas and smaller cities), the training of medical personnel, and increased support from local and national governments and international agencies. Above all, social changes are needed that promote the status of women and lead to the recognition that family violence is unlawful and unacceptable.[53]

"women's issue," the vast majority of victims of domestic violence are women. The private nature of this form of violence—the shame, guilt, and social taboos associated with it—means that much remains hidden, not only from the public, but from family, friends, and health care practitioners. This makes accurate information on the prevalence of domestic violence difficult to obtain.

Despite this, it is estimated that domestic violence and rape account for approximately 5% of the global health burden for women in the reproductive years.[54] Severe and ongoing domestic violence has been documented in almost every country in the past decade. Table 8.4 presents an overview of findings from selected recent studies.

Although detailed epidemiological data linking psychiatric disorders with domestic violence is scant for most regions, research from North America points to the power of the association. A recent study found that battered women are four to five times more likely to require psychiatric treatment and five times more likely to attempt suicide than nonbattered women.[55] Other research links major depression, alcohol and drug dependency, and post-traumatic stress syndromes with a history of abuse and domestic violence.[56] Ethnographic data from Oceania, South America, and China corroborate these associations with evidence that wife beating is directly related to depression and suicide.[57]

Domestic violence resulting in death deserves special mention here. Of particular concern, due to their apparent recent increase, are "dowry death" or "bride-burning" in India and female infanticide in India and China.

Traditionally, dowry was a Hindu practice that made it possible for parents to confer wealth upon their daughters, who were not allowed to inherit property. In recent years, however, it has developed into a form of exploitation in which the relatives of married sons demand large sums in material goods from the families of their daughters-in-law, sometimes continuing for years after the marriage has taken place. If the required wealth is not forthcoming, the situation may end in death. A woman may either be murdered by her in-laws or commit suicide herself. The most

Table 8.4 Violence Against Women

Source	Place, Population	Findings
Sonali, 1990	Sri Lanka	60% of a random sample of women from a low-income neighborhood had been beaten
Stewart, 1989	Bangladesh	Husbands killing their wives account for 50% of all murders
Toft, 1986	Papua New Guinea	Survey data reveal 60% of rural women "beaten"; 56% urban low-income women "beaten"; 62% urban elite women "beaten"
Valdez and Shrader-Cox, 1991	Nezahualcoyotl, Mexico	Survey showed 1 in 3 women were victims of family violence; 20% reported blows to the stomach during pregnancy
World Bank, 1993a	Thailand	50% of women living in Bangkok's largest slum are beaten regularly

common form of dowry death is by burning. "Cooking accidents," in which women die from ignited kerosene, are so commonly recognized to be dowry deaths that the term is routinely used as a euphemism by women's groups attempting to combat the practice.[58] Yet these deaths are rarely prosecuted, despite the existence of laws designed to protect women from harassment and abuse.

India had 999 registered cases of dowry death in 1985, 1,319 in 1986, 1,786 in 1987, and 5,157 in 1991.[59] However, women's groups argue that these deaths are grossly underreported. In 1990, 4,835 cases were officially recorded; a local women's organization estimated that 1,000 women burn to death in "cooking accidents" every year in the state of Gujarat alone.[60]

Female infanticide (which must be distinguished from sex-selective abortion) has been reported to be increasing in parts of Asia over the past decade. A flurry of media and government reports appeared in China in the early 1980s documenting resurgence of the practice and attributing it to the remnants of feudal ideology.[61] As noted above, a recent study carried out by the Community Services Guild in Madras, India, indicated that of 1,250 women surveyed, more than half had at some time killed a baby daughter.[62]

While female infanticide is widely recognized to be an extreme abuse of women, it is important as well to acknowledge the effects of this practice on the mental health of mothers and other family members. Mothers are not without feelings of grief but rather are forced by family pressures and agonizing circumstances to make desperate moral choices. These choices are neither forgotten nor made without remorse. Infanticide can be viewed as a routine form of domestic violence in which females are, in two senses, victims.

The Downside of Development

Women have always been economically productive. Until recently, however, their contributions have been rendered largely invisible by assessment procedures that underestimate or ignore the work women do and the goods they produce. Definitions of economic goods and services that exclude all those that are not income-generating, and measures of labor force participation that define participation in terms of paid wages or "principal occupation" (even women who earn wages often report their principal occupation as "housewife"), systematically discount a set of economic activities that, if adequately represented in national accounting, would raise estimated global output by at least 25% to 30%.[63] Failure to recognize women's productive roles is one reason that, generally speaking, their needs have yet to be satisfactorily addressed by those who plan and implement development policies.

Formal acknowledgment of the importance of women's roles for achieving economic development came with the 1973 Percy Amendment to the U.S. Foreign Assistance Act, which called for their full integration into all subsequent development projects. At the time, development policy tended to focus on improving the lives of poor people through direct interventions aimed at meeting basic needs while at the same time attacking what was considered to be the primary cause of poverty: overpopulation. As principal suppliers of basic needs, and the social actors most directly responsible for shaping population trends, women became the recipients of welfare programs that focused, for example, on maternal and child health and family planning. In turn, projects designed to alleviate poverty through significant increases in income and economic productivity tended to be reserved for men.[64] Although well-intended, the effect of many such initiatives has been to render women poorer, more marginal, and more dependent (see Box 8.4).

Box 8.4 Women and Development

The Mahaweli River Development Scheme in Sri Lanka, funded by the World Bank, combines two approaches to agricultural development—cash cropping and resettlement. The centerpiece of an effort to make Sri Lanka self-sufficient in rice production, the project involved irrigating large portions of the dry zone of the country with water from the Mahaweli River by constructing a massive dam. The some 645,000 acres of newly arable land would be cultivated by approximately 1.5 million settlers organized into nuclear family units and required to run their farms according to instructions from the government. Each family was allocated 2.5 acres of paddy land on which to grow rice, and a half-acre homestead with which to provide food for domestic consumption by the family.

The project transformed relations between the sexes in a number of ways. Traditional Sinhalese custom dictates that sons and daughters inherit equal shares of land and other properties. To preclude fragmentation of land plots in the Mahaweli Scheme, however, special legislation was passed requiring that only one child inherit the family farm. Because paddy rice cultivation is defined as a male responsibility, the single heir was almost always a son.

The Mahaweli project also radically reorganized gender roles in the division of labor. Accustomed to working alongside men in the slash-and-burn system of agriculture that served to complement rice paddy cultivation in the predevelopment era, women now found themselves relegated to the home, where they were encouraged to improve their knowledge of health and nutrition, and their skills in needlework, animal-raising, and ironically, "home gardening," by attending courses at the "Home Development Center" established by the project. The driving force behind this arrangement was a "male-as-breadwinner; female-as-wife-and-mother" gender ideology imposed on the project by the Western developers. Critics of the model call this process "housewifization."

This is the way the project "developed" for women. Only a few men were actually able to earn enough to support their families. Thus, rather than devoting all their time to domestic pursuits, most women worked all day as unpaid agricultural laborers in their husband's rice paddies, then came home to confront their responsibilities as "housewive"—food preparation, cooking, cleaning, and child care. Instead of learning needlework and nutrition, women were working a double day.

Even so, rice production for most settler families was insufficient to cover the costs of food and agricultural supplies. Economic conditions in the country worsened, the price of rice increased, male "breadwinners" could not be counted on to use all of their earnings to provide for their families, and women, now with almost no land at their disposal, had no means of alleviating the situation by growing food. The result was hunger and malnutrition at the center of an economy founded on the production of food. While the Mahaweli River Project was also flawed in other ways, its devastating effect on women could have been avoided had the developers been able to transcend Western ideologies prescribing domesticity for women, and leave local gender divisions of labor intact.[65]

The decollectivization of agriculture in China, which began in the late 1970s, is an example of this pattern. After the death of Mao Zedong, Chinese political leaders put in place a new program of economic and social reforms, part of which was a set of rural "economic readjustment policies" designed to promote agricultural growth. The new agricultural policies define the family, rather than the work team or brigade, as the unit of production. There are essentially three policies.

First is the "family responsibility system," whereby plots of land are allocated by communes to individual households to grow particular crops. The family is free to organize its own system of labor but is obligated to meet a production quota or compensate the commune in the amount of the difference. If production exceeds the designated quota, the family can keep the surplus and can sell it, consume it, or arrange for it to be applied as a "credit" in the commune's system of accounting. In turn, the private garden plots that families have traditionally maintained near their homes have been expanded, allowing people to raise larger amounts of vegetables, animals, and cash crops for sale on the open market. The third policy is a new emphasis on so-called sideline production, such as small cottage industries.

As a result of these new policies, women's labor has become largely invisible. Whereas under the collective system, both men and women earned workpoints (although not at an equal rate) that accrued to them as individuals, under the new system women's labor is subsumed under the rubric of the household, whose total income is most often controlled by the senior male. The absence of an identifiable economic contribution tends to erode personal control over the nature and number of tasks to be performed and to decrease women's power in decision-making in the family.

The agricultural policies have apparently brought with them renewed emphasis on the importance, for women, of focusing their attention on housework and child care. However, this is not viewed as incompatible with full-time involvement in home-based production, such as sideline activities or the tending of family garden plots.

Finally, with the new agricultural policies, women's work burden has increased. Whereas under collectivization some effort was made to liberate women from full-time domestic duties, the new system, with its emphasis on traditional female roles *and* its incentives to increase income through hard work and expanded productivity, has meant a return to the double day. As one field researcher who observed family life in a number of rural households in the early 1980s reports:

> In all of these houses, women got up early, started work at 4 A.M. or earlier and worked for 10 to 12 hours in the sideline production. Men also worked, but the women's situation was different in the following respects. First, in addition to the 10 or 12 hours work in sideline production, women were responsible for cooking, washing, and childcare, carrying nightsoil to the pit in the field and bringing the wooden pots back to the houses after adequate cleaning. Surprisingly, men did none of these tasks; "These are always a woman's work," I was told, and if a man were to do it, others would say, "Your wife is lazy."[66]

Structural adjustment refers to a relatively consistent program of economic reforms in countries with heavy burdens of international debt. The reforms have been prescribed by lending institutions, such as the International Monetary Fund and the World Bank, as a condition for receiving loans. The loans are intended to help governments manage an economic crisis situation in the short term. The reforms seek to transform recession into economic growth over the long term through what one author calls "deflation, devaluation, decontrol, and privatization."[67] Thereby, reformers seek to improve human conditions over the long term. Typically, they involve lifting subsidies on food and other basic commodities, deregulating local currencies, decreasing investment in social services, such as health and education, denationalizing state-sponsored production activities, and shifting from production for domestic use to production for export.

These adjustments often result, in the short term at least, in rising prices and the loss of jobs. As the cost of living rises and jobs disappear, women must look for opportunities to earn income in export-oriented manufacturing or in the informal sector. Women often succeed in finding jobs where men fail, because the labor force is strictly sex-segregated in many societies and women work for lower wages. In short, women must work harder, both outside and inside the home.[68] The United Nations estimates that in many of the countries hard hit by the economic crisis of the 1980s, women are now working sixty to ninety hours a week to maintain the often inadequate standard of living of a decade before.[69]

Structural adjustment policies have also resulted in the intensification of domestic work. Cutbacks in social services have meant that, if services are to be provided at all, they must be provided at home, by women. In Mexico, one of the countries that has suffered most from the economic crisis, tight budgets have turned shopping for food from a weekly into a daily activity. More sewing and mending is done at home, as there is no money for store-bought clothes. Women perform all these tasks. Daughters with full-time jobs, but not their brothers, are being pressed into service to ease the burden on mothers, leading to a pattern known as the "oldest-daughter syndrome," whereby daughters threaten early marriage or migration to escape their new role in the family.[70]

Unemployment stemming from structural adjustment also strikes hard at women. In Nicaragua, state-sponsored women's cooperatives that produced textiles, bread, jewelry, and furniture have been decimated as a result of privatization. They cannot successfully compete with foreign industry, and the removal of price subsidies has greatly reduced access to raw materials. Workers have coped by retreating to the informal economy; instead of going to a steady job, they now sell sodas and used clothing out of their homes. As the major beneficiaries of the establishment of cooperative businesses, Nicaraguan women have been hit especially hard by their decline.[71]

While women are working harder as a result of structural adjustment, they are also becoming less well-nourished. Rising food prices and falling wages mean that people eat less and less well—fewer fresh fruits and vegetables, less protein, cheaper sources of calories in general. Again, women and girls are disproportionately affected, as preference is given to male "breadwinners."[72]

Development policy in the 1970s cast women as adjuncts to men—as homemakers and mothers rather than as economic producers in their own right. To the extent that they earned income, it was assumed to be supplementary—"pin money" to buy "extras" for the family. Women's development programs that emphasized the honing of domestic skills or trained women to be able to earn income by producing goods related to traditionally female tasks (sewing, handicrafts, food processing) were consistent with this basic concept. But they failed to meet the real needs of women for full integration into economic life.

It took the United Nations' "Decade for Women" to begin to make women's productive, as well as their reproductive, roles visible to the world. As a result of this global consciousness-raising, attempts to reformulate measures of economic output to include what women do began to appear. In this spirit, new approaches to assessing productivity count time as well as money and estimate the value of time devoted to unpaid work.

The Decade for Women also spawned a small number of successful development assistance projects for women based on the premise that what women need is not lessons in being housewives or training to earn pin money but access to the kinds of resources—like money and technical supports—that will help them become successful, independent entrepreneurs. Examples are Women's World Banking and the Association for the Development and Integration of Women (ADIM), both of which were founded around 1980 by delegates to the International Women's Year Conference in Mexico City. Women's World Banking provides supports to aspiring businesswomen around the world in the form of technical assistance and credit. ADIM makes loans to marketwomen and women who already have small businesses. As of the late 1980s, it had made more than 10,000 loans to 3,000 borrowers; the repayment rate was more than 90%.[73]

Enabling women to be productive, to control their own labor, their means of production, and their earnings, is an issue of health as well as economic development. Control over resources has a direct and beneficial effect on mental health and well-being. It also has indirect effects, buffering women from oppressive conditions that place them at risk for mental illness and allowing them to escape situations of violence and abuse. Control over resources enables women to protect and to provide for their children. In the face of policies that encourage women to become housewives and consumers, the importance of supporting women in traditional economies and entrepreneurial activities needs to be asserted. The potential hazards for women's lives of development policies that increase women's dependency need to be evaluated.

Toward Research on the Social Origins of Women's Ill Health

An appreciation of the burdens that women of poor countries endure on a day-to-day basis is a critical first step in understanding their distress. To the extent that current economic reforms, such as structural adjustment, work to intensify women's suffering, we may expect to see this reflected in their deteriorating mental health. And yet the task of analyzing the impact of development policies and practices on women from a perspective that emphasizes the interaction of economic and cultural forces has only just begun. Two examples of how economic and cultural forces may interact to erode women's well-being are presented in the following paragraphs.

Take, for instance, the "missing women" that demographers have recently documented.[74] Boys and girls are born in roughly equal proportions (about 105 male for every 100 female births), and females in all age groups are more likely to survive, and survive longer, than males under conditions of equal care. Yet in India, the results of a national census released in 1991 show only 920 women for every 1,000 men in that country (down from 972 at the beginning of the century).[75] In China, information provided by the State Statistical Bureau reveals male-to-female sex ratios of 108.47 to 100 for 1981, 110.94 for 1986, and 113.8 for 1989.[76] According to information provided by the United Nations, the proportion of women to men is as low as 84 for every 100 men in Saudi Arabia, 67 per 100 men in Bahrain, and 48 per 100 men in the United Arab Emirates.[77] Based on these and similar calculations, Amartya Sen contends that over 100 million women are "missing" in the world today.[78]

Sen explains how economic reforms might interact with cultural values to contribute to the "missing women" phenomenon in China.[79] For example, the one-child population policy, while ostensibly gender-neutral, in fact works to intensify the traditionally strong preference for sons in Chinese society; if families are allowed only one child, it becomes more important that the child be a boy. Similarly, the replacement of communal agriculture with the family-responsibility system has placed a premium on health services, as rural health programs relied on the collective system for a large share of their funding. With resources restricted, families may be forced into choices about who receives health care and who does not. Again, the higher value placed on males means they would be more likely to be afforded needed care.

In the case of India, Agarwal has proposed that certain forms of economic development will result in the intensification of gender subordination, with possibly devastating consequences for women.[80] In India, development has emphasized agricultural growth through the application of modern technology to bring about the so-called "green revolution." Those with the money to invest in seeds, fertilizers, wells, and mechanical equipment had some success in mounting a green revolution. Most others did not. Success led landowners who had leased out land to tenants to take it back in order to increase profits, thereby creating a new cohort of landless farmers. New wells dug for irrigation permanently lowered the water table, leaving those without the money to dig wells of their own with barren land. In short, the rich have become richer, and the poor poorer, as a result of India's green revolution; class distinctions have been sharpened by economic development. The expectation is that, as poverty increases, it will have a disproportionate effect on women through the resurgence and exacerbation of gender-discriminatory practices in this region.

A small body of scholarly literature now exists that critiques structural adjustment policies for the disproportionately heavy burden they place on women.[81] Some of this work touches on specific issues glossed here as aspects of women's suffering. The adverse effect of structural adjustment policies on women's nutritional status has been pointed out, as has the increase in the burden of unrewarding work.

More-detailed information is needed, however, to reach an adequate understanding of the meaning of current economic reforms for women's health, so that their adverse effects can begin to be rectified. Specifically, research is needed that emphasizes the *interaction* of cultural and economic factors in an analysis of the social origins of women's suffering. Future research might begin by asking: Does increasing poverty lower the status of women? If so, in what ways does it do so, and how does it affect the well-being of women?

What Can Be Done?

Just as important as an understanding of the social origins of women's ill health is a recognition of what can and is being done to improve women's status and well-being.

The development of policies and programs consistent with broader definitions of health require listening to the women whom such programs are designed to serve, at all stages of planning, implementation, and management. Listening to women who will use and staff programs maximizes the likelihood that services provided will fit well in local settings, and as a result be acceptable and used. The myth that poor women cannot, or will not, speak for themselves must be dispelled.[82]

Much local listening work, that is, going into communities and talking with women about how they live and what their health needs are, remains to be done. In the meantime, we may listen to the voices of contributors to the 1991 National Council for International Health's (NCIH) Conference on Women's Health.[83] Consistent with the definition of health as general well-being, the recommendations produced at the conference are directed toward women's overall empowerment. Specifically, these include: (1) establishing baselines for women's health and well-being and then measuring progress toward those standards; (2) developing ways of monitoring the impact of structural adjustment programs on women's welfare and establishing programs to mitigate their adverse effects; (3) enforcing or enacting legislation to improve women's status; (4) addressing women's need for equitable employment and economic development; and (5) expanding education for women and girls.[84]

Building local movements and enhancing grass-roots strengths offer another path through which the status of women and of women's health may be improved. The following series of examples illustrates the resourcefulness of women in confronting the social roots of mental illness and ill health.

Less than a year ago, women in a literacy group in the Indian state of Andra Pradesh read a story in their primer about how a group of village wives, fed up with their husbands' habit of spending large portions of meager family funds on alcohol instead of food, organized and forced the local liquor shop to close. The women in the group started talking and soon realized they shared this and other problems related to alcohol use by men. In Andra Pradesh, the rate of alcoholism can climb to as high as 90% for males in some villages, where men earn pitiful daily wages performing agricultural labor. After work, they stop off with their male friends at the local liquor establishment and spend more than half of their earnings on drinks, while women leave the fields to collect firewood, then go home to prepare the family dinner. After dinner, drunken husbands beat their wives.

Before long, this cluster of women learning to read had ignited what is being called the first large-scale grass-roots women's movement in India's history. They stormed the liquor shop in their village, poured barrels of alcoholic beverage into the street, and shaved the heads of several unsuspecting customers who were slouching, intoxicated, over the bar. A group of women in another village did the same, and another, until 6,000 liquor shops in Andra Pradesh had been destroyed. Having confronted drunkenness, the women moved on to curtail prostitution, literally battering to pieces a number of brothels where husbands and fathers were in the habit of spending the night.[85]

Women in Asia, Africa, and Latin America are organizing to resist oppression and confront the causes of ill health. Zapotec women in San Cristóbal, Mexico, empowered through newly found economic independence as successful vendors of handmade crafts, kicked out deadbeat and abusive husbands and organized a system to protect each other from sexual assaults in the marketplace.[86] In a poor section of Lima, Peru, women carry whistles to warn each other of impending attacks.[87]

"Barefoot lawyers," respected local women who have received basic training in legal rules and procedures as these relate to women's issues, advocate for women's rights in the judicial and political systems of rural Uganda.[88] The National Association of Nurses and Nurse-Midwives in Nigeria has provided training for its membership in the health hazards of female circumcision, and has developed educational materials in the form of songs, comic books, and theater in an attempt to raise the consciousness of the public.[89]

In a village outside Banda Aceh in Sumatra, local women organized (with governmental assistance) and continue to operate a primary health care clinic, where they are actively involved in the acquisition and distribution of resources such as oral contraceptives, oral rehydration solution, and medical supplies. Many Indonesian government programs rely on women to mobilize community support and to lead community efforts in health.[90]

In India, the Self-Employed Women's Organization (SEWA), a registered trade union, organizes women workers in the informal sector and assists them in advocating for their rights in legal and political venues. Among SEWA's accomplishments has been the organization of a women's cooperative bank, which provides much-needed credit and a source of financial support during strikes. A cooperative of trained health workers has also been established through SEWA to provide primary care. The goal of increasing women's self-reliance underlies all SEWA's activities.[91]

Initiatives such as these deserve support in whatever form is needed—money, technical expertise, or legitimation. New initiatives that address women's mental health issues in a locally meaningful way can build on these grass-roots efforts and models. In Indonesia, women physicians who are committed to providing and expanding mental health services are promoting programs that would be incorporated into the village primary health care program, where local women would be trained and paid to provide screening, support, and elementary therapy.[92]

These grass-roots efforts suggest models for the development of mental health programs that address women's needs for economic opportunities and local needs to design, staff, and control services. Cadres of health workers—women who would serve children and men as well as women—may be trained in a repertoire of skills appropriate to abilities, needs, and setting. Issues salient for a particular community could be identified and constitute the focus of training and program response.

Efforts at the international and local levels are both crucial, but to be maximally effective, the two must connect. This may take several forms. One is the "listening exercise" mentioned above; exogenous donor agencies seeking to promote health and "development" should do so having listened, heard, and acted upon the agendas set forth by those destined to be the beneficiaries of programs. For women, this means being partners in the development process. International support for local initiatives is another connecting mechanism, but again, that support must be relevant to real needs. A third possible mechanism is replication of local programs. Not all programs are transferable, however, and they cannot be transposed without careful attention to problems of adaptation to different social, cultural, and political contexts.

Health policies can be distinguished from "healthy" policies at the level of the state.[93] "Healthy" policies are those government programs that, while not specifically aimed at fighting illness and disease, nonetheless have positive consequences for health. Healthy policies for women are supported by state gender ideologies that enhance the cultural, political, and legal status of women by legitimizing equitable public investment in and protection of females as well as males. Countries with equitable gender ideologies are far more likely to educate females at approximately the same rate as men and to provide women legal protection and economic opportunities than are those that do not promote such equity. Although furthering gender equity in state ideologies requires the mobilization of political will and political action, the impact on women's well-being, and therefore the well-being of society, should be considerable. Indonesia, which now has progressive policies designed to enhance women's status, is a case in point. The involvement of women as well as men in carrying out development projects is sanctioned by the state, and educational levels of Indonesian women approximate those of men; 83% of females and 90% of males are literate.

Healthy policies for women are those formulated to increase women's personal and political power, to help lift them out of poverty and oppression, and to assure their access to, and control over, economic resources. Women's poverty can be addressed through economic initiatives that increase the productivity of women farmers (through access to technology and credit), provide equitable income-earning opportunities for wage earners, and ensure access to and continued enrollment in school for all girls. Oppression of women can be addressed through economic or other incentives to enforce existing laws that protect women, such as those outlawing dowry in India and Bangladesh. If, for example, the World Bank can make future loans for health services in Kenya contingent upon the government's adoption of its preferred program of health financing,[94] they can also be made contingent on improving the status of women.

Health policies that incorporate mental health into public health and address women's needs and concerns from childhood to old age can be developed in numerous ways. Ethical considerations and competence of practitioners are central to the formulation of integrated health programs capable of redressing the trauma of rape, the stigma of sexual or domestic violence, the depression of isolation or gender oppression, and the anxiety of scarcity. Although the social roots of many of these problems cannot be simply patched over with medical care, to ignore the potential of the health care system's role to attend to needy women would imply that a society does not want to invest its resources in women's health.

Institutions of health education, such as medical schools and training programs for health workers, need to be evaluated and barriers to treating mental illness or consequences of violence addressed. Communication among health workers, physicians, and women patients is notoriously paternalistic in many places in the world, regardless of the sex of the physician or health worker, making a patient's disclosure of psychological distress or consequences of sexual violence often difficult, at times stigmatized. Evaluation of training and enhancing competence of primary care physicians and health workers to treat the consequences of domestic violence, rape, and psychological distress commonly experienced by women may occur in tandem with a review of what women ideally want from their health care providers.

Health policies must also face the challenge of formulating moral but "culturally sensitive" responses to practices hazardous to the health of women and girls (such as female genital mutilation, female infanticide, gender-specific abortion, and feeding practices that discriminate against girl children). Such dilemmas can be partially resolved by offering support to local public health movements and grass-roots efforts.

We can use health policies and accompanying programs of health research as leverage to mobilize political will and promote change in policies controlled by other sectors of government. Continued documentation of the powerful relationship between the health of the whole society and female education is but one example. Similar analyses of links between legal inequities (such as gender discrimination in family and criminal law) and sexual and domestic violence and their health consequences for women (and their families) is another. A third example would be to emphasize the link between health and access to and control of economic resources and opportunities.

Health policies and "healthy" policies that address the depth and breadth of women's suffering in less privileged communities of Asia, Africa, the Middle East, and Latin America will be required if there is to be real progress in improving the health of women.

Conclusions

- Until very recently, women's health has largely been defined in terms of maternal and child health. As a result, maternal and child health programs in poor countries have often emphasized the needs of children over those of mothers. To address this problem, we need broader definitions of women's health that encompass not only reproductive functions (including fertility control) but also other aspects of physical health, emotional well-being, and general quality of life. Services consistent with these definitions must then be implemented. Examples include routine screening for cancer and sexually transmitted diseases; mental health services (especially those designed to deal with physical and sexual violence against women); and nutrition and feeding programs. Priorities need to be set, and services designed, to address the most pressing needs and specific circumstances of particular geographic regions.

- Besides reviewing existing data concerning the prevalence of psychiatric disorder and psychological distress in women, this chapter posits social origins for observed (and as yet unidentified) morbidity. This means that to improve women's health, a two-pronged approach is required that attacks the sources of female suffering and provides services to deal with the negative consequences of gender inequality. Among the social roots of poor health for women are widespread discrimination against females in employment, education, food distribution, health care, and resources for economic development. Women's relative powerlessness also renders them vulnerable to exploitation in many forms, from physical and sexual violence to murder. The social roots of poor mental and physical health for women are numerous and deeply entangled; hence the strategies needed to address the problem must be multifaceted.

- While systematic and reliable international prevalence data are lacking, it is clear that violence directed against women in their homes and elsewhere (as in the case of refugee women) is extremely widespread. Rape and beatings of women by male relatives are common and considered unremarkable in many parts of the world. The problem is complicated by the shame and stigma attached to these events, which not only inhibit victims from seeking help but also ruin lives. However, women are now beginning to fight back, organizing their own forms of protection against male violence in the form of shelters, "all-female" police, and various mechanisms for alerting others who will come to a victim's aid in the case of attack. These efforts must be affirmed and supported. However, the international health community must also generate its own initiatives to combat violence against women. These include, but are not limited to, (a) research, to produce more accurate estimates of the prevalence and incidence of gender violence; (b) services to treat and protect victims and to empower women in general through information and education; and (c) training to enable health workers to identify, counsel, and refer women who are the objects of physical or sexual abuse.

- Women throughout the world are limited, both economically and politically, by a lack of education comparable to the levels attained by men. To reduce this disparity, girls must stay in school regardless of the constraints imposed by structural adjustment.

- The quality of women's lives is deeply related to their economic status. Women must therefore have access to fairly compensated employment. In addition, development efforts should target women directly in ways that will increase their economic independence and productivity. For example, women farmers should receive technical assistance such as fertilizers and machinery. Crops grown by women should be the focus of agricultural research. Businesswomen should have access to credit.

- A range of practices in many countries contribute to both direct and indirect discrimination against women. Existing laws prohibiting discrimination against women must be enforced.

- State resources must be mobilized to promote gender ideologies that enhance the economic, legal, political, and cultural status of women. Examples are the implementation of "healthy policies" for women, such as equitable public investment in, and protection of, females as well as males.

- Women have too frequently been ignored or trivialized by mainstream economic development efforts. In imposing concepts of gender roles familiar to, or preferred by, outside developers, these efforts have removed women from positions of relative economic power and independence. Meaningful progress has also been inhibited by the seemingly widespread, but inaccurate, assumption that women (especially poor women) are incapable of articulating their own needs. In light of this, future initiatives, whether focused on health services, education, or economic development, must incorporate the voices of women, building on their own vision of what is required and what is feasible in any given local context. This means listening and then acting on what is heard, and supporting local organizations where they exist. Support includes providing material resources, training for women, and linkages with relevant national and international organizations.

- Communication among physicians and other health workers and women patients is paternalistic in many parts of the world. Women are often neither encouraged nor permitted to voice their feelings and complaints. When they do, they are likely to be discounted or dismissed. Health care professionals must therefore be trained to empower women in the clinical encounter. This means authorizing, and even encouraging, disclosure of routine information as well as experiences that are shameful and threatening, such as physical or sexual assault. Women patients must be given information about disease processes and options for care, and insofar as possible, authorized to participate in making treatment decisions. Formulators of policy must take time to consider how such training programs might best be developed, funded, and implemented in their respective countries.

9

The Elderly

The number of aged in the world population will more than double from 500 million in 1990 to over one billion by 2025.[1] The majority of this growth will occur in Africa, Asia, and Latin America.[2] In 1990, 250 million people in these regions were over the age of sixty; by 2025 this number will grow to over 800 million. Health care systems and government institutions will have to struggle hard to provide for their needs, as some of the social systems that traditionally have provided care for the elderly are beginning to weaken and the numbers of needy aged are increasing.

These demographic changes influence mental health in several ways. The growth in the elderly population means an inevitable increase in age-related diseases, such as the dementias. In addition, changes in social patterns will alter the role of the elderly and the ways they are valued. These changes can lead to poor mental health outcomes, such as depression, anxiety, suicide, and serious constraints on the quality of life among elderly individuals. In addition, the high prevalence of multiple coexisting physical conditions, such as incontinence, hip fracture, and sensory loss influence mental health through the loss of self-esteem and independence. Finally, families will also be affected by the increased demand for caregiving (see Box 9.1).

Given the serious problems that many countries in Africa, Asia, and Latin America now face, the mental health problems of the elderly are likely to be a low priority in the short to medium term. Beginning to anticipate these problems, however, will help countries plan for the inevitable strains of rapid population and social change and their impact on elderly mental health.

Demographic Changes

A combination of high fertility and increases in longevity has led to an increase in both absolute and relative numbers of elderly people in Africa, Asia, and Latin America. The growth in older age groups is due primarily to a process in which large cohorts of children, born in the past under conditions of high fertility in these regions, progress into old age.[4] Also, contributing somewhat to this "momentum" in population aging is the fact that, over the last generation, life expectancy in these areas of the world as a whole rose by almost ten years.[5] According to the United Nations, in 1950 the 200 million people aged over 60 in the world were evenly dis-

---

Box 9.1 Aging and Dementia in China

The plight of Mrs. Kwong, who has been chronically ill for a number of years and requires around-the-clock care, illustrates the new dilemmas Chinese families must confront as the population in China ages.

In 1987, Mrs. Kwong was brought home from the hospital after a stroke, despite the need for additional care, because it became too expensive to keep her there any longer. The 84-year-old Mrs. Kwong was looked after by family members, particularly her daughter Mrs. Lam. She initially made a good recovery, although she needed assistance in washing, dressing, and using the toilet. A lively conversationalist, Mrs. Kwong nevertheless had trouble understanding what was going on around her.

Over the next three years, her mental and physical state deteriorated to such an extent that she was virtually bedridden. In addition to a lack of strength to sit up in bed by herself, Mrs. Kwong was incontinent, quarrelsome, and stubborn. She had also lost her ability to remember well.

Mrs. Lam still provided the majority of care for her mother but found it increasingly difficult to cope. Two grandsons helped in moving Mrs. Kwong when necessary and two of her sons made some financial contribution. However, the money was not enough to hire outside help to provide ongoing care. Mrs. Lam, in her mid-fifties, was desperate to find alternates to ease the burden of family obligation. "Even if you have the money," she said, "it is still difficult to get people to look after an old person, to do all the dirty things . . . Old people live much longer now."

China's population is aging and the elderly are living longer. Chronic illnesses, such as dementia, are on the rise and limited state and family resources are available to handle some of the severe manifestations of the disease. The traditional Chinese custom of caring for retired parents is becoming more demanding as these parents live longer and succumb to physical and mental disabilities.

The experience of mild dementia in China is less disruptive for the elderly and their families than it is in some other countries. A certain "childishness" is accepted in Chinese culture as a normal part of being very old. Yet dementia in its advanced states is more troublesome; there are fewer options available for caregivers. The cost of hiring people to care for chronically ill family members can be prohibitive. Further, there are few assisted living environments or homes for the aged in China. They are usually chosen as a last resort.

New needs for the elderly are coming at a time when the state is focusing more on acute than on chronic diseases, and is reducing its commitment to funding health care. Partly as a result, the moral and legal responsibility of families to attend to aging and needy parents can become an emotional and financial hardship.[3]

---

tributed between "developed" and "developing" countries. By 2000 the total will have grown to 614 million, with 62% living in "developing" countries, and by 2025 there will be 1.2 billion people over age 60 in the world, 72% of whom will be living in "developing" countries.[6]

Throughout Africa, Asia, Latin America, and the Pacific, there is a wide range in population age structure (see Figure 9.1). Hong Kong and China, for example, have a greater proportion of older people than do other Asian nations. Africa tends to have a smaller proportion of elderly than the other regions, yet Northern African

Median Population Age

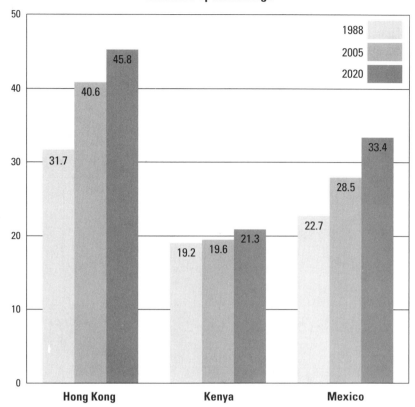

Figure 9.1 Population Age Structures for 1988, 2005, and 2020 (*Source:* Kinsella, 1988)

nations have higher proportions of older members as compared to sub-Saharan Africa.

Over the next three decades, percent growth in the older populations of Africa, Asia, and Latin America will range from 25% in Uruguay to 282% in Costa Rica (Figure 9.2). The absolute numbers of persons aged 55 and over will more than double by 2020 in all of the nations in Figure 9.2 except Uruguay (which has already reached high rates), and will more than triple in 10 of the 22 countries. China alone will witness an increase of 75 million persons aged 55 and over by the year 2005, and another 139 million from 2005 to 2020. India's older population will increase 123 million by 2020.

Throughout the world, the oldest old (persons 85 and over) are the most rapidly increasing age group of the older population. The growth rate of the oldest old is higher than that for all other older ages in Asia, Latin America, and the Caribbean, and will soon become so in Africa as well. The oldest old will increase more than twice as fast as the young old in China, Indonesia, and Uruguay.

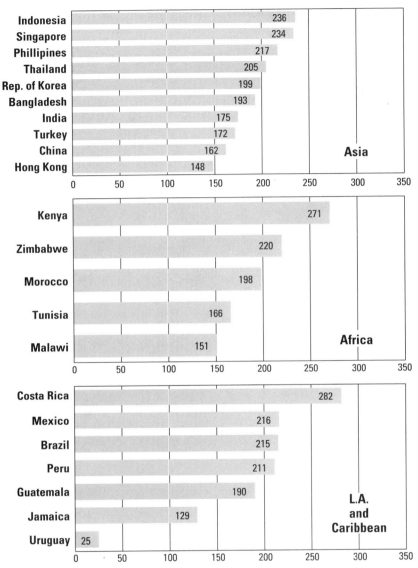

Figure 9.2 Percent Increase in Older Populations (Aged 55 and Over), 1988–2020
(*Source:* U.S. Bureau of the Census; Kinsella, 1988)

Economics, Social Change, and the Elderly

Dramatic economic and structural changes are influencing the lives of the elderly
and their families throughout the world. Industrialization and "modernization"
involve changes such as the shift from a subsistence to a money economy, the
movement of labor from rural to urban centers, and the growth in urban and peri-

urban slums and shantytowns. Two broad effects can be expected. First, the dislocations and disturbances might increase rates of psychiatric morbidity, including behavioral disturbances and suicide, problems that will be exacerbated by the concomitant destruction in traditional mechanisms for buffering distress.[7] Second, the changes will undermine social structures that have developed to ensure care for the elderly and mentally ill. Table 9.1 outlines a model that identifies the major forces driving changes that affect the mental health of the elderly, listing secondary social and economic effects caused by these changes and possible mental health outcomes.

As countries have modernized, the value of agricultural produce and related assets like agricultural land has fallen relative to manufactured goods. These shifts in relative prices have major implications for the social and material well-being of the elderly who own agricultural assets such as land or cattle. In rural communities, social status and financial security depends importantly upon these assets. If they become devalued, the elderly person is vulnerable to both social marginalization and financial troubles. However, price changes need not only have negative impacts. Economic upheaval can bring benefits to the elderly in terms of status and material well-being if they have any form of pension or guaranteed income. An index-linked old-age pension gives a relatively stable income and may provide an important source of income for the children of the pensioners.[8] Moreover, the elderly may have the resources to play an active role in rural credit associations.

Rural areas remain disproportionately older in most African countries because migration of the economically active to cities has turned villages into homes for the very young and very old, who then must carry responsibility for farming as well as maintenance of the household.[9] Patterns of increasing urbanization do not always bring unmitigated negative changes for the elderly. For example, when the young family members of the Sherpa in Nepal move from the villages to urban centers, and so become unavailable to share the household and take care of the elderly, the old resist traditional methods of dividing up property and are beginning to keep their sons' share of the family land for themselves. By doing this, they maintain their economic security.[10]

Education in early life has a major effect on the well-being of the elderly. Longevity correlates positively with education because it enhances both a person's economic prospects and adaptability in the face of massive socioeconomic change.[11] Literacy rates vary from country to country. In the poorest countries, more than two-thirds of the population is functionally illiterate. Illiteracy is almost always higher among women than men. When the younger members of the society have received formal education, they often feel that they have no role in the agriculture based traditional society. This encourages them to migrate to cities.[12] Moreover, when younger members are educated, elderly uneducated members often find themselves in a society that no longer values their knowledge and experience in the same way as before. This leads to a disorienting loss of meaning as well as a loss of respect from their younger family members and neighbors that can create lowered levels of self-confidence, self-esteem, and well-being.[13]

Table 9.1 Factors Potentially Affecting the Mental Health of the Elderly

Primary Causes	Secondary Causes	Potential Mental Health Outcomes
Life expectancy increases throughout the population, followed by a decline in fertility levels.	A greater absolute number and proportion of elderly in the population.	An increase in age-related diseases such as the dementias.
Economic changes cause the price of agricultural products to decline relative to manufactured goods.	Social structures that ensured care for the elderly through inheritance of agricultural land or animals begin to break down as the assets to be inherited become less valuable. The elderly lose respect and care, and, in the extreme, face isolation or abandonment.	Increased depression, substance abuse, suicide, feelings of worthlessness, and low-self esteem.
Rural-urban migration continues to increase.	For the elderly that move to the cities or grow old in the cities, living in crowded shantytowns without basic sanitation and with the constant risk of eviction poses substantial threats to physical and mental health.	Increased stress, leading to anxiety, depression, and increased rates of substance abuse and suicide.
	The majority of migrants to the city are in their reproductive years and may return to the countryside when they become elderly. Thus, the villages are populated predominantly by the elderly and the very young. A result is the isolation and lack of adequate care for the remaining elderly.	Increased loneliness and decreased sense of self-worth.
Increased education of young.	When the young are formally educated and their parents and grandparents are not, this can result in the young not valuing their elderly relatives or their traditions and customs. This can lead to the elderly feeling useless and to abandonment by their families.	Increased depression, anxiety, and decreased sense of self-worth.
Increased education of elderly.	When the elderly are educated, they tend to be somewhat better off financially as well as being better able to cope with the sweeping social changes around them.	Buffer to depresson, anxiety, and feelings of worthlessness.
Per capita income rises in some countries and health care improves.	This will reduce mortality, particularly in men, who tend to die younger than women, resulting in fewer single elderly women, and a higher availability of care for elderly.	Decreased loneliness, buffer to depression, anxiety, and feelings of worthlessness.

Mental Health of the Elderly

Organic Disorders

The senile dementias (the gradual loss of cognitive function resulting from diseases that appear late in life) have assumed great importance in public health because of the larger number of persons living into the age of risk. The World Health Organization has defined dementia as an acquired impairment of higher mental functions, including memory, the capacity to solve everyday living problems, the performance of learned skills, the correct use of social skills, all aspects of language, and the control of emotions.

The two principal kinds of dementia in the elderly are Alzheimer's disease (AD) and vascular or multi-infarct dementia. Brain injury leading to presenile dementia is a major problem in many countries because of increasing road-accident rates as well as increasing numbers of strokes. Multiple other causes of dementia exist, but they are far outnumbered by cases of AD and vascular dementia. The diagnosis of AD has two basic criteria: (1) evidence of dementia, and (2) the absence of other diseases that can produce dementia. The following features are typical: multiple cognitive defects (both memory impairment and language disorder or impaired executive function), and gradual onset with continuing decline resulting in significant social or occupational impairment without delirium. AD also causes change in affect and personality. This may be especially salient in some societies where cognitive decline may be less culturally marked. The second major category, vascular or multi-infarct dementia, is diagnosed when dementia is characterized by an uneven distribution of intellectual defects *and* when there is evidence of focal brain damage and significant cerebrovascular disease demonstrated by history, clinical examination, or brain imaging.

Although the ultimate criterion for distinguishing AD from vascular dementia is autopsy, it is still important to differentiate these entities from one another. The justification is practical. Progression in vascular dementia can sometimes be halted or delayed by treating underlying causes: hypertension, transient ischemic attacks, elevated hematocrit, cardiac disease, and sickle-cell disease. There is yet no treatment for Alzheimer's-type dementia, although recent pharmacologic interventions show modest improvements in certain groups. As for protection against the disease, the findings from an epidemiological study in New York suggest that increased educational and occupational attainment can reduce the risk of incidence of Alzheimer's disease, either by decreasing ease of detection or by imparting a "reserve" that delays onset of clinical manifestations.[14]

Another important diagnostic task is to differentiate the pseudodementia caused by depression in the elderly from senile dementia, because appropriate treatment of depression will lead to the disappearance of the symptoms of cognitive impairment. Treating depression in the elderly requires attention to drug dosage (therapeutic levels are often lower) and careful monitoring for side effects; properly done, treatment yields excellent results.

Almost all studies on the prevalence of dementia have been undertaken in industrialized societies; in recent years, important surveys have been conducted throughout the world (see Table 9.2 and Table 9.3). AD is reported to be more common than vascular dementia in North America and Europe; the contrary has been reported from Japan and China (Table 9.3). In general, prevalence doubles with every five-year increase in age from about 60 to 90. The point prevalence of dementia found in a collaborative study in Europe rose from 1.4% in 65-to-69-year-olds to 32% in those aged 90 to 94. Because rates increase steadily with age, average figures on prevalence above age 60 or age 65 are of limited utility; the rates computed

Table 9.2 Prevalence of Dementia in Different Geographic Regions

Region	Age Surveyed	Number Surveyed	Prevalence	Diagnostic Methods
China				
Shanghai	55 +	5,055	4.6	Clinical, MMSE
Beijing	60 +/65 +	1,331	1.3/1.8	Clinical, MMSE
Taiwan	60 +	1,113	0.5	Clinical
Singapore	65 +	612	1.8	Clinical, GMS
United States				
Baltimore, MD	24–95	6,000	4.0	Autopsies
Boston, MA	65 +	3,623	10.3	Clinical, neuropsychological
England				
Liverpool	65 +	1,070	5.2	Clinical, GMS
All Areas	30 +/65 +	8,000	1.8/6.7	Clinical health interview and examinations in selected samples
Japan				
Nagoya	65 +	3,106	5.8	Clinical
Italy				
Appignano	59 +	778	6.2	Clinical, MMSE

MMSE = Mini-mental State Exam; GMS = Geriatric Mental State.

Source: See Chang et al. (1993) for authors of original studies.

will depend heavily on the number of individuals in the older age cohorts included in a given study (i.e., the more oldest old in the sample, the higher the rates). This phenomenon is reflected in the wide variability of prevalence data reported in different studies within one country or between countries; for example, from 4.5 to 10.3 per hundred in the U.S., from 1.1 to 4.8 in Japan, and from 4.6 to 7.2 in the People's Republic of China.[15]

In field surveys of elderly persons living in the community, rates for dementia are much higher among those with little education. In a Shanghai study, the rate of dementia among illiterates was recorded at five times the rate among those who had attended elementary school and eighteen times that among those who had attended college.[16] In part, such findings reflect the dependence of test items themselves on skills learned at school. Nonetheless, there may be a real gradient in the incidence of dementia across educational levels. Some investigators believe that lack of education slows brain development in the early years so that loss of brain cells in late life has more serious consequences for function (i.e., "lack of reserve").[17]

In some societies, dementia is treated as an expected or at least understandable part of aging. As such, it is not constructed publicly as a major health problem and families respond to it as they do to other aspects of aging, such as physical disable-

Table 9.3 Percentage of Diagnosed Dementias in Patients with Dementia in Different Countries

Region/Ethnicity	Alzheimer's Disease	Multi-infarct Dementia	Parkinson's Dementia	Other Dementias
Chinese				
Shanghai, China	64.7	26.8	Not specified	8.5
Beijing, China	33.0	61.0	0.0	6.0
Singapore	63.6	36.4	0.0	None
New York, USA	12.1	75.9	4.6	7.5
Japan				
Nagoya	41.4	48.3	Unknown	10.3
Tokyo	18.0	70.0	Unknown	12.0
Americans (caucasians)				
Boston, MA	84.1	4.4	0.0	11.5
Americans (blacks)				
Baltimore, MD	18.2	22.7	1.5	57.6
British				
Cambridgeshire (rural)	52.0	31.0	0.0	17.0
Italy				
Appignano	42.0	35.0	Unknown	23.0

Source: See Chang et al. (1993) for authors of original studies.

ment. Neki suggests that senile dementia is less frequent or less severe in India either due to lower longevity or because there is a better tolerance for the demented aged in India than in the West.[18] Makanjuola suggests that low rates of the dementias in Nigeria, especially of the Alzheimer's type, may be due to the fact that families are relatively tolerant of all but the most extreme mental disturbances in the elderly, and thus fail to seek care from medical facilities.[19] In some cultures, "childishness" is an expected accompaniment of old age and the condition is tolerated rather than regarded as pathological; in others, demented old women are at risk of being denounced as witches and of being stoned to death if the accusation is widely believed.[20] In general, changes in personality (pathological suspiciousness), in mood (depression and irritability), in the appropriateness of behavior (neglect of personal hygiene), and in spatial orientation (wandering off and getting lost) are more conspicuous than cognitive loss in family descriptions of senile relatives in many of these countries (see Box 9.2).

Uncertainties about accurate diagnosis of mild cases of dementia should not obscure the fact that moderate or severe dementia is incapacitating in any setting; patients are disoriented, cannot care for themselves, and require constant supervision. In both the United States and the United Kingdom, approximately half the persons in nursing homes have been admitted because of dementia. In Beijing, cases of dementia are cared for in the community, often with a very considerable burden for the patient's family.

Box 9.2 Somita, a "Madwoman" in Calcutta

Somita Bose married an educated man and moved from her village to Calcutta well over half a century ago. Her husband was a professor who had little in common with her; he rarely spent time with her after their marriage. They had one son, Mithun, who became the primary outlet for the unhappy woman's affections. Mithun became an artist and eventually married Sharmila, a librarian.

Sharmila resented her mother-in-law's dependence on Mithun. Mithun, for his part, could not find steady work as an artist and grew increasingly depressed. Sharmila, who worked full-time in a library in central Calcutta, supported the family, but when Mithun's father died, the three—mother, son, and daughter-in-law—were forced to move to a downstairs flat in Sharmila's parents' house.

Soon after the move, Somita began to wander off and get lost in the neighborhood, an embarrassment to Sharmila. Mithun began spending most of his time at home to watch his mother and stopped looking for work. One day Somita called out the window for the police, accusing her family of maltreating her. Sharmila then accused Somita of destroying Mithun's career to keep him home with her. The strains among the three in their one-bedroom flat were enormous.

Mithun eventually put his mother in an old-age home. Three days after Somita was admitted, the superintendent sent word that she was unacceptable for the home. Mithun and Sharmila arrived at the institution to find Somita sitting outside, her eyes flashing and her hair in wild disarray. "You lied to me," the superintendent angrily accused them. "She is crazy. She is your responsibility." Crazy people do not belong in old-age homes, according to the superintendent, for they challenge the institution's image of benevolence.

Sharmila then sought out psychiatric care with the hope of diagnosing her mother-in-law as mad and having her admitted to a psychiatric nursing home. The couple took Somita to the clinic of one of Calcutta's best-known psychiatric families. A doctor there told Sharmila that her mother-in-law had Alzheimer's. He recommended a CT-scan of the brain to enable him to make a more definitive diagnosis. Though CT-scans are neither necessary nor sufficient tools for diagnosing dementia, the doctor used the test results to confirm his opinion.

Armed with a diagnosis of Alzheimer's—a complex biological disease—and a drug called Dasovas, Sharmila was relieved: Somita was diseased and thus a legitimate candidate for a psychiatric nursing home. The couple began investigating homes, but only one rather expensive home accepted Somita; it was a two-hour commute in Calcutta traffic, and her family could visit only rarely.

What was wrong with Somita? It is difficult to say for sure. As Somita moved from home to old-age home to a psychiatric facility, family tensions, institutional forms of care, and new "advances" in biomedical knowledge contributed to changing assessments of her actions. The diverse interpretations of these actions point to the complex cultural and social issues that underpin any behaviors seen as deviant or different. Any assessment of illness or pathology in the elderly, from madness to Alzheimer's disease, is a contested one, marked by competing political and social interests.[21]

Other Mental Health Problems

Data on other mental health disorders, such as depression and anxiety among the aged in Africa, Asia, and Latin America, are limited. Studies indicate the following rates of disorders:

A survey of psychiatric disorders among the hospitalized aged in India found 27% suffering from depression, as compared to 12% for dementia, 35% for chronic schizophrenia, and 25% for other nonspecified disorders.[22] Another survey among a sample of fifty-one elderly Nigerians attending a psychiatric clinic hospital found a lower rate of depression (9.8%) compared to late-onset paranoid disorders, which were diagnosed in 55% of cases (of which twenty cases fulfilled criteria for paranoid schizophrenia).[23] In Lesotho, Hollifield and colleagues found 3.2% prevalence of panic disorder and generalized anxiety disorder among elderly surveyed.[24]

Results from a sample of 111 community-dwelling elderly aged 65 years and older in São Paulo, Brazil, found a 29.7% prevalence of psychiatric problems, with the following distribution: dementia, 5.5%; depression, 14.3%; neuroses, 7.7%; personality disorders, 15.3%; substance-abuse disorders, 3.3%; and adjustment reactions, 6.6%.[25] When the authors compared these data to a similar sample of community-dwelling elderly from Mannheim, Germany, they observed much higher rates of symptoms of "minor" psychiatric morbidity in the São Paulo sample, including symptoms such as sleep disorder, irritability, anxiety, depression, and lack of concentration. They believe that these high symptom counts in São Paulo relative to those in Mannheim reflect "stresses associated with rapid acculturation, poverty, difficult housing conditions, and low or non-existent retirement pensions for the elderly."[26]

In a four-country study designed to examine aging in the West Pacific region (Fiji, Malaysia, the Philippines, and the Republic of Korea), Andrews and his colleagues report on the presence of five symptoms indicative of psychiatric disorders.[27] These include sleep difficulties, worry and anxiety, loss of interest, tiredness, and forgetfulness. Their data demonstrate that, in general, the level of all problems remained static or increased with age.

In Fiji, older subjects documented loss of interest and forgetfulness more often than did younger subjects, with no sex differences. In the Republic of Korea, 30% to 50% of the study population complained of sleep difficulties, worry and anxiety, loss of interest, and tiredness; these proportions changed very little with age. In Malaysia, there was an increase with age in the reporting of all five mental problems in the male population and an increase in reporting loss of interest, tiredness, and forgetfulness in the female population. These increases were greatest for loss of interest. Eighteen percent of men and 29% of women aged 60 to 64 years said that they were not as enthusiastic about doing things that they used to care about, compared with 76% of men and 77% of women aged 80 years and over. In the Philippines, the prevalence of all five mental health problems increased with age. The largest differences between youngest and oldest age groups were noted for loss of interest (about 30% difference for both sexes), tiredness (29% difference for men), and forgetfulness (48% difference for men).

Other mental health problems relate to lack of food. The World Bank estimates that some 780 million people of all age groups worldwide are energy-deficient.[28] The elderly, particularly women, are disproportionately poor and therefore more likely than the general population to be malnourished. Lack of food can lead to problems such as confusion and forgetfulness. These reversible dementias could cause problems in diagnosis. For example, a patient exhibiting symptoms of confusion could be assumed to have an organic disorder when he or she is really suffering from malnutrition. Thus, no effort would be made to treat a reversible condition. Another scenario might be that the community, expecting the elderly to be confused and slow as normal accompaniments of aging, will not recognize the symptoms of malnutrition, and thus not encourage the elderly to seek treatment. Perhaps more prevalent an effect, however, are problems caused by malnutrition that mask symptoms of organic disorders and leave patients undiagnosed.

Many mediating factors contribute to mental illnesses and exaggerate any conditions that already exist. Studies indicate that the elderly can avoid some mental health problems if they maintain an active role in society.[29] Social changes associated with industrialization often isolate the elderly from their previous roles and increase dependency.[30] Studies show that social changes result in problems for the elderly such as declining social participation, loss of dignity and self-respect, and weakening filial support networks, all of which can take their toll on mental health.[31]

Rethinking the Myths of Care

The stereotypical view among laypeople (and supported in most of the gerontology literature) is that many "traditional" societies revere their elderly and that families care for them, whereas societies in the most highly industrialized countries neglect their older members. According to this view, rapid social change leaves older people behind. The generalization holds that the elderly tend to have high status in agricultural societies, where the extended family is the norm, and lower status in urbanized societies, where the nuclear family structure is more prevalent.[32] These persistent myths echo throughout the policy debate. People arguing against providing formal care and publicly funded services for the elderly in Africa, Asia, and Latin America, for example, use these preconceptions to support their arguments.[33]

This view is oversimplified for several reasons. First, the traditional situation where the village lives in awe of a much-respected elder, who officiates at ceremonies, and gives out advice and judgments, is only possible where a few exceptional individuals reach old age. Thus, old age is seen as a privilege for those who achieve it. Now that more people are becoming elderly, old age itself becomes less unusual and there are increasing numbers of sick and disabled among the elderly. It may therefore not be basic respect for the elderly that is diminishing, but rather, as incomes rise and medical care improves, the proportion of unusual and remarkable people in the elderly population declines. The elderly as a group then command less respect.

Second, the extended family, key to the traditional view, may exist more out of economic necessity than choice. According to Nydegger, co-residence is determined more by economic conditions, and many older family members would prefer to live alone.[34] In Shanghai, China, for example, three-quarters of the elderly live with their families. This may only be a reflection of the acute lack of housing, because rates are much lower in Beijing and Tianjin, where much more housing stock is available.

Third, in some countries, gerontocracy reflects economic structures. Expectations of inheritance ensures that families care for their elderly members. In societies that do not have a strong industrial base, the elderly maintain control over their resources, as they die before physical disability is pronounced. Elsewhere, the aged may relinquish authority over the property but keep ownership and let their families work the land. The elderly then rely on the power of inheritance to bequeath assets or to ensure that their families care for them properly.[35] If the children can make more money in the city than by inheriting all of their father's assets, they may be less willing and certainly less able to care for their parents.

In the course of recent policy debates, the danger of creating a new myth has emerged. In an attempt to counter the Western reliance on models of institutional care, some authors swing too far in the other direction and imply that all care for the elderly can and should take place within the family. This could burden the family without necessarily increasing financial aid to allow it to undertake these tasks. By emphasizing how families can support elderly relatives, this claim also overlooks the positive contributions, both emotional and financial, that the elderly can make to family life.[36]

Informal Care Systems

The informal care system is prevalent in most countries of Africa, Asia, and Latin America, as the burden of caring for the elderly falls predominantly on their children. In one study in Indonesia, 80% of the elderly in need of care received it only from their families, whereas sick younger people were considered the responsibility of the community.[37] Data from a study in Kenya show that 92% of elderly women and 88% of elderly men received help from at least one child.[38] In industrialized countries, similar rates of family care exist for the elderly that have become frail and dependent on others for the functional activities of daily living.[39] The high cost of hospitals and technology and the great increases in elderly populations mean that the family is likely to remain the chief caregiver to the elderly throughout the world.[40]

In general, cultural change in China, Japan, sub-Saharan Africa, and parts of Muslim India[41] are resulting in declining family care for the elderly. Moreover, the family is expected to deal with the increasing challenges of aging at precisely the time when it is coming under severe pressure from other social and economic forces.

Four principal sources of stresses will impinge on the family's ability to care for their elderly. First, employment opportunities will draw the younger generations to work in the cities and leave the elderly in the villages with no one to take care of them. Although migrants usually send money back to their relatives in the villages, the care of the elderly in the villages will become more problematic with increased migration. Second, lower birth rates will mean that one or two children will bear the burden of looking after their parents, when previously that burden was split among several children. In some countries such as China, strict rules govern which child shall take care of the parents in their old age. Third, it is likely that migration and agricultural transformations will break down patron-client relationships (in which a group of peasant workers are tied to a landlord or trader). Left with no patron and no formal medical system, former sharecroppers may possess few resources in times of emergency. Fourth, economic development will increase the number of women in the work force in many countries. As women tend to provide the bulk of the care for the elderly, this change will further reduce possibilities for informal care for the elderly mentally ill.

These stresses on the family and the increase in situations where a complete family does not exist to care for the elderly is likely to increase the need for formal care systems.[42] The burden of care falls heavily on women, as they are usually the primary caregivers, and on the poor, who do not possess adequate resources.[43] Furthermore, childless elderly and especially widows (who account for a large percentage of the elderly in some societies) may depend on a relative for care. In many cases, this is a sibling, most often a sister who is slightly younger than the old person in need of care. Especially in those situations where larger family networks are nonexistent and the caregivers may be old themselves, the caregivers may succumb to frustration, hopelessness, and depression.

Formal Care Systems

Formal care systems are inadequate in most low-income countries, both in extent of coverage and quality of care. For example, of the 12 million elderly people in need of assistance in their daily life in China, only 0.05% are cared for in an institutional setting. Many societies are opposed to institutionalization even where it exists as a practical option.[44] Information on the countries of Africa, Asia, and Latin America is scarce, but according to the United Nations some 4% to 6% of the elderly in "industrialized" countries are in some sort of institution.[45] There are great differences in rates of institutionalization among these countries, which can be explained by a complex interaction of demographic factors, cultural perceptions, and environmental factors such as climate. In most countries, however, institutionalization remains a last resort, usually for cases of severe dependence.[46] It is unclear whether the social changes discussed earlier will force countries in Africa, Asia, and Latin America to follow the patterns of institutionalization in other countries, as families become unable to cope with caring for increasing numbers of the mentally ill elderly. If this occurs, with luck it will coincide with an increase in the quantity and quality of institutional care.

Policy Recommendations

There is little information on which to evaluate specific policies and programs designed to help care for the elderly with mental health problems. Moreover, the World Bank notes that health care accounts on average for only 4% of the total budgets in "developing" nations, compared to over 12% in the United States, and total health expenditures are about $41 per person per year in the "developing" world.[47]

Thus, "developing" nations are unable to allocate large investments to meeting the needs of the elderly and mentally ill elderly. Many policies designed for other purposes will affect the general well-being and the mental health conditions of the elderly. Pension policies, for example, will increase economic stability, and housing policies will affect the establishment of multigenerational families. Thus, we focus on programs and policies that facilitate the ability of families to provide care within existing community structures but that can also be easily and inexpensively incorporated into existing programs. Also, we consider broader policies that could potentially address mental health problems of the elderly.

Two key themes dominate our recommendations for policies. The first theme is that government intervention should complement and improve the care already given to the elderly by their families. The second theme is that policies should be developed that integrate programs serving the elderly's physical and mental health care needs.

Budgetary constraints give many countries a strong incentive to explore the possibilities of complementing or improving care given to elderly people within the family, both promoting and maintaining good health in old age. Experience in industrialized countries suggests that they should not invest in high-cost capital equipment and specialized training as a matter of course. By adopting diffuse policies aimed to support family care, rich elites will not as easily capture the benefits of the government intervention. Investment in formal health care technology, on the other hand, often serves only the rich sectors of society. The optimal policy will respond to the nation's cultural traditions, will involve individuals and communities in health education, and will maximize the informal support and services to the aged from family and neighbors.

Experience in advanced industrialized countries suggests that government intervention for the elderly has not diminished the willingness of families to provide economic and social support to older members in need.[48] In fact, quite the opposite may be true. When there is no support from the government available, informal care mechanisms can break down more quickly and in some cases ultimately force the government to assume all responsibility for care.[49] In many cases, families care for their elderly out of necessity rather than by choice, so the ideal government policies will make it easier for families to provide care for their elderly relatives.

Policies that governments might take to enhance family care fall into three groups. First, there is the "obligation approach," where the family is viewed as obliged to provide care and the government's role is to provide formal support for those who do not have families. The emphasis in this approach is on incentives to encourage families to meet their obligations. Second, in the "willingness approach" the state supplements the assistance that the family is willing to provide. In this approach, the government has to help the elderly and their families define what they are willing and able to do by themselves. Third, in the "compensation approach" the government provides assistance (financial support) to the elderly irrespective of the family's ability to provide for them. Of course, combinations of these approaches are possible.[50]

The precise form of these policies will vary in different situations, but some policies that could help family providers include:

- Multipurpose day-care centers that offer recreational activities and other services, such as medical screening and counseling both for the elderly and their families. This provides some respite for the caregivers. Countries such as the Republic of Korea, Sri Lanka, Thailand, and Hong Kong, as well as parts of Latin America, are organizing centers along these lines.[51]
- Programs that teach the caregivers of demented elders strategies to manage the difficult behavioral disturbances that occur during the progression of the disease. These types of programs should be modified to build upon local realities.
- Housing and social policies that do not discourage multigenerational families. In Hong Kong, for example, previous public housing policies required married children to move out of their parents' public housing unit. Now the rules have been changed to allow one married child to stay on when the parents are elderly and need care. Preference is given to new applicants who are willing to include their elderly parents in the household. Singapore public housing authorities give priority to married children and their parents who apply for adjoining apartments; similar policies exist in Malaysia.[52] Both Lesotho and Botswana are considering giving people loans to upgrade their houses to provide shelter for elderly relatives.[53]
- Support for any employer-sponsored benefits that assist families. With the increasing numbers of women in the work force, employers are beginning to give assistance, time off work, or flexible schedules to employees with obligations to children or elderly parents.
- Income tax relief for people caring for an elderly dependent. This is in place or under consideration in many countries, including Singapore, Gabon, Kenya, Botswana, Morocco, the Republic of Korea, the Philippines, Iran, and Kuwait.[54]

The reliance on families makes care for the childless extremely difficult. Certain policies aim to reduce the vulnerability of those people who have no children, such as:

- In China, where there is a policy to provide financial support for the childless elderly who have no way to earn a living and no other means of support. The government found this very successful, both because the elderly childless are few in number, so the policy is not cripplingly expensive, and because it encouraged the government's family planning program.[55] There is a similar policy for the destitute elderly in Maharashtra state in India, and Zimbabwe has a program to provide residential care for the destitute elderly.[56]
- Support for nongovernment organizations (NGOs) to provide residential care, as the governments of Malaysia, India, and China are currently attempting. A voluntary agency has started a training course in Uruguay for middle-aged and older women who want to care for the elderly at home.[57] Ideally, residential homes should be small and have strong links to the community, in order to avoid the asylum connotations prevalent in the Western world (see Box 9.3).

Box 9.3 Caring for the Elderly in Zimbabwe

One of the drawbacks of rapid social change in many places is the effects that changing institutions have on the lives of the aged. The tribal peoples of Zimbabwe, for instance, have traditionally respected their elders, particularly for their control of economic and political structures within the society. Local communities are largely based on gerontocracies, in which the elderly wield considerable power and control much of the land, food, and cattle.[58]

In recent years, however, Zimbabwe has experienced rapid gains in industrial development and commercialization. The mining and modern agricultural industries, set up under the colonial government, have prompted an exodus of the population from rural areas, leaving behind the traditional ways of life and family. Unable to keep up with these rapid changes, the elderly are often left alone—destitute and dependent on outside sources for their care.

The challenges for communities burdened with caring for the destitute elderly include providing inexpensive housing along with adequate support services. A study of two separate housing projects in Zimbabwe, carried out by Andrew Chad Nyanguru, a social worker from the Harare School, illustrates the benefits of developing alternative housing.[59]

Kudzai Old People's Home and the Dambudzo Old People's Cooperative are both designed as hostel accommodations that allow elderly residents to maintain their independence of daily living while providing them with food, laundry, and general care services. Located in rural areas, both facilities house male and female members. Kudzai is a larger facility and has fewer residents. The residence offers amenities such as indoor bathrooms, beds, and dining room, along with an on-site health clinic. In contrast, Dambudzo is more primitive and crowded. Residents eat and bathe outdoors, are five to a bedroom, sleep on mattresses on the floor, and rely on once-a-month visits from a doctor. The daily operations of Kudzai and Dambudzo are also distinct. Dambudzo is self-sufficient, with residents actively involved in growing, gathering, and preparing food. The residents participate in a governing body that plans and administers the household rules. Residents are typically involved in moneymaking endeavors such as weaving mats. The residents are free to come and go as they please. In contrast, Kudzai is run by a religious organization that employs a staff to cook, clean, and care for the residents. While some residents are working at moneymaking projects, such practices are not encouraged. The residents are required to check in with staff members when they wish to leave the facility or have guests visit them.

When the residents of each home were interviewed, they indicated that while they felt that their need for shelter, food, and companionship were met, the quality of life differed substantially. Members of the Dambudzo home said they were more satisfied, primarily because of sustained social contact and their ability to actively participate in the daily operation of the home and maintain their independence. Residents of Kudzai said they were satisfied with the amenities offered them but were not as positive about the overall quality of life there.

As Nyanguru observes: "The results of this [Zimbabwe] study serve to underline that provision of food, clothing, and shelter is insufficient to ensure a satisfactory quality of life for the elderly in residential care facilities. Policy should emphasize continuity in the conditions of life, opportunities for self-help, participation in the day-to-day running of the home, all of which contribute to the individual's sense of self-worth and dignity."

A report by the United Nations concludes: "The experience of these two facilities in Zimbabwe for destitute elderly persons indicates that relatively inexpensive and less institutionalized approaches may provide more, not less, satisfaction among the old people they serve."[60] This point needs to be heeded in other places where the elderly find themselves without traditional means of support.

- A matchmaking service to encourage remarriage among the elderly to reduce the number of elderly people living alone. This has been tried in China and Korea.[61]

The second theme of the recommendations is the integration of care for both the physical and mental needs of the elderly. Because the elderly tend to suffer from multiple pathologies, it is likely that anyone with a mental disorder will also be suffering from some other chronic physical disorder. Since the elderly are more likely to seek treatment for physical disorders than for mental problems,[62] any attempt to treat mental disorders will be most effective if it is part of the existing system to treat physical ailments. This policy has the added advantage of being cheaper to establish than an independent, formal system aimed specifically at the mental health needs of the elderly.

Strategies to integrate mental health needs in the formal care system include:

- Developing gerontopsychiatry components within community health centers and in acute-care hospitals.
- Including a gerontopsychiatry component in barefoot-doctor programs in which paramedics conduct house-to-house visits for screening of physical and mental health problems.

In general, anything that reduces older people's sense of social and economic marginality is likely to help reduce the prevalence of mental health problems and will provide a financial cushion for care and medical help later in life. Pension schemes are key to reducing the vulnerability of the aged. Pensions for those employed in the formal sector now exist in most regions of the world, especially Latin America, the Caribbean, and most of Africa. Progress toward universal coverage in Asia has been slower.[63] Some have argued that pension schemes serve mainly to redistribute income to elite segments of the population, since those employed in the formal sector tend to be a privileged minority (30% of the population in Gabon, for example).[64] Coverage is sparse for rural populations and for those who work in the informal sector, who are usually some of the poorest members of a society. In countries with high inflation, private savings become riskier and formal pension schemes grow in importance because they grow with inflation, whereas savings often do not.

Where these schemes can increase a person's sense of self-worth and value, they are particularly helpful. In Ecuador, a nongovernmental organization with help from the United Nations has set up a pilot scheme to provide employment for the elderly. This is problematic, because the most needy are often the frailest and the least able to be retrained to fill available jobs. In one village, however, the organization noticed that there was no bakery within forty kilometers, and set up an old people's bakery using simple local technology. This provided employment for the elderly and a product valued by the community. The organization then set up a related sewing workshop for women and a plot of land for men to cultivate medicinal herbs. In Colombia, elderly people are running a recycling program in collaboration with the city, by sorting recyclable waste materials that residents deliver to recycling centers around the city. The program has provided enough money to give the elderly people a small salary.[65] These programs all have the potential to increase the well-being of the elderly, leading to positive mental health.

It is important to keep in mind that there is oftentimes conflict between the delivery of care in rural versus urban populations. Government intervention can reach the urban populations much more easily and usually much more cheaply. This may be troublesome in some countries where the majority of elderly live in rural areas. But in rural areas, the tendency to remain in the work force until physical incapacity prevents it, the high proportion of self-employed or unpaid family workers, close-knit family support mechanisms, and the less concentrated populations make it more difficult and in some senses less necessary for the public sector to intervene with programs specifically for the aged.

In summary, policy interventions should fall into two broad categories. First, policies should take advantage of the care currently provided for the elderly by their families, by promoting their ability to care for the aged relatives. Second, formal health care systems should integrate mental and physical care, particularly by incorporating geriatric care aspects into existing community initiatives. The precise mix of optimal policies for each country will vary and cannot be generalized. The challenge for all nations is to learn from each other and to develop policies that are realistic and sensitive to local conditions.

Research Recommendations

Research recommendations fall into four broad categories, which directly parallel the sections of this chapter: (1) those related to the future demand and utilization of health care services, given the widespread demographic changes resulting in population aging; (2) those related to identifying the major forces affecting mental health of the elderly and to specifying the structural changes that could be implemented to provide for mechanisms for improving elderly mental health; 3) those related to the epidemiology of mental illnesses in the elderly; and 4) those related to the family's continuing ability to provide care for the elderly amid rapidly occurring economic and social changes and population aging.

First, the rapid growth in the numbers of elderly throughout the world will likely lead to strains on existing health care systems. Research is needed on the development of acceptable models of care to meet the demands for long-term care, including home care and institutional care.

A second area of research would examine the major forces affecting mental health of the elderly, with a focus on how structural changes, such as pensions, labor force participation, and intergenerational transfers (including money, shared housing, and help with daily living) could be implemented to enhance the quality of life for mentally ill elderly in the countries of Africa, Asia, and Latin America.

Third, the development of comparable epidemiological studies on the prevalence and incidence of the major illnesses of the elderly in Africa, Asia, and Latin America is recommended. Such studies could be coordinated and implemented by numerous countries.

A fourth area of research would document how the family's traditional arrangements for support of the elderly are being affected by rapid social and economic changes. What will take the place of the traditional social structures that have ensured care for the elderly and mentally ill elderly as social and economic changes undermine them?

Research needs to focus on specifying the nature, extent, and impact of caregiving for family caregivers of elderly mentally ill patients, particularly those with dementia. Given our earlier observations that dementia is not always construed as a major health problem among the peoples of some nations, a research focus on family caregiving must be modified to be consistent with the local responses of these people.

Other specific research recommendations parallel many of the policy recommendations proposed. For example, research should be conducted to evaluate the effectiveness of caregiver support groups and family caregiver training programs that teach the caregivers of demented elders how to manage the difficult behavioral disturbances that accompany the progression of dementing illness. Such programs will need to be shaped by the local culture and availability of resources. Additional promising interventions should be piloted.

Conclusions

- Countries in Africa, Asia, and Latin America are currently witnessing and will continue to witness large increases in the numbers and proportions of elderly members in their populations. Since organic dementias are age-related, a heavier burden of these disorders will appear as the populations age. Furthermore, the elderly are particularly vulnerable to economic and social changes that result from industrialization and modernization. The elderly often suffer as a result of the decline in value of agricultural assets, migration of younger family members from rural to urban environments, and the access of younger family members to education. Correspondingly, the prevalence among the elderly of mental disorders such as depression and anxiety is likely to increase.

- The family is still the primary caregiver in most areas of the world, and it is under stress at exactly the time when the numbers of elderly are undergoing unprecedented increases. Migration, lower birth rates, the breakdown of patron-client relationships, and the participation of more women in the labor force all influence the ability of family members to provide care for their elderly. Older persons depending on poor, female, old, and solitary caregivers are at particular risk.

- The reliance on stereotypes of modern and traditional societies can result in dangerous policy orientations. By assuming that families in the countries of Africa, Asia, and Latin America confer more respect on their elders and are more inclined to care for them, the role of the state in implementing useful policy may be downplayed. However, given the demographic transition and social, cultural, and economic changes, careful planning is needed to originate policies that strengthen informal and formal care systems.

- Since many countries in Africa, Asia, and Latin America are financially burdened and face other serious social and political problems, inexpensive targeted and universal policies are desirable. Programs and policies helping family care-providers that the government can support include day-care centers, home help, education programs on dementia, housing policies that encourage multigenerational families, promotion of employer-sponsored benefits for families with obligations to elder members, and income tax relief for families caring for an elderly person. Examples of policies aimed at the elderly without children or other caregivers are direct financial transfers to those elderly who cannot support themselves, provision of formal care through group residential facilities, and matchmaking services to encourage remarriage or establishment of friendships. Universal policies that benefit the elderly will still reach those who become demented. For example, pensions provide a steady source of income and can be indexed against inflation; coverage should be expanded where possible. Finally, the mental needs of the elderly should be addressed, when possible, simultaneously with their physical needs. All of these policy ideas have been successfully implemented in different countries throughout the world.

- Future research should ideally address the following questions of interest. What are the prevalence and incidence rates of mental disorders among the elderly in different areas of the world, and what are the implications for care in different cultures? What can be learned from successful models of formal care systems (which would, ideally, be community-based), and how cost-effective are they? How will informal family care systems be influenced by ongoing social and economic changes? How can universal policies be adapted to benefit the demented elderly? Answers to such questions will be increasingly important as the number of elderly in the world rapidly grows.

10

Behavior and Health

In the late nineteenth and early twentieth century, the discovery of the specific infectious agents (bacteria and parasites) that cause acute diseases so preempted medical attention that the role of behavior as a mediator between disease risk and host exposure largely disappeared from view. The demographic transition has brought renewed attention to the behavioral link between risk and exposure. Industrialized nations have shifted from an era of death from pestilence and famine to an era of sickness from degenerative diseases and behavioral pathology. When mortality was very high and life expectancy at birth was low, population increase was held in check by the death rate. Now that death rates have declined sharply (life expectancy at birth is twice what it was at the turn of the century), fertility has become the principal determinant of population growth.[1] Degenerative diseases (heart disease, stroke, cancer, dementia) have become the main public health problems.[2]

In contrast, low-income countries are in the midst of a protracted epidemiologic transition. Citizens suffer from a triple burden of morbidity and mortality from infectious diseases, degenerative diseases, and behavioral problems (substance abuse, violence, etc.). In addition, there are ever-sharper differences between the health status of the upper and lower social classes in many societies; that is, the health of the upper classes has begun to resemble that of today's industrialized populations, whereas the lower class suffers from chronic disease as well as infection and parasitism.

In these processes of change, behavior is crucial. The way people behave plays an important role in determining whether they stay well or become ill, and if they become ill, whether and how fast they recover. This may seem hard to believe when many diseases are known to have specific causes: genes, germs, poisons, physical trauma, etc. The point is that behavior determines whether a particular person is exposed to disease-causing agents (as in the case of sexually transmitted diseases); furthermore, even when an effective treatment for the illness exists, a person must decide to seek care for the illness; if the illness is long-term, he or she must continue with the treatment (as with the many months needed for the treatment of tuberculosis or leprosy). Thus, behavior influences the risk of getting sick and the likelihood of getting better.

Why include health behaviors in a report on mental health? For one, they are major determinants of physical, mental, and public health; these behaviors directly connect the domain of mental health to general well-being. Secondly, health behaviors illustrate practical preventative and therapeutic measures that can be applied in even the poorest of societies. There are impressive examples of how behavioral transformations can improve the health of society.

The combined impact of behavioral factors on health is evident in the startling difference in the female/male population ratio in Europe and North America, versus that in India, China, North Africa, and South and West Asia. In Europe and North America, the ratio is 1.05 to 1; in the other countries noted, it is 0.94 to 1 or less. Amartya Sen calculates that 100,000,000 women are "missing" if the 1.05 ratio is applied to various parts of Asia and North Africa.[3] The biological advantage in longevity lies with the female, but that advantage is overridden and reversed by actions stemming from bias in favor of males. As set out in Chapter 8, the difference reflects the combined effect of sex discrimination in: infanticide and abortion; differential access to nutrition, education, and medical care; the inability of women to control their own reproductive function; and their lack of economic independence.

In all, behavior is deeply related to well-being. A sizable amount of suffering in the world today could be prevented if systematic changes in behavior were implemented. (Figure 10.1) shows the portion of behavior-related disability in the world today, as adapted from the World Bank's 1993 estimates of disability-adjusted life years. Roughly one-third of the global burden of illness could be readily prevented by changes in behavior, including: improved sanitation and better nutrition to prevent diarrheal diseases, malnutrition, and nutritional deficiencies; immunizations to prevent childhood diseases; the prevention and treatment of tuberculosis; the prevention of sexually transmitted diseases; and the reduction of violence and motor-vehicle accidents. The point is that behaviors as seemingly straightforward as washing or not washing hands, starting or stopping smoking, deciding what and when to eat, having sex when, with whom, and how often, and working safely or not have a profound influence on health. All of these behaviors are constrained by poverty, powerlessness, and beliefs.

Behaviors that have an impact on health are commonly referred to as "lifestyle." This term implies that, like styles of clothing, a person is "free" to choose his own. While middle- and upper-class persons have the means to choose the environment for their homes, the quality and type of food they consume, and the medical options they elect for the treatment of disease, the choices of those living in poverty are sharply restricted by their limited resources, including limited schooling. Behavior is so rooted in social contexts, so inflected by social differences, and so at the mercy of social resources that behaviors must be thought of as primarily social. They are subject to individual variation at the margins only.

The ability of people to decide what to do to protect health and cope with illness is limited by social resources available to them. Those resources include local knowledge, networks of communication, and culturally approved modes of action as much as disposable income, education, and available services. It is never a simple matter of beliefs causing behaviors. Local contexts make certain health options more available and others less so for certain categories of persons. Cultural orientations toward risk and suffering, influenced by gender, class, age cohort, and religious differences, create different expectations about health and health care. In their

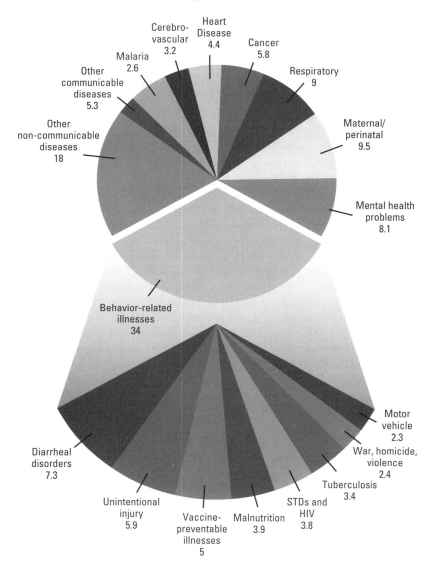

Figure 10.1 Behavior-related Disability (*Source*: Adapted from the World Bank, 1993). *DALY = Disability-Adjusted Life Year

interactions with social institutions, people work out distinctive patterns of health and illness behavior. In a setting of rapid industrialization, for instance, changes in diet can cause increased rates of cerebrovascular and coronary artery disease. In other places, communal water-use patterns contribute to parasitic infections.

Some behavioral interventions can rely on a classical model of modifying behaviors, and others can take medical forms, as if behavioral changes were analogous to treatments. Yet many of the most serious problems reviewed in this book cannot be effectively handled in this manner. They require a unique framework in which political economy and social structure—including the politics and economics and procedures of the health sector—must be the focus for interventions.

In simplest terms, supplying a shantytown with safe water and sewage disposal would yield greater health benefits than teaching inhabitants about building latrines, boiling water, washing hands, and so on. However, to abandon education (labor-intensive and partially effective as it is) while awaiting the political decision to commit the resources needed for sanitary engineering is to condemn millions of persons to needless illness. On the other hand, to focus only on educating victims and *not* to fight for municipal services is to allow avoidable suffering to persist indefinitely.

The success or failure of a public health program ultimately turns on the local context of behavior. The behaviors that contribute to health include those of policy-makers and service providers, so these too must be considered, and may be part of the problem. The extent of risk from a behavior may also depend on environmental conditions; if sanitation and water purification are at a high level, poor personal hygiene confers less risk.

The behaviors that put health at risk vary from those that may be common-place but risky (failure to wash hands), to those that are taken up only by some in a given society (cigarette smoking), to those that are pathological in any society and exhibited by few citizens (chronic and persistent drunkenness). It also includes behaviors that stem from the ubiquity of automobiles and television sets: what is now termed the "sedentary lifestyle." According to the Centers for Disease Control, nearly 60% of the adult population in the United States reported little or no leisure time physical activity in 1991, a disposition thought to increase the risk for heart disease.[4]

Cigarette Smoking: A Behavioral Risk for Death

Cigarette smoking puts health at risk in every community. There is a risk for non-smokers if they share a common indoor environment with smokers, because of the effects of passive smoke inhalation. Although behavior is often taken to represent voluntary choice (one argument is that no one is "forced" to smoke and everyone is "free" to stop), the situation is much more complex. Education and social class are powerful predictors of the likelihood that a person will smoke. More years of schooling, higher income, and higher social status are inversely related to the probability of becoming a smoker. All citizens are subject to a steady barrage of propaganda. Because adolescence is a prime time for picking up new social habits, cigarette companies target youth in their advertising schemes. For example, "Joe Camel," the cartoon logo for Camel cigarettes, has been shown to have high recognition value among elementary 12-to-19-year-old public school students in the United States.[5] Cigarette advertisements are ubiquitous. Because tobacco is a source of foreign exchange, the production of tobacco and the manufacture of cigarettes are subsidized by governments of almost every stripe.

Table 10.1 Causes of Death Related to Smoking Among British Male Doctors
(per 100,000 per year)

Causes of Death	NON-S	EX-S	C-S	C-S>25	C-S>25 NON-S
Ischemic heart disease	553	661	870	999	1.8 X
Cerebrovascular disease	249	273	371	441	1.8 X
Other cardiovascular disease	201	221	310	402	2.0 X
Pneumonia	73	87	134	161	2.2 X
Lung cancer	14	58	205	347	24.8 X
Chronic obstructive lung disease	10	56	124	218	22.0 X

NON-S = Non-Smoker; EX-S = Ex-Smoker; C-S = Continuing Smokers; C-S>25 = more than 25 daily.
Source: Adapted from Sharp, 1993:486.

Table 10.1, which compares death rates among nonsmokers, ex-smokers, and continuing smokers in a study of 40,000 male British doctors followed for forty years, shows just how injurious cigarette smoking is to health.[6] The benefits of quitting as well as the hazards of continuing smoking are clearly demonstrated. Nonetheless, smoking persists in the face of overwhelming evidence of the fatal long-term outcomes associated with it. Peto et al. estimate that 20% of all deaths in industrialized countries is attributable to smoking.[7] Tobacco is currently responsible the world over for 3 million premature deaths each year, a figure that will reach 10 million by the year 2025 if present trends are not halted. Per capita tobacco consumption is continuing to rise in many countries and is expected to increase by 12% between 1990 and 2000. The problem is not simply a matter of ignorance. Although physicians in England and the United States have sharply reduced their own smoking rates in response to these facts, physicians in the rest of the world continue to smoke at high rates. Changing behavior clearly requires more than making information available.

Thus, powerful forces are arrayed to increase the probability that people will smoke; the success of the propaganda is greater among those who have fewer independent sources of information and who are under greater social stress. Cigarette advertising is designed to lure preadolescent and adolescent youngsters to start smoking. By depicting smoking as a symbol of strong, sexually potent men and smart, sophisticated women, the lure becomes irresistible to adolescents not yet confident of their own identity. Once the habit is picked up, the addictive properties of nicotine (now classified as a psychoactive substance) make it difficult for the smoker to stop because of the side effects caused by withdrawal.

In a 1994 report on tobacco use among young people, the U.S. Surgeon General reports that nearly all first use occurs before high school graduation; if adolescents can be kept tobacco free until that time, most will never start smoking.[8] The Surgeon General's report notes that community-wide efforts, including tobacco-tax increases, enforcement of limits to access by minors, youth-oriented mass media campaigns, and school-based prevention programs, have been successful in reducing use of tobacco. The decision to smoke and to continue to smoke is therefore hardly "free"; it is made under the pressure of powerful constraints. At the same time, the remarkable fact that some 50 million Americans have given up smoking is the result of a fundamental shift in cultural practices.[9]

Eating Behaviors

What and how much we eat, and when and how we eat, are shaped by social forces. Eating depends on access to food, on the culinary practices of a particular society, on local beliefs about nutritional value, and on personal choice. When there is famine, choice disappears; there is only an unremitting search for food of any kind. As Dreze and Sen point out, famines rarely are just the result of crop failure, but rather are based in the politics of food distribution.[10] Under ordinary conditions, income determines the availability of food; the poor can consume only the least expensive foods, which are often the least complete. Even when nutritious food is potentially available (fish in the ocean, for example), it may be disdained by a given community; in turn, a given food may be eaten even though it is associated with risk for some members of the population (fava bean consumption by those whose blood cells are destroyed by it). Food that may be safe to eat when it is ripe may be toxic before ripening (as with cassava), but may be eaten when other foods are short.

The act of eating is under strong social control. Many cultures have strict food taboos that have important health consequences. Some foods are designated as improper for children or unmarried women, but may be regarded as essential for men. The age at which supplementary solid foods are added to an infant's diet has important health consequences. What is considered the right age for supplementation varies from group to group. It can be changed to conform to a science-based nutritional practice by making education available to women in such fashion as to minimize conflicts with local beliefs. In distributing food to family members, rural Bangladeshi mothers give more calories to sons than to daughters; in an environment in which rural nutrition is marginal, these differences lead to greater rates of female malnutrition.[11] When food is scarce, mothers everywhere give preference to their own over foster children. This presents a problem of growing magnitude in Africa in view of the projected size of the AIDS orphan population.

With modernization, imported foods often take precedence over traditional ones. Thus, polished white rice, which is identified with modernity and "refinement," becomes preferred to brown rice with its outer shell intact; the result is thiamine deficiency. Just as inherited biological traits that might be advantageous (or neutral) for survival in one environment can become entirely negative in a second, dietary customs, carried from one geographic region to another, can become hazardous. Pakistani immigrants to England suffer from rickets, a disease now almost completely eliminated in the rest of the English population. Traditional Pakistani diet employs ghee (rendered butter) in place of table butter. Rendering destroys its vitamin D content. That practice has no health effects in Pakistan, where sunlight converts precursors present in human skin into vitamin D. When exposure to the sun is sharply restricted by cloud cover and smog, as in English industrial towns, this alternate source of vitamin D is missing. Rickets appears in those with reduced vitamin D intake.[12]

An aspect of eating behavior that has major disease consequences the world over is the increase, as affluence increases, in consumption of animal fats. Cardio-vascular disease (CVD) is the leading cause of death in the industrialized coun-tries and an ever more common cause of death in other parts of the world. The conjunction of too much animal fat and salt in the diet, insufficient exercise, and smoking, which continues in Eastern European countries, has led to increasing death rates from CVD and stroke in those countries, whereas rates have fallen by 30% in North America.[13] There has been a continuing increase in blood lipid lev-els in Eastern Europe and a decline in North America, where public health cam-paigns have reduced fat consumption, increased exercise, reduced cigarette smok-ing, and increased treatment of hypertension.[14] While many industrializing nations stand on the threshold of a CVD epidemic, public policy to favor grain rather than meat consumption, to discourage smoking, to encourage exercise, and to increase access to primary health care can slow an already visible increase in cardiovascular mortality.

A diet can be appropriate in calories, protein, and the ratio of carbohydrates to fat and still be deficient in micronutrients such as iodine, iron, and vitamin A. Iodine deficiency can lead to goiter, to miscarriage in women, and to stillbirth, cre-tinism, and mental deficiency in their offspring. Iodine deficiency is common in Asia, Africa, and some areas of Europe wherever rainfall or floods leach the ele-ment from the soil. The clinical problem is entirely preventable by adding iodine to the diet. For rural populations, alternatives include periodic injections of iodized oil, potassium iodide tablets, or iodine capsules.[15] Inadequate vitamin A intake causes irreversible blindness and results in vulnerability to infections, anemia, and poor growth in children.[16] At a minuscule cost (less than 2 U.S. cents per capsule), the vitamin can be distributed to children with a diet inadequate in green leafy vegeta-bles, yellow fruits, and dairy products. Iron deficiency is the most common micronutrient disorder. It is more common in women because of blood loss (and hence, iron loss) via menstruation and childbearing; iron-deficiency anemia increases the risk of death from hemorrhage in childbirth. In children, iron defi-ciency is associated with diminished capacity to learn.[17] Distribution of ferrous sul-fate tablets can prevent iron-deficiency anemia and cure it when it does occur. Alternatively, iron can be added to powdered milk, to flour, and to other foods. Unfortunately, the connection between the diseases resulting from micronutrient deficiency and their nutritional causes is not recognized in many "traditional" com-munities. Public education is essential in the campaign to prevent these disorders. At times, minor changes in diet can have significant health benefits (Box 10.1).

Personal Hygiene

Hygienic practices also have enormous health effects. More than one billion people in low-income countries are without access to safe water to drink and almost twice that number lack access to sanitation.[19] This remains the case even though the 1980s were designated by the World Health Organization as the "International Drinking Water Supply and Sanitation Decade." The situation is unlikely to change in the

Box 10.1 Reduction of Child Deaths and Pneumonia Cases in Nepal

Low-cost primary care measures can reduce child morbidity and mortality in even the least-hospitable of areas served.

Jumla, one of the most remote and inaccessible districts in Nepal, is such an area, with few modern amenities and, for the most part, no electricity. The literacy rate is low, with barely one in three men, and one in twenty women, able to read and write. Jumla is further characterized by long, dry winters and a short growing season, resulting in a high level of malnutrition. Outside of a small administrative center there were no modern health facilities prior to 1986. At that time child mortality was extraordinarily high, with nearly one of every five children dying within the first year of life, and nearly one in three dying by the age of five. Pneumonia and diarrhea were the leading causes of child death.

In 1986 the Resources for Child Health (REACH) Project began a phased low-cost program to reduce child mortality. The first phase, from 1986 to 1989, focused exclusively on pneumonia detection and treatment in Jumla's more than 13,000 children five years or younger. Eighty health workers were selected on the basis of community reputation, willingness and ability to walk to all the houses in their service area, and basic literacy skills. They received nine days of training in pneumonia standard case management, and supervisory visits every two weeks. They were taught to make a presumptive diagnosis of pneumonia based on indrawing of the chest on breathing, or a breathing rate of 50 breaths per minute or more for children up to five years of age. They were also taught to treat all children so diagnosed with cotrimoxazole syrup. Finally, they were taught how to keep basic records and how to educate mothers about the danger signs of pneumonia.

Each health worker visited each of the 160 households in their areas at least once every two weeks. During these visits they educated the mothers and examined the children under five for pneumonia. In the event that a child was diagnosed with pneumonia, the mother was provided with a five-day supply of cotrimoxazole and taught to administer the syrup to the child. The health worker followed up on each sick child after two days and at the end of the treatment course. In the rare event that the child failed to respond to cotrimoxazole, the child was given oral chloramphenicol.

A separate data-collection system, with different workers and supervisors, was set up to assess mortality rates. By 1989, the third year of the project, the pneumonia case management services had reduced total child deaths by 28%. This decline was observed not only in pneumonia-specific deaths (which declined 30%) but in deaths ascribed to numerous other causes, particularly measles and diarrhea.

In 1989, REACH implemented the second phase of the program—vitamin A supplementation—again with the primary goal of reducing child mortality. In each village, all the children five years or younger were assembled on the same day. The program supervisors then administered a high dose of vitamin A capsules. This was repeated every five months. The supplementation was organized into two rounds. Communities that received supplementation within the initial round were matched with villages with comparable presupplementation child mortality rates. In the first five months, the child mortality rate was 26% lower in those villages that had received vitamin A supplementation. By age group, the reduction was greatest in children between 6 and 12 months, as their risk of death was cut nearly in half. By cause of death, the reduction was greatest for diarrhea deaths, which decreased by a third. Morbidity was also significantly reduced: those communities that received early dosing with vitamin A showed a 33% lower rate of pneumonia cases. And all this was the effect of one dose of vitamin A.

At this writing, the pneumonia case management and vitamin A supplementation services continue throughout the Jumla district. The remarkable mortality reductions noted here have been sustained and are being further augmented by a set of complementary services directed at the early treatment of childhood diarrheas and the promotion of support of the government's immunization services.

The continuing success of primary health care services in Jumla has been attributed to several factors. First, the initial services provided—pneumonia case management— gave such tangible and rapid results that the community health workers gained substantial credibility and authority in the villages. This made it much easier to introduce additional programs and procedures that might have been less credible, or produced less rapid results. Second, the phased approach prevents overload of the health workers, allowing them to be more effective providers. The health workers' effectiveness was, and is, further complemented by adequate training and supervision and the simple diagnostic criteria and treatment regimen. Finally, the low cost of the programs allow them to be easily implemented with minimal financial support. The total cost of the pneumonia program per child covered (including salaries of the community workers, supervisory and management costs, and antibiotic costs) was less than $4 per year. Similarly, the dramatic impact of vitamin A supplementation on child mortality in Jumla resulted in an estimated cost of less than $11 for every life saved.[18]

near term because of the vast resources needed. Therefore, emphasis on hygienic washing, sanitation, and drinking behaviors is central to good public health.

Women and children are particularly affected by the unavailability of water. Carrying water home from remote sources, a task assigned to women, exacts great time and energy costs. Because available water for domestic use is contaminated, diarrheal diseases are the third-leading cause of disease burden in children under five.[20] Although the immediate causes of diarrhea are ingested bacteria or viruses that multiply in the gut and cause fluid loss, the proximate causes include exposure to contaminated water, food, and nonedible substances that the child mouths and swallows. Contributing causes include measles, respiratory infections, and malnutrition, which, separately and together, increase morbidity and mortality from diarrhea; in turn, infections and diarrhea exacerbate malnutrition. Protecting child health, then, includes immunization, prompt treatment of respiratory infections, and measures to prevent and treat diarrhea.[21]

The behavior of the caretaker, both in feeding the child and supervising its immediate environment, is a key link in the chain of events. The more years of education mothers have, the less the child's risk of death from diarrhea and other diseases.[22] Greater maternal education may lead to greater child survival by the following mechanisms.[23] Women with more education marry later, have their first child later, and have fewer children; thus, far fewer die in childbirth. They are therefore less likely to leave their children orphaned; the magnitude of this effect in low-income countries where maternal mortality is high can reduce risk of orphaning to less than one-fifth of the rate among uneducated mothers. Educated mothers are more likely to receive prenatal care, to have been given tetanus toxoid before delivery, and to have trained birth attendants at delivery. Therefore, perinatal morbidity and mortality is reduced. Their children are less likely to get diarrhea and more likely to be treated adequately for it if they do, because educated mothers are more responsive to modern hygienic practices. They are likely to marry more-educated men, a further benefit to their children although the effect of paternal education is less than that of maternal education.

Behaviors that reduce risk include breast feeding, maintaining cleanliness, prompt and appropriate disposal of feces, and the proper preparation and storage of nursing and weaning food. Studies in Bangladesh and Guatemala have shown that improving personal and domestic hygiene, especially through hand washing, reduces diarrheal morbidity.[24] (Box 10.2) provides a description of an intervention that decisively reduced the episodes of diarrhea and improved general nutrition in a rural area of Bangladesh.

When diarrhea does develop, its immediate life threatening consequence is

---

Box 10.2 Reducing Diarrhea in Infants

Diarrheal diseases are among the leading causes of illness and death in infants and children in low-income countries. Over the long term, the provision of safe water and effective sewage disposal in every community constitute the best solution for this problem. Are there methods in the near term that can reduce diarrhea rates?

Nutritionist Nasar Ahmed and his coworkers evaluated the effectiveness of a community-based intervention designed to improve personal hygiene, reduce diarrheal morbidity, and enhance the development of 0-to-18-month-old children at rural sites along the Padma River, 100 km northwest of Dhaka, Bangladesh.[25] The public health measures were designed after a careful survey (a) to identify the behaviors associated with childhood morbidity, and (b) to understand community organization. Local field-workers (high school graduates from the study communities) were recruited on the basis of interest and ability and were paid for their participation. The support and cooperation of village leaders were solicited for the health program. Lectures were delivered to villagers at weekly Friday prayer gatherings at mosques (most households were Muslim). Islam's stress on cleanliness was congruent with the basic public health message.

Proposed interventions were tested and revised through iterative trials at homes, first by the project workers, then by volunteer mothers, and then by twenty-five of the poorest community mothers. The measures that proved feasible under village conditions were included in the intervention. The field workers trained and supervised community volunteer mothers, who in turn taught the remaining mothers in the community.

The most powerful impetus for behavior change was interactive teaching in small groups (three to five members) of mothers twice a week. Mothers were taught the rudiments of germ theory of disease so that they were able to understand the logic of the interventions. Hygiene and sanitation behaviors were actively demonstrated by the volunteers and dramatized through group participation to show graphically how they affect health.

There were three principal targets for change. The first, toward ground sanitation, was to keep babies from touching and eating contaminated matter from the dirt surface of the village compound. Techniques included: sweeping the baby's play area; using an inexpensive trowel to remove animal or human feces immediately; constructing a feces pit to receive this matter; and keeping crawling babies in a rudimentary playpen. The second, toward personal hygiene, was to reduce the transmission of germs. Techniques included: hand-washing with ashes or soap after defecation as well as before eating; cleaning the baby immediately after its defecation; keeping nails short by frequent cutting; and drying hands on a clean rag. The third target, toward food hygiene, was to reduce germ transmission during supplementary and bottled feeding. Techniques included: discouraging the use of feeding bottles; preparing only that food and drink which the baby can consume at one time; washing caretaker's and baby's hands and utensils before food preparation and eating; keeping food protected from flies and animals.

Field workers collected data in successive months after the completion of the intervention from February to July. Outcomes studied were the degree to which mothers understood the theory behind cleanliness, direct observation of the cleanliness of the child and its play area, mother's report of episodes of diarrhea, and anthropometric measures of the child's development. The mother's understanding correlated *directly* with the cleanliness score and with the child's weight for age, and *inversely* with the diarrhea score. Cleanliness indicators in the intervention site were dramatically better than those in the control site by the end of the study period. The prevalence of diarrhea at the intervention site was consistently lower, and the percentage of severely malnourished children was reduced. Furthermore, there was a sharp decrease in the rate of bottle feeding at the intervention site. The findings strongly support the utility of community-based interventions to improve knowledge about hygiene, to modify relevant behaviors, to lower the diarrheal disease rate, and to reduce malnutrition even in an impoverished setting.

As might be expected, there are limits to such interventions at times of extreme environmental contamination. During the periodic severe floods in Bangladesn, sewage is swept directly into contact with water sources; hygienic behaviors cannot be maintained when homes and villages must be abandoned. Flood control is beyond local initiative and, in this instance, beyond the national government of Bangladesh alone. It requires a multilateral effort by India, Nepal, and Bangladesh, whose farming, logging, water-use patterns, and population growth must be rationalized with the goal of flood control. In July 1993, a wave of flooding killed more than 2,000 in South Asia and displaced 10,000,000, but narrow conceptions of national self-interest have thus far impeded agreement on steps to control floods.[26]

dehydration; its near-term effect is malnutrition. Prompt and appropriate replacement of fluids and salts with oral rehydration treatment (ORT) can be lifesaving. However, giving fluid under these circumstances challenges local understandings; the response of almost all mothers to such a child is to restrict fluids in order to "rest the bowel." Moreover, the initial response to ORT can be increased diarrhea. Yet fluids are essential for saving lives. Therefore, systematic education of each community is essential for the prompt and sustained use of ORT; locally prepared rice or cereal gruels as alternatives to prepackaged ORT preparations have the advantage of immediate availability, supplying more calories, and slowing diarrhea. There is no question about the effectiveness of oral rehydration or about the ability of educational campaigns to increase its use, but use of ORT is far from adequate and education requires reinforcement. ORT programs must be built into primary health care services in order to make them sustainable over the long term. However, neither ORT nor any other technology can be effective in preserving child health indefinitely in settings of repeated reinfection owing to the intolerable conditions under which the poorest shantytown inhabitants live: to wit, in makeshift housing, without access to clean water or sewage disposal, without means to store water or food safely, and without municipal services of any kind.

Sexual Behavior: Childbearing

Sexual activity has at least three major consequences for health: childbearing, sexually transmitted diseases (STDs), and cancer of the liver and probably of the cervix as well.

Pregnancy and childbirth carry a significant risk for maternal health, particularly when mothers are very young or relatively old and have borne many children; when mothers have been ill-nourished as adolescents so that the pelvic outlet is small; when interbirth intervals are short; or when prenatal and obstetrical backup care is inadequate. For example, in "developing" countries, death in childbirth is three times as likely for women under age 18 and five times as likely for those over age 34 than for women between 20 and 29. For all these reasons, maternal mortality is some twenty-five times higher in low-income countries than in prosperous countries; about 1 in 100 women in low-income countries die as a consequence of complications of pregnancy and childbirth, compared with only 1 in 2,700 in established market economies (and 1 in 12,000 in the United States).[27] The tragedy does not end there. The death of the mother increases the likelihood that her child will not survive till age five by 50%.[28]

Unwanted pregnancies may lead women to have abortions. In those countries where abortion is legal and accessible, it is remarkably safe; where it is not, the hazards are remarkably high. The World Health Organization estimates that more than half of the better than 100,000 maternal deaths caused by induced abortion each year occur in South and Southeast Asia and sub-Saharan Africa. When abortion was banned in Romania in 1966 for political reasons (the birth rate was regarded as too low), maternal deaths rose to a rate ten times higher than that in any other European country, the rate declined rapidly when the law was revoked.[29]

A major new social problem has arisen. Amniocentesis and ultrasonography permit prenatal sex determination. These methods are now in use for selective abortion of female infants in India and in China. As a result, the male/female birth ratio in China has increased from the expected 105 boys to 100 girls to an unprecedented 118.5 to 100. Thus, one out of nine female fetuses are being aborted. Sex selective abortion, although illegal, is extremely difficult to intercept; sonography equipment is now widely dispersed in China, even in rural areas.[30]

The need for abortion can be markedly reduced by the systematic use of contraception, but it cannot be altogether eliminated because of method failures. In addition to better maternal and child health resulting from planned, properly spaced, and desired pregnancies, the benefits to many countries from lower fertility rates lends investment in family planning programs one of the highest benefit-to-cost ratios of any health program. Field studies have demonstrated that trained midwives can safely provide oral contraceptives and intrauterine devices (IUDs), can implant depot medroxy progesterone acetate, and can perform postpartum tubal ligations. Recently, a large field trial in Vietnam demonstrated the remarkable safety and effectiveness of sterilization by the nonsurgical transcervical implantation of pellets of quinacrine, which can be put in place by trained health workers.[31] The most efficient reversible methods of birth control are the use of hormones by mouth (the Pill) or by injection of slow-release hormone. Unfortunately, neither hormones (nor the IUD) confer protection against STDs. The one method of contraception that serves both purposes is the use of a condom with a spermicidal jelly.

Box 10.3   A Tale of Two Cities: Poverty and Maternal Mortality

F.A. died during labor in a small district hospital in an African country. The pathologist diagnosed her death as due to antepartum hemorrhage resulting from placenta praevia. She was admitted in shock because of blood loss; only half a liter of blood was available for transfusion; three hours passed before a cesarean section could be started. She died on the operating table.

At 39, F.A. had borne seven children; five were still alive. She did not want more children, but had no access to family planning information or services. She had two minor episodes of bleeding during the last month of her pregnancy (a sign of placenta praevia), but they were ignored. She suffered from chronic iron-deficiency anemia because of parasites; it was untreated. She had never had antenatal care. It took four hours to reach the district hospital after the onset of bleeding.

She need not have died. With access to family planning, she might not have become pregnant. With access to antenatal care, her parasitic disease and her chronic anemia could have been effectively treated; the bleeding episodes would have led to referral to the district hospital and early admission before delivery. Had that not occurred, the availability of rapid emergency transport, an adequate blood supply, and prompt surgical services at the district hospital would have prevented her death.

Was F.A.'s death from placenta praevia due to medical or to social pathologies?

C.R., a 33-year-old Hispanic mother of four, died in New York City when her uterus was perforated in a botched abortion performed by a doctor whose license had been suspended once and who was under investigation by the Board of Registration. The pathologist ascribed her death to intraabdominal bleeding. Because she did not want her Roman Catholic family and friends to know about her intention to have an abortion, C.R. went to another borough of the city to a doctor's office that had been advertised in a local Spanish newspaper. She did not know how to assess the competence of the physician or the adequacy of the office facility where the abortion was done. Because she was an immigrant, she was not aware that reliable abortion centers were available in New York at less cost and with full assurance of confidentiality. She felt compelled to abort because she feared that her pregnancy might cause the loss of her job as a nurses' aide, a job that provided needed family income.

Had maternity leave with job protection been provided, had the state licensing authority stopped the incompetent physician from practicing, had information about confidential and safe abortion been made available to all city residents in Spanish as well as English, had abortion not carried so great a stigma that she felt it necessary to keep it secret from her husband, her friends, and her doctor, the scenario would have been radically different.

Was C.R.'s death the result of hemorrhage from a perforated uterus or was it the result of neglect and stigma?

As different as the national settings are, the problems for women who live in poverty are remarkably similar: limited access to health care, often of dubious quality; insufficient information about health care options; and lack of control over their bodies. Just as lessons learned in the North can be applied to the South, so solving the problems of women in the South in a serious and urgent fashion, and forging solutions through collaboration, will benefit nations of the North as well.[32]

Sexual Activity and Cancer

Hepatitis B, a disease that can be transmitted sexually and by blood, can lead to hepatocellular carcinoma, an untreatable malignancy of the liver. Fortunately, there is a remarkably effective recombinant vaccine that protects against hepatitis and therefore immunizes against this liver cancer. The vaccine can be administered in childhood and is now being included in vaccination routines in some industrialized countries. The need for immunization is greatest in many low-income countries where hepatitis B is endemic.[33] However, cost remains a deterrent to widespread use.

There is accumulating evidence that cancer of the cervix is related to age at which heterosexual activity begins, to the frequency of such activity over a lifetime, and to the number of male partners a woman has. There is increasing evidence that a virus transmitted through sexual intercourse is responsible for cancer development.[34] There is as yet no protective vaccine, but behavior change can diminish the risk for cervical cancer—that is, by delaying the age of onset, by limiting the number of partners, and by using condoms.

Birth-control pills and tubal ligation both lead to a substantial lowering of risk from ovarian cancer.[35]

Sexually Transmitted Diseases

High rates of sexually transmitted diseases (STDs) in low-income countries reflect the disruption of traditional folkways governing sexual behavior.[36] The number of partners for both men and women has increased markedly; as a result, STDs spread rapidly within communities. Because transport between town and village is more rapid and more frequent, STDs spread more readily between them. The new patterns of sexual activity stem from major social changes.

East Africa exemplifies this trend. The benefits of development and foreign investment have been unequally distributed; a small elite has grown richer; little has trickled down to the majority. Most citizens struggle to survive, the sexual divisions of labor sharpen, traditional female support structures crumble, and male dominance is accentuated. Because male inheritance prevails in many tribes, women have no more than cultivation rights on land they hold for succession to their sons. Whereas women once produced crops for domestic consumption, today their labor may be devoted mostly to export crops; the money earned reverts to husbands.[37]

For all too many women in East Africa, sex work is the only way to survive. Twenty years ago, prostitution was severely stigmatized. Now sex workers who accumulate savings from their earnings acquire respect in the village when they return with wealth. Although sex workers have begun to use condoms, married couples rarely do. Wives are afraid that they will be beaten or abandoned if they refuse sex without a condom.[38] The result of all of these changes in sexual behavior patterns is a disturbingly high rate of STD transmission.

In Thailand and the Philippines, sex has become big business with high profits. Prostitution is perpetuated by predatory criminal syndicates organized to exploit sex tourism. Young women, some prepubertal, are bought from their parents by cash advances for their "services." They are obliged to pay back the "loan" by some years of indentured service before they are allowed to retain any of their earnings. Others are shanghaied off the streets or bought from criminal gangs in Myanmar (Burma), after being kidnapped, raped, and sold into slavery. The brothels of Thailand are a major source of an epidemic that has transformed that country within five years from a low-HIV prevalence to a high-HIV prevalence nation.[39]

The STDs include gonorrhea, syphilis, chancroid, chlamydia, and human immunodeficiency (HIV) infection. STDs are extremely common; as many as 250 million new cases occur each year.[40] STDs can have severe consequences, including pelvic inflammatory disease with sterility, central nervous system pathology, and death. STDs victimize women disproportionately, because male-to-female transmission is more efficient and because the early stages of STDs in women often do not produce symptoms of illness. Because prevention requires either monogamy for both partners in the sex act or the use of a condom, prevention is under male control (a female condom is on the market and is being perfected). In many societies, women have little say about the conditions under which sexual intercourse occurs. Studies in East Africa report that married *monogamous* women are being infected with HIV despite knowing about AIDs *and* having access to condoms. Why is this so? They are unable to control their husband's extramarital sex and unable to deny him unprotected sexual intercourse. Efforts to reduce STDs, therefore, necessitate improving the social status of women.

Diagnosis and treatment of syphilis have been shown to be cost effective in field trials in sub-Saharan African countries. Until now, the diagnosis of disease caused by chlamydia has been difficult. A new laboratory test based on the polymerase chain reaction has proved both sensitive and specific; treatment with a single dose of the antibiotic azithromycin is highly effective.[41] Unfortunately, both methods are prohibitively expensive.

HIV infection is the most virulent of the STDs. In 1981, when the disease was first recognized, there were perhaps 100,000 infected persons in the world; a decade later, the number had reached 12 million, 8 million of whom live in Africa (see Table 10.2). The Kenyan government, initially unwilling to acknowledge the existence of AIDS in that country, now estimates that there will be 900,000 deaths from AIDS and 2 million HIV persons by the year 2000 in a country whose current population is 22 million.[42] As of 1990, 80% of HIV-infected persons lived in low-income countries. The disease produces tragedy for families and catastrophe for nations, because it typically strikes down adults in their economically most productive years.

Because there is a seven-to-ten year lag between HIV infection and clinical disease (acquired immunodeficiency syndrome, or AIDS), transmission is silent. Infection is lifelong (the virus integrates its genetic instructions into human host cells). Without getting a blood test, those with HIV do not know they are infected and they cannot be identified by those they solicit for sex or for sharing drug-using equipment or when they donate blood. In consequence, the disease spreads like wildfire. To make matters worse, the virus mutates (changes) at a very rapid rate, so that it escapes elimination by host antibody defenses.

Table 10.2 Estimated HIV Infections by Region and by Gender

Region	Total	Male/Female Ratio
North America	1,200,000	8.5/1
Western Europe	725,000	5/1
Oceania	28,000	7/1
Latin America	1,035,000	4/1
Sub-Saharan Africa	8,772,000	1/1
Caribbean	325,000	1.5/1
Eastern Europe	27,000	10/1
South East Mediterranean	35,000	5/1
North East Asia	42,000	5/1
Southeast Asia	700,000	2/1
WORLD	**12,900,000**	**1.5/1**

Source: Adapted from Mann et al., 1992:30–31. Reprinted by permission of the publishers from *AIDS in the World* by Jonathan Mann, Daniel J. M. Tarantola and Thomas W. Netter, Cambridge, Mass.: Harvard University Press. Copyright © 1992 by the President and Fellows of Harvard College.

Persons who are infected with HIV are at high risk for a psychiatric disorder during the course of their illness.[43] Table 10.3 lists the prevalence of lifetime mental disorders in subjects evaluated in health centers in Brazil, Zaire, Kenya, and Thailand.[44] Subjects with symptomatic HIV infection (S/HIV-1+) have substantially higher rates of functional mental disorder (e.g., depressive disorder, dysthymia, and generalized anxiety disorder) than subjects who were seronegative (HIV-1−). At the same time, subjects with asymptomatic HIV infection (A/HIV-1+) also display evidence of functional psychiatric disorder. Indeed, in several centers, asymptomatic subjects reported higher rates of generalized anxiety disorder than did persons with AIDS-related symptoms. In the early stages of infection, before any clinical symptoms of AIDS are present, the knowledge of being infected is in itself a severe stressor. In effect, the patient has been given a death sentence from a disease that has no cure, is severely stigmatized, and has a chronic downhill path. Reaction to the bad news may lead to an acute stress reaction, depression, or an anxiety disorder. Learning that one has a positive HIV test increases the risk for suicide by a factor of twenty or more.[45] In the later stages of HIV disease (clinical AIDS), people have increasing rates of dementia because brain cells have been destroyed (see Table 10.4).

The virus enters the central nervous system in most infected persons shortly after systemic infection occurs. This has been shown by antibodies and by virus isolation from cerebrospinal fluid. Although the brain infection usually remains asymptomatic for long periods (months and years), almost all patients who die from AIDS have multiple brain lesions at autopsy; many exhibit dementia before they die.[46] In addition to the damage from direct infection by the HIV virus, the patient may contract uncommon infections (such as toxoplasmosis, cryptococcal meningitis, tuberculosis, cytomegalovirus, and herpes zoster) that produce severe brain lesions.

The causal chain works in both directions. Persons who abuse alcohol, who mis-

Table 10.3 Prevalence of Lifetime* Mental Disorders in Persons with HIV in Centers in Africa, Asia, and South America

	HIV-1−	A/HIV-1+	S/HIV-1+	HIV-1−	A/HIV-1+	S/HIV-1+
	Kinshasa, Zaire			Nairobi, Kenya		
ICD-10 Diagnosis (Percent)	(n=85)	(n=52)	(n=68)	(n=65)	(n=66)	(n=72)
Depressive episode/recurrent depressive disorder	2.3	3.8	7.3	4.6	7.5	11.1
Dysthymia	1.2	0	0	0	1.5	0
Generalized anxiety disorder	0	1.9	1.5	1.5	1.5	1.4
Any mental disorder	4.7	7.6	10.3	6.1	10.5	12.5
	Bangkok, Thailand			São Paulo, Brazil		
ICD-10 Diagnosis (Percent)	(n=59)	(n=89)	(n=38)	(n=77)	(n=55)	(n=46)
Depressive episode/recurrent depressive disorder	16.9	22.5	26.3	19.5	21.8	26.1
Dysthymia	0	1.1	0	1.3	1.8	2.2
Generalized anxiety disorder	0	0	2.6	3.9	5.4	6.5
Any mental disorder	16.9	24.7	34.1	24.7	30.8	37.0

* Excluding current.

HIV-1 = Human immunodeficiency virus type 1; HIV-1− = HIV-1 type 1-seronegative subjects; A/HIV-1+ = Asymptomatic HIV type 1-seropositive subjects; S/HIV-1+ = Symptomatic HIV type 1-seropositive subjects; ICD-10 = International Classification of Diseases, 10th Revision.

Source: Maj et al., 1994a. WHO Neuropsychiatric AIDS Study, Cross-Sectional Phase I. Arch. Gen. Psychiatry, 51:39–49. © Copyright 1994, American Medical Association.

use drugs, and who have antisocial personality disorders are more likely to become infected because they engage in high-risk behaviors. Indeed, persons who have been exposed, but not infected, may develop hypochondriacal syndromes and even delusions of having AIDS.

HIV infection can be transmitted by heterosexual and male homosexual intercourse; transfer from mother to fetus in the uterus, from mother to infant during

Table 10.4 Prevalence of Dementia in Persons with HIV in Four Health Centers

	ICD-10 Diagnosis of Dementia (%)		
Center	HIV-1−	A/HIV-1+	S/HIV-1+
Kinshasa, Zaire	0	0	5.9
Nairobi, Kenya	0	0	6.9
Bangkok, Thailand	0	0	0
São Paulo, Brazil	0	0	6.5

ICD-10 = International Classification of Diseases, 10th Revision; HIV-1 = Human immunodeficiency virus type 1; HIV-1− = HIV type 1-seronegative subjects; A/HIV-1+ = Asymptomatic HIV type 1-seropositive subjects; S/HIV-1+ = Symptomatic HIV type 1 seropositive subjects.

Source: Maj et al., 1994b. WHO Neuropsychiatric AIDS Study, Cross-Sectional Phase II. Arch. Gen. Psychiatry, 51:51–61. © Copyright 1994, American Medical Association.

childbirth, or by breast feeding, intravenous drug use, or through infected blood products (such as transfusions). Of all infections to date, about 75% have been sexually transmitted (with a heterosexual to homosexual ratio of 7:1), 10% by drug use, 10% perinatally, and 5% by blood used for transfusion or blood products used for treatment. Worldwide averages, however, obscure striking differences between regions (see Table 10.5).

Infection by sexual intercourse can be prevented by monogamy, by the use of condoms, and by eliminating the riskiest sexual behavior (anal intercourse). STDs markedly increase the risk of infection because they disrupt the integrity of skin and mucosal surfaces. Thus, treatment of other STDs is an important step in HIV prevention. Preventing spread by transfusion requires discouraging those who engage in risky behaviors from donating blood and by screening donated blood for HIV antibodies. Blood products can be made safe by manufacturing procedures that ensure the destruction of the virus. HIV infection from injected drugs has been reduced by diminishing drug abuse, by enrolling IV users in treatment programs, and by making clean needles and syringes available for users who refuse treatment. Although passive transfer from mother to infant could in theory be reduced by cesarean section and by stopping breast feeding, cesarean section is still unproven as a preventive measure and is impractical in countries with limited obstetrical services; the hazards of formula feeding for infants where water is not pure far exceed the potential contribution of breast feeding to HIV transmission.

There is as yet no cure for AIDS. There are drugs that retard the progress of the disease and others that are effective in controlling otherwise fatal secondary infections. These drugs are costly and largely unavailable in many countries. Social

Table 10.5 Distinguishing Features of HIV Infection in Major Geographic Areas

Factors	North America	Western Europe	Latin America	Sub-Saharan Africa	Caribbean	Mediter-ranean	Southeast Asia
			Major Modes of HIV Transmission				
Blood/blood products	L	L	M	M/L	L	L	M
Homosexual/ bisexual men	H	M	M	M	L	L	L
Injection drug use	H	H	M	L	M	M/H	H
Heterosexual	M/L	M/L	M	H	H	L	M/H
Urban/rural ratio	3.2:1	5:1	2.3:1	3.6:1	3.6:1	12:1	6:1
Prevalence of HIV in the general population	0.005–3.0	0.007–2.8	0.0007–0.8	0.9–7.3	0.5–20	0.0001–0.5	0.01–0.29

H = high; M = medium; L = low.

Source: Modified from Mann et al., 1992:20–21. Reprinted by permission of the publishers from *AIDS in the World* by Jonathan Mann, Daniel J. M. Tarantola, and Thomas W. Netter. Cambridge, Mass.: Harvard University Press. Copyright © 1992 by the President and Fellows of Harvard College.

forces determine the likelihood of acquiring HIV infection, the rapidity with which infection produces AIDS, and the duration of AIDS. Infection is more widespread in sub-Saharan Africa and the progression of clinical disease in infected people is more rapid, because general health is poor and treatment is available only to the privileged few. When candidate vaccines become available for large-scale trials, countries with high rates of disease transmission are likely to be the sites, because high rates make it easier to demonstrate vaccine efficacy. If this becomes the case, then those who are asked to give consent to participate in an experiment from which the rest of the world will benefit must have access to treatment; the vaccine, if successful, must be made available free of charge to those in the placebo arm of the trial and at affordable prices to other citizens.[47]

Reactivation of widespread latent *Mycobacterium tuberculosis* infection among HIV-infected persons has resulted in an accelerating tuberculosis epidemic that has also spread to those without HIV. Tuberculosis (TB) has been and remains the most important microbial disease in the world. It has infected an estimated 1.7 billion persons, about 4.5 million of whom also have HIV. Local variability is, however, marked. In Haiti, half of patients with AIDS have TB as their initial opportunistic infection; the seroprevalence of HIV among TB patients can be as high as 40%.[48]

Rates of tuberculosis had been rapidly declining in Europe and North America for the past century and a half because of increased host resistance (resulting from improved health), less crowded housing, public health control measures, and, in recent decades, chemotherapy. The declining morbidity curve turned upward in the mid-1980s and has continued to rise for the last decade. Rates in low-income countries, which had remained high, have doubled in many in the past five years. AIDS and TB interact synergistically: persons infected with either are not only more susceptible to the other but they experience greater clinical disease severity from each when they are infected by both. People with HIV are vulnerable to developing multidrug-resistant TB organisms. The diagnosis of TB is more difficult in the presence of HIV, because the standard tuberculin skin test often yields false negatives. Extrapulmonary forms of TB are more common in such people and chest X rays are less reliable. Because HIV infection is worse in patients with TB, chemoprophylaxis for TB may extend the life expectancy of dually infected individuals.[49] In Haiti, isoniazid prophylaxis in symptom-free HIV-infected persons lowered the incidence of TB and delayed the onset of HIV-related disease in a controlled trial.[50] Both TB and HIV infection are social diseases, despite differences in modes of transmission. Both tend to attack the most disadvantaged populations. Elite groups are not immune, but they can protect themselves by avoiding environments in which risk is high. Those without resources tend not to have this choice (see Box 10.4).

The first target for HIV prevention are members of high-risk groups: sex workers, long-distance truck drivers, soldiers, migrants, intravenous drug users, and government officials who travel frequently. Sex education must be explicit and graphic in language appropriate to each audience. Because world tourism is a major source of HIV infection, information directed at tourists and those who serve them is essential. Euphemisms guarantee failure. It is essential to spell out what it is safe to do while also flagging what is unsafe. Giving up a habitual behavior, particularly one associated with pleasure, is difficult at best; it is almost impossible if alternate

---

Box 10.4   Poverty and Risk for Tuberculosis in Haiti

Jean Dubuisson lives in a small village in Haiti's central plateau, where he farms a tiny plot of land. He shares his two-room hut with his wife and their three children. In the fall of 1989, Jean began coughing. For a couple of weeks, he simply ignored his persistent hack (there is no clinic or dispensary in or near his village). When he began having night sweats and losing weight, he drank herbal teas known for their efficacy for the *grip*, or "cold." In December, Jean had an episode of hemoptysis, which led him to the clinic closest to his home village. For two dollars he received multivitamins and was told to eat well, drink clean water, sleep in an open room away from others, and go to a hospital. Because he lacked the finances, he was unable to follow this advice.

Two months later, a second, massive episode of hemoptysis sent Jean to a church-affiliated hospital. Still coughing, he was admitted to an open ward, where he stayed for a full two weeks before being referred to a sanatorium. During his stay, Jean was charged $4 per day for his bed, and any prescriptions written there had to be paid for before the medication was administered. Jean therefore received less than half of what was prescribed. Because the hospital did not serve food, the only meals Jean received were those prepared by his wife. The cough persisted, as did night sweats and an intermittent fever. Jean continued to lose weight and discharged himself from the hospital when he ran out of money. He did not go to the sanatorium.

Jean's recurrent health problems point to the force of poverty in the inability of Haiti's poor to recovery from such illnesses. For instance, while over 95% of all those with tuberculosis can be cured, many do not adequately recover because of limited resources. In fact, a recent study in Haiti shows how minor and inexpensive changes in a person's life can lead to significant changes in his or her state of health.

Proje Veye Sante, a small community-health program founded in 1984 that serves a peasant population living around a reservoir in rural Haiti, had great success in diagnosing tuberculosis, but found that detection of new cases did not lead to cure, in spite of the fact that their 80-cent fee was waived for any patient carrying a diagnosis of TB and all TB medications were free of charge. They therefore developed a program in 1989 to improve services to fifty patients with TB to see how they then fared in comparison with fifty other patients who did not receive the supplemental health care.

Patients from "Sector 1," a catchment area that rings the reservoir, participated in a treatment program that featured daily visits from village health workers during the first month following diagnosis. These patients received financial aid of $30 per month for at least the first three months, and were also eligible for nutritional supplements. They also received a monthly reminder from their village health worker to go to the clinic, and "travel expenses" (such as renting a donkey) were defrayed with a $5 honorarium upon attending the clinic. When a Sector 1 patient did not attend, a physician or nurse visited his home.

Patients from "Sector 2," a catchment area that consisted of a larger number of villages and towns beyond the reservoir, also received free care, but did not benefit from the same community-based services and financial aid offered to Sector 1 patients. Mean age of patients (42.5 years) and sex ratio (approximately 2:1 were women) did not vary significantly between the two groups.

A comparison of treatment outcomes of the two groups of patients revealed striking differences (see Table 10.6). Only one patient in the Sector 1 group died in the year following diagnosis, compared to six from Sector 2. None of the patients from Sector 1 were sputum-positive at six months after the start of antituberculosis therapy, whereas

Table 10.6 Characteristics of Tuberculosis in Sector 1 versus Sector 2

Patient Characteristics	Sector 1 (N = 50)	Sector 2 (N = 50)
Mortality from TB during 18 months after diagnosis	1 (2%)	6 (12%)
Sputnum positive after six months of treatment	0	9 (18%)
Persistent pulmonary symptoms after one year of treatment	3 (6%)	21 (42%)
Average weight gained/patient/year (lbs.)	9.8	1.9
Return to work after one year of treatment	46 (92%)	24 (48%)
One-year disease-free survival	49 (98%)	24 (48%)

Source: Paul Farmer, Department of Social Medicine, Harvard Medical School.

nine were sputum-positive in Sector 2 after six months. Three of the Sector 1 group reported persistent pulmonary symptoms (e.g., cough, hemoptysis, dyspnea) after a full year of treatment, and two of these patients had developed asthma during the course of their convalescence. Twenty-one of those in Sector 2 continued to complain of cough or other symptoms consistent with persistent or partially treated tuberculosis.

Sector 1 patients gained an average of 9.8 pounds during the first year of their treatment (correcting for fluctuations associated with pregnancy); patients from Sector 2 had a mean weight gain of 1.9 pounds per person per year. One year after diagnosis, 46 of the Sector 1 patients said they were able to return to their work activities. In Sector 2, less than half (24 patients) were able to do so—a significant finding given that most patients from both groups were peasant farmers or market women whose families relied on their ability to perform physical labor.

Removing barriers to "compliance," when coupled with financial aid, thus dramatically improved outcome in poor Haitians with tuberculosis. This fact sheds light on the plight of Jean Dubuisson, who was told by biomedical practitioners to eat well, drink clean water, and sleep in an open room, away from others, and go to a hospital, but "refused." Most important, he was also instructed to go to a hospital, which he did not do until two months later. In the end, Jean Dubuisson was forced to relocate to become eligible for the community-based anti-TB program described above. Apparently cured of tuberculosis, he remains a pulmonary invalid to this day.

Risk for tuberculosis, then, is strongly influenced by economic factors. If there are going to be effective local programs to combat tuberculosis, they must address those factors. More important, when behavior is strongly constrained by social forces, as was the case with Jean Dubuisson, it is not always illuminating to group these forces in catch-all categories such as "behavioral factors." Indeed, a new research agenda would do more than stress the importance of socioeconomic status. It would seek to define the precise mechanisms by which such large-scale forces, such as poverty, powerlessness, and gender inequality, come to be embodied in patients. Such research would ascribe relative weights to various social factors and would link variations in incidence or prevalence to socioeconomic status, gender, and factors as diverse as racial discrimination, sexism, and political upheaval.[51]

sources of pleasure (or means for earning a livelihood) are not available. The message should be delivered by credible spokespersons from the population whose behavior must be changed. It must be feasible for the target population to make the changes urged upon them. The anti-AIDS slogan in Uganda—"Zero Graze"—is widely broadcast and widely understood by women, but women remain at high risk when they cannot control their husbands' "grazing" and cannot deny them sex. Maintaining change, once it is achieved, is no less a challenge. Safe-sex messages require constant reinforcement.

Mandatory, population-wide screening is poor public policy.[52] Where sero-prevalence is low, false positives exceed true positives. An intrusive and costly police apparatus would be necessary to ensure compliance. Persons fearing they are seropositive would be the ones most likely to avoid screening in a public system lest they be stigmatized, whereas many now seek the information for themselves when it is confidential.

Because the changes in behavior needed to intercept the epidemic require confronting controversy about sexual and drug-using behavior, governments defer large-scale interventions in the hope that an effective vaccine will appear by magic to control the disease. Whatever the long-term prospects may be (and they are not promising because of the high mutation rate of the virus and its incorporation into the genetic apparatus of cells), no such vaccine is on the near-term horizon. Tests to determine the efficacy of a candidate vaccine will in themselves take three to five years. Basing public policy on the expectation that a vaccine will avert the need to face controversy is shortsighted. Thailand, which had relatively few infections a few years ago, now has at least 400,000 and the epidemic continues to accelerate. Religious objections to public discussion of sexuality, denial that sex tourism exists even though it is widespread, inadequate treatment services for intravenous drug users, and political hesitation to provide condoms and clean needles and syringes, all persist the world over, despite an epidemic of HIV infection. By the year 2000, WHO projects the HIV epidemic to reach at least 38 million, and perhaps as many as 100 million, if effective public health measures are not applied forcefully now (see Table 10.7).

Disease Control and Human Rights

Public health programs to contain HIV infection have three essential components: information adapted to the needs of the target population; health and social services closely linked with the educational messages, such as counseling, voluntary testing, drug treatment, and condoms; and social support and legal protection against discrimination for infected persons. As Jonathan Mann points out, the public health rationale for protecting human rights and dignity became self-evident from experience in trying to control the epidemic.[53]

The vulnerability of populations to the spread of HIV is strongly influenced by the nature, scope, and intensity of discrimination that exists within their communities. People's capacity to learn about and to respond to AIDS depends on their social role and status. The HIV pandemic flourishes where a person's ability to learn and to respond is constrained by belonging to a marginalized group.

Table 10.7 Estimates of Cumulative Adult HIV Infections by
Region in the Year 2000

Region	Estimates	
	Low	High
North America	1,800,000	8,150,000
Western Europe	1,200,000	2,330,000
Oceania	22,000	45,000
Latin America	1,600,000	8,550,000
Sub-Saharan Africa	20,800,000	33,600,000
Caribbean	540,000	7,000,000
Eastern Europe	2,000	20,000
South East Mediterranean	890,000	3,530,000
North East Asia	6,000	490,000
Southeast Asia	11,300,000	45,000,000
Total	**38,100,000**	**108,800,000**

Source: Modified from Mann et al., 1992:107. Reprinted by permission of the
publishers from *AIDS in the World* by Jonathan Mann, Daniel J. M. Tarantola, and
Thomas W. Netter. Cambridge, Mass.: Harvard University Press. Copyright © 1992
by the President and Fellows of Harvard College.

In 1948, the Universal Declaration of Human Rights was adopted by nations as
a fundamental set of values.[54] It has five basic features. First, human rights inhere in
people simply because they are human; therefore, these rights are *inalienable*. Second, they are *universal*, applying equally to all people, regardless of time or place.
Third, these are the *rights* of individuals. Societies must satisfy the claims that
result from these rights. Fourth, human rights are generally *inviolable*. Fifth, human
rights are a legitimate concern of all people, without regard to national sovereignty.

Every right in the document has an important impact on health, including civil
and political rights (such as the rights to security of person, to privacy, to due
process, and to prohibitions against torture and arbitrary arrest) and economic and
social rights (such as the rights to the highest attainable standard of health, to work,
to social security, to adequate housing, and to education).

In order to understand the linkage between health and human rights, we need
some key health definitions. According to the World Health Organization, health is
a "state of complete physical, mental, and social well-being." Public health ensures
"the conditions in which people can be healthy." Combining the two, public health
seeks to ensure the conditions in which people can best achieve physical, mental,
and social well-being. Public health can be a justification for a deviation from
human rights. This privileged status derives from the history of traditional commu-
nicable disease control that relied on quarantines to halt the spread of epidemics.

Yet modern public health is principally concerned with behavior—personal and
collective—expressed in problems such as tobacco, alcohol and other substance use
and abuse, injuries, child abuse, cardiovascular disease, collective violence, sexually
transmitted diseases, and unwanted pregnancies. In these contexts, a careful analysis of
existing policies and programs frequently uncovers a lack of respect for human rights

and of hidden discrimination in the way policies are developed, designed, and implemented.

At the same time, human rights violations have health impacts. Clearly, the victims of torture or imprisonment under inhumane conditions suffer severe health effects, as do civilians whose rights of neutrality are violated during conflicts. How many preventable cancers result from marketing of tobacco while violating the right to information about its dangerous consequences? How many children have died as a result of violations of the right to education? What is the health cost of violating the child's right to be protected from economic exploitation and from performing work that is hazardous?

In short, fighting for human rights and dignity for all is a necessary condition for promoting public health.

Non-intentional Injuries

Non-intentional violence refers to injuries and death from motor vehicles (by far the largest single source), poisoning, falls, fires, drowning, and occupational injuries. In everyday terminology, non-intentional injuries are called "accidents." This implies that they are random, unpredictable, and unpreventable. The fact is that non-intentional injuries display remarkable statistical regularities; most stem from identifiable and preventable causes. Therefore, the word "accident" should be dropped from the public health lexicon.

Motor vehicle injuries are a major cause of adult mortality in the "developing" world, resulting in about 500,000 deaths, a like number of permanent injuries, and 2.5 million hospitalizations. In North America and Europe, motor vehicle fatality rates are highest among males from 15 to 24 years of age, whereas in "developing" countries vehicle fatality rates are higher after age 25 because of differences in car ownership and travel patterns. Data from India for 1986 indicate that one in five male and one in six female deaths between ages 15 and 54 were due to violence; of the unintentional injuries in men, half were due to motor vehicles. Similar rates are reported from a rural district (Machakos) in Kenya, where one in six deaths from all causes resulted from injury. Data from China, based on special surveillance districts, reveal that 38% of male and 35% of female age-standardized adult years of potential life lost were the result of injuries. For women, mortality from injuries is increasing in the face of a decline in overall female mortality.[55] The principal debate in the field of injury prevention is between those who emphasize interventions to make the environment relatively "fail-safe" in the face of inevitable human error versus those who emphasize reducing the human contribution to injury by changing behavior. Proponents of the first position argue, in the case of vehicular accidents, for wider highways with median divider strips, better lighting and maintenance of road surfaces, safer car construction with collapsible steering wheels and mandatory automatic air bags, and so on. Proponents of the second position argue for driver education, lowering maximum highway speed limits with strict enforcement, laws mandating helmets for motorcyclists, stiff penalties for drunk driving, and so on. There is, of course, no contradiction between the two positions; the most prudent course is to move on both fronts as rapidly as possible. In the United States, the reduction of highway speed limits from 65 to 55 miles per hour (dictated not by safety considerations, but by the need to conserve fuel at the time of the sharp price increase in OPEC oil) proved to be the most effective single public health measure introduced in the 1970s. In many poor societies, the roads are in abysmal condition, vehicles are not maintained properly because funds are lacking, and taxi drivers and long-range truckers often drive while sleep-deprived because they work such long hours. These are all "preventable" sources of motor vehicle collisions, but *only if* adequate resources are made available.

With increasing pesticide use, the risk of poisoning becomes ever greater: among those who mix and spray pesticides, those who are exposed to spray drifts, those who eat contaminated foods, and those who consume pesticides to commit suicide (an ever more common method in countries dependent on agriculture). Suicide attempts using pesticides are estimated at 2 million and completed suicides at 200,000.[56] Children who have access to chemicals of any kind in the household may ingest them and be severely injured or killed. This risk can be sharply reduced by storing chemicals in safe places, by mandating childproof safety caps on containers necessary for use in the household, and by proper adult supervision of children, much of which may not be feasible under conditions of severe poverty.

Deaths from workplace injuries in agriculture, construction, transport, mining, and manufacturing are estimated to be ten times as common in "developing" countries. The annual number of injuries at work leading to impairment (more than 3 million per year) is about the same as the number of new cases of tuberculosis. Hazards in farming include falls, pesticide exposure, tractor and harvesting injuries, and drownings. In industry, risks include exposure to lead, organic solvents, corrosives and silica, and asbestos dust. Workplace safety measures and laws mandating compliance with safety regulations are lacking in many countries. Even where equipment is made available to workers (goggles, masks, etc.), it may not be used because of insufficient education on its proper use and on its value in protecting health. Safety equipment is often uncomfortable to wear. If using it slows down the pace of work, this will be a major deterrent to use for workers on a piece-work wage. Active worker involvement in equipment design and training for use is essential to the success of health and safety programs in the workplace.

Health and Illness Behaviors

Health-enhancing behaviors are behaviors undertaken when one is well in order to maintain health and prevent future illness. Some folk practices are fully compatible with Western scientific knowledge; others may bring false assurance and injure health. Examples of the first are dietary habits that assure healthy growth and development. Cultures have evolved their own mixtures of complementary proteins: in the Middle East, wheat bread, which is deficient in lysine, is eaten with cheese, which has a high lysine content; in Mexico, corn is treated with limewater in preparing food, a step that releases essential niacin, otherwise biologically unavailable. An example of a culturally sanctioned unhealthy behavior is the consumption of a high-salt diet (because it is traditional) by people with high blood pressure for whom it is toxic.

In many tropical diseases, behavior is a key link in the chain of causation. Schis-

---

Box 10.5   Warning Workers Is Not Enough

As part of his study of the work environment in the industrial areas surrounding Mexico City, a specialist from the Pan American Health Organization inspected a plant producing asbestos. Work conditions were appalling. The atmosphere was so befouled by clouds of asbestos dust that no refined test equipment was needed to recognize its hazard. His efforts to persuade management to change operating procedures were unavailing, and he discovered that there were no occupational safety laws that governed the dangerous situation he had identified. Moreover, union officials were no more interested than management in changing work conditions because of the job threat.

At a hastily assembled meeting of the work force, the pulmonary medicine specialist explained as forcefully as he could the risks for lung cancer, mesothelioma, and obstructive lung disease from prolonged exposure to so heavy a concentration of asbestos. When he invited questions, he was greeted by a long silence. At length, a worker stood up and asked the doctor how long it might take before he died of lung disease. The visitor stated that the interval might be as short as ten or as long as thirty years. The worker then asked the doctor if he knew how long it would take him to die of starvation if he quit or lost his job in a town where there was no other way to earn a living wage.

Although it should be obligatory that workers be told about job-related risks as a matter of occupational safety law, such information will be useless if workers have no other ways of earning a livelihood. Society must make the decisions about the risk to which it is permissible that workers be exposed in order to meet community needs. Such issues arise in connection with mining, logging, nuclear energy plants, manufacturing operations using toxic materials, and so on.[57]

---

tosomiasis is acquired when larval stages of the organism penetrate the skin of persons standing in water. Risk of infection is, of course, eliminated by staying out of irrigation ditches, rivers, and lakes altogether. But this is impossible for fishermen, farmers, women washing clothes, and children seeking relief from heat. However, the twenty-four-hour rhythms governing the life cycle of the parasite are such that release of free-swimming cercariae peaks between 10:00 A.M. and 3:00 P.M. Risk of infection is reduced if humans enter the water only before and after these hours.[58]

Malaria is caused by a parasite transmitted by a biting mosquito; yet the regular use of bed netting impregnated with a pyrethroid insecticide can markedly reduce the likelihood of acquiring malaria. Despite demonstrations of effectiveness in China and in Africa, use is irregular even though costs are low. Netting is uncomfortable to use in hot climates and must be carefully tucked in before sleep. Populations that live in malaria-infested areas acquire a degree of relative biologic immunity to the parasite. Unprotected and previously unexposed populations are highly vulnerable. When Brazilian workers from other areas of the country moved into the Amazon region because of encouragement by government economic policy, the result was an explosion of malaria infections.[59] Without health-protective measures appropriate to the new environment, movement of populations can result in disease epidemics.

The vaccines against the principal childhood infections included in the WHO Expanded Program on Immunization (such as measles, diphtheria, pertussis, tetanus, tuberculosis, and polio) are the most effective health-maintaining biomed-

---

Box 10.6   Dracunculiasis

Guinea worm disease (dracunculiasis) is a human parasitic infestation that comes from drinking water containing Cyclops, an aquatic crustacean that acts as an intermediate host for the larvae produced by the guinea worm. The adult female worm grows to 20 to 50 inches in length inside the human host. It then bores through flesh to the skin of the leg, where a blister develops. The bursting of the blister releases a new generation of larvae. If they enter into water containing Cyclops, the cycle is repeated when another person drinks the water. Dracunculiasis is painful and exhausting but not fatal. It can be totally prevented by filtering water to remove Cyclops before drinking it and by keeping infected persons from contaminating water sources.

In 1988, the President of Ghana launched a public health campaign against the disease. Many doubted it would be effective. However, disease prevalence was reduced by 30% in the first year of the program. Four years later, the number of cases in Ghana had been reduced from 180,000 to 30,000. A remarkable degree of behavior change was achieved by a committed cadre of primary health care workers who educated villagers to change how water was treated. As an additional measure, the government provided training for health workers to perform minor surgery to extract the worm from patients rather than waiting for the mature worm to burrow its way through the skin.[60]

---

ical technologies. The package can be extended to include hemophilus B, hepatitis B, and pneumococcus where appropriate. The Program can be combined with vitamin A and iodine supplements (where deficiency is endemic) and with anthelminthics (where worm infestation is common). The benefit-to-cost ratio is enormous. In 1970, less than 5% of children in most "developing" countries were immunized. Today, coverage approaches 80%. Poliomyelitis, for example, appears to have been eliminated in Latin America. Paradoxically, many poor countries cooperating with EPI have attained immunization rates for preschool children higher than those in the United States.[61]

There is, however, a dark side to immunization; in some instances, all inhabitants of a village have been rounded up and compelled to be vaccinated despite their objections, whether religious or political. This apparently occurred during the enormously successful WHO campaign to eliminate smallpox and during successive waves of EPI.[62] If obtaining consent for health interventions is a matter of principle for some countries, strongarm tactics should not be employed against the inhabitants of remote villages. In the United States, immunization is required as a condition for entry into school (which is compulsory), but people with religious objections can apply to the courts for relief from this requirement.

Illness Behavior

Illness behavior constitutes that set of activities and meanings which people, families, and communities exhibit when bodily changes (pain, shortness of breath, rash, or fatigue) are perceived as symptoms of illness. The process begins when a person who experiences these changes interprets them as meaning he or she is ill and seeks remedy for them. Help may at first be sought from family, friends, and only later from folk or professional healers. If those who are sick are children, their mothers are the key providers of care and serve as the decision makers about seeking outside help. This is one reason the health of children varies directly with the years of education their mothers have received. The decision to consult healers depends upon the extent to which the illness episode is perceived as a threat, the ease of access to the healer, the cost of securing his or her services, the perceived effectiveness of the healer, the reputation of the healer, and local cultural meanings.[63]

For a peasant family, "free care" at a government clinic may be costly, because it requires time in travel and in waiting to take a family member to the clinic. Even when biomedical medicine would otherwise be sought, a visit to the clinic may not take place if clinic personnel humiliate and demean patients. Because costs are entailed, decisions to seek help require belief that the illness carries a significant risk and that the treatment will reduce that risk. Persons in most countries take a pluralistic view of healing; that is, they will frequently consult physicians and traditional healers at the same time. Traditional medicine may be viewed as more effective than biomedicine for certain conditions (chronic diseases and infertility, in particular). Patients are pragmatists seeking results, not purists following a theory. When local village healers migrate into an urban setting, they, like their patients, are subject to commercialization in the new environment. Healers may be corrupted (as are some professionals) and exploit their clients. Cultural differences in the ways illness and cure are interpreted make the evaluation of effectiveness more than a matter of counting symptoms.

Financial barriers to effective health care can have disastrous results. China made great progress during the 1960s and 1970s in reducing rates of infection from tuberculosis by providing public care. The pattern of steady improvement underwent a tragic reversal in the 1980s when the government decreed that health services must become self-supporting. Because of higher charges for diagnosis and treatment, many patients with tuberculosis dropped out of care, and more than one million people who could have been rendered bacillus-free remained infectious. The result was tens of millions of new infection via person-to-person spread. Many of the 3 million TB deaths recorded in China during the 1980s could have been averted.[64] An erroneous public health policy has had bitter results; more than another decade will be required to repair the damage in China. Similar results have followed upon the "structural adjustments" (user fees) imposed by external agencies on debt-ridden countries in order to reduce deficits from subsidized public services. In 1990, six weeks after the introduction of user charges for inpatient care, the *Nation*, a leading Kenyan daily, reported: "General hospitals across the country once notorious for overcrowding now find themselves in the unfamiliar position of being deserted . . . The introduction of cost-sharing . . . made . . . illness a luxury. People simply chose not to seek treatment." Similar effects were observed in outpatient settings where even a small increase in fees reduced use by 50%.[65]

The health transition also implies a transition in the way health services are used. Whereas many pharmaceuticals are available only by prescription in industrialized countries, such drugs are available on the open market elsewhere. The proliferation of biomedical pharmaceuticals in many regions is radically changing how care is sought. Prescription drugs in the form of injections and pills are popular because they are easily available and thought to have powerful therapeutic effects. Often they are misdispensed by poorly trained physicians, "pharmacists," or traditional healers. Unsupervised self-medication with pharmaceuticals is common practice; the outcomes can be devastating. Inadequate antibiotic treatment promotes the spread of drug-resistant germs. Appropriation of medicines by enterprising hospital workers who then sell them for profit to the general public has been documented in Uganda; these "practitioners" develop reputations as informal medical experts in local communities.[66] Yet in some settings this practice, though illegal, is the only way medications are actually delivered to patients who need them.

A major issue for health services the world over is the degree to which patients adhere to therapeutic recommendations. Adherence is of particular importance in the care of patients with chronic disease. When the ailment is acute and a single injection (as in certain STDs) or a single surgical procedure (as in appendectomy) is curative, nothing more is required of the patient than to permit the initial intervention. However, in the treatment of hypertension, diabetes, epilepsy, or cancer, the patient must not only agree to begin, but keep on with the treatment—despite its cost, its inconvenience, or its side effects. Yet any benefits may not be evident for weeks or months, and the health consequences of *not* taking the treatment may not be obvious until weeks or months have gone by if the disease is relatively silent (as in hypertension). Unless health workers are alert to the importance of asking about adherence, the behavior of the patient in not taking his medicine will be invisible to the caretakers. The problem is a major one in all health care settings. It is especially significant in the treatment of mental illness and epilepsy, where the problem of nonadherence is particularly high. In fact, the problem has received insufficient attention in the training of health workers at all levels.[67]

Medical illnesses can increase rates of mental illness, especially risk for depression. The physical handicap, pain, loss of gainful employment, and lowered social status caused by chronic illness are severe assaults against the integrity of the self and may result in depression. Moreover, members of that patient's family, faced with the responsibility of taking care of the patient, are themselves subject to depression because of the additional burden they must carry. Thus, mental health care is important in the treatment of arthritis, diabetes, coronary heart disease, and other chronic medical problems, just as the effective treatment of the primary disease will reduce the risk for secondary depression. Making primary care available in the community *and* reaching out to ensure that citizens benefit from its services will help to reduce the burden of mental illness in the community among medical patients and their families.

Rehabilitation programs can have an enormous impact, often at relatively low cost, on the quality of life for physically impaired individuals, who are handicapped in the absence of prostheses or other measures. Impaired persons are estimated to number not less than 250 million worldwide. Yet eyeglasses can restore functional vision, hearing aids can permit communication, and functional locomotion can be restored by limb prostheses or motorized wheelchairs. Such interventions make an enormous contribution to the welfare of people otherwise condemned to handicap. In fact, the Division of Mental Health of the World Health Organization has introduced an initiative to provide eyeglasses to nearsighted schoolchildren on the

grounds that they promote mental health by improving vision and classroom participation and hence a sense of competence.

It is difficult to change habitual behaviors. To undertake the sizable effort to
unlearn the old and learn new behaviors, a person must be persuaded that the risk to
health is substantial and that the new behavior will pay off in reduced disease risk.
Educational materials must take into account local understandings and practices in
order to fit in with the goals of the community.

Conclusions

- Behavior is a major influence on whether people stay well or become sick.
  The behaviors with the greatest effect on health status are patterns of eating
  and drinking, personal hygiene, sexual activity, smoking, substance abuse,
  driving, and occupational activities. These behaviors affect both physical and
  mental health, often revealing that the two are inseparably linked. They are
  also governed by social rules, by social class position within a given society,
  by level of education, and by personal history. Because they are habitual and
  deeply ingrained, they are not easy to change. Yet, unless high-risk behaviors
  are changed, unnecessary sickness and premature death will persist.
- Assuring everyone pure water and proper sewage disposal will diminish the
  risk from poor hygienic practices. We are still decades away from the time
  when these health-protective measures will be present in all countries. Until
  that time, people can learn to reduce their own health risks by boiling water
  before drinking it, by cooking food thoroughly, by washing hands thoroughly,
  and by setting aside segregated areas for urination and defecation, away from
  sources of drinking water and from areas for food preparation. Teaching such
  behaviors can become a basic goal of public schooling.
- Severe malnutrition leading to the stunting of physical growth and of mental
  development in children is almost entirely limited to low-income countries.
  Diets deficient in micronutrients can be found the world over and reflect local
  characteristics of the soil and of dietary practices. The consumption of diets
  overly rich in calories and proteins, which contribute to heart disease, stroke,
  and metabolic disorders, are more common in high-income countries but they
  are also seen among the elite in other countries. National agricultural and tax
  policies in combination with public education on nutritional needs can be
  used to make dietary patterns healthier.
- Patterns of sexual behavior have decisive consequences for health. Adolescent pregnancy, short interpregnancy intervals, and multiple pregnancies are
  associated with higher risks of maternal mortality as well as higher risks for a
  developmentally compromised infant and child. Sexual intercourse without
  the use of condoms can lead to bacterial and viral diseases, including fatal
  HIV infection. STDs, including HIV infection, can be prevented by a monogamous relationship with an uninfected partner or by the use of barrier contraceptives (male or female condoms). Despite the relatively low cost of condoms, religious, cultural, and chauvinistic practices keep their use at low

levels. Sex education is labor intensive, requires constant reinforcement, and is undercut by disinformation. Nonetheless, it provides the only available method for controlling STDs.

- Cigarette smoking is a major environmental health hazard. Risks for cancer of the respiratory system, for heart disease and stroke, for peripheral vascular disease, for other cancers, and for many other diseases are higher among smokers. For most of these diseases, available methods of treatment are of limited effectiveness. Preventing the young from beginning to smoke and helping those who are smokers to quit constitute the basis of public health. Tax policy, agricultural policy, and controls on advertising can help to control smoking.

- Exposure to toxic hazards, to risks from machinery, and to physical problems from repetitive motions at work are key determinants of occupational health. Many of these risks are subject to control by decontaminating the workplace, by the use of safety guards on machinery, by having workers wear protective equipment, and by redesigned work movements. The costs of these measures is an essential part of the agricultural or manufacturing process. Strong occupational health and safety legislation, together with methods of active surveillance, are essential components of national health policy.

- Modern biomedicine, despite its limitations, can bring many, though not all, diseases under control. Nations should make the best of modern treatments available to their citizens. However, the mere availability of medical care does not ensure its consistent use unless patients can understand the options available to them and exercise intelligent choices. Failures of communication and lack of trust between health workers and patients too often result in inconsistent therapeutic programs, which not only fail to bring about the expected cures, but may actually endanger health by causing complications. Programs of education directed at health workers and patients are essential to bring about mutual understanding and thus better health.

11

Conclusions and an Agenda for Action

This volume was undertaken with a sense of deep concern about the magnitude of mental health problems in the societies of Africa, Asia, Latin America, and the Middle East. For too long, social, behavioral, and mental health problems have been inadequately addressed by scholars and agencies committed to health and international development.

The World Bank's 1993 World Development Report *Investing in Health* offers an example. The Bank's decision to focus its annual development report on health and health care in low- and middle-income countries is enormously welcome. The Report reflects a growing awareness among policymakers that particular strategies of development have important consequences for health, and that health indicators rank with economic indicators as markers of the benefits of development policies. Furthermore, the authors of that report recognize that since ill health has negative consequences for a society's economic development, "investing" in health is crucial for development as well as for alleviating human misery.

Our own investigations were stimulated by our belief that reports such as that of the World Bank leave a crucial portion of the story untold. *Investing in Health* focuses quite properly on classic problems of public health, advocating increased investment in primary health care and public health measures as the most cost-effective means of improving health in poor countries. It goes beyond this to analyze the health benefits of policies that reduce poverty and promote the development of human resources—the empowerment of women and the expansion of schooling, in particular—and provides strong policy recommendations in these areas. However, in this and similar reports, mental health is given little attention, even though the figures cited demonstrate the enormous burden of neuropsychiatric illnesses. Furthermore, many of the most profound issues for the health and well-being of communities and individuals—violence, alcoholism and drug addiction, exploitation of children, homelessness, discrimination and abuse against women, ethnic or political violence, and dislocation of whole communities—are barely touched on. Despite the expressed concern for a broad definition of health, reports such as this rely almost exclusively on the prevalence of disease or on mortality rates as indicators of health. Many of the most crucial sources of ill health and human suffering are thus largely neglected by researchers and have little place in policy development. In this context, mental health care is seldom viewed as belonging to essential health services.

Scholars and activists can no longer fail to address these difficult issues. The problems associated with the new morbidities are central to the health and well-being of vast portions of the globe. They should be recognized as key challenges to public health and be granted new priority among those institutions and governing bodies concerned with international health and development.

These problems are obviously daunting. However, they should not provoke despair. For some problems, cost-effective solutions are available and directions for policy initiatives are relatively clear. For others, experimental programs have shown promising results. And for some, the very enormity and lack of ready answers argue for the urgency of discovering solutions.

The primary goal of this report has been to investigate the scope and magnitude of problems of social, behavioral, and mental health in societies of Africa, Asia, and Latin America, and where possible, to provide information on innovative programs for prevention and clinical care. We have not attempted to provide an overarching analysis of the social origins of psychiatric and social morbidity, nor to examine in detail the consequences of particular economic development policies. Even with these limited goals, the task has been more formidable than might be apparent. The problems we have examined do not fit neatly into disciplinary boundaries or statistical categories; information is often available only in the "gray literature" of government and agency reports. No directory of innovative programs aimed at prevention and treatment exists, and analyses of successful and failed programs and policies have to be assembled from a wide range of journals and unpublished reports sometimes containing conflicting information. The lack of reliable data, the inadequacy of current theoretical frameworks, and the lack of research centers or training programs that address these problems speak to the challenge that stands ahead.

Fortunately, the analytic tools, technologies, and collective experience available for understanding and responding to these conditions have grown along with the scope of the problems themselves. It is our hope that the findings of this report will serve as a provocation to action.

What, then, are our most important findings? What conclusions can be drawn from this report? What are the immediate priorities for action, and what broad strategy should guide action?

The Scope and Magnitude of the Problems

Perhaps the most startling finding is the extent of the overall health burden of mental illnesses. *Investing in Health* estimates that neuropsychiatric diseases make up 6.8% of the global burden of disease for men, women, and children in "demographically developing economies." For adults aged 15 to 44, neuropsychiatric diseases are 12% of the global burden of disease; when "intentional, self-inflicted injuries" are added, the total constitutes 15.1% of the global burden of disease for women, 16.1% for men. Depressive disorders are the most prevalent neuropsychiatric disorders (fifth in overall disease burden among women, seventh among men); they constitute the largest proportion of community burden and, together with anxiety disorders, have been found in a number of studies to be responsible for between a quarter and a third of all primary health care visits.[1] Since the most common neuropsychiatric disorders have their onset during adulthood, the demographic transition will result in a sharp increase in overall burden of such disorders in the immediate future. For example, it is estimated that the total number of cases of schizophrenia in less-developed countries will increase from 16.7 million in 1985 to 24.4 million in 2000, a 45% increase simply as a result of demographic changes.[2] For certain societies, there is also evidence that the rates of depression have risen as a result of social change in the last four decades.[3]

The overwhelming conclusion of this report, however, is that formally defined neuropsychiatric disorders are responsible for only a portion of the overall burden of social and psychological morbidity. Alcoholism, drug addiction, suicide and suicide attempts, violence against women, abuse and abandonment of children, forced prostitution, crime and street violence, ethnic warfare and state violence, dislocation and forced migration—all of these constitute a substantial burden in societies of Africa, Asia, Latin America, and the Middle East. While it is impossible to provide country-by-country estimates of the burden from each of these problems, they are among the most urgent problems in our shrinking world.

Where data are relatively accessible, figures indicate what further investigations are likely to find. Alcohol-related diseases, for example, affect 5% to 10% of the world population. The sale of narcotics and drugs is one of the world's largest businesses and a major source of morbidity. Rates of domestic violence against married women vary from 20% to as high as 75%. Nearly 20 million persons are officially recognized as refugees today, many of whom suffer clusters of psychosocial and psychiatric problems. For all the limits to the database, the problems surveyed in this report constitute a profound challenge to health and well-being and exact a large human and economic toll.

Mental Health and "Development": The Global Distribution of Psychosocial Disorders

Our second broad conclusion is that the problems reviewed in this report cannot easily be parceled out between "developed" and "developing" nations. Unlike diarrheal diseases, which still account for high levels of infant mortality in many poorer countries but are almost completely controlled in the industrial nations of Europe and North America, many of the problems examined in this report are shared by nations rich and poor, North and South. Chronically high levels of violence are deadly on the streets of Los Angeles, in the working-class neighborhoods of Belfast, and in the slums of Caracas. Women within abusive relationships face physical and emotional hardship, even death, whether they live in Sydney, Boston, or Nairobi. Sexual exploitation of young women is found in Japan, Thailand, and East Africa, causing suffering and a serious risk of HIV infection. These pressing problems do not fit into a simple, progressive framework of maturing market economies inexorably transforming the societies to which they are attached.

Thus, while it is tempting to argue that the conditions discussed in this report have their origins in "underdevelopment" and lack of wealth per se (which would imply that economic development in a society leads not only to reductions in infant mortality but to reductions in global mental health problems), it is clear that such a model would fail to account for the range and distribution of distress. For many mental and behavioral health problems, there is little evidence of decline with a rise in a society's wealth. For some, such as schizophrenia and dementia, there is evidence of an increase because of demographic changes themselves. For others, such as alcohol abuse, violence, depression, and suicide, the complex social changes of the current epoch appear to worsen their numbers.

By the same token, most social and mental health problems are not a simple *result* of economic development, whereby development processes "produce" psychological symptoms or the social pathologies discussed in this volume. The general hypothesis that "modernization" results in the breakdown of coherent cultures and communities and leads to increased mental health problems has a long history in the social sciences, but it has not stood up well to empirical investigation.[4] Exploitative development that destroys aboriginal cultures has disastrous effects on mental health and should be fiercely resisted on both moral and health grounds. However, "development" is not a single linear and progressive (or retrogressive) process but an extremely complex interaction of diverse global and local processes. Population growth, urbanization, increased literacy and education, economic restructuring, changes in the technologies of production, the "information revolution," the distribution of military hardware, the weakening of the state, fundamentalist religious movements, the breakdown of family structures, and a vast array of changes in local cultures and practices are inseparable from development processes. Each has implications for global mental health, some positive, some negative, and the result is a complex social distribution of social and psychological morbidity. Simple models ascribing social ills to either underdevelopment or rapid development fail to further understanding.

Although research does not indicate a simple, direct relationship between economic development and mental health, poverty and profound inequities are clearly key risk factors for nearly all forms of social and psychiatric morbidity. Poverty exacerbates existing problems and leaves individuals and communities with limited resources to cope with new difficulties. The profound poverty found in parts of Africa, Latin America, the Caribbean, and Asia is particularly destructive of health and well-being. Unfortunately, rapid economic development is no certain cure. Development often creates poverty side by side with wealth, producing the social origins of suffering for many as well as rising living standards for some. The new forms of poverty, along with the social ills they produce, are challenges to social justice and human rights. Only when economic development is linked to a global concern for equity and human rights can it eliminate a key source of the new morbidities.

The problems reviewed in this report are thus truly global ones, shared by all nations, rich and poor. They are found in greater numbers in settings of poverty and desperation, but none are limited to the poorest nations or to poor communities. They are problems of the human community and require new thinking and new responses on a global scale.

Social Origins of Mental and Behavioral Ill Health

A third overall finding of this report is that, although no single, overarching theory or model can account for all social, behavioral, and mental health problems, researchers have identified a number of causal pathways that may be useful in developing intervention strategies. Five dimensions of these pathways stand out as major conclusions of our work.

- First, *current research on mental illnesses provides strong evidence that neuropsychiatric disorders are biosocial—that both biological and social factors are involved.* Mental disorders are not simply symptoms of broader social conditions. They also reflect inherited vulnerabilities and are mediated by neurophysiological processes. Nonetheless, the quality of a person's social environment is closely linked to the risk for suffering a mental illness, to the triggering of an illness episode, and to the likelihood that such an illness will become chronic. For example, micronutrient deficiency in childhood in association with malnutrition, poverty, and dislocation leads to neurological deficits and brain dysfunction. Schizophrenia is not a "social disease"; however, social and cultural factors strongly influence the course of the disease and the likelihood of recovery. Epilepsy results from pathology in the brain; why 90% of epileptic patients in a number of Asian and African societies do not receive biomedical treatment that has proven efficacy is a social question. Although neurotransmitters are implicated in major depression, trauma in childhood, such as the loss of a parent, increases lifelong vulnerability for depression; and significant losses, violence, and trauma play an important role in triggering particular episodes of depression, especially when experienced by relatively powerless persons with few personal and social resources.
- Second, *causal pathways for behavioral disorders and social problems also involve multiple factors interacting in subtle, but ultimately understandable, ways.* Suicide, for instance, is much more likely in persons with mental illness, particularly depression; it is also linked to availability of means for suicide (guns, poisons), to particular cultural meanings and pathways, and to intolerable social conditions. Use of addictive drugs usually has its onset in youth; it is associated not only with the social and cultural environment of adolescents but also with organization of the drug trade. Still other problems, such as the exploitation of children, are linked to rapid economic change as it affects the most vulnerable segments of a society. For example, the selling of young girls into sexual servitude in Thailand followed changes in agriculture, the migration to cities of rural populations, and the development of domestic and foreign markets for sex tourism. The consequences, as well as the origins, of commercial sex are global, as the explosive growth of HIV infection makes clear.
- Third, *the problems reviewed singly in separate chapters are in fact most typically found in clusters of psychosocial problems.* Substance abuse, violence toward women and children, psychiatric sequelae such as depression, and health risks in adulthood for children so victimized are closely associated

with one another. Community violence is linked to post-traumatic stress disorders, dislocation, and depression. These clusters need to be identified and investigated if we are to design effective strategies of prevention and treatment.

- Fourth, for many of the problems described in this report, *"cause" is best understood as a vicious spiral* rather than as simply a chain of conditions or discrete events (e.g., poverty leading by specific steps to mental illness and social pathology). Complexes of problems reproduce themselves in the life histories of individuals and families and in communities. Abused children are more likely to become abusers. Communities of poverty and violence reproduce clusters of social and mental health problems, and in turn are reproduced by political and economic conditions. In South Africa, for example, the violence in the shantytowns and townships stemmed from apartheid; yet these problems are likely to persist into the new era. However democratic, the new South African government will confront communities burdened with the terrible consequences of apartheid. New measures will be needed to prevent violence from reproducing itself, rather than just interrupt its initiating factor.

- Fifth, this report identifies several *key social forces that recur as sources of social and psychiatric morbidity*. Repressive gender practices have widespread devastating consequences; empowerment and education of women, and support for families and youth, are crucial for diminishing most of the problems we have examined. Ethnic conflict breeds violence, displacement, trauma, and depression. Relative and absolute poverty has broad effects; increased investment in poor communities is critical in breaking cycles of social and psychiatric morbidity. Economic policies that lead to great inequities in wealth and social resources, that isolate communities from political power and economic opportunity, and that remove security systems for those most in need spawn cycles of poverty and desperation associated with ill health.

The Role of Economic Development Policies in Mental Health

A fourth overall conclusion of this report is that economic policies and mental, behavioral, and social health problems are intimately linked. Distinctions between improving health, stimulating economic development, and enriching society are artificial. Neither health nor mental health is a luxury, something to be afforded at the point where a society has generated enough wealth to pay for it. To the contrary, the health of populations is, over the long run, a major determinant of their economic productivity.

Concern for the mental health impact of development strategies dictates that we think through what we mean by development. If development is understood primarily in terms of foreign-exchange balances, and rebalancing requires competitive commodity prices, which in turn requires the driving down of wages, increasing unemployment, lowering the standard of living, and stringently curtailing social spending, then any health policy generated in the aftermath of such "adjustments" is attempting to correct problems in a piecemeal fashion that are in fact being generated at a systems level.

Efforts to "restructure" an economy—that is, devalue its currency and withdraw social spending supports—are meant to improve the economic basis of human conditions. It is usually an abstract matter for an economist at the World Bank or the International Monetary Fund, and its effects are often remote from the national leaders who implement reform from the confines of a capital. But for those at the bottom of the socioeconomic pyramid, such changes are often a practical matter of life and death. "Competitiveness in the global market," then, should not become a watchword for policies friendly to those with wealth and Malthusian with respect to human suffering. If investment in health and well-being is a serious goal, those who formulate and implement economic and health policy must constantly bear in mind that what is being "developed" in poorer nations is precisely *the human potential of a given society*. As the best development projects have always reflected, and as many in development circles now argue, the critical issue must be how to promote the positive human aspects of economic growth while ameliorating its negative consequences. At a practical level, public health and mental health specialists should be involved in the review of development projects and policies to assess their likely impact on the health and mental health of those concerned.

Mental health services are deeply affected by restructuring policies. Too often the World Bank has accepted the shamefully small budgets for health services in poorer countries and the gross disparities in wealth between advanced and underdeveloped economies as facts of life impervious to human will in the face of global fiscal austerity. Governments are instructed to "target" their health care resources, with the very poorest societies being told to all but abandon tertiary care and advanced medical technology. The World Bank's *Investing in Health* can be read as suggesting that mental health services should be viewed as "discretionary," outside of the package of "essential" clinical services, and left largely to the private sector.[5] This view stands in sharp contrast to the one advocated in these pages.

The Role of Culture and Local Institutions

This report has stressed the critical importance of focusing on *culture*, and on local social institutions and cultural worlds, in efforts to understand the complex problems and responses under discussion. The categories we have employed—suicide, violence against women, abuse of children, use of alcohol or addictive drugs, depression—have distinct meanings in different societies. They point to issues that are often sharply debated within local cultural, religious, and political contexts. And people respond to these issues with local resources. We have therefore cautioned against the attacks on "traditional beliefs and practices" that have been all too common among health initiatives.

At the same time, we do not romanticize "tradition." Many traditional practices serve local power and patriarchal interests and lead to local forms of oppression and

misery. "Traditional" forms of caring for the mentally ill or responding to those suffering from epilepsy can be as oppressive as some traditional forms of treating new
brides or widows. Challenges to such traditions by individuals and groups advocating human rights should be supported by national and international policies.

Nonetheless, solutions to the problems we have discussed can only be developed in relation to local institutions and community resources. Some of the most
innovative programs we have canvassed, such as the village-structured care of children in Eritrea orphaned in the war for independence, the program to stimulate
interaction between mental health professionals and healers in Mali, and factory-
based rehabilitation programs for mentally retarded and mentally ill adults in China,
stem from inspired collaboration between the state and local communities. Similar
efforts aimed at providing culturally appropriate mental health care have gained a
sympathetic hearing in North America; prime examples are the aboriginal spirituality programs for the treatment of American Indians with substance-abuse problems
in some American and many Canadian prisons.[6] For the foreseeable future, the
paucity of trained mental health and social service professionals will be a fact of life
for much of the world. Therefore, efforts to build systems of care will have to recognize the importance of local modes of healing as well as to train professionals and
paraprofessionals in cultural awareness.

The best solutions will have certain qualities in common wherever they are
found.

- Insofar as possible, they will recognize cultural and ethnic diversity, and will
  be locally controlled and administered.
- They will build on local strengths and resources, while attempting to repair
  local weaknesses.
- They will attempt to mitigate the worst of economic and structural inequalities and promote human rights.
- And they will take seriously the fundamental connection between the well-
  being of individuals and the well-being of communities.

Successful Models and Directions for Change

Finally, although the problems facing many of the poorest societies of the world are
daunting, this report concludes that opportunities for effective interventions are far
greater in the area of mental and social health than many observers have assumed.
Advances in psychosocial and pharmacological therapies for psychiatric illnesses
offer cause for hope. Programs of prevention have proven promising. And new
approaches to mental health services have shown the kinds of advances that can be
achieved at relatively low cost.

The many innovative programs noted throughout the chapters of this volume
offer important models to be supported in future work. The community-based psychiatric rehabilitation services in China, discussed in Chapter 2, show how
guardianship networks can improve the efficacy of clinical services while reducing
the costs of such services. Dr. Lambo's program in Western Nigeria illustrates the

advantages of treating the mentally ill in the community. Dr. Guinness's innovative pairing of a mental health program with the primary care health system in Swaziland suggests the cost-effective value of training mental health nurses to care for patients in the community. And for more than a decade, the World Health Organization has supported projects in countries as diverse as India, Tanzania, and the Philippines that demonstrate ways for improving mental health care in primary care settings in a cost-effective manner.

Similarly effective programs have helped communities to combat violence, to treat recovering drug addicts, and to improve the lives of the elderly. The success of programs that deter domestic violence and rape in Mexico, noted in Chapter 8, has been a catalyst for different countries to develop similar programs. The success of folk healers and "drug bomohs" in Malaysia, based largely on the bomohs' ability to reinstill traditional values and help the person to reestablish a personal identity, points to the effectiveness of traditional approaches to substance abuse. In Zimbabwe, low-cost, cooperative residential facilities are helping destitute elderly to manage their daily lives and maintain a sense of independence and self-worth; these facilities are less expensive to run and offer better quality of life than more institutionally based programs. And in Ecuador, a nongovernment organization has set up a program to provide employment for the elderly and enable them to earn a modest income while contributing to their well-being (see Chapter 9).

Other interventions at the behavioral level have helped to eliminate unnecessary deaths and suffering. In 1988, the President of Ghana launched a public health campaign to eliminate dracunculiasis by filtering water sources and keeping infected people from contaminating purified water sources. By the end of the first year of the program, there was a 30% reduction in the disease. Four years later, the number of cases in Ghana had been lowered from 180,000 to 30,000 (see Chapter 10). In Haiti, the research by Proje Veye Sante shows that the chronicity of tuberculosis can be substantially reduced with minimal financial support and nutritional supplements (see Chapter 10). A recent project in Jumla, Nepal (noted in Chapter 7), showed that child morbidity and mortality can be drastically curtailed through low-cost measures; a pneumonia case-management service reduced total child deaths in the area by 28%, and a program designed to give vitamin A supplements to children reduced mortality by 26% and diarrhea deaths by a third. The death rate of children aged 6 to 12 years was thus cut in half. Similarly, a community-based intervention to improve personal hygiene, reduce diarrheal morbidity, and enhance the development of infants along the Padma River in Bangladesh reduced the prevalence of diarrhea and the number of severely malnourished children. Greater knowledge of personal hygiene and modification of behaviors leads to lower diarrheal-disease rates and reduced malnutrition even in impoverished settings. Not only are lives saved, but mothers and families are spared the grief and suffering associated with deaths of children.

Experimental programs such as these provide crucial models for a new generation of mental health services. Quite often, commitments from individuals, communities, and governments, coupled with minimum financial outlays, can go a long way in contributing to mental health. Mobilizing rural populations, empowering people with the skills to understand and care for their mentally ill members, and supporting people with adequate resources to provide care all contribute to effective ways of treating mental illness and improving the quality of life in general. If implemented on a larger scale, these approaches could save institutions tens of millions of dollars over the long term. Indeed, sophisticated, expensive treatment strategies are not always necessary when sound, effective, and culturally appropriate programs are developed to deal with problems.

Enthusiasm should be tempered by two observations. Whereas successful demonstration projects have been shown to be beneficial and feasible in local contexts, few have been generalized, systematically developed, and expanded to serve increasing portions of the society in a sustainable fashion. Too often projects remain dependent upon agency funding, the charisma of a single person or a small team of care providers, or the enthusiasm of a small region. Thus, in addition to developing and evaluating innovative demonstration programs, special attention must be given to the diffusion of successful programs and the building of sustainable systems of care. This is an enormous challenge. Second, both bureaucratic inefficiencies and economic restructuring can rob a society of the resources necessary to develop and follow through on innovative programs. Governments should be encouraged to invest in mental health, to recognize such services as essential to the social and economic well-being of their societies. An international commitment to investments in mental health care will be required if such systems of care are to take root.

What Is to Be Done? Meeting the Challenge

The health problems reviewed in these pages cry out for a concerted response. They are substantial in scope and not amenable to easy solutions. In many societies, the resources available for responding to them are extraordinarily limited. How can we conceptualize these problems in a way that provokes action rather than dismay? What are the priorities, and how should we proceed?

We suggest a conceptual frame to help map the territory and organize action. The problems of global mental health can be addressed, we argue, in three ways:

1. through *health services and appropriate medical technologies*;
2. through *a new generation of public health interventions*; and
3. through relevant *national and international policy innovations.*

This framework allows us to identify the knowledge bases and technologies available, and encourages systematic thinking about the development and evaluation of interventions for the problems that we have canvassed.

Mental Health Services

Contrary to prevailing myths, mental health problems can be effectively treated, and treatment and prevention can be made affordable. Effective mental health services thus have a crucial role to play in meeting the challenge outlined by this report. Advances in available psychotropic agents have made it possible to provide medical

---

Box 11.1 The Promise of Mental Health Care in Mali

Recent innovations in mental health care in Mali, an impoverished and isolated country of 8 million people in Western Africa, underscore both the changes that many African countries are making and the economic constraints on those changes.

Professor Baba Koumare, one of two fully trained Malian-born psychiatrists who work in the country, has been an instrumental leader of a new psychiatric movement. After eliminating an archaic practice of imprisoning the mentally ill without psychiatric care, he and his colleagues spearheaded a movement to develop guidelines and procedures for the delivery of mental health services throughout the country. In 1983, the government of Mali adopted the National Program in Mental Health, which promoted a hierarchical structure of psychiatric care, ranging from ritual practices in villages to psychiatric services in the capital city. With this system, mental health care was to be integrated into existing primary health services and primary health care nurses and other workers were to be trained in all aspects of mental health, including knowledge of the sociocultural aspects of mental distress. Local health committees were to act as liaisons in all rural and urban communities, and traditional healers (under the supervision of health professionals) were to continue their ritual practices in the villages.

The promotion of self-reliance, the support of traditional healers, and an integrated health care system rooted in primary health care characterized this new system of care, which, in tandem with the liberalization of health care in general, had three tenets: each patient and a family member were to be given a traditional hut in the village constructed on the hospital grounds; clinicians were to rely on a traditional form of the Bambara theater called a "koteba" as one of the regular therapeutic procedures[7]; and stabilized patients who had no family, and patients resistant to psychiatric care, were to receive care from traditional healers working under the psychiatrists' supervision.

Although the Malian government has supported the changes in mental health care in principle, inability to provide financial support has left them in limbo, and the policies have not been fully executed due to scarcity of personnel and problems in traveling and communicating from one region to another. Like other African countries, Mali is in serious economic decline due to lack of infrastructure and resources; it does not have the financial capacity to carry out many essential public services. Thus, despite the best intentions, and the potential for sophisticated, culturally sensitive care, financial constraints provide an insurmountable barrier. International agencies can make an enormous contribution by providing funds to implement and sustain such innovative programs.[8]

---

treatment for conditions previously thought unresponsive. Advances in psychoeducational interventions and psychosocial rehabilitation provide complementary treatment modalities to enhance outcomes. Two decades of demonstration and research projects by the World Health Organization have led to a broad consensus about the basic principles that should guide the development of mental health services. This consensus embodies a vision of health and mental health as indivisible, and of mental health care as an integral part of essential health services. As new efforts to upgrade primary care and health services get under way in many societies, it is crucial to strengthen, develop, and upgrade the quality of comprehensive, community-based mental health services.

Public Health Interventions

In recent years, innovative efforts have been made to adapt public health models to mental health problems. Micronutrient deficiencies and infectious diseases of infants and children are susceptible to traditional programs of prevention, and can contribute to the prevention of neuropsychiatric disorders, as outlined by a recent WHO task force.[9] New public health models have been introduced: epidemiological models for research and risk evaluation, anthropological and community research aimed at assessing the social and cultural context of particular behaviors (such as intravenous drug use), and community approaches to prevention (e.g., of street violence) and to health promotion.[10] In many cases, intersectoral interventions are required—that is, programs that cut across disciplines and across ministries of health, public housing, labor, finance, security, and social welfare, as well as the legal system. The challenge is now to give new priority to these problems, to develop additional strategies, and to replicate successful efforts in a wider variety of settings in culturally appropriate ways.

Public Policy Interventions

While the development of health policies for prevention and health services is essential, it is equally necessary to develop what Dr. Julio Frenk of Mexico calls "healthy policies" at the national and international level for progress to be made in addressing many of the most significant problems of our time.[11]

Explicit attention should be paid to the mental health consequences of social and economic policies—by researchers, national governments, private foundations, and international agencies. Policies that encourage gainful employment, reduce poverty, protect the environment, improve the quality of leisure, and provide universal basic education, primary health care, decent housing, and adequate nutrition are all prima facie beneficial. They are not merely a concession to an abstract vision of social justice; they have real effects on the health of individuals and communities.

Other policies have specific impacts on mental health. Universal education for women, from primary through secondary school, might at first glance seem removed from such issues as infant mortality and substance abuse. Yet the evidence is overwhelming that the education of women is the single most important factor in improving the health of infants and children. It is even a factor in reducing alcohol consumption by husbands (which, in turn, reduces male abusive behavior); the more education a woman has, the more resources she will have and the less likely she is to tolerate substantial portions of the family income being spent on alcohol.[12]

Recent approaches to the analysis of policy formulation and implementation and to the assessment of costs and benefits of particular policies provides an opportunity for advancing our understanding of mental health policies and placing policy recommendations on a solid empirical foundation.

The problems described in the chapters of this volume cannot be addressed separately through clinical services, public health activities, or broad social policies. Each requires some combination of these approaches. This general categorization, however, provides a framework for identifying knowledge bases and for organizing actions most appropriate for particular problems.

Recommendations for Specific Initiatives

Several issues are of the highest priority. They call for concerted attention from the research community, international agencies, and local governments. The following instances do not propose formulas for the development of specific solutions, but rather suggest a way of thinking about problems that recognizes both their complexity from a policy perspective and the fact that, ultimately, those most interested in becoming allies of positive change in their local world are those very people most affected by the problems in question.

1. We recommend a major initiative to upgrade the quality of mental health services in countries of Africa, Asia, Latin America, and the Middle East.

Mental health services have a crucial role to play in alleviating the suffering associated with neuropsychiatric illnesses, emotional distress, and behavioral pathology. Troubled children, abused women, the elderly, those traumatized by political violence, those who have attempted suicide or are addicted to alcohol or narcotics, and especially those who suffer from acute or chronic mental illnesses can be helped substantially by competent mental health care. With recent advances in psychiatric medications and specialized forms of psychosocial intervention, the potential for benefit is greater than at any time in history.

Yet mental health services in most societies are inadequate. Well-trained practitioners are scarce, drugs and psychosocial interventions are unavailable or of poor quality, and even where expertise and resources exist, they seldom reach into the communities where the needs are greatest. The human rights of the mentally ill are often severely compromised, and mental health care is too often associated with social control. Obstacles to the development of high-quality, comprehensive, and broadly distributed mental health services are great. Innovative programs are too seldom generalized, and mental health programs are particularly difficult to sustain. Financial investment is required, and creativity is needed to build programs that join local resources with professional knowledge.

The rehabilitation efforts in China noted in Chapter 2 (see Box 2.6) are of special interest because innovations have occurred in a number of large cities and rural areas and have been largely self-sustaining. Programs such as these deserve careful study, and expertise developed in the conduct of such projects should be made available to mental health specialists in other societies. The creation of new regional and international centers for research and training may be critical if the evaluation and diffusion of the best of a new generation of mental health services are to succeed.

The basic principles that should guide the development of community-based services are now reasonably clear. The care of the mentally ill should be specifically discussed in national and regional health plans, including clear description of activities to be undertaken and appropriate budgetary allocation. Mental health services need to be based in communities and adapted to local settings if they are to be sustained. They should address the most important problems of particular settings. Primary health care, the de facto mental health system in many communities, needs to be upgraded in order to improve the treatment of neuropsychiatric disorders. The promotion of mental health care for the mentally ill should be officially recognized as an essential aspect of primary health care (as stated in the Alma Ata Declaration), and reports about the effectiveness of primary health care activities should consider mental health issues. Improvements in mental health systems require rational drug policies for psychotropic medications and the reliable provision of adequate supplies of selected generic antidepressant, antipsychotic, and anticonvulsant drugs. Formal mental health services must be complemented by nonmedical support groups, consumer groups and healing institutions that provide crucial care in many communities. The human rights of patients require protection in mental health legislation.

2. We recommend systematic efforts to upgrade the amount and quality of mental health training for health workers at each level of training, from medical students to graduate physicians and from nurses to village health workers. Task-appropriate mental health modules should be introduced into student curricula and into continuing education programs in order to develop skills in the recognition, management, and referral (when needed) of mental health problems.

Essential to mental health programs is a small cadre of well-trained mental health professionals: psychiatrists, psychologists, social workers, and psychiatric nurses. They are the ones who must lead efforts to establish the priority of mental health in medical education and health policy. They also are responsible for designing and implementing training programs, for providing consultation to general health workers when complex problems arise, and for supervising the care of chronically mentally ill patients. Support is needed to upgrade the quality of training for these specialists and to introduce current concepts and improve standards of care— from psychopharmacology to specialized treatment of drug users or victims of violence to new approaches to community rehabilitation services. In addition to knowledge developed in international settings, findings of local and regional researchers and experiences of local communities, care providers, and policy specialists need to be systematically integrated into ongoing programs.

Along with improving the quality of training for specialists, however, new efforts are needed to increase the understanding of psychiatric conditions among general physicians and other specialists, to upgrade the quality of behavioral science teaching in medical education, and to provide new training for practicing primary care practitioners. New forms of training are needed if general physicians are to play a major role in providing mental health care and clinical responses to distress. Attention to psychosocial aspects of care are necessary in medical and nursing education if the new morbidities are to be seen as legitimate and treatable conditions, and training in doctor-patient communication, medical ethics, and community and social medicine is important if physicians are to take on new roles. Specific training in the diagnosis and management of neuropsychiatric conditions is required to improve the quality of mental health services offered in primary care. And since community practitioners often depend almost exclusively on pharmaceutical-company agents for new information on medications, new initiatives in continuing medical education are needed to provide more basic training in the safe and effective use of psychotropic medications.

With appropriate training and supervision, nonphysician primary care health workers can learn to diagnose, treat, and organize follow-up programs for a substantial fraction of cases of depression, anxiety, and epilepsy, and can, with appropriate supervision, manage many patients with chronic schizophrenia in the community if their social welfare is provided for.[13] The World Health Organization has developed training programs and shown that they can be effectively employed in societies as diverse as India, the Philippines, and Tanzania. In societies in which nonphysicians provide a substantial portion of primary care, specialized training activities are a cost-effective means of improving and extending mental health services.

3. We recommend that a coordinated series of efforts be directed toward improving state gender policies, toward interdicting violence against women, and toward empowering women economically. Research on these efforts should be directed toward evaluating the mental health consequences of these programs—for women, for children, and for men.

Investing in the health, education, and well-being of women is of high priority for improving the mental health of the population in low- and middle-income countries. The World Bank's 1993 World Development Report clearly demonstrates that educating women to primary-school level is the single most important determinant of both their own and their children's health. Our report indicates women's education is an equally valuable investment for the *mental* health of women, men, and children. Such education also renders women less likely to tolerate substantial portions of the family income being spent on drinking or gambling by their spouses, as well as making them more receptive to (and presumably more engaged as equal partners with) public health programs.

The mental health of women should be a primary concern for policymakers. Along with promoting the well-being of women for its own sake, which should be the first order of business, helping to improve the social and economic standing of women has various implications. The necessity of supporting women both economically and socially seriously affects both the conceptualization and implementation of formal services for many of the conditions analyzed in this report. For better or worse, women throughout much of the world constitute the vast majority of caretakers of first and last resort for chronically disabled family members, including mentally retarded children, demented elderly, and adults suffering a major mental illness. Minimally, it is in a community's long-term social interests to assist with this burden.

One of the more troubling mental health consequences of general health problems is the effect on mothers of high infant-mortality rates, where desperate decisions have to be made urgently about apportioning the family's meager resources in order to save one child by denying others. No mother should be placed in a position where she has to make such a choice. The provision of adequate family resources so that women can support the family's health is a fundamental human right and a crucial element of women's mental health.

Women are critical to the success of any particular health policy and to economic policies in general. Women should be enabled to participate formally in political and economic structures in their societies. The policies of governments, international aid agencies, and nongovernment organizations should have defined avenues for female voices and offer opportunities for women to exercise leadership roles. Local support networks, women's groups, and initiatives in maternal health should be prioritized. Such policies should be in part evaluated on the basis of their impact on women. Those that tend to increase access of women to education and economic opportunities (that is, those that empower women to control their own destinies, including control over their reproductive destinies) tend to increase the health not only of women but of the entire community and are deserving of the name "healthy policies".[14] It follows, then, that policies that retard such access are, according to our best evidence, destructive of the health of populations and should be opposed.

4. We recommend improvements and innovations in mental health services for children and adolescents, in early detection and prevention of mental disorders, and in educational programs.

The future prosperity of all countries depends on the health, education, and training of young people. Unfortunately, trends in mental disorders among children and adolescents have worsened in both rich and poor countries.

To counter these trends, mental health services for children, especially those that stress early detection of problems, must be integrated into all forms of health care. As with other mental services, priority should be given to cost-effective services that meet local needs. For example, early detection of epilepsy and appropriate medication to control seizures enables a child with the disorder to participate fully in school and community life and to avoid the secondary complications (burns, injuries, educational failure, stigma) that would otherwise blight his development. A second example of the benefit of early identification is the use of home visitors trained to recognize the potential for abuse and neglect and to summon community resources before an infant is damaged beyond repair.

The limited effectiveness of existing child psychiatric treatments, as well as their costliness, emphasize the importance of innovating and testing new local programs (particularly preventative ones) through support for family life. Prevention of mental disability in children and adolescents is achievable through birth planning, the provision of prenatal and perinatal care, immunization, the provision of optimal nutrition (in terms of calories, protein, and micronutrients), home visiting and day care, child safety measures, school-based programs on family life and human sexuality, and appropriate treatment for common childhood neuropsychiatric disorders, such as epilepsy.

Public schools are the principal social institution in the community for furthering the cognitive and emotional development of children. The goal should be full educational opportunity for each child. What is practical in a given community at a given time will be determined by its resources. Schooling should be available for girls and boys on the same terms. When feasible, the school-leaving age should be raised to 16. Young adults, particularly those whose early education has been insufficient, must receive training in vocational skills. The goals of public schooling are not only basic literacy and numeracy but also the norms of social behavior and the ability to cooperate with others. Teachers should be trained to recognize signs and symptoms of mental illness, to manage early problems as they arise in the classroom, and to refer to primary care facilities those children who need more assistance. Peer counseling programs in public schools can diminish risk for substance use and antisocial behavior. Success in school is a major source of self-esteem.

As mental health services are made available, they should be targeted at those children who are at the highest risk for disturbance: children without parents or in shattered families, children among refugee and displaced populations, children living in a continued atmosphere of violence, and children living on the streets or in squatter colonies.

5. We recommend systematic efforts to assess the global burden of substances (alcohol and drugs) with the potential for abuse, to reduce the demand for these substances, and to develop effective treatment and prevention programs.

Substance abuse is intertwined in complex ways with some of the most pressing problems currently facing the human community. Glue-sniffing among homeless children compromises the health and well-being of a population whose very day-to-day survival is tenuous; the ingestion of alcohol vastly increases the likelihood that forms of violence, such as domestic abuse, will take place; and the violence associated with the illegal trade in cocaine and heroin disrupts the social stability of many societies. Indeed, of all the problems investigated in this report, substance use and abuse is the one most clearly intertwined with broader social and economic issues. Alcohol and tobacco policies, for example, reap high profits for both private enterprise and governments in both developed and less developed economies. Economies of scale have also grown up around the trade in illegal substances.

Yet the costs of these policies, in terms of community distress, compromised population health measures, hospital and other social services, and legal and punitive systems, are obscured. Trade in illegal substances generates revenues large enough to compromise national governments in many places in the world (e.g., Colombia). In general, the lack of reliable, systematic data on substance-abuse problems has impeded an understanding of the severity and magnitude of the problems and undermined effective policy strategies. The true economic costs of the ingestion of legal substances have to be understood by electorates and their representatives, and the enormous economic incentives around the trade in illegal substances must be addressed. We must also better understand how poverty, social inequalities, and economic and cultural marginalization place specific groups at special risk. International bodies need to enhance their capacity for meaningful, comparable data-gathering on substance abuse, and governments should elucidate the negative economic and social consequences of substance abuse in terms that will lead to initiatives to stop the tide of drug production and distribution in their countries. These should be regarded as essential data for mental health planning.

Combating the abuse of both licit and illicit substances is a tall order. Nonetheless, the current data suggests that some strategies are better than others. Interventions aimed at reducing the supply of illicit drugs rarely work effectively; they are expensive both in terms of resources and the character of a society, and tend not to significantly curb the supply of illicit drugs, the number of users, or the amounts they consume. Governments must therefore develop stronger policies to reduce the demand for drugs if the problem is to be meaningfully addressed. This requires enhanced public education that includes messages on prevention that are meaningful to youth and that notes the dangers associated with the more casually accepted use of tobacco and apparently less potent liquors. The most successful educational campaigns tend to be locally administered, culturally meaningful, and relevant for all youths. Governments should also enhance and support culturally relevant prevention efforts. This requires that prevention and treatment interventions be systematically evaluated in a culturally sensitive manner. Consistent with the efforts of the World Health Organization, a focus on dependence, as an enduring health problem, should replace the negative connotations of "abuse" to lead to more support for effective prevention and intervention efforts.

Addressing this problem also requires an expansion of treatment capacities with particular attention to culturally sensitive means of intervention. Adequate treatments and treatment capacity are essential to provide a means to help those who seek help, and thus prevent the resignation that commonly perpetuates epidemic drug use. Traditional and nontraditional approaches, at both the community and personal level, can succeed if systematically developed, implemented, and rigorously evaluated. This work should become an iterative process that generalizes what works and eliminates what fails.

6. We recommend that broad initiatives be developed to attend to the causes and consequences of collective and interpersonal violence.

Collective and interpersonal violence is one of the most pressing problems in the world today. Wars, prolonged conflicts, ethnic strife, and political repression often lead to a range of social, economic, and psychological problems that undermine well-being. Damage ranges from physical disabilities to psychological trauma to the breakdown of local ways of life. Some of the most harmful aspects of violence relate to the aftermath of conflicts: the disruption of local economies, shortages of food and drinking water, dislocation, and separation from family members.

While only profound changes in international and national politics will reduce the frequency and severity of armed conflicts, peace and security initiatives that target violence as the major threat to health and social well-being globally should be strongly encouraged. In addition, mental health concerns should be more widely understood in peace and security programs. For ethnic conflict, for instance, mental health issues, from the effect of racism on ethnic identity to the vicious cycles of revenge, should become the target of new policies and programs, such as education in schools on these issues.

Several other modest but effective steps can be taken to reduce the suffering associated with collective violence. First, trauma from collective violence can be better attended to if transnational initiatives are developed that anticipate regional or intrastate conflicts and quickly aid victims of violence. Second, culturally sensitive treatment centers in refugee camps and other safe havens can be systematically developed and implemented. These therapeutic interventions must work at the cultural as well as the psychological level to reestablish a secure moral ground for everyday life. They must also work in tandem with local values. For instance, while some communities might be best served by programs that help to communicate the experience of traumatic events and the consequences of violence in words, the cultivation of a new reality, rather than reiteration of former traumas, might be the best approach for others. Since therapy for individuals is rarely available to many residents in poor countries (where most conflicts presently take place), community-oriented programs are the most realistic options in many settings. Furthermore, it is extremely beneficial to help families, villages, and social networks to stay intact whenever possible.

Research has shown that these interventions have beneficial effects.[15] The problem is that the health and mental health services in many poor countries are severely limited in terms of finances and potential manpower. In turn, the present range of international services designed to attend to these problems are helpful but inadequate. There is therefore an urgent need for a concerted, systematic effort, in both national and international circles, to establish programs of therapy and triage to counter the traumatic effects of violence at both the personal and community level.

The burden of distress resulting from domestic violence requires address in each country in a way specific to its culture and its mode of governance. Prevention will ultimately demand gender equality, but this is a distant horizon. In the near term, progress toward that goal requires repealing laws that deny rights to women (for example, to the inheritance of property) and community education that stresses respect for women. Deterrence requires laws that make violence against women a crime and enforcement mechanisms that assure the punishment of perpetrators. Women who are threatened with violence should receive immediate protection by the police and by the courts. Medical care for physical wounds and mental health care for psychological wounds can mitigate long-term suffering. And finally, community-based group programs for women who have been victimized through rape and spousal abuse can enable them to avoid self-blame and to take a more active stance in demanding their full rights as human beings. Greater attention in human rights programs to these specific abuses of women will be important.

7. We recommend that a specific effort be directed to make the primary prevention of mental, neurological, behavioral, and psychosocial disorders a major focus in the field of health.

Such an effort would survey the scientific knowledge base, examine primary prevention activities around the world, address the cross-cultural relevance of prevention programs, and define training needs and other relevant activities. Successful prevention programs call for the integration of biological and psychosocial factors, and the active promotion of known preventive programs (immunization, needed nutrients, alleviation of known organic causes). Of particular importance is the potential for developing generic prevention models that would take into account the co-morbidity of many disorders and the multiple outcomes of risk factors. For poor societies in particular, prevention programs require an understanding of protective factors that are a part of local cultures.

The Next Step: A Provocation for Action

The recommendations outlined here grow directly out of our analysis of the research and practical experiences of social scientists, public health specialists, the designers of innovative mental health programs, and many others. However, rather than a simple statement of where we see consensus to lie on these issues, we take these recommendations as a provocation for action. Ultimately, the findings and recommendations of this report will only have meaning and value when they are debated, challenged, adapted to local conditions, drawn upon by advocacy groups in local societies, used to rethink educational or mental health service policies, and used to promote international and national collaboration to bring about change.

One thing is clear. For these recommendations to be taken seriously and implemented, there must be an *international movement that prioritizes mental health*. There is no question that global consensus such as that organized around democratization brings substantial pressure to bear on all societies to rethink priorities and practices. It is essential to draw similar international attention to mental health concerns in international agencies such as the United Nations, the World Bank, the World Health Organization, and in regional organizations such as ASEAN, the Organization of African Unity, and the Organization of American States. It is essential, in short, to raise the international level of awareness that will affect the priority that policymakers and program developers in countries worldwide assign to mental health. Such a global campaign for mental health should involve the media, businesses, educational institutions, and networks of health and social-policy makers. We are now in the United Nations Year of Indigenous Peoples. There soon needs to be a United Nations Year of Mental Health.

12

An Agenda for Research

Why Do Research?

Research requires the commitment of substantial human and financial resources. During a worldwide recession that has left many low-income societies heavily in debt and high-income countries struggling to maintain their economic growth and prosperity, why should research be done? The answer is that ignorance is more costly than knowledge. The cost is economic; but it is also a cost in the burden of social misery and in the abridgment of human potential.

Sound research enables countries to spend their health care funds more efficiently. For example, research tools now exist to analyze the cost-effectiveness of specific clinical interventions. A study in mainland China found that innovative family- and community-based rehabilitation programs for people with chronic mental illness decreased symptoms, improved functioning, and reduced the rate of rehospitalization; such approaches carried out on a national scale could save tens of millions of dollars while also improving care and reducing suffering.[1] Studies examining the quality of existing care can identify sources of substandard care that are also very costly. For example, studies of physician practices and patient compliance reveal that doctors often prescribe antidepressant medication in suboptimal amounts and that patients do not take medication as prescribed[2]; medication is wasted; depression often continues unabated; the result is further work and social disability. While few studies have examined their cost-effectiveness, approaches that prevent mental illness have enormous potential to save money while reducing suffering[3]; as many as half of all mental and neurological disorders are amenable to primary prevention.[4]

A research database is required to set priorities for action, evaluate the effects of policies, monitor the quality and efficacy of services, and respond to changing social and health conditions. The critical question is not *whether* to do research, but rather *what kind* of research to carry out. Which research questions should receive priority? What kinds of epidemiological, ethnographic, clinical science, and health services data are needed as a first step? Which public health interventions and public policies should receive priority for research evaluation?

Great progress has been made over the past twenty years in developing more rigorous and theoretically grounded approaches to research. Advances have been made in the fields of psychiatric epidemiology, biological psychiatry, health services research, psychiatric and medical anthropology, public health, health economics, and health care policy research. Examples of new research technologies include

279

a more valid and reliable psychiatric nosology, improved methods to assess out-comes, more rigorously designed clinical trials, innovative prevention and interven-tion strategies, cost-benefit analyses, systematic program evaluation strategies, and ethnographic approaches to studying psychiatric disorders.

However, a great deal of work still needs to be done. New technologies, methodologies, and treatments must be adapted for use in diverse cultural settings. Innovative interdisciplinary approaches to problems must be developed. Research agendas need to cross the artificial boundaries that divide health policy from social policy. Social policies have profound consequences for health; health problems have social sources and powerfully affect the social world. A crucial issue for research is deciding whether to respond to a population's mental and behavioral health problems through health services, public health interventions, or "healthier" social policies.

This report shows that, despite many similarities, mental health problems and services also take shape in particular cultural patterns. Ethnographic research plays a key role in our vision of the future, because ethnography can better describe and interpret these local patterns. A surprisingly large body of cross-cultural psychiatric and anthropological information is available at present to guide such local efforts. The upshot of local research should be culturally informed studies that yield infor-mation that is highly specific to particular communities. Such information will then enable local cultural knowledge to inform practice and prevention in a way that both has been missing and has been an obstacle to the development and sustainabil-ity of culturally appropriate programs. The development of culturally informed knowledge should be an extra contribution of a report that combines the perspec-tives of anthropology with those of the health sciences.

Because low- and high-income societies share many problems, the knowledge generated by research can benefit all societies. For example, effective community approaches to violence worked out in Bogotá can contribute to the development of programs in Boston. High-income countries such as the United States, which have become more ethnically diverse, are searching for solutions to inner-city poverty, substance abuse, and violence. Knowledge from low-income societies helps them to provide better policies, services, and prevention programs for their own popula-tions.

Research Development and the Challenge of Diversity

Though many societies face similar mental and social health concerns, diversity across nations and within nations must be taken into account to set priorities for research, build research capacity, and conduct research. Research programs that do not consider these sources of diversity are likely to be less successful. The sources of diversity are material, cultural, political, historical, and epidemiological. A few examples will illustrate their importance for research.

Material resources available on the ground, such as health care services, research infrastructure, and trained research personnel, differ dramatically. Thai-land, for example, has a well-developed research infrastructure and formal system of mental health care services, whereas Eritrea has virtually none. The extent and nature of informal services—traditional healing and family-based care—also varies widely. Epidemiological variation in the types, rates, co-morbidities, and distribution of mental and behavioral health problems, will influence local priorities for research. For example, developing innovative services for trauma-related conditions may be a high priority in war-torn Somalia but much less of a concern in Samoa.

Local and culturally based norms, values, and practices will influence local priorities for research and action. Conflicts may occur between the priorities of researchers, who often base their decisions on epidemiological data, and laypersons, who draw upon local knowledge. In Thailand, for example, lay perceptions of health priorities differed dramatically from those based on survey data.[5] Since community support for projects is vital, conflicts need to be recognized and resolved in a fashion that respects both lay and professional perspectives.

We recommend six general principles to help research development meet the challenge of diversity. Because of ethnic, class, and urban-rural differences within countries, these principles apply to researchers from Shanghai undertaking studies in rural parts of China, for instance, just as they do to researchers from Boston conducting research in Tanzanian shantytowns or in American inner cities. Together, these principles will make research development more locally relevant and sustainable:

1. Focused ethnographic studies should precede epidemiological and intervention studies to provide descriptive maps of local problems, perspectives, social realities, and resources. Ethnographic studies will be cost-effective in the long run because they are relatively inexpensive to conduct and produce vital data to make research development more culturally appropriate.
2. The most successful intervention approaches will be community-based and build on local institutions, traditions, and values.
3. Citizens and researchers from the areas being studied must have substantial control over the research process itself, from the setting of priorities to the carrying out of projects. Local investment in and support for research is critical.
4. The cultural relevance of new technologies and treatments should be evaluated using ethnographic data on local values, patterns of use, resources, and priorities. Promising approaches can then be adapted for use elsewhere.
5. Ethical issues in mental health research should be monitored from the outset, considering both local and international perspectives. Engaging issues from both perspectives can usually resolve conflicts or establish more-valid grounds for mediation.
6. Interdisciplinary research approaches will be more helpful than those based on a single disciplinary perspective.

An Inclusive Framework for Research

World Mental Health emphasizes the intimate connection between social processes and mental health. Violence, displacement, abuses of human rights, the social conditions of vulnerable and marginal groups, problems in the different developmental phases of the life cycle—all have a place in this view of mental health as a broad, inclusive index of social well-being. Yet this report recognizes that mental and behavioral health is at once a social, psychological, and biological process inseparable from general health. Any adequate research framework will need to address the biological, psychological, and social determinants of mental and behavioral health; it will need to take into account both social policies and individual biologies.

Mental health problems such as depression, domestic violence, and substance use represent a combination of protective and undermining influences at the level of individuals, families, communities, and societies. These influences include macrosocial forces, local social contexts, interpersonal processes, and the biological and psychological endowments of individuals. An understanding of the interaction among these influences is vital. Similarly, the interaction of large-scale economic and political forces, local institutional structures, and cognitive and interpersonal coping processes shapes the kinds of services available to people, how people use these services, and how they respond to treatments. To study these interactions, interdisciplinary methods are essential so that the approaches of social sciences and health sciences can be applied to problems at particular levels of analysis as well as across levels. This integrative, biocultural framework stands behind our suggestions for developing research agendas, operationalizing research approaches, building and sustaining a cadre of researchers, and relating research to policy.

An example of the kind of framework that we have in mind is presented by Julio Frenk in an article titled "The New Public Health." With some modification, his typology of health research is a useful and inclusive framework for research on mental and behavioral health problems (see Table 12.1).[6] The typology has two dimensions: the level of analysis, which includes the individual/subindividual level

Table 12.1 Typology of Research on Mental and Behavioral Health Problems

Level of Analysis	Object of Analysis	
	Conditions (mental and behavioral health problems and their determinants)	**Responses** (mental health systems, clinical trials, policies, programs)
Individual/subindividual	Biomedical research	Clinical and behavioral research; evaluation of efficacy
	Behavioral research	
		Prevention research
		Ethnographic research
Populations	Epidemiological research	Mental health services research
	Ethnographic research	Ethnographic research
	Social policy research	Prevention research
		Mental health policy research

Source: Adapted from Frenk, 1993b. Adapted, with permission, from the *Annual Review of Public Health*, Volume 14. © 1993, by Annual Reviews Inc.

and the population level; and the object of analysis, referring to mental conditions and their determinants or to the organized social responses to those conditions. The major types of research relevant to mental health can be located within this matrix (for example, biomedical, epidemiological, ethnographic, clinical, mental health systems, mental health policy, and social policy research). Some types of research move across levels and objects of analysis. For example, ethnographic research, depending on the questions being asked, considers data at both the aggregate level and the individual level. Prevention research, one type of response to mental health conditions, often begins with pilot projects examining efficacy at the individual level and is later generalized to entire communities or populations.

This typology illustrates that relating data from distinct levels of research and deciding when one level has a comparative advantage over another are important issues in research development. In addition, it highlights the potential for combining different disciplinary perspectives at specific levels of research in planning and carrying out research programs. For example, the methods and findings of two research paradigms—ethnography and epidemiology—can together provide a more effective knowledge base for understanding the burden of mental and behavioral health conditions in a particular population and for designing public health or services interventions. Why is this so? Because while epidemiological research considers data at the aggregate level, ethnographic research describes the contextual forces at work in the processes that underpin those problems and provides information about culturally valid approaches to intervention.

Essential National Mental Health Research

In this section we specify five domains of research that merit priority funding (see Table 12.2). The list of research questions and approaches is not exhaustive. For the sake of conciseness, we do not attend to certain problems and refer the reader to earlier chapters of this report for specific recommendations for research in these areas. This report raises far more research questions than could possibly be investigated even in high-income countries. The research areas and approaches described below are "first steps" toward addressing the problems described in this report. They are a partial list of *essential national mental health research*. We note them here in order to stimulate discussion and debate in ministries of health and various nongovernmental organizations.

Five areas that merit priority funding are (1) developing culturally informed epidemiological databases, (2) improving research on mental health services,

Table 12.2 Essential National Mental Health Research

1. Culturally informed databases

2. Research on mental health services

3. Research on violence

4. Research on women's mental health

5. Evaluation of prevention approaches

(3) preparing a research agenda for violence, (4) preparing a research agenda for women's mental health, and (5) evaluating prevention programs. The first two are examples of research where studies are under way, methods are well established, and we are more certain of how results can be used. The last three are examples of areas where research is just beginning, where new approaches must be developed, and where it is still unclear how findings will be applied in policy and programs.

Culturally Informed Databases

Basic epidemiological data on the prevalence and distribution of mental and behavioral health conditions is still lacking for many low-income countries. Data is also lacking for particular age groups, such as children and youth, and for particular mental health problems, such as violence and substance abuse. Without valid databases, it will be impossible to gauge the magnitude of the problems, the adequacy of existing mental health services, and the groups at highest risk. Clinic and community epidemiological studies are needed to fill these gaps. These studies should tabulate basic sociodemographic and mental health data (see Table 12.3). To maximize their usefulness, studies must meet scientific standards of reliability and validity, be culturally appropriate, and be standardized enough to allow for cross-national comparisons.

A series of epidemiological studies sponsored by the World Health Organization can serve as a starting point.[7] The methodology of these studies, which rely on standardized instruments and methods of data collection, is sound. Future research studies should go beyond these valuable studies to produce a new generation of more culturally informed epidemiological studies that more accurately represent how distress takes form at the local community level. To accomplish this, deeper collaboration between epidemiologists and social scientists is needed.

The following specific recommendations will help improve future epidemiological studies. First, cultural validity should be enhanced by incorporating local patterns of distress. The clinical implications of local categories can then be compared with DSM-IV or ICD-10 categories. For example, a study on Puerto Rican mental health examined the relationship of the folk illness category "*ataques de nervios*" to DSM-III-R categories.[8] Persons who reported experiencing "*ataques*" were much more likely to meet criteria for depressive or anxiety disorders and to report suicide attempts. Second, studies need to examine the cultural patterning of coping, care-

Table 12.3 Variables to Be Covered in Epidemiological Research

---

1. Basic Sociodemographic characteristics
2. Neuropsychiatric diagnoses
3. Local manifestations of distress
4. Behavioral and social pathologies
5. Disability and physical health status
6. Care-seeking and coping responses

---

seeking, and meaning-making responses to mental and behavioral disorders. Initially, this can be done through clinic-based studies, such as the WHO study of psychological problems in primary care, which are relatively inexpensive and yield much valuable data.[9] Third, epidemiological studies need to tabulate data on behavioral pathologies such as substance abuse and violence. The co-morbidity of substance-abuse disorders and other mental and behavioral health conditions deserve special attention: for example, alcoholism and depression, substance abuse and violence. This "clustering" of conditions needs to be more systematically described, both in relationship to individual psychological and biological variables as well as to social variables. Fourth, data should be routinely collected on the relationship between mental and behavioral health problems and general health status.

Research on Mental Health Services

Research can play a major role in efforts to upgrade the quality of existing mental health services by: (1) enhancing the quality of mental services in primary care and in psychiatric treatment settings; (2) developing and evaluating community-based treatment and psychiatric rehabilitation programs; and (3) improving the balance, continuity of care, and integration of mental health systems.

1. *Improving the quality of mental health services in primary care and psychiatric settings.* Because there are so few mental health professionals in most low-income societies, the design, funding, and evaluation of cost-effective training programs for auxiliary mental health personnel should be a high priority. There are numerous excellent models of such programs. For example, a WHO-sponsored study conducted by Timothy Harding and his associates illustrates the improvement in recognition rates when health care workers are adequately trained to identify mental health conditions.[10] After being trained, mental health care workers' ability to recognize mental disorders (expressed as the percentage of those with disorder who were accurately identified) improved two- to threefold at most sites. Results were similar for adults and children.

Future demonstration projects must train health care workers to identify and intervene skillfully in situations of domestic violence, suicidal behavior, or substance abuse—all of which are common in primary care settings. A more comprehensive treatment approach to family, network, and community problems is necessary to avoid harmful "medicalization" of social problems. For example, diagnosing a woman with major depression and treating it with a medication is inadequate if a physically abusive husband is contributing to her distress.

Studies in primary care and psychiatric settings can also effectively examine the appropriateness of psychotropic-drug-prescribing practices. This is an area of vital importance, because drugs are an expensive component of outpatient treatment in many low-income countries. Studies of physician prescribing practices and of factors that lead to patient nonadherence are equally important.

Demonstration projects of clinical services that provide culturally sensitive treatment and community outreach should be given priority. In Zimbabwe, Jeremy Broadhead and his colleagues relied on key-informant interviews with community leaders, community outreach and education, and knowledge of local idioms of distress to develop depression treatment services in a primary care setting.[11] First, these investigators interviewed local traditional healers and other key informants in order to elicit local expressions of distress and community ideas about the nature and treatment of mental health problems. Local idioms of distress were then used to design a screening instrument and treatment protocol for depression. Nurses were trained to use the screening instrument to help them identify and then treat persons with depression. Community outreach and education were conducted to advertise these services. Data are not available on the efficacy of this intervention—precisely the research required to close the gap between demonstration projects and general programs.

2. *Community-based psychiatric treatment and rehabilitation programs.* Many neuropsychiatric disorders are chronic conditions associated with significant disability, such as impaired occupational and social functioning. Thirty years ago, the customary treatment for chronically ill patients was institutional-based custodial care, often alienating and long term. Even in countries with limited resources, there are now examples of affordable, humane, and effective community-based psychosocial rehabilitation programs that can sustain patients in family and work settings. One such study, the family-based community treatment by Xiong Wei and her colleagues in China, was described in Chapter 2 (see Box 2.6).[12] From a research perspective, this study was exemplary because of its rigorous methodological approach and its comprehensive assessment of outcome, which went beyond symptoms to assess social and occupational functioning. Researchers need to adapt this and comparable approaches in other cultural settings and evaluate them by valid and reliable methods.

3. *Evaluating local systems of mental health care.* Research must examine more broadly the range of mental health services at the community level, including the "informal" sector of care (especially the family and traditional healers) as well as the "formal" sector of care, which includes primary care, general hospitals, and formal psychiatric services.[13] Basic descriptive data on existing services within low-income countries is often lacking altogether, is limited to "formal" services, or is too superficial to be useful to policymakers.

In low-income countries, the "informal" sector of care plays a major role in the care of the mentally ill and must be more rigorously described and evaluated to determine its strengths, limitations, and relationship to "formal" sectors of care. Informal sources of care deserve more systematic description and evaluation. What sorts of treatments are employed to treat conditions like "depression," "anxiety," and "soul loss"? Are these treatments effective? For whom? Under what conditions? What models might be developed to link these practitioners to the formal primary health care system? How does the family's response to mental illness influence its course and outcome?

Ethnographic observation, surveys of institutions and government agencies, and community epidemiological data should be used to construct maps of the structure and integration of local systems of mental health care. The responses to persons with mental and behavioral disorders within family, community, and care sectors should be part of that description. Once the nature of the system is known, it can be evaluated in terms of five criteria: how adequately it meets basic mental and behavioral health needs; how decentralized it is; how integrated it is; how it balances various sectors and types of services; and how continuous is the care.[14]

Collective and Interpersonal Violence

While much previous research on violence has focused on treating the consequences of violence at the individual level, we need research that (1) describes the distribution, types, social contexts, and health consequences of interpersonal and collective violence in populations; (2) describes and compares successful and unsuccessful community responses to violence; and (3) evaluates social initiatives and public health interventions to prevent interpersonal and collective violence.

Epidemiological data on violence can be tabulated as part of the development of culturally informed databases. This data collected in clinics and in community surveys would help to define the pervasiveness, patterns, and consequences of particular forms of violence (e.g., domestic violence, ethnic or racially motivated violence, violence related to substance abuse or crime). Ethnographic studies carried out before and during the collection of epidemiological data are essential to help develop survey instruments, to understand the local meanings and practices for violence, and to understand the impact of violence at the community level. The ultimate goal of this research is to improve our understanding of the complex interactions of social, political, and cultural forces that lead to high rates of interpersonal, criminal, and domestic violence in particular settings, such as the interplay of poverty, racism, absence of effective gun controls, gang culture, drugs, and the breakdown of families in American inner cities. What, for example, is the social epidemiology and ethnographic context of the relationship between interpersonal violence and substance abuse? If these forces can be better understood through research, we will be in a better position to develop community prevention strategies and broader social policy initiatives to reduce violence in cities, in streets, and in households.

Many communities have successfully responded to violence through innovative local programs both within and outside the formal health care system. For example, a community-based intervention program in a Guatemalan Mayan community helps heal the psychological wounds of war in children through workshops aimed at building personal self-esteem.[15] In other cases, the response may involve particular institutions within the community. An ethnographic study of ethnic violence in India and Sri Lanka revealed that police and local governments played a central role: ethnic riots were averted when the police took a firm, public stand against such behavior and politicians indicated no tolerance for any level of violence or cycles of revenge.[16] A systematic comparison of these community responses might reveal general principles to guide policy and public health interventions in other settings. Knowledge obtained in Asia and Africa may have relevance to areas at high risk in North America and Western Europe.

A third major area for research is the evaluation of social policies and public health interventions to prevent violence. For example, social policies that restrict firearms or change the police response to ethnic conflicts should be evaluated. A complex set of variables exerts an influence early in the life cycle to cause violent interpersonal behavior later; research is needed to develop and evaluate prevention programs for children and families at increased risk.[17] In her work with South African youth, Mamphela Ramphele emphasizes the need for programs for high-risk youth. She designed a program that accomplished this through the involvement of township youth in outdoor activities with local mentors.[18] Media campaigns to reduce the acceptability of violence and promote nonviolent lifestyles also need to be developed and evaluated.

Women's Mental Health

Social policy and public health research is needed to inform and evaluate public policy and public health interventions that enhance the mental health of women across the life cycle. Although research should include the role of women as care-takers of the mentally ill, of children, and of elders, improving the status of women's health and well-being is an important goal in and of itself. The data marshaled here show that poverty, hunger, overwork, violence, powerlessness relative to men, and some economic development policies have negative effects on women's mental health. The overall goals of research should be (1) to examine how these social forces influence women's mental health in particular cultural contexts and (2) to identify social policy interventions, community-based programs, and other alternatives that empower women and raise their status in societies. Research in these areas is most likely to lead to interventions that reduce the incidence of certain mental disorders that occur disproportionately in women, such as depression and anxiety disorders. To be effective, interventions must speak to the concerns of women in low-income societies and engage them as active collaborators.

As for the worldwide epidemic of domestic violence, basic epidemiological research and innovative public health interventions can make a difference. Epidemiological data is needed to document the extent and patterning of the problem, as well as its "clustering" with other mental and behavioral pathologies, such as substance abuse and depression. To be valid, such surveys must be preceded by focused ethnographic studies that elicit the particular situations and perspectives of women within the community so that subjects can be approached and questions asked in a culturally valid format. Basic epidemiological data combined with ethnographic information on women's perspectives can inform the design of practical community-based intervention programs such as women's groups and shelters. Program evaluation research should be an integral part of these interventions. The development and evaluation of community programs to prevent violence against women is perhaps the most important long-term solution to this ubiquitous problem.

Programs of development too often have a mental health "downside" for women that makes preexisting gender inequalities worse. One hypothesis highlighted in these pages deserving further investigation is that economic restructuring programs, often based on patriarchal definitions of gender roles, interact with local cultural factors to negatively impact women's mental health. In countries where economic restructuring is already under way, research is needed to study how it effects women's mental health. Where restructuring is now being contemplated, research can anticipate its effects on women and on other vulnerable groups. Initiatives designed to increase recognition of women's productive activities and provide appropriate remuneration should be promoted and the results evaluated in both health and economic terms.

Prevention Research

New social policies, public health interventions, and clinical services are needed to prevent mental and behavioral distress. Research is central to this effort. Prevention research, as we use the term, is research that evaluates interventions occurring before the onset of mental or behavioral health problems.[19]

Prevention approaches can be either universal, selective, or indicated.[20] Universal approaches are applied to entire populations, communities, or groups, without regard to individual risk factors. Evaluations of social policy interventions, such as enacting laws to restrict the availability of firearms to prevent violence, or public health interventions, such as adding iodine to all salt to prevent childhood mental retardation, are examples of this kind of research. Selective approaches target particular subgroups at higher risk because of biological, psychological, or social risk factors. For example, families with characteristics that put children at risk for violence could be the target of intervention research. Finally, indicated prevention refers to intervention in those who may have signs or symptoms of mental or behavioral disorders but do not yet meet full criteria for those conditions. For example, persons who experience some (but not all) symptoms of post-traumatic stress disorder or major depression following a disaster could be the target of prevention efforts.

Prevention research can be conceptualized as a process that begins with review of the relevant literature on risk factors and protective factors, moves on to carefully designed and evaluated pilot projects, and eventually results in large-scale implementation. Given its potential, we recommend a major international initiative to review the interdisciplinary knowledge base, identify priority areas and promising strategies, and organize a series of coordinated small-scale prevention projects. Universal interventions falling outside of the domain of mental illness per se, such as social policy and public health interventions, should receive priority along with selective or indicated interventions. Areas most likely to benefit from prevention approaches include initiatives directed at interpersonal violence, women's health, children's health, and substance abuse. For example, a better understanding of the epidemiology and ethnographic context of substance abuse bring into sharp relief local points of intervention for community-based programs.

Ethical Issues

Resolving ethical issues must be at the heart of the international research agenda.[21] For example, those who participate in research in low-income nations must benefit from that research. Informed consent and confidentiality must be assured. Do international ethical standards adequately protect the rights of research participants? What is the proper balance in any given case between national, local, or international ethical perspectives? How, for example, are the voices of women, minority ethnic groups, the poor, and the politically powerless to be kept from being erased in ethical deliberations? How are plural concepts and practices regarding personhood, privacy, social responsibility, and clinical relationships to be taken into account? How is the larger framework of North-South disparity in resources and opportunities to be taken into account with respect to the application of ethical principles such as equity and justice?

A second set of ethical questions emerges from control of the process of research itself, from the formulation of questions to the interpretation of data and publication of results. Who should control the various phases of this process? How can misuses of data—including research by outsiders that has no local benefit—be discouraged and prevented?

A third set of issues involves the relationship between the research community and powerful interest groups, such as the pharmaceutical industry, other multinational corporations, and health professionals themselves. How do these groups currently exercise control over local research agendas? What constitutes misuse of elite control? When do researchers have an ethical obligation to conduct research strongly opposed by certain interest groups (in the case of industrial disasters, for instance, multinational corporations can thwart the collection of certain kinds of data used in litigation)? What controls can be put in place to assure that research is in the best interest of an entire society as well as minorities and other marginalized groups within that society? Although answers will be neither simple nor universally applicable, recognition of the ethical dilemmas should promote more responsible research.

Strengthening the Capacity for Research

Research requires qualified and well-trained researchers, supportive institutional environments, and international collaborative networks.

Recruiting, training, and supporting mental health researchers in low-income societies is crucial. Recruitment must begin with increased exposure of students to the relevant mental health fields and the social sciences in medical schools and in graduate programs. Adequate training opportunities must also be available at the doctoral and postdoctoral levels. Training opportunities should be available in a wide variety of disciplines, including the biomedical sciences, public health, mental health services, and the social sciences. If these are not available at home institutions, regional, national, and international institutions should offer training programs tailored to the needs of foreign students. Conversely, there is much to be gained by encouraging scholars in the mental health field in wealthy countries to travel to poor societies (where in fact the greatest proportion of mental health problems are to be found) in order to alert them to the way in which mental health problems are rooted in local cultural systems and local health care systems.

To develop a cadre of mental health experts in low-income countries, postdoctoral training programs should provide biomedical and health services researchers with training in relevant social science disciplines and vice versa. The ideal for training should be the transdisciplinary model.[22] This requires that researchers combine expertise in a primary discipline with competence in one or more additional disciplines. Competence entails more than simply being familiar with different methods; a deep engagement with the history and major theoretical constructs of other disciplines is necessary.[23] Once students have finished their training, attractive academic positions must be available to avoid the "brain drain" of qualified researchers to high-income countries or into better-paying administrative positions in their own countries.

Institutional environments should encourage interdisciplinary approaches by bringing together faculty from biomedical, public health, and social science disciplines. In certain situations, this work can be accomplished by developing innovative cross-disciplinary programs within existing medical institutions or through institutional strengthening programs that foster cooperation and dialogue between social science and medical faculty. The international efforts sponsored by the social science division of the WHO Tropical Disease Program, the Harvard Institute of International Development's Applied Diarrheal Disease Research Project, and the International Clinical Epidemiology Network (INCLEN) to link social science research to public health institutions through mission-oriented collaborations should also be considered as models. Whenever possible, officials from ministries of public health and other governmental sectors should participate in the planning phases of research to make it more relevant to policy questions and to encourage its dissemination. More-effective links between the world of policy-makers and researchers will ensure that research findings are translated into programs and policies to address at least some of the social forces that influence social and mental health.[24]

A third element in strengthening research capacity worldwide is to form better international and regional networks of investigators and policymakers, institutional representatives, and training directors. Effective network building should be modeled on programs such as the new International Forum for Social Sciences in Health, which seeks to create a global colloquy of social and health scientists to advance the relevance of social science to health. One goal of such programs is to facilitate communication and collaboration across disciplines regionally and internationally. Other examples of collaborative international networks include the International Clinical Epidemiology Network. The World Health Organization Mental Health Unit's Collaborating Centers are models of the kinds of programs that are needed. These networks already cover behavioral and population studies, but other issues—such as violence, displacement, substance abuse, and the wider set of mental health problems of women, children, and the elderly—need to be addressed systematically.

Because mental health and social science research communities are much more developed in high-income nations, connections across continents are crucial. The flow of knowledge, too often imagined as flowing exclusively from rich to poor, must be understood as bidirectional. Mechanisms for facilitating this two-way exchange must be developed more fully (such as opening leading international journals to more contributions by investigators from low-income countries).

Funding for Research

In an influential report titled *Health Research; Essential Link to Equity in Development*, the Commission on Health Research for Development proposed that each nation allocate two percent of their health budget for "Essential National Health Research."[25] Because of the magnitude and urgency of the problems facing low-income countries, we recommend that two percent also be set aside for "Essential National Mental Health Research." This will only be a start.

Funds for mental health research in Asia, Africa, and Latin America are inadequate to support even the preliminary research activities outlined in this chapter. Substantial support must come from governments, international agencies, private foundations, and other nongovernmental organizations. The development of national databases is so fundamental to a state's responsibilities that ministries of health and social welfare should be expected to provide much of the support for epidemiological and survey research. Where they cannot, international agencies should assist.

Because of serious resource constraints and competing demands, health and welfare agencies in low-income countries often neglect mental health research. This is an inadequate response, given the magnitude and cost of mental health problems. Yet institutional inattention has become so mundane it may well require an international campaign to change the status quo. We recommend that international agencies and nongovernmental organizations seriously consider undertaking a campaign to diminish bias against, and to raise the priority of, mental health research. Central to this challenge is the need to reduce bias that is also present against the use of local knowledge. A response to this bias must also receive support from agencies and programs if we are to assure that programs are culturally relevant.

Mental Health Research Policy Units

Mental health problems have a range of effects on numerous pubic agencies, such as health, welfare, public security, and disaster-relief agencies. Yet there is little coordination among them, so that multiple projects often overlap and compete with one another. This is a strikingly inefficient use of already limited resources. We recommend, therefore, the creation of mental health research policy units that cut across various ministries at the national level. These units will assist in giving priority to, and coordinating, regional research efforts, more efficiently distributing funds to support projects, and monitoring their ongoing progress and results. Mental health research and policy units should be established in each nation. Funding for such units should be provided by ministries of health, with the assistance of other agencies whose mission is oriented to mental, behavioral, and social health.

The Translation of Findings

The global interdependence of societies, including the shared mental health burden for many of the problems reviewed in this report, mandates a need to translate findings from mental health policy research in high-income societies to low-income societies and vice versa. The international community needs a process through which concepts, methods, and data are systematically collected and shared. This clearinghouse function can best be undertaken by a consortium of international agencies linked with regional and national mental health policy research programs. Collection, dissemination, and follow-up will become increasingly necessary as local research generates the knowledge we have listed as essential, and as some societies generate policy-relevant research findings that others can adapt. The absence of such an international process means that there is an obstructing divide between knowledge creation and its dissemination and application in the mental health field.

A second process of translation is also crucial. As in the health and social welfare sectors generally, it is often difficult to directly convert research findings into policy initiatives. There should be an iterative process that tests and refines new knowledge through program development and policy applications followed by rigorous evaluation; too often today there is an unbridged gap between research and policy. To overcome this obstacle mental health researchers must learn to formulate their findings in ways more accessible to policymakers, and policymakers must acquire a basic understanding of mental health research that will enable them to make more effective use of research contributions. Although national mental health policy research units should give priority to this objective, a campaign by international agencies must urge policymakers to become more informed consumers of the relevant mental and social health research literature. Mental health researchers also need to receive advanced training in policy-relevant applications so that they can participate more effectively in interactions with policymakers.

In sum, the objective should be to give priority to mental health research, to move it from the margin to the center of health and social policy, to recruit and train social scientists and health researchers, and to increase the numbers of health and social policymakers who are knowledgeable about mental health findings and committed to the improvement of mental health problems.

A Call to Action

Why should the reader pay attention to one more crisis, to one more claim on resources, and to one more set of problems? We think he or she should do so because these problems come as close as any to getting at what is most at stake in being human, because these problems directly prevent our flourishing, and because the relative silence surrounding these problems is shameful inasmuch as there are things that can now be done about them.

This report is in no sense the last word on the subject of mental health, but rather the beginning of a process. In these pages, we describe the global burden of mental and behavioral health problems. We address the complex social, political, and economic forces that contribute to these problems. We recommend innovative and cost-effective ways to improve the well-being of peoples facing serious mental health problems throughout the world. And we note the major policy and research initiatives that must now be undertaken.

All this has been done in broad strokes, in part because only so much can be said in a summary report prepared for the general public, but principally because so much more needs to be known about the causes and consequences of mental health problems, and because so much more needs to be done to develop effective responses to these problems. In effect, we propose an agenda for action and research that the international community must pursue. Governments, nongovernmental agencies, research institutes, international agencies, and local communities must now work together to develop this blueprint for change and make it a reality. The precondition for action is the need for national governments and international agencies to give priority to mental, behavioral, and social health. The next step in this effort is to engage in a series of conversations that will help to develop feasible and culturally significant policies that, when implemented at both national and local levels, can improve the mental health of peoples throughout the world.

Notes

Introduction

1. UNICEF, 1993.

2. The World Bank's estimates of lost years of quality life hinges on the concept of Disability-Adjusted Life Years (DALYs), which is a measure of the burden produced by specific diseases; it combines the impact of the premature deaths and of the disablements that result from those diseases. In taking death at a given age into account, the number of *years of life lost* is evaluated by using the expectation of life remaining at that age to individuals in low-mortality countries. Years of life do not have the same value throughout the life span; thus, most people value a year in their twenties as worth three or four times what a year in their eighties is worth. This differential evaluation is taken into account in the calculation. To measure the disability resulting from disease, each surviving year is modified according to the expected *duration* and *severity* of the disability. Duration is simply the years (or fractions thereof) that the disability lasts. Severity represents the comparative disadvantage of a given handicap on a scale from 0, for perfect health, to 1, for death. For example, expert panels have rated blindness at a severity of 0.6, and disease of the female reproductive system at a severity of 0.22. Losses from death and disability are combined. In calculating DALYs, the formula takes into account the age at which the specific disease is acquired, the years of life expectancy lost (and the relative value of those years), and the years compromised by handicap.

Of course, this measure is, at the moment, a crude and provisional one. But it does offer a new way to think about health and disability. We recognize the cultural assumptions motivating the measurement, though this is not the place to offer a cultural interpretation of DALYs as a socially constructed index.

3. Rice et al., 1992. In the case of mental illness, direct costs (for hospital days, medical consultation, drugs, etc.) constitute 45% of total costs, the remainder being due to loss of productivity because of illness or death. In the case of alcohol abuse, direct costs are only 13% of the total, with costs from crime and motor vehicle crashes exceeding that percentage. In the case of drug abuse, the costs stemming from crime and motor vehicle crashes are twice as great as the direct medical costs for treating drug users.

4. Greenberg et al., 1993.

5. Kramer, 1989.

6. Lin et al., 1969; Yeh et al., 1987; Cross-National Collaborative Group, 1992.

7. Cross-National Collaborative Group, 1992.

8. See Chapter 9, which notes that approximately 10% of people over the age of 65 in low-income countries suffer from dementia.

Chapter 1

1. Head, 1989.
2. Sadik, 1992.
3. Jones and Kiguel, 1994.
4. World Bank, 1993b.
5. Brooke, 1993b, 1993c.
6. Durning, 1991.
7. Ibid.
8. Chang, 1993.
9. Head, 1989.
10. World Bank, 1993b:52.
11. Ravenhill, 1990.
12. World Bank, 1993b:49.
13. *The Economist*, Sept. 25, 1993.
14. Jolly, 1988; World Bank, 1993b.
15. United Nations, 1991a:15.
16. Jolly, 1988; Ware, 1993.
17. Sadik, 1992.
18. Jazairy et al., 1992:1.
19. Kutzner, 1991:1.
20. Sullivan, 1991:167.
21. Jazairy et al., 1992:52.
22. World Bank, 1993a.
23. Sen, 1981; Scrimshaw, 1987.
24. Scheper-Hughes, 1992.
25. Scrimshaw, 1991.
26. *Time* magazine, June 21, 1993, p. 51.
27. Brooke, 1993a.
28. See Brooke, 1993a; Ennew, 1981; Masland, 1992; Khan, 1993; and various reports by the Anti-Slavery Society.
29. Harpham et al., 1988.
30. Mari, 1987.
31. Santana, 1982.
32. Almeida-Filho, 1982, 1993.
33. Webb, 1984; Marsella, 1993; Cheng, 1989.
34. Almeida-Filho et al., 1992; Harpham, 1992; Mari, 1987.
35. Smith and Rutter, 1994; Rutter, n.d.
36. Rutter, forthcoming.
37. Maynes, 1993:5.
38. Ibid.: 11.
39. Helman and Ratner, 1992/93.
40. Nietschmann, 1987.
41. Harff and Gurr, 1987.
42. Gleick, 1989; Homer-Dixon, 1991.
43. UNHCR, 1993.
44. Jacobson, 1989.
45. World Bank, 1993a.
46. Ibid.
47. Sadik, 1990.
48. Maddox, 1993.

49. Tyler, 1993.

50. de Girolamo and McFarlane, n.d.

51. Lima et al., 1991b.

52. See Cohen, 1987; Lima et al., 1990; and International Federation of Red Cross and Red Crescent Societies, 1993.

Chapter 2

1. World Bank, 1993a.

2. Eisenberg, 1986b.

3. The material on Argentina was culled from articles in various Argentinean newspapers; the material on the Dominican Republic was drawn from ethnographic research conducted by Anna Ortiz, Department of Anthropology, Harvard University

4. Phillips, 1993.

5. For example, Leighton et al., 1963; Beiser et al., 1972.

6. Kleinman, 1977.

7. See Murphy (1982) and Kleinman (1988) for reviews of this work.

8. Kleinman, 1988.

9. World Health Organization, 1993c.

10. Kramer, 1989.

11. World Health Organization, 1993c.

12. American Psychiatric Association, 1994.

13. Jablensky, 1993.

14. Phillips, 1993.

15. Eisenberg, 1986b.

16. Eisenberg, 1990.

17. Dohrenwend et al., 1992.

18. World Health Organization, 1979; Waxler, 1977.

19. Jablensky et al., 1992b.

20. See Hopper (1991) for a review.

21. Harding et al., 1987:479.

22. Ibid.: 483.

23. Waxler, 1977.

24. Brown et al., 1962; Leff et al., 1985.

25. Warner, 1985.

26. Estroff, 1981, 1989.

27. Sartorius et al., 1993.

28. Fransen, 1990.

29. Gruenberg, 1967.

30. World Health Organization, 1993c.

31. Brent et al., 1988.

32. Robins and Regier, 1992.

33. Almeido-Filho, 1993.

34. Rice et al., 1992.

35. Kleinman and Good, 1985.

36. von Korff et al., 1990; Goldberg and Huxley, 1992.

37. Eisenberg, 1992.

38. Wells et al., 1989.

39. Kupfer et al., 1992.

40. Brown, 1993.

41. Lin et al., 1969; Yeh et al., 1987.

42. Cross-National Collaborative Group, 1992.
43. Kupfer et al., 1992.
44. Goldberg and Huxley, 1992.
45. Almeida-Filho, 1993.
46. Kleinman and Good, 1985.
47. Compton et al., 1991.
48. Weiss, 1985.
49. Panicker et al., n.d.
50. Carr and Vitaliano, 1985.
51. From Desjarlais, 1992.
52. See Kleinman, 1980, 1988.
53. Kleinman, 1988; Csordas and Kleinman, 1990.
54. See, for instance, Kleinman and Song, 1979; Kleinman and Gale, 1982; Jilek, 1974; Ness, 1980; Finkler, 1985; and Desjarlais, 1992.
55. Jenkins, 1993.
56. Phillips, 1993.
57. From Pedersen, 1993.
58. Cited in Kilonzo, 1993.
59. Kilonzo, 1993.
60. Bibeau and Corin, 1993.
61. Iacoponi et al., 1991.
62. Government of India, 1984.
63. Tan and Lipton, 1988.
64. Wig, 1993; see also Franke and Chasin, 1992.
65. Kilonzo, 1993; Dorwart, 1993.
66. Glara Rabinowitz, Deputy Medical Director, American Psychiatric Association, personal communication, 1994.
67. Center for Mental Health Services, 1992.
68. Christian, 1990.
69. United Nations, 1991b.
70. Bibeau and Corin, 1993.
71. World Health Organization, 1984:33.
72. Sartorius and Harding, 1983; see also Jablensky, 1993; Kilonzo, 1993.
73. Leighton et al., 1963.
74. Personal communication, 1993.
75. This box was drawn from Guinness (1992), and from materials provided by Dr. Guinness.
76. Phillips et al., 1994.
77. Xiong Wei et al., in press.
78. See Phillips et al., in press.
79. Nunley, 1993.
80. Xiong Wei et al., in press.
81. From Nunley, 1993.

Chapter 3

1. World Bank, 1993a.
2. Diekstra and Gulbinat, 1993.
3. Diekstra, 1993.
4. Banerjee et al., 1990.

5. Shukla et al., 1990.

6. Lester, 1982.

7. Van Winkle and May, 1993; Kraus and Buffler, 1979.

8. Ackerman, 1993.

9. Diekstra, 1993; Klerman, 1987.

10. Garrison et al., 1991.

11. National Center for Health Statistics, 1992.

12. Reuter Textline, 1993.

13. Rubinstein, 1983:658.

14. Rubinstein, 1984:91–92.

15. Johnson, 1981:326.

16. Rubinstein, 1983:660.

17. Hezel, 1984:200–02.

18. Finau and Lasalo, 1985:103.

19. Finau and Lasalo, 1985; Hezel, 1984; Johnson, 1981; Macpherson and Macpherson, 1984; and Rubinstein, 1983, 1984. This box was drawn from research by Anne Becker, Department of Social Medicine, Harvard Medical School.

20. See Gould and Shaffer, 1986; Eisenberg, 1986a; Schmidtke and Hafner, 1988; Taiminen et al., 1992; Jonas, 1992, Gould et al., 1990.

21. Gould and Shaffer, 1986.

22. Murphy and Wetzel, 1990.

23. Henriksson et al., 1993.

24. Rich et al., 1986.

25. Marzuk et al., 1992.

26. Goldacre et al., 1993. Other psychologically oriented theories of suicide continue to be influential. Biological psychiatrists continue to search optimistically for correlates of suicide, focusing on the role of serotonin and other monoamines (Traskman-Bendz et al., 1993). Freud's 1917 study "Mourning and Melancholia" explained suicidality as turning hostility against oneself. Psychoanalysts now tend to explain suicide with reference to object relations theory (Buie and Maltsberger, 1983).

27. Guze and Robins, 1970.

28. Rutz et al., 1989.

29. Rimer et al., 1990.

30. Schneidman, 1993.

31. Durkheim, 1951.

32. Bloor, 1980.

33. Morrell et al., 1993.

34. Kreitman and Platt, 1984.

35. Pritchard, 1992.

36. Platt et al., 1992.

37. Counts, 1990b.

38. Ibid. :160–61.

39. Banerjee, 1990; Shukla et al., 1990.

40. Pitchford, 1991.

41. *Economist*, 1992.

42. Kearney and Miller, 1985.

43. Straus and Straus, 1953.

44. Silva, in press.

45. O'Ballance, 1989.

46. Silva and Pushpakumara, in press.

47. Ganesvaran and Rajarajeswaran, 1988.
48. From Silva and Pushpakumara, in press.
49. Soni Raleigh, 1993.
50. Murphy et al., 1986.
51. Tatai and Tatai, 1991.
52. Fishbain and Aldrich, 1985.
53. Joseph, 1991.
54. Basham, 1959.
55. Shaffer, 1993.
56. Nowak, 1992.
57. Jeffery et al., 1984; Patel, 1989.
58. *India Today*, 1990.
59. Adapted from Tukol, 1976.
60. Berger, 1988.
61. Bowles, 1985.
62. Berger, 1988.
63. Other examples may be cited from New Guinea and elsewhere; see Bowles, 1985.
64. Tousignant and Mishara, 1981.
65. Eferakeya, 1984.
66. Loftin et al., 1991.
67. Meehan et al., 1991.
68. Kellerman et al., 1992.
69. Shetty and Nikam, 1993.
70. Glatt, 1987.
71. Kleinman, 1991.
72. Diekstra and Gulbinat, 1993.

Chapter 4

1. World Bank, 1993a.
2. Adapted from World Health Organization, 1993c.
3. Ibid.
4. Heggenhougen, 1979.
5. Brenner, 1975.
6. Engels, 1969 [1854].
7. Belsasso, 1978.
8. Ortiz et al., 1992.
9. Argandoña, 1993.
10. Babor, 1993; Sugar et al., 1992.
11. Coombs and Globetti, 1986.
12. Engels, 1969 [1854].
13. Singer, 1986.
14. Ibid.
15. Doyal, 1979.
16. Wolcott, 1974.
17. This box was prepared by Michael and Susan Whyte, Institute of Anthropology, University of Copenhagen.
18. See Lin and Lin, 1982.
19. Shen, 1987.
20. Ibid.

21. Shen et al., 1992.
22. Agahi and Spencer, 1982; Aldy et al., 1985; Suwanwela and Poshyachinda, 1986.
23. Asuni, 1964.
24. Schenker and Speeg, 1990.
25. Ray and Chandrashekhar, 1982.
26. Royal College of Physicians, 1987.
27. From Edwards et al., 1994.
28. Obot, 1989, cited in Obot, 1990.
29. Obot and Olaniyi, 1989; cited in Obot, 1990.
30. Babor, 1993.
31. Acuda, 1985.
32. Kua and Ko, 1991.
33. Cherpitel, 1993; Cook, 1990; Gureje and Olley, 1992; Rosovsky and Lopez, 1986.
34. Sugar et al., 1991.
35. Ibid.
36. Kua and Ko, 1991.
37. Finkler, 1993.
38. Adapted from Montenegro, 1993.
39. Pakistan Medical Association, 1987.
40. Aslam, 1992.
41. Aslam, 1993.
42. Mufti, 1986.
43. Ebie and Pela, 1982.
44. Baasher, 1989.
45. Smart et al., 1981.
46. Oviasu, 1976.
47. Baasher, 1989; Belsasso, 1978.
48. Cameron and Debelle, 1984.
49. Belsasso, 1978.
50. Ibid.
51. Cravioto et al., 1992.
52. The Study on Youth and Drugs and the 20th Expert Committee on Drug Dependence, cited in Argandoña, 1993.
53. World Bank, 1993.
54. Solis and Wagner, 1992; cited in NIDA, 1992.
55. World Health Organization, Programme on Substance Abuse, 1993b.
56. Pope and Katz, 1990.
57. See Ebie and Pela, 1982.
58. Odiase, 1980, cited in Ebie and Pela, 1982.
59. Asuni, 1964; Boroffka, 1960.
60. Nevadomsky, 1982; Ebie and Pela, 1982.
61. Nahas, 1971.
62. Dhadphale and Omolo, 1988.
63. Ibid.
64. Kalix, 1987.
65. Kennedy, 1987.
66. Omolo and Dhadphale, 1987.
67. World Bank, 1993a.
68. Senay, 1991.
69. World Health Organization, Programme on Substance Abuse, 1992.

70. NIDA, 1992. Substance use and subsequent abuse does not begin "de novo" with each new drug. A process of "graduation" from the use of one drug to another can often be detected. As reported in the overwhelming number of studies from almost all cultures, nicotine (cigarette smoking) is the first habit-forming substance consumed in the majority (88.7%) of the heroin population. This finding, along with other data underscoring the significant role of tobacco as a "gateway" drug, emphasizes the continuum of addictive substance abuse (Navaratnam and Foong, 1989). Alcohol (8.9%), cannabis (2.0%), and heroin (0.4%) are much less frequently reported as first drugs than is tobacco. In second-drug-use ranking, alcohol (37.1%) and cannabis (38.7%) are dominant, while the opiates (heroin and morphine) represent 13.7%. Heroin addicts show a strong correlation between the age at first use and the type of drug used (Navaratnam and Foong, 1989). First drug use most often occurred in adolescence. Opiates were usually experimented with by heroin addicts in their early twenties. Information of this sort not only offers an understanding of patterns of progression of use that makes more meaningful the available data, but gives guidance to aspects of developing effective prevention programs.

71. Montagne, 1991.
72. Ibid.: 278; citing the President's Commission on Organized Crime, 1986:343.
73. Cravioto et al., 1992.
74. Cohen, 1964.
75. Oetting et al., 1988.
76. Aslam, 1989; Gossop, 1989.
77. Carlini-Cotrim and Carlini, 1988.
78. Baasher, 1981.
79. Inciardi, 1987.
80. For example, the British High Commission has reported that 65% of all heroin (50g or more) seized in British airports in 1986 was from Nigeria (Obot, 1990). From one seizure of cocaine in 1982 by Nigeria's Department of Customs and Excise, the figure rose to 123 in 1982.
81. Asuni and Bruno, 1984.
82. Heather et al., 1993.
83. McGlothlin, 1980.
84. Suwanwela and Poshyachinda, 1980; see Edwards and Arif (1981) for a review of other examples of national programs for the reduction of drug and alcohol use.
85. World Health Organization, 1991b.
86. Pickens and Fletcher, 1991.
87. Bourne, 1975; Heggenhougen, 1984.
88. Westermeyer, 1973, 1979.
89. Vichai et al., 1978.
90. Wen and Cheung, 1973.
91. Patterson, 1974; Sainsbury, 1974.
92. Gimlette and Thomsen, 1939.
93. Heggenhougen, 1984.
94. Belsasso, 1978.
95. World Health Organization, 1990.
96. Solis and Wagner, 1992.
97. Carlini-Cotrim and Aparecida de Carvalho, 1983.
98. Montagne and Scott, 1993.

Chapter 5

1. Nietschmann, 1987.
2. Summerfield and Toser, 1991; Cliff and Noormahomed, 1988; Nordstrom, 1992.
3. The Arms Project and Physicians for Human Rights, 1993.

4. Santiago, 1990.
5. Das and Nandy, 1985.
6. Santiago, 1990.
7. Ibid.: 293.
8. Dowdall, 1992:453–54.
9. Liddell et al., 1991.
10. Das, 1990; Tambiah, 1993.
11. See Tambiah, 1993.
12. Agudelo, 1992:370.
13. Martin-Baro, 1989.
14. León, 1987.
15. Bourque and Warren, 1989.
16. Nordstrom, 1992.
17. O'Donnell, 1983; Corradi et al., 1992; Jenkins, 1991:149.
18. Straker, 1988.
19. Salimovich et al., 1992:74–75.
20. Martin-Baro, 1989:5.
21. Allodi and Rojas, 1985.
22. Allodi, 1980.
23. Barudy, 1989:719.
24. Amnesty International, 1983:5.
25. Ibid.: 11.
26. Katz, 1982; Foster, 1987:110.
27. Foster, 1987.
28. Vesti et al., 1992.
29. Allodi and Rojas, 1988.
30. Allodi, 1991:5.
31. Comitá de Defensa de los Derechos del Pueblo, 1989.
32. Acuna, 1989.
33. Cohn et al., 1980; Weile et al., 1990.
34. Dawes, 1990:17.
35. Kanji, 1990.
36. Melville and Lykes, 1992.
37. Save the Children, 1991.
38. Martin-Baro, 1989.
39. Jenkins, 1991.
40. Richards, 1992; Nordstrom, 1992:269.
41. Jenkins, 1991; Jenkins and Valiente, in press.
42. Straker, 1992.
43. Turton et al., 1991.
44. Straker, 1992.
45. Ramphele, 1993.
46. See Ramphele, 1993.
47. Nordstrom, 1992:269.
48. León, 1987.
49. Martin-Baro, 1989.
50. Farias, 1991:170.
51. Suarez-Orozco, 1992.
52. Kusnetzoff, 1986; Suarez-Orozco, 1990:368.
53. Suarez-Orozco, 1992:249.
54. Mollica, 1987:299.

55. Cienfuegos and Monelli, 1983.
56. Mollica, 1987.
57. Barudy, 1989; Becker et al., 1989.
58. Somnier and Genefke, 1986.
59. Willigen, 1992:290.
60. Boehnlein et al., 1985; Muecke, 1992:520.
61. Barudy, 1989; Becker et al., 1989.
62. Lykes, 1994.
63. Beristain and Riera, 1992; Shaw and Harris, 1991.
64. Kanji, 1990; Melville and Lykes, 1992.
65. Bourbeau, 1993.
66. Pan American Health Organization, 1993.
67. Earls, Slaby, Spirito et al., 1992.
68. Earls et al., 1992.
69. Earls, 1991:65.
70. Sadowski et al., 1989.
71. Earls et al., 1993:294.
72. Earls et al., 1992.
73. Pan American Health Organization, 1993; Earls et al., 1992; Earls et al., 1993.
74. Earls et al., 1993.
75. Nordstrom, 1992:270.
76. Nordstrom, 1992.

Chapter 6

1. Statements of Mozambican refugees interviewed during the course of the UNHCR-funded study reported in Ager et al. (1991).
2. From Lumsden, 1993.
3. Canadian Task Force, 1988.
4. From Lovell, 1992.
5. Mollica et al., 1991.
6. Athey and Ahearn, 1991; citing Carlin and Sokoloff, 1985.
7. Rumbaut, 1991.
8. Ressler et al., 1988.
9. McCallin, 1992.
10. Eisenbruch, 1990b.
11. Eisenbruch, 1990a, 1990b, 1992.
12. Beiser et al., 1989.
13. de Girolamo et al., 1989.
14. Goffman, 1961.
15. Jareg, 1987.
16. The material for this box was provided by Lindsay French, Department of Anthropology, Harvard University.
17. Westermeyer, 1991.
18. Freud and Burlingham, 1943.
19. Ressler et al., 1988.
20. McCallin and Fozzard, 1990; McCallin, 1992.
21. Shisana and Celentano, 1985.
22. McCallin and Fozzard, 1990.
23. McSpadden, 1987.

24. Beiser et al., 1989.
25. McCallin and Fozzard, 1990; Pines, 1989.
26. Reynell, 1989.
27. Punamaki, 1987.
28. Eisenbruch, 1990b.
29. Kanaaneh and Netland, 1992.
30. Reynell, 1989.
31. Kinzie and Sack, 1991.
32. Westermeyer, 1991.
33. See Morgan et al., 1984.
34. Westermeyer, 1991.
35. Mollica, 1989.
36. Kinzie et al., 1984.
37. Punamaki, 1992.
38. Bustos, 1992.
39. Silove, 1992.
40. Egli et al., 1991.
41. Tout, 1989:281-89.
42. Godfrey and Kalache, 1989.
43. WHO/UNHCR, 1992.
44. Jablensky et al., 1992a.
45. See Wilson, 1992a; 1992b.
46. Rumbaut, 1991; Westermeyer et al., 1983.
47. Chavez, 1992:74.
48. The material for this box was drawn from Chavez, 1992; Chavez et al., 1985; Mobed et al., 1992; Moore, 1986; and Palerm, 1992.
49. WHO/UNHCR, 1992.

Chapter 7

1. Brooke, 1993b.
2. Carnegie Commission, 1992.
3. Liddell, 1993.
4. WHO, 1951.
5. Gruber, 1978; Rein et al., 1974.
6. Wolff et al., forthcoming.
7. Wolff et al., forthcoming.
8. Toole and Waldman, 1993.
9. Yip and Sharp, 1993.
10. See Aptekar, 1988; Balanon, 1989; Ribadeneira, 1993; and World Health Organization, 1992b.
11. Cliff and Noormahomed, 1993.
12. Richman et al., 1990a.
13. Richman et al., 1990b.
14. Gargan, 1992.
15. See Burra, 1988; Ennew and Brian, 1989; Gargan, 1992; Lee-Wright, 1990; International Labor Office, 1991; and World Health Organization, 1987.
16. Andersen, 1988; cited in Lee-Wright, 1990.
17. Cited in Simons, 1993. See also Anderson (1988) and Lee-Wright (1990).
18. Raffaelli et al., 1993.

19. Reuters, 1994.
20. Grantham-McGregor et al., 1991.
21. World Health Organization, 1993c.
22. Stein et al., 1986.
23. Rutter et al., 1994:620.
24. Jones and Smith, 1973.
25. Abel and Sokol, 1987.
26. Streissguth et al., 1983.
27. Centers for Disease Control, 1992; Werler et al., 1993.
28. Ramphele, 1993.
29. Isaac, 1987.
30. Shorvon and Farmer, 1988.
31. Ellenberg et al., 1986.
32. Matuja, 1990.
33. Jilek-Aall and Rwiza, 1992.
34. Shorvon and Farmer, 1988.
35. Feksi et al., 1991.
36. Tekle-Haimanot et al., 1991.
37. Lai et al., 1990.
38. Kleinman et al., in press.
39. Graham, 1981; Earls, 1985; Joffe et al., 1988.
40. Rutter et al., 1975.
41. Shen et al., 1985.
42. Rahim and Cederblad, 1984; Cederblad and Rahim, 1986.
43. Matsuura et al., 1993.
44. See Odejide et al., 1989; Al-Issa, 1989; Ganesvaran et al., 1984; and Maniam, 1988.
45. Giel et al., 1981.
46. Institute of Medicine, 1994.
47. Mackwardt and Ochoa, 1993.
48. National Research Council, 1987; Population Council, 1989.
49. DaVanzo et al., 1990.
50. Institute of Medicine, 1985.
51. Sosa et al., 1980; Klaus et al., 1986.
52. Hetzel, 1983.
53. Ramalingaswami, 1973.
54. Sommer et al., 1986; West et al., 1991.
55. Lozoff et al., 1991.
56. Warren, 1991.
57. Dobbing, 1987.
58. Grantham-McGregor et al., 1991.
59. Wagenaar et al., 1990.
60. Thompson et al., 1989.
61. Olds and Kitzman, 1990.
62. Eisenberg and Earls, 1975.
63. Berrueta-Clement et al., 1984.
64. Bell et al., 1993.
65. Giel et al., 1981.
66. Pless and Wadsworth, 1989.
67. Stein and Jessop, 1991.
68. World Health Organization, 1993b.
69. Robb, 1981.

Chapter 8

1. Raikes, 1989.
2. Rosenfield and Maine, 1985.
3. Van der Kwaak et al., 1991:2.
4. World Bank, 1993a.
5. Orley et al., 1979:515.
6. Gureje et al., 1992.
7. Chakraborty, 1990.
8. Finkler, 1985.
9. World Bank, 1993a.
10. Das, 1994.
11. Finkler, 1985; Malik et al., 1992; Naeem, 1992; Nations and Rebhun, 1988; Scheper-Hughes, 1987, 1992.
12. Davis and Low, 1989.
13. Jenkins, 1991; Farias, 1991.
14. Good and Good, 1982.
15. Boddy, 1989.
16. Lewis, 1986:32.
17. Ibid.: 39.
18. See Ong, 1987; Boddy, 1989.
19. Kapferer, 1983.
20. Explanations proposed for gender differences in psychiatric morbidity in Asia, Africa, the Middle East, and Latin America echo established associations among poverty, isolation, and psychiatric morbidity for women in Western Europe and the United States (see Dennerstein et al., 1993). In a now classic study by Brown and Harris (1978), depression was found to be more prevalent among working-class than middle-class women living in London. There is evidence that poor women experience more and more severe life events than does the general population (Brown et al., 1975; Makosky, 1982); they are more likely to have to deal with chronic sources of social stress in the form of low-quality housing, dangerous neighborhoods, etc. (Makosky, 1982; Pearlin and Johnson, 1977); they are at higher risk for becoming victims of violence (Belle, 1990; Merry, 1981); and they are especially vulnerable to encountering problems in parenting and child care. (Belle et al., 1988). Poverty also erodes intimate and other personal relationships (Cherlin, 1979; Wolf, 1987). In fact, social networks can represent additional stress for poor women as well as sources of support (Belle, 1990).
21. Scheper-Hughes, 1992.
22. World Health Organization, 1993d.
23. Leslie, 1991; Merchant and Kurz, 1993.
24. United Nations, 1991d; Merchant and Kurz, 1993.
25. Chen et al., 1981.
26. Batliwala, 1983.
27. Sen and Sengupta, 1983.
28. Anderson and Moore, 1993.
29. Rosenfield, 1980, 1989; Good, 1992b.
30. Boylan, 1991.
31. The material for this box was provided by Violet Gaturu Kimani, Department of Community Health, University of Nairobi.
32. Preston, 1993.
33. Ibid.
34. *Time* magazine, August 12, 1991.

35. Mollica and Son, 1989.

36. See Adanda and Shaman, 1985; Kelkar, 1991; Asian and Pacific Women's Resource and Collection Network, 1989; and Russel, 1991.

37. Heise, 1993.

38. Shamim, 1985.

39. Faveau and Blanchet, 1989:1125.

40. Heise, 1993.

41. Duncan, 1990.

42. Barry, 1981.

43. Moore and Anderson, 1993.

44. This box was prepared by Elizabeth Miller, Department of Anthropology, Harvard University.

45. Levine, 1993.

46. Dalsimer and Nisonoff, 1987.

47. Kristof, 1993a.

48. WuDunn, 1993.

49. Anderson and Moore, 1993.

50. Heise, 1993.

51. Kristof, 1993b. Data revealing that girl children die more frequently than boys must be added to evidence of excess female mortality before birth. Death rates have been found to be strikingly higher for young girls in a number of countries in the Middle East, North Africa, and the Indian subcontinent (Jacobson, 1993). One Indian health specialist estimates that 330,000 more girls than boys die in that country every year (Chatterjee, 1991). Recent U.N. statistics place the number of deaths per 1,000 population in children aged 2–5 at 54.4 for girls vs. 36.9 for boys in Pakistan, 68.6 vs. 57.7 in Bangladesh, and 14.9 vs. 9.3 in Syria (U.N., 1991d).

52. Institute of Medicine, Committee to Study Female Morbidity and Mortality in Sub-Saharan Africa, 1994; Christopher P. Howson, personal communication on a work in progress, 1994.

53. From Finkler, 1993.

54. World Bank, 1993.

55. Stark and Flitcraft, 1991.

56. Koss, 1990; Leidig, 1992.

57. Counts, 1987, 1990a; Gilmartin, 1990.

58. Hodge-McKoid, 1989.

59. United Nations, 1991d; Anderson and Moore, 1993.

60. Kelkar, 1992.

61. See Kelkar, 1987.

62. Anderson and Moore, 1993.

63. United Nations, 1991d. The same study mentions that, in one study of a Nepalese village, estimates of household income based solely on wages placed women's contribution at 20%; when their subsistence production activities were taken into account, this figure increased to 53%.

64. Buvinic, 1983.

65. See Schrijvers, 1987.

66. Kelkar, 1987.

67. Elson, 1992:30.

68. Chinnery-Hesse, 1989.

69. United Nations, 1991d.

70. Beneria, 1992.

71. Babb, 1992.
72. Buvinic and Yudelman, 1989; Safa and Antrobus, 1992.
73. Buvinic and Yudelman, 1989.
74. Banister, 1985; Sen, 1989, 1990; Hull, 1990.
75. *New York Times*, March 26, 1991, p. A10.
76. Hull, 1990; WuDunn, 1993.
77. United Nations, 1991d.
78. Sen, 1990.
79. Sen, 1989.
80. Agarwal, 1987.
81. UNICEF, 1989; Beneria and Feldman, 1992.
82. Brems and Griffiths, 1993.
83. Koblinsky et al., 1993.
84. Jacobson, 1993.
85. Moore and Anderson, 1993.
86. Sullivan, 1992.
87. Heise, 1993.
88. M. Whyte, personal communication, 1993.
89. Adebajo, 1991; Heise, 1993.
90. Mary-Jo DelVecchio Good, personal communication.
91. Buvinic and Yudelman, 1989.
92. Dr. N. Mboi, personal communication.
93. Dr. Julio Frenk, personal communication.
94. Dahlgren, 1991.

Chapter 9

1. United Nations, 1991c.
2. Ibid.
3. See Ikels, 1993.
4. Jamison and Mosley, 1991.
5. Gibson, 1992:89.
6. United Nations, 1991c.
7. Sugar et al., 1991; Sugar et al., 1992.
8. Keith, 1985.
9. Kinsella, 1992; Apt, 1990.
10. Goldstein and Beall, 1981.
11. Kinsella, 1992.
12. Apt, 1975.
13. Twumasi, 1987.
14. Stern et al., 1984.
15. Henderson, 1993.
16. Yu et al., 1989.
17. Katzman, 1993.
18. Neki, 1987a.
19. Makanjuola, 1985.
20. See Carstairs (1983) and Fiske (1990), for instance.
21. Cohen, 1992.
22. Neki, 1987a.
23. Makanjuola, 1985.

24. Hollifield et al., 1990.
25. Blay et al., 1991.
26. Ibid.: 250.
27. Andrews et al., 1986.
28. World Bank, 1993.
29. Chen-I et al., 1985; Logue, 1990.
30. Cowgill, 1974; Kendig et al., 1991; Phillips, 1990.
31. Sharma and Dak, 1987.
32. Kendig et al., 1991; Martin, 1990; Neki, 1987b.
33. Gibson, 1992.
34. Nydegger, 1983.
35. Ibid.
36. Gibson, 1992.
37. Manton et al., 1986.
38. Cattell, 1990.
39. United Nations, 1991c.
40. Ogawa, 1990.
41. Chultoo, 1990.
42. Martin, 1988.
43. Chen and Jones, 1989.
44. Phillips, 1990.
45. United Nations, 1991c.
46. Gibson, 1992.
47. World Bank, 1993a.
48. Gibson, 1992; United Nations, 1991c.
49. Gibson, 1992; Chappell, 1990.
50. United Nations, 1991c.
51. Gibson, 1992.
52. United Nations, 1991c:89.
53. Gibson, 1992.
54. United Nations, 1991c:93; Gibson, 1992:101.
55. Sankar, 1990.
56. Nyanguru, 1987.
57. Pons de O'Neill, 1986.
58. Clarke, 1977.
59. Nyanguru, 1987.
60. Center for Social Development and Humanitarian Affairs, 1991.
61. *Ageways,* 1987; Fang, 1987.
62. Levkoff et al., 1988.
63. Jliovici, 1990.
64. United Nations, 1991c.
65. Ibid.

Chapter 10

1. Frenk, 1992.
2. Feachem et al., 1992.
3. Sen, 1990.
4. Centers for Disease Control, 1993.
5. Di Franza et al., 1991.

6. Sharp, 1993.

7. Peto et al., 1992.

8. U.S. Department of Health and Human Services, 1994.

9. Mechanic, 1994.

10. Dreze and Sen, 1991.

11. Chen et al., 1981.

12. *The Lancet*, 1981.

13. Uemura and Piza, 1988.

14. Johnson et al., 1993.

15. Hetzel, 1983.

16. Sommer et al., 1986.

17. Lozoff et al., 1991.

18. From Daulaire, 1993.

19. World Bank, 1992:47.

20. World Bank, 1993a:222.

21. Taylor and Greenough, 1989.

22. Caldwell, 1986.

23. Hobcraft, 1993.

24. Taylor and Greenough, 1989.

25. Ahmed et al., 1993.

26. Hazarika, 1993.

27. World Bank, 1993a: 300–301.

28. World Bank, 1993a:82–85.

29. Ibid.: 86.

30. Kristof, 1993b.

31. Hieu et al., 1993.

32. Khanna et al., 1992; Bernstein, 1993.

33. Fortuin et al., 1993.

34. Rotkin, 1973; Skegg et al., 1982.

35. Grimes, 1992; Hankinson et al., 1993.

36. Levine, 1993.

37. Ibid.

38. Ibid.

39. Mann et al., 1992; Mastro et al., 1994.

40. World Bank, 1993:115.

41. Centers for Disease Control, 1993.

42. Lorch, 1993.

43. Maj et al., 1993.

44. Maj et al., 1994a, 1994b.

45. Marzuk et al., 1988.

46. Price et al., 1988.

47. Lurie et al., 1994.

48. Pape et al., 1993.

49. Mukadi et al., 1993.

50. Pape et al., 1993.

51. The material for this box was contributed by Paul Farmer, Department of Social Medicine, Harvard Medical School.

52. Eisenberg, 1989.

53. Mann, 1993.

54. United Nations, 1948.

55. Murray et al., 1992.
56. Kjellstrom et al., 1992:236–37.
57. See Levy and Wegman, 1988.
58. Tameim et al., 1985.
59. Sawyer and Sawyer, 1992.
60. *The Lancet*, 1992.
61. Freed et al., 1993.
62. Greenough, 1993.
63. Christakis et al., 1994.
64. World Bank, 1993:58.
65. Dahlgren, 1991.
66. Whyte, 1991.
67. Roter and Hall, 1992.

Chapter 11

1. See Almeida-Filho, 1993.
2. See Kramer, 1989.
3. See the Introduction, note 6.
4. See Almeida-Filho (1993), for instance.
5. George and Pandya, 1993.
6. See Waldram, 1993.
7. Koumare et al., 1992.
8. From Bibeau and Corin, 1993; see also Koumare et al., 1992.
9. World Health Organization, 1993e.
10. See Chapter 2, and Earls (1991), for instance.
11. Frenk, 1993a.
12. World Bank, 1993a.
13. Harding et al., 1980; Harding et al., 1983.
14. See Chapter 8.
15. See Chapter 2.

Chapter 12

1. Phillips et al., in press.
2. Katon et al., 1993.
3. Institute of Medicine, 1994.
4. Sartorius and Henderson, 1992.
5. Commission on Health Research for Development, 1990.
6. Frenk, 1993a.
7. Sartorius, 1993.
8. Guarnaccia et al., 1993.
9. Gater et al., 1991; Sartorius et al., 1993.
10. Harding et al., 1983.
11. Broadhead and Abas, 1993.
12. Xiong et al., in press.
13. Kleinman, 1980.
14. Dorwart, 1993.
15. Lykes, 1994.
16. Tambiah, 1993.

17. Earls et al., 1993.
18. Ramphele, 1993.
19. Institute of Medicine, 1994.
20. Ibid., 1994.
21. Christakis, 1992.
22. Rosenfield, 1992.
23. Good, 1992a.
24. Frenk, 1993b.
25. Commission on Health Research for Development, 1990.

References

Abel, E.L. and R.J. Sokol. 1987. Incidence of fetal alcohol syndrome and economic impact of FAS-related anomalies. *Drug and Alcohol Dependence* 19:51–70.

Ackerman, G.L. 1993. A congressional view of youth suicide. *American Psychologist* 48:183–184.

Acuda, S. 1985. International Review Series: alcohol and alcohol problems research. I. East Africa. *British Journal of Addiction* 80:121–126.

Acuna, J.E. 1989. *Children of the Storm*. Philippines: Children's Rehabilitation Center.

Adanda, L. and I. Shaman. 1985. *Women and Violence: A Comparative Study of Rural and Urban Violence Against Women in Bangladesh*. Dhaka, Bangladesh: Women for Women: A Research and Study Group.

Adebajo, C. 1991. A grassroots project by nurses and midwives in Nigeria to eradicate female circumcision. Paper presented at 18th Annual NCIH International Health Conference, Arlington, VA.

Agahi, C. and C. Spencer. 1982. Patterns of drug use among secondary school children in post-revolutionary Iran. *Drug and Alcohol Dependence* 9:235–242.

Agarwal, B. 1987. Neither sustenance nor sustainability: agricultural strategies, ecological degradation and Indian women in poverty. In *Structures of Patriarchy*, edited by B. Agarwal, pp. 83–120. London: Zed Books.

Ager, A., Ager, W., and L. Long. 1991. *A Case Study of Refugee Women in Malawi: A Report for the United Nations High Commissioner for Refugees*. Zambia: Centre for Social Research.

Ageways. 1987. Newsletter for Help Age International, September, London.

Agudelo, S.F. 1992. Violence and health: preliminary elements for thought and action. *International Journal of Health Services* 22:365–376.

Ahmed, N., Zeitlin, M., Beiser, A., Super, C., and S. Gershoff. 1993. A longitudinal study of the impact of behavioral change intervention on cleanliness, diarrheal morbidity and growth of children in rural Bangladesh. *Social Science and Medicine* 37:159–171.

Al-Issa, I. 1989. Psychiatry in Algeria. *Psychiatric Bulletin* 13:240–245.

Aldy, D. et al. 1985. Ganja smokers among the freshman at the University of North Sumatera-Indonesia. *Paediatrica Indonesiana* 25:67–70.

Allodi, F. 1980. The psychiatric effects in children and families of victims of political persecution and torture. *Danish Medical Bulletin* 22:229–232.

———. 1991. Assessment and treatment of torture victims: a critical review. *The Journal of Nervous and Mental Disease* 179:4–11.

Allodi, F. and A. Rojas. 1985. The health and adaptation of victims of political violence in Latin America (psychiatric effects of torture and disappearance). In *Psychiatry: The State of the Art*, edited by P. Pichot, P. Berner, R. Wolf, and K. Thau, Volume 6, pp. 243–248. New York: Plenum Press.

Allodi, F. and A. Rojas. 1988. Arauco: the role of a housing cooperative community in the mental health and social adaptation of Latin American refugees in Toronto. *Migration World* 16:17–21.

Almeida-Filho, N. 1982. The psychosocial costs of development: labor, migration, and stress in Bahia, Brazil. *Latin American Research Review* 17(3):91–118.

———. 1993. Becoming modern after all these years: social change and mental health in Latin America. Working paper, International Mental and Behavioral Health Project, Center for the Study of Culture and Medicine, Harvard Medical School, Boston, Massachusetts.

Almeida-Filho, N., Mari, J., Coutinho, E., et al. 1992. Estudo multicêntrico de morbidade psychiátrica em áreas urbanas brasileiras (Brazilia, São Paulo, Porto Alegre). *Revista da ABP-APAL* 141:93–104.

Amazigo, U. Forthcoming. Nutrition. In *In Her Lifetime: Female Morbidity and Mortality in Sub-Saharan Africa*, edited by C. Howson, D. Hotra, and M. Law. Institute of Medicine, Washington, DC: National Academy Press.

American Psychiatric Association. 1994. *Diagnostic and Statistical Manual of Mental Disorders* (4th Edition). Washington, DC: American Psychiatric Press.

Amnesty International. 1983. *Mental Health Aspects of Political Imprisonment in Uruguay*. Amnesty International Special Briefing, June 7.

Anderson, A. 1988. *Throwaway Children*. Soundtrack. Norway.

Anderson, J.W. and M. Moore. 1993. Born oppressed: women in the developing world face cradle-to-grave discrimination, poverty. *The Washington Post*, February 14, A1.

Andrews, G.R., Esterman, A.J., Braunack-Mayer, A.J., and C.M. Rungie. 1986. *Aging in the Western Pacific: A Four-Country Study*. Western Pacific Reports and Studies No.1, World Health Organization.

Apt, N. 1975. Urbanization and the aged. In *Changing Family Studies, Legon Family Research Papers*, edited by C. Oppong, pp. 177–183. Institute of African Studies.

———. 1990. Cited in American Association of Retired Persons. *Network News* 5(2), p. 29.

Aptekar, L. 1988. *Street Children of Cali*. London: Duke University Press.

Argandoña, M. 1993. *Drug Users' Treatment and Care: A Draft Review of WHO Reports*. Geneva: Program on Substance Abuse, World Health Organization.

Arms Project and Physicians for Human Rights. 1993. *Landmines: A Deadly Legacy*. New York: Human Rights Watch.

Asian and Pacific Women's Resource and Collection Network. 1989. *Asian and Pacific Women's Resource and Action Series: Health*. Kuala Lumpur, Malaysia: Asian and Pacific Development Centre.

Aslam, A. 1989. Drug addiction in Pakistan. Paper presented to the Commission on Health Research for Development. Cambridge, Massachusetts, May 17.

———. 1992. Drug addiction in Pakistan. *Specialist* 6(3):104–108.

———. 1993. A drug demand reduction project in a squatter settlement of Karachi, Pakistan. Working paper, International Mental and Behavioral Health Project, Center for the Study of Culture and Medicine, Harvard Medical School, Boston, Massachusetts.

Asuni, T. 1964. Socio-psychiatric problems of cannabis in Nigeria. *Bulletin on Narcotics* 16:27.

Asuni, T. and F. Bruno. 1984. Summary of an eleven-country study of socio-legal measures to combat drug abuse and related crime. *Bulletin on Narcotics* 36:3–8.

Athey, J. and F.L. Ahearn. 1991. The mental health of refugee children: an overview. In *Refugee Children: Theory, Research, and Services*, edited by F.L. Ahearn and J.L. Athey, pp. 3–19. Maryland: Johns Hopkins University Press.

Baasher, T. 1961. Survey of mental illness in Wadi Halfa. *World Mental Health* 13:1–5.

———. 1981. The use of drugs in the Islamic world. *British Journal of Addiction* 76:233–243.

———. 1989. Drug and alcohol problems and the developing world. *International Review of Psychiatry* 1:13–16.

Babb, F. 1992. From co-ops to kitchens. *Cultural Survival Quarterly* 16(4):41–43.

Babor, T.F. 1993. Alcohol use and abuse in developing countries: implications for public health and social welfare. Working paper, International Mental and Behavioral Health Project, Center for the Study of Culture and Medicine, Harvard Medical School, Boston, Massachusetts.

Balanon, L. 1989. Street children: strategies for action. *Child Welfare* 68(2):159–66.

Banerjee, G., Nandi, D.N., Nandi, S., Sarkar, S., Boral, G.C., and A. Ghosh. 1990. The vulnerability of Indian women to suicide: a field-study. *Indian Journal of Psychiatry* 32:305–308.

Banister, J. 1985. Surprises and confirmations in the results of China's 1982 census. *International Population Conference, Florence 1985*, Volume 4, pp. 465–78. Liege: IUSSP.

Barbosa, J. and N. Almeida-Filho. 1986. Prevalence of emotional disorders in a rural area of Bahia, Brazil. Paper presented at the 11th World Congress of Social Psychiatry, Rio de Janeiro.

Barragan Alvarado, L. et al. 1992. Proyecto educativo sobre violencia de genero en la relación domestica de pareja. Centro de Planificatión y Estudios Sociales. CEPLAES: Quito, Ecuador.

Barry, K. 1981. *Female Sexual Slavery*. Englewood Cliffs, NJ: Prentice-Hall.

Barudy, J. 1989. A programme of mental health for political refugees: dealing with the invisible pain of political exile. *Social Science and Medicine* 28:715–727.

Basham, A.L. 1959. *The Wonder That Was India: A Survey of the Culture of the Indian Sub-Continent before the Coming of the Muslims*. New York: Grove Press.

Batliwala, S. 1983. Women in poverty: The energy, health and nutrition syndrome. Paper presented at a workshop on "Women and Poverty" at the Centre for Studies in Social Sciences, Calcutta, March 17–18.

Becker, D., Castillo, M., Gomez, E., Kovalskys, J., and E. Lira. 1989. Subjectivity and politics: the psychology of extreme traumatization in Chile. *International Journal of Mental Health* 18:80–97.

Beiser, M. et al. 1972. Assessing psychiatric disorder among the Serer of Senegal. *Journal of Nervous and Mental Disease* 154:141–151.

Beiser, M., Turner, R.J., and S. Gandsen. 1989. Catastrophic stress and factors affecting its consequences among Southeast Asian refugees. *Social Science and Medicine* 28:183–195.

Bell, R.M., Ellickson, P.L. and E.R. Harrison. 1993. Do drug prevention effects persist into high school? How Project ALERT did with ninth graders. *Preventive Medicine* 22:463–483.

Belle, D. 1990. Poverty and women's mental health. *American Psychologist* 45:385–389.

Belle, D., Dill, D., Longfellow, C. and V. Makosky. 1990. Stressful life conditions and mental health of mothers. In *Women and Depression: Research Gaps and Priorities*. Symposium presented at the Annual Meeting of the American Psychological Association, Atlanta, Georgia, (August), N. Russo (Chairman).

Belsasso, G. 1978. The international challenge of drug abuse: the Mexican experience. In *The International Challenge of Drug Abuse*, edited by R.C. Pedersen, NIDA Research Monograph Series No. 19, pp. 26–40. Rockville, MD: Department of Health, Education, and Welfare.

Beneria, L. 1992. The Mexican debt crisis: restructuring the economy and the household.

In *Unequal Burden: Economic Crises, Persistent Poverty and Women's Work*, edited by L. Beneria and S. Feldman, pp. 83–104. Boulder, CO: Westview Press, Inc.

Beneria, L. and S. Feldman, eds. 1992. *Unequal Burden: Economic Crises, Persistent Poverty, and Women's Work*. Boulder, CO: Westview Press, Inc.

Berger, L.R. 1988. Suicides and pesticides in Sri Lanka. *American Journal of Public Health* 78:826–828.

Beristain, C.M. and F. Riera. 1992. *Salud Mental: La Comunidad como Apoyo*. Barcelona: Virus Editorial.

Bernstein, E.M. 1993. A lesson in one woman's decision: in choosing clinics for abortions, knowledge is key. *The New York Times*, July 19, B1.

Berrueta-Clement, J.R., Schweinhart, L.J., Barnett, W.S., et al. 1984. *Changed Lives: The Effects of the Perry Preschool Program on Youths Through Age 19*. Ypsilanti, MI: The High Scope Press.

Bibeau, G. and E. Corin. 1993. Organizational models, local knowledge and socioeconomic constraints in the building of mental health policies in African countries. Working paper, International Mental and Behavioral Health Project, Center for the Study of Culture and Medicine, Harvard Medical School, Boston, Massachusetts.

Blay, S.L., Bickel, H., and B. Cooper. 1991. Mental illness in a cross-national perspective. *Social Psychiatry Epidemiology* 26:245–251.

Bloor, M. 1980. Relationships between unemployment rates and suicide rates in eight countries, 1962–1976. *Psychological Reports* 47:1095–1101.

Boddy, J. 1989. *Wombs and Alien Spirits: Women, Men, and the Zar Cult in Northern Sudan*. Madison, WI: University of Wisconsin Press.

Boehnlein, J.K., Kinzie, J.D., Rath B., and J. Fleck. 1985. One-year follow-up study of posttraumatic stress disorder among survivors of Cambodian concentration camps. *American Journal of Psychiatry* 142:956–959.

Boroffka, A. 1960. Mental illness and Indian hemp in Lagos. *East African Medical Journal* 43:377.

Bourbeau, R. 1993. Analyse comparative de la mortalité dans les pays développés et dans quelques pays en développement durant la période 1985–1989. *World Health Statistics Quarterly* 46:4–33.

Bourne, P.G. 1975. Non-pharmacological approaches to the treatment of drug abuse. *American Journal of Chinese Medicine* 3(3):318–384.

Bourque, S. and K.B. Warren. 1989. Democracy without peace: the cultural politics of terror in Peru. *Latin American Research Review* 24:7–34.

Bowles, J.R. 1985. Suicide and attempted suicide in contemporary Western Samoa. In *Culture, Youth and Suicide in the Pacific: Papers from an East-West Center Conference*, edited by F.X. Hezel, D.H. Rubinstein, and G.H. White, pp. 15–35. Honolulu: East-West Center.

Boylan, E., ed. 1991. *Women and Disability*. London: Zed Books.

Bradley, C. 1988. The problem of domestic violence in Papua New Guinea. In *Guidelines for Police Training on Violence Against Women and Child Sexual Abuse*. London: Commonwealth Secretariat, Women and Development Programme.

Brems, S. and M. Griffiths. 1993. Health women's way: learning to listen. In *The Health of Women: A Global Perspective*, edited by M. Koblinsky, J. Timyan, and J. Gay, pp. 255–273. Boulder, CO: Westview Press, Inc.

Brenner, H. 1975. Trends in alcohol consumption and associated illness. *American Journal of Public Health* 65:1279.

Brent, D.A., Kupfer, D.J., Bromet, E.J., et al. 1988. The assessment and treatment of patients at risk for suicide. *Review of Psychiatry* 7:353–385.

Broadhead, J.C. and M. Abas. 1993. Defeating depression in the developing world. Working paper, International Mental and Behavioral Health Project, Center for the Study of Culture and Medicine, Harvard Medical School, Boston, Massachusetts.

Brooke, J. 1993a. Slavery on rise in Brazil, as debt chains workers. *The New York Times*, May 23, A3.

———. 1993b. A hard look at Brazil's surfeits: food, hunger and inequality. *The New York Times*, June 6, C20.

———. 1993c. Inflation saps Brazilians' faith in democracy. *The New York Times*, July 25, I10.

Brown, G.W. 1993. Life events and affective disorder: replications and limitations. *Psychosomatic Medicine* 55(3):248–259.

Brown, G.W., Monck, E.M., Carstairs, G.M., et al. 1962. Influence of family life on the course of schizophrenic illness. *British Journal of Preventive and Social Medicine* 1:55–68.

Brown, G.W., Bhrolchain, M., and T. Harris. 1975. Social class and psychiatric disturbance among women in an urban population. *Sociology* 9:225–257.

Brown, G.W. and T.O. Harris. 1978. *Social Origins of Depression: A Study of Psychiatric Disorder in Women*. New York: The Free Press.

Buie, D.H. and J.T. Maltsberger. 1983. *The Practical Formulation of Suicidal Risk*. Cambridge: Firefly Press.

Burra, N. 1988. Exploitation of children in Jaipur gem industry II: health hazards of gem polishing. *Economic and Political Weekly* 23(4):131–138.

Bustos, E. 1992. Psychodynamic approaches in the treatment of torture survivors. In *Torture and Its Consequences: Current Treatment Approaches,* edited by M. Basoglu, pp. 333–347. Cambridge: Cambridge University Press.

Buvinic, M. 1983. Women's issues in third world poverty: a policy analysis. In *Women and Poverty in the Third World,* edited by M. Buvinic, M.A. Lycette, and W.P. McGreevey, pp. 14–31. Baltimore: Johns Hopkins University Press.

Buvinic, M. and S.W. Yudelman. 1989. *Women, Poverty and Progress in the Third World.* New York: The Foreign Policy Association.

Caldwell, J.C. 1986. Routes to low mortality in poor countries. *Population and Development Review* 12:171–220.

Cameron, F.J. and G.D. Debelle. 1984. No more Pacific Island paradises. *The Lancet* June 2:1238.

Canadian Task Force on Mental Health Issues Affecting Immigrants and Refugees. 1988. *Review of the Literature on Migrant Mental Health.* Canada.

Canino, G., Bravo, M. Rubio-Stipec, M., and M. Woodbury. 1990. The impact of disaster on mental health: prospective and retrospective analyses. *International Journal of Mental Health* 19:51–69.

Carlin, J.E. and B.Z. Sokoloff. 1985. Mental health treatment issues for Southeast Asian refugee children. In *Southeast Asian Mental Health: Treatment, Prevention, Services, Training, and Research,* edited by T.K. Owan, pp. 91–112. U.S. Department of Health and Human Services. Bethesda, MD: National Institute of Mental Health.

Carlini-Cotrim, B. and V. Aparecida de Carvalho. 1983. Extracurricular activities: are they an effective strategy against drug consumption? *Journal of Drug Education* 23:97–104.

Carlini-Cotrim, B. and E.A. Carlini. 1988. The use of solvents and other drugs among children and adolescents from a low socioeconomic background: a study in São Paulo, Brazil. *International Journal of Addiction* 23(11):1145–1156.

Carnegie Commission. 1992. *Partnerships for Global Development: The Clearing Horizon.* New York, Carnegie Commission on Science, Technology and Government, December, p. 31.

Carr, J. and P. Vitaliano. 1985. The theoretical implications of converging research on depression and culture-bound syndromes. In *Culture and Depression*, edited by A. Kleinman and B. Good, pp. 244–266. Berkeley: University of California Press.

Carrillo, R. 1991. Violence against women: an obstacle to development. In *Gender Violence: A Development and Human Rights Issue*, edited by C. Bunch and R. Carrillo, pp. 19–41. New Brunswick, New Jersey: Center for Women's Global Leadership, Douglas College, Rutgers University.

Carstairs, G.M. 1983. *Death of a Witch: A Village in North India, 1950–1981.* London: Hutchinson.

Castillo, D. et al. 1992. *Violencia Hacia la Mujer en Guatemala.* Report prepared for the First Central American Seminar on Violence Against Women as a Public Health Problem, Managua, Nicaragua, March 11–13.

Cattell, M. 1990. Models of old age among the Samia of Kenya: family support of the elderly. *Journal of Cross-Cultural Gerontology* 5:375–394.

Cederblad, M. and S.I.A. Rahim. 1986. Effects of rapid urbanization on child behavior and health in a part of Khartoum, Sudan—I. Socio-economic changes 1965–1980. *Social Science and Medicine* 22(7):713–721.

Center for Mental Health Services. 1992. *Mental Health, United States, 1992*, edited by R.W. Manderscheid and M.A. Sonnenschein, DHHS Pub. No. (SMA) 92-1942. Washington, DC: U.S. Government Printing Office.

Center for Social Development and Humanitarian Affairs. 1991. *The World Aging Situation.* Vienna: United Nations.

Centers for Disease Control. 1992. Recommendations for use of folic acid to reduce the number of cases of spina bifida and other neural tube defects. *Mortality and Morbidity Weekly Report* 41(RR14):1–7.

———. 1993. Prevalence of sedentary life-style—behavioral risk factor surveillance system, United States, 1991. *Morbidity and Mortality Weekly Report* 42:576–579.

Chacon, K. et al. 1990. Characteristicas de la mujer agredida entendida en el Patronato Nacional de la Infancia (PANI). In *La Violencia Contra la Mujer en la Familia Costarricense: Un Problema de Salud Publica,* by Batres Giocanda and C. Claramunt. San Jose, Costa Rica: ILANUD.

Chakraborty, A. 1990. *Social Stress and Mental Health: A Social-Psychiatric Field Study of Calcutta.* New Delhi: Sage Publications.

Chang, L-Y. 1993. Mental health care in Taiwan. Working paper, International Mental and Behavioral Health Project, Center for the Study of Culture and Medicine, Harvard Medical School, Boston, Massachusetts.

Chang, L., Miller, B.L., and K.M. Lin. 1993. Clinical and epidemiologic studies of dementias: cross-ethnic perspectives. In *Psychopharmacology and Psychobiology of Ethnicity*, edited by K.M. Lin, R.E. Poland, and G. Nakasaki, pp. 223–252. Washington, DC: American Psychiatric Press.

Chappell, N. 1990. Aging and social care. In *Handbook of Aging and the Social Sciences*, edited by L. George, pp. 438–454. New York: Academic Press.

Chatterjee, M. 1991. Indian women: their health and productivity. *World Bank Discussion Paper 109.* Washington, DC: The World Bank.

Chavez, L.R. 1992. *Shadowed Lives: Undocumented Immigrants in American Society.* Fort Worth: Harcourt Brace Jovanovich College Publishers.

Chavez, L.R., Cornelius, W.A., and O.W. Jones. 1985. Mexican immigrants and the utilization of U.S. health services: the case of San Diego. *Social Science and Medicine* 21:93–102.

Chen, A.J. and G. Jones. 1989. *Ageing in ASEAN, Its Socio-Economic Consequences.* Singapore: Institute for Southeast Asian Studies.

Chen, L., Huq, E. and S. D'Souza. 1981. Sex bias in the family allocation of food and health care in rural Bangladesh. *Population and Development Review* 7:55–70.

Chen-I, W.U., Zu-En, T., Jing-Guang, Y. and D. Rong-San. 1985. Evaluation of the family system and its influence on the mental health of the aged in China, 147–155. In *Mental Health Planning for One Billion People: A Chinese Perspective*, edited by T. Lin and L. Eisenberg, pp. 147–155. Vancouver: University of British Columbia Press.

Cheng, T.A. 1989. Urbanization and minor psychiatric morbidity. *Social Psychiatry and Psychiatric Epidemiology* 24:309–316.

Cherlin, A. 1979. Work life and marital dissolution. In *Divorce and Separation: Context, Causes and Consequences*, edited by G. Levenger and O. Moles. pp. 156–166. New York: Basic Books.

Cherpitel, C.J. 1993. Alcohol and injuries: a review of international emergency room studies. *Addiction* 88:923–937.

Chinnery-Hesse, M. 1989. *Engendering Adjustment for the 1990s: Report of the Commonwealth Expert Group on Women and Structural Adjustment*. London: Commonwealth Secretariat Publications.

Christakis, N.A. 1992. Ethics are local: engaging cross-cultural variation in the ethics for clinical research. *Social Science and Medicine* 35:1079–1091.

Christakis, N.A., Ware, N.C., and A. Kleinman. 1994. Illness behavior and the health transition in the developing world. In *Health and Social Change in International Perspectives*, edited by L.C. Chen, A. Kleinman, and N.C. Ware, pp. 275–302. Boston, MA: Harvard Series on Population and International Health, Department of Population and International Health, Harvard School of Public Health.

Christian, S. 1990. Argentina deaths bring focus on health care. *The New York Times* (International Edition), August 11, 5.

Chultoo, S. 1990. A sociological study of certain aspects of disease and death: a case study of Muslims in Kashmir. Unpublished Ph.D. dissertation, University of Delhi.

Cienfuegos, A.J. and C. Monelli. 1983. The testimony of political repression as a therapeutic instrument. *American Journal of Orthopsychiatry* 53:43–51.

Clarke, D. 1977. *The Distribution of Income and Wealth in Rhodesia*. Gweru: Mambo Press.

Cliff, J. and A.R. Noormahomed. 1988. Health as a target: South Africa's destabilization of Mozambique. *Social Science and Medicine* 27:717–722.

———. 1993. The impact of war on children's health in Mozambique. *Social Science and Medicine* 7:843–848.

Cohen, A.K. 1964. *Delinquent Boys—The Culture of the Gang*. Glencoe: The Free Press.

Cohen, L. 1992. *No Aging in India*. Ph.D. dissertation, Department of Anthropology, Harvard University.

Cohen, R.E. 1987. The Armero tragedy: lessons for mental health professionals. *Hospital and Community Psychiatry* 38(12):1316–1321.

Cohn, J., Holzer, K.I., Koch, L., and B. Severin. 1980. Children and torture: an investigation of Chilean immigrant children in Denmark. *Danish Medical Bulletin* 27:238–239.

Comité de Defensa de los Derechos del Pueblo. 1989. The effects of torture and political repression in a sample of Chilean families. *Social Science and Medicine* 7:735–740.

Commission on Health Research for Development. 1990. *Health Research: Essential Link to Equity in Development*. Oxford: Oxford University Press.

Compton, W.M., Helzer, J.E., Hwu, H-G., et al. 1991. New methods in cross-cultural psychiatry: psychiatric illness in Taiwan and the United States. *American Journal of Psychiatry* 148:1697–1704.

Conyer, R.C.T., Sepulveda, A.J., Medina, M.M.E., Caraveo, J., and J.R. De La Fuente.

1987. Prevalencia del sindrome de estres postraumatico en la poblacion sobreviviente a un desastre natural. *Salud Publica Mexicana* 29:406–411.

Cook, P. 1990. The social cost of drinking. In *The Negative Social Consequences of Alcohol Use*, edited by O. Aasland, pp. 49–81. Oslo, Norway: Norwegian Ministry of Health and Social Affairs.

Coombs, D.W. and G. Globetti. 1986. Alcohol use and alcoholism in Latin America: Changing patterns and sociocultural explanations. *International Journal of Addiction* 21:59–81.

Corradi, J., Weiss Fagen, P., and M. Garreton. 1992. *Fear at the Edge: State Terror and Resistance in Latin America*. Berkeley: University of California Press.

Counts, D.A. 1987. Female suicide and wife abuse: a cross-cultural perspective. *Suicide and Life-Threatening Behavior* 17:194–204.

————. 1990a. Beaten wife, suicidal woman: domestic violence in Kaliai, West New Britain. *Pacific Studies* 13:151–169.

————. 1990b. Domestic violence in Oceania: introduction. *Pacific Studies* 13:1–5.

Cowgill, D.O. 1974. Aging and modernization: a revision of the theory. In *Late Life: Communities and Environmental Policy,* edited by J.F. Gubrium, pp. 123–146. Springfield, IL: Charles C. Thomas.

Cravioto, P., Anchondo, R-L, de la Rosa, B., Rojas, G., and R. Tapia-Conyer. 1992. Risk factors associated with inhalant use among Mexican juvenile delinquents. In *Epidemiological Trends in Drug Abuse*, NIDA, pp. 472–477. Rockville, MD: National Institutes of Health.

Cross-National Collaborative Group. 1992. The changing rate of major depression. *Journal of the American Medical Association* 268:3098–3105.

Csordas, T. and A. Kleinman. 1990. The therapeutic process. In *Medical Anthropology: A Handbook of Theory and Method*, edited by T.M. Johnson and C. Sargent, pp. 11–25. New York: Greenwood Press.

Dahlgren, G. 1991. Strategies for health financing in Kenya: the difficult birth of a new policy. *Scandinavian Journal of Social Medicine* (supplement) 46:67–81.

Dalsimer, M. and L. Nisonoff. 1987. The implications of the new agricultural and one-child family policies for rural Chinese women. *Feminist Studies* 13:583–607.

Das, V. 1994. Moral orientations to suffering: legitimation, power and healing. In *Health and Social Change in International Perspective*, edited by L. Chen, A. Kleinman and N. Ware. pp. 139–170. Boston: Harvard Series on Population and International Health.

————, ed. 1990. *Mirrors of Violence: Communities, Riots and Survivors in South Asia*. Oxford: Oxford University Press.

Das, V. and A. Nandy. 1985. Violence, victimhood, and the language of silence. *Contributions to Indian Sociology* 19:177–195.

Daulaire, N.M.P. 1993. The children of Jumla, Nepal: reduction of child deaths and pneumonia cases through pneumonia case management and vitamin A supplementation at the community level. Draft, September.

DaVanzo, J., Parnell, A.M., and W.H. Foege. 1990. Health consequences of contraceptive use and reproductive patterns. *Journal of the American Medical Association* 265:2692–2696.

Davis, D.L. and S.M. Low, eds. 1989. *Gender, Health, and Illness: The Case of Nerves*. New York: Hemisphere Publishing.

Dawes, A. 1990. The effects of political violence on children: a consideration of South African and related studies. *International Journal of Psychology* 25:13–31.

de Girolamo, G. and A. McFarlane. (No date). Epidemiology of post-traumatic stress disorders: a comprehensive review of the literature. Unpublished paper.

de Girolamo, G., Diekstra, R., and C. Williams. 1989. *Report of a Visit to Border*

Encampments on the Kampuchea-Thailand Border. Geneva: World Health Organization: MNH/PSF/90.1.

Demographic and Health Survey (DHS Colombia). 1991. Colombia: Encuestra de Prevalencia Demographia y Salud. Columbia, MD: Institute for Resource Development.

Dennerstein, L., Astbury, J., and C. Morse. 1993. *Psychosocial and Mental Health Aspects of Women's Health*. Geneva: World Health Organization.

Desjarlais, R. 1992. *Body and Emotion: The Aesthetics of Illness and Healing in the Nepal Himalayas*. Philadelphia: University of Pennsylvania Press.

Dhadphale, M. and O.E. Omolo. 1988. Psychiatric morbidity among khat chewers. *East African Medical Journal* 65:355–359.

Di Franza, J.R., Richards, J.W., Paulman, P.M., et al. 1991. RJR Nabisco's cartoon camel promotes camel cigarettes to children. *Journal of the American Medical Association* 266:3149–3153.

Diekstra, R.F.W. 1993. The epidemiology of suicide and parasuicide. *Acta Psychiatrica Scandinavica* 371(supplement):9–20.

Diekstra, R.F.W. and W. Gulbinat. 1993. The epidemiology of suicidal behavior: a review of three continents. *World Health Statistical Quarterly* 46:52–68.

Dobbing, J., ed. 1987. *Early Nutrition and Later Achievement*. London: Academic Press.

Dohrenwend, B., Levav, I., et al. 1992. Socioeconomic status and psychiatric disorders: the causation-selection issue. *Science* 255:946–951.

Dorwart, R.A. 1993. Balance in organizing and financing of mental health services: perspectives from developed and developing countries. Working paper, International Mental and Behavioral Health, Center for the Study of Culture and Medicine, Harvard Medical School, Boston, Massachusetts.

Dowdall, T. 1992. Torture and the helping professions in South Africa. In *Torture and Its Consequences: Current Treatment Approaches*, edited by M. Basoglu, pp. 452–471. Cambridge: Cambridge University Press.

Doyal, L. 1979. *The Political Economy of Health*. London: Pluto Press.

Dreze, J. and A. Sen. 1991. *Hunger and Public Action*. New York: Oxford University Press.

Duncan, A.A. 1990. Women in the non-formal economic sector in Pakistan. In *Women in Health and Development: Report of the International Seminar at The Aga Khan University*, edited by K.Y. Qureshi and A.F. Qureshi, pp. 49–56. New York: UNICEF and Norad.

Durkheim, E. 1951 [1897]. *Suicide: A Study in Sociology*, translated by J.A. Spaulding and G. Simpson, ed. Glencoe, IL: Free Press.

Durning, A. 1991. Asking how much is enough. In *State of the World 1991*, A Worldwatch Institute Report, Washington, DC, pp. 153–169. New York: Norton.

Earls, F. 1985. Epidemiology of psychiatric disorders in children and adolescents. In *Psychiatry*, Volume 3, edited by J.O. Cavenar, Chapter 12. Philadelphia: J.B. Lippincott Company.

―――. 1991. A developmental approach to understanding and controlling violence. *Theory and Research in Behavioral Pediatrics*, Volume 5, edited by H.E. Fitzgerald et al., pp. 61–88. New York: Plenum Press.

Earls, F., Slaby, R., Spirito, A., et al. 1992. Prevention of violence and injuries due to violence. *Morbidity and Mortality Weekly Report* 41:5–7.

Earls, F., Cairns, R., and J. Mercy. 1993. The control of violence and the promotion of nonviolence in adolescents. *Promoting the Health of Adolescents: New Directions for the 21st Century*, edited by S. Millstein, A. Petersen, and E. Nightingale, pp. 285–304. New York: Oxford University Press.

Ebie, J.C. and A.O. Pela. 1982. Drug abuse in Nigeria: a review of epidemiological studies. *Bulletin on Narcotics* 34:91–99.

The Economist. 1992. Sri Lanka's other killing ground. Nov. 28, p. 38.

————. 1993. Third-world finance: new ways to grow. Sept. 25, 1993, pp. 5–44.

Edwards, G. and A. Arif. 1981. *Drug Problems in the Socio-Cultural Context: A Basis for Policy and Programme Planning.* Geneva: World Health Organization.

Edwards, G., Anderson, P., Babor, T.F., et al. Alcohol and the public good. New York: Oxford University Press. Forthcoming.

Eferakeya, A.E. 1984. Drugs and suicide attempts in Benin City, Nigeria. *British Journal of Psychiatry* 145:70–73.

Egli, E.A., Shiota, N.K., Ben-Porath, Y.S., and J.N. Butcher. 1991. Psychological interventions. In *Mental Health Services for Refugees*, U.S. Dept. of Health and Human Services, pp. 157–188. Maryland: NIMH.

Eisenberg, L. 1986a. Does bad news about suicide beget bad news? (Editorial). *New England Journal of Medicine* 315(11):705–707.

————. 1986b. Mindlessness and brainlessness in psychiatry. *British Journal of Psychiatry* 148:497–508.

————. 1989. Health education and the AIDS epidemic. *British Journal of Psychiatry* 154:754–767.

————. 1990. Benefits and risks of biological paradigms for psychiatry. In *Psychiatry: A World Perspective*, Volume 2, edited by C.N. Stefanis, pp. 3–9. Amsterdam: Elsevier Science Publishers.

————. 1992. Treating depression and anxiety in primary care. *New England Journal of Medicine* 326:1080–1084.

Eisenberg, L. and F.J. Earls. 1975. Poverty, social depreciation and child development. In *American Handbook of Psychiatry*, edited by D.A. Hamburg, pp. 275–291. New York: Basic Books.

Eisenbruch, M. 1990a. The cultural bereavement interview: a new clinical research approach for refugees. *Psychiatric Clinics of North America* 13:715–737.

————. 1990b. Cultural bereavement and homesickness. In *On the Move: The Psychology of Change and Transition*, edited by S. Fisher and C.L. Cooper, pp. 191–205. Chichester: Wiley.

————. 1992. Toward a culturally sensitive DSM: cultural bereavement in Cambodian refugees and the traditional healer as taxonomist. *The Journal of Nervous and Mental Disease* 180:8–10.

Ellenberg, J.H., Hirtz, D.G., and K.B. Nelson. 1986. Do seizures in children cause intellectual deterioration? *New England Journal of Medicine* 314:1085–1088.

Elson, D. 1992. From survival strategies to transformation strategies. In *Unequal Burden: Economic Crises, Persistent Poverty, and Women's Work*, edited by L. Beneria and S. Feldman, pp. 26–48. Boulder, CO: Westview Press, Inc.

Engels, F. 1969 [1854]. *The Condition of the Working Class in England.* Grenada, London.

Ennew, J. 1981. *Debt Bondage: A Survey.* London: Anti-Slavery Society.

Ennew, J. and M. Brian. 1989. *The Next Generation: Lives of Third World Children.* London: Zed Books.

Estroff, S.E. 1981. *Making It Crazy: An Ethnography of Psychiatric Clients in an American Community.* Berkeley: University of California Press. (2nd edition, 1985).

————. 1989. Self, identity, and subjective experience of schizophrenia: in search of the subject. *Schizophrenia Bulletin* 15:189–196.

Fairley, M., Langeluddecke, P., and C. Tennant. 1986. Psychological and physical morbidity in the aftermath of a cyclone. *Psychological Medicine* 16:671–676.

Fang, Y. 1987. The status and role of the Chinese elderly in families and society. In *Aging China: Family, Economics and Government Policies in Transition*, edited by J.

Schultz and D. Davis-Friedman, pp. 36–46. Proceedings of the International Forum on Aging, Beijing, China, May 20–23, 1986, the Gerontological Society of America, Washington, DC (out of print).

Farias, P. 1991. Emotional distress and its socio-political correlates in Salvadoran refugees: analysis of a clinical sample. *Culture, Medicine and Psychiatry* 15:167–192.

Faveau, V. and T. Blanchet. 1989. Deaths from injuries and induced abortion among rural Bangladeshi women. *Social Science and Medicine* 29:1121–1127.

Feachem, R.G.A., Phillips, M.A., and R.A. Bulato. 1992. Introducing adult health. In *The Health of Adults in the Developing World*, edited by R.G.A. Feachem, T. Kjellstrom, C.J.L. Murray, M. Over, and M.A. Phillips, pp. 1–22. New York: Oxford University Press.

Feksi, A.T., Kaamugisha, J., Sander, J.W.A.S., Gatti, S., and S.D. Shorvon. 1991. Comprehensive primary health care antiepileptic drug treatment programmes in rural and semi-urban Kenya. *The Lancet* 337:406–409.

Finau, S. and P. Lasalo. 1985. Suicide and parasuicide in Paradise. *New Zealand Family Physician* 12:101–104.

Finkler, K. 1985. Symptomatic differences between the sexes in rural Mexico. *Culture, Medicine and Psychiatry* 9:27–57.

———. 1993. Gender, violence and sickness in Mexico. Working paper, International Mental and Behavioral Health Project, Center for the Study of Culture and Medicine, Harvard Medical School, Boston, Massachusetts.

Fishbain, D.A. and T.E. Aldrich. 1985. Suicide pacts: international comparisons. *Journal of Clinical Psychiatry* 46:11–15.

Fiske, A.P. 1990. Relativity within Moose ("Mossi") culture: four incommensurable models for social relationships. *Ethos* 18:180–204.

Fortuin, M., Chotard, J., Jack, A.D., et al. 1993. Efficacy of hepatitis B vaccine in the Gambian expanded program on immunization. *The Lancet* 341:1129–1131.

Foster, D. 1987. *Detention and Torture in South Africa*. Capetown: David Philip.

Franke, R.W. and B.N. Chasin. 1992. Kerala State, India: radical reform as development. *International Journal of Health Services* 22:139–156.

Fransen, V., ed. 1990. *Mental Health Services in the United States and England: Struggling for Change*. Selected papers prepared for the joint United States–England Conference on Mental Health Services, Princeton, NJ: Robert Wood Johnson Foundation.

Freed, G.L., Bordley, W.C., and G.H. DeFriese. 1993. Childhood immunization programs: an analysis of policy issues. *Milbank Quarterly* 71:65–96.

Frenk, J. 1992. The health-care transition. Unpublished manuscript.

———. 1993a. The new public health. *Annual Review of Public Health* 14:469–490.

———. 1993b. Balancing relevance and excellence: organizational responses to link research with decision-making. *Social Science and Medicine* 35:1397–1404.

Freud, A. and D.T. Burlingham. 1943. *War and Children*. New York: Ernst Willard.

Freud, S. 1917. Mourning and melancholia. In *The Standard Edition of the Complete Psychological Works*, edited by J. Strachey, Volume 14, pp. 243–258. London: Hogarth Press.

Ganesvaran, T., Subramaniam, S., and K. Mahadevan. 1984. Suicide in a northern town of Sri Lanka. *Acta Psychiatrica Scandinavica* 69:420–425.

Ganesvaran, T. and R. Rajarajeswaran. 1988. Fatal deliberate self-harm seen in a Sri Lankan hospital. *British Journal of Psychiatry* 152:420–423.

Gargan, E. 1992. Bound to looms by poverty and fear, boys in India make a few men rich. *The New York Times* (International Edition), July 9, A8.

Garrison, C.Z., Addy, C.L., Jackson, K.L., McKeown, R.E., and J.L. Waller. 1991. A longitudinal study of suicidal ideation in young adolescents. *Journal of the American Academy of Child Adolescent Psychiatry* 30:597–603.

Gater R., Almeida, E., Sousa B.D., Barrientos G., et al. 1991. The pathways to psychiatric care: a cross-cultural study. *Psychological Medicine* 21:761–774.

George, T. and S.K. Pandya. 1993. The World Development Report 1993: An unhealthy prescription. *Medicine and Society* 6:279–282.

Gibson, M. 1992. Public health and social policy. In *Family Support for the Elderly: The International Experience*, edited by H. Kendig, A. Hashimoto, and L. Coppard, pp. 88–111. Oxford: Oxford University Press.

Giel, R., de Arango, M.V., Climent, C.E., et al. 1981. Childhood mental disorders in primary health care: results of observations in four developing countries. *Pediatrics* 68:677–683.

Gilmartin, C. 1990. Violence against women in contemporary China. In *Violence in China: Essays in Culture and Counterculture*, edited by J. Lipman and S. Harrell, pp. 203–225. New York: State University of New York Press.

Gimlette, J.D. and H.W. Thomsen. 1939. *A Dictionary of Malayan Medicine*. Singapore: Oxford University Press.

Glatt, K.M. 1987. Helpline: suicide prevention at a suicide site. *Suicide and Life-Threatening Behavior* 17(4):299–309.

Gleick, P.H. 1989. The implications of global changes for international security. *Climatic Change* 15:309–325.

Glickman, T., Golding, D., and E. Silverman. 1992. *Acts of God and Acts of Man: Recent Trends in Natural Disasters and Major Industrial Accidents*. Washington, DC: Center for Risk Management.

Godfrey, N. and A. Kalache. 1989. Health needs of older adults displaced to Sudan by war and famine: questioning current targetting practices in health relief. *Social Science and Medicine* 28:707–713.

Goffman, I. 1961. *Asylums*. Chicago: Aldine.

Goldacre, M., Seagroatt, V., and K. Hawton. 1993. Suicide after discharge from psychiatric inpatient care. *The Lancet* 342:283–286.

Goldberg, D. and P. Huxley. 1992. *Common Mental Disorders: A Biosocial Model*. London, Routledge.

Goldstein, M.C. and C.M. Beall. 1981. Modernization and aging in the third and fourth world: views from the rural hinterland in Nepal. *Human Organization* 40(1):48–55.

Good, B. and M-J.D. Good. 1982. Toward a meaning centered analysis of popular illness categories: "fright illness" and "heart distress" in Iran. In *Cultural Conceptions of Mental Health and Therapy*, edited by A. Marsella and G. White, pp.141–166. Dordtrecht: Reidel.

Good, M-J.D. 1992a. Local knowledge: research capacity building in international health. *Social Science and Medicine* 35:1359–1368.

———. 1992b. Work as a haven from pain. In *Pain as Human Experience: An Anthropological Perspective*, edited by M-J.D. Good, P. Brodwin, B. Good, and A. Kleinman, pp. 49–76. Berkeley: University of California Press.

Gossop, M. 1989. The detoxification of high dose heroin addicts in Pakistan. *Drug and Alcohol Dependence* 24:143–150.

Gould, M.S. and D. Shaffer. 1986. The impact of suicide in television movies: evidence of imitation. *New England Journal of Medicine* 315(11):690–694.

Gould, M.S., Wallenstein, S., Kleinman, M.H., O'Carroll, P., and J. Mercy. 1990. Suicide clusters: an examination of age-specific effects. *American Journal of Public Health* 80:211–212.

Government of India. 1984. *National Mental Health Plan for Bangladesh*.

Graham, P. 1981. Epidemiological approaches to child mental health care in developing countries. In *Psychopathology of Children and Youth: A Cross-cultural Perspective*, edited by E.F. Purcell, pp. 28–45. New York: Josiah Macy, Jr., Foundation.

Grantham-McGregor, S.M., Powell, C.A., Walker, S.P., et al. 1991. Nutritional supplementation, psychosocial stimulation and mental development of stunted children: the Jamaican study. *The Lancet* 338:1–5.

Greenberg, P., Stiglin, L., Finkelstein, S., et al. 1993. Depression: a neglected major illness. *Journal of Clinical Psychiatry* 54:419–424.

Greenough, P. 1993. Intimidation, resistance and coercion in the final stages of the South Asian smallpox eradication campaign, 1973–75. Workshop on Global Immunization and Culture. Iowa City, University of Iowa, unpublished manuscript.

Grimes, D.A. 1992. The safety of oral contraceptives. *American Journal of Obstetrics and Gynecology* 166:1950–1954.

Gruber, A.R. 1978. *Children in Foster Care*. New York: Human Sciences Press.

Gruenberg, E.M. 1967. The social breakdown syndrome: some origins. *American Journal of Psychiatry* 123:1481–1489.

Guarnaccia, P.J., Canino, G., Rubio-Stipec, M., and M. Bravo. 1993. The prevalence of ataques de nervios in the Puerto Rico disaster study: the role of culture in psychiatric epidemiology. *Journal of Nervous and Mental Disorders* 181:157–165.

Guinness, E.A. 1992. Lecture at Annual Meeting of Royal College of Psychiatrists, London.

Gureje, O. and D. Olley. 1992. Alcohol and drug abuse in Nigeria: a review of the literature. *Contemporary Drug Problems* (Fall):491–504.

Gureje, O., Obikoya, B., Ikuesan, B.A. 1992. Prevalence of specific psychiatric disorders in an urban primary care setting. *East African Medical Journal* 69:282–287.

Guze, S.B. and E. Robins. 1970. Suicide among primary affective disorder. *British Journal of Psychiatry* 117:437–438.

Hall, L.A., Williams, C.A., and R.S. Greenberg. 1985. Supports, stressors, and depressive symptoms in low-income mothers of young children. *American Journal of Public Health* 75:518–522.

Handwerker, W.P. 1991. Gender power difference may be STD risk factors for the next generation. Paper presented at the 90th Annual Meeting of the American Anthropological Association, Chicago, Illinois.

Handwerker, P. 1993. Power, gender violence, and high risk sexual behavior: AIDS/STD risk factors need to be defined more broadly. Department of Anthropology, Humboldt State University, Arcata California (private communication cited in L. Heise, 1993).

Hankinson, S.E., Hunter, D.J., Colditz, G.A., et al. 1993. Tubal ligation, hysterectomy and risk of ovarian cancer. *Journal of the American Medical Association* 270:2813–2818.

Harding, T.W. et al. 1980. Mental disorders in primary health care: a study of their frequency and diagnosis in four developing countries. *Psychosocial Medicine* 10:231–241.

Harding, T.W., Bushnello, E.D., Climent, C.E., Diop, M., El-Hakim, A., Giel, R., Ibrahim, H., Landrido-Ignacio, L., and N. Wig. 1983. The W.H.O. collaborative study on strategies for extending mental health care III: evaluative design and illustrative results. *American Journal of Psychiatry* 140:1481–1485.

Harding, C.M., Zubin, J., and J.S. Strauss. 1987. Chronicity in schizophrenia: fact, partial fact, or artifact? *Hospital and Community Psychiatry* 38:477–486.

Harff, B. and T.R. Gurr. 1987. Genocides and politicides since 1945: evidence and anticipation. In *Internet on the Holocaust and Genocide*, Jerusalem: Institute of the International Conference on the Holocaust and Genocide. Special Issue 13.

Harpham, T. 1992. Urbanisation and mental disorder. *Principles of Social Psychiatry*, edited by D. Bhugra and J. Leff, pp. 346–354. New York: Blackwell.

Harpham, T., Lusty, T., and P. Vaughan. 1988. *In the Shadow of the City: Community Health and the Urban Poor*. Oxford: Oxford University Press.

Hazarika, S. 1993. Bangladesh faces dispute on floods. *The New York Times*, August 1, A7.

Head, I. 1989. South-North dangers. *Foreign Affairs* 68(3):71–86.

Heather, N., Wodak, A., Nadelmann, E., and P. O'Hare, eds. 1993. *Psychoactive Drugs and Harm Reduction*. London: Whurr Publishers.

Heggenhougen, H.K. 1979. Modernization, drug addiction and traditional palliatives. Paper presented to the Ninth Annual Conference of the Canadian Council for Southeast Asian Studies, Vancouver, November 8–11.

———. 1984. Traditional medicine and the treatment of drug addicts: three examples from Southeast Asia. *Medical Anthropology Quarterly* 16:3–7.

Heise, L. 1993. Violence against women: the missing agenda. In *The Health of Women: A Global Perspective*, edited by M. Koblinsky, J. Timyan, and J. Gay, pp. 171–195. Boulder, CO: Westview Press, Inc.

Helman, G. and S. Ratner. 1992/93. Saving failed states. *Foreign Policy* 89:3–20.

Henderson, A.S. 1993. *Dementia: A World Mental Health Situation Report*. Geneva, Division of Mental Health, World Health Organization.

Henriksson, M.M., Aro, H.M., Marttunen, M.J., Heikkinen, M.E., Isometsä, Kuoppasalmi, K.I., and J.K. Lönnqvist. 1993. Mental disorders and comorbidity in suicide. *American Journal of Psychiatry* 150:935–940.

Hetzel, B.S. 1983. Iodine deficiency disorders (IDD) and their eradication. *The Lancet* ii:1126–1129.

Hezel, F.X. 1984. Cultural patterns in Trukese suicide. *Ethnology* 23:193–206.

Hieu, D.T., Tan, T.T., Tan, D.N., et al. 1993. 31,781 cases of non-surgical female sterilization with quinacrine pellets in Vietnam. *The Lancet* 342:213–217.

Hinton, L.W., Chen, Y-C.J., Du, N., Tran, C.G., Lu, F.G., Miranda, J., and S. Faust. 1993. DSM-III-R disorders in Vietnamese refugees: prevalence and corrolates. *The Journal of Nervous and Mental Disease* 181:113–122.

Hobcraft, J. 1993. Women's education, child welfare and child survival. *Health Transition Review* 3:159–175.

Hodge-McCoid, C.H. 1989. Dowry deaths in India: a materialist analysis. Women in International Development, Working paper #188, Michigan State University.

Hollifield, M., Katon, W., Spain, D., and L. Pule. 1990. Anxiety and depression in a village in Lesotho, Africa: a comparison with the United States. *British Journal of Psychiatry* 156:343–350.

Homer-Dixion, T.F. 1991. On the threshold: environmental changes as causes of acute conflict. *International Security* 6(2):76–116.

Hopper, K. 1991. Some old questions for the new cross-cultural psychiatry. *Medical Anthropology Quarterly* 5:299–330.

Hornblower, M. 1993. *Time* magazine, June 21, 1993, p. 44–45.

Hull, T. 1990. Recent trends in sex ratios at birth in China. *Population and Development Review* 16:63–83.

Iacoponi, E., Laranjeira, R.R., and J. Mari. 1991. Brazil: a giant worker wakes up to progress and inequality. In *Mental Health Services in the Global Village*, edited by L. Appleby and R. Araya, pp. 131–148. London: Gaskell.

Ikels, C. 1993. The experience of dementia in China. Working paper, International Mental and Behavioral Health Project, Center for the Study of Culture and Medicine, Harvard Medical School, Boston, Massachusetts.

Inciardi, J.A. 1987. Beyond cocaine: basuco, crack, and other coca products. *Contemporary Drug Problems* (Fall):461–492.

India Today. 1990. Organ bazaar: health. July 30, pp. 30–37.

Indian Council of Medical Research. 1986. Ansari nagar, New Delhi, India.

Institute of Medicine. 1985. *Preventing Low Birth Weight*. Washington, DC: National Academy Press.

————. 1994. *Reducing Risks for Mental Disorders: Frontiers for Preventive Intervention Research*. Washington, DC: National Academy Press.

————. Forthcoming. *In Her Lifetime: Female Morbidity and Mortality in Sub-Saharan Africa*. Edited by C. Howson, D. Hotra, and M. Law. Institute of Medicine, Washington, D.C.: National Academy Press.

International Labor Office. 1991. Child labor: law and practice. *Conditions of Work Digest* 10(1). Geneva.

International Federation of Red Cross and Red Crescent Societies. 1993. *World Disasters Report 1993*. Dordrecht: Martinus Nijhoff.

Isaac, M.K. 1987. *Collaborative Study on Severe Mental Morbidity*. New Delhi, Indian Council of Medical Research and Department of Science and Technology.

Jablensky, A. 1993. Schizophrenia in the thirld world: an epidemiological perspective. Working paper, International Mental and Behavioral Health Project, Center for the Study of Culture and Medicine, Harvard Medical School, Boston, Massachusetts.

Jablensky, A., Marsella, A., Ekblad, S., Levi, L., and B. Jansson. 1992a. The International Conference on the Mental Health and Wellbeing of the World's Refugees and Displaced Persons, Stockholm, Sweden, October 6–11, 1991. *Journal of Refugee Studies* 5(2):172–183.

Jablensky, A., Sartorius, N., Ernberg, G., et al. 1992b. *Schizophrenia: Manifestations, Incidence and Course in Different Cultures*. A World Health Organization ten-country study. Psychological Medicine Monograph Supplement 20. Cambridge: Cambridge University Press.

Jacobson, J. 1989. Abandoning homelands. *State of the World 1993*. New York: Norton.

————. 1993. Women's health: the price of poverty. In *The Health of Women: A Global Perspective*, edited by M. Koblinsky, J. Timyan, and J. Gay, pp. 3–32. Boulder, CO: Westview Press.

Jamison, D.T. and W.H. Mosley. 1991. Disease control priorities in developing countries: health policy responses to epidemiological change. *American Journal of Public Health* 81:15–22.

Jareg, E. 1987. *Psychosocial Factors in Relief Work During Famine and Rehabilitation*. Oslo: Redd Barna.

Jazairy, I., Alamgir, M., and T. Panuccio. 1992. *The State of World Rural Poverty: An Inquiry into Its Causes and Consequences*. New York: International Fund for Agricultural Development.

Jeffery, R., Jeffery, P., and A. Lyon. 1984. Female infanticide and amniocentesis. *Social Science and Medicine* 19:1207–1212.

Jenkins, J.H. 1991. The state construction of affect: political ethos and mental health among Salvadoran refugees. *Culture, Medicine and Psychiatry* 15:134–165.

————. 1993. Anthropology, expressed emotion, and schizophrenia. *Ethos* 19:387–431.

Jenkins, J.H. and M. Valiente. Forthcoming. Bodily transactions of the passions: *El calor* (the heat) among Salvadoran women. In *The Body as Existential Ground: Studies in Culture, Self, and Experience*, edited by T.J. Csordas. Cambridge: Cambridge University Press.

Jilek, W. 1974. *Indian Healing*. Surrey: Hancock House.

Jilek-Aall, L. and H.T. Rwiza. 1992. Prognosis of epilepsy in a rural African community: a 30-year follow-up of 164 patients in an outpatient clinic in rural Tanzania. *Epilepsia* 33(4):645–650.

Jliovici, J. 1990. Contribution of social security to the well-being of the elderly. In

Improving the Health of Older People: A World View, edited by R.L. Kane, J.G. Evans, and D. Macfedyen, pp. 659–666. Oxford: Oxford University Press.

Joffe, R.T., Offord, D.R., and M.H. Boyle. 1988. Ontario Child Health Study: suicidal behavior in youth age 12–16 years. *American Journal of Psychiatry* 145(11):1420–1423.

Johnson, P.L. 1981. When dying is better than living: female suicide among the Gainj of Papua New Guinea. *Ethnology* 20:325–334.

Johnson, C.L., Rifkind, B.M., Sempos, C.T., et al. 1993. Declining serum cholesterol levels among U.S. adults. *Journal of the American Medical Association* 269:3002–3008.

Jolly, R. 1988. A UNICEF perspective on the effects of economic crises and what can be done. *Health, Nutrition, and Economic Crises: Approaches to Policy in the Third World*, edited by D. Bell and M. Reich, pp. 81–101. Dover, MA: Auburn House.

Jonas, K. 1992. Modelling and suicide: a test of the Werther Effect. *British Journal of Social Psychology* 31(part 4):295–306.

Jones, C. and M. Kiguel. 1994. *Adjustment in Africa*. Washington, DC: World Bank.

Jones, K. and D.W. Smith. 1973. Recognition of the fetal alcohol syndrome in early infancy. *The Lancet* ii:999–1001.

Joseph, A. 1991. Political parties and "sati." *Economic and Political Weekly* (April 20):1025–1026.

Kaaya, S.F. and M.T. Leshabari. 1993. Depressive illness and primary care in developing countries. Unpublished manuscript. University of Dar es Salaam, Tanzania.

Kalix, P. 1987. Khat: scientific knowledge and policy issues. *British Journal of Addiction* 82:47.

Kanaaneh, M. and M. Netland. 1992. *Children and Political Violence*. Jerusalem: Early Childhood Resource Centre.

Kanji, N. 1990. War and children in Mozambique: is international aid strengthening or eroding community-based policies? *Community Development Journal* 25:102–112.

Kapferer, B. 1983. *A Celebration of Demons: Exorcism and the Aesthetics of Healing in Sri Lanka*. Bloomington: Indiana University Press.

Katon, W., Von Korff, M., Lin, E., Bush, T., and J. Ormel. 1992. Adequacy and duration of antidepressant treatment in primary care. *Medical Care* 30:67–96.

Katz, G. 1982. The attitudes and feelings of South African former detainees during their detention. Unpublished B.A. Honors thesis, University of the Witwatersrand.

Katzman, R. 1993. Education and the prevalence of Alzheimer's disease. *Neurology* 43:13–20.

Kearney, R.N. and B.D. Miller. 1985. The spiral of suicide and social change in Sri Lanka. *Journal of Asian Studies* 45:81–101.

Keith, J. 1985. Age in anthropological research. In *Handbook of Aging and the Social Sciences*, 2nd Edition, edited by R. Binstock and E. Shanas, pp. 91–105. New York: Van Nostrand Reinhold Company.

Kelkar, G. 1987. . . . Two steps back? New agricultural policies in China and the woman question. In *Structures of Patriarchy: State, Community and Household in Modernising Asia*, edited by B. Agarwal, pp. 121–150. London: Zed Books.

———. 1992. Stopping the violence against women: fifteen years of activism in India. In *Freedom from Violence: Women's Strategies from around the World,* edited by M. Schuler, pp. 75–99. Washington, DC: OEF International.

Kellerman, A.L., Rivara, F.P., Somes, G., Reay, D.T., Francisco, J., Banton, J.G., Prodzinski, J., Fligner, C., and B.B. Hackman. 1992. Suicide in the home in relation to gun ownership. *New England Journal of Medicine* 327(7):467–472.

Kendig, H., Hashimoto, A. and L. Coppard. 1991. *Family Support for the Elderly*. Oxford Medical Publications, Oxford University Press.

Kennedy, J.G. 1987. *The Flower of Paradise—The Institutionalized Use of the Drug Qat in North Yemen*. Dordrecht: D. Reidel.

Khan, E.U. 1993. *Report Given to UN Working Group on Contemporary Forms of Slavery*.

Khanna, J., Van Look, P.F.A. and P.D. Griffin, eds. 1992. *Reproductive Health: A Key to a Brighter Future: Biennial Report 1990–1991*. Geneva: World Health Organization.

Kilonzo, G.P. 1993. Development of mental health services in Tanzania. Working paper, International Mental and Behavioral Health Project, Center for the Study of Culture and Medicine, Harvard Medical School, Boston, Massachusetts.

Kinsella, K.G. 1992. Population aging in Africa—the case of Zimbabwe. In *Changing Population Age Structures: Demographic and Economic Consequences and Implications*, pp. 391–398. Geneva: United Nations Population Fund.

———. 1988. *Aging in the Third World*. International Population Report Series No. 79. Washington, DC: U.S. Bureau of the Census, Center for International Research.

Kinzie, J.D., Fredrickson, R.B., Ben, R., Fleck, J., and W. Karls. 1984. Post-traumatic stress disorder among survivors of Cambodian concentration camps. *American Journal of Psychiatry* 141:645–650.

Kinzie, J.D. et al. 1986. The psychiatric effects of massive trauma on Cambodian children: I. The children. *Journal of the Academy of Child and Adolescent Psychiatry* 25:370–376.

Kinzie, J.D. et al. 1990. The prevalence of posttraumatic stress disorder and its clinical significance among Southeast Asian refugees. *American Journal of Psychiatry* 147:913–917.

Kinzie, J.D. and W. Sack. 1991. Severely traumatized Cambodian children: research findings and clinical implications. In *Refugee Children: Theory, Research, and Services*, edited by F.L. Ahearn and J.L. Athey, pp. 92–105. Baltimore, MD: The Johns Hopkins University Press.

Kjellstrom, T., Koplan, J.P. and R.B. Rothenberg. 1992. Current and future determinants of adult health. In *The Health of Adults in the Developing World*, edited by R.G.A. Feachem, T. Kjellstrom, C.J.L. Murray, M. Over, and M.A. Phillips, Chapter 5, pp. 209–260. New York: Oxford University Press.

Klaus, M.H., Kennell, J.H., Robertson, S.S., et al. 1986. Effects of social support during parturition on maternal and infant morbidity. *British Medical Journal* 293:585–587.

Kleinman, A. 1977. Depression, somatization and the new cross-cultural psychiatry. *Social Science and Medicine* 11:3–10.

———. 1980. *Patients and Healers in the Context of Culture*. Berkeley: University of California Press.

———. 1988. *Rethinking Psychiatry: From Culture Category to Personal Experience*. New York: The Free Press.

Kleinman, A. and L.H. Song. 1979. Why do indigenous practitioners successfully heal?: a follow-up study of indigenous practice in Taiwan. *Social Science and Medicine* 130:7–26.

Kleinman, A. and J. Gale. 1982. Patients treated by physicians and folk healers: a comparative outcome study in Taiwan. *Culture, Medicine and Psychiatry* 6:405–423.

Kleinman, A. and B. Good. 1985. *Culture and Depression*. Berkeley: University of California Press.

Kleinman, A. and J. Kleinman. 1991. Suffering and its professional transformation: toward an ethnography of interpersonal experience. *Culture, Medicine and Psychiatry* 15:275–301.

Kleinman, A., Wang, W., Li, S., Cheng, X., Dai, X., Li, K. and J. Kleinman. Forthcoming. The social course of epilepsy: chronic illness as social experience in interior China. In *Social Science and Medicine*.

Klerman, G.L. 1987. Clinical epidemiology of suicide. *Journal of Clinical Psychiatry* 48 (supplement):33–38.

Koblinsky, M., Trimyan, J., and J. Gay, eds. 1993. *The Health of Women: A Global Perspective*. Boulder, CO: Westview Press, Inc.

Koss, M.P. 1990. The women's mental health research agenda. *American Psychologist* 45:374–379.

Koumare, B., Coudray, J.P., and E. Miquel-Garcia. 1992. L'assistance psychiatrique au Mali. A propos du placement des patients psychiatriques auprès des tradipaticiens. *Psychopathologie africaine* 24:135–148.

Kramer, M. 1989. Barriers to prevention. In *Epidemiology and the Prevention of Mental Disorders*, edited by B. Cooper and T. Helgason, pp. 30–55. London: Routledge.

Kraus, R.F. and P.A. Buffler. 1979. Sociocultural stress and the American native in Alaska: an analysis of changing patterns of psychiatric illness and alcohol abuse among Alaska natives. *Culture, Medicine and Psychiatry* 3:111–151.

Kreitman, N. and S. Platt. 1984. Suicide, unemployment, and domestic gas detoxification in Britain. *Journal of Epidemiology and Community Health* 38:1–6.

Kristof, N.D. 1993a. China's crackdown on births: a stunning, and harsh, success. *The New York Times*, Sunday, April 25, 1:12.

―――. 1993b. Peasants of China discover new way to weed out girls. *The New York Times*, July 23, A1.

Kroll, J. et al. 1989. Depression and posttraumatic stress disorder in Southeast Asian refugees. *American Journal of Psychiatry* 146:1592–1597.

Kua, E.H. and S.M. Ko. 1991. Family violence and Asian drinkers. *Forensic Science International* 50:43–46.

Kupfer, D.J., Frank, E., Perel, J.M., et al. 1992. Five-year outcome for maintenance therapies in recurrent depression. *Archives of General Psychiatry* 49:769–773.

Kusnetzoff, J.C. 1986. Renegacion, desmentida, desaparicion y percepticido como technicas psicopaticas de la salvacion de la patria (Una vision psicoanalitica del informe de la Conadep). In *Argentina Psicoanalisis Represion Politica*, edited by O. Abudara et al., pp. 95–114. Buenos Aires: Ediciones Kargieman.

Kutzner, P. 1991. *World Hunger: A Reference Handbook*. Santa Barbara, CA: ABC-CLIO.

Lai, C-W., Huang, X., Lai, Y-H.C., et al. 1990. Survey of public awareness, understanding, and attitudes toward epilepsy in Henan Province, China. *Epilepsia* 31(2):182–187.

The Lancet. 1981. Asian rickets in Britain (Editorial). 2:402.

―――. 1992. Guinea worm: good news from Ghana (Editorial). 340:1322–1323.

Larrain, S. 1993. Estudio de frecuencia de la violencea intrafamiliar y la condicion de la mujer en Chile. Santiago, Chile: Pan Amerian Health Organization.

Lee-Wright, P. 1990. *Child Slaves*. London: Earthscan Publications.

Leff, J., Kuipers, L., Berkowitz, R., et al. 1985. A controlled trial of intervention in the families of schizophrenic patients: a two-year follow-up. *British Journal of Psychiatry* 146:594–600.

Leff, J., Wig, N., Bedi, H., et al. 1990. Relatives' expressed emotion and the course of schizophrenia in Chandigarh: a two-year follow-up of a first-contact sample. *British Journal of Psychiatry* 156:351–356.

Leidig, M.W. 1992. The continuum of violence against women: psychological and physical consequences. *Journal of American College Health* 40:149–155.

Leighton, A.H., Lambo, T.A., Hughes, C.C., Leighton, D.C., Murphy, J.M., and D.B. Macklin. 1963. *Psychiatric Disorders among the Yoruba: A Report of the Cornell-Aro Mental Health Project in the Western Region, Nigeria*. Ithaca: Cornell University Press.

León, C. 1987. Observing violence: the case of Colombia. Presented as the Simon Bolivar Lecture to the 140th Meeting of the American Psychiatric Association. Chicago, May 13.

Leslie, J. 1991. Women's nutrition: the key to improving family health in developing countries. *Health Policy and Planning* 6:1–19.

Lester, D. 1982. The distribution of sex and age among completed suicides: a cross-national study. *International Journal of Social Psychiatry* 28(4):256–260.

Levav, I., Lima, B.R., Lennon, M.S., Kramer, M., and R. Gonzalez. 1989. Mental health for all in Latin America and the Caribbean: epidemiological basis for action. *Boletin de la Oficina Sanitaria Pan Americana* 107(3):196–219.

LeVine, S. 1993. Women and mental health in the developing world: East Africa. Working paper, International Mental and Behavioral Health Project, Center for the Study of Culture and Medicine, Harvard Medical School, Boston, Massachusetts.

Levkoff, S.E., Cleary, P.D., Wetle, T. and R.W. Besdine. 1988. Illness behavior in the aged: implications for clinicians. *Journal of the American Geriatrics Society* 36:622–629.

Levy, B.S. and D.H. Wegman, eds. 1988. *Occupational Health: Recognizing and Preventing Work-Related Disease*, 2nd Edition. Boston: Little, Brown, and Company.

Lewis, I.M. 1986. *Religion in Context: Cults and Charisma*. Cambridge: Cambridge University Press.

Liddell, C. 1993. Diversities of childhood in developing countries. Working paper, International Mental and Behavioral Health Project, Center for the Study of Culture and Medicine, Harvard Medical School, Boston, Massachusetts.

Liddell, C., Kemp, J., and M. Moema. In Press. *The Young Lions—South African Children and Youth in Political Struggle*.

Lima, B.R., Santacruz, H., Lozano, J., Chavez, H., Samantiego, N., Pompei, M.S., and S. Pai. 1990. Disasters and mental health: experience in Colombia and Ecuador and its relevance for primary care in mental health in Latin America. *International Journal of Mental Health* 19(2):3–20.

Lima, B.R., Pai, S., Santacruz, H., and J. Lozano. 1991a. Psychiatric disorders among poor victims following a major disaster: Armero, Colombia. *The Journal of Nervous and Mental Disorders* 179(7):420–427.

Lima, B.R. Pai, S., Caris, L., Haro, J.M., Lima, A.M., Toledo, V., Lozano, J., and H. Santacruz. 1991b. Psychiatric disorders in primary health care clinics one year after a major Latin American disaster. *Stress Medicine* 7:25–32.

Lin, T.Y. et al. 1969. Mental disorders in Taiwan, fifteen years later. In *Mental Health Research in Asia and the Pacific*, edited by W. Caudill and T.Y. Lin, pp. 66–91. Honolulu: East-West Center Press.

Lin, T-Y. and D.T.C. Lin. 1982. Alcoholism among the Chinese: further observations of a low risk population. *Culture, Medicine and Psychiatry* 6:109–116.

Lin, T., Chu, H., Rin, H., Hsu, C., Yeh, E.K., and C. Chen. 1989. Effects of social change on mental disorders in Taiwan: observations based on a 15-year follow-up survey of general populations in three communities. *Acta Psychiatrica Scandinavica* 79 (supplement) 348:11–34.

Loftin, C., McDowall, D., Wiersema, B., and T.J. Cottey. 1991. Effects of restrictive licensing of handguns on homicide and suicide in the District of Columbia. *New England Journal of Medicine* 325(23):1615–1620.

Logue, B.J. 1990. Modernization and the status of the frail elderly: perspectives on continuity and change. *Journal of Cross Cultural Gerontology* 5(4):345–374.

Lorch, D. 1993. After years of ignoring AIDS epidemic, Kenya has finally begun facing up to it. *The New York Times*, December 18, I5.

Lovell, A.M. 1992. Mental and behavioral issues and the immigration of West African women residing in France. Working paper, International Mental and Behavioral Health Project, Center for the Study of Culture and Medicine, Harvard Medical School, Boston, Massachusetts.

Lozoff, B., Jimenez, E., and A.W. Wolf. 1991. Long-term developmental outcome of children with iron deficiency. *New England Journal of Medicine* 325:689–694.

Lumsden, D.P. 1993. Dams, Dis-placement, and mindful distress. Working paper, International Mental and Behavioral Health Project, Center for the Study of Culture and Medicine, Harvard Medical School, Boston, Massachusetts.

Lurie, P., Bishaw, M., Chesney, M.A., et al. 1994. Ethical, behavioral and social aspects of HIV vaccine trials in developing countries. *Journal of the American Medical Association* 271:295–301.

Lykes, M.B. 1994. Terror, silencing, and children: international, multidisciplinary collaboration with Guatemalan Maya communities. *Social Science and Medicine* 38:543–552.

Mackwardt, A.M. and L.H. Ochoa. 1993. Population and health data for Latin America. Washington, DC: DHS/Macro International Inc., Pan American Health Organization.

Macpherson, C. and L. Macpherson. 1984. Suicide in Western Samoa: a sociological perspective. In *Culture, Youth and Suicide in the Pacific: Papers from an East-West Conference*, edited by F. Hezel et al., pp. 36–73. Honolulu: University of Hawaii.

Maddox, J. 1993. Social science and the new world order. *Nature* 366:403.

Mahajan, A. 1990. Instigators of wife battering. In *Violence Against Women*, edited by Sushman Sood, pp. 1–10. Jaipur, India: Arihant Publishers.

Maj, M., Starace, F., and N. Sartorius. 1993. *Mental Disorders in HIV-1 Infection and AIDS*. Seattle: Hogrefe and Huber Publishers.

Maj, M., Janssen, R., Starace, F., Zaudig, M., Satz, P., Sughondhabirom, B., Luabeya, M., Riedel, R., Ndetei, D., Calil, H., Bing, E., St. Louis, M., and N. Sartorius. 1994a. WHO neuropsychiatric AIDS study, cross-sectional phase I. *Archives of General Psychiatry* 51:39–49.

Maj, M., Satz, P., Janssen, R., Zaudig, M., Starace, F., D'Elia, L., Sughondhabirom, B., Mussa, M., Naber, D., Ndetei, D., Schulte, G., and N. Sartorius. 1994b. WHO neuropsychiatric AIDS study, cross-sectional phase II. *Archives of General Psychiatry* 51:51–61.

Makanjuola, R.O.A. 1985. Psychiatric disorders in elderly Nigerians. *Tropical and Geographic Medicine* 37:348–351.

Makosky, V. 1982. Sources of stress: events or conditions? In *Lives in Stress: Women and Depression*, edited by D. Belle, pp. 35–53. Beverly Hills, California: Sage Publications.

Malik, I.A., Bukhtiari, N., Good, M-J.D., et al. 1992. Mothers' fear of child death: a study in urban and rural communities in Northern Punjab, Pakistan. *Social Science and Medicine* 35:1043–1053.

Maniam, T. 1988. Suicide and parasuicide in a hill resort in Malaysia. *British Journal of Psychiatry* 153:222–225.

Mann, J. 1993. Health and human rights. Unpublished. Presented at Children's Hospital, Boston, October 20.

Mann, J., Tarantola, D.J.M., and T.W. Netter. 1992. *AIDS in The World: A Global Report*. Cambridge: Harvard University Press.

Manton, K.G., Dowd, J.E., and M.A. Woodberry. 1986. Conceptual and measurement issues in assessing disability cross-nationally: analysis of a WHO-sponsored survey of the disablement process in Indonesia. *Journal of Cross Cultural Gerontology* 1:339–362.

Mari, J. 1987. Psychiatric morbidity in three primary medical care clinics in the city of São Paulo. *Social Psychiatry* 22:129–138.

Mari, J., Almeida-Filho, N., Coutinho E., et al. 1993. The epidemiology of psychotropic use in the City of São Paulo. *Psychological Medicine* 23:467–474.

Marsella, A. 1993. Urbanization and mental disorders. Working paper, International Mental and Behavioral Health Project, Center for the Study of Culture and Medicine, Harvard Medical School, Boston, Massachusetts.

Martin, L.G. 1988. The aging of Asia. *Journal of Gerontology* 43(4):S99–113.

Martin, L.G. 1990. The status of South Asia's growing elderly population. *Journal of Cross Cultural Gerontology* 5(2):93–117.

Martin-Baro, I. 1989. Political violence and war as causes of psychosocial trauma in El Salvador. *International Journal of Mental Health* 18:3–20.

Marzuk, P.M., Tardiff, K., Leon, A.C., Stajic, M., Morgan, E.B., and J.J. Mann. 1992. Prevalence of cocaine use among residents of New York City who committed suicide during a one-year period. *American Journal of Psychiatry* 149(3):371–375.

Marzuk, P.M., Tierney, H., Tardiff, K., et al. 1988. Increased risk of suicide in persons with AIDS. *Journal of the American Medical Association* 259:1333–1337.

Masland, T. 1992. Slavery. *Newsweek* 119(18):30–36.

Mastro, T.D., Satten, G.A., Nopkesorn, T., et al. 1994. Probability of female-to-male transmission of HIV-1 in Thailand. *The Lancet* 343:204–207.

Matsuura, M., Okubo, Y., Kojima, T., Takahashi, R., Wang, Y-F., Shen, Y-C., and C-K. Lee. 1993. A cross-national prevalence study of children with emotional and behavioral problems—a WHO Collaborative Study in the Western Pacific Region. *Journal of Child Psychology and Psychiatry and Allied Disciplines* 34:307–315.

Matuja, W.B.P. 1990. Psychological disturbance in African Tanzanian epileptics. *Tropical and Geographical Medicine* 42:359–364.

Maynes, C.W. 1993. Containing ethnic conflict. *Foreign Policy* 90:3–21.

McCallin, M. 1992. The impact of current and traumatic stressors on the psychological well-being of refugee communities. In *The Psychological Well-Being of Refugee Children: Research, Practice and Policy Issues*, edited by M. McCallin, pp. 68–89. Geneva: International Catholic Child Bureau.

McCallin, M. and S. Fozzard. 1990. *The Impact of Traumatic Events on the Psychological Well-Being of Mozambican Refugee Women and Children*. Geneva: International Catholic Child Bureau.

McGlothlin, W.H. 1980. The Singapore heroin control programme. *Bulletin on Narcotics* 32:1–14.

McSpadden, L.A. 1987. Ethiopian refugee resettlement in the western United States: social context and psychological well-being. *International Migration Review* 21:796–819.

Mechanic, D. 1994. Promoting health: implications for modern and developing nations. In *Health and Social Change in International Perspective*, edited by L.C. Chen, A. Kleinman, N. Ware. pp. 471–490. Harvard Series on Population and International Health, Harvard School of Public Health. Cambridge: Harvard University Press.

Meehan, P.J., Saltzman, L.E., and R.W. Sattin. 1991. Suicides among older United States residents: epidemiologic characteristics and trends. *American Journal of Public Health* 81:1198–1200.

Melville, M. and M.B. Lykes. 1992. Guatemalan Indian children and the sociocultural effects of government-sponsored terrorism. *Social Science and Medicine* 34:533–548.

Merchant, K.M. and K.M. Kurtz. 1993. Women's nutrition through the lifecycle: social and biological vulnerabilities. In *The Health of Women: A Global Perspective*, edited by M. Koblinsky, J. Timyan, and J. Gray, pp. 63–90. Boulder, CO: Westview Press, Inc.

Merry, S. 1981. *Urban Danger*. Philadelphia: Temple University Press.

Mobed, K. et. al. 1992. Occupational health problems among migrant and seasonal farm workers. *Western Journal of Medicine* 157:367–373.

Mollica, R.F. 1987. The trauma story: the psychiatric care of refugee survivors of violence and torture. In *Post-Traumatic Therapy and Victims of Violence*, edited by F. Ochberg, pp. 295–314. New York: Brunner/Mazel.

―――. 1989. Developing effective mental health policies and services for traumatised refugee patients. In *Crossing Cultures in Mental Health*, edited by D.R. Koslow and E.P. Salett, pp. 101–115. Washington, DC: Sietar International.

Mollica, R.F., Wyshak, G. and J. Lavelle. 1987. The psychological impact of war trauma and torture on Southeast Asian refugees. *American Journal of Psychiatry* 144:1567–1572.

Mollica, R.F. and L. Son. 1989. Cultural dimensions in the evaluation and treatment of sexual trauma: An overview. *Psychiatric Clinics of North America* 12:363–379.

Mollica, R.F., Donelan, K., Tor, S., Lavelle, J., Elias, C., Frankel, M., Bennett, D., and R.J. Blendon. 1991. Repatriation and disability: a community study of health, mental health and social functioning of the Khmer residents of Site Two. A Working Document of the Harvard Program in Refugee Trauma, The Harvard School of Public Health, and the World Federation for Mental Health.

Montagne, M. 1991. Descriptive epidemiology on international cocaine trafficking. In *The Epidemiology of Cocaine Use and Abuse*, edited by S. Schober and C. Schade, NIDA Research Monograph Series No. 110, pp. 275–296. Rockville, MD: Department of Health and Human Services.

Montagne, M. and D.M. Scott. 1993. Prevention of substance abuse problems: models, factors and processes. *International Journal of the Addictions* 28:1177–1208.

Montenegro, H. 1993. Alcohol abuse in Chile. Working paper, International Mental and Behavioral Health Project, Center for the Study of Culture and Medicine, Harvard Medical School, Boston, Massachusetts.

Moore, E. 1986. Issues in access to health care: the undocumented Mexican resident in Richmond, California. *Medical Anthropology Quarterly* 17(3):65–70.

Moore, L.J. and J.K. Boehnlein. 1991. Posttraumatic stress disorder, depression, and somatic symptoms in U.S. Mien patients. *Journal of Nervous and Mental Disease* 179:728–733.

Moore, M. and J.W. Anderson. 1993. Women, fed up and fighting back. *The Washington Post*, February 18, A1.

Morgan, M.C., Wingard, D.L., and M.E. Felice. 1984. Subcultural differences in alcohol use among youth. *Journal of Adolescent Health Care* 5:191–195.

Morrell, S., Taylor, R., Quine, S., and C. Kerr. 1993. Suicide and unemployment in Australia 1907–1990. *Social Science and Medicine* 36:749–756.

Muecke, M. 1992. New paradigms for refugee health problems. *Social Science and Medicine* 35:515–523.

Mufti, K.A. 1986. Community programme in Pakistan aimed at reducing drug abuse. *Bulletin on Narcotics* 38:121–127.

Mukadi, Y., Perriens, J.H., St. Louis, M.E., et al. 1993. Spectrum of immunodeficiency in HIV-1-infected patients with pulmonary tuberculosis in Zaire. *The Lancet* 342:143–146.

Murphy, E., Lindesay, J., and E. Grundy. 1986. Sixty years of suicide in England and Wales. *Archives of General Psychiatry* 43:969–976.

Murphy, G.E. and R.D. Wetzel. 1990. The lifetime risk of suicide in alcoholism. *Archives of General Psychiatry* 47:383–392.

Murphy, H.B.M. 1982. *Comparative Psychiatry: The International and Intercultural Distribution of Mental Illness*. New York: Springer-Verlag.

Murray, C.J.L., Yang, G. and X. Qiao. 1992. Adult mortality: levels, patterns and causes. In *The Health of Adults in the Developing World*, edited by R.G.A. Feachem et al., pp. 23–111. The World Bank, New York: Oxford University Press.

Naeem, S. 1992. Vulnerability factors for depression in Pakistani women. *Journal of the Pakistan Medical Association* (June):137–138.

Nahas, G.G. 1971. Lethal cannabis intoxication. *New England Journal of Medicine* 284(14):792.

Nandi, D.N., Ajmany, S., Ganguli, H., Banerjee, G., Boral, G.C., Ghosh, A., and S. Sarkar. 1975. Psychiatric disorders in a rural community in West Bengal. *Indian Journal of Psychiatry* 17:87–99.

National Center for Health Statistics. 1992. *Health United States 1991*. Hyattsville, MD: Public Health Service.

National Crime Records Bureau. 1992. Government of India.

National Institute of Drug Abuse. 1992. *Epidemiological Trends in Drug Abuse*. Proceedings of the Community Epidemiology Work Group, December. Rockville, MD: National Institutes of Health.

National Research Council. 1987. *Risking the Future: Adolescent Sexuality, Pregnancy and Childbearing*. Washington, DC: National Academy Press.

Nations, M.K. and L.A. Rebhun. 1988. Angels with wet wings won't fly: maternal sentiment in Brazil and the image of neglect. *Culture, Medicine and Psychiatry* 12:171–200.

Navaratnam, V. and K. Foong. 1989. Sequence of onset of different drug use among opiate addicts. *Current Medical Research and Opinion* 11:600–609.

Neki, J. 1987a. Psychosocial stressors in ageing and old age in various subcultures in India. In *Society, Stress and Disease*, Volume 5: *Old Age*, edited by L. Levi, pp. 85–93. Oxford: Oxford University Press.

————. 1987b. Health promotion for the elderly from the viewpoint of developing countries. In *Society, Stress and Disease*, Volume 5: *Old Age,* edited by L. Levi, pp. 275–281. Oxford: Oxford University Press.

Ness, R. 1980. The impact of indigenous healing activity: an empirical study of two fundamentalist churches. *Social Science and Medicine* 14:167–180.

Nevadomsky, J. 1982. Self-reported drug use among secondary school students in two rapidly developing Nigerian towns. *Bulletin on Narcotics* 34:21–32.

Census in India counts 844 million people. *New York Times*, March 26, 1991, p. A10.

Nietschmann, B. 1987. The third world war. *Cultural Survival Quarterly* 11(3):1–16.

Nordstrom, C. 1992. The backyard front. In *The Paths to Domination, Resistance, and Terror*, edited by C. Nordstrom and J. Martin, pp. 260–274. Berkeley: University of California Press.

Nowak, R. 1992. Final ethics: Dutch discover euthanasia abuse (news). *Journal of the NIH Research* 4:31–32.

Nunley, M. 1993. Families in Indian psychiatry. Working paper, International Mental and Behavioral Health Project, Center for the Study of Culture and Medicine, Harvard Medical School, Boston, Massachusetts.

Nyanguru, A.C. 1987. Residential care for the destitute elderly: a comparative study of two institutions in Zimbabwe. *Journal of Cross-Cultural Gerontology* 2:345–357.

Nydegger, C.N. 1983. Family ties of the aged in cross-cultural perspective. *The Gerontologist* 23:26–32.

O'Ballance, E. 1989. *The Cyanide War: Tamil Insurrection in Sri Lanka, 1973–88*. London: Brassey's.

Obot, I.S. 1989. Alcohol and drug abuse in Nigeria: the Middlebelt Study. Preliminary Report, University of Jos.

————. 1990. Substance abuse, health and social welfare in Africa: an analysis of the Nigerian experience. *Social Science and Medicine* 31:699–704.

Obot, I.S. and A. Olaniyi. 1989. Drug-induced psychiatric disorders in four Nigerian Hospitals. Unpublished manuscript.

Odejide, A.O., Oyewunmi, L.K., and J.U. Ohaeri. 1989. Psychiatry in Africa: an overview. *American Journal of Psychiatry* 146(6):708–716.

Odiase, G.I. 1980. Marital status and mental illness among psychiatric inpatients treated at University of Benin Teaching Hospital over a six-year period (1973–1979). Unpublished manuscript.

O'Donnell, G. 1983. La cosecha del miedo. *Nexos* 6.

Oetting, E.R., Edwards, R.W., and F. Beauvais. 1988. Social and psychological factors underlying inhalant use. In *Epidemiology of Inhalant Abuse: An Update,* edited by R.A. Crider and B.A. Rouse, NIDA Research Monograph Series No. 85, pp. 172–203. Rockville, MD: Department of Health and Human Services.

Ogawa, N. 1990. Economic factors affecting the health of the elderly. In *Improving the Health of Older People: A World View*, edited by R.L. Kane, J.G. Evans, and D. Macfadyen, pp. 627–645. Oxford: Oxford University Press on behalf of the World Health Organization.

Olds, D.L. and H. Kitzman. 1990. Can home visitation improve the health of women and children at environmental risk? *Pediatrics* 86:108–116.

Omolo, O.E. and M. Dhadphale. 1987. Prevalence of khat chewers among primary health clinic attenders in Kenya. *Acta Psychiatrica Scandinavica* 75:318–320.

Ong, A. 1987. *Spirits of Resistance and Capitalist Discipline: Factory Women in Malaysia*. Albany: State University of New York Press.

Orley, J., Blitt, D.M., and J.K. Wing. 1979. Psychiatric disorders in two African villages. *Archives of General Psychiatry* 36:513–520.

Ortiz, A., Romero, M., and E. Rodriguez. 1992. Information reporting system on drugs data: cocaine use trends—two border cities and Mexico City. In *Epidemiological Trends in Drug Abuse*, NIDA, pp. 532–543. Rockville, MD: National Institutes of Health.

Oviasu, V.O. 1976. Abuse of stimulant drugs in Nigeria. *British Journal of Addiction* 71:51–63.

Padmavathi, R., Rajkumar, S., Kumar, N., Manoharan, A., and S. Kamath. 1987. Prevalence of schizophrenia in an urban community in Madras. *Indian Journal of Psychiatry* 31:233–239.

Pakistan Medical Association. 1987. *Report of Committee on Drug Addiction in Pakistan*. Karachi: Pakistan Medical Association.

Palerm, J.V. 1992. A season in the life of a migrant farm worker in California. *Western Journal of Medicine* 157:362–366.

Pan American Health Organization. 1993. *Violence and Health*. Provisional Agenda Item 5.11. Washington, DC: PAHO.

Panicker, K.N., Vijaya Kumar, K.N., and S. Sabesan. (No date). Psycho-social and economic consequences of lymphatic filariasis in Shertallai, Kerala State, India. Vector Control Research Centre, Indira Nagar, Pondicherry, India.

Pape, J.W., Jean, S.S., Ho, J.L., et al. 1993. Effect of isoniazid prophylaxis on incidence of active tuberculosis and progression of HIV infection. *The Lancet* 342:268–272.

Patel, V. 1989. Sex-determination and sex-preselection tests in India: modern techniques for femicide. *Bulletin of Concerned Asian Scholars* 21:1–11.

Patterson, M.A. 1974. Electro-acupuncture in alcoholism and drug addiction. *Clinical Medicine* 81:9–13.

Pearlin, L.I. and J.S. Johnson. 1977. Marital status, life-strains and depression. *American Sociological Review* 82:652–663.

Pedersen, D. 1993. Mental health amongst the Indigenous Peoples of Latin America. Working paper, International Mental and Behavioral Health Project, Center for the Study of Culture and Medicine, Harvard Medical School, Boston, Massachusetts.

Peto, R., Lopez, A.D., Boreham, J., et al. 1992. Mortality from tobacco in developed countries: indirect estimation from National Vital Statistics. *The Lancet* 339:1268–1278.

Phillips, D.R. 1990. *Health and Healthcare in the Third World.* London: Longman Press.

Phillips, M. 1993. The influence of social, political, and economic factors on the evolution of mental health services in China. Working paper, International Mental and Behavioral Health Project, Center for the Study of Culture and Medicine, Harvard Medical School, Boston, Massachusetts.

Phillips, M., Pearson, V., and R. Wang, eds. 1994. Psychiatric rehabilitation in China: models for change in a changing society. Special issue of *The British Journal of Psychiatry* Suppl. 24, Vol. 165,

Pickens, R.W. and B.W. Fletcher. 1991. Overview of treatment issues. In *Improving Drug Abuse Treatment,* edited by R.W. Pickens, C.G. Leukefeld, and C.R. Schuster, NIDA Reseach Monograph Series No. 106, pp. 1–19. Rockville, MD: Department of Health and Human Services.

Pines, R. 1989. Why do Israelis burn out?—the role of the Intifada. Paper presented at the International Conference on Psychological Stress and Adjustment, Tel Aviv, Israel, January 1989.

Pitchford, R. 1991. India reports 11,000 "dowry deaths" in three years. *Reuter Library Report,* July 31.

Platt, S., Micciolo, R., and M. Tansella. 1992. Suicide and unemployment in Italy: description, analysis and interpretation of recent trends. *Social Science and Medicine* 34:1191–1201.

Pless, I.B. and M.E.J. Wadsworth. 1989. Long-term effects of chronic illness on young adults. In *Caring for Children with Chronic Illness,* edited by R.E.K. Stein, pp. 147–158. New York: Springer.

Pons de O'Neill, D. 1986. Reported in *Network News* 1(2):6–7.

Pope, H.G. and D.L. Katz. 1990. Homicide and near homicide by anabolic steroid users. *Clinical Psychiatry* 51:28–31.

Population Council. 1989. *International Conference on Adolescent Fertility in Latin America and the Caribbean: Overview.* Oaxaca, Mexico.

President's Commission on Organized Crime. 1986. *America's Habit: Drug Abuse, Drug Trafficking and Organized Crime.* Washington, DC: Superintendant of Documents, U.S. Government Printing Office.

Preston, J. 1993. For rural women, a millstone of poverty. *The Washington Post,* February 15, A33.

Price, R.W., Brew, B., Sidtis, J., et al. 1988. The brain in AIDS: central nervous system HIV-1 infection and AIDS dementia complex. *Science* 239:586–592.

Pritchard, C. 1992. Is there a link between suicide in young men and unemployment? A comparison of the UK with other European Community Countries. *British Journal of Psychiatry* 160:750–756.

Punamaki, R-L. 1992. "Natural healing processes" and experiences of political violence. Paper presented at the meeting "Refugee Children Exposed to Violent Environments." Refugee Studies Programme, Oxford, January.

———. 1987. Psychological stress of Palestinian mothers and their children in conditions of political violence. *The Quarterly Newsletter of the Laboratory of Comparative Human Cognition* 9:116–119.

Radloff, L. 1975. Sex differences in depression: the effects of occupation and marital status. *Sex Roles: A Journal of Research* 1:249–266.

Raffaelli, M., Campos, R., Merritt, A.P., et al. 1993. Sexual practices and attitudes of street youth in Belo Horizonte, Brazil. *Social Science and Medicine* 37:661–670.

Rahim, S.I.A. and M. Cederblad. 1984. Effects of rapid urbanization on child behavior in a part of Khartoum, Sudan. *Journal Child Psychology and Psychiatry* 25(4):629–641.

Raikes, A. 1989. Women's health in East Africa. *Social Science and Medicine* 28:447–459.

————. 1990. *Pregnancy, Birthing and Family Planning in Kenya: Changing Patterns of Behavior*. Copenhagen: Centre for Development Research.

Raj-Hashim, R. 1993. Summary of a survey research Malaysia (SRM) study on women and girlfriend battery. Asia-Pacific Resource and Research Centre for Women, Kaula Lumpur, Malaysia.

Ramalingaswami, V. 1973. Endemic goiter in Southeast Asia: new clothes on an old body. *Annals of Internal Medicine* 78:277–283.

Ramirez Rodriguez, J.C., and G. Uribe Vasquez. Forthcoming. Mujer y violencia: un hecho cotidiano. *Salud Publica de Mexico*. Cuernavaca: Instituto Nacional de Salud Publica.

Ramphele, M. 1993. Adolescents and violence in South Africa. Working paper, International Mental and Behavioral Health Project, Center for the Study of Culture and Medicine, Harvard Medical School, Boston, Massachusetts.

Ravenhill, J. 1990. The North-South balance of power. *International Affairs* 66:731–748.

Ray, R. and K. Chandrashekhar. 1982. Detection of alcoholism among psychiatric inpatients. *Indian Journal of Psychiatry* 24:389–394.

Reichenheim, M. 1988. Child health in an urban context: risk factors in a squatter settlement of Rio de Janeiro. Unpublished Ph.D. dissertation, London University.

Rein, M., Nutt, T.E., and H. Weiss. 1974. Fostering family care: myth and reality. In *Children and Decent People*, edited by A. L. Schorr, pp. 24–52. New York: Basic Books.

Ressler, E.M., Boothby, N., and D.J. Steinbock. 1988. *Unaccompanied Children*. New York: Oxford University Press.

Reuter Textline. 1993. *South China Morning Post*, July 12.

Reuters. 1994. 5,000 children slain in Brazil from '88 to '91, rights unit says. *Boston Globe*, February 1, p. 12.

Reynell, J. 1989. *Political Pawns: Refugees on the Thai-Kampuchean Border*. Oxford: Refugee Studies Programme.

Ribadeneira, D. 1993. Guatemala street children in battle for survival. *Boston Globe*, July 25, 10.

Rice, D., Kelman, S., and L.S. Miller. 1992. Estimates of economic costs of alcohol and drug abuse and mental illness, 1985 and 1988. *Public Health Reports* 106:280–291.

Rich, C.L., Young, D., and R.C. Fowler. 1986. San Diego suicide study. I. Young vs. old subjects. *Archives of General Psychiatry* 43(6):577–582.

Richards, P. 1992. Famine (and war) in Africa. *Anthropology Today* 8:3–5.

Richman, N., Ratilal, A., and A. Aly. 1990a. *The Effects of War on Mozambican Children: Preliminary Findings*. Maputo: Ministry of Education.

Richman, N., Ratilal, A. and Aly, A. 1990b. *The Effects of War on Teachers in Mozambique: Preliminary Findings*. Maputo, Ministry of Education.

Rimer, Z., Barsi, J., Veg, K., et al. 1990. Suicide rates in Hungary correlate negatively with reported rates of depression. *Journal of Affective Disorders* 20:87–91.

Robb, P. 1981. *Epilepsy: A Manual for Health Workers*. Bethesda, MD: United States Department of Health and Human Services.

Robins, L.N. and D.A. Regier, eds. 1992. *Psychiatric Disorders in America: The Epidemiologic Catchment Area Study*. New York: The Free Press.

Rosenfield, A. and D. Maine. 1985. Maternal mortality—a neglected tragedy. Where is the "M" in MCH? *The Lancet* 2(8446):83–85.

Rosenfield, P.L. 1992. The potential of transdisciplinary research for sustaining and extending linkages between the health and social sciences. *Social Science and Medicine* 35:1343–1358.

Rosenfield, S. 1980. Sex differences in depression: do women always have higher rates? *Journal of Health and Social Behavior* 21:33–42.

Rosenfield, S. 1989. The effects of women's employment: personal control and sex differences in mental health. *Journal of Health and Social Behavior* 30:70–91.

Rosovsky, H. and J.L. Lopez. 1986. Violencia y accidentes relacionados con el consumo de alcohol en la poblacion registrada en una agencia investigadora del Ministerio Salud Publico del D.F. *Salud Mental* 9(3):72–76.

Roter, D.L. and J.A. Hall. 1992. *Doctors Talking With Patients/Patients Talking With Doctors: Impriving Communication in Medical Visits*. Westport, CT: Auburn House.

Rotkin, I.D. 1973. A comparison review of key epidemiologic studies in cervical cancer related to current searches for transmissable agents. *Cancer Research* 33:1353–1367.

Royal College of Physicians. 1987. *The Medical Consequences of Alcohol Abuse: A Great and Growing Evil*. London: Royal College of Physicians.

Rubinstein, D.H. 1983. Epidemic Suicide among Micronesian Adolescents. *Social Science and Medicine* 17:657–665.

———. 1984. Suicide in Micronesia. *Culture, Youth and Suicide in the Pacific: Papers from an East-West Conference*, edited by F.X. Hezel et al., pp. 88–111. Honolulu: University of Hawaii.

Rumbaut, R.G. 1991. The agony of exile: a study of the migration and adaptation of Indochinese refugee adults and children. In *Refugee Children: Theory, Research, and Services*, edited by F.L. Ahearn and J.L. Athey, pp. 53–91. Baltimore, MD: The Johns Hopkins University Press.

Russel, D. 1991. Rape and child sexual abuse in Soweto: an interview with community leader Mary Mabaso. Seminar presented at the Centre for African Studies, University of Cape Town, South Africa, March 26.

Rutter, M. et al. Forthcoming. Report on poverty and adolescent health. London: Academia Europaea Study Group.

Rutter, M., Yule, B., Quinton, D., Rowlands, O., Yule, W., and M. Berger. 1975. Attainment and adjustment in two geographical areas: III—some factors accounting for area differences. *British Journal of Psychiatry* 126:520–533.

Rutter, M., Taylor, E., and Hersov, L., eds. 1994. *Child and Adolescent Psychiatry*, 3rd Edition. Oxford: Blackwell Scientific Publications.

Rutz, W., Von Knorring, L., and J. Walinder. 1989. Frequency of suicide on Gotland after systematic post-graduate education of general practioners. *Acta Psychiatrica Scandinavica* 80:151–154.

Sadik, N. 1990. *The State of World Population*. New York: United Nations Population Fund.

———. 1992. Global development challenges: the population dimension. *Change: Threat or Opportunity*, Volume 4, Social Change. Editor Unar Kirdar. UNDP.

Sadowski, L.S., Cairns, R.B., and J.A. Earp. 1989. Firearm ownership among nonurban adolescents. *American Journal of Diseases of Children* 143:1410–1413.

Safa, H.I. and P. Antrobus. 1992. Women and the economic crisis in the Caribbean. In *Unequal Burden: Economic Crises, Persistent Poverty, and Women's Work*, edited by L. Beneria and S. Feldman, pp. 49–82. Boulder, CO: Westview Press, Inc.

Saigh, P.A. 1991. The development of post-traumatic stress disorder following four different types of traumatization. *Behavioural Research and Therapy* 29:213–216.

Sainsbury, M.J. 1974. Acupuncture in heroin withdrawal. *Medical Journal of Australia* 2:102–105.

Salimovich, S., Lira, E., and E. Weinstein. 1992. Victims of fear: the social psychology of repression. *Fear at the Edge: State Terror and Resistance in Latin America*, edited by J. Corradi, P.W. Fagen, and M.A. Garreton, pp. 72–89. Berkeley: University of California Press.

Sankar, A. 1990. Gerontological research in China. *Journal of Cross-Cultural Gerontology* 4:199–224.

Santana, V. 1982. Estudo epidemiológico das doenças mentais em um bario de Salvador. *Série de Estudoes em Saúde* (Secretaria de Saúde da Bahia), 3:1–122.

Santiago, D. 1990. The aesthetics of terror, the hermeneutics of death. *America*, March 24.

Sartorius, N. 1993. WHO's work on the epidemiology of mental disorders. *Social Psychiatry and Psychiatric Epidemiology* 28:147–155.

Sartorius, N. and T.W. Harding. 1983. The WHO collaborative study on strategies for extending mental health care. I: The genesis of the study. *American Journal of Psychiatry* 140:1470–1473.

Sartorius, N., de Girolamo, G., Andrews, G., et al., eds. 1993. *Treatment of Mental Disorders: A Review of Effectiveness*. Washington: American Psychiatric Press.

Sartorius, N. and A.S. Henderson. 1992. The neglect of prevention in psychiatry. *Australian and New Zealand Journal of Psychiatry* 26:550–553.

Sartorius, N., Ustun, B., Costa e Silva, J., Goldberg, D., Lecrubier, Y., Ormel, J., Von Korff, M., and H. Wittchen. 1993. An international study of psychological problems in primary care: preliminary report from the world health organization collaborative project on "Psychological Problems in General Health Care." *Archives of General Psychiatry* 50:819–824.

Save the Children. 1991. *Helping Children in Difficult Circumstances: A Teacher's Manual*. London.

Sawyer, D.R. and D.O. Sawyer. 1992. The malaria transition and the role of social science research. In *Advancing Health in Developing Countries: The Role of Social Research*, edited by L. Chen, A. Kleinman, and N. Ware, pp. 105–122. New York: Auburn House.

Schenker, S. and K.V. Speeg. 1990. Risk of alcohol intake in men and women: all may not be equal. *New England Journal of Medicine* 322:127–129.

Scheper-Hughes, N. 1987. Culture, scarcity and maternal thinking: mother love and child death in northeast Brazil. In *Child Survival*, edited by N. Scheper-Hughes, pp. 187–208. Dordrecht: Reidel.

———. 1992. *Death Without Weeping: The Violence of Everyday Life in Brazil*. Berkeley: University of California Press.

Schmidtke, A. and H. Hafner. 1988. The Werther Effect after television films: new evidence for an old hypothesis. *Psychology of Medicine* 18(3):665–676.

Schneidman, E.S. 1993. Suicide as psychache. *Journal of Nervous and Mental Disease* 181:145–147.

Schober, S. and C. Schade, eds. 1991. *The Epidemiology of Cocaine Use and Abuse*. NIDA Research Monograph Series No. 110. Rockville, MD: Department of Health and Human Services.

Schrijvers, J. 1987. Blueprint for undernourishment: The Mahaweli River development scheme in Sri Lanka. In *Structures of Patriarchy: State, Community and Household in Modernising Asia*, edited by B. Agarwal, pp. 29–51. London: Zed Books.

Scrimshaw, N. 1987. The phenomenon of famine. *Annual Review of Nutrition* 7:1–21.

———. 1991. The consequences of hidden hunger. *Commonweal* 58(5):138–144.

Seager, J. and A. Olson. 1986. *Women in the World: An International Atlas*. London: Pluto Press Limited.

Sen, A. 1981. *Poverty and Famine*. Oxford: Oxford University Press.

———. 1989. Women's survival as a development problem. *Stated Meeting Report of the American Academy of Arts and Sciences* 43(2):14–29.

———. 1990. More than 100 million women are missing. *New York Review of Books*, December 20, 37(26):61–67.

Sen, A. and S. Sengupta. 1983. Malnutrition of rural children and the sex bias. *Economic and Political Weekly*, Annual Number 18.

Sen, B., Nandi, D.N., Mukherjee, S.P., Mishra, D.C., Banerjee, G., and S. Sarkar. 1984. Psychiatric morbidity in an urban slum-dwelling community. *Indian Journal of Psychiatry* 26:185–193.

Senay, E.C. 1991. Drug abuse and public health: a global perspective. *Drug Safety* 6(supplement):1–65.

Shaffer, D. 1993. Suicide: risk factors and the public health (Editorial). *American Journal of Public Health* 83(2):171–172.

Shamim, I. 1985. Kidnapped, raped, killed: recent trends in Bangladesh. Paper presented at the International Conference on Families in the Face of Urbanization, New Delhi, December 2–5.

Sharma, M.L. and T.M. Dak. 1987. *Aging in India, Challenge for the Society*. New Delhi: Ajanta Publications.

Sharp, D. 1993. Cancer prevention tommorrow. *The Lancet* 341:486.

Shaw, J. and J. Harris. 1991. Child victims of terrorism in Mozambique. In *Individual and Community Response to Trauma and Disaster*, edited by R. J. Ursano, B.G. McGaughey, and C. Fullerton, pp. 287–305. England: Cambridge University Press.

Shen, Y. 1981. The psychiatric services in the urban and rural areas of People's Republic of China. *Bulletin of Neuroinformation Laboratory*, Nagasaki University 8:131–137.

Shen, Y. 1987. Recent epidemiological data of alcoholism in China. *Chinese Mental Health Journal* 1(6):251–252.

Shen, Y., Weixi, Z., Liang, S., Xiaoling, Y., Yuhua, C., Dongfeng, Z., Hengyao, S., and S. Entao. 1981. Investigation of mental disorders in Beijing suburban district. *Chinese Medical Journal* 94:153–156.

Shen, Y., Yu-feng, W., Xiao-ling, Y. 1985. An epidemiological investigation of minimal brain dysfunction in six elementary schools in Beijing. *Journal of Child Psychology and Psychiatry* 26(5):777–787.

Shen, Y., Weixi, Z., Yuegin, H., et al. 1992. Epidemiological survey on alcohol dependence in population of four occupations in nine cities of China. (1) Methodology and prevalence. *Chinese Mental Health Journal* 6(3):112–115.

Shetty, K. and G. Nikam. 1993. Hogenakal: the last resort. *India Today*, January 31, p. 13.

Shinfuku, N. 1993. Mental health care in the Western Pacific Region. *International Journal of Mental Health*, 22(1):6.

Shisana, O. and D.D. Celentano. 1985. Depressive symptomology among Namibian adolescent refugees. *Social Science and Medicine* 21:1251–1257.

Shorvon, S.D. and P.J. Farmer. 1988. Epilepsy in developing countries: a review of epidemiologic, sociocultural, and treatment aspects. *Epilepsia* 29(supplement 1) S36–S54.

Shukla, G.D., Verma, B.L., and D.N. Mishra. 1990. Suicide in Jhansi city. *Indian Journal of Psychiatry* 32(1):45–51.

Silove, D. 1992. Psychotherapy and trauma. *Current Opinion in Psychiatry* 5:370–374.

Silva, K.T. and W.D.N.R. Pushpakumara. Forthcoming. Suicide, anomie and powerlessness among the Mahaweli settlers in Sri Lanka. *Journal of Asian Studies*.

Silva, K.T. Forthcoming. Suicide, self-destructive violence and armed conflict in Sri Lanka. *Studies in Conflict and Terrorism*.

Simons, M. 1993. The sex market: scrounge on the world's children. *The New York Times*, April 9, A3.

Singer, M. 1986. Toward a political-economy of alcoholism: the missing link in the anthropology of drinking. *Social Science and Medicine* 23:113–130.

Skegg, D.C.G., Corwin, P.A., Paul, C., et al. 1982. Importance of the male factor in cancer of the cervix. *The Lancet* 2:581–583.

Smart, R.G., Mora, M.E., Terroba, G., and V.K. Varma. 1981. Drug use among non-students in three countries. *Drug and Alcohol Dependence* 7(2):125–132.

Smith, D.J. and M. Rutter. 1994. Time trends in psychosocial disorders of youth. Unpublished manuscript.

Solis, V.A.C. and F. Wagner. 1992. Epidemiology of drug abuse in the Mexican Republic: a panoramic comparison with the United States. In *Epidemiological Trends in Drug Abuse*, NIDA, pp. 462–471. Rockville, MD: National Institutes of Health.

Sommer, A., Tarwotjoi, I., Djunaedi, E., et al. 1986. Impact of vitamin A supplementation on child mortality. *The Lancet* 1(8491):1169–1173.

Somnier, F.E. and I.K. Genefke. 1986. Psychotherapy for victims of torture. *British Journal of Psychiatry* 149:323–329.

Sonali, D. 1990. *An Investigation into the Incidence and Causes of Domestic Violence in Sri Lanka*. Colombo, Sri Lanka: Women in Need (WIN).

Soni Raleigh, V. 1993. Suicide and Asian religions (letter). *British Journal of Psychiatry* 162:124.

Sosa, R., Kennell, J., Klaus, M., et al. 1980. The effect of a supportive companion on perinatal problems, length of labor and mother-infant interaction. *New England Journal of Medicine* 303:597–600.

Stark, E. and A. Flitcraft. 1991. Spouse abuse. In *Violence in America: A Public Health Approach*, edited by M. Rosenberg and M. Fenley, pp.123–157. New York: Oxford University Press.

Stein, Z., Durkin, M., and L. Belmont. 1986. Serious mental retardation in developing countries: an epidemiologic approach. *Annals of the New York Academy of Sciences* 477:8–21.

Stein, R.E.K. and D.J.J. Jessop. 1991. Long-term mental health effects of a pediatric home care program. *Pediatrics* 88:490–496.

Stern, Y., Gurland, B., Tatemichi, T.K., et al. 1994. Influence of education and occupation on the incidence of Alzheimer's disease. *Journal of the American Medical Association* 271:1004–1010.

Stewart, D. 1989. *The Global Injustice*. Ottawa: Canadian Council on Social Development.

Straker, G. 1988. Post-traumatic stress disorder: A reaction to state supported child abuse and neglect. *Child Abuse and Neglect* 12:383–395.

————. 1992. *Faces in the Revolution: The Psychological Effects of Violence on Township Youth in South Africa*. Cape Town: David Philip.

Straus, J.H. and M.A. Straus. 1953. Suicide, homicide, and social structure in Ceylon. *American Journal of Sociology* 63(5):461–469.

Streissguth, A.P., Darby, B.L., Barr, H.M., Smith, J.R. and D.C. Martin. 1983. Comparison of drinking and smoking patterns during pregnancy over a six-year interval. *American Journal of Obstetrics and Gynecology* 145(6):716–724.

Suarez-Orozco, M.M. 1990. Speaking of the unspeakable: toward a psychosocial understanding of responses to terror. *Ethos* 18:353–383.

————. 1992. A grammar of terror: psychocultural responses to state terrorism in dirty war and post-dirty war Argentina. In *The Paths to Domination, Resistance, and Terror*, edited by C. Nordstrom and J. Martin, pp. 219–259. Berkeley: University of California Press.

Sugar, J.A., Kleinman, A., and H.K. Heggenhougen. 1991. Development's downside: Social and psychological pathology in countries undergoing social change. *Health Transition Review* 1:211–220.

Sugar, J.A., Kleinman, A., and L. Eisenberg. 1992. Psychiatric morbidity in developing countries and American psychiatry's role in international health. *Hospital and Community Psychiatry* 43:355–360.

Sullivan, K. 1992. Protagonists of change. *Cultural Survival Quarterly* 14(4):38–40.

Sullivan, M. 1991. *Measuring Global Values: The Ranking of 162 Countries*. New York: Greenwood.

Summerfield, D. and L. Toser. 1991. "Low intensity" war and mental trauma in Nicaragua: a study in a rural community. *Medicine and War* 7:84–99.

Suwanwela, C. and V. Poshyachinda. 1980. Primary health care in hill tribe villages. In *Drug Problems in the Socio-cultural Context*, edited by G. Edwards and A. Arif, pp. 183–188. Geneva: World Health Organization.

Suwanwela, C. and V. Poshyachinda. 1986. Drug abuse in Asia. *Bulletin on Narcotics* 38:41–53.

Taiminen, T., Salmenpera, T., and K. Lehtinen. 1992. A suicide epidemic in a psychiatric hospital. *Suicide and Life-Threatening Behavior* 22(3):350–363.

Tambiah, S.J. 1993. Friends, neighbors, enemies, strangers: aggressor and victim in civilian ethnic riots. Working paper, Center for the Study of Culture and Medicine, Harvard Medical School, Boston, Massachusetts.

Tameim, O., Abdu, K.M., El Gaddal, A.A., et al. 1985. Protection of Sudaneses irrigation workers from schistosome infection by a shift to earlier working hours. *Journal of Tropical Medicine and Hygiene* 88:125–130.

Tan, E-S. and G. Lipton. 1988. *Mental Health Services in the Western Pacific Region. A Report on a Ten-Country Survey*. World Health Organization, Regional Office for the Western Pacific, Manila, Philipines.

Tao, K.-T. 1988. Mentally retarded persons in the People's Republic of China: review of epidemiological studies and services. *American Journal on Mental Retardation* 93:193–199.

Tatai, K. and K. Tatai. 1991. Suicide in the elderly: a report from Japan. *Crisis* 12(2):40–43.

Taub, B. 1992. Calling the soul back to the heart: soul loss, depression and healing among Indigenous Mexicans. Unpublished Ph.D. dissertation, University of California at Los Angeles.

Taylor, C.E. and W.B. Greenough. 1989. Control of diarrheal diseases. *Annual Review of Public Health* 10:221–244.

Tekle-Haimanot, R., Abebe, M., Forsgren, L., et al. 1991. Attitudes of rural people in Central Ethiopia toward epilepsy. *Social Science and Medicine* 32(2):203–209.

Thompson, R.S., Rivara, F.P., and D.C. Thompson. 1989. A case-control study of the effectiveness of bicycle helmets. *New England Journal of Medicine* 320:1361–1367.

Toft, S., ed. 1986. *Domestic Violence in Papua New Guinea*. Law Reform Commission Occasional Paper No. 19, Port Moresby, Papua New Guinea.

Toole, M.J. and R.J. Waldman. 1993. Refugees and displaced persons: war, hunger and public health. *Journal of the American Medical Association* 270:600–605.

Tousignant, M. and B.L. Mishara. 1981. Suicide and culture: a review of the literature (1979-1980). (Overview). *Transcultural Psychiatric Research Review* 18(1):5–32.

Tout, K. 1989. *Ageing in Developing Countries*. Oxford: Oxford University Press.

Traskman-Bendz, L., Alling, C., Alsen, M., Regnell, G., Simonsson, P., and R. Ohman. 1993. The role of monoamines in suicidal behavior. *Acta Psychiatrica Scandinavica* 371(supplement):45–47.

Tukol, T.K. 1976. *Sallekhanā Is Not Suicide*. Ahmedabad: LD Institute of Indology.

Turton, R.W., Straker, G., and F. Moosa. 1991. Experiences of violence in the lives of township youths in "unrest" and "normal" conditions. *South African Journal of Psychology* 21:77–84.

Twumasi, P.A. 1987. Ageing and problems of old age in Africa: a study in social change and a model for its solutions. In *Society, Stress and Disease,* edited by L. Levi, Volume 5, pp. 85–93. New York: Oxford University Press.

Tyler, P. 1993. China lacks water to meet its mighty thirst. *The New York Times*, November 7, I1.

Uemura, K. and Z. Piza. 1988. Trends in cardiovascular disease mortality in industrialized countries since 1950. *World Health Statistical Quarterly* 41:155–178.

Ullrich, H.E. 1987. A study of change and depression among Havik Brahmin women in a South Indian village. *Culture, Medicine and Psychiatry* 11:261–287.

———. 1988. Widows in a South India society: depression as an appropriate response to cultural factors. *Sex Roles* 19:169–188.

United Nations. 1948. Universal Declaration of Human Rights. New York, United Nations, General Assembly, December 10.

———. 1991a. *International Cooperation for the Eradication of Poverty in Developing Countries: Report by the Secretary-General*. Fifty-Sixth session, Agenda item 80.

———. 1991b. *The Protection of Persons with Mental Illness and the Improvement of Mental Health Care*. Report of the Third Committee, Resolution UN/GA/46/119. New York, United Nations, December 17, 1991.

———. 1991c. *The World Ageing Situation*. United Nations Office at Vienna, Centre for Social Development and Humanitarian Affairs.

———. 1991d. *The World's Women 1970–1990: Trends and Statistics*. New York: United Nations.

UNHCR. 1993. *The State of the World's Refugees 1993: The Challenge of Protection*. New York: Penguin.

UNICEF. 1989. *The Invisible Adjustment: Poor Women and the Economic Crisis*. Santiago: Regional Office for the Americas and the Caribbean.

———. 1993. *The State of the World's Children, 1993*. New York: Oxford University Press.

United States Department of Health and Human Services. 1994. *Preventing Tobacco Use among Young People: A Report of the Surgeon General*. Washington, DC: U.S. Government Printing Office.

Valdez, S. and E. Shrader-Cox. 1991. Estudio Sobre la Incidencia de Violencia Domestica en una Microregion de Ciudad Nezahualcoyotl, 1989. Mexico City: Centro de Investigacion y Lucha Contra la Violencia Domestica.

Van der Kwaak, A., Van den Engel, M., Richters, A., et al. 1991. Women and health. *Vena Journal* 3:2–33.

Van Winkle, N.W. and P.A. May. 1993. An update on American Indian suicide in New Mexico, 1980–1987. *Human Organization* 52(3):304–315.

Verghese, A., Beig, A., Senseman, S.A., Rao, S.S., and V. Benjamin. 1973. A social and psychiatric study of a representative group of families in Vellore town. *Indian Journal of Medical Research* 61:609–620.

Vesti, P., Somnier, F., and M. Kastrup. 1992. *Psychotherapy with Torture Survivors: A Report of Practice from the Rehabilitation and Research Centre for Torture Victims, Copenhagen, Denmark*. Copenhagen: International Rehabilitation Council for Torture Victims.

Vichai, P. et al. 1978. *Evaluation of Treatment Outcome at the Buddhosh Treatment Center*. Tam Krabor, Bangkok: Institute for Health Research, Chiklongkorn University.

von Korff, M., Katon, W., and E. Lin. 1990. Psychological distress, physical symptoms, utilization and the cost-offset effect. In *Psychological Disorders in General Medical Settings*, edited by N. Sartorius, D. Goldberg, G. deGirolamo, et al., pp. 159–169. Toronto: Hogreff and Huber Publishers.

Wagenaar, A.C., Streff, F.M., and R.H. Schultz. 1990. Effects of the 65 MPH speed limit on injury morbidity and mortality. *Accident Analysis and Prevention* 22:571–585.

Waldram, J. 1993. Aboriginal spirituality: symbolic healing in Canadian prisons. *Culture, Medicine and Psychiatry* 17:345–362.

Ware, N. 1993. Structural adjustment and women's mental health. Working paper, International Mental and Behavioral Health Project, Center for the Study of Culture and Medicine, Harvard Medical School, Boston, Massachusetts.

Warner, R. 1985. *Recovery from Schizophrenia: Psychiatry and Political Economy*. London: Routledge and Kegan Paul.

Warren, K.S. 1991. Helminths and health of school-aged children. *The Lancet* 338:686–687.

Waxler, N.E. 1977. Is outcome for schizophenia better in non-industrial societies? The case of Sri Lanka. *Journal of Nervous and Mental Disease* 167:144–158.

Webb, S.D. 1984. Rural-urban differences in mental health. *Mental Health and the Environment*, edited by H. Freeman, pp. 226–249. London: Livingstone-Churchill.

Weile, B., Wingender, L.B., Bach-Mortensen, N., and P. Busch. 1990. Behavioral problems in children of torture victims: a sequel to cultural maladaptation or to parental torture? *Journal of Developmental and Behavioral Pediatrics* 11:79–80.

Weiss, M.G. 1985. The interrelationship of tropical disease and mental disorder: conceptual framework and literature review (part I—malaria). *Culture, Medicine and Psychiatry* 9:121–200.

Wells, K.B., Stewart, A., Hays, R.D., et al. 1989. The functioning and well-being of depressed patients. *Journal of the American Medical Association* 262:914–919.

Wen, H. and S. Cheung. 1973. Treatment of drug addiction by acupuncture and electrical stimulation. *American Journal of Acupuncture* 1:71–75.

Werler, M.M., Shapiro, S., and A.A. Mitchell. 1993. Periconceptional folic acid exposure and risk of occurrent nural tube defects. *Journal of the American Medical Association* 269:1257–1261.

West, K.P., Pokhrel, R.P., Katz, J., et al. 1991. Efficacy of vitamin A in reducing preschool child mortality in Nepal. *The Lancet* 338:67–71.

Westermeyer, J. 1973. Folk treatment of opium addiction in Laos. *British Journal of Addiction* 68:345–349.

———. 1979. Medical and non-medical treatment of narcotic addicts: a comparative study from Asia. *Journal of Nervous and Mental Disorders* 167:205–211.

———. 1991. Psychiatric services for refugee children. In *Refugee Children: Theory, Research, and Services*, edited by F.L. Ahearn and J.L. Athey, pp. 127–162. Baltimore, MD: The Johns Hopkins University Press.

Westermeyer, J., Vang, T.F., and J. Neider. 1983. Refugees who do and do not seek psychiatric care: an analysis of premigratory and postmigratory characteristics. *The Journal of Nervous and Mental Disease* 171:86–91.

Whyte, S. 1991. Medicines and self-help: the privatization of health care in eastern Uganda. In *Changing Uganda: The Dilemmas of Structural Adjustment and Revolutionary Change,* edited by H.B. Hansen and M. Twaddle, pp. 130–148. London: James Curry.

Wig, N. 1993. Mental health in Kerala. Working paper, International Mental and Behavioral Health Project, Center for the Study of Culture and Medicine, Harvard Medical School, Boston, Massachusetts.

Wijesinghe, C.P., Dissanayake, S.A.W. and P.V.L.N. Dassanayake. 1978. Survey of psychiatric morbidity in a semi-urban population in Sri Lanka. *Acta Psychiatrica Scandinavica* 58:413–441.

Willigen, L. 1992. Organization of care and rehabilitation services for victims of torture and other forms of organized violence: a review of current issues. In *Torture and Its Consequences: Current Treatment Approaches*, edited by M. Basoglu, pp. 277–298. Cambridge: Cambridge University Press.

Wilson, K.B. 1992a. *Internally Displaced Refugees and Returnees From and In Mozambique*. SIDA Studies on Emergencies and Disaster Relief, Report No. 1. Oxford: Refugee Studies Programme.

———. 1992b. Cults of violence and counter-violence in Mozambique. *Journal of Southern African Studies* 18:527–582.

Wolcott, H.P. 1974. *The African Beer Gardens of Bulawayo*. New Brunswick, N.J.: Rutgers Center of Alcohol Studies.

Wolf, B. 1987. Low-income mothers at risk: the psychological effects of poverty-related stress. Unpublished dissertation, Harvard Graduate School of Education, Cambridge, Massachusetts.

Wolff, P.H., Bereket, T., Habtab, E., and T. Aradom. Forthcoming. The orphans of Eritrea: a comparison study. *Journal of Child Psychology and Psychiatry*.

World Bank. 1992. *World Development Report 1992: Development and the Environment*. New York: Oxford University Press.

———. 1993a. *World Development Report 1993: Investing in Health*. New York: Oxford University Press.

———. 1993b. *Global Economic Prospects and the Developing Countries*. Washington, DC: World Bank.

World Health Organization. 1951. *Expert Committee on Mental Health, Report on the Second Session 1951*. Technical Report Series #31. Geneva: World Health Organization Monograph.

———. 1979. *Schizophrenia: An International Follow-Up Study*. Geneva: World Health Organization.

———. 1984. *Mental Health Care in Developing Countries*. Technical Report Series, 698. Geneva: World Health Organization.

———. 1987. *Children at Work: Special Health Risks*. Geneva: World Health Organization.

———. 1990. *Preventing Alcohol Problems: Local Prevention Activity and the Compilation of "Guides to Local Action."* Geneva: World Health Organization (WHO/MNH/ADA/90.4).

———. 1991a. *Statistics Annual, 1991 [for 1989]*. Geneva: World Health Organization.

———. 1991b. *Action to Reduce Health Problems Associated with Alcohol and Drug Abuse: A Framework for National Programme Development*. Geneva: World Health Organization (WHO/MNH/ADA/91.1).

———. 1992a. *Women and Substance Abuse, 1992 Interim Report*. Geneva: WHO, Programme on Substance Abuse.

———. 1992b. *Street Children Project*. Geneva: World Health Organization.

———. 1993a. *Guidelines for the Primary Prevention of Mental Retardation*. Geneva: World Health Organization, WHO/MNH/MND/93.22.

———. 1993b. *Guidelines for Primary Prevention: 3—Epilepsy*. Geneva: World Health Organization, WHO/MNH/MND/93.23.

———. 1993c. *The ICD-10 Classification of Mental and Behavioral Disorders*. Geneva: World Health Organization.

————. 1993d. World health assembly calls for the elimination of harmful traditional practices. Press release: May 12. Geneva: World Health Organization.

————. 1993e. *Guidelines for the Primary Prevention of Mental, Neurological and Psychosocial Disorders. 1. Principles for Primary Prevention.* Geneva: WHO, Division of Mental Health (WHO/MHN/MND/93.21).

World Health Organization, Programme on Substance Abuse. 1992. *ATLAS Report.* Geneva: World Health Organization.

————. 1993a. *Report on the 1992 Programme Activities.* Geneva: World Health Organization (WHO/PSA/93.1).

————. Abuse. 1993b. *Drug Use and Sport: Current Issues and Implications for Public Health.* Geneva: World Health Organization (WHO/PSA/93.3).

World Health Organization/United Nations High Commissioner for Refugees. 1992. *Refugee Mental Health: Draft Manual for Field Testing.* Geneva: WHO, Division of Mental Health/UNHCR.

World Notes. A night of madness. *Time* magazine, August 12, 1993, p. 43.

WuDunn, S. 1993. Births punished by fine, beating or ruined home: crackdown by family planning authorities in China. *The New York Times*, April 25, 6N, 12L.

Xiong, W. Phillips, M.R., Hu, X. Wang, R.W., et al. 1994. Family-based intervention for schizophrenic patients in China: a randomized controlled trial. *British Journal of Psychiatry.* 165:239–247.

Yeh, E.K. et al. 1987. Social changes and prevalence of specific mental disorders. *Chinese Journal of Mental Health* 3:31–42.

Yip, R. and T.W. Sharp. 1993. Acute malnutrition and childhood mortality related to diarrhea: lessons from the 1991 Kurdish refugee crisis. *Journal of the American Medical Association* 270:587–590.

Yu, E.S.H., Liu, W.T., Levy, P., Zhang, M., Katzman, R., Lung, C., Wong, S., Wang, Z., and Q.G. Ya. 1989. Cognitive impairment among elderly adults in Shanghai, China. *Journal of Gerontology and Social Sciences* 44:597–106.

APPENDIX 1

International Advisory Board

Name and Affiliation	*Area of Expertise*
Naomar Almeida–Filho, M.D., Ph.D Universidade Federal da Bahia Canela, Salvador, Bahia, Brazil	Mental Health in Latin America
Prof. Tolani Asuni, M.D. Private Clinician Lagos, Nigeria, Africa	Mental health in Nigeria
Prof. Taha Baasher, FRCPsych Department of Psychiatry Faculty of Medicine University of Khartoum Khartoum, the Sudan	Mental health in Sudan
Prof. Eugene B. Brody, M.D. Secretary General World Federation for Mental Health The Sheppard and Enoch Pratt Hospital Baltimore, Maryland USA	World mental health
Prof. Ly-yun Chang, Ph.D. Institute of Ethnology Academia Sinica Nankang, Taipei, Taiwan	Mental health policy in Taiwan's political economy
Prof. Jorge Alberto Costa e Silva, M.D. Director Division of Mental Health World Health Organization Geneva, Switzerland	Mental health in Brazil and globally
Prof. Veena Das, Ph.D. Head Department of Sociology Delhi School of Economics University of Delhi New Delhi, India	Sociology of health and suffering

Name and Affiliation	***Area of Expertise***
Prof. Almaz Eshete, Ph.D. Dept. of Educational Psychology Addis Ababa University Addis Ababa, Ethiopia	Mental health in Ethiopia
Prof. Julio Frenk M.D. Director del Proyecto "Economia e Salud in Mexico" Fundacion Mexicana Para la Salud Martir, Tlalpan 14560 Mexico, D.F. Mexico	Health and health care in Mexico and low-income societies
Rodrigo Guerrero Velasco, M.D. Mayor of Cali School of Medicine Universidad del Valle Cali, Colombia	Health aspects of urban life in South America
Prof. Françoises Heritier, Ph.D. College de France 11 Place Marcelin-Berthelot 75231 Paris, France	Anthropological perspectives on AIDS and other health problems in Africa and France
Violet Kimani, Ph.D. Department of Community Health College of Health Sciences University of Nairobi Nairobi, Kenya	Mental health issues in Kenya, including status of women
Thomas Lambo, M.D. Lambo Foundation for the Advancement of Biomedical and Bio-Behavioral Sciences Lagos, Nigeria	Mental health in Nigeria and globally
Carlos León, M.D. Director, WHO Centre for Research and Training in Mental Health Hospital Universitario del Valle Cali, Colombia	Epidemiology of mental health in South America; women's mental health in Latin America
Itzhak Levav, M.D. Regional Adviser in Mental Health Health Promotion Program Pan American Health Organization Washington, DC USA	International mental health
Shichuo Li, M.D. Deputy Director Department of Foreign Affairs Ministry of Public Health Beijing, China	Public health in China

Name and Affiliation	*Area of Expertise*
Prof. Tsung-yi Lin, M.D. Emeritus Department of Psychiatry University of British Columbia Honorary President World Mental Health Federation Vancouver, B.C.	International psychiatry, and mental health in Asia
Dr. Nafsiah Mboi Member of Parliament Kompleks A.D. No. G11 Jakarta, Indonesia	Women's mental health
Tsunetsugu Munakata, Ph.D. Assoc. Prof. of Health Sociology and Behavioral Health Tsukuba University Tsukuba, Japan	Global health and behavior
Jane Mutambirwa, Ph.D. Department of Psychiatry University of Zimbabwe Medical School Harare, Zimbabwe	Mental health in Africa
Prof. Paul Nkwi, Ph.D. President Association Pan Africaine de l'Anthropologie B.P. 1862 Yaounde, Cameroon, Africa	Anthropological approaches to health in Africa
Prof. B.O. Osuntokun, M.D. Department of Medicine University of Ibadan Ibadan, Nigeria	Neurological and neuropsychiatric conditions in sub-Saharan Africa
Mamphela Ramphele, M.D., Ph.D. Deputy Vice Chancellor University of Cape Town Cape Town, South Africa	Health and social change; violence
Prof. Sir Michael Rutter, M.D. Department of Child and Adolescent Psychiatry Institute of Psychiatry MRC Unit Denmark Hill, London, UK	Child psychiatry and child development
Norman Sartorius, M.D. President, World Psychiatric Association Former Director, Division of Mental Health World Health Organization Geneva, Switzerland	International mental health

Name and Affiliation	***Area of Expertise***
Shridhar Sharma, M.D. Deputy Director-General of Health Services New Delhi, India	Mental health and health care in India
Jaime Arroyo Sucre, M.D. Psiquiatra Clinica San Fernando Norte Panama City, Panama	Mental health in Panama
Sir Crispin Tickell Warden Green College at the Radcliffe Observatory Oxford, UK	International environmental problems and policies
Prof. Wen-Shing Tseng, M.D. Department of Psychiatry John A. Burns School of Medicine University of Hawaii at Manoa Honolulu, Hawaii	International psychiatry
Prof. Luzviminda B. Valencia, Ed.D. University of the Philippines System College of Social Sciences and Philosophy Department of Sociology, CSSP Quezon City 1101, Philippines	Mental health in the Philippines
Dr. Mariam K. Were, MBchB Representative to Ethiopia and Chief of Mission World Health Organization Addis Ababa, Ethiopia	Health in Africa
Narendra N. Wig, M.D. Consultant in Mental Health Panchkula, India	Mental health in Eastern Mediterranean and India

APPENDIX 2

Consultants

Name and Affiliation	*Area of Expertise*
Mohan Agashe, M.D. Professor and Head Department of Psychiatry BJ Medical College Pune, Maharashtra, India	Community psychiatry; mental health in India
Miguel Cherro Aguirre, M.D. Director Children and Adolescent Psychiatry Clinic Universidad de la Republica Montevideo, Uruguay	Child and adolescent mental health in Latin America
Prof. Ronald Angel, Ph.D. Department of Sociology University of Texas Austin, Texas USA	Refugee and migrant mental health
Roberta Apfel, M.D. Associate Clinical Professor Department of Psychiatry Harvard Medical School Boston, Massachusetts USA	Children and violence
Mario Argandona, M.D. Chief, Treatment and Care Unit Programme on Substance Abuse World Health Organization Geneva, Switzerland	Substance abuse
Kunihiko Asai, M.D. Regional Vice President World Federation of Mental Health Director, Asai Hospital Togane City, Japan	International mental health policy
Asif Aslam, M.P.H. Faculty of Health Sciences Aga Khan University Medical College Karachi, Pakistan	Substance abuse in Pakistan

Name and Affiliation	*Area of Expertise*
Ernaldi Bahar, Ph.D. Jalan Musi I Blok B14 Palembang, Indonesia	Mental health in Indonesia
Carlos Martin Beristain, M.D. Bedia-Bizkaia Basque Country, Spain	Mental health and political violence
Prof. Philippe Bourgois, Ph.D. Department of Anthropology San Francisco State University San Francisco, California USA	Social change and drug abuse in Central America
Jack Carr, Ph.D. Department of Psychiatry and Behavioral Sciences University of Washington Medical School Seattle, Washington USA	Mental health in Malaysia
Mark Connolly, MPH Consultant to UNICEF New York, NY USA	Street children in Latin America Africa, and Asia
Hanteng Dai, M.D. Shenzhen Municipal Bureau of Public Health Shenzhen City, China	Mental health in China
Prof. M.P. Deva, Head Department of Psychological Medicine Faculty of Medicine University of Malaya Kuala Lumpur, Malaysia	Mental health in Southeast Asia
Prof. William Dressler, Ph.D. College of Community Health Science Department of Behavioral and Community Medicine University of Alabama School of Medicine Tuscaloosa, Alabama USA	Relationship between social status, depression, psychophysiology, and social change
Prof. Felton Earls, M.D. Professor of Human Development and Behavior Professor of Child Psychiatry Harvard School of Public Health Harvard Medical School Boston, Massachusetts USA	Antecedents of violence; child development
Hans Emblad, M.D. Director, Programme on Substance Abuse World Health Organization Geneva, Switzerland	International substance abuse problems

Name and Affiliation	*Area of Expertise*
Prof. Sue Estroff, Ph.D. Medical Anthropology Department of Social Medicine University of North Carolina at Chapel Hill Chapel Hill, North Carolina USA	Research on schizophrenia
Prof. Ruthbeth Finerman, Ph.D. Department of Anthropology Memphis State University Memphis, Tennessee USA	Mental health of women in Latin America
Hugh Freeman, M.D. Editor Emeritus *British Journal of Psychiatry* London, UK	International environmental issues and mental health
Prof. Allan German, M.D. Department of Psychiatry University of Western Australia Perth, Australia	Mental illness and services in Africa
Pauline E. Ginsberg, Ph.D. Associate Professor of Psychology Division of Behavioral Studies Utica College of Syracuse University Syracuse, New York USA	Mental health services in Kenya
Prof. Mitzy Goheen, Ph.D. Department of Anthropology and Sociology Amherst College Amherst, Massachusetts USA	Women's mental health in West Africa
Prof. Peter Guarnacia, Ph.D. Department of Human Ecology Cook College Rutgers University New Brunswick, New Jersey USA	Hispanic mental health
E.A. Guinness, M.D. Adolescent Unit The Bethlem Royal Hospital London, UK	Mental health services in Africa
Robert Hahn, Ph.D. Epidemiologist Centers for Disease Control Atlanta, Georgia USA	Racial, ethnic and cultural indexes in epidemiology
Trudy Harpham, M.D. Professor of Urban Development and Policy School of Urban Policy South Bank University London, UK	Urbanization and mental health; mental health problems in Brazil

Name and Affiliation	*Area of Expertise*
B.E. Harrell-Bond, Ph.D. Director, Refugees Studies Programme University of Oxford Oxford, UK	Refugee health
Prof. Gail Henderson, Ph.D. Department of Social Medicine University of North Carolina at Chapel Hill Chapel Hill, North Carolina USA	Health and social change in China
Francis X. Hezel, S.J. Micronesian Seminar Pohnpei, Federated States of Micronesia	Suicide in Micronesia
Nick Higginbotham, Ph.D. Center for Clinical Epidemiology and Biostatistics Royal Newcastle Hospital New South Wales, Australia	International mental health policy
Lawrence Hipsham, M.D. Assistant Clinical Professor in Psychiatry Yale Medical School New Haven, Connecticut USA	Mental health in Zimbabwe
Mario Hollweg, M.D. Director, Mental Health Center Santa Cruz de la Sierra, Bolivia	Mental retardation in Bolivia; mental health problems in Latin America
Prof. Charlotte Ikels, Ph.D. University Center on Aging and Health Case Western Reserve University Cleveland, Ohio USA	Senile disorders and disability in China
Sushrut Jadhav, M.D. Department of Academic Psychiatry Middlesex Hospital Editor, *British Medical Anthropology* *Review* London, UK	Mental health aspects of migration and cultural adaptation in India
Prof. Janis Jenkins, Ph.D. Department of Anthropology Case Western Reserve University Cleveland, Ohio USA	Mental health of refugees from Central America
Mercedes Juarez, M.D. Primary Health Care Unit Royal Dutch Tropical Institute Amsterdam, The Netherlands	Social change and mental health; mental health of women in developing countries

Name and Affiliation	*Area of Expertise*
Prof. Keh-Ming Lin, M.D., M.P.H. Director of Research Center for the Study of Ethnicity and Psychobiology UCLA Medical Center Torrance, California USA	International psychiatric research
Ravindra Khare, Ph.D. Department of Anthropology University of Virginia Charlottesville, Virginia 22903	Violence, health, and society
Alexander H. Leighton, M.D. Professor of Psychiatry Emeritus Dalhousie University Halifax, Nova Scotia	Epidemiology of mental illness
Charles Leslie, Ph.D. Professor of Anthropology, Emeritus Center for Science and Culture University of Delaware Newark, Delaware USA	Health and society in India and internationally
Robert LeVine, Ph.D. Roy Edward Larson Professor of Education and Human Development Professor of Anthropology Harvard Graduate School of Education Cambridge, Massachusetts USA	Culture and child development in Africa, Mexico, and South Asia
M. Brinton Lykes, Ph.D. School of Education Boston College Chestnut Hill, Massachusetts USA	Children and political violence

Margaret Lock, Ph.D.
Professor, Department of Social Studies
  of Medicine and Department of
  Anthropology
McGill University
Montreal, Canada
	Women's health and mental health

Prof. Setha Low, Ph.D.
Ph.D. Program in Psychology:
  Environmental Psychology
The Graduate School and
  University Center of
  The City University of New York
New York, NY USA
	Women's mental health in Latin
	America

Name and Affiliation	*Area of Expertise*
Prof. David Paul Lumsden, Ph.D. Department of Anthropology York University Toronto, Ontario Canada	International mental health policy
Prof. Carol MacCormack, Ph.D. Department of Anthropology Bryn Mawr College Bryn Mawr, Pennsylvania USA	Health problems associated with chronic and infectious disease in Africa
Roger Makanjuola, M.D., Ph.D. Professor of Psychiatry and Chief Medical Director University Teaching Hospital Obafemi Awolowo University Oshun State, Nigeria, Africa	Mental health in Nigeria
Masuma Mamdani, Ph.D. London School of Hygiene and Tropical Medicine Keppel Street London, UK	Reproductive health in low-income countries
Kitikorn Meesapya Institute of Mental Health Nonthaburi, Thailand	Mental health in Thailand
Juan Mezzich, M.D., Ph.D. Professor of Psychiatry and Epidemiology University of Pittsburgh Chairperson, Task Force on Culture and DSM-IV Pittsburgh, Pennsylvania USA	International mental health; culture and psychiatric classification
Neva Milicic Pontificia Universidad Catolica de Chile Santiago, Chile	Women's mental health
Darci Neves dos Santos, M.D. Institute of Psychiatry London, UK	Schizophrenia in Brazil
Kayode Ogunremi, M.D. Professor of Psychiatry University of Ilorin Kwara State, Nigeria, Africa	Mental illness in Nigeria
Prof. Michael Olatawura, M.D. University College Hospital Department of Psychiatry Ibadan, Nigeria, Africa	Mental illness in Nigeria

Name and Affiliation	*Area of Expertise*

Terry O'Nell, Ph.D.
National Center for American
   Indian and Alaska Native
   Mental Health Resource
Denver, Colorado USA
	Mental health consequences of
	dislocation, depression, and suicide
	among ethnic minorities

Shubhangi R. Parkar, M.D. Psychiatrist Department of Psychiatry K.E.M. Hospital Bombay, India	Suicide in India
Kok Lee Peng, M.D. Department of Psychological Medicine Faculty of Medicine National University of Singapore Singapore	Mental health in Singapore
Asma Fozia Qureshi, M.D. Associate Professor Department of Community Health Sciences Aga Khan University Medical College Karachi, Pakistan	Mental health and women's well- being in Pakistan
R. Raguram, M.D. Associate Professor of Psychiatry National Institute of Mental Health and Neuro Sciences Bangalore, India	Clinical aspects of mental health care in India
A. Venkoba Rao, M.D. Emeritus Professor of Psychiatry Head, Institute of Psychiatry Madurai Medical College Madurai, India	Suicide and depression in India
David Reynolds, Ph.D. Medical Anthropologist Constructive Living Coos Bay, Oregon USA	Suicide in psychiatric care facilities
Richard Rothenberg, M.D. Assistant Director for Science National Center for Chronic Disease Prevention and Health Promotion Centers for Disease Control Atlanta, Georgia USA	Behavioral risk factors for chronic disease in the developing world
Donald H. Rubinstein, M.D. Micronesian Area Research Center University of Guam UOG Station Mangilao, Guam	Suicide in Micronesia

Name and Affiliation	*Area of Expertise*
Prof. Sermsri Santhat, Ph.D. Faculty of Social Sciences and Humanities Mahidol University Bangkok, Thailand	Mental health problems and policy in Thailand
Bennett Simon, M.D. Associate Clinical Professor Department of Psychiatry Harvard Medical School Boston, Massachusetts USA	Children and violence
Jonathan Sugar, M.D. Assistant Professor of Child Psychiatry University of Michigan Medical Center Ann Arbor, Michigan USA	Mental health of children
Eng-Seong Tan, M.D. Professorial Associate Department of Psychiatry St. Vincents Hospital Victoria Parade Victoria, Australia	Mental health services in the Western Pacific region
Bonnie Taub, Ph.D. Project Director Adolescent Stress and Coping Study UCLA School of Public Health Los Angeles, California USA	Women's mental health in Central and South America
Ming Tsuang, M.D., Ph.D. Professor of Psychiatry Harvard School of Public Health and Harvard Medical School Boston, Massachusetts USA	International epidemiology of mental disorders
Prof. Anthony Ugalde, Ph.D. Department of Sociology University of Texas Austin, Texas USA	Economic and political forces affecting mental health in developing countries
Helen Ulrich, M.D., Ph.D. Assistant Professor Department of Psychiatry and Neurology Tulane University Medical School New Orleans, Louisiana USA	Depression among women in India
Nancy Warwick, M.A. Department of Anthropology UCLA Los Angeles, California USA	Domestic violence

Name and Affiliation	*Area of Expertise*
Unni Wikan, Ph.D. Professor of Anthropology University of Oslo Oslo, Norway	Women's mental health in Bali, Egypt, and Bhutan
James Wilce, M.A. Department of Anthropology UCLA Los Angeles, California USA	Mental health and women's well-being in Bangladesh
Lawrence Wilson, M.D. Associate Professor Department of Psychiatry and Behavioral Sciences University of Washington Seattle, Washington USA	Mental health services in Micronesia
Sir Gordon Wolstenholme, M.D. Chairman, Board of Governors Action in International Medicine London, UK	International health
A. Michael Wylie, Ph.D. Associate Professor Department of Psychology University of Guam UOG Station Mangilao, Guam	Chronic mental illness in Micronesia

Allan Young, Ph.D.
Professor, Department of Social Studies
   of Medicine and Department of
   Anthropology
McGill University
Montreal, Canada
	Culture and post-traumatic stress disorder

APPENDIX 3

Additional Readers

Robert Bates, Ph.D.
Professor of Government
Harvard University
Fellow, Harvard Institute of
    International Development
Cambridge, Massachusetts USA

Gilles Bibeau, Ph.D.
Professor of Anthropology
Department of Anthropology
Université de Montréal
Montreal, Canada

Herbert P. Ginsburg, Ph.D.
Professor of Psychology
Teachers' College
Columbia University
New York, NY USA

Margaret Levi, Ph.D.
Professor of Political Science
University of Washington
Seattle, Washington USA

Beverly Long
President-Elect
World Federation of Mental Health
Atlanta, Georgia USA

David Mechanic, Ph.D.
University Professor and Director
Institute of Health, Health Care
    and Aging
Rutgers University
New Brunswick, New Jersey USA

Samuel Preston, Ph.D.
Professor of Sociology and Demography
Director, Center for Population Studies
University of Pennsylvania
Philadelphia, Pennsylvania USA

Robert Scott, Ph.D.
Associate Director
Center for Advanced Study in the
    Behavioral Sciences
Stanford, California USA

Kenneth Shine, M.D.
President, Institute of Medicine
National Academy of Sciences
Washington, DC USA

Working Papers

Alastair Ager, Department of Management and Social Sciences, Queen Margaret College, Edinburgh, Scotland:
Mental Health Issues in Refugee Populations: A Review

Naomar de Almeida-Filho, Departmento de Medicina Preventiva, Universidade Federal da Bahia, Brazil:
Becoming Modern Twenty Years Later: Social Change and Mental Health in Latin America

James Anthony, Department of Mental Hygiene, The Johns Hopkins University School of Hygiene and Public Health, Baltimore, MD:
Drug Dependence Databases

Thomas Babor, Alcohol Research Center, The University of Connecticut Health Center, Storrs, CT:
Alcohol Use in Developing Countries

Anne Becker, Department of Psychiatry, Massachusetts General Hospital, Boston, MA:
Suicide in the South Pacific

J.M. Bertolote, Division of Mental Health, World Health Organization, Geneva, Switzerland:
Trends in the Development of Mental Health Services

Gilles Bibeau and Ellen Corin, Department of Anthropology, Université dé Montréal, Departments of Psychiatry and Anthropology, McGill University, Montreal, Canada:
Organizational Models, Local Knowledge and Socioeconomic Constraints in the Building of Mental Health Policies in African Countries

Jeremy Broadhead and Melanie Abas, The Maudsley Hospital, London:
The Presentation and Management of Mental Illness at the Primary Care Level in Developing Countries

Ly-yun Chang, Institute of Ethnology, Academia Sinica, Taiwan:
The Mental Health Delivery System in Taiwan

Robert Desjarlais, Department of Social Medicine, Harvard Medical School, Boston, MA:
Political Violence and Mental Health

Robert Dorwart, Division of Health Policy Research and Education, Harvard University, Cambridge, MA:
Balancing International Mental Health Systems

Kaja Finkler, Department of Anthropology, University of North Carolina, Chapel Hill:
Gender, Violence and Sickness in Mexico

Ruth Fischbach and Elizabeth Donnelly, Department of Social Medicine, Harvard Medical School, Boston, MA:
Domestic Violence Against Women; A Contemporary Issue in International Health

Dwight Heath, Department of Anthropology, Brown University, Providence, RI:
Beverage Alcohol in Developing Regions: An Anthropological and Epidemiological Perspective on Public Health Issues

Charlotte Ikels, Department of Anthropology, Case Western Reserve University, Cleveland, OH:
The Experience of Dementia in China

Assen Jablensky, University Department of Psychiatry and Behavioral Science, Royal Perth Hospital, Perth, Australia:
Schizophrenia in the Third World: An Epidemiological Perspective

Sylvia Kaaya and Melkizedeck Leshabari, Muhimbili University College of Health Sciences, Dar es Salaam, Tanzania:
Depressive Illness and Primary Health Care in Developing African Countries, with Special Reference to Tanzania

Richard Laing, Management Sciences for Health, Boston, MA:
Water Use Behavior and Consequences for Health

Sarah LeVine, Graduate School of Education, Harvard University, Cambridge, MA:
Women and Mental Health in the Developing World: East Africa

Christine Liddell, Department of Psychology, University of Ulster at Coleraine, Ireland:
Diversities of Childhood in Developing Countries

Roland Littlewood, Department of Anthropology and Psychiatry, University College, London U.K.
Caribbean Immigrants to Britain: Migrants and their British-born Families

Anne Lovell, University of Toulouse le Mirail, France:
Mental and Behavioral Health Issues and the Immigration of West African Women to France

David Paul Lumsden, Norman Bethune College, York University, Canada:
Dam and Resettlement Projects and Mental Health

Anthony Marsella, Department of Psychology, University of Hawaii at Manoa:
Urbanization and Mental Disorders: An Overview of Issues, Theories and Research

Hernan Montenegro, Department of Psychiatry, Catholic University, Santiago, Chile:
Alcohol Abuse in Chile

Michael Nunley, Cecil G. Sheps Center for Mental Health Services Research, University of North Carolina at Chapel Hill:
Families in Indian Psychiatry

K.N. Panicker, Vector Control Research Centre, Pondicherry, India:
Economic and Psycho-social Consequences of Filariasis

Duncan Pedersen, Departmento Medicine Preventiva, Universidad Federal da Bahia, Brazil:
Mental Health amongst the Indigenous Peoples of Latin America

Michael Phillips, Research Center of Clinical Epidemiology, Shashi Psychiatry Hospital, Hubei, China:
The Influence of Social, Political and Economic Factors on the Evolution of Mental Health Services in China

Mamphela Ramphele, Deputy Vice-Chancellor, University of Cape Town, South Africa:
Adolescents and Violence in South Africa

Shridhar Sharma, Deputy Director-General of Health Services, New Delhi, India:
The History and Development of Mental Health Services in India

Stanley Tambiah, Department of Anthropology, Harvard University, Cambridge, MA:
Friends, Neighbors, Enemies, Strangers: Aggressor and Victim in Civilian Ethnic Riots

Norma Ware, Department of Social Medicine, Harvard Medical School, Boston, MA:
Structural Adjustment and Women's Mental Health

Mitchell Weiss, Culture, Community, and Health Studies, University of Toronto, Canada;
and Shubhangi Parkar, Department of Psychiatry, K.E.M. Hospital, Bombay, India:
Suicide and Social Change in Developing Countries

Narendra Wig, Mental Health Consultant, World Health Organization, New Delhi, India:
Mental Health in Kerala: A Study of the Impact of Social Change on Mental and Behavioral Health in a Society

APPENDIX 5

Brief Reports

Pablo Farias, Centro de Investigaciones Ecologicas del Sureste, Chiapas, Mexico: "The Impact of Refugee Women's Social Status on Psychosocial Health, Child Mortality and Malnutrition"

Paul Farmer, Department of Social Medicine, Harvard Medical School, and Port au Prince, Haiti: "Poverty and the Risk of Tuberculosis in Haiti"

Lindsey French, Department of Anthropology, Harvard University: "Mental Health among Displaced Khmer on the Thai-Cambodian Border"

Charlotte Ikels, Department of Anthropology, Case Western Reserve University: "The Impact of Population Aging in China"

Gad P. Kilonzo, Department of Psychiatry, Muhimbili University College of Health Sciences: "The Development of Mental Health Services in Tanzania"

Violet Kimani, Department of Community Health College of Health Sciences, University of Nairobi: "A Day in the Life of a Kenyan Woman"

Elizabeth Miller, Department of Anthropology, Harvard University: "The Trafficking of Women in Asia"

Paul Nkwi, Pan African Association of Anthropologists, Yaounde, Cameroon: "Ethnographic Assessment of Mental Health in Cameroon: The Social, Economic and Cultural Issues"

Anna Ortiz, Department of Anthropology, Harvard University: "Psychiatric Care in the Dominican Republic"

Michael Whyte and Susan Whyte, Institute of Anthropology, University of Copenhagen: "Drinking and Drunkenness—Reflections from East Africa"

Unni Wikan, Department of Anthropology, University of Oslo: "Women and Poverty in Egypt"

Jim Wilce, Department of Anthropology, University of California, Los Angeles: "The Burden of Women in Bangladesh"

Peter Wolff, Department of Psychiatry, Harvard Medical School, Boston, MA; and Tesfay Aradom, Roxbury Community College, Department of Early Childhood Education, Boston, MA: "The Care of Orphans in the Third World: An Eritrean Case Study"

APPENDIX 6

Directory of Mental Health Agencies

ASIA

Indian Council of Medical Research
Government Rajaji Hospital and
Madurai Medical College
Madurai-625 020, India

Indian Psychiatric Society
Krishna Niwas, 3rd Floor
Junction Chani Road and Queens Road
Bombay 4, India

Institute of Mental Health
Bejing Medical University
Hawyuan beilu,
Beijing 100083, China

Japan Association for Mental Health
Neuropsychiatric Research Institute
#162 91 Bentencho
Shinjuku-Ku Tokyo, Japan

Malaysian MHA
No 42 Jalan Masjid, 3/69
46200 Petaling Jaya, Malaysia

Mental Health Association of Hong Kong
Duke of Windsor Social Service Building
Room 92 15 Hennesy Road
Hong Kong

Mental Health Association in Taiwan
Department of Psychology
National Taiwan University
Taipei, Taiwan

Mental Health Association of Thailand
356/10 Sri Ayudhaya Road
Bangkok 10400, Thailand

National Institute of Mental Health and
  Neurosciences
B.P. 2900, Bangalore 560029
Bangalore, India

Philippine Mental Health Association
P.O. Box 40 18 East Ave.
Quezon City 1100, Philippines

Shanghai Mental Health Centre
600 Wan Ping Nan Road
Shanghai, China

Singapore Association for Mental Health
APT Block 69
Lorong 4 Toa Payoh
#01-365 1231
Singapore

SANJIVINI
Society for Mental Health
A-6 Satsang Vihar Marg
Institutional Area
New Delhi, India 110 067

AUSTRALIA

Australian National Association for Mental
  Health
Tweedie Place, Richmond
Victoria 3121, Australia

Mental Health Foundation of New Zealand
POB 37-438 Parnell
Auckland 1, New Zealand

World Federation
  of Psychiatric Users
POB 46-018
Herne Bay
Auckland, New Zealand

367

CANADA

Canadian International Development
  Association (CIDA)
200 Promendie du Portage
Hull, Quebec, Canada K1A 0G4

Canadian Mental Health Association
2160 Yonge Street, 3rd Floor
Toronto, Ontario, Canada M4S 2Z3

Canadian Psychiatric Association
294 Albert St., Suite 204
Ottawa, Ontario, Canada KIP 6E6

International Council on Women's
  Health Issues
RR 2 Stewiacke Col County
Nova Scotia, Canada BON 2J0

International Development Research
  Council
Box 8500
Ottawa, Canada K1G 3H9

International Organization of
  Psychophysiology
P.O. Box 1614, Station H
Montreal, Quebec, Canada H3G 2N5

World Schizophrenia Fellowship
238 Davenport Road, Ste. 118
Toronto, Ontario, Canada M5R 1J6

EUROPE

Asociación de Enfermeria
En Salud Mental
Carretera De Chinchon
28350 Ciiempozuelos, Madrid, Spain

Center for Mental Health
58 Notara Street
Athens 106 83, Greece

Central Institute of Mental Health
P.O. Box 5970, D-W-6800 Mannheim-1
Mannheim, Germany

Committee of Control on Narcotic
  Drugs
Ministry of Health of the Russian
  Federation
Rylyleyva d.20
Moscow 121879, Russia

Danish Society for Mental Health
Bremerholm 6, 4 1065
Copenhagen K, Denmark

Foundation for European
  Cooperation in Psychological
  Reform and Cultural
  Integration of Mental Health
P.O. Box 88 6200 AB
Maastricht, The Netherlands

High Commissioner for Refugees
P.O. Box 2500 CH-1211
Geneva 2 Depot, Switzerland

Mental Barnehjelp
Arbeinsgate 1
0253 Oslo 2, Norway

National Institute of Health and Medical
  Research
Centre Collaboraeur de l'OMS pour la
  Recherche et la Formation en Santé
  Mental
INSERM Centre Paul Broca
2ter Rue d'Alésia 75014
Paris, France

NED Centre for Mental Health
Stichting Nederlands Centrum
P.O. Box 5103
Utrecht 3502 JC, The Netherlands

Portuguese Association for Mental
  Health
Rua Joao Rodrigues
Cabrilho, 108 Apartado 1504
P-4108 Porto Codex, Portugal

Prague Psychiatric Centre
Ustavni 91, 18103 Praha
Czech Republic, Prague

Rights and Humanity
27 ch des Cretes de Pregny
1218 Grand Saconnex, Switzerland

Societá Italiana di Riabilitazione
Psicosociale
Via Adva 6
37121 Verona, Italy

EUROPE (*continued*)

Hungarian Psychiatric Association
Voroshadsereg u. 116, P.O. Box 1
H-1281 Budapest, Hungary

Icelandic Mental Health Association
Gedverndarfelag Islands
10 Hatun
Reykjavik 105, Iceland

International Association for Suicide
Prevention
Institut for Medical Psychologie
Severingasse 9 A-1090
Vienna, Austria

International Federation of
Psychoanalytic Societies
Lansitie 9 SF-02160 ESP00
Finland

International Union of Psychological
Science
University of Hamburg
Von-Melle-Park 11
D-20146, Hamburg, Germany

Joint Commission on International
Aspects of Mental Retardation
248 Avenue Louise, BTE17
1050 Brussels, Belgium

L'Association Nationale des C.M.P.P.
Rue Gaston Michineau Petit Par
97100 Basse Terre
Guadeloupe, France

Swedish National Association
for Mental Health
Box 45246
Stockholm s-104 30, Sweden

Swiss Foundation Pro Mente Sana
Freiestrasse 26
CH-8570 Weinfelden, Switzerland

United Nations International Drug
Control Programme (VIENNA)
International Center
P.O. Box 500 A-1400
Vienna, Austria

World Association of Psychosocial
Rehabilitation
"Mario Negi" Institute of Pharmacological
Research
Via Enitrea 62, 20157
Milan, Italy

World Federation for Mental Health
WHO Residence Cologny Park
Plateau de Froutenex 9C
1208 Geneva, Switzerland

World Health Organization
Mental Health Unit
CH-1211 Geneva 27, Switzerland

World Psychiatric Association
Clinica Lopez Ibor
Avenida Nueva Zelanda
44 E-28035 Madrid, Spain

LATIN AMERICA

Asociacion Cubana de Salud Mental
Consejo de Sociedades Cientificas
Calle L entre 23 Y 25 Vedado
Plaza C, Havana, Cuba

Casa de Proteccion de la Salud
Mental, A.C.
Javier Mina #7
Edificiolxpalia, Zona del Rio
Tijuana, B.C. Mexico

Chilean Society of Mental Health
Av. La Paz 841
Santiago, Chile

Federacion Mexicana de Salud
Fresnos 46 San Angelinn
C.P. 01060
Mexico D.F. Mexico

Foundation for Mental Health
Aguero 1287 (1425)
Capital Republica, Argentina

Mexican Institute of Psychiatry
Calzada México-Xpchimilco 101
Col. San Lorenzo Huipulco
Delegación Tlalpan, 14370 Mexico, DF

Sociedad Mexicana de Salud Mental A.C.
Apartado Postal 63-205
Mexico 02800 D.F., Mexico

MIDDLE EAST

AMAAN
Palestinian Association of Mental
    Health
P.O. Box 2516
Cairo 11361, Egypt

ENOSH, Israel Mental Health
Association
Box 1593
Ramat Hasharon 47113, Israel

Mental Health Department
Ministry of Health
1st floor, 1st May Building
#2, Flat #110, El Nasr St.
Nasr City, Cairo Egypt

World Islamic Assn. for Mental Health
Nasr City, Cairo Egypt

Yemen Neuro-Psychiatric Association
P.O. Box 1224
Sana, Yemen Arab Republic

UNITED KINGDOM

British Psychological Society
St. Andrews House
48 Princess Road
E. Leicester, LE17DR UK

International League against Epilepsy
Department of Neurology
King's College Hospital
Denmark Hill
London, SE5 9R5 UK

National Association for
    Mental Health
15-19 Broadway
Stratford
London, E15 4BQ UK

Scottish Association for Mental Health
Atlantic House
38 Gardners' Crescent
Edinburgh, EH3 8DQ Scotland

Social Science and Medicine
Glengarden, Ballater
Aberdeenshire, AB35 5UB Scotland

The Mental Health Association
    of Ireland
6 Adelaide St.
Dun Laoghaire, Dublin Co., Ireland

The Northern Ireland Association for
    Mental Health
80 University Street
Belfast, BT7 1HE Northern Ireland

UNITED STATES

American Mental Health Foundation
2 East 86th Street
New York, NY 10028

American Orthopsychiatric Association
19 W. 44th Street, Suite 1616
New York, NY 10036

American Psychiatric Association
1400 K Street, NW
Washington, DC 20005

American Psychiatric Nurses' Association
1101 Connecticut Ave, NW
Washington, DC 20036

National Association of Social Workers
750 1st Street, NE
Washington, DC 20002-4241

National Community Mental Healthcare
    Council
12300 Twinbrook Parkway, 320
Rockville, MD 20852

National Institutes of Health
National Institute of Mental Health
Parklawn Building
5600 Fishers Lane
Rockville, MD 20857

UNITED STATES (*continued*)

American Psychological Association
1200 17th Street, NW
Washington, DC 20036

American Schizophrenic Association
900 N. Federal Highway, Suite 330
Boca Raton, FL 33432

Bazelon Center for Mental Health Law
1101 15th Street, NW
Washington, DC 20036

Institute for Victims of Trauma
6801 Market Square Drive
McLean, VA 22101

International Association for Child and
Adolescent Psychiatry and Allied
Professions
Yale Medical School
P.O. Box 3333
New Haven, CT 06510

International Clinical Epidemiology
Network (INCLEN)
3600 Market Street, Suite 380
Philadelphia, PA 19104-2644

International Committee Against Mental
Illness
P.O. Box 1921 Grand Central Station
New York, NY 10163

International Psychogeriatric Association
3127 Greenleaf Avenue
Wilmette, IL 60091

International Society for Adolescent
Psychiatry
24 Green Valley Road
Wallingford, PA 19086

Mental Health Policy Resource Center,
Inc.
1730 Rhode Island Avenue, NW
Washington, DC 20036

National Alliance for the Mentally Ill
2101 Wilson Boulevard, Suite 302
Arlington, VA 22201

National Alliance for Research on
Schizophrenia and Affective Disorders
(NARSAD)
60 Cutter Mill Road
Great Neck, NY 11021

National Mental Health Association
1900 Central Trust Tower
1 West 4th Street
Cincinnati, OH 45202

One World Productions
847A 2nd Avenue, Suite 361
New York, NY 10017

Pan American Health Organization
525 23rd Street, NW
Washington, DC 20037

Society for Traumatic Street Studies
435 N. Michigan Avenue, #1717
Chicago, IL 60611-4008

The Carter Center
Task Force on Mental Health
1 Copenhill Drive
Atlanta, GA 30307

UNESCO
2 United Nations Plaza
New York, NY 10017

UNICEF, United Nations Children's Fund
3 United Nations Plaza
New York, NY 10017

United Nations High Commissioner
for Refugees (Liaison Office)
United Nations Headquarters
New York, NY 10017

World Bank, Health Policy Unit
1818 H Street, NW
Washington, DC 20433

World Federation for Mental Health
1021 Prince Street
Alexandria, VA 22314-2971

Youth at Risk Project
National Development and
Research Institutes
11 Beach Street
New York, NY 10013

Index

Aboriginal peoples: extermination of, 119; dislocation of, 137
Abortion, and amniocentesis: in China, 239; deaths from, 239; and involuntary/forced, 239; and sex determination: in China, 239, in India, 239; as population control, 239; in Romania, 239; and sex selective abortions: in China, 239, in India, 239; and statistics; and ultrasound, 239
Abuse Trends Linkage Altering System (ATLAS), 102
Academia Euripaea Study Group, 24
Acculturation: and children, 143; and elderly, 143; and families, 143–45; and refugees; and women, 143; and youth, 147
Acuda, S., 94
Acuna, J. E., 125
Acupuncture, 109
Adolescents: and depression, 24; and psychosocial disorders, 172; and rates of suicide in the U.S., 69; and suicide, 72; and substance abuse, 89, 91. *See also* Children
Africa: elderly in, 208–11; famine in, 29; refugee statistics in, 136; settlement patterns in, 142; women in, 180, 185–89, 191–92, 202–3
African-Americans, rates of suicide, 71
Agarwal, Bina, 200
Agudelo, Silva F., 119, 121
Ahearn, Frederick L., 140
Ahmed, Nasar, 237
AIDS: and blood transfusion, 245; and education: in Uganda, 249; and child prostitution, 162; and eating behaviors, 233; and HIV and anal intercourse, 242–45; and human rights, 249–51; and infection rates, 242–46 (*see also* Table 10.2, 243; Table 10.5, 245; Table 10.7, 250); in Haiti, 247–48; and high risk groups, 246, 249; in Kenya, 242–44; and prevention: in high risk groups, 245–46; and psychiatric disorders, 243; and public health programs, 249; and public policy, 249; and statistics, 242–49; and stigma, 243; in sub-Saharan Africa, 246; and substance abuse, 243–44; and suicide, 243; in Thailand, 242–44, 249; and tourism, 246–47; transmis-

sion of, 244–45; treatment of: cost of, 245–46; and tuberculosis, 246; and women, 191–92, 242, 246. *See also* HIV
Alcohol/alcoholism, and abuse of: in Africa, 92; in Chile, 96; in China, 92; and cirrhosis of the liver, 94; and control of labor in Zimbabwe, 92; as a commodity, 91; and consequences of, 91–92; and economics, 91; effects of, 91; and fetal alcohol syndrome, 94; and homicides, 95; and human costs, 95; in India, 94; and mental health, 92; in Nigeria, 92, 94; in Papua, New Guinea, 95; and public health, 93; and social change, 90; and suicide, 74; and traffic accidents, 95; and violence, 95; and wife-beating, 95; and women, 95. *See also* Substance abuse
Allodi, F., 124
Almeida-Filho, Naomar, 23
Alzheimer's disease, 34, 213
American Indians, rates of suicide, 71
Amphetamines, effects of, 99. *See also* Substance abuse
Anderson, J. W., 185
Andrews, Gary R., 217
Anemia, 185, 234
Angola, literacy rates, 156
Anticonvulsant treatment/drugs, 169, 272
Antidepressant drugs, 46, 272
Antipsychotic drugs, 272
Anxiety disorders: characteristics of, 46; consequences of, 47; diagnosis of, 47, 50; and idioms of distress, 46; types of 46–47
Apartheid, 26: and violence, 118–19, 127; adolescent criminality, 167
Argentina, 59: and the disappeared, 37, 129; and healing from violence, 129; and mental health services, 36; and suicide: Gran Chaco (Matako people), 81, 83
Armed Conflicts in 1987, Table 5.1, 117
Arms Project of Human Rights Watch and Physicians for Human Rights, The, 117–18
Asia: and the elderly, 207–10, and population control, 239; and prostitution, 162–63, and refugees, 136
Aslam, Asif, 98